Rachel Carson

McFarland Literary Companions

Rachel Carson

A Literary Companion

MARY ELLEN SNODGRASS

McFarland Literary Companions, 20

McFarland & Company, Inc., Publishers
Jefferson, North Carolina

ALSO BY THE AUTHOR (AND SEE PAGE ii) AND FROM MCFARLAND

Television's Outlander: A Companion, Seasons 1–5 (2021; *Edwidge Danticat: A Companion to the Young Adult Literature* (2021); *Marion Zimmer Bradley: A Companion to the Young Adult Literature* (2020); *Coins and Currency: An Historical Encyclopedia*, 2d ed. (2019); *Gary Paulsen: A Companion to the Young Adult Literature* (2018); *World Epidemics: A Cultural Chronology of Disease from Prehistory to the Era of Zika*, 2d ed. (2017); *Settlers of the American West: The Lives of 231 Notable Pioneers* (2015); *Who's Who in the Middle Ages* (2001; paperback 2013); *Encyclopedia of World Scriptures* (2001; paperback 2011); *Coins and Currency: An Historical Encyclopedia* (2003; paperback 2007); *World Shores and Beaches: A Descriptive and Historical Guide to 50 Coastal Treasures* (2005)

ISBN (print) 978-1-4766-8312-6
ISBN (ebook) 978-1-4766-4129-4

LIBRARY OF CONGRESS AND BRITISH LIBRARY
CATALOGUING DATA ARE AVAILABLE

Library of Congress Control Number 2021009004

Front cover image of Rachel Carson (Rachel Carson Council/Photofest); *background* Maine coastline © 2021 Shutterstock

Printed in the United States of America

McFarland & Company, Inc., Publishers
Box 611, Jefferson, North Carolina 28640
www.mcfarlandpub.com

Acknowledgments

Special thanks go to these sources:

Appalachian State University Library, Boone, North Carolina
Boyd Library, Sandhills Community College, Pinehurst, North Carolina
Central Carolina Community College, Sanford, North Carolina
L.C. Coonse, chemist, Granite Falls, North Carolina
Marsha Fanning, biology professor, Lenoir Rhyne University, Hickory, North Carolina
Martin Otts, reference librarian, Patrick Beaver Library, Hickory, North Carolina
Burl McCuiston, reference librarian, Lenoir Rhyne University, Hickory, North Carolina
Montreat College Library, Montreat, North Carolina
Renfro Library, Mars Hill University, Mars Hill, North Carolina
Special thanks go to my publicist and consultant Joan Lail, a voice of reason in my ear.

We each have our turn at this earth.
—Pearl Buck, *The Good Earth*

Every human being in the world is now subjected to contact
with dangerous chemicals, from the moment of conception until death.
—Rachel Carson, *Silent Spring*

Table of Contents

Preface

For the environmentalist, teacher, scientist, literary historian, reviewer, and feminist reader, *Rachel Carson: A Literary Companion* presents the themes and messages of a serious biologist endowed with reverence for life. The 107 alphabetically arranged topics cover her major essays and orations along with commentary on critical response and congressional testimony. Individual subjects—fish, waterfowl, land, eels, birds, whales, sea, mammals, wetlands, waterways—locate insights into areas of nature that dominated her laboratory and field research.

Specific phenomena—wind, temperature, tides, topography, fossils—identify Rachel's overview of the powers that shaped creation. Themes—World War II, carcinogens, sport hunting, endangered species, death, the future—inform readers of Rachel's private thoughts, including fears for her own mortality. Additional entries view the author's interest in details, diction, literature, folklore, and history, especially her respect for the canon of English naturalist Charles Darwin. A detailed genealogy refutes notions that she lived the isolation and disengagement of a lone spinster rather than the high moral principles of her grandfather, Irish-American minister Daniel McLean.

Glossing specifies 198 terms and phrases that attest to Rachel's expertise, as with these topical examples:

abbreviations Ce^{137} AEC, NAS, CCC, FIFRA, I^{131}, Sr^{90}

anatomy macerate, Krebiozen, metabolite, germ plasm, evisceration, enzyme, cortin, mesentery, coracoid process

chemical terms cobalt, radioiodine, polysaccharide, purpurin, radioisotope, hydrocarbon

descriptors adipose, atrophy, diurnal, ichthyological, obsolescence, sessile, vitreous, phosphorescence, serrate, viviparous, lenticular, crepuscular, commensal

fauna grilse, opercula, poult, radula, ambergris, brant, eyrie, guano, milt, crustacea, cochineal, foraminifera, capris, byssus, copepod, spelt

flora graminoid, stipe, phaeocystis, understory, chara, duff, rock tripe, lichen, inflorescence, holdfast, chlorophyll, glasswort, diatom, buck brush

history Laurentian Era, Cambrian Era, Silurian, trilobite, nummulites, Mohorovicic discontinuity, alchemy

scientific terms echogram, dynamometer, toxicology, mitosis, ultraviolet light, mitochondria, nanocurie, necrosis, protoplasms, mutagenic, synthesis, vector, sub stratospheric, symbiosis, phosphorylation, monograph, atomic fission, hydrophone, fallout, echogram, back siphonage

seafaring terms beam to the wind, dory, haul seine, neap tide, winch, cull, derrick, gunwales, lee, Tonger, fathom, brush weir

topographical terms zonda, fallow, humus, freshet, gneiss, ilmenite, marl, rutile, monadnock, tundra, Oyashio, redd, spindrift, moraine, foehn wind, continental margin, chinook, estuary, biosphere, convection

A glossary of terms found in Rachel's work is provided in the first appendix; for discussion, research, and writing, the appendix "A Guide to Writing, Art, and Research Topics" suggests 17 ideas for glossing, speech topics, biographical and historical background, comparative literature, and education. A bibliography of primary and secondary sources, both print and electronic, precedes the index, which points readers to fundamental titles, issues, and cultural and scientific subjects, particularly presidents and congressional acts. The overall work explicates and honors Rachel Carson as an ethicist for all times.

Introduction

A model of female persistence and commitment at a time when women counted for little in academe or government, Rachel Louise Carson turned a career in biology into worldwide fame in ecology. Although biographers tend to reduce her writings to a few major titles, she authored influential newspaper articles, essays on food from the sea, correspondence with scientists, book reviews, speeches, and testimonies to legislative authorities. Her works demonstrated a patient humility with the power-hungry military-industrial complex, which sought license to churn out contaminants that threatened life on earth. Ironically, her existence depended on radiation treatments for breast and bone cancer while she concealed her declining health from the public and continued making inroads against a dire planetary threat from atomic power and biocides.

Historians credit Carson with initiating environmentalism and ecofeminism, a mustering of female volunteers to do battle with local, national, and international polluters. By yoking women advocates to the complex issue of planetary health, she motivated an ongoing crusade that continues over half a century later. Her name attaches to awards, honoraria, citizen campaigns, and sanctuaries where animals and plants exist in balance with humankind.

Rachel's writings progressed from journalistic features and government brochures to melodic tokens of love to the wild. From her sea trilogy—*Under the Sea Wind, The Sea Around Us,* and *The Edge of the Sea*—writers, journalists, spiritualists, and monarchs extract aphorisms rich in comfort and pert scoldings to dwellers on earth who privilege themselves above other life forms. To prepare a new generation for wiser stewardship, she evolved a hands-on curriculum in *The Sense of Wonder,* a guide to adult-led ventures in the outdoors that introduced children to natural phenomena as simple as butterflies, as grand as star clusters.

The decisive point in Carson's work coincided with ebbing strength. As she fought cancer with meager mid–twentieth century treatments, her heart and mind committed to a duty to earth. From informed reading before and after World War II, she recognized hubris in the agrochemical industry that encouraged patenting and selling biocides without testing their menace to life. By compiling *Silent Spring,* a subversive prophecy of planetary apocalypse issued on September 27, 1962, she scourged the radioactive and chemical killers that had already begun eating away at the future. After studying the possibilities of chromosomal damage, she alerted readers to imperiled genes still *in utero.* Some turned away from her jeremiad in terror;

others fostered a hateful screed that condemned her excellence as ill-intentioned and self-aggrandizing.

In retrospect of a remarkable career, Carson's imprint on earth's survival refuses to dim. Rather, her impact gains credence daily with news of exterminated species, shrinking public lands, nuclear accidents, and the detritus that chokes the seas. Students seek her works as beacons to sense. Lawmakers pay homage to her efforts by monitoring weaponry, the outdoors, drinking water, and foodstuffs. Ethicists cite passages that revive to their former primacy reverence and humility toward creation.

Key to Carson's prominence in twentieth-century philosophy lies her prediction that the environmental campaign will never end—must never end. Each new generation must relearn the lessons of Hiroshima and Nagasaki, Bikini Atoll, the Dust Bowl, DDT, Chernobyl, and Three Mile Island. For its tenacity and vigor, *Silent Spring* remains fresh in human minds as a guide to what could happen and will happen if humankind abandons its guardianship of planet earth.

A Chronology of Rachel Carson's Life and Works

In an era when males dominated government, capitalism, and science, Rachel Louise Carson made a resonant career as a pioneering aquatic biologist, artful nature writer and lecturer, ecologist, and ethicist. From awareness of harsh environmental truths, she accepted the onus to bear witness. She became a global celebrity for compiling and defending a seminal jeremiad warning readers of threats to earthly life from fertilizer, radioactivity, and biocides. As both educator and earth keeper, the author influenced U.S. legislators to take responsibility for damage to nature and abnormalities in the food chain. After introducing a lucid masterwork, *Silent Spring*, on September 27, 1962, she survived only a year and a half.

Time magazine lauded Rachel as "one brave woman and her very brave book," a model of clarity, conviction, and objectivity ("Rachel," Moyers, 2007). In 1991, an editorial in the *Baltimore Sun* reflected on the author's contributions to the newspaper: "That writing not only educated and inspired our readers, it also honed the skills and expertise that soon thereafter produced *Under the Sea Wind*, *The Sea Around Us*, and *Silent Spring*" (Sterne, 1991, 8A). Into the 21st century, her legacy still ignites controversy. Her work enables farmers in developing countries to produce sustainable crops and fosters respect for the beauties of the wild in all parts of the globe.

1870

Rachel claimed ancestry among British immigrants from Ireland and Scotland to Pennsylvania. After a year at Steubenville and four years ministering to Presbyterians in Erie, Pennsylvania, her 30-year-old maternal grandfather, Daniel M.B. McLean, began a decade of pastoral service to Chartiers United Presbyterian Church of Canonsburg. Sickened during his last year, he died at age 40 of tuberculosis. His legacy influenced the McLean clan to adopt a profound ethos—to honor God's creation for its mystery and everyday beauty and to avoid the pride and recklessness of corporate profiteers and scientists.

The author treasured nature as a divine miracle deserving reverence. Book critic and White House correspondent Frances Lewine declared that the Scots-Irish heritage endowed the author with a fighter's punch. Scholarly author Andrew Wadsworth stated that "much of her writing resonates with Christian beliefs regarding the sacred nature of life, man's stewardship over the earth, and man's relationship with his fellow man" (Wadsworth, 2016).

1901

In west central Pennsylvania east of the Monongahela River, the Carsons, Robert Warden and Maria Frazier McLean Carson, and their two-year-old son Robert McLean and three-year-old daughter Marian Frazier settled at a two-story, two-bedroom frame cottage on a hillside at 613 Marion Avenue. The four-room log residence, erected in 1870 in Springdale Borough on 65 acres, cost the family $11,000. It had no electricity or plumbing. Rachel's mother, a teacher, pianist, and alto soloist, profited from a classical education southwest of Pittsburgh at Washington Female Seminary, a Presbyterian academy of 150 students studying core curriculum, art, elocution, and music. Out of respect for nature, she owned no flyswatter and carried pesky insects out of her house by hand.

The region flourished from the Pittsburgh and Steubenville and the Pittsburgh & Lake Erie railroads, Iron City Brewery, and Darr bituminous coal mine. The family relied on coal fireplaces, Maria's vegetable garden, a lean-to kitchen, springhouse, horse stable, and two privies. Their windows looked out on white pines, apple and pear trees, meadows, Robert's rose bed, and the smoky bilge of processed horseflesh at the American Glue Factory, a producer of fertilizer. Malodorous smoke from Edgar Thomson Steel Works, Heinz glass company, Alcoa aluminum factory, and American Iron Company smelting despoiled the countryside.

May 27, 1907

Born Rachel Louise Carson in Springdale, the writer bore the first name of her maternal grandmother, Rachel Frazier McLean, and an Irish great-aunt, Rachel Alexander Niblock. As described in "A Fable for Tomorrow," an allegory beginning the classic work *Silent Spring,* the author grew up around a horse, pig, and sheep and tramped wetlands of the Allegheny River at Parnassus 18 miles from Pittsburgh, where barges ferried lumber and oil to the Ohio River and west to the Mississippi. The family introduced the children to Protestant beliefs, including Jesus' parables, and entertained them with games of Parcheesi, storytelling, songs sung by the piano, and readings from children's magazines and James Fenimore Cooper's *The Last of the Mohicans.*

At Springdale Grammar School, Rachel searched for data in science books on natural phenomena and animal nest and den building. On her own, by kerosene lantern, she read Beatrix Potter's Peter Rabbit fantasies, Kenneth Grahame's *Wind in the Willows,* and memoirs of Gene Stratton-Porter, an Indiana naturalist. After school, she fed the chickens and viewed her surroundings. Because of her respect for living things, her older brother Robert gave up hunting rabbits.

Like rural-reared authors Leslie Marmon Silko, Willa Cather, and Barbara Kingsolver, Rachel valued the outdoors as both fun and constant learning experience.

Exploring with her dogs Pat and Candy, she imitated Maria's use of the five senses to absorb beauty by examining leaves and bugs and listening to a conch shell, which her mother kept on the mantel. Maria assured her that God created all life. From the song "Rocked in the Cradle of the Deep," Rachel imagined the sea's grandeur, the essence of life's wholeness. Her mounting spirituality evolved from respect for the mystic in nature.

1910

To retire debts, the Carsons sold lots from their acreage, which Robert advertised in the *Springdale Record* for $300. Rachel grieved for family land that he sold.

1913 September

Scarlet fever impeded Rachel's attendance at School Street School. While Maria coordinated homeschooling in Anna Botsford Comstock's *Handbook of Nature Study*, Robert introduced his youngest to the town library. 6 yrs old

1914

During World War I, nature coursework like Rachel's lost ground in school curricula. From September to November, she attended only three weeks of classes. Her writing about pure forest air and unspoiled wildflowers stood in stark "contrast to the stink of town, the gash of the coal mine" ("Education," 2009, G6). 7 yrs old

1915

At age eight, the future author composed a tale of Mr. and Mrs. Wren entitled "The Little Brown House."

1915 November

After sister Marian, a tenth-grace dropout and stenographer, married 21-year-old Lee Frank Frampton, she kept books amid coal piles at the West Penn power plant, a shameless polluter of water and air. Contributing to the area's contamination, the stench of the glue factory added to the odor and smog. Rachel conducted outings in the wild and expressed views on country life in original drawings, verse, and animal stories featuring nesting wrens. She had no experience with the ocean and never learned to swim, but disclosure of fossil fish and spiral shells near Springdale convinced her that the land was once under sea.

1916

Rachel missed one month of the fourth grade because of illness. She wrote and illustrated for her father a book of verse entitled "The Sleeping Rabbit" based on Beatrix Potter's animal stories and painted glimpses of a wildflower—the red catchfly (*Silene dioica*)—in bud and bloom.

1918 spring

During World War I, brother Robert McLean Carson, a tenth-grade dropout and radio repairman, entered the Army Air Corps. At age 19, he served in northeastern France at the battles of Champagne on July 15, St.-Mihiel on September 12–15, and Meuse-Argonne on September 26 until November 11, the end of the war. On mustering out, he related the bravery of a Canadian pilot who hung on to the wing of a damaged plane to give it balance. Because of his courage, German aviators respected the enemy flier and did not fire on him.

1918 September

Enlightened by the respect for living things modeled by Maria, Rachel wrote verse and fiction and submitted five original works to *St. Nicholas Magazine,* founded in 1873. For the aviator's story "A Battle in the Clouds" that she wrote in May, the fourth grader won a silver medal. The prize placed her in league with poets Stephen Vincent Benet and Edna St. Vincent Millay, essayist E. B. White, humorists Mark Twain and Joel Chandler Harris, short story author Eudora Welty, children's writer Frances Hodgson Burnett, autobiographer Laura Ingalls Wilder, and novelists Louisa May Alcott, William Faulkner, and F. Scott Fitzgerald.

1919 January

The author's second story to *St. Nicholas,* "A Young Hero," returned to themes of soldiers in World War I. The next month, Rachel advanced to a gold badge and ten dollars for publishing "A Message to the Front."

1919 August

St. Nicholas magazine accepted a fourth story, "A Famous Sea Fight."

1921

At age 14, Rachel began earning a penny a word for a story that *St. Nicholas* used as a model of reader interest. Her themes incorporated quail, pheasants, orioles, cuckoos, and hummingbirds. While her appreciation of birds increased, her sensitivity to the defilement of the outdoors by industrial expansion made her dubious that progress extended to citizens and nature.

1922

The writer attended Springdale High School in tenth grade, earned a 93.7 average, and contributed to the newspaper and literary magazine, the *Hamilton.*

1922 May *around her 15ᵗ BD*

Rachel learned skywatching from her mother, collected caterpillars and cocoons to follow their development, and photographed the nest of a yellowthroat, a warbler that bred in marshy thickets. Karen F. Stein, a teacher of English and women's studies at the University of Rhode Island, commented on girlhood field work: "Her love of nature was shaped by a pedagogy that advocated direct experience and avoided rote learning and memorization of facts" (Stein, 2014, 81).

1922 July

Rachel's six-paragraph memoir "My Favorite Recreation" earned $3.00 from *St. Nicholas* for its detailed narrative about hiking the western Pennsylvania hills with a camera and her dog Pal. A day's walk put her in sight of the Maryland yellow-throat, bobwhite, oriole, hummingbird, ovenbird, wood thrush, and vesper sparrow.

1923 September *16 yrsold*   *high school*

After transferring to Parnassus High School in New Kensington for her junior year, Rachel traveled two miles to class. She took a speech course and managed to walk to French club and the oratorical society. Out of an obsession with the sea, she consumed the works of Robert Louis Stevenson, Herman Melville, Mark Twain, W.H. Hudson, and Joseph Conrad and found inspiration in the verse of Algernon Swinburne, Gerard Manley Hopkins, Robinson Jefferson, and John Masefield. She internalized A.E. Housman's "Loveliest of Trees" and Alfred Lord Tennyson's poem "Locksley Hall." In a speech sponsored by the *New York Herald-Tribune,* she lovingly recalled "great poets of the sea" and described a tendency to turn class compositions into marine topics and themes (Carson, speech, 1951).

1925 May

Submitting a senior paper on "Intellectual Dissipation" extolling quality literature, the author disclosed an academic mindset and graduated valedictorian from Parnassus.

September 15, 1925

A freshman at age 18 in Pittsburgh at the Pennsylvania College for Women, later Chatham University, Rachel "Ray" Carson traveled from home with her parents in a borrowed Model T Ford and moved into Berry Hall, a three-story brick residence. She enrolled on funds from two scholarships—$100 for academic excellence, which paid for tuition, and $100 from a state exam to underwrite room and board. Her parents sold part of their land and mortgaged the rest to secure the remaining $600 for college. Maria earned spare cash by teaching piano lessons. Rachel sought loans based on family property as collateral.

No longer living in poverty, Rachel enjoyed electric lights, plumbing, and meals at the dining hall tables set with china, crystal, and silver. In retreat from campus socials, she earned honors by reading in the library, surveying stuffed birds in a natural history exhibit, and submitting verse to *Atlantic, Good Housekeeping, Collier's, Harper's, Ladies Home Journal, Poetry,* and *Saturday Evening Post.* She maintained observations of the wild in spiral-bound notebooks and enjoyed intramural field hockey, baseball, and basketball.

In addition to majoring in English composition, Rachel reported for the newspaper, the *Arrow.* She wrote a first essay, "Who I Am and Why I Came to PCW," which characterized idealism as the "vision splendid" (Quaratiello, 2010, 6). A subsequent essay on "The Golden Apple" analyzed the Greek myth about women who sought the good opinion of men, a suggestion of feminist stirrings.

1926

A first biology course introduced Rachel to her life's work, causing her to abandon composition as a career. In the essay "Nature Fights Back" in *Silent Spring,* she reflected on the miracle of paramecia cultured in a jar of water and hay, "all multiplying without restraint in their temporary Eden" (Carson, 2002, 247). She later realized, "It never occurred to me that I was merely getting something to write about" (Carson, 1954). In a book review of *The Sea Around Us* for the London *Guardian,* poet Billy Mills extolled the bestseller for "[marrying] her early ambition with her skills as a researcher and synthesiser" (Mills, 2014).

1926 February

An announcement in the school paper listed Rachel among the ten top academically ranked freshmen.

1926 spring

To make up the tuition and board still owed the college, benefactors contributed tuition and fees. Rachel's mother marketed chickens and apples and sold the family china and silver.

April 30, 1926

Rachel's lighthouse story in *The Englicode*, "The Master of the Ship's Light," earned positive comments for dialogue and clarity.

1926 summer

The Carson household became so crowded with nine residents that Rachel's brother pitched a tent on the lawn.

November 19, 1926

College paper

Rachel joined the staff of *The Arrow* and, by November 19, headed alumnae news coverage until March 11, 1927. In addition, she composed a poem about a butterfly and "Why I Am a Pessimist" about a cat's isolation from the family.

November 26, 1926

The Allegheny County Department of Public Works began a two-year project engineering the Ninth Street Bridge at uptown Pittsburgh, a self-anchored steel suspension bridge over the Allegheny River later named for the author on Earth Day, April 22, 2006. In her teens she viewed riverbank damage caused by industrial contaminants. Her biographer, Linda Lear, remarked, "She observed here, as she could nowhere else, the contamination of the environment" (Sherman, 2006).

1927

Rachel's social life admitted a few outings into her packed schedule. She sledded on dining hall trays in the snow and dated Bob Frye, going to a prom and basketball game. After one more date, she abandoned flirtations and pairing off with boys.

February 11, 1927

The *Englicode* published "Keeping an Expense Account," Rachel's admission of dislike for finance.

May 27, 1927

Her short story "Broken Lamps" in the *Englicode* won an Omega Club award.

1928

A loner and contributor to *The Arrow*, Rachel composed in longhand, often at night, and subjected the text to rigorous self-editing and her mother's proofreading. Students isolated her for unsightly acne and homemade dresses and ridiculed her mother's weekend visits to type papers on a portable Olivetti.

1928 January

College
Ecology
Studies
✗

Enthusiasm for science altered Rachel's college plans from a major in English to Professor Mary Scott Skinker's biology course in Dilworth Hall. Skinker stressed the interconnection of life since its beginning. The syllabus emphasized environmental studies of the finfish and shellfish, shorelines, tides, coral reefs, thermal vents, and subsurface kelp and seagrass. The blend yielded what the *New York Times* journalist Nancy F. Koehn termed "a scientist with a lyrical bent" and leader of fellow researchers, who were openly hostile to female scientists (Koehn, 2012).

Rachel hoped to continue studies at Cornell in New York or Baltimore's Johns Hopkins University. Lacking funds, she had to spend the senior year at her alma mater despite early admission to Johns Hopkins. While taking genetics, histology, organic chemistry, physics, and German, she served *The Arrow* as grammarian. She co-formed a science club, Mu Sigma Sigma, the initials honoring Professor Skinker.

1928 summer

Rachel earned summer funds by tutoring high school students.

June 10, 1929

With a B.A. in biology and a *magna cum laude* diploma, Rachel left college owing $1,600. She had an introductory experience at the seacoast after traveling to New York Harbor and New Bedford, Massachusetts. In 1953, she stated, "I loved the ocean with a purely vicarious love long before I had seen it" (Steingruber, 2018, 331).

1929 July

Rachel took a bus to Luray, Virginia, and visited Professor Skinker at a family retreat in the Great Smoky Mountains. Amid ongoing discussions of careers in science, Rachel played tennis, rode horseback, and hiked into bird-watching territory in the Shenandoah Valley. She expected an academic world where teachers were male and jobs for female scientists rare.

1929 August

On a $200 scholarship, the author entered graduate studies in genetics and zoology at Johns Hopkins. She found no dormitory space open to women and settled at a rented house in Stemmers Run, a few miles from the edge of the Chesapeake Bay. While living east of campus at a Homewood Terrace apartment, she enrolled in botany and chemistry classes and genetics and physiology labs. In the most dreaded field, organic chemistry, where she competed against 70 male students, she was satisfied to earn an 85.

In the zoology lab at Gilman Hall, the four-story intellectual core of the campus, Rachel could access symposia, library collections, and her adviser, revered zoologist Rheinart Parker Cowles. With a special interest in the American eel, she kept an eel tank and collected turtles and investigated reptile nerves in crocodiles, lizards, and rattlesnakes, venomous pit vipers that arrived in the mail. To her annoyance, she found male students better trained and more familiar with scientific protocols.

Rachel studied live specimens of fish and swans for six weeks at the Woods Hole Marine Biological Laboratory, an affiliate of the University of Chicago in southwestern Cape Cod. On a small dredging boat, she seined Buzzards Bay and Vineyard Sound for seaweed, shells, and crustaceans, the impetus to the book *The Sea Around Us,* which appeared under "R.L. Carson."

1930 spring

To support a sickly father and ease the cost of the family's rented three-story house at Old Philadelphia Road northeast of Baltimore, Rachel supported two siblings, parents, and two nieces. When tuition rose 50 percent to $300, she limited coursework to part-time and earned cash as a laboratory assistant at the medical school. She assisted with rats and fruit flies (*Drosophila*) at the genetics lab of Raymond Pearl, a specialist in bio-gerontology or lifespans at the Institute for Biological Research at Johns Hopkins School of Hygiene and Public Health. She groused, "I've just put in a tough day at the lab. Getting the lab ready for 45 students is no fun" (Archer, 2016). Her work involved washing test tubes and equipping lab tables with the appropriate containers.

1930 summer

As a classroom assistant and part-time instructor, Rachel taught zoology in summer school at Johns Hopkins. On her own, she studied fish roe under the microscope.

1931 September

At College Park east of Washington, Rachel began teaching zoology at the Dental and Pharmacy School at the University of Maryland, where she commuted by bus or train.

1932

The biologist abandoned a mullet roe project and research into the cranial nerves of pit vipers and embryonic African (*Anomalurus*) squirrels before initiating a 108-page master's thesis. Her paper, "The Development of the Pronephros during the Embryonic and Early Larval Life of the Catfish," explored the emergence of pronephros (kidneys) in young catfish (*Ictalurus punctatus*). The daily task of staining embryonic tissue required use of the camera lucida, a bioscope that flashed an image on drawing paper.

June 14, 1932

A year later than the author intended, she earned an M.S. in marine zoology from Johns Hopkins. To pay tuition debts, she deeded Springdale land to Pennsylvania College.

1934 winter

The Great Depression ended Rachel's quest for a doctorate in zoology. The failing health of her father and sister Marian caused the Carson family to elude debt by fleeing creditors in Springdale. Instead of postgraduate work, she took a full-time classroom appointment at the University of Maryland and submitted short stories and fiction unsuccessfully to literary magazines.

1935

The naturalist wrote of a mounting imbalance in nature. Alterations jeopardized wildlife across the Northern Hemisphere by plowmen uprooting frontier prairie grass, draining bogs, and promoting topographical changes that initiated topsoil erosion and the Dust Bowl. Gabriel Popkin, a science writer for *Johns Hopkins Magazine,* noted the shift in style and method—"Not to conduct scientific research but to illuminate it, contextualize it, and share it with the public" (Popkin, 2013).

1935 April

At the urging of President Franklin D. Roosevelt, congress passed the Soil Conservation Act to rebuild land scored by drought and the Dust Bowl and to replace topsoil from the Rio Grande to the Ontario border.

July 6, 1935

Rachel's father, a courteous 70-year-old traveling salesman for the Great American Insurance Company, collapsed and died in the backyard at Stemmers Run northeast of Baltimore. Rachel began supporting her widowed mother, who aided her daughter as secretary and housekeeper.

1935 October

At the urging of mentor Mary Scott Skinker, Rachel submitted three test assignments to prove her expertise at writing scientific prose for the U.S. Bureau of Fisheries, a federal conservation office organized in 1903. During two-days-per-week employment as one of the first two women hired under the New Deal, she resided on Flower Avenue near Sligo Creek Park in Silver Spring, Maryland, on a pay scale of $6.50 per day. The tenor of the times relegated female intellectuals to women's work—writing and editing, but not field exploration. *Sexism*

Elmer Higgins, chief of the U.S. Bureau of Fisheries, hired her as a radio writer of public education essays. Marginalized as a composer of press releases and features on the complexities of marine biology, the author/editor issued "Romance under the Waters," field research on fish populations in 52 seven-minute weekly radio scripts for CBS Radio. She also composed a first brochure, "The World of Waters," an 11-page study of sea creatures on the ocean floor. In reference to the importance of federal pamphlets on natural resources, she expected the reports "to hold the interest of people who are not management specialists—the people whose support of our program is very important" (Klinger, 2007, 33).

1936 January

The first female to pass civil service exams, Rachel outscored the competition in aquatic biology, parasitology and wildlife, and gained a post at College Park, Maryland, which she reached by streetcar. On her days off, under the byline R.L. Carson, she submitted essays to the *Baltimore Sun, Richmond Times-Dispatch,* Charleston *News and Currier, Collier's, Nature, Holiday, Reader's Digest,* and *Sun Magazine* on *Sexism* the intricate life cycles of sea creatures of the Chesapeake Bay, Nova Scotia, and south to the North Carolina Outer Banks. Tom Horton, a journalist for the Salisbury (MD) *Daily Times,* concluded that she obscured her real name and home "to avoid pigeonholing her writing as 'local' or 'regional'" (Horton, 2019, A4). Bulgarian writer Maria Popova explained the need for a pseudonym because of Rachel's "era-calibrated fear that her writing wouldn't be taken as seriously if her gender was known" (Popova, 2017).

For information, Rachel interviewed watermen, shrimpers, crabbers, fish merchants, and trawler and whaling crews and toured factories, hatcheries, and conservation efforts. As her message grew more urgent, magazine editors rejected articles that threatened advertisers. Male professionals defamed her reputation. Autumn Nieves, an ecological biologist at Tulane University, explained the gender gap: "Women must defend the quality of their work, while also proving that the nature of being a woman does not make them unable to perform well" (Nieves, 2018).

March 1, 1936

The *Baltimore Sun* paid Rachel $20 for the 12-page article "It'll Be Shad Time Soon," published under the byline R.L. Carson. The 4,000-word essay revealed the U.S. Bureau of Fisheries' compilation of the degree to which sewage destroyed mid–Atlantic habitats for spawning shad. She followed with data on oyster farms, clamming, ducks, starlings, and waterfowl in the Chesapeake Bay, eel migration from the Sargasso Sea, and the bluefin tuna industry of Nova Scotia.

topics

1936 April

With confidence in a science writing career, the biologist upped her minimum salary request to $1,800.

May 26, 1936

The *Baltimore Sunday Sun* issued Rachel's article "Numbering the Fish of the Sea," which opened with a citation from John Masefield's poem "Roadways." She allowed images to magnify the erratic mackerel migration, comparing it to an "iridescent, streamlined sea rover" that vanished each fall into the deep (Carson, 1936, 5).

August 17, 1936

On the first full-time job, the scientist accepted a bureau appointment to junior aquatic biologist, for which she determined fish ages and reported on conservation for the Division of Scientific Inquiry. The weekly salary of $38.48 supported a family of five.

1937

While composing six more media articles in 1937, Rachel began postgraduate research as a junior aquatic biologist at the oceanographic institute in Woods Hole, Massachusetts, a global project sponsored by the Rockefeller Foundation.

1937 January

The death of Marian Frazier Carson Williams from pneumonia at age 39 orphaned two daughters, 12-year-old Marian Virginia and 11-year-old Marjorie "Marjie" Louise, whose father deserted them. The pre-teens passed to the care of their grandmother Maria in Tacoma Park, Maryland, and to Rachel, who resided in a two-story house in the Woodside neighborhood of Silver Spring along with Persian cats Buzzie and Kito.

January 3, 1937

The *Baltimore Sunday Sun* featured winter commercial croaker, trout, scup, and flounder runs in the article "The Northern Trawlers Move South." Through new data on wintering sanctuaries off coastal North Carolina and Virginia, Rachel promoted commercial prosperity for the Atlantic fleet at the new port of Ocean City, Maryland. The even-handed article incorporated complaints that recent winter sources of fresh seafood lowered spring prices for commercial fishermen and threatened fish populations, a problem that assailed New England haddock. She concluded with a rhetorical question: "Can man devise protective measures" to shield the fishing industry? (Carson, 1937, 7).

January 24, 1937

Rachel issued another essay in the *Baltimore Sun,* "Farming under the Chesapeake," an overview of the value of oysters, which produced the second highest fishing profit after salmon. The research anticipated greater artificial oyster beds propagated by private investors in Louisiana, Massachusetts, New Jersey, and Virginia.

February 14, 1937

Rachel sold the essay "Shad Going the Way of the Buffalo" to the *Charleston News and Courier,* which reported results of the Atlantic States Shad Conference in Atlantic City, New Jersey, of 11 states from Maine south to the Carolinas. The narrative spoke knowledgeably of coastal rivers—St. John's, Edisto, Neuse, Potomac, James, Susquehanna, Delaware, and Savannah. She outlined research data on shad—"their years at sea, their migrations, their enemies and the factors that bring them back … at spawning time" (Carson, 1937, 8C). Her prose classic *Under the Sea Wind* returned to the subject of human violation of seasonal patterns governing shad runs.

February 28, 1937

The *Baltimore Sun* reprinted Rachel's essay for the Charleston *News and Courier* under the title "Sentiment Plays No Part in the Save the Shad Movement."

March 28, 1937

The *Baltimore Sun* continued supporting Rachel's essays by printing "Chesapeake Oystermen See Stars and They Don't Like It," an exposé on predatory starfish.

April 25, 1937

More media articles included "Oyster Dinners at the Bottom of the Chesapeake," a reprint for the *Richmond Times Dispatch Sunday Magazine.*

July 18, 1937

Rachel's article "It's Tick Time in Maryland," on tick bite and spotted fever, alerted readers of the *Baltimore Sun* to the dangers of sucking insects common to mouse-infested meadows and underbrush. She reported a total of 18 incidents in Maryland, Virginia, and the District of Columbia.

1937 September

[handwritten: about "Sea Creatures on the Ocean floor." See Oct 1935]

[handwritten margin: Dbl check ?? '']

The naturalist waited a year to see her 11-page essay "The World of Waters," issued in the *Atlantic Monthly* under the title "Undersea." Reduced to four pages, it earned $100. The publication introduced the author by a female name, Rachel Carson, rather than the coy R.L. Carson. It mused on the food chain inhabiting "those six incomprehensible miles" into a fluid milieu forever battling at the edge of beach and dune (Quaratiello, 2010, 24). Although the essay ventured beyond lyricism to pedantic tutorial in the last six paragraphs, the eloquent tone impressed Quincy Howe, editor-in-chief at Simon & Schuster.

September 10, 1937

Dutch polymath Hendrik Van Loon, a Jules Verne fan and Newbery Medalist, wrote a letter from Greenwich, Connecticut, inviting Rachel to come for a meeting with Quincy Howe to discuss her nonfiction. His own regard for marine life derived from wanting "to read something about that mysterious world" (Van Loon, 1937).

The article inspired the core of *Under the Sea Wind,* a portrait of salty depths that offered no lasting shelter for humans. Rachel composed in longhand on National Recovery Administration stationery at the rate of 500–1,500 words per night. On a $250 advance, she focused on the perspective of a mackerel and sanderling and divided data into chapters on the Arctic, plankton hunters, seaways, fishing and seining, and seasonal cycles.

1938

The freelancer upped her media output in 1938 with seven more articles, concluding with an overview of seasonal whaling. Her expertise and reviews for *Atlantic Monthly* established respect among naturalists.

January 16, 1938

Rachel began the new year with a waterfowl essay for the *Baltimore Sun* "Ducks Are on Increase, But the Short Hunting Season Will Continue." Her rationale affirmed both conservationist and shooter by emphasizing major loses of acreage needed for nesting, breeding, and resting along flyways.

February 13, 1938

The *Baltimore Sunday Sun Magazine* issued Rachel's "Baltimore New Mecca for Nation's Sportsmen and Conservationists," which reported on the Sports, Garden, and Outdoor Life Show at the Fifth Regiment Armory.

February 14–17, 1938

The author attended the Third North American Wildlife Conference sponsored by the American Wildlife Institute at the Lord Baltimore Hotel in south central Baltimore. Speakers discussed pollution, antelope and deer management, pond fish, game animals, mosquito control, irrigation, fish crops, night shooting, waterfowl market hunting and illegal trapping of canvasback ducks, and a wildlife census. Research by D.R. Coburn and E.R. Quortrup revealed western duck illness from botulinus toxin, which can cause head droop and drowning.

March 20, 1938

For the *Richmond Times-Dispatch Sunday Magazine*, Rachel's article "Fight for Wildlife Pushes Ahead," overviewed the declines since Europeans arrived of the North American passenger pigeon, heath hen, canvasback and redhead ducks, elk, pronghorn antelope, moose, grizzly, mountain goat, and shad.

1938 July

At a rented cabin with Maria and nieces Marjorie and Virginia Williams, Rachel prepared for a job at the Pivers Island fisheries station at Beaufort in the Morehead City Channel. On the south end of North Carolina's Outer Banks, she viewed the museum and aquarium and read surveys of aquaculture and commercial fishing at Bird Shoal. At Nags Head, she shopped for the rare Janthina snail shell, which a boutique owner refused to sell. Under a full moon by flashlight, she toured the Shackleford Banks barrier islands and salt marshes on the Cape Lookout National Seashore, compared mollusk shells, and inhaled shore fragrance at Ship's Shoal while she took notes on sand fleas and crabs. On private time, she chatted with pier fishermen and gathered details of a comprehensive ocean environment as far from shore as Frying Pan Shoal, the infamous Graveyard of the Atlantic.

August 3, 1938

The *Baltimore Sunday Sun* published Rachel's views on "Giants of the Tide Rip Off Nova Scotia Again," a survey of fishing for bluefin tuna and herring in the waters around northeastern Canada. She named Chicagoan Thomas Howell a champion fisherman off Liverpool, Nova Scotia, for landing a tuna weighing nearly a half ton. She reviewed fairness rules limiting rod tip weight, thickness of lines, and the number of people participating.

August 21, 1938

Rachel continued freelance writing for the *Baltimore Sun* with "Walrus and Carpenter Not Oysters' Only Foe," which revealed damage done by sea snails and "an army of starfish" in the Chesapeake Bay (Carson, 1938, 2). She ended the piece with announcement of chemical control of snails introduced by the federal government.

1938 September

Under the pseudonym R.L. Carson, Rachel reviewed six scholarly papers for the *Progressive Fish-Culturist*. The journal issued her comments in November on "Lake Management Reports, Horseshoe Lake Near Cairo, Illinois," revealing that the analyst expressed greater expertise than the original authors.

September 13, 1938

"Mass Production for Diamond-Back Terrapins," a farming feature in the *Baltimore Sunday Sun Magazine,* summarized Rachel's observation of government turtle propagation in Beaufort, North Carolina.

October 9, 1938

The freelancer completed the essay "Chesapeake Eels Seek the Sargasso Sea" for the *Baltimore Sun*. The tone and style anticipated later writings about the mysterious behavior and migration of eels.

November 20, 1938

The *Sun* published Rachel's essay "Whalers Ready for New Season," which identified the massing of vessels as "harbingers of spring" (Carson, 1938, 2). The article reviewed international restrictions on licensing, supervision by a Coast Guard officer, and limitation of the season to 90 days. She promoted regulations as a means of saving whales from extermination.

1939

Busy at editing pamphlets on "Our Aquatic Food Animals," Rachel reduced her media writing to three articles.

March 5, 1939

The *Baltimore Sunday Sun Magazine* printed the essay "Starlings a Housing Problem," a tongue-in-cheek examination of problems with bird litter and noise. As spokesperson for the U.S. Department of Agriculture, she judged the seasonal migrant a friend of the farmer for gobbling insects.

March 26, 1939

Rachel's piscatorial article "Shad Catches Declining as 1939 Season Opens" appeared in the *Baltimore Sun*. She maintained empathy for fishermen and concern for a valuable food fish.

April 2, 1939

At the opening of trout season, the *Baltimore Sun* featured "A New Trout Crop for Anglers." Her reportage covered size limits and daylight hours for fishing. She warned Maryland residents that Gunpowder Falls, the Youghiogheny River, and Little Falls were too contaminated and Western Run too warm in summer to support trout stocking. Details of natural pollution from selenium in Western soils characterized the element as "death-dealing" (Carson, 1939, 3). Overfishing and epidemic disease further muddled issues of stocking by depleting adult fish before spawning season.

1939 summer

At the Woods Hole Station in southeastern Massachusetts, Rachel scanned beach, harbor, and wharf after completing work at the library and laboratory.

1939 June

At a time that Rachel advanced to Assistant Aquatic Biologist, DDT (dichlorodiphenyltrichloroethane) gained credence as the first modern insecticide.

1939 June–July

The author published a first-person essay in *Nature*, "How About Citizenship Papers for the Starling?," a foreign bird that she identified as a useful part of North

American ecology from Ontario to the Gulf Coast. She reviewed its ancestry among migrators from Great Britain to the Indian Ocean and plateaus of the Himalayas and its stability in New York after 1890. Within a decade, it had acclimated to Connecticut, Massachusetts, New Jersey, Pennsylvania, and Rhode Island.

1939 September   *Starts writing Book 1*

Rachel began outlining a book on sea life for Simon & Schuster based on her discussion with Quincy Howe in September 1937. She limited writing to "evenings and Saturday afternoons and Sundays" until a contract set a deadline (Carson, "Memo," 1942).

1940

A relaxed photo pictured Rachel on the steps of her Silver Spring home with the family dog Rags.

1940 Spring

Rachel posted five chapters of *The Sea Around Us* to Quincy Howe for approval.

1940 May

The author's output included a review of "Spawning Induced Prematurely in Trout with the Aid of Pituitary Glands of Carp and the Use of Hormones for the Conservation of Muskellunge, *Esox Masquinongy Immaculatus Garrard*," a book commentary for the *Progressive Fish-Culturist*.

1940 June

A contract from Simon & Schuster advanced Rachel another $250 until she completed the manuscript in November.

June 30, 1940

The U.S. Bureau of Fisheries became the U.S. Fish and Wildlife Service, a maker of conservation policy, enforcer of wildlife law, and protector of wetlands, hatcheries, endangered species, and migratory birds. All became significant themes in Rachel's speeches and writings.

1940 July   *US F & W (New Name)*

A major development placed Rachel in the newly formed U.S. Fish and Wildlife Service, which expanded outdoor sanctuaries and monitored the health and populations of flora and fauna. On vacation, she visited the wetlands and fisheries station at Woods Hole, Massachusetts, and sailed Buzzards Bay and Vineyard Sound on a U.S. Bureau of Fisheries research dredger, the *SS Phalanthrop*. Her observations of predatory squid and mackerel at the stone breakwater began answering her questions about the deep.

December 31, 1940

With time stolen from weekends, days off, and night writing, Rachel completed a manuscript for Simon & Schuster just as the year ended. Baltimore artist Howard Frech, a staff artist at the *Baltimore Sun*, drew the line art featuring dunes, nereid worms, hermit crab, gulls, and jellyfish. For its insouciant look at teeming coastal organisms, *The Sea Around Us* became her favorite work compiled at a contented time in her life. The unassuming style resulted from assiduous reading aloud and self-editing, requiring seven versions for the chapter "Spring Flight."

November 1, 1941

Under the Sea Wind: A Naturalist's Picture of Ocean Life won fans for lyric presentation of a scientist's observations of eels, fish, seafowl, and other ocean residents of a watery world. The narrative detailed their appearance, behaviors, salt tolerance, and diet. With a touch of drama, she chose Beaufort, North Carolina, as a setting for its large elver population and anthropomorphized whimsical creatures under individual names:

- Scomber the mackerel
- Blackfoot and Silverbar the sandpipers
- Ookpik the snowy owl
- Rynchops the skimmer
- Nereis the clamworm
- Anguilla the eel.

Illustrator Howard Frech added line drawings, which reappeared in the 2007 edition with action shots of a fox on the prowl, a heron gobbling a mouse, a clam worm undulating in eel-grass, and an osprey, talons extended, splashing the surf in search of mullet.

The treatise reaped praise from *New York* magazine, *Christian Science Monitor,* and *New York Times*. The *New York Herald Tribune* commended the work for its unrelenting drama; the Chicago *Tribune* marveled at the clarity of Rachel's prose. Reviewers lauded her ability to describe the wild with accuracy, energy, and lyricism. The Scientific Book Club named the work a November selection. However, the bombing of Pearl Harbor reduced sales to a mere 2,000. Rachel salvaged remaindered copies of her favorite book to give to friends.

1941 December

Oceanographer William Beebe, an underwater explorer by bathysphere, declared impeccable Rachel's research for *Under the Sea Wind*. His survey in *Saturday Review of Literature* labeled the text an enduring classic.

December 7, 1941

Throughout U.S. involvement in World War II, the writer/editor/zoologist issued tutorial pamphlets to the public on *Conservation in Action,* a 12-part series for the U.S. Fish and Wildlife Service. The brochures promoted wildlife sanctuaries through maps and illustrations by Shirley A. Briggs, Bob Hines, and Kay Howe. The author introduced citizens to six national wildlife refuges—Bear River, Chincoteague, Mattamuskeet, National Bison Refuge, Parker River, and Red Rocks Lake. Her editorial plan incorporated personal surveys of sanctuaries in Utah, Virginia, the North Carolina Outer Banks, Montana, and Massachusetts. She oversaw the accuracy of illustrations and insisted that the government printing office add color to black and white pages.

For 30 months, research into poison gas for military use informed Rachel of the expansion of organic herbicides and pesticides such as malathion and parathion to promote the war effort.

1942 March

Rachel spoke on eel research over a Washington radio program.

1942 May

As newly appointed assistant aquatic biologist at the Fishery Biology department of the U.S. Fish and Wildlife Service, the author acquired an office on the third floor and earned $216.67 a month for analyzing research and editing the marine journal *Progressive Fish-Culturalist*.

1942 August

During a governmental shuffling of posts to ease cramped Washington war offices, Rachel transferred to Chicago to work for a year in rented space for the Bureau of Fisheries of the U.S. Department of the Interior. Along with instruction in first aid and air raids, her assignment involved production of illustrated pamphlets on "Food from the Sea" covering 100 species.

1943

The military's proliferation of synthetic biocides raised Rachel's concern for environmental toxicity. She published a first brochure, "Fish and Shellfish of New England," which opened on the centrality of New England to colonial history and the fishing industry. The text introduced the home cook to anglerfish, wolffish, alewife, launce, dab, fluke, tautog, butterfish, scup, rosefish, squirrel hake, blackback flounder, yellowtail, and cusk along with the more familiar lemon sole, herring, mackerel, swordfish, cod, tuna, skate, haddock, pollock, mussels, shrimp, crabs, scallops, oysters, conch, lobsters, and clams.

1943 May

As associate aquatic biologist, Rachel relocated to Washington, worked in the information office of the U.S. Department of the Interior, and settled at Takoma Park, Maryland, with her mother. The new position carried a raise of $50 a month.

1943 July

The author published "Fishes of the Middle West," a 44-page pamphlet in the "Food from the Sea" series. To enlarge the wartime diet during shortages and rationing of meat and poultry, the text featured freshwater meat sources—buffalo fish, carp, burbot, bowfin, gar, pike, whitefish, sunfish, herring, trout, chub, perch, crappie, bluefin, sucker, catfish, bullhead, smelt, and sheepshead—from the Great Lakes and Mississippi River. She listed nutritional advantages of fish and shellfish in the diet and informed readers on preparation and storage.

1944

As an information specialist on fish and ocean wildlife, Rachel studied the underwater sounds of sea organisms and radar to help the navy identify submarines. She compiled a third brochure, "Fish and Shellfish of the South Atlantic and Gulf Coasts," which featured mullet, grouper, red snapper, bluefish, kingfish, pompano, grunt, black drum, redfish, pigfish, menhaden, snook, blue runner, crevalle, hard shell crab, and spiny lobster. The appendix followed her patterns of advocating consumption of seafood for its mineral value to the body. An essay on bats, "Ace of Nature's Aviators," received a rejection from *Reader's Digest,* which also denied the naturalist the post of science editor.

1944 March

Rachel's article "Ocean Wonderland" for the London *Transatlantic* required research at the Library of Congress. The feature reported on sea communities and predation at the Marineland aquarium south of St. Augustine, Florida, and appeared in reprint as "Indoor Ocean" in the June 1946 issue of *This Month*.

September 4, 1944

For *This Week*, the author wrote "Lifesaving Milkweed."

November 18, 1944

Collier's Weekly issued "The Bat Knew It First," Rachel's study of echolocation, nature's original sonar. She traced the winged mammal to the Eocene Era (60,000,000 BCE), but noted a previous ancestor, the clawed bat (*Onychonycteris finneyi*), that jumped, rather than flew, from tree to tree.

June 1, 1945

Rachel advanced to supervisor of staff writers for the U.S. Fish and Wildlife Service and moved to a larger house. Along with the revamping of tedious, ungrammatical prose for the series *Conservation in Action*, she wrote and distributed "Fish and Shellfish of the Middle Atlantic Coast." The 74-page bulletin, the last of the four "Food from the Sea" series, featured a map of the Atlantic coastline from New York to Cape Hatteras, North Carolina, and advice on 60 edible species, notably, oysters, crab, mackerel, menhaden, croaker, bass, porgy, shad, spot, herring, eel, whiting, kingfish, bonito, clam, and kingfish. Demand for her work limited creative writing and the advance of a career in freelance nonfiction. She barely had time to heat water for tea.

June 5, 1945

On a windy day, a government pilot's spraying of 17-acre Patuxent Wildlife Refuge on the north shore of Redington Lake, Maryland, northeast of Washington spread DDT. The project caused overspray and drift, imperiling some 20 fish species and unknown quantities of bird life. Reports alarmed Rachel with details of destruction and the illogic of food fish processors who fogged factories with insecticide. She composed press releases warning of the dangers of organic biocides.

July 7, 1945

Reader's Digest refused her proposal of an article on the effects of biocides because the topic was too grim. While attempting to reach a broad audience, she collected more rejection letters from *Coronet, Holiday, Science Digest, Ladies Home*

Journal, Tomorrow, Harper's, Scientific American, Town and Country, Saturday Evening Post, and *National Geographic.*

1945 August

During international acclaim over high-tech physics and chemistry, pesticide manufacturers heralded DDT as an "insect bomb," an allusion to the atomic explosions over Hiroshima on August 6 and Nagasaki on August 9, 1945. Exuberance for quick kills linked factory output and use of pesticides to patriotism. *Reader's Digest* reprinted "The Bat Knew It First," for which Rachel earned $500. The U.S. Navy reprised the article as training for radar operators.

1945 October

travel

The naturalist began a series of field trips to Hawk Mountain Sanctuary, a prize vantage lookout on hawks and bald eagles in east central Pennsylvania, where ancient seas once deposited the skeletons of small life forms. In a letter to the editor of the monthly *Outdoor Life,* she specified ornithology as her main hobby. She began the essay "Road of the Hawks," an unfinished survey that examined the Appalachian flyway as far back as the Paleozoic Age (542,000,000–251,000,000 BCE). The Carsons worried that intense research threatened Rachel's health.

health issues

1945 November

Coinciding with an appendectomy, submission to *Coronet* of "Sky Dwellers" on chimney swift migration became the author's second freelance sale in 1945. It earned $55. Initially refused by *Reader's Digest,* the article described migration of the chimney swift, which she originally called "The Ace of Nature's Aviators." Job requests to the National Audubon Society, *Reader's Digest,* and the New York Zoological Society received no offers.

1946 January

Rachel submitted to *Outdoor Life* the 1,000-word ecology essay "Why America's Natural Resources Must Be Conserved." Using maps and diagrams of flight patterns, she described a proactive restoration of wildlife on the Atlantic, Mississippi, Central, and Pacific flyways as investments in commerce and sport hunting. Her devotion to history of the wild featured avian migration as one of earth's most ancient and mysterious phenomena. To build consensus, she embedded pamphlets with appeals to groups of divergent interests and views on nature—hikers, bird watchers, fishers, hunters, campers, aesthetes, artists, and photographers.

March 31, 1946

After failing to sell an article on tern banding to *Saturday Evening Post* and *National Geographic,* the author issued "Long-Range Bird Migration" in *Holiday,* which paid her $500.

1946 April

Researching the new National Refuge System, Rachel went birding in Seneca, Maryland, and viewed migratory flyovers at Chincoteague on the south end of Assateague Island, a barrier isle on the Virginia shore. She typed up field notes on an upright Underwood typewriter. Her field work investigated Parker River in the Massachusetts marshland, home of the American black duck, snowy owl, Hudsonian godwit, and piping plover. The habitat provided foragers with plums, salt hay, and clams.

May 18, 1946

For the U.S. Department of the Interior Division of Information, Rachel composed a press release warning about DDT, which violated her sense of justice and propriety.

1946 June   *Maine vacation 1month*

With freelance writing still stalled by the war, Rachel sold only "Indoor Ocean," a five-page article for *This Month.* In a rented cabin, she and her mother enjoyed a month's accumulated vacation on Samoset Road along the Sheepscot River west of Boothbay Harbor, Maine. She reviewed lobster research at a federal hatchery overlooking Indiantown Island northeast of Portland. The respite initiated Rachel's 12 summer pilgrimages, which ecologist Stephanie Kaza compared to cyclical bird and fish migrations. In love with regional rambles, Rachel limited her observations to seaweeds and tidal pool invertebrates. She dreamed of owning a shore cottage where her soul could be "nourished and restored by the sea" (Kaza, 2010, 291).

1946 July

The author wrote in a letter her longing to buy land on the Maine shore and "spend a great deal of time in it—summers at least!" (*ibid.,* 291). She composed the ode "An Island I Remember," which remained unsold. A personal reverie on the passage of a day and movements of seals, warblers, herons, and cormorants amid spruce and huge hemlocks, the narrative reached a height of mystery at sunset with "broken, silvery cadences" of birdsong (Carson, "Island," 1946). She incorporated appreciation of commercial fishing and "the men who handle the nets [and] lived by their own toil" (*ibid.*)

September 28, 1946   *travel*

Accompanied by illustrator Kay Howe, Rachel surveyed wildlife and duck banding at Plum Island on the Parker River Refuge along the Atlantic Flyway in Montana and Utah and researched data in the Massachusetts Audubon Society library in Boston. She continued field work at the Oregon fish hatcheries and on the Merrimack River estuary in Lowell, Massachusetts. In a description of her work to the editor of *Outdoor Life,* she declared a love of tramping the wild, especially at the seashore, but admitted, "I suffer over writing, but do it anyway" (Steingruber, 2018, 318–319).

1946 December

The writer won second place and $1,000 for submitting to *Outdoor Life* a four-page essay on the Conservation Pledge. Maria Carson entered a hospital before Christmas for intestinal surgery.   *health*

1947

Rachel co-founded the Maine Nature Conservancy and directed the Washington, D.C. Audubon Society, for which she organized birdwatching field trips and denounced blood sport and steel animal traps. Rather than fill children's heads with facts and phyla, she encouraged curiosity about natural cycles and outrage at killing for sport, a prominent issue with members of the Society for the Prevention of Cruelty to Animals.

late January–February 2, 1947   *NC*

The author and artist Kay Howe surveyed the Mattamuskeet refuge on the Pamlico Sound in Hyde County, North Carolina, to observe hundreds of Canada geese and the whistling swan, an endangered species. The rain-fed lake, viewed by Sir Walter Raleigh in 1585, offered a natural habitat to tundra swans, snow geese, 18 species of ducks, largemouth and striped bass, catfish, and crappie.

1947 June

Unlike bleak federal leaflets, the author's 18-page illustrated pamphlet "Chincoteague: A National Wildlife Refuge" lauded protection of biodiversity on a migratory flyway of ducks, geese, and other waterfowl. A second bulletin, the 23-page

"Parker River: A National Wildlife Refuge," described recreation, bird watching, and photography. For the *Massachusetts Audubon Society Bulletin,* Rachel recycled her research as a 10-page article, "Parker River—A New England Conservation Project."

1947 July

Before traveling west, Rachel was hospitalized for a hemorrhoidectomy. Her subsequent pamphlet, "Mattamuskeet: A National Wildlife Refuge," a nine-page introduction to Mattamuskeet Lake, Pea Island, and Swanquarter, North Carolina, described mallards, pintails, goldeneyes, Canada geese, snow geese, and whistling swans inhabiting ancestral Algonquin lands.

September 21, 1947

On a month's train trip through heavy snow, Rachel and Kay Howe assessed the trumpeter swan migrations at the Red Rock Lakes wildlife sanctuary in Centennial Valley, Montana. Rachel also enjoyed views of moose, flickers, and bluebirds and photographed a porcupine before traveling on to Butte and Missoula.

September 29–30, 1947

From Ronan, Montana, Kay and Rachel explored Columbia River dams, fish ladders, and hatcheries and the Bear River refuge in Utah, noting the importance of protecting waterfowl. Despite constant work, Rachel feared "My life isn't at all well ordered and I don't know where I'm going" (Archer, 2016).

1948

In the year that the formulator of DDT won a Nobel Prize, at Orwigsburg north of Reading, Pennsylvania, Rachel continued monitoring raptors at the Hawk Mountain Sanctuary. At this point in her career, the U.S. Fish and Wildlife Service involved 120 biologists in marine surveillance and solving the problems of conservation.

1948 January

A bout of shingles slowed the author's work.

1948 February

For *Field and Stream,* Rachel wrote "The Great Red Tide Mystery," a discussion of the invasion in November 1947 of Captiva Island off Florida's gulf coast by *Gymnodinium* algae that flourished in sewage and farm runoff. The marine plankton produced algae blooms yielding natural toxins that killed herring, flounder, salmon, cod, pollock, manatee, dolphins, sea turtles, and coastal birds. Devastation extended 130 miles from Naples to Boca Grande.

1948 spring

To increase income from stand-alone essays, the author hired New Yorker Marie Freid Rodell as literary agent and executor of the Rachel Carson Trust for Living Environment. Rodell compiled the book *The Sense of Wonder* for Harper & Row containing touches of fairyland in lichens and an elfin bell ringer. Meanwhile, the author worked on the 46-page bulletin "Guarding Our Wildlife Resources," featuring the importance to citizens of fisheries, big game antelope and bison, beaver, whales, and bird families of dove, barn swallows, whooping cranes, Canada geese, trumpeter swans, and terns. Rachel's belief in hands-on outdoor experience impacted school curricula and endorsed field trips as a teaching alternative to lecture. Karen F. Stein, on staff at the University of Rhode Island, explained that "Facts, names, dates, and other details will follow once the child—or indeed any individual—has formed a personal relationship to a subject and is motivated to learn more" from "spiritual adventure" (Stein, 2014, 81).

December 19, 1948

The author visited her college mentor, Mary Scott Skinker, before the former professor died of cancer.

1949 May

After adopting a plan to sell individual chapters as she finished them, Rachel contributed "Lost Worlds: The Challenge of the Islands" to *Wood Thrush*, a publication issued by influential scientists at the Washington, D.C. Audubon Society.

June 28, 1949

Following a rejection by Simon & Schuster, Oxford University Press sent Rachel an advance of $1,000 for writing *The Sea Around Us*. Originally titled *Return to the Sea*, the narrative sensitized readers to the dynamics of the shores and the worth of marine fowl. Artist Kay Howe provided illustrations of ancient sea serpents and a chart of geologic eras. Rachel could not afford the rest of the drawings, which remained unpublished.

1949 July

Appointed editor-in-chief over a staff of six assistants, during a 15-year career with the U.S. Fish and Wildlife Service, the naturalist had less time for field research because she managed bureau publications, reviewed field reports for the *Fishery Bulletin*, outlined congressional testimony, ghost-wrote speeches, and super-intended the bureau library. Sailing off Miami on the 27-foot research vessel S.S. *Nauplius,* owned by the University of Miami, with net and specimen bucket, Rachel accomplished shallow dives. Climbing down the ship's ladder and clinging to the rungs, she equipped herself with an 84-pound copper helmet, lead boots, and an air hose. The plunges introduced her to shifting colors under the sea.

1949 late July

With a chaperone, agent Marie Rodell, Rachel sailed on the U.S. Fish and Wild-life trawler S.S. *Albatross III* around the Georges Banks fishing grounds through Nan-tucket Channel 200 miles off Boston and southwest of Nova Scotia. At first, agency policy allowed only men on their research voyages. As a crew member with 50 males, Rachel managed a 10-day North Atlantic field study using underwater lighting. Amid noise, fog, and damp, she examined with an echo sounder the causes of cod deple-tion and prowled the five-acre Boothbay Harbor for data on water temperatures. She rejected a job offer to join the New York Zoological Society.

1949 October

On a Eugene Saxton Memorial Fellowship of $2,250 commemorating the editor-in-chief at Harper & Brothers, Rachel enjoyed a month's leave to write on ocean waves and currents, tide patterns, sea floor topography, and islands. She con-tinued leave time in December and early 1950 with investigation of tidal ecology from northern New England to Florida. Her personae included a one-legged sand-erling, ghost crabs, sand dollars, plume worms (*Diapatra*), egrets, willets, and mud shrimp (*Callianassa*).

1950 mid–February

With input from specialists at Harvard and Yale, the author completed the pre-liminary text of *The Sea Around Us.* A first view of galleys for Oxford University Press raised issues of sans serif type and font size. She preferred Baskerville, Garamond, or its offshoot, Granjon.

1950 summer

Rachel traveled to Island Beach on New Jersey's Barnegat Peninsula east of Phil-adelphia to view birds on the barrier island and petition for its preservation. Her research into surf and wind resulted in specific wave data on whitecaps, swells, seas, and fetches: "How long it will live, how far it will travel, to what manner of end it will come" (Carson, 1951, 111).

1950 June

Rachel's book outsold Norwegian explorer Thor Heyerdahl's *Kon-Tiki*. In addition to selling 250,000 copies of *The Sea Around Us*, she submitted segments to *Science Digest, Popular Science,* and *Yale Review*. The *New Yorker* paid her $7,200 for nine chapters, which helped spike sales into the best seller range. *Atlantic Monthly* was prominent among the 15 magazines that rejected Rachel's submission.

Rachel issued a 13-page conservation booklet, "Bear River: A National Wildlife Refuge," featuring a map of the territory around the Great Salt Lake explored in winter 1824–1825 by Jim Bridger. Her perusal revealed the convergence of two bird migration paths, the Central and the Pacific, and the area's worth to culture, recreation, the economy, and wildlife. With Shirley A. Briggs, Rachel's survey of the Florida Everglades Refuge off the Tamiami Trail covered flat land and "upthrust masses of jagged coral rock" that once formed the basin of an ancient sea (Carson, 1951, 99). Her research extended to a dive of 15 feet, a landmark of aquatic investigation. At Nags Head, North Carolina, she tracked sanderlings.

1950 September

Yale Review paid Rachel $75 for the essay "The Birth of an Island," a chronology of the volcanic origins of Bermuda. The article, illustrated by a photo of an ash column arising from sea, won widespread academic regard.

September 21, 1950

Rachel underwent surgical removal of a tumor on her breast and convalesced at Nags Head on North Carolina's Outer Banks.

1950 October

The author sold "Wealth from the Salt Seas" to *Science Digest* and "The Global Thermostat" to *Vogue,* which introduced to readers the subject of climate change.

1950 December

In Cleveland, Ohio, the American Association for the Advancement of Science presented Rachel the $1,000 George Westinghouse Science Writing Prize for science magazines for one chapter, "The Birth of an Island."

1951 January

The author made *The Sea Around Us* the centerpiece of an ocean trilogy she had mentally compiled over much of her adult life, "although the actual writing of the book occupied only about three years" (Zwinger, 1989, xxi). In addition to dedicating the text to Harvard oceanographer Henry Bryant Bigelow, she acknowledged a network of associates and fellow scientists who corroborated and advanced her research. She consulted specialists at Harvard, Yale, Columbia, George Washington University, and the universities of Miami and Michigan along with the U.S. Coast and Geodetic Survey, American Museum of Natural History, U.S. Geological Survey, New York Public Library, and Scripps Institution of Oceanography. The narrative earned the praise of botanist Francis Raymond Fosberg, a researcher of atoll formation, for covering the birth of the oceans, tidal flow of New York's Bay of Fundy, ocean deterioration, and extinction of marine life. Similar respect came from global scientists in Goteborg, Sweden, and Oslo and Bergen, Norway, and at the International Council for the Exploration of the Sea.

1951 March

Rachel won a Simon Guggenheim Fellowship. The $1,000 purse underwrote a year's sabbatical. Because of mounting royalties, she returned the stipend to assist another applicant.

1951 May

Nature magazine published Rachel's eight-page essay "The Shape of Ancient Seas."

1951 early June

At a favorite shore, Bird Shoal in Beaufort, North Carolina, Rachel climbed over barnacles and waded in the Atlantic to view horseshoe crabs and sea anemones.

June 16, 1951

The *New Yorker* became what Gary Kroll termed a "conduit for transmitting environmental ideas" by serializing nine chapters of *The Sea Around Us,* the magazine's first non-human profile (Kroll, 2001, 404). Intended for an educated urban readership of some 5,000, the text, subtitled "A Profile of the Sea," earned Rachel $5,200 for introducing "that great mother of life, the sea" (Madera, 2017, 294).

June 20, 1951

The Women's National Press Club invited Rachel to its Willard Hotel headquarters at 14th and Pennsylvania NW as honored guest. At a time when the men-only National Press Club refused females entrance to banquets and limited their presence to the balcony, she allied with press women and female government employees and scientists. Gendered friendships and advice became integral to ecofeminism and preservation of the global landscape.

July 1, 1951

The *New York Times Book Review* featured *The Sea Around Us*. A physical description of the author in the Boston *Globe* refuted rumors that she was male. *Motor Boating* furthered Rachel's notoriety with the four-page excerpt "Moving Tides."

July 2, 1951

Oxford University's *The Sea Around Us,* an oceanographic biography and a *New York Times* bestseller, sold 250,000 copies in six months and remained a top seller for 86 weeks. In the most successful editions in 40 languages, the German translation sold 130,000 copies. The French compared Rachel's damning of pesticides to the dilemma of the sorcerer's apprentice and released excerpts on radio and in *Paris-Match*. At its 86-week height, the book brought Rachel literary respect and fame as a maven of natural history and financed a new binocular microscope.

July 7, 1951

Saturday Review editor Norman Cousins placed Rachel's picture on the cover, refuting rumors that she was a hardy aged male. To journalists from the *Washington Post* and the *Washington Daily News,* the author repined the loss of endangered species: "What has taken centuries to develop is being destroyed in a few years" (Lear, 1997, 202).

July 14, 1951

Brentano's book store in New York incorporated *The Sea Around Us* alongside taxidermied fish, coral, and seashells from the American Museum of Natural history in its window display.

1951 July–August

Rachel returned to Woods Hole to intensify marine research and gather data for a book on human fascination with waves and tides.

1951 mid–August

Rachel rented a cabin on Linekin Bay at Wall Point overlooking Lewis Cove and invited illustrator Robert "Bob" Hines and editor Marie Rodell to join her and her mother. In breaks from project work, the biologist inspected sea life across the channel at Ocean Point.

1951 fall

Book-of-the-Month Club featured *The Sea Around Us* as an alternate choice.

September 9, 1951

The Sea Around Us reached top spot on the *New York Times* bestselling nonfiction list.

September 11, 1951

Look magazine featured the author and her successful *The Sea Around Us.*

September 25, 1951

In company with Bess and Harry Truman at Washington's Mayflower Hotel, Rachel addressed a benefit lunch for the National Symphony Orchestra with remarks about the impact of oceans and sky on the writing of Finnish musician Jean Sibelius and Russian composer Nikolai Rimsky-Korsakov and on French impressionist Claude Debussy's symphonic masterwork *La Mer*. She extolled a marine influence on survivors of difficulties: "People everywhere are desperately eager for whatever will lift them out of themselves" and restore their hope (Carson, "National," 1951). She viewed art and music as necessary to people coping with the atomic age and the possibility that more A-bombs would end the Korean War. On the liner notes of Arturo Toscanini's performance of *La Mer,* she found comfort in "the implacable, inexorable power" of ancient seas (Carson, "Liner," 1951).

October 16, 1951

On an invitation from Irita Van Doren, the editor of the *New York Herald Tribune Book Review,* Rachel addressed 1,500 attendees at the Books and Authors Luncheon at the Astor Hotel, from which WNYC broadcast the event. Hydrophone recordings of sounds from porpoises, shrimp, fish, and whales illustrated her 20-minute talk. The topic enlarged on female contributions to science and mused on "the great antiquity of the earth" from the Silurian Era (440,000,000 BCE), when tide pools housed "those early pioneers from the sea" (Carson, speech, 1951).

1951 November

Popular Science printed the naturalist's views on "Why Our Winters Are Getting Warmer," which pictured Manhattan inundated by the Atlantic Ocean. She credited deep sea tides with influencing climate change.

December 2, 1951

Rachel's "A Treasure Chest of Favorite Sea Books" appeared in the *Washington Post*.

December 7, 1951

The author made a guest appearance on the Cunard line's RMS *Mauretania,* the world's largest ocean liner, where she presented the captain an autographed copy of *The Sea Around Us.*

December 17, 1951

Newsweek profiled Rachel Carson and the success of her bestseller.

December 25, 1951

Oxford Press paid Rachel $20,000 for permission to reissue *The Sea Around Us.* The outpouring of respect and notoriety coincided with her worry about Marjie's affair with a married man and the birth of illegitimate son Roger Allen Christie two months later.

1952

"The Birth of an Island," an excerpt of *The Sea Around Us,* appeared in *Reader's Digest, Pageant,* and *Saturday Review.* Among its themes, she rebutted notions that humankind could control nature via chemicals, bombs, or space exploration. The book won a *New York Times* best nonfiction of 1951 citation.

1952 January

Glamour magazine spotlighted shell-decked and sand-toned accessories, hats, and jewelry spun off from *The Sea Around Us.*

January 9, 1952

From the Geographical Society of Philadelphia, the writer became the first woman to achieve the Henry Grier Bryant Gold Medal for distinguished service to oceanography and a cash prize. The Associated Press named her "Woman of the Year in Literature."

January 27, 1952

After scrutiny by a panel of writers, Rachel's second nature compendium beat 16 competitors for a $10,000 National Book Award for Nonfiction from the National Book Foundation. Along with fellow winners—poet Marianne Moore and James Ramon Jones, author of the novel *From Here to Eternity*—Rachel appeared at the Hotel Commodore in New York. Her acceptance speech deflated the notion that scientists were elite experts who dwelt apart, "isolated and priest-like in their laboratories" (Lear, 1997, 218). To the audience, she exemplified the juncture of a double major in English composition and biology. She stressed, "No one could write truthfully about the sea and leave out poetry" (Carson, 1952, 128).

February 17, 1952

The *New York Herald Tribune* extolled *The Sea Around Us* for appearing on 60 lists of notable books compiled by the American Library Association.

April 7, 1952

To her complete satisfaction, Rachel received a John Burroughs Medal for nature writing from New York's American Museum of Natural History. Her acceptance speech "Design for Nature Writing," reminded hearers of the audacity and self-adulation that caused humankind to experiment with destruction, an allusion to the bombing of Hiroshima and Nagasaki, Japan, on August 6 and August 8, 1945. In place of anthropocentric science, she advocated individual curiosity and professional humility. For distinguished service to conservation, the Garden Club of America presented her the Frances K. Hutchinson Medal, named for Frances Kinsley Hutchinson, the founder of the Lake Geneva Garden Club.

April 13, 1952

A second release of *Under the Sea Wind* by Oxford University Press resulted in a bestseller that buoyed Rachel to public and academic acclaim.

April 14, 1952

Along with articles on photojournalist Margaret Bourke-White, author Truman Capote, and atomic artillery, *Life* magazine excerpted *Under the Sea Wind* in the 18-page entry "The Edge of the Sea," featuring original illustrations by Maryland artist Rudolph Freund.

April 17, 1952

Rachel's evening trek on Saint Simon Island, Georgia, past the Coast Guard Station extended a broad swathe of sand to view. As dark approached at 7:30 p.m., her thoughts turned to sounds of wind, gentle surf, and the birds of the open sea and salt marsh.

April 27, 1952

The *New York Times* declared Rachel's two books a literary phenomenon as unusual as a total eclipse of the sun.

1952 early May

Rachel's alma mater, Pennsylvania College for Women, presented her a Distinguished Service Alumnae Award. She was pleased to be named an authority on biology whom others cited as an expert. The *Atlantic Naturalist* published the author's advice in the three-page speech "Design for Nature Writing."

With wildlife illustrator Bob Hines, Rachel collected specimens from a three-week dive in the Florida Keys. At Ohio Key three-quarters of the way down the island string, she encountered a sea hare (*Dolabella auricularia*), a sea mollusk. After Bob's detailed examination and pencil sketching, she returned each living organism to the water. Pushing physical limits in a mangrove ghost swamp left her depleted.

May 16, 1952

"The Harbor," an excerpt from *The Sea Around Us,* appeared in the *Falmouth Enterprise.*

May 25, 1952

This Week featured one of Rachel's more poetic meditations, "The Exceeding Beauty of the Earth—Words to Live By" the same day that the New York *Herald-Tribune* published "The Land Around Us." She reprised a belief that nature's mystic tides, seasons, and bird migrations eased human stress over global tensions.

1952 June

In mid-career, the marine biologist left her federal service post as chief editor of U.S. fisheries publications to become a full-time freelance science writer and speaker on issues of wilderness conservation. Little of her office records remained, only her magnifying glass. No immediate relative asked for her agency files. Recovery of office memoranda in 1970 retrieved a comment about trumpeter swans. At commencements, Rachel received honorary Ph.Ds from Oberlin College in Oberlin, Ohio, and the Drexel Institute of Technology in Philadelphia. At a luncheon, she thanked the Drexel faculty for acknowledging and encouraging science writers.

1952 July

The scientist arranged a sabbatical to Woods Hole to begin defining coastal bird life in marshes, shallows, and tide pools in *The Edge of the Sea*. Wading the Atlantic coast from Maine rock pools as far south as mangrove forests in the subtropics gave her intense joy. On Dogfish Head, a rocky ascent above Sheepscot Bay at West Southport, Maine, she built an island cottage across from Georgetown Island. The purchase included "my own small tract of woodland" and access to the Atlantic Ocean, where she browsed the 140-foot shoreline each summer (Carson, 1965, 14). From observation of seals and whales along the eastern seaboard, she gleaned a unique scan of marine life.

1952 November

The Sea Around Us sold 100,000 copies at the rate of 28,000 per week and reached 250,000 copies before the New Year. Readers could purchase it in 32 languages. The National Institute of Arts and Letters in the United States, established in 1898, named her the second female to be honored after poet Julia Ward Howe.

December 25, 1952

The author toured Sanibel and the Marco Islands on the gulf shore of Florida and, at Ten Thousand Islands, combed barrier shoals for shells. She continued examining coastal communities at the tidal flats of St. Simons Island, Georgia, and Bears Bluff and Myrtle Beach, South Carolina, and filled notebooks with natural backdrops.

Author Irwin Allen revamped Rachel's *The Sea Around Us* into a 62-minute color documentary film for RKO. The finished work accentuated the world's dependence on sea species for 30 percent of human food. Although limited by budget constraints, the movie featured underwater camerawork donated by expeditioners, librarians, and oceanographers examining microscopic biota plus sharks, octopi, and whales from Marineland and Tarpon Springs, Florida, seals on Alaska's Pribilof Islands, and corals on Australia's Great Barrier Reef. Textual conclusions warned of global warming, glacial melting, a rise of oceans 100 feet, and a global cataclysm in world climate, which the tides controlled.

The winner of an Academy Award, the film listed 2,341 sources and earned reviews from *Time, Newsweek,* and the *New York Times* and *Los Angeles Daily News* but not the approval of the *Washington Post* or the author. Because the documentary corrupted her text with praise for sea sports and speargun hunting and with archaic thinking and cartoonish voiceovers for cormorant, dolphin and porpoise, octopus, and shark, she rebuffed future contracts for cinematic versions of her work. She considered a lawsuit charging RKO with errors and distortions.

January 14, 1953

At the Barclay Hotel in Philadelphia, the celebrity author accepted a gold medal from the New York Zoological Society, which had previously rejected her application for a job.

January 20, 1953

Rachel feared that the election of President Dwight D. Eisenhower threatened conservation projects completed by the previous earth-friendly administration of four-term president Franklin D. Roosevelt.

1953 March

The author vacationed at Myrtle Beach, South Carolina.

April 22, 1953

While Rachel conducted studies of shore life and ecosystems off Maine, the Carolinas, and Florida, she responded to the Republican backlash against ecological protection. In a letter to the editor of the *Washington Post,* she protested the replacement of Secretary of the Interior Albert M. Day, a 35-year veteran, with one of a series of inexperienced political appointees. Her message claimed that government hiring policies favored party cronies, lumbermen, and mining concerns rather than competent professionals. The unwise choice portended a "raid upon our natural resources that is without parallel within the present century" (Carson, 1953, A26). Three months later, *Reader's Digest* reissued the letter, which warned of "unrestrained exploitation and destruction" and called for national defense from within (Steingruber, 2018, 326).

1953 June

From Smith College in Northampton, Massachusetts, Rachel added a fourth Ph.D. to her honoraria.

1953 July

While living with her mother on West Southport Island, Maine, Rachel bought the cottage Silverledges overlooking Boothbay Harbor and viewed the Atlantic underwater from a diving helmet. Her home exhibited shells, sea glass, and books on the sea. Readings to her two-year-old great-nephew Roger included the Beatrix Potter works she had loved in childhood. Recordings taught him to identify birdsong. Rachel formed a long-lived relationship and a 12-year correspondence with a Maine couple, Dorothy and Stanley Freeman, parents of a son, Stanley Freeman, Jr.

1953 September

In one self-revelation, Rachel admitted to being overwrought by a demanding manuscript that required extensive rewriting and expansion. Family responsibilities left her housebound: "It's the feeling that there is no way out that gets me down" (Freeman, 1995, 45). The letters remain at the Ladd Library, Bates College, in Lewiston, Maine.

1953 mid–October

The author and foster mother began exposing great-nephew Roger at age 20 months to visual, auditory, tactical, and olfactory elements of the outdoors. Wrapped in a blanket, he enjoyed a first encounter with the Atlantic Ocean by night. Two nights later, she guided him by flashlight on a search for periwinkles and "ghos" crabs (Carson, 1965, 10). Rachel intended to instill an awareness of nature's daily renewal.

October 26, 1953

After condensation in the *New Yorker, The Edge of the Sea,* a new version of *Under the Sea Wind: A Naturalist's Picture of Ocean Life,* completed Carson's oceanographic trilogy. She dedicated the work to the Freemans. Saks Fifth Avenue chose the marine theme for window decor on leisurely beach togs.

November 5–6, 1953

In a letter from Myrtle Beach, South Carolina, Rachel described seeing porpoises and helping Roger find shore treasures—reef sponges, worm tubes, sea squirts, starfish, urchins, an octopus, and horseshoe crabs.

December 29, 1953

At The Hub, a prestigious Boston hotel, Rachel made a presentation on the sea frontier at a six-day symposium "Water for Industry" hosted by the American

Association for the Advancement of Science. She ventured into academic diction in a scholarly 13-page paper, "The Edge of the Sea." The topic itemized changes to marine propagation from the steady rise of water temperature. She concluded, "Nothing lives to itself," a controlling theme of her later works (Carson, 1953).

1954

The Royal Society of Literature in England named Rachel a fellow; the U.S. Department of the Interior conferred on her a medal for distinguished service. In a review for the *Western North American Naturalist,* John D. Rothlisberger, a biologist at Notre Dame, observed how she developed a "network of support, likened to an interdependent ecological network, ... through her familial, educational, professional, and platonic relationships" (Rothlisberger, 2009, 145). He declared scientific collegiality "crucial to her persistence and success" (*ibid.*).

1954 January

Rachel described correspondence with Dorothy as "appearing in your mail practically every day" (Steingruber, 2018, 333).

April 9, 1954

In Bloomfield Hills, Michigan, at the Cranbrook Institute of Science, the author presented a slide show at her lecture on "The Edge of the Sea."

April 21, 1954

In "The Real World Around Us," an address in Columbus, Ohio, at the Matrix Table Dinner of Theta Sigma Phi, a national sorority of female journalists, Rachel stated a childhood assumption that she would be a writer. To some 1,000 attendees, she summarized her spiritual response to nature. In an era of "man-made ugliness," her credo valued outdoor beauty as integral to the soul's integrity (Carson, 1954).

Of the growth of humanity during youth, the author reflected on childhood solitude, a time to observe waterways, flowers, birds, and insects. The narrative remarked on an "absolute fascination for everything related to the ocean" (*ibid.*). In reference to urban artificiality and concrete infrastructure, she reminded the audience of the importance of woodlands and streams to ease overwork and heal the troubled spirit.

May 11, 1954

The Limited Editions Club awarded the author the Jubilee Silver Medal and proclaimed her an American writer whose work would survive with the classics.

1954 December

Rachel presented a lecture with slides to Audubon Society Members in Washington, D.C.

1955

On Southport Island, Maine, the naturalist surveyed tide pools and catalogued specimens from a constantly shifting milieu.

1955 May

To extend observation with photos, the author bought an Exakta, a 35 mm. German camera adaptable to microscope and medical use. She learned to shoot landmarks, moss, and flowers as well as organisms up to five feet under the surface of the sea.

May 13, 1955

The author used Stanley Freeman's slides to illustrate a benefit lecture at the Lincoln County Cultural and Historical Association in Wiscasset, Maine.

1955 June

Incorporating research from beaches to global ocean depths, *The Edge of the Sea* completed the author's marine trilogy. The third volume faced competition on the *New York Times* bestseller list from poet Anne Morrow Lindbergh's *Gift from the Sea*. Rachel's bestseller became a Book-of-the-Month Club alternate and a Penguin Nature Classic and gained the author interviews and requests for speeches. By late in the month, Rachel could retreat to Maine with her mother to await publication of her book.

1955 July

The author scripted "Something about the Sky" for CBS-TV *Omnibus,* continued submitting articles to magazines, and proposed a book on evolution and an environmental monograph called *Remembrance of the Earth*. During activities for the Maine Nature Conservancy, she and Dorothy proposed buying the "Lost Woods," a 78-acre tract near the beach cottage.

August 20 and 27, 1955

Two weekly excerpts of *The Edge of the Sea* appeared in the *New Yorker.* By purchasing an adjacent lot, Rachel extended her Maine shoreline to 350 feet.

October 26, 1955

With the aid of a housekeeper and assistant Dorothy Algire, the author was able to publish *The Edge of the Sea* complete with a taxonomic appendix. Well wishers applauded the work in Manhattan at a book release party on West 52nd Street at the 21 Club.

November 8, 1955

The Boston Museum of Science named Rachel an honorary fellow. Later in the month, *The Edge of the Sea* reached the level of bestseller.

November 27, 1955

In New York City, the author accepted the annual nonfiction award from the National Council of Women of the United States.

December 13, 1955

Rachel agreed to lecture to the Washington, D.C., Audubon Society.

1956 February

Reader's Digest condensed *The Edge of the Sea* under the title "The Mystery of Life at the Seashore."

March 11, 1956

CBS-TV broadcast on *Omnibus* Rachel's documentary "Something about the Sky," an engaging introduction to cloud types and significance that she and her family viewed on her brother's television.

1956 April

While the author vacationed with friends in Radnor, Pennsylvania, she planned to purchase forested property adjacent to her beach house in Southport, Maine.

June 22, 1956

Before receiving an achievement award at a state presidents' conference in Washington Sheraton-Park Hotel, Rachel wrote a four-page letter to Mrs. Boyette, president of the American Association of University Women. She declared a break-through in biology: "The old, man-made barriers between the sciences are breaking down, and it is now acknowledged that, whatever else life may be, it is to an important extent a chemical and physical process" (Carson, 1956). She addressed the Social and Economic Issues Committee on a book about new frontiers in biology that she planned to write with the $2,500 stipend. She observed, "The subject chooses the writer, not the other way around" ("Rachel Carson Wins," 1956, 19). The book she had in mind evolved into *Silent Spring*.

1956 late July

Arriving late to the cottage because of Maria's arthritis, Rachel arranged her day's work at a lap board in bed with a tape deck for recording edited changes. In the afternoon, she read mail and left responses for her secretary. Telephone messages from nephew Roger's principal demanded attention. The author had to refuse an oceanographic expedition to Tonga planned for Christmas 1956.

As a source of renewal, the author's outpouring of essays included "Help Your Child to Wonder" for *Woman's Home Companion*, an autobiographical subject that detailed her enthusiasm for nature and the satisfaction that strengthened her. To express a mounting ecological catastrophe, Rachel's essay "On the Biological Sciences" for *Good Reading* identified the interconnections of human life and nature—Dutch elm trees, insect and avian life, rodents, waterways, pastures, and dairy herds.

August 8, 1956

During a stirring tide, Rachel aided a firefly caught in the flickering surge and considered writing a children's story about the insect's confusion.

1956 September

Reader's Digest issued a condensed version of "Help Your Child to Wonder."

November 26, 1956

To protect the Maine wilds, the author became honorary board chair of the Maine Nature Conservancy. Established in 1951 in Arlington, Virginia, the environmental crusade fostered renewable energy, climate change adaptation, imperiled species, coral reefs, lakes, and rivers through the action of 600 scientists worldwide.

December 12, 1956

Rachel yearned to invest in the Lost Woods on Southport Island between Deep Cove and Dogfish Head in coastal Maine. In a letter to Curtis and Nellie Lee Bok, she rhapsodized on the intricacy of a mile-long beachhead restored from a forest fire by natural forces and swathed in mosses and lichen: "It is a treasure of a place to which I have lost my heart completely" (Carson, letter, 1956). She ended her 49th year with upbeat hopes for her career and royalties of $100,000 and requested advice on establishing a foundation as a tax shelter.

January 30, 1957

At the death of 31-year-old niece Marjorie Williams from anemia, pneumonia, and diabetes, Rachel, approaching age 50, adopted her five-year-old great-nephew, Roger Allen Christie. Though fearful of her lack of knowledge about little boys, she reared him at home on 204 Williamsburg Drive in Quaint Acres, Silver Spring, Maryland. He required treatment for respiratory ills and an eye disease. Meanwhile, the author planned on enlarging her Maine getaway with a study, bedrooms, and a porch where she could experience tidal vibrations.

March 11, 1957

CBS *Omnibus* presented "Clouds," a program that Rachel scripted for the Ford Foundation TV-Radio Workshop. She highlighted the dynamics of water and wind in forming sky cover in all seasons of the year. The broadcast revived her concern for world climate change.

June 20, 1957

Rachel and friend Olga Owens Huckins, a bird watcher, organic gardener, and writer for the media, joined members of Duxbury, Massachusetts, Committee Against Mass Poisoning. The advocates posted letters to newspaper editors in Long Island and New England about an eco-crisis—aerial spraying of DDT, which killed birds. Huckins considered the invasions of private property vicious and unconstitutional.

1957 July

Rachel designed a brick ranch house at 11707 Berwick Road, Montgomery County, in Colesville, Maryland, west of Chesapeake Bay, featuring built-in book shelves, a display of seashells in the birch-paneled office, a stone fireplace, and a mirror over the kitchen sink that facilitated birdwatching while she washed dishes. After its completion in 1956, she surrounded her home with pink and white azaleas, spruce, white pine, hemlock, Maine birch, Dutch iris, and daffodil beds.

1957 October–November

The flights of Sputnik I and II violated Rachel's views on space and introduced new possibilities for war.

1958

While writing and reading lines aloud in the Colesville den, Rachel enjoyed her cat Jeffie and listening to Beethoven's "Violin Concerto." Simon & Schuster convinced her to expand the outreach for nature with *The Sea Around Us: A Special Edition for Young Readers,* co-authored by Anne Terry White, a Ukrainian children's book author, to suit the interests of middle and high school readers. The layout of maps, line drawings, 150 coastal photos increased visual appeal. Rachel earmarked profits to support the Carson family and to purchase as a refuge nearby forested land that she dubbed the "Lost Woods." In private dealings with William Shawn, editor of the *New Yorker,* she accepted an assignment to compose a 50,000-word article on DDT.

1958 January

After a letter to the *Boston Herald* from Olga Owens Huckins alerted the author to avian death in Plymouth County, Massachusetts, from pesticide spray, Rachel gathered data from Washington libraries on genetics, physiology, and biochemistry and discovered that "a lot of isolated pieces of the jigsaw puzzle have suddenly fallen into place" (Koehn, 2012). She hired pre-med student Bette Haney, a biology major at Bryn Mawr College, as research assistant to comb resources in scientific libraries and at the Audubon Society, National Institutes of Health, and Smithsonian Institution and to compile 55 pages of endnotes substantiating the research. The project aroused opposition from the U.S. Department of Agriculture and the U.S. Department of the Interior.

January 27, 1958

Rachel notified the editor of *Reader's Digest* that a proposed pro-pesticide article courted danger by advocating killing with aerial spray such useful insects as bees and grasshoppers. On her way to an epoch-making cautionary tale, she realized, "Nothing I could do would be more important" (Woods, Johnson, Fellows, 2007, 12).

In a pine-scented room, Rachel began the 64-month compilation of *Silent Spring*, the landmark eco-manifesto on synthetic herbicide and pesticide damage that she tentatively entitled "Man Against the Earth." Robert McCrum, a London journalist for *The Guardian,* called her warnings "a classic of American advocacy" for exposing half-truths and the sugarcoating of scientific horror stories, especially the widespread death of robins (McCrum, 2016). She considered collaborating with *Newsweek* and the *New Yorker.*

February 1, 1958

Rachel's letter to Dorothy Freeman admitted that the nagging fears of human extinction required action "to acknowledge what I couldn't help seeing" and couldn't shut out (Carson, 1958).

1958 mid–July

To relieve a duodenal ulcer, the author took a vacation from work before returning to interviews and adding articles and letters from experts to her files. For the six-page essay "Our Ever-Changing Shore" in a special issue of *Holiday,* she wrote of the sea's sublimity and its existence apart from human strivings.

1958 fall

Maria's stroke forced Rachel into full-time caregiving at home. On free time, she taught Roger how to identify birdsong. The pressure of balancing work with home duties raised "conflict that just tears me to pieces" (Quaratiello, 2010, xiv). She incurred a bout of pneumonia.

December 1, 1958

At age 89, Rachel's mother died at Silver Spring of pneumonia, stroke, and cardiac disease. Within months, Rachel's great nephew became sick with a respiratory infection. She warned her editor that compilation was slow, but acknowledged to Dorothy Freeman that "there would be no future peace for me if I kept silent" (Koehn, 2012). Meanwhile, she worked harder for herself than she ever did for a boss. Editor Paul Brooks suggested a title: *Silent Spring.* The blockbuster, according to nature writer Bill McKibben, began "knocking the shine off modernity" (McKibben, 2019, 73).

1959

Rachel delved into the multiple aspects of insect control by researching details at the National Institutes of Health and National Cancer Institute and by corresponding with doctors, geneticists, and specialists in organic farming, bird and insect survival, and water quality.

1959 February

The researcher gained broader insight in New York by attending sessions of the National Wildlife Federation.

February 14, 1959

The author decided to concentrate on the threat to human health that pesticides "inflicted upon us [from] slow, cumulative and hard-to-identify long term effects" (Carson, letter, 1959). In correspondence with editor William Shawn, she balanced hard facts about infants fed on contaminated milk with hopeful experiments replacing pesticides with insect sterilization and natural predators.

April 10, 1959

In response to an editorial printed on March 30, 1959, with data from the National Audubon Society, Rachel's letter "Vanishing Americans" to the *Washington Post* alerted readers to a drop in bird populations and less interaction between middle-class homeowners and nesting songbirds, a passion she shared with Lady Bird Johnson. The author connected a "rain of death" with the post–World War II nerve gases consisting "of highly poisonous hydrocarbons and of organic phosphates" (Carson, 1959, A26).

April 12, 1959

In a letter to friend Beverly Knecht, Rachel considered dedicating her major work to Albert Schweitzer, who believed, "Modern man has lost the capacity to foresee or to forestall. He will end by destroying the earth" (Carson, "Knecht," 1959).

April 16, 1959

Rachel's correspondence with Lois Crisler, author of *Arctic Wild,* charged the U.S. Fish and Wildlife Service with creating a "black picture" by labeling animals as "vermin" and poisoning such desert creatures as prairie dogs to rid the area of predators (Cafaro, 2002, 73).

May 20, 1959

A letter from Rachel to R.D. Radeleff, a specialist at the Animal Disease and Parasite Research Division of the U.S. Agricultural Research Service, sought the particulars about heptachlor and its part in killing livestock and poultry.

October 17, 1959

The author showed Stan's slides as part of her address to the Washington, D.C., Audubon Society, at the Brookings Institution, a research consortium on Dupont Circle in Washington, D.C.

November 9, 1959

In Washington, D.C., Arthur Sherwood Flemming, Secretary of the U.S. Department of Health, Education, and Welfare, announced significant cranberry contamination from aminotriazole, a carcinogenic herbicide. Before Christmas, the U.S. Department of Agriculture removed tainted cranberries from grocery stores.

November 18, 1959

At a public hearing, Rachel viewed efforts by industrial chemists to deny dangers by refuting scientific evidence. She anchored her research to data from the medical library of the National Institutes of Health on carcinogens and neurological and immune system toxins. As she investigated, she asked scientists to corroborate her findings. When she requested a legislator's statement about food contamination, his office worker quivered, "You frighten me" (Carson, letter, 1959).

December 3, 1959

Rachel began to feel "my thinking on [the health hazards of pesticides] has begun to fit together" (Carson, letter, 1959). She believed that the public was ready to hear the facts.

1960

For the Animal Welfare Institute, the author wrote "To Understand Biology," a four-page preface published in the 41-page pamphlet *Humane Biology Projects*. The ethical guide advised educators to remove from classroom study and science fairs the brutal, unconscionable treatment of specimen and laboratory animals. Rachel based her philosophy on Albert Schweitzer's advocacy of respect for life. As part of the child's humanity, she recommended "awareness and reverence for the wholeness of life" (Carson, 1960, iv). The commentary sought to rid biological science of artificiality, callousness, and "unnatural conditions" that encouraged disrespect and prejudices in students for animal rights and feelings, such as the blinding and starving of birds, frog vivisection, and the launching of rockets containing mice (*ibid.*).

1960 January

Viral pneumonia, sinus infection, more breast lesions, and a duodenal ulcer plus Roger's virus sidelined Rachel and interrupted completion of *Silent Spring*.

1960 February

The aerial proliferation of weed and insect killers mixed with fuel oil killed birds, causing the author "anger at the senseless, brutish things that were being done" (Koehn, 2012). She requested that a major advocate, *New Yorker* essayist and editor Elwyn Brooks White, attack the issue, which he agreed "starts in the kitchen and extends to Jupiter and Mars" (Doyle, 2012). At his refusal to write about biocides, she accepted the challenge of leading an environmental revolution.

April 4, 1960

Although one of the two cysts on Rachel's left breast required a radical mastectomy in Washington's Doctor's Hospital, a ten-story complex at 1815 I Street NW, she found doctors unwilling to provide an outlook for survival to an unmarried woman. She began a private study of physiological changes caused by cancer and documented a possible link between tumors and chemical poisons.

April 11, 1960

Before the biologist left the hospital April 9, her surgeon, Dr. Fred Sanderson, ordered no further radiation and concealed from her that the malignancy had spread to lymph nodes on the left pectoral muscle. Lest chemical companies renew attacks, Rachel concealed from the press the cancer and treatment with Krebiozen, a useless drug comprised largely of creatinine from horse blood and mineral oil and sold for $170,000 per gram. In October 1964, a court charged promoter Stephan Durovic, a Yugoslav refugee, with violating interstate law in marketing his bogus cure throughout the United States.

June 8, 1960

Despite overwork and time restraints that Rachel compared to climbing Everest, she volunteered to aid the Democratic National Committee in formulating a platform issue for U.S. Senator John F. Kennedy's presidential campaign. Her advice covered pollution control of radiation in the sea and rescuing natural areas for wildlife conservation and recreation.

June 12, 1960

At the office of William Shawn, editor of the *New Yorker*, Rachel made her case for a world-changing manuscript. His reply: "One doesn't condone murder" (Carson, 1958). He hired her as "Reporter at Large" and a prime source on ecology for the average reader. She composed a chapter on the rifling of oceans for profit, then omitted the theme of wealth from marine resources lest readers use her words to justify overfishing.

1960 November

Discovery of an aggressive growth in the left ribs forced Rachel to seek diagnosis from Dr. George Crile at the Cleveland Clinic, where she learned that previous physicians had not reported metastatic cancer. On the flight home, she pondered mortality and the time she had left to finish her project.

1960 mid–November

Sick with flu, the author missed the Water Pollution Conference on November 18, 1960, at Michigan State University, Ann Arbor. At home, she continued cross-discipline readings in biology, chemistry, medicine, and physiology and returned to Hawk Mountain, Pennsylvania, to analyze changes in raptor migrations.

1960 December

Metastatic cancer in the lymph nodes and radiation treatment further slowed Rachel's work on a second edition of *The Sea Around Us,* to which she added footnotes and an updated preface. Her work reported advances in oceanography by the bathyscaphe *Trieste,* a two-person submersible that had plumbed earth's lowest point on January 23, 1960, to observe the Mariana Trench east of Guam at a depth of 30,000 feet. For the chapter "Surface Waters and Underground Seas," she incorporated data from the U.S. Fish and Wildlife Service on the accumulation of DDT in fish from contaminated groundwater.

1961

Early in the year, Rachel learned from the Welder Wildlife Foundation in Sinton, Texas, about DDD (dichlorodiphenyldichloroethane) that accumulated in plankton specimens from Clear Lake, California. She also gathered research on biocides in KIamath Lake, Oregon, and Tule Lake, California, where toxic DDE (dichlorodiphenyldichloroethylene) killed pelicans, cormorants, and other fish-eating waterbirds.

1961 January

Two months of cobalt radiation sapped and nauseated the biologist and reduced her immunity, resulting in learning to walk again because of rheumatoid arthritis of the ankles and knees. She suffered a urinary tract infection, staph infection and phlebitis in her lower limbs, and a resurgence of the duodenal ulcer. Iritis threatened her vision and limited office hours each day. She prayed to return to Maine and, a year later, confided to Dorothy Freeman, "Such a catalogue of illness! If one were superstitious it would be easy to believe in some malevolent influence at work" (Carson, letter, 1962).

January 18, 1961

At John F. Kennedy's inauguration, Rachel joined supporters for a reception of Distinguished Ladies on the Washington Mall at the National Gallery of Art.

1961 late spring

Persistent sickness compromised Rachel's ability to concentrate and write until late spring, when she propped on pillows and continued her book. Reliance on a wheelchair left unresolved her ability to walk again.

1961 summer

The author enjoyed a physical restoration and once more trekked to New England. According to ecologist Stephanie Kaza, "The cottage in Maine was crucial to Carson's urgent need to finish the massive piece of work she had undertaken" (Kaza, 2010, 296). Her letter to the *Boothbay Register* informed Maine residents of the danger of spraying the region to quell Dutch elm disease. The letter caused a mild frisson nationwide when other media reprised her warning.

1961 December

Although a corneal infection interrupted Rachel's schedule in November, she submitted much of her text to Shawn. His admiration for her research brought tears of satisfaction that the job was nearly complete.

1962

Rachel acquired from the Food Safety Committee of the League of Women Voters in Swarthmore, Pennsylvania, a pamphlet warning of chemical contaminants in edibles consumed by humans and domestic pets. She persisted in demanding data on the concentrations of pesticides in human tissue. Her loss of patience with extremists resulted in criticism: "They often start off excellently … but they always go too far" (Free, 1963, A17).

1962 January

Dickering between continuing research or using her last months to write a shorter book, Rachel chose to follow the original outline, which she posted to the *New Yorker*. Shawn considered it beautiful, moving, and brilliant; Elwyn Brooks White valued it above any other article in the magazine. Happy at the accomplishment, she arrived at the office to watch the final edit and issued proofs to ecofeminists at the Children's Bureau, National Council of Jewish Women, National Federation of Women's Clubs, and U.S. congresswoman from Oregon Edith Starrett Green, U.S. senator from Oregon Maurine Brown Neuberger, and U.S. congresswoman Leonor Kretzer Sullivan, the first female legislator from Missouri.

February 8, 1962

In a letter to wilderness writer Lois Brown Crisler, an instructor at the University of Washington, Rachel commented on the tone of *Silent Spring*: "I myself never thought the ugly facts would dominate, and I hope they don't" (Carson, letter, 1962). The author also doubted that "one book could bring a complete change," evidence of undervaluation of her activism on global science (*ibid.*).

1962 March

Radiation treatment continued at the Cleveland Clinic.

May 15, 1962

To shield citizen rights to a safe home, Rachel attended a White House Conference on Conservation that issued a report, "The Uses of Pesticides."

May 19, 1962

A busy evening in Washington, D.C., began with dinner with the National Parks Association trustees and a post-dinner Conservation Forum gathering addressed by U.S. Supreme Court Justice William Orville Douglas. He identified Rachel's *Silent Spring* as something everyone should read.

May 28, 1962

To the Association of Librarians, Rachel spoke on "Man and Nature in a Chemical Age."

1962 June

Velsicol Chemical Company threatened lawsuits against Houghton Mifflin because of Rachel's editorial in *Audubon* criminalizing pesticides. To recuperate from attack, Rachel retreated to Maine's Audubon Camp and in Washington, D.C., to the Audubon Society.

June 12, 1962

"Of Man and the Stream of Time," a commencement address for Scripps College in Claremont, California, expressed Rachel's admiration for John Muir, a Scots-American conservationist and proponent of the first U.S. national park. She alerted graduates to two obstacles to successful conservation: ignorance and evading the truth that humankind posed earth's most serious threat.

June 16, 1962

The *New Yorker* issued *Silent Spring* in three weekly installments, completed over June 23 and June 30. The abridged text targeted DDT, aldrin, dieldrin, endrin, heptachlor, malathion, and parathion and legitimized her censure. Her writing caught the attention of President John F. Kennedy and continues to sell 25,000 copies annually.

1962 July

The U.S. Department of Agriculture acknowledged the theories that misapplication of organic biocides posed risks to people and animals.

July 1, 1962

The *New York Times Book Review* made *The Sea Around Us* a front page feature. In a book review for the *Los Angeles Times*, Susan Salter Reynolds characterized the book as a "unique blend of the sober and the provocative" (Reynolds, 2007, R4).

July 14, 1962

Commentary from *Chemical Week* implied that Rachel had a diabolical purpose in her anti-pesticide screed.

July 22, 1962

The *New York Times* bruited the headline "SILENT SPRING IS NOW NOISY SUMMER." Journalist John M. Lee's lead sentence stated: "The $300,000,000 pesticides industry has been highly irritated by a quiet woman author whose previous works on science have been praised for the beauty and precision of the writing" (Lee, 1962, 87). Media photos tended to picture her calmly viewing birds through binoculars or mentoring children in the outdoors rather than sailing on research vessels and studying specimens through a binocular microscope.

August 2, 1962

Louis A. McLean, lawyer for Velsicol Chemical, wrote Houghton Mifflin that Rachel inaccurately criticized chlordane and heptachlor. The publisher sought an independent toxicology report, which exonerated Rachel of false statements. The National Agricultural Chemicals Association invested a quarter million dollars in pamphlets, ads, letter blitzes, and media inserts to discredit *Silent Spring* and defame Rachel Carson and the Audubon Society.

August 29, 1962

President John F. Kennedy respected Rachel's thorough and accurate rationale in charging physicians and government agencies with complacency. After he held a 4:00 p.m. press conference announcing a government inquiry, he empaneled 17 men and Rachel on the Science Advisory Committee to collect further information about the pesticide industry and its relationship with farming and public health.

1962 September

Audubon magazine issued a section of *Silent Spring* entitled "Poisoned Waters Kill Our Fish and Wildlife."

September 8, 1962

Business Week reviewed Rachel's research under the title "Are We Poisoning Ourselves?"

September 27, 1962

Issuance of *Silent Spring* outraged industrial chemists, who demeaned Rachel as an hysterical female, a spinster, a popularizer of science, and a communist and lesbian, but her warnings of indiscriminate application of synthetic poisons aroused citizen concern for ecology. To answer a scholarly need for research space and ongoing correspondence with fellow academics, the author began spending more time at her Silver Spring home and indulging a love of watching veeries and terns.

1962 October

As a first choice, Book-of-the-Month Club selected *Silent Spring* for a 150,000-copy press run; *National Parks* magazine excerpted the treatise "Beyond the Dreams of the Borgias."

October 5, 1962

At the Audubon Society Naturalist Dinner, Rachel reported on positive and negative critiques of her work from a growing counterculture. She joined Frances Oldham Kelsey, the pharmacologist who rejected thalidomide in the U.S., in a session with the Washington Audubon Naturalist Society. Rachel compared the terrors of thalidomide to effects of DDT on the unborn. In the analysis of children's author and illustrator Stephanie Roth Sisson, the author deserved respect for "courageously speaking truth to an often hostile world" (Sisson, 2018). Diatribes increased book publicity and recognition for its author.

October 11, 1962

In the first two weeks since publication, *Silent Spring* sold 65,000 copies. Rachel delivered the address "Tomorrow's Spring" to the All-Women Conference of the National Council of Women. She stressed the pivotal role of females in superintending household health, welfare, and child rearing and reminded them that ecology reached into future generations.

October 12, 1962

Journalist Jane Howard's review "The Gentle Storm Center" in *Life* magazine pictured the author with her camera in the woods teaching three boys about nature. In a portrait pose, Rachel sat at a stream in Glover Archbold Park, a 221-acre valley northwest of Georgetown University in Washington, D.C. Howard considered Rachel a feminist and a "formidable adversary," but the author denied launching a "Carrie Nation crusade" (Howard, 1962, 105).

October 16, 1962

The 12-day Cuban Missile Crisis permeated the media and public conversations with militant vocabulary that carried over to criticisms of Rachel's philosophy. Advertising pictured a crisis of crawling bugs in phalanxes mowed down by a squirt from an aerosol can.

October 24, 1962

Cleveland's Museum of Natural History honored Rachel with a reception.

1962 November

Audubon magazine raised the fright level of *Silent Spring* with an excerpt called "Beetle Scare, Spray Planes and Dead Wildlife."

November 12, 1962

Far from defeated by snipers and trolls, Rachel found herself a public icon in rock and jazz lyrics and cartoons, notably, Charles Schulz's *Peanuts*. First Lady Jacqueline Kennedy honored Rachel with membership in the Women's Committee for New Frontiers, a distinction the author shared with First Lady Eleanor Roosevelt and U.S. Secretary of Labor Frances Perkins, the first female member of a presidential cabinet. Bulgarian analyst Maria Popova named Rachel a "poet of science" and the "Copernicus of biology" (Popova, 2017).

December 2, 1962

In a personal essay, "On the Reception of Silent Spring," to the National Parks Association, the author summarized the timing of *Silent Spring* and its value to humanity "doing very badly in his self-imposed role of master of this planet" (Carson, Reception, 1962). Rachel identified her treatise as "a rallying point for an awakened public" (Carson, 1962). She summarized letters from citizens, both male and female and some physicians who condemned pesticides and demanded action from the military-industrial complex.

December 5, 1962

With droll self-deprecation, Rachel delivered a keynote address to the Women's National Press Club at the Willard Hotel headquarters at 14th and Pennsylvania NW, Washington, D.C. She concluded with a jab at greedy industrialists and exploiters.

December 10–12, 1962

The author attended the 1,400-member National Conference on Air Pollution in Washington, D.C., where she heard remarks by biologist Barry Commoner, founder of modern ecology. A cold prevented her presentation.

December 20, 1962

More radiation treatment of cancer in Rachel's neck, shoulder, and clavicle preceded completion of back treatments on December 31 and an additional round of x-rays in February 1963.

1963

For *World Book,* Rachel completed the 13 page entry "Mother of Life" for a section entitled "The Living Ocean."

1963 January

Specialists diagnosed Rachel's cardiac problem as angina and reported the spread of cancer to vertebrae and pelvis. She relied on a wheelchair and slept in a hospital bed. To Dorothy Freeman, she confided a wish to die of heart disease because it might limit more suffering from cancer. Meanwhile, sales of *Silent Spring* reached $500,000 and translations progressed to 30 languages.

January 7, 1963

The author received from the Animal Welfare Institute in New York the Albert Schweitzer Medal and the Izaak Walton League of America Founders Award for outstanding conservation of outdoor recreation. In defiance of human arrogance, she saluted Schweitzer for defining civilization as "the relation of man to all life" (Quaratiello, 2010, xii).

January 8, 1963

In New York City, Rachel accepted a special commendation from the Garden Club of America and delivered an address praising women's organizations for educating families and neighborhoods on threats to their districts. Her oration, published five months later in *Bulletin of the Garden Club of America,* saluted club committees for promoting ecology. She warned that tainted money from chemical firms and compromised university grants favored "those who seek to block remedial legislation" (Gore, 1994). She delivered a subsequent speech to the Federation of Homemakers, activists in Arlington, Virginia, demanding stronger food regulation. To the assembly in Bethesda, Maryland, she suggested that women contact congressmen and state and local authorities about the pesticides poisoning soil, killing wildlife, and threatening future generations with birth defects.

January 17, 1963

The New England Wildflower Preservation Society honored Rachel, who delivered the address "A Sense of Values in Today's World," which *New Englander Magazine* published in April 1963.

February 12, 1963

A blizzard and serious joint inflammation from a staph infection sent Rachel for six days to Washington Hospital Center on Irving Street, the city's largest private facility.

February 15, 1963

The Women's National Book Association gave Rachel the Constance Lindsay Skinner Award. Her reception speech asserted an ecological principle: that earthly life is interwoven, species with species.

February 17, 1963

After more medical tests, the author wrote Dr. George "Barney" Crile about her difficulties with nighttime angina pain, which limited exertion and stair climbing. Additional lymph node problems above the left clavicle demanded thrice weekly radiation. She anticipated future metastasis in the coracoid process, a bony stabilizer of the left shoulder blade, evidence of a spread of breast cancer to bone.

February 21, 1963

Rachel's agent accepted recognition in her name from the Rod and Gun Association.

1963 March

British readers turned *Silent Spring* into a bestseller, eliciting a cartoon in *Punch*. To the General Federation of Clubwomen, Rachel delivered the address "Are Pesticides Threatening the Nation's Health?" Her essay "Make Spring Silent" appeared in *News* of the Garden Club Federation of Pennsylvania. Because of advancing cancer, she canceled a keynote speech in Detroit to the annual assembly of the National Wildlife Federation.

March 6, 1963

Punch issued a droll cartoon about a dead dog above the line "This is the dog that bit the cat that killed the rat that ate the malt that came from the grain that Jack sprayed" (Harrison, 2009, 134).

March 20, 1963

British geographer Edward Arthur Shackleton led a debate on pesticides in England's House of Lords.

March 27, 1963

Daily treatment of bone cancer in her back sapped Rachel's strength and preceded evenings in bed. Of immortality, she revealed, "I have never formulated my own belief and feeling in words" (Carson, letter, 1963).

March 28, 1963

The National Wildlife Federation proclaimed Rachel the Conservationist of the Year and presented her a bronze plaque on walnut.

April 1, 1963

Rachel won the Spirit of Achievement Award from the Albert Einstein College of Medicine. In a letter to Dorothy Freeman, she complained of pain in the pelvis from the injection of Krebiozen, which later proved useless against cancer.

April 3, 1963

CBS Reports with Eric Sevareid broadcast "The Silent Spring of Rachel Carson," a one-hour television special on Rachel's treatise. Camera shots pictured her as a storyteller in a rocking chair and characterized her male critics as arrogant and patronizing toward women. She charged advertisers of organic chemicals with concealing the hazards, faults, and inefficiencies of modern pesticides. Her thoughts on humankind tended to label people naive rather than evil.

The airing on a Wednesday evening at 7:30 reached close to 15,000,000 homes with the message of a voice crying in the wilderness. She attested that scientists had made egregious, life-ending mistakes by tampering with nature. Eric Sevareid further stirred fears with reports of an annual application of 450,000 tons of DDT. Because of Rachel's conclusions about poisoned ecosystems, Lehn and Fink, Ralston Purina, and

Standard Brands, makers of Lysol, canceled their advertising of products incompatible with Rachel's themes.

May 15, 1963

More critical commentary marked a one-hour CBS Reports documentary, *The Verdict of the Silent Spring of Rachel Carson,* also hosted by Eric Sevareid. Analyst Charles Musser, a professor of film and media studies at Yale University, stated, "It was the depth and analysis of Carson's argument that convinced people that she was discussing what chemical corporations and the like were eager to keep hidden from view" (Musser, 2015, 49).

Before President Kennedy's Science Advisory Committee, Rachel testified about the long-term effects of toxic biocides and other hazardous substances such as those targeting fire ants, gypsy moths, Japanese beetles, and white-fringed weevils, a despoiler of potatoes, soybeans, onions, white clover, peanuts, strawberries, and grapevines. According to refuge manager Ward Feurt, the biologist reverted to a successful method of bombarding the opposition with facts: "Most powerfully, she presented the science in such a manner that it spoke for itself" (Feurt, 2007, 35).

For defending data with unwavering confidence, Rachel earned the title "Mother of Modern Environmentalism." The presidential consortium, chaired by Jerome Bert Wiesner, president of Massachusetts Institute of Technology, issued the 47-page report "The Use of Pesticides," which compared toxic chemicals to radioactive fallout. The panel cautiously declined to ban biocides, but, instead, to cease constant reliance on toxins.

May 16, 1963

For the Chicago *Sun-Times,* Rachel composed "Man's Great Peril—Pesticide Poisons."

1963 June

The National Council of Women named the author their first Woman of Conscience. Rachel's acceptance speech rallied activists on behalf of future generations.

June 4, 1963

Before Connecticut Senator Abraham Ribicoff and the Committee on the Senate Government Operations Subcommittee in the New Senate Office Building, Rachel delivered from typed notecards the 40-minute address "Environmental Hazards: Control of Pesticides and Other Chemical Poisons." Her speech indicted the chemicals that built agribusiness: "The contamination of the environment with harmful substances is one of the major problems of modern life" (Vail, 2018, 97). She advised congress on the formation of a Pesticide Commission and urged authorities to stop the sale of chemical biocides and halt aerial spraying.

June 6, 1963

Despite backache, fractures in the left pelvis, and the alopecia caused by radiation, Rachel appeared before the U.S. Senate Commerce Committee as the citizen-scientist, sedate and composed in a brown wig before dignitaries. She dismissed her cane as an aid to arthritic joints. Her testimony advocated formation of a cabinet-level commission to regulate sale and use of environmental hazards. She stressed that the agency should function free of input from the litigious chemical industry. By month's end, she found the strength to return to her summer cottage one last time, but couldn't maneuver down the incline to the shore.

1963 July

Motor Boating featured "Moving Tides," an excerpt from *The Sea Around Us.*

August 5, 1963

John F. Kennedy's signing of the Limited Nuclear Test Ban Treaty with Russia and Great Britain bolstered Rachel's hope that the atomic weapons race would end before it poisoned earth's waters.

October 18, 1963

Ill health did not prevent Rachel from presenting an hour-long address, "The Pollution of Our Environment," to 1,500 physicians attending the Kaiser-Permanente symposium *Man Against Himself* in San Francisco. In a last public appearance, she identified her career as ecologist. The famed radical biologist cited Barry Commoner's philosophy of waste control. In free time, she allowed a park ranger to guide her wheelchair to Muir Woods. She viewed old-growth redwoods in the 2,700-acre Bohemian Grove campground in Monte Rio and Cathedral Grove, Mill Valley, where trees had lived up to 1,200 years.

October 21, 1963

On the flight home from San Francisco, the author declared her love for the city and her enjoyment of a wheelchair ride through the giant sequoias of Muir Woods above the Golden Gate Bridge. Although seriously depleted from cancer and pancreatitis, she continued to read and study nature through the writings of John Muir, Stewart Udall, Irston Barnes, Edwin Way Teale, and George Stewart.

1963 November

A fish kill over millions of Mississippi River denizens substantiated Rachel's claim that endrin was dangerous.

December 3, 1963

In an address accepting her second Paul Bartsch Medal, a conservation citation from the National Audubon Society for contribution to natural history, Rachel defined the protection of nature as an ongoing obligation. In the same week, responders to *Silent Spring* awarded her a membership in the American Academy of Arts and Letters.

December 5, 1963

Upon receipt of the Cullum Geographical Medal from the American Geographical Society for the advancement of global science, Rachel mustered more volunteerism by individuals and citizen groups.

December 17, 1963

The Clean Air Act of 1963 bore the impact of Rachel Carson's *Silent Spring*. One of the first U.S. environmental laws, it initiated hearings and legal actions against contaminants at a national level. In November 1985, author Jack Lewis declared the Environmental Protection Agency "the extended shadow of Rachel Carson" (Lewis, 1985).

December 18, 1963

While Christmas shopping for electronics for Roger, Rachel collapsed in Woodward & Lothrop's, a Chevy Chase department store opened at Western and Wisconsin avenues in 1950. Her doctor reported a fast heart rate as the cause.

1964

Rachel continued the crusade for nature by appending a preface to Ruth Harrison's *Animal Machines: The New Factory Farming Industry,* published in London by Vincent Stuart. Rachel's detailed analysis of crowded hen cages, filthy pigpens, and anemic veal calves challenged practitioners of intensive farming to examine moral rights to torment animals.

1964 January

A virus sickened Rachel, causing her to seek treatment incognito.

1964 February

Radiation therapy for metastatic cancer caused anemia, which Dr. George Crile treated.

1964 March

Because cancer spread to Rachel's liver, radiologists at the Cleveland Clinic implanted a radioactive device to quell metastasis to major organs.

April 6, 1964

Although cancer spread to the brain, Rachel was able to leave the Cleveland Clinic. She revealed a comforting thought: "I can feel that I have achieved most of what I wished to do" (Freeman, 1995, 542). When Dorothy Freeman made a final visit to her bedside, Rachel barely responded to her friend.

April 14, 1964

At evening, Rachel died at age 56 at home in Silver Spring, Maryland, from cancer and heart attack, the result of cardiac weakness from radiation. She left undone four proposed works on ecology, climate change, and evolution. In her honor President Lyndon B. Johnson named April as Cancer Control Month and requested more research and earlier diagnosis and treatment. Columnist Hedwig Michel of the Fort Myers, Florida, *News Press* declared, "Rachel Carson was a friend to humanity" (Michel, 1964, 27).

April 17, 1964

After a service held at Washington's National Cathedral and a small memorial at All Souls Unitarian Church, half of Rachel's cremated remains joined Maria's grave in Rockville at Parklawn Memorial Cemetery. The rest graced the shores of Southport, Maine, off Cape Newagen, where Dorothy sprinkled them. A plaque noted Rachel's dates and demise, "at last returned to the sea—to Oceanus, the ocean river, like the ever-flowing stream of time, the beginning and the end" (Kaza, 2010, 315).

Rachel willed her estate to Roger, who became a computer engineer. Montgomery County authorities began acquiring 650 acres at Brookeville in Olney, Maryland, for a hiking and equestrian greenway to commemorate the ecologist.

May 22, 1964

The *Falmouth Enterprise* reprised Rachel's essay "The World of Waters."

September 3, 1964

The American conservation movement began accomplishing Rachel's goals with the Wilderness Act, signed by President Lyndon B. Johnson to protect and manage primeval American lands.

1965

Rachel's agent issued *The Sense of Wonder,* a posthumous meditation published by HarperCollins and featuring the photos of Charles Pratt. She dedicated the work to nephew Roger. Shirley A. Briggs's research on pesticides and her establishment of the Rachel Carson Council extended the biologist's efforts to inform citizens of widespread poison. Nonetheless, public attention wavered, leaving the campaign to organic farmers, gardeners, and nature activists.

1965 May

Rachel entered the Women's Hall of Fame Gallery at the New York World's Fair. Chosen by a panel of women, she shared the honor with birth control advocate Margaret Sanger, singer Marion Anderson, painter Grandma Moses, combat photographer Margaret Bourke-White, and poet Edna St. Vincent Millay.

October 20, 1965

Martina G. Vijver, an environmentalist at Leiden University, declared the biologist "ultimately responsible for getting stipulations included in major U.S. policy documents on air quality, nature conservation, and the broad environment" by making the public aware of "the dark side of progress" (Vijver, 2019, 369). Upon signing the Clean Air Act amendments and the Solid Waste Disposal Act on October 20, 1965, President Lyndon B. Johnson quoted Rachel's assertion that "no organism before man has deliberately polluted its own environment" (Johnson, 1965, 51).

1966

The Beinecke museum at Yale University received Rachel's papers, correspondence, and manuscripts. The issuance of U.S. Senator from Connecticut Abraham Ribicoff's "Ribicoff Report" vindicated *Silent Spring* with an admission that DDT threatened ecology.

October 15, 1966

The National Historic Preservation Act rescued historic properties such as Mount Vernon, Walden Pond, Thomas Jefferson's gardens and plantings at Monticello, Virginia, and photographs of extinct species.

1967

The Environmental Defense Fund harbored the osprey, raptors, coral reefs, river banks, and fisheries. The effort launched a crusade to ban DDT, a defense of citizen rights to a clean environment. Meanwhile, protesters cited Agent Orange, napalm, and oil and chemical spills as proof of Rachel's predictions. In Sweden, authorities impaneled the Environmental Protection Board and began legislating protective statutes.

November 13, 1968

ABC-TV featured Helen Hayes in a one-hour documentary of excerpts from *The Sense of Wonder* and *The Edge of the Sea.*

1969

Incorporating a 50-mile shoreline from Cape Elizabeth to Kittery, Maine, the U.S. Fish and Wildlife Service established the Rachel Carson National Wildlife Refuge on 5,300 acres, which extends along Port Road at Wells, Maine. Later acquisitions increased the conservancy to 9,125 acres, a sanctuary for plovers, terns, peregrine falcons, loons, eagles, egrets, and blue herons and a watershed for the Webhannet River. A small plot, the Salt Pond Preserve at New Harbor, contained the pine-edged Carson Trail, wetlands, salt marsh, and beach.

A burst of stewardship followed the ecologist's example. The first orbit of the moon yielded photos of spaceship earth. An oil spill in Santa Barbara increased demands for contaminant controls. The same year that saw the formation of Greenpeace, David R. Brower established Friends of the Earth. Feminists linked Rachel's cancer struggle with a polluted environment and its effects on the women's health initiative.

1970

The empaneling of the National Resources Defense Council coincided with the founding of Zero Population Growth and amendments to the Clean Air Act.

January 1, 1970

The Senate Committee on Interior and Insular Affairs and the House Committee on Science and Astronautics began formulating the National Environmental Policy Act. It spread to all federal agencies responsibility for shielding the ecosystem and influenced a similar ecological enhancement in 100 countries.

April 22, 1970

Conservationists celebrated the first Earth Day simultaneous with the founding of the National Oceanic and Atmospheric Administration.

December 2, 1970

Following President Richard M. Nixon's federalizing of the Environmental Protection Agency (EPA), members met in hearings for seven months. Rachel's concepts of sound scientific motivation and necessary regulation impacted subsequent laws governing industrial and radioactive waste and untreated sewage.

1971

With photos by Charles Pratt and the illustrations of Bob Hines, Rachel's *The Rocky Coast,* a 118-page outtake from *The Edge of the Sea,* revealed "A Magical Journey in Words and Pictures to the Timeless World Where Sea and Shore Meet."

January 31, 1972

A domestic U.S. ban on indiscriminate application of DDT derived from the Federal Insecticide, Fungicide, and Rodenticide Act. Legislation reversed previous laws and promoted a resurgence in bald eagle populations from a low of 500 pairs to 100,000, primarily on California's Channel Islands. Alligators, brown pelicans, gray whales, and peregrine falcons, which had neared extinction, also rebounded. As a result, the falcons returned to nest at the Gulf Tower and the Cathedral of Learning at the University of Pittsburgh. Nonetheless, the pesticide industry continued exporting biocide.

March 14, 1973

The U.S. Migratory Bird Conservation Commission opted to save 370 acres of marshland within the Rachel Carson Wildlife Refuge. The parcels retained included tracts at Spurwink River, Well Marsh, Little River, Smith Brook, and 189 acres at Goose Fare Brook.

December 27, 1973

The Endangered Species Act identified rare varieties of amphibians, fish, reptiles, insects, birds, mammals, crustaceans, wildflowers, grasses, and trees and safeguarded habitats, especially the migratory lanes of bluefin and Bigeye tuna and fin whales, colonies of sea lions and polar bears, and nesting grounds of the hawksbill and green sea turtle. The legislation extended Rachel's influence over positive change to prevent extinction of animal species. For its breadth, naturalist Edward Osborn Wilson declared it "the most important piece of conservation legislation in the nation's history" (McCrum, 2016).

1978

Discovery at Love Canal near Niagara River, New York, of buried industrial waste—BHC (*beta-hexachlorocyclohexane*), benzylchlorides, chlorobenzenes, carbon tetrachloride, chloroform, toluene, dioxin, phthalates, disulfides, naphthenes, sulfides, sulfhydrates—raised concerns for citizen health.

1979

An accident at a nuclear generator in Three Mile Island, Pennsylvania, threatened radioactive contamination from a meltdown releasing cesium-137, iodine-131, xenon, and krypton.

June 9, 1980

President Jimmy Carter awarded Rachel a posthumous Presidential Medal of Freedom.

September 29, 1980

The Fish and Wildlife Conservation Act added to financial and technical protections non-game species—wood bison, fox squirrel, walrus, California condor, peregrine falcon, elk, snapping turtle, tundra rabbit, red fox, snowy and burrowing owls, caribou, hermit crab, wood duck, sockeye salmon, Florida panther, snow leopard, mule deer, diamondback terrapin, Canada lynx, sperm whale, ruddy duck, tufted puffin, eider, moose, bobcat, beaver, harbor seal, black skimmer, spotted bat, coyote, nuthatch, curlew, sandpiper, phalarope, paddlefish, black bear, manatee, pileated woodpecker, tufted titmouse, black-footed ferret, monitor gecko, loon, speckled dace, tern, mussel, falcon, sandhill crane, Laysan albatross, goldfinch, sea otter, eel, Merriams turkey, beach mouse, arboreal toad, magpie, tundra swan, scorpion, shagreen snail, rusty blackbird, indigo bunting, kestrel, salamander, roadrunner, monarch butterfly, softshell turtle, shrike, red-tailed hawk, alligator gar and musk ox.

1981

The organization of Earth First! involved more citizens in volunteer efforts.

The U.S. Postal Service honored Rachel with a 17¢ Great American portrait stamp.

1983 September

Mother Earth News ranked Rachel's activism alongside that of naturalist John James Audubon, author John Muir, and national parks founder Theodore Roosevelt in the Environmental Hall of Fame.

1986

A nuclear disaster at Chernobyl outside Kiev, Ukraine, contaminated groundwater in Russia, Austria, Finland, and Sweden with radiation from strontium-90, cesium-137, cesium-143, ruthenium-106, plutonium-239, plutonium-240, and americium-241.

1988

The Chemical Manufacturers Association announced Responsible Care, a program intended to teach factory owners the safe manufacture of organic substances and the disposal of wastes.

1989

The Rachel Carson Institute at Chatham College focused the attentions of scholars, scientists, and government authorities on the sustainability of air, biodiversity, forests, soil, and water.

March 24, 1989

At Prince William Sound east of Anchorage, Alaska, oil leaking from the Exxon *Valdez* outraged citizens.

1990 Fall

On the recommendation of 150 scholars, *Life* magazine listed Rachel among the 100 most important people of the twentieth century.

June 7, 1991

The U.S. National Park Service added Rachel's Silver Spring home in Maryland to the National Register of Historic Places.

1993

As a segment of *The American Experience*, the PBS-TV documentary "Rachel Carson's Silent Spring" from Peace River Films for WGBH Boston surveyed opposition to Rachel's book from Dr. Robert White Stevens, a biochemist who labeled the text absurd.

1994

Vice President Al Gore composed an introduction to a new edition of *Silent Spring*.

1995

Beacon Press compiled 900 letters in *Always, Rachel: The Letters of Rachel Carson and Dorothy Freeman: An Intimate Portrait of a Remarkable Friendship*, a collection edited by Martha Freeman, Dorothy's granddaughter.

1996

Theo Colborn's *Our Stolen Future* alerted readers to one of Rachel's concerns—the altered hormones in fish, birds, and people.

1997 September

Linda Lear issued a biography, *Rachel Carson: Witness for Nature,* winner of the Best Book on Women in Science.

May 26, 1998

Supporters posted www.RachelCarson.org on the internet.

1998 June

Biographer Linda Lear published 31 of Rachel's lesser essays, letters, and newspaper articles in *Lost Woods: The Discovered Writing of Rachel Carson.*

2001 January

Blackstone Audio issued a recording of *Under the Sea Wind,* read by C.M. Hébert. The 7.5-hour production took the form of a "diary of a food chain," a contemplative subject featuring what reviewer Sandy Bauers reduced to "life—and, inevitably, death—at its rawest and most beautiful" (Bauers, 2001, E6).

2004

Florida Gulf Coast University launched the Rachel Carson Distinguished Lecture Series featuring literary and ethical themes about life on earth.

May 17, 2004

The Stockholm Convention on Persistent Organic Pollutants outlawed global reliance on DDT and organochlorine biocides except for control of malaria-bearing mosquitoes.

2006

Discover magazine named *Silent Spring* one of the world's top 25 science texts.

2007

CBS-TV broadcast Caitlin A. Johnson's *The Price of Progress,* which celebrated the restoration of bald eagles on Catalina Island. A children's competition, "The Sense of Wonder: Rachel Carson Intergenerational Poetry, Essay, Photo and Dance Contest," awarded winners in four categories.

May 27, 2007

Pennsylvanians honored the centennial of Rachel's birth.

September 21, 2007

Bill Moyers Journal commemorated Rachel's life and work with mention of adapter Kaiulani Lee, the narrator of *Silent Spring* for Recorded books. Lee wrote and performed a one-act play *A Sense of Wonder,* which she has presented at some 100 universities, the Albert Schweitzer Conference, the United Nations, the Smithsonian, the Sierra Club Centennial, and the 150th anniversary of the U.S. Department of the Interior. The actor cited Rachel's lyric love of Earth: "To stand here at the edge of the sea, to sense the ebb and flow of the tides, to feel the breath of the mist over the great salt marsh, to watch the flight of shorebirds that have swept up and down these continents for untold thousands of years, to see the running of the old eels and the young shad to the sea, is to have knowledge of things that are as nearly eternal as any earthly life can be" (Curwood, 2005). The one-woman performance has toured Canada, England, India, Italy, and Japan.

2008 October

The Linda Lear Center archives supported research from Rachel's papers and manuscripts at Connecticut College in New London. With 50 collections of art, books, and manuscripts, the archive incorporated botany and post-war philosophy exhibits on animal rights activism, animal welfare advocacy, photos, documents, landscapes, Asian painting, and Lear's research into the writing and art of British children's writer Beatrix Potter. Additional writings reside at the Thoreau Institute outside Walden Pond, Massachusetts.

2009

International scholars studied ecology at the Rachel Carson Center for Environment and Society in Munich, Germany.

2012

The American Chemical Society proclaimed *Silent Spring* a National Historic Chemical Landmark. Simultaneously, the Cato Institute issued a rebuttal of Rachel's warnings of a creeping apocalypse, calling her "over-simplified" warnings "false crises" that promoted government control of chemical application (Meiners, Desrochers, & Morris, 2012). Editors Roger Meiners, Pierre Desrochers, and Andrew Morriss, issuers of the book *Silent Spring at 50: The False Crises of Rachel Carson,* charged Rachel with launching a health scare, chemical federalization, and a secular religion.

February 17, 2012

The Pittsburgh Symphony debuted *Silent Spring,* a symphony commissioned to honor the work's fiftieth anniversary. Written by Steven Stucky, the city's composer of the year, the piece gradually reduced sounds of nature to "Rivers of Death" and the silence of a bleak prophecy.

2015 November

The Academic Book of the Future, a project of the British government, selected *Silent Spring* among the world's most influential works.

May 11, 2016

At the Ames Library, the Illinois Grand Prairie Master Naturalists screened a documentary, "The Power of One Voice: A 50-Year Perspective on the Life of Rachel Carson."

January 24, 2017

Michelle Ferrari's two-hour documentary film *Rachel Carson* summarized the genius of the modern environmental movement. The voice-over of Mary-Louise Parker incorporated Rachel's friends, nephew Roger Allen Christie, writers, and learned associates in interviews.

2017 December

In a Republican reversal of Rachel's conservation movement, President Donald Trump limited federal protection of bird migration.

March 22, 2018

The film *Rachel Carson: Voice of Nature* honored the scientist's impact on Pennsylvania's preservation activism.

Sources

Archer, Jules. *To Save the Earth: The American Environmental Movement*. New York: Simon & Schuster, 2016.

Bauers, Sandy. "'Under the Sea Wind' Takes Listeners on a Rich Journey." *Orlando Sentinel* (31 January 2001): E6.

Bowes, Catherine. "An Evening with Rachel Carson." *Conservation Matters* 7:2 (Summer 2000): 48.

Cafaro, Philip. "Rachel Carson's Environmental Ethics." *Worldviews* 6:1 (2002): 58–80.

Carson, Rachel. "Beyond the Dreams of the Borgias." *National Parks* (October 1962).

_____. "Books and Authors Luncheon." https://www.wnyc.org/story/148408-rachel-carson-1951/.

_____. "Design for Nature Writing." *Atlantic Naturalist* (May–August 1952): 232–234.

_____. "The Edge of the Sea" (speech), American Association for the Advancement of Science, Boston (December 29, 1953).

_____. "Essay on the Biological Sciences." *Good Reading* (1958).

_____. "An Island I Remember," unpublished elegy, July 1946.

_____, "Letter to Beverly Knecht" (12 April 1959).

_____. "Letter to Curtis and Nellie Lee Bok" (12 December 1956).

_____. "Letter to Dorothy Freeman" (1 February 1958).

_____. "Letter to Dorothy Freeman" (12 June 1958).

_____. "Letter to Dorothy Freeman" (19 November 1959).

_____. "Letter to Dorothy Freeman" (6 January 1962).

_____. "Letter to Dorothy Freeman" (27 March 1963).

_____. "Letter to Lois Crisler" (8 February 1962).

_____. "Letter to Morton S. Biskind" (3 December 1959).

_____. "Letter to Mrs. Boyette" (12 June 1956).

_____. "Letter to William Shawn" (14 February 1959).

_____. "Liner Notes." Claude Debussy's *La Mer,* RCA Victor, 1951.

_____. "Memo to Mrs. Eales," Rachel Carson papers, 1942.

_____. "Mr. Day's Dismissal." *Washington Post* (22 April 1953): A26.

_____. "National Book Award Acceptance Speech." *House of Life* (27 January 1952): 127–129.

_____. "National Symphony Orchestra Benefit Luncheon," Washington, D.C. (25 September 1951).

_____. "On the Reception of *Silent Spring.*" *National Parks Association Magazine* (2 December 1962).

_____. "The Real World Around Us," address to the Theta Sigma Phi Matrix Table Dinner (21 April 1954), Columbus, Ohio.

_____. *The Sea Around Us.* New York: Oxford University Press, 1951.

_____. *The Sense of Wonder.* New York: Harper & Row, 1965.

_____. *Silent Spring.* Boston: Houghton Mifflin, 40th Anniversary Edition, 2002.

_____. speech, *New York Herald Tribune Book Review,* Astor Hotel (1 October 1951).

_____. "To Understand Biology." *Humane Biology Projects.* Washington, D.C.: Animal Welfare Institute, 1960, i–iv.

_____. "Vanishing Americans." *Washington Post* (10 April 1959): A26.

Carson, R.L. "A New Trout Crop for Anglers." *Baltimore Sun* (2 April 1939): 3.

_____. "The Northern Trawlers Move South." *Baltimore Sunday Sun* (3 January 1937): 6–7.

_____. "Numbering the Fish of the Sea." *Baltimore Sunday Sun* (24 May 1936): 5, 7.

_____. "Shad Going the Way of the Buffalo." *Charleston News and Courier* (14 February 1937): 8C.

_____. "Starlings a Housing Problem." *Baltimore Sunday Sun Magazine* (5 March 1939): 1.

_____. "Walrus and Carpenter Not Oysters' Only Foe." *Baltimore Sun* (21 August 1938): 2.

_____. "Whalers Ready for New Season." *Baltimore Sunday Sun* (20 November 1938): 2.

Curwood, Steve. "Living on Earth." *PRI Environmental News Magazine* (22 April 2005).

Doyle, Jack. "Power in the Pen." https://www.pophistorydig.com/topics/tag/rachel-carson-senate-hearings/ (22 February 2012).

Druckenbrod, Andrew. "The Sound of Silence." *Pittsburgh Post-Gazette* (12 February 2012): E1, E3.

"The Education of Rachel Carson." *Pittsburgh Post-Gazette* (2 May 2006): G6.

Fellows, Valerie, and Joshua Winchell. "Returning to the Water." *Fish & Wildlife News* (Spring 2007): 26–28.

Feurt, Ward. "A Living Trust." *Fish & Wildlife News* (Spring 2007): 35.

Free, Ann Cottrell. "Silent Spring Stir: 'I Never Thought Uproar Would Be So Tremendous.'" *Baltimore Evening Sun* (8 January 1963): A17.

Freeman, Martha, ed. *Always, Rachel: The Letters of Rachel Carson and Dorothy Freeman, 1952–1964.* Boston: Beacon Press, 1995.

Gore, Al. "Introduction" to *Silent Spring.* Boston: Houghton Mifflin, 1994, xiii.

Griswold, Eliza. "How *Silent Spring* Ignited the Environmental Movement." *New York Times Magazine* (21 September 2012).

Harrison, Brian. *Seeking a Role: The United Kingdom.* Oxford, UK: Oxford University Press, 2009.

Horton, Tom. "Rachel Carson No Stranger to Chesapeake, Its Creatures." *Salisbury* (MD) *Daily Times* (3 November 2019): A4.

Howard, Jane. "The Gentle Storm Center: A Calm Appraisal of *Silent Spring.*" *Life* 53:5 (12 October 1962): 105.

Johnson, Lyndon B. "Remarks by President Johnson upon Signing the Clean Air Act Amendments and the Solid Waste Disposal Act" in *Health, Education, and Welfare Indicators.* Washington, D.C.: U.S. Government Printing Office, 1965.

Kaza, Stephanie. "Rachel Carson's Sense of Time: Experiencing Maine." *ISLE* 17:2 (Spring 2010): 291–315.

Klinger, David. "Rachel Carson's Hidden Treasures." *Fish & Wildlife News* (Spring 2007): 33.

Koehn, Nancy F. "From Calm Leadership, Lasting Change." *New York Times* (27 October 2012).

Kroll, Gary. "The 'Silent Springs' of Rachel Carson: Mass Media and the Origins of Modern Environmentalism." *Public Understanding of Science* 10:4 (1 October 2001): 403–420.

Lawlor, Laurie. *Rachel Carson and Her Book That Changed the World.* New York: Holiday House, 2014.

Lear, Linda J. *Rachel Carson: Witness for Nature.* New York: Henry Holt, 1997.

Lee, John M. "'Silent Spring' Is Now Noisy Summer." *New York Times* (22 July 1962): 87, 97.

Lewis, Jack. "The Birth of EPA." *EPA Journal* (November 1985).

Madera, Judith. "The Birth of an Island: Rachel Carson's *The Sea Around Us.*" *Women's Studies Quarterly* 45:1/2 (Spring/Summer 2017): 292–298.

Marco, Gino J., et al., eds. *Silent Spring Revisited*. Washington, D.C.: American Chemical Society, 1987.

McCrum, Robert. "The 100 Best Nonfiction Books: No 20—*Silent Spring* by Rachel Carson (1962)." *The Guardian* (13 June 2016).

McKibben, Bill. *Falter: Has the Human Game Begun to Play Itself Out?* New York: Henry Holt, 2019.

Meiners, Roger, Pierre Desrochers, and Andrew Morris. *Silent Spring at 50: The False Crises of Rachel Carson*. Washington, D.C.: Cato Institute, 2012.

Michel, Hedwig. "Ideas and Ideals Are Not Lost." (Fort Myers, FL) *News-Press* (19 April 1964): 27.

Mills, Billy. "A Book for the Beach." *The Guardian* (28 July 2014).

Musser, Charles. "Trauma, Truth, and the Environmental Documentary" in *Eco-Trauma Cinema*. New York: Routledge, 2015.

Narine, Anil, ed. *Eco-Trauma Cinema*. New York: Routledge, 2015.

Nicklin, Emmy. *What We Owe to Rachel Carson*. https://www.cbf.org/blogs/save-the-bay/2019/03/what-rachel-carson-gave-us.html.

Nieves, Autumn. "Rachel Carson: Proving the Competency of Femininity." *Women Leading Change* 3:2 (10 October 2018).

Popkin, Gabriel. "Right Fish, Wrong Pond." *Johns Hopkins Magazine* (Summer 2013).

Popova, Maria. "Undersea: Rachel Carson's Lyrical and Revolutionary Masterpiece Inviting Humans to Explore Earth from the Perspective of Other Creatures." /www.brainpickings.org/2017/02/28/undersea-rachel-carson/

_____. "The Writing of *Silent Spring*: Rachel Carson and the Culture-Shifting Courage to Speak Inconvenient Truth to Power." https://www.brainpickings.org/2017/01/27/rachel-carson-silent-spring-dorothy-freeman/.

Quaratiello, Arlene Rodda. *Rachel Carson: A Biography*. Amherst, NY: Prometheus, 2010.

"Rachel Carson," *Bill Moyers Journal*, https://www.pbs.org/moyers/journal/09212007/profile.html (21 September 2007).

"Rachel Carson Wins Achievement Award." *AAUW Journal* (December 1956): 19.

Reynolds, Susan Salter. "It's the End of the World As We Know It." *Los Angeles Times* (25 February 2007): R4.

Rothlisberger, John D. "The Gentle Subversive: Rachel Carson and the Rise of the Environmental Movement." *Western North American Naturalist* 69:1 (2009): 144–146.

Routhier, Ray. "Documentary Looks at Life, Work of Rachel Carson," *Portland* (ME) *Press Herald* (22 January 2017): E5.

Sherman, Jerome L. "Environmentalist Rachel Carson's Legacy Remembered on Earth Day," *Pittsburgh Post-Gazette* (23 April 2006).

Sisson, Stephanie Roth. *Spring After Spring: How Rachel Carson Inspired the Environmental Movement*. New York: Roaring Book, 2018.

Stein, Karen F. "The Legacies of Rachel Carson." *English Journal* 103:6 (2014): 81–84.

Steingruber, Sandra, ed. *Rachel Carson: Silent Spring & Other Writings on the Environment*. New York: Library of America, 2018.

Sterne, J.R.L., ed. "Silent Spring." *Baltimore Sun* (10 January 1991): 8A.

Vail, David D. *Chemical Lands: Pesticides, Aerial Spraying, and Health in North America's Grasslands Since 1945*. Tuscaloosa: University of Alabama Press, 2018.

Van Loon, Hendrik. "Letter" (10 September 1937).

Vijver, Martina G. "The Choreography of Chemicals in Nature; Beyond Ecotoxicological Limits." *Chemosphere* 227 (2019): 366–307.

Wadsworth, Andrew. "Carson's Christianity and Environmental Crises." *Criterion* 9:1 (Winter 2016).

Woods, Bruce, Philip Johnson, and Valerie Fellows. "Sounding the Alarm." *Fish & Wildlife News* (Spring 2007): 12–13.

Zwinger, Ann H. "Introduction." *The Sea Around Us*. New York: Oxford University Press, 1989.

The Carson Genealogy

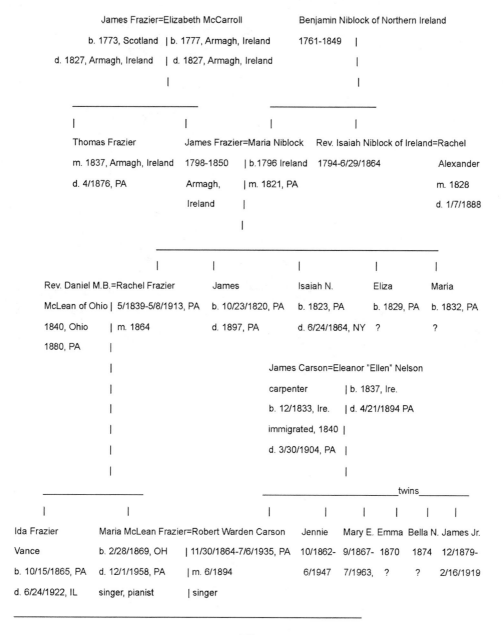

James Frazier=Elizabeth McCarroll　　　Benjamin Niblock of Northern Ireland

b. 1773, Scotland | b. 1777, Armagh, Ireland　　1761-1849 |

d. 1827, Armagh, Ireland | d. 1827, Armagh, Ireland |

|　　　　　　　　　　　　　　　　　　　　|

_____　　_____

| | | |

Thomas Frazier　　James Frazier=Maria Niblock　Rev. Isaiah Niblock of Ireland=Rachel

m. 1837, Armagh, Ireland　1798-1850 | b.1796 Ireland　1794-6/29/1864　　Alexander

d. 4/1876, PA　　Armagh, | m. 1821, PA　　　　　　　　　　m. 1828

　　　　　　　　　Ireland |　　　　　　　　　　　　　　　　d. 1/7/1888

　　　　　　　　　　　　 |

_____

| | | | |

Rev. Daniel M.B.=Rachel Frazier　James　　Isaiah N.　　Eliza　　Maria

McLean of Ohio | 5/1839-5/8/1913, PA　b. 10/23/1820, PA　b. 1823, PA　b. 1829, PA　b. 1832, PA

1840, Ohio | m. 1864　　d. 1897, PA　　d. 6/24/1864, NY　?　　?

1880, PA |

| 　　　　　　　　　　　James Carson=Eleanor "Ellen" Nelson

| 　　　　　　　　　　　carpenter | b. 1837, Ire.

| 　　　　　　　　　　　b. 12/1833, Ire. | d. 4/21/1894 PA

| 　　　　　　　　　　　immigrated, 1840 |

| 　　　　　　　　　　　d. 3/30/1904, PA |

|

_____　　_____twins_____

| | | | | | | |

Ida Frazier　　Maria McLean Frazier=Robert Warden Carson　Jennie　Mary E. Emma Bella N. James Jr.

Vance　　b. 2/28/1869, OH | 11/30/1864-7/6/1935, PA　10/1862-　9/1867-　1870　1874　12/1879-

b. 10/15/1865, PA　d. 12/1/1958, PA | m. 6/1894　　6/1947　7/1963, ?　?　2/16/1919

d. 6/24/1922, IL　singer, pianist | singer

79

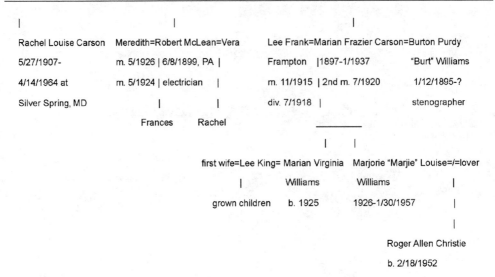

Rachel Louise Carson	Meredith=Robert McLean=Vera		Lee Frank=Marian Frazier Carson=Burton Purdy	
5/27/1907-	m. 5/1926 | 6/8/1899, PA |		Frampton |1897-1/1937	"Burt" Williams
4/14/1964 at	m. 5/1924 | electrician |		m. 11/1915 | 2nd m. 7/1920	1/12/1895-?
Silver Spring, MD			div. 7/1918 |	stenographer
	Frances	Rachel		

first wife=Lee King= Marian Virginia   Marjorie "Marjie" Louise=/=lover

Williams   Williams

grown children   b. 1925   1926-1/30/1957

Roger Allen Christie

b. 2/18/1952

The Literary Companion

"Address" to the Women's National Press Club

In an afternoon address to the Women's National Press Club at the Willard Hotel headquarters at 14th and Pennsylvania NW, Washington, D.C., on December 5, 1962, Rachel chose droll repeats of criticisms of *Silent Spring* by Pennsylvanians who had not read the book and by Vermont readers who countered statements she didn't make. Taking the high road, she affirmed the classic treatise by citing public response as "a tidal wave of letters" to the author, congress, media editors and columnists, and federal agencies (Carson, "Reception," 1962). Her comments on criticism from agribusiness and the chemical industry described a rush to issue propaganda to "repair the somewhat battered image of pesticides" (*ibid.*). Modestly, her text acclaimed contemporary gains "toward a saner policy of pest control" (*ibid.*).

Without rancor, Rachel's speech listed *ad hominem* attacks collected by a clipping service on a "bird lover—a cat lover—a fish lover" and "priestess of nature—a devotee of a mystical cult" designed to discredit her person rather than her research (*ibid.*). More insidious, critiques charged her with demanding "abandonment of chemical control," a position she never took (*ibid.*). Pincus Rothberg, president of Montrose Chemical of California, dismissed her as a fanatic. With a quick riposte, she charged appraisers of *Silent Spring* with favoring "a rather low level of scientific thinking" lacking appropriate sophistication (*ibid.*). Applying the "soft sell," apologists for biocide manufacturers implied that the examples in Rachel's text consist of outdated reports no longer applicable to the status of pesticides.

Calm Candor

The speaker wisely adopted a journalist's approach to argumentation by citing cases of pesticide poisoning in Framingham, Massachusetts, Canada, and Turkey and the crashing of 873 crop dusting planes. The Federal Aviation Agency assumed that the cumulative disaster that killed 135 pilots illustrated the lethal accumulation of toxins in the body. Rachel listed eight incidents of careless employment of biocides and named the poisons: aldrin, dieldrin, highway herbicides, lawn sprays, seeds permeated with fungicide, DDT (dichlorodiphenyltrichloroethane), and heptachlor, a treatment for fire ants. A quick aside in the seventh item reminded the audience that, if fish in Framingham, Massachusetts, contain 10 times the tolerable level of DDT, so too did drinking water. The eighth item interpreted the freakish inward growth of sprouts on New York potatoes, an alert to savvy journalists of the hellish repercussions of chemicals not thoroughly tested for use on consumables.

At a peak in tone and detail, Rachel's speech hammered the audience with fearful alerts to suspicious pesticides still in use, cattle inexplicably felled by spray, pilots asphyxiated while crop dusting, and parathion poisoning in California, Florida, India, and Japan. To the quibblers who accused the author of name dropping and padding the bibliography, she specified post–B.S. "training in the scientific method at Johns Hopkins," a vindication to which she added an exclamation point (*ibid.*). A charge of insidious influence on universities censured the chemical firms of Monsanto, Velsicol, Diamond Black-Leaf, and Shell Chemical with offering grants to researchers at the University of Wisconsin, Kansas State, University of California, and the Illinois Natural History Survey at Urbana. At a climactic point, the author drew the audience to attention with two rhetorical questions—"Whose voice do we hear—that of science? or of the sustaining industry?" (*ibid.*).

Pinpointing the Moneymakers

In calm, unemotional concluding remarks, Rachel incriminated profiteers by enlarging on the insidious nature of "hard cash" (*ibid.*). She denounced chemical and trade guilds that influenced a report on wildlife from the National Academy of Sciences, a conflict of interest that journalists branded as "fronts for the industry" (*ibid.*). A reviewer made a veiled complaint of "some segments of the public that are causing trouble," a gibe that Rachel ignored (*ibid.*). By comparing the infiltration of "the gods of profit and production" into the science lab, an intrusion that happened in Soviet Russia under Josef Stalin in the 1920s, she backhanded accusations that the author posed a Communist threat to America's food supply.

Rachel confided, "I never thought the uproar would be so tremendous" (Free, 1963, A17). Her candid dealings with astute news mavens helped to clear her name of scurrilous smears, but did not endear her to the U.S. Department of Agriculture or the National Academy of Sciences, which colluded with major biocide manufacturers to exonerate pesticides. She also angered the American Medical Association for criticizing their apathetic response to biocidal threats. In the estimation of activist Marcy Jane Knopf-Newman, Rachel believed that the AMA chose "a relationship with industry" and that "it kept alternative medical remedies from the public," a suggestion of the author's concern for denial of treatments for breast cancer (Knopf-Newman, 2004, 40–41).

Sources

Carson, Rachel. "Address," Women's National Press Club (5 December 1962), Washington, D.C.
_____. "On the Reception of *Silent Spring*." (2 December 1962).
Free, Ann Cottrell. "Silent Spring Stir: 'I Never Thought Uproar Would Be So Tremendous,'" *Baltimore Evening Sun* (8 January 1963): A17.
Knopf-Newman, Marcy Jane. *Beyond Slash, Burn, and Poison: Transforming Breast Cancer Stories into Action.* Piscataway, NJ: Rutgers University Press, 2004.

Aerial Spraying

In Rachel's version of human rights, citizens deserved healthful surroundings unsullied by industry, agribusiness, or science. For the uncontrollable overspray and drift on air currents, she gathered data on aerial dispersal of poisons, a post–World War II practice over the Great Plains to quell bindweed, musk thistle, mosquitoes, and corn borers. In the words of David D. Vail, an historian at the University of Nebraska, she "did not look kindly on agricultural aviation" or on the honcho ag pilots who zoomed over property boundaries (Vail, 2018, 3). Her reply to an editorial in the *Washington Post* in April 1959 impugned insecticides from the skies for permeating soil and coating flora with lethal hydrocarbons that turned earthworms into death traps for robins and their offspring. One aerial assault polluted a wide area for months and lingered in living organisms, water, and soil.

The U.S. government fostered expanded biocide use by selling decommissioned military planes to private pilots. Many of them developed chronic ills from inhaling and touching the dust of DDT (dichlorodiphenyltrichloroethane), especially inexperienced crop dusters flying on windy days. On January 27, 1958, she alerted DeWitt Wallace, publisher of *Reader's Digest,* that the U.S. Department of Health, Education and Welfare questioned the consumption of drinking water bearing aerial pesticides. More fearful, the new poison dieldrin, an aerosol organochloride aimed at fire ants, tested at many times the toxicity level of DDT and caused seizures, convulsions, liver necrosis, and death.

Anti-Spray Activism

An assault by the U.S. Department of Agriculture on invasive fire ants, tent caterpillars, mites, and gypsy moths in the South in 1957 raised threats of massive dispersal of dieldrin and heptachlor, another organic chemical that attacked liver, kidneys, and nervous system and caused cancer. The toxic organophosphates and chlorinated hydrocarbons accumulated in mammal tissue, tainting breast milk. Aerial spraying on private property for mosquitoes and Dutch elm disease required mixing DDT with fuel oil, which clung to limbs and leaves and floated on creeks and streams. Long Islanders—ornithologist Robert Cushman Murphy and Archibald Roosevelt, Theodore Roosevelt's son—filed suit to stop the project, gaining support from the National Wildlife Federation and the National Audubon Society. Rachel kept current on the U.S. Supreme Court response to the aerial dispersal. Justices mooted the spraying after the fact, but granted citizen rights to injunctions in future assaults on ecosystems and human physiology.

The author received a call to action in 1958 from a friend, journalist Olga Owens Huckins, a nature preservationist in Duxbury, Massachusetts. Olga had complained in a letter to the *Boston Herald* that mosquito control involved an aerosol from a plane buzzing marshlands, recreational parks, and her two-acre wildlife sanctuary. As a citizen, she considered invasion from the skies a violation of privacy by a deadly poison. She warned, "YOU CAN NEVER KILL DDT" (Huckins, 1958). Rachel learned that the same aerial strategy had poisoned salmon, trout, and birds along the

Miramichi River, New Brunswick, after planes crisscrossed balsam stands to spew DDT over the spruce budworm. She added that pilots had no control of the drift of DDT in oil, which coated watersheds. In February 1960, Rachel proposed organic farming and biological pest control as an alternative to routine spraying of synthetic killers.

Stopping a Menace

Rachel's plan of action mobilized the people aware of the danger and the uninformed. In reply to readers of the *Silent Spring* series in the *New Yorker,* on August 2, 1962, she composed a form letter urging citizen action demanding that authorities justify the need for all aerial spraying. Her brisk tone implied that halting the spread of toxins from the air constituted a national emergency requiring a patriot riposte. *Audubon* magazine raised the ante with the chilling outtake in the November 1962 issue entitled "Beetle Scare, Spray Planes and Dead Wildlife," an implication of cause and result. Environmentalist Al Gore noted that Los Angeles was already swathed in fog in 1962, but the danger to citizens of trapped gases earned little or no citizen dialogue. From his own experience as a harbinger of change, he recognized the cause of "a fierce—and sometimes foolish—reaction" from profiteers (Matthiessen, 2007, 64).

The completed study "Use of Pesticides," a 47-page report from President John Kennedy's Science Advisory Committee on May 15, 1963, opened on the dangers of "aerial drift" (Carson, 1963). The uncontrolled spread of poisons via wind currents contaminated much of earth's surface. When Rachel testified for 40 minutes before congress on June 4, 1963, she reported the drift of 60 percent of forest spraying, sending the herbicide 2,4-D (Agent Orange or 2,4-Dichlorophenoxyacetic acid) up to 20 miles from its intended site. Because of Rachel's death 18 months later from metastatic breast cancer and heart attack, Gore declared she "was literally writing for her life" (*ibid.,* 65).

On October 18, 1963, Rachel's speech at San Francisco's Fairmont Hotel to a consortium of 1,500 physicians from Kaiser-Permanente emphasized emerging information on air contaminants. She cited an example in summer 1962 in Washington State of a temperature inversion that kept aerial spray adrift. Far from the farmlands the pilot intended to cover, the droplets sickened 30 people and poisoned cows. A second model, from Long Island in winter 1962, characterized potato protection with insecticide dust that drifted into school windows. Before flying home on October 21, she spent part of the weekend traveling Muir Woods by wheelchair and enjoying "such a wonderful freshness in the air there!" (Carson, letter, 1963). In a thank you for the Audubon Medal delivered in mid-town Manhattan on December 3, 1963, the author reiterated her concern for contaminated air, water, and forests.

Media attention to Rachel's warning began a groundswell of citizen concerns for urban yards, gardens, children's classrooms and playgrounds, athletic fields, agricultural grassland, and water reservoirs. In 1965, the Illinois Pesticide Control Committee required licensing of crop dusters. New Zealand and Sweden prohibited the spread of biocides and fertilizer from the air. In 2009, the European Union banned aerial sprays. Six years later, Oregon and Colorado citizens placed citizen rights above corporate profit in a war on helicopter spraying of herbicides over creeks, lakes, and rivers. The same equipment targeted budworms in Washington state forests, West Nile-carrying mosquitoes in North Dakota, and 800 acres of Lake Okeechobee, Florida, with herbicidal deterrents to cattails, maidencane, and spikerush. In India in November 2019, district sprayers added drones to the equipment spewing biocides over cornfields beset by fall armyworms.

See also DDT; *Silent Spring: Indiscriminately from the Skies.*

Sources

Carson, Rachel. "Acceptance Speech," National Audubon Society, New York (3 December 1963).
_____. "Environmental Hazards: Control of Pesticides and Other Chemical Poisons." Statement before the Subcommittee on Reorganization and International Organizations of the Committee on Government Operations (4 June 1963): 206–219.
_____. "Letter to correspondents" (2 August 1962).
_____. "Letter to DeWitt Wallace" (27 January 1958).
_____. "Letter to Dorothy Freeman" (21 October 1963).
_____. "The Pollution of Our Environment," address to the Kaiser-Permanente Symposium *Man Against Himself*, San Francisco (18 October 1963).
_____. "She Started It All—Here's Her Reaction." *New York Herald Tribune* (19 May 1963).
_____. *Silent Spring.* Boston: Houghton Mifflin, 40th Anniversary Edition, 2002.
_____. "Vanishing Americans." *Washington Post* (10 April 1959): A26.
Cook, Christopher D. "The Spraying of America." *Earth Island Journal* 20:1 (2005): 34–38.
Huckins, Olga. "Letter to the Editor." *Boston Herald* (January 1958).
Matthiessen, Peter, ed. *Courage for the Earth: Writers, Scientists, and Activists Celebrate the Life and Writing of Rachel Carson.* New York: Mariner, 2007.
Murphy, Tom. "Are You Being Poisoned?" (De Kalb, Illinois) *Daily Chronicle* (2 June 1965): 20.
Vail, David D. *Chemical Lands: Pesticides, Aerial Spraying, and Health in North America's Grasslands Since 1945.* Tuscaloosa: University of Alabama Press, 2018.

Amphibians

Rachel incorporated amphibians into a worldview that treasured small creatures as a vital part of global biodiversity. For field work, she and colleague Shirley A. Briggs monitored the cold-blooded vertebrates in June 1950 in a swamp buggy exploration of the Florida Everglades Refuge. Off the Tamiami Trail, amphibians lived on invertebrates and other amphibians and fed fish, birds, and small mammal predators. In a paean to seasonal change in *The Sea Around Us,* she featured the croaking of frogs in swamplands, a token of spring awakenings. In *Sense of Wonder,* she exulted in a life-affirming sound "infinitely healing in the repeated refrains of nature—the assurance that dawn comes after night, and spring after winter" (Carson, 1965, 100).

The author valued amphibians as proof of earth's resilient life forms. Investigations dated the fishy creatures to fossil evidence in sandstone from the Devonian Era (400,000,000 BCE). During North American glaciation in Africa, Australia, India, and South America, amphibians suffered a decline until the lowering of sea depths covering central North America. She explained the metamorphosis of the amphibian from fish to land animal: "Over the thousands of years its fins became legs, and instead of gills it developed lungs" and permeable skin and clustered in wetlands for a habitat (Carson, 1951, 13).

Published on September 27, 1962, the classic alarum *Silent Spring* acknowledged the risk to groundwater, fishing streams and ponds, and amphibian habitats from biocides and fertilizer in farm and city runoff. More menace by air derived from aerial DDT (dichlorodiphenyltrichloroethane) drift and lake treatment with DDD (dichlorodiphenyldichloroethane), a biocide linked with human lung tumors, damaged adrenal glands, and liver and thyroid disease. At greatest risk were tadpoles, frogs, newts, and salamanders that lived their whole lives in water and depended on its purity. By feeding on poisoned butterflies, dragonflies, mites, and insect larvae, newts and frogs increased their intake of organic contaminators, which lodged in their tissues the same as in fish, birds, and reptiles.

The treatise compiled dates and locations of fish kills on North American farmland and the annihilation of frogs in Florida by agrarian use of heptachlor, which also exterminated fish, rabbits, muskrats, and opossums. Chapter Nine, "Rivers of Death," revealed interaction in 1958 between the U.S. Department of Agriculture and the American Society of Ichthyologists and Herpetologists to protect reptiles and amphibians from the effects of aerial sprays of heptachlor and dieldrin, a biocide that wiped out songbirds, quail, pheasants, and squirrels. The Society highlighted delicate balances of nature in the southeastern U.S., where amphibians "occupy only small areas and therefore might readily be completely exterminated" (Carson, 2002, 141). More information about complex cell activity in Chapter Thirteen, "Through a Narrow Window," connected oxygen deprivation with the death of embryonic frogs and sea urchins during ovum division. In 1996, Ron Seely, a columnist for the *Wisconsin State Journal,* corroborated her concerns by reporting deformities in frog eyes and limbs in habitats over California, Iowa, Minnesota, Missouri, Quebec, South Dakota, Texas, and Vermont.

Amphibians faced extermination, especially in the southeast, and incurred decreased reproduction as high as 60 percent. Of the metamorphosis of amphibians from an egg mass into sprightly creatures, Rachel pursued a rhetorical question: "Did the eggs … of the laboratory frogs stop developing" because of a lack of energy molecules to finish their development (*ibid.,* 206). Her personal response involved willing 9,125 acres of her Maryland shoreline property as a habitat for piping plover, New England cottontail, spring peeper (*Pseudacris crucifer*), and wood frog (*Rana sylvatica*), which flourished in a small nearby stream and as far north as Alaska, the Yukon, and Labrador. In pools, ponds, and cattail marshes, biologists surveyed green and pickerel frogs, bullfrogs, gray tree frogs, salamanders, and eastern newts. Because of her intense crusade to rescue living things, protection of U.S. wildlife saved 250 amphibians and reptiles among 2,000 organisms and preserved them as compromised species.

Sources

Carson, Rachel. *The Sea Around Us.* New York: Oxford University Press, 1951.
_____. *The Sense of Wonder.* New York: Harper & Row, 1965.
_____. *Silent Spring.* Boston: Houghton Mifflin, 40th Anniversary Edition, 2002.
Rohr, J.R. "Atrazine and Amphibians: A Story of Profits, Controversy, and Animus." *The Encyclopedia of the Anthropocene.* Oxford: Elsevier, vol. 5, (2018): 141–148.
Seely, Ron. "Nature Is Giving Us Dire Warnings." *Wisconsin State Journal* (3 November 1996): 3C.

Awards

Achievement marked Rachel's life from childhood to posthumous regard around the globe for ecology and ethics. At age 11, she began making a name for herself as a writer in September 1918, when *St. Nicholas Magazine* published her aviation hero tale "A Battle in the Clouds," winner of a silver medal. After a second publication, "A Young Hero," in January 1919, the magazine awarded her 10 dollars and a gold badge in February for "A Message to the Front." A fourth submission, the memoir "My Favorite Recreation," received $3.00 in July 1922.

The gift for excellence resulted in two $100 scholarships, which assured matriculation on September 15, 1925, at the Pennsylvania College for Women in Pittsburgh. By February 1926, she ranked among the top scholars in her class. Her short fiction "Broken Lamps" for *The Englicode* won recognition from the Omega Club. Rated *magna cum laude* at age 22, she enrolled in graduate work at Johns Hopkins University on full scholarship. Writing continued to remunerate the biologist on May 1, 1936, when the *Baltimore Sun* paid her $20 for the feature story "It'll Be Shad Time Soon."

IN PRINT

Rachel's literary acumen earned advances for future publications. In November 1941, the Scientific Book Club chose *Under the Sea Wind* as its monthly selection. A second place prize of $1,000 in December 1946 from *Outdoor Life* honored her four-page essay on the Conservation Pledge. In October 1949, she gained $2,250 from the Eugene Saxton Memorial Fellowship, a windfall that financed field work on sea waves and tides, currents, and sea floor topography. In December 1950, the $1,000 George Westinghouse Science Writing Prize hailed Rachel's essay "The Birth of an Island," a chapter of *The Sea Around Us*.

The author's winning streak continued in March 1951 with a $1,000 Simon Guggenheim fellowship to underwrite a year's sabbatical and, on July 7, her picture on the cover of *Saturday Review*. At the topping of the *New York Times* bestseller list on September 9, *The Sea Around Us* became the Book-of-the-Month-Club alternate. Two days later, she received feature credit in *Look* magazine. On December 7, Rachel made a guest appearance aboard the Cunard line SS *Mauretania*. She achieved a profile in the December 17 *Newsweek* and a *New York Times* best 1951 nonfiction.

PERSONAL ACCLAIM

1952 was a stellar year for Rachel, who accepted the Henry Grier Bryant Gold Medal for accomplishments in oceanography and a woman of the year citation from the Associated Press. On January 27, she earned from the National Book Foundation $10,000 National Book Award for Nonfiction. A month later, the American Library Association and the *New York Herald Tribune* commended *The Sea Around Us* for placement on 60 listings of notable books. Her personal delight on April 7 for presentation of a John Burroughs Medal for nature writing from the American Museum of

Natural History in New York coincided with the Frances K. Hutchinson Medal from the Garden Club of America. In the same week, a reissue of *Under the Sea Wind* again placed her work on the bestseller list and inspired the *New York Times* to name Rachel a literary phenomenon and the Pennsylvania College for Women to bestow a Distinguished Service Alumnae Award. At June graduations, she received honorary doctorates from Oberlin College in Oberlin, Ohio, and the Drexel Institute of Technology in Philadelphia, followed a year later with a third Ph.D. from Smith College. In November, she joined poet Julia Ward Howe as the second female honoree of the U.S. National Institute of Arts and Letters. A film documentary of *The Sea Around Us* won an Oscar.

More kudos marked the next 24 months, beginning on January 14, 1953, with a gold medal from the New York Zoological Society and, in 1954, Royal Society of Literature in England selection of Rachel as a fellow and a U.S. Department of the Interior distinguished service medal. On May 11, the Limited Editions Club Silver chose the author to receive the Jubilee Medal. By June 1954, *The Edge of the Sea*, a *New York Times* bestseller, became Book-of-the-Month Club's alternate and an excerpt in *New Yorker*. In a speech, "The Real World Around Us," on April 21, 1954, to the Theta Sigma Phi Matrix Table Dinner, in Columbus, Ohio, Rachel confided that public clamor surprised her. A private person, she found herself the object of curiosity as to what a bestselling author looked like, even in a beauty salon and motel room.

Another fellowship honored Rachel on November 8, 1955, from the Boston Museum of Science; on November 27, the National Council of Women of the U.S. presented its nonfiction citation.

Winning awards dominated Rachel's public profile and her platform speeches. On June 22, 1956, the American Association of University Women voted her an Achievement Award of $2,500. As cancer gobbled her time and energy, she retreated from the public eye. John F. Kennedy's inauguration on January 18, 1961, restored her to celebrity at a reception of Distinguished Ladies on the Washington Mall at the National Gallery of Art. On July 1, 1962, *The Sea Around Us* appeared on the front page of the *New York Times Book Review*. By October, it was a Book-of-the-Month Club first choice. *Life* magazine featured Rachel on October 12, 1962; 12 days later, she appeared at a reception hosted by Cleveland's Museum of Natural History.

LAST DAYS

With little time left to live, on January 7, 1963, Rachel received from the Animal Welfare Institute in New York the Albert Schweitzer Medal and the Izaak Walton League of America commendation, followed the next day by a citation from the Garden Club of America. On January 17, she accepted an honorarium from the New England Wildflower Preservation Society. A month later, the Women's National Book Association selected the author to receive the Constance Lindsay Skinner Award. On March 28, 1963, the National Wildlife Federation named Rachel the Conservationist of the Year. Within days, Albert Einstein College of Medicine chose her to receive the Spirit of Achievement Award. For defending scientific facts, in mid–May, the author earned the title "Mother of Modern Environmentalism." In June, she accepted the title "Woman of Conscience" from the National Council of Women.

Rachel's last months placed a strain on her declining stamina. On December 3, 1963, the National Audubon Society presented her a second Paul Bartsch Medal for conservation. The same week brought membership in the American Academy of Arts and Letters and, on December 5, the Cullum Medal from the American Geographical Society. Her death on April 14, 1964, inspired President Lyndon B. Johnson to designate April as Cancer Control Month.

In Memoriam

Posthumous acclamations continued in May 1965 with installation in the Women's Hall of Fame Gallery at the New York World's Fair. Advocates credited Rachel's influence with passage of the National Historic Preservation Act on October 15, 1966, and foundation of the Environmental Defense Fund in 1967. Two years later, the U.S. Fish and Wildlife Service designated the Rachel Carson National Wildlife Refuge.

Observance of the original Earth First day on April 22, 1970, extended the biologist's fame, as did the founding of the National Oceanic and Atmospheric Administration on the same day. On January 31, 1972, the Federal Insecticide, Fungicide, and Rodenticide Act promoted a resurgence of bald eagles, alligators, brown pelicans, gray whales, and peregrine falcons. The Endangered Species Act of December 27, 1973, identified rare varieties of fish, reptiles, insects, birds, mammals, crustaceans, flowers, grasses, and trees.

Commendations took a variety of types and styles, including the Presidential Medal of Freedom from President Jimmy Carter on June 9, 1980. In September 1983, *Mother Earth News* enshrined Rachel in the Environmental Hall of Fame. In autumn 1980, *Life* magazine named Rachel of the 100 most importance people of the 1900s. Random House listed *Silent Spring* at fifth place among the 100 top nonfiction works of the twentieth century. *The Guardian* staff in London listed it among 50 Books to Change the World. More lists from *National Review* and *Time* to *Discover* magazine placed Rachel's classic among the most trenchant nonfiction titles. Chatham University established the Rachel Carson Healthy Planet Award to identify ecology-minded teens. In November 2015, the Academic Book of the Future, a project of the British government, selected *Silent Spring* among the world's most influential books.

Sources

Archer, Jules. *To Save the Earth: The American Environmental Movement.* New York: Simon & Schuster, 2016.
Carson, Rachel. "The Real World Around Us," address to the Theta Sigma Phi Matrix Table Dinner, Columbus, Ohio (21 April 1954).
Griswold, Eliza. "How *Silent Spring* Ignited the Environmental Movement." *New York Times Magazine* (21 September 2012).
Koehn, Nancy F. "From Calm Leadership, Lasting Change." *New York Times* (27 October 2012).
Lear, Linda J. *Rachel Carson: Witness for Nature.* New York: Henry Holt, 1997.

Beauty

More than just a lab scientist and science editor, Rachel was an esthete who coordinated life's complexities with grace, tranquility, and fascination with diversity.

She spoke of the human lack of awareness of earth's "beauties, its wonders, and the strange and sometimes terrible intensity of the lives that are being lived about us" (Carson, 2002, 249). Her pamphlet series *Conservation in Action,* for the U.S. Department of the Interior, extolled protected areas for "their value in our modern life" (Carson, 1948, 1). She justified her philosophy with a comparison to fine art: "Contemplation of the color, motion, and beauty of form in living nature yields esthetic enjoyment of as high an order as music or painting" (*ibid.*).

In "How about Citizenship Papers for the Starling?," a feature in the June 1939 issue of *Nature 32* magazine, she admitted joy in watching "aerial maneuverings" that "wheel and turn, ... patterning the evening sky with intricate designs ... black as Poe's raven" (Carson, 1939, 318). Her famous essay "The Birth of an Island" in *The Sea Around Us* concluded on the precious species networks on Laysan, Trinidad, and St. Helena and the rapidity of their destruction by exotic newcomers such as rats, cattle, and goats. Of the extinction of pampas birds in Argentina, she quoted novelist W.H. Hudson's plaint in *Exploring the Deep Pacific* (1923) for fragile life forms: "The beautiful has vanished and returns not" (Carson, 1951, 96).

New England's Splendors

In nine summers of tidepooling at Southport, Maine, Rachel shared with neighbors Dorothy and Stan Freeman the many moods of the coastline. Small ponds "[held] the stars and [reflected] the light of the Milky Way" (Carson, 1971, 101). The pellucid backwater contained its own stars, "shining emeralds of tiny phosphorescent diatoms" (*ibid.*). She dissected their appeal as "simple elements—color and form and reflection" and the impression that algal branches portray forests (*ibid.*). In occluded coves, the biologist searched out watery caves, where rays of sunlight sparked color shows in baby anemones and sponges, "a mesh of fine threads—a web of starched lace made to fairy scale" (*ibid., 116*).

For RCA Victor, in 1951, the author composed liner notes to introduce French composer Claude Debussy's symphony *La Mer.* The narrative accounted for the mesmerizing quality of dawn light on waves as "the shimmering beauty of the face of the sea and the sparkle of sun on water" (Carson, "Liner," 1951). Her thoughts in *The Edge of the Sea* in 1955 found elegance and grace in "the poignant beauty of things that are ephemeral," brushed daily by the tides and winds that feed and jeopardize them (Carson, 1955, 3). She welcomed the mystic connection between walks on a moonlit shoreline and "occasional flashes of insight" into the source and continuance of life (*ibid., 7*). To educate her nephew, Roger, on evanescence, she pointed out clouds in the sky, constellations, and the transition to daybreak and sunset. In December 1956, a letter to Curtis and Nellie Lee Bok, founders of the Bok Tower, hoped for the creation of sanctuaries of natural appeal to enhance "the peace and spiritual refreshment that our 'civilization' makes too difficult to achieve" (Carson, letter, 1956).

The author's personal and professional writing found occasions to rejoice in what poet Gerard Manley Hopkins's nature poem "Inversnaid" called "wildness and wet." Between Deep Cove and Dogfish Head, she made regular pilgrimages to rugged beaches and steep declivities of the Lost Woods on Southport Island, Maine, and viewed the crash of waves on rocks from her deck. The essay "Our Ever-Changing Shore" for the July 1958 issue of *Holiday* celebrated the unpredictable shaping of tide and wind on the Maine coast, "sculpturing it into forms that are often beautiful, sometimes bizarre" (Carson, 1958, 71). In a treatise for the October 1963 issue of *Audubon,* she extolled living species as "not only beautiful but full of meaning and significance" (Carson, 1963, 262). Of her uniqueness, John Burnside, a literary critic for the London *Guardian,* declared, "No other writer speaks so unabashedly about beauty and wonder; no other writer gets away with it so well" (Burnside, 2014, 55).

VALUING EARTH

Rachel pinpointed roadside wildflowers as examples of valuable plantings and questioned charges of sentimentality for "[caring] whether the robin returns to our dooryard and the veery sings in the twilight woods" (*ibid.*). Her criticism of soullessness in the mid-twentieth century pitted casual destruction of the irreplaceable with material dazzle intended to earn dollars. She rebuked period greed: "Beauty—and all the values that derive from beauty—are not measured and evaluated in terms of the dollar" (Carson, 1954, 325). Estelle C. Tappen, a book critic for the *Verona-Cedar Grove Times,* respected Rachel's earth ethic for its authenticity: "It is a wholesome and necessary thing for us to return again to earth and in the contemplation of her beauties to know the sense of wonder and humility" (Tappen, 1952, 16).

Notes of elegance in bird life balanced the horrors in *Silent Spring,* an alarm issued on September 27, 1962, about global contamination by pesticides and radiation. To contrast the grace of waterfowl with tainted waterways, Chapter Four, "Surface Waters and Underground Seas," summoned portraits of the gliding swan grebe and strings of migrating geese over Clear Lake, California. By picturing fleecy baby grebes, the imagery correlated descriptions of vulnerable animals and human babies in previous chapters. The underlying message, that the smallest, most precious beings faced imminent death from poisons, stirred the public to action to preserve delicate beings. In *Sense of Wonder,* she asserted that "Those who contemplate the beauty of the earth find reserves of strength that will endure as long as life lasts" (Carson,1965, 100).

See also Birds; Maine.

Sources

Burnside, John. "A Fish Called Wonder." *Guardian* 143:5205 (11–17 April 2014): 54–55.
Carson, Rachel. *The Edge of the Sea.* Boston: Houghton Mifflin, 1955.
_____. "Guarding Our Wildlife Resources: A National Wildlife Refuge." #5. Washington, D.C.: U.S. Department of the Interior, 1948.
_____. "How About Citizenship Papers for the Starling?" *Nature* 32 (June/July 1939): 317–319.
_____. "Letter to Curtis and Nellie Lee Bok" (12 December 1956).
_____. "Liner Notes." Claude Debussy's *La Mer,* RCA Victor, 1951.
_____. "Our Ever-Changing Shore." *Holiday* 24 (July 1958): 70–71, 117–120.
_____. "Rachel Carson Answers Her Critics." *Audubon* 65 (September/October 1963): 262–265, 313–315.
_____. "The Real World Around Us," address to the Theta Sigma Phi Matrix Table Dinner, *House of Life* (21 April 1954): 324–326.
_____. *The Rocky Coast.* New York: McCall, 1971.
_____. *The Sea Around Us.* New York: Oxford University Press, 1951.

_____. *The Sense of Wonder.* New York: Harper & Row, 1965.
_____. *Silent Spring.* Boston: Houghton Mifflin, 40th Anniversary Edition, 2002.
"Rachel Carson." *Calliope* 21:4 (January 2011): 32–33.
Tappen, Estelle C. "Review: *Under the Sea Wind.*" *Verona-Cedar Grove* (NJ) *Times* (5 June 1952): 16.

Birds

A protector of avian biodiversity and habitats, from preschool age, Rachel adopted her mother's example of reverence for living creatures. The author advocated the restoration of birds to landscapes and forests, where owls and woodpeckers reduced the influx of insects. She witnessed the life cycles of birds, including the song of veeries in Rock Creek Park in the nation's capital, fall flights of Maine ducks over Merrymeeting Bay, and migratory Canada geese at Mattamuskeet, North Carolina. In the essay "Nature Fights Back," she credited swallows with speedy capture of insects in the air.

Rachel's essay on avian life found a cooperative publisher in *Nature* magazine, which issued "How About Citizenship Papers for the Starling?" in June 1939. The summation covered the bird's value as an insect reducer as well as the detriments of noise maker and fouler of buildings. In Baltimore, Maryland, and Harrisburg, Pennsylvania, citizens reverted to gunfire, balloons, tin cans, and squirts of water to drive off "nightly encampments" (Carson, 1939, 318). Annoyance at starling infestation illustrated the author's description of urban hostility toward nature.

BIRD STORIES

In the opening chapter of *Under the Sea Wind,* in 1941, Rachel applied storytelling skills to admire the athleticism of the blue heron searching for mullet on the North Carolina Outer Banks. The long-legged stalker celebrated success by tossing the fish and catching the head in his bill for a quick gulp. The author intuited pleasure in mockingbirds, which spent the day listening to curlew, plover, and sandpiper cries. The next day, the imitators had "many new notes in their rippling, chuckling songs," which she described as delights to themselves and their mates.

With a natural bent for theater, Rachel envisioned the growth of shorebird families over the Arctic tundra and the mustering of flocks to begin the bicoastal flight to the southern hemisphere by way of Labrador and Nova Scotia. As though reporting bird cries in urgent dialogue, she followed the golden plover exodus, admiring the migrants' "strength and grace and beauty in every stroke of the pointed wings ... a river of birds" (Carson, 1941, 48). The narrative credited tenacity and stamina to a "racial urge" imprinted over millennia that guided each species to its ancestral home (*ibid.,* 50).

Rachel's immersion in the outdoors focused on avian movements and sounds. Her ode "An Island I Remember," composed in July 1946, opened on daylight observations of herons, cormorants, and thrushes and an evening survey of gulls fishing for herring. As light diminished, she noted from her dock a half mile away, "It was possible to do a good deal of birding by ear alone" (Carson, "Island," 1946). Acute interpretations of sounds identified osprey, kingfisher, phoebe, redstart, and parula warbler. In her 1947 summation of herons, thrushes, ducks, swans, and geese of Mattamuskeet nature sanctuary along North Carolina's Pamlico Sound, she delighted in the relaxation of elderly and disabled birders, some in wheelchairs, viewing ample flocks "within good binocular or camera range" (Carson, 1947, 3).

The author's curiosity piqued "The Birth of an Island," a stave of *The Sea Around Us*. She charted the survival and extinction of avian species by exotic fauna introduced by outsiders. Rachel returned to bird life in the final segment, "The Restless Sea," by depicting the Humboldt Current's unique "abundance of sea life perhaps unparalleled anywhere else in the world" (Carson, 1951, 135). Because of the millions of birds inhabiting the western coast of South America, merchants profited from rich deposits of guano, exported for fertilizer.

BIRD KILLERS

Significant to Rachel's avian investigations, the effects of DDT (dichlorodiphenyltrichloroethane) prevented calcium release in the female's body and thinned eggshells, causing embryos to die before hatching. Researcher Pedro Ramirez of Cheyenne, Wyoming, examined an American avocet egg and found an embryo left freakish by selenium, which deformed the cranium, crossed the bill, and deprived the unhatched skeleton of toes and wings. At Michigan State University in 1959, robin corpses pocked the campus from consumption of as few as 11 tainted earthworms. Those that survived convulsion remained sterile. The loss prodded observers to conclusions about the ethics of pesticides and the need for earth advocacy.

Other proofs of harm compelled the author to become a scientist advocate. She composed "Vanishing Americans" in the April 10, 1959, issue of the *Washington Post*, in which she posed a rhetorical question: "If this 'rain of death' has produced so disastrous an effect on birds, what of other lives, including our own" (Carson, 1959, A26). In January 1960, she confided to neighbor Dorothy Freeman, "I could never again listen happily to a thrush song if I had not done all I could" (Carson, 1960). The result of her unrest, *Silent Spring*, revealed on September 27, 1962, to readers worldwide the specific loss of swan grebes in Clear Lake, California, the drop in robin populations in East Lansing, Michigan, and bald eagles everywhere from toxic accumulations in their bodies. To advance one step from the objective laboratory scientist, she linked bird loss to human esthetics and the yearning for beauty in everyday life.

In Chapter Four, "Surface Waters and Underground Seas," Rachel reported the demise of egrets from plumage hunters, of songbirds in Illinois from aldrin and heptachlor spray, and of fish-eating swan grebes and gulls in California the previous two years by 97 percent from DDD (dichlorodiphenyldichloroethane) emulsion alone. The 30 remaining nesters produced no viable young. In southeastern England in 1961, toxins killed pigeons, owls, hawks, and small mammals. Biocides reduced populations of ospreys and Scots raptors and turned herons into rigid statues. The herons' wobbly stance and vomiting preceded their final tumble to earth.

A CALL TO RESCUE

In Chapter Thirteen, "Through a Narrow Window," the biologist alerted readers to the unhatched eggs of robins, eagles, pheasants, and chickens. After significant support from the Kennedy administration turned opinion in Rachel's favor, in summer 1962, she vacationed in Maine with neighbor Dorothy Freeman. From a beachfront porch, she recovered from radiation therapy while observing gulls, parula warblers, and terns. Under England's Protection of Birds Acts, the Department of Environment for Britain initiated sanctuaries to support breeding, nesting, and fledging and to halt mass die-offs.

Within a quarter century of conservation law and volunteerism, ornithologists found that pelicans, broadbills, kingfishers, rails, cardinals, crows, falcons, swiftlets, condors, storks, and murrelets had a greater chance of survival. In an address to the Women's National Press Club on December 5, 1962, Rachel pinpointed the poisoning of bald eagles with DDT and New Brunswick woodcocks with heptachlor, making the carcasses dangerous for Canadian hunters to eat. A subsequent speech to the Garden Club of America on January 8, 1963, warned of the dieldrin in East St. Louis, Illinois, where insecticide dispersal against Japanese beetles in a game preserve killed hundreds of quail and songbirds. Deliberate misinformation by the Virginia Department of Agriculture in Norfolk claimed to drill poisons into the soil rather than spew them from the sky. The use of helicopters, blowers, and seeders produced the same mayhem as in Illinois—the extermination of brown thrashers, meadowlarks, and robins.

GOVERNMENT INQUIRY

On May 15, 1963, President John F. Kennedy's Science Advisory Committee reported the loss of 80 percent of songbirds and a serious reduction in viable quail eggs and chicks tainted with aldrin or dieldrin. A more disturbing discovery of the U.S. Fish and Wildlife Service near the Arctic Circle at Yellowknife, Canada, found DDT in the soil and vegetation of an area that used no pesticides, yet migratory birds and their young exhibited residues. On October 18, 1963, to a San Francisco symposium of 1,500 physicians at Kaiser-Permanente, Rachel reprised the central issue of "Man Against Himself" with the example of long range effects of death-dealing chemicals.

On June 6, 1963, the biologist's testimony before congress, "Environmental Hazards: Control of Pesticides and Other Chemical Poisons," asserted the role of the woodcock in carrying heptachlor from its application to southern fire ant infestations as far north as the Canadian maritimes. The treatment of Big Bear Lake, California, with toxaphene resulted in a food chain migration from plankton to pelicans, with the concentration from .2 parts per million burgeoning to 1,700 parts or 8,500 times the original saturation. Her hour-long oration at San Francisco's Fairmont Hotel alerted the audience to high mortality among fish-eating birds at sanctuaries on Tule Lake and Klamath National Wildlife Refuge and the near extinction of the western grebe at Clear Lake, California.

Rachel informed the public of nature's unity and the inability of polluters to limit the extent of damage to one area, state, or nation. In fall 1963, woodcock (*Scolopax minor*) poisoned with heptachlor during fire ant extermination in the southeastern U.S. carried the carcinogen north in spring to New Brunswick, where people valued the game birds for food. Still an avid bird-watcher in her last six months, Rachel proposed to friend Dorothy Freeman a January trek to Mattamuskeet, North Carolina, to inspect the condition of Canada Geese.

In correspondence with Dorothy on October 26, 1963, Rachel regretted dependence on a wheelchair and the inability to tramp the wild and monitor birds in fall migration. She found encouragement on the large number of blackbirds and grackles. At Rachel's passing in April 1964, nearly 99 percent of bird eggs revealed poisons. Sparrow hawks presented symptoms of reproductive failure because of DDE (dichlorodiphenyldichloroethylene), which caused variance in infancy and growth; peregrine falcons declined in number. The 9,125-acre Maryland sanctuary she willed to the public preserved habitats of the piping plover, loon, teal, merganser, hawk, sandpiper, herring gull, thrush, warbler, and scarlet tanager. In 1982, a former colleague, Shirley A. Briggs, director of the Rachel Carson Council, saluted her friend for precipitating the ban on DDT for agrarian purposes. As a result, the bald eagle and brown pelican began their rebound from the endangered species list.

See also "A Fable for Tomorrow"; Pesticide Alternatives; *Silent Spring: The Other Road*; Waterfowl.

Sources

Brinkley, Douglas. "Rachel Carson and JFK, an Environmental Tag Team." *Audubon* (May–June 2012), https://www.audubon.org/magazine/may-june-2012/rachel-carson-and-jfk-environmental-tag-team.

Carson, Rachel. "Address," Women's National Press Club (5 December 1962), Washington, D.C.

_____. "Environmental Hazards: Control of Pesticides and Other Chemical Poisons." Statement before the Subcommittee on Reorganization and International Organizations of the Committee on Government Operations (4 June 1963): 206–219.

_____. "How About Citizenship Papers for the Starling?" *Nature* 32 (June/July 1939): 317–319.

_____. "An Island I Remember," unpublished ode, July 1946.

_____. "Letter to Dorothy Freeman" (January 1960).

_____. "Letter to Dorothy Freeman" (26 October 1963).

_____. "Mattamuskeet: A National Wildlife Refuge." #4. Washington, D.C.: U.S. Department of the Interior, July 1947.

_____. "A New Chapter in *Silent Spring*," address to the Garden Club of America, New York City (8 January 1963).

_____. "The Pollution of Our Environment," address to the Kaiser-Permanente Symposium *Man Against Himself*, San Francisco (18 October 1963).

_____. "Rachel Carson Answers Her Critics." *Audubon* 65 (September/October 1963): 262–265, 313–315.

_____. "She Started It All—Here's Her Reaction." *New York Herald Tribune* (19 May 1963).

_____. *Under the Sea Wind: A Naturalist's Picture of Ocean Life.* New York: Simon & Schuster, 1941.

_____. "Vanishing Americans." *Washington Post* (10 April 1959): A26.

Doffey, Philip M. "Environment, Two Decades after *Silent Spring*." *Rutland Daily Herald* (29 May 1982): 17.

Ramirez, Pedro. "Everything Is Connected." *Fish & Wildlife News* (Spring 2007): 16.

"Use of Pesticides," Washington, D.C.: White House (15 March 1963): 1–25.

Carcinogens

Rachel knew from laboratory experience the pending danger of mutagenic-carcinogenic chemical agents, which interrupted cell respiration. She vilified the U.S.

Department of Agriculture for the widespread spraying of dieldrin and heptachlor against fire ants and gypsy moths. The substances caused human tumors, especially to migrant pickers, produce packers, and agribusiness workers. Similar effects of the fish killer toxaphene afflicted pond cleaners and toxin handlers with bronchial cancer. In California, Clear Lake fishermen who ate their catch incurred adrenocortical carcinoma, a rare adrenal cancer caused by buildup of DDD (dichlorodiphenyldichloroethane) in fish. The biocides joined DDT (dichlorodiphenyltrichloroethane) on her list of noxious chemicals.

The author extended an examination of carcinogens to post–Hiroshima radioisotope technology, a source of strontium-90, a byproduct of nuclear fission. Thirteen nations began jettisoning radioactive vessels and nuclear fuel from nuclear plants, with the Soviet Union leading the dumping in 1959. Into the Atlantic Ocean from July 15, 1946, to June 1961, U.S. detritus in 55-gallon drums tumbled 300 at a time from the U.S.S. *Calhoun County* off the continental shelf up to 2.3 miles deep. In addition to ocean contamination, Rachel scrutinized biocidal threats from the gamma rays emitted by five bomb tests in Yucca Flat, Nevada, beginning July 6, 1962. The dispersal of radiation on air currents altered DNA and imperiled citizens as far away as Idaho and Utah. Her perusal of experimental A-bomb testing and atomic fallout detailed tainted of dairy animals and food products with ultraviolet radioactivity that was more likely to cause disease in children than adults.

In September 1962, Rachel's treatise *Silent Spring* implicated the toxicity of radioactive particles and organic insecticides in human cancer. She opened the topic with commentary on arsenic dust and spray, an environmental carcinogen studied by Wilhelm Carl Hueper, a specialist in occupational carcinogens at the National Cancer Institute in Bethesda, Maryland. To connect contamination with the ordinary grocery store, the author reprised the cranberry scare from the 1957, 1958, and 1959 harvests, which resulted from illicit application of aminotriazole, a virulent herbicide linked to throat and thyroid cancer. She saluted Austrian and English authorities for outlawing biocides that mutated cells.

Delayed Reactions

The theme of carcinogens in the atmosphere demonstrated Rachel's concern for future generations. The title of Chapter Twelve, "The Human Price," focused on exposure to multiple industrial chemicals that spawned anatomical mutations, some of which did not appear in the body for decades. In Chapter Fourteen of *Silent Spring*, "One in Every Four," the biologist reflected on the toxicity of soot and heavy metals in Europe and Great Britain from the beginning of the Industrial Age. She classified six insecticides in eastern Florida as causes of bladder cancer and cited as examples in everyday life the bone tumors in painters of radium dial watches and the carcinogens that passed through the human placenta to the fetus.

On October 10, 1963, at a Kaiser-Permanente symposium in San Francisco on *Man Against Himself*, the orator described the growth of the post–World War II chemical industry. She denounced DDT as "a grim experiment never before attempted" (Carson, 1963, 314). Her speech castigated the products as lethal and cumulative in the body. One example, iodine in milk, compromised the thyroid glands of babies and children. In the opinion of Lisa H. Sideris, an environmentalist at Indiana University, and Kathleen Dean Moore, a philosopher at Oregon State University, the author's sufferings with metastatic breast cancer "made her an icon of women's health movements and others seeking to draw attention to the links between cancer and the environment" (Sideris and Moore, 2008, 1).

POSTHUMOUS INFLUENCE

As a result of Rachel's unorthodox and disturbing texts and speeches, the government impaneled the Environmental Protection Agency in Washington, D.C., on December 2, 1970. Federal regulations required the review, registration, and standards of use for pesticides, fungicides, and rodenticides, including narrow-spectrum biocides of high toxicity that threatened the health of rural laborers with neurological damage and malignancies. Ecology activist Al Gore corroborated Rachel's wise advice—"Americans received short-term gain at the expense of long-term tragedy" (Matthiessen, 2007, 71). Ecofeminists took up the challenge of an array of issues, specifically environmental harm. Author Joni Seager, an activist at the University of Vermont, applauded the wellness rally as a "take-it-to-the-streets movement" (Seager, 2003, 945).

Over a quarter century ago in 1993, the *New York Times* exposed 68 synthetic ingredients that caused cancer. Facts proved unnerving to readers:

- 10 percent of community well water bore pesticide contamination.
- Farmers who handled herbicides died of cancer at six times the average rate.
- Children of pesticide users developed leukemia at seven times the average rate.

In a Carsonian defense of ecology, Sandra Steingraber's *Living Downstream* questioned the global dependence on nightmarish substances that bolstered agribusiness and the economy.

See also Radiation; *Silent Spring: One in Every Four.*

Sources

Bailey, Ronald. "*Silent Spring* at 40: Rachel Carson's Classic Is Not Aging Well." *Reason* (12 June 2002).

Carson, Rachel. "Rachel Carson Answers Her Critics." *Audubon* 65 (September/October 1963): 262–265, 313–315.

_____. *Silent Spring*. Boston: Houghton Mifflin, 40th Anniversary Edition, 2002.

Matthiessen, Peter, ed. *Courage for the Earth: Writers, Scientists, and Activists Celebrate the Life and Writing of Rachel Carson.* New York: Mariner, 2007.

Seager, Joni. "Rachel Carson Died of Breast Cancer: The Coming of Age of Feminist Environmentalism." *Signs* 28:3 (Spring 2003): 945–972.

Sideris, Lisa H., and Kathleen Dean Moore, eds. *Rachel Carson: Legacy and Challenge.* Albany: State University of New York, 2008.

Steingraber, Sandra. "Living Downstream," www.LivingDownstream.com.

ten Have, Hank. *Wounded Planet: How Declining Biodiversity Endangers Health and How Bioethics Can Help.* Baltimore: Johns Hopkins University Press, 2019.

Chemical Industry

Rachel studied changes in nature at a boom time for chemical and pharmaceutical factories, which employed 98 percent of the researchers who formulated biological controls of natural phenomena. In the mid–1950s, David D. Vail, an historian at the University of Nebraska, revealed falsehoods and semi-truths in the media:

> To convince landowners and agricultural leaders to buy their pesticides, chemical companies generated advertisements that championed local crop health, mixture accuracy, livestock safety, and a chemical-farming "'way of life" that kept fields healthy and productive [Vail, 2012, 170].

These "economic entomologists" spread their obfuscations by bankrolling graduate studies in universities, such as the world's largest chemical conglomerate, BASF, the German sponsor of research at ten California schools (Carson, 2002, 259). Proponents blazoned "Better living through chemistry" and touted the synthetics found in pharmaceuticals, cosmetics, toys, cars, human and livestock food, and plastics (Lytle, 2007, vi).

The author gained a personal knowledge of chemical pollutants in childhood. She grew up in an industrial ring around Pittsburgh, Pennsylvania, where capitalism exonerated profligate factory owners for smoke, soot, and odor. Her family complained that industry ignored the corruption of Springdale's air, water, and land and avoided responsibility for pollutants. For her "grace and fierce intelligence," writer Terry Tempest Williams, a conservationist in the American West, validated Rachel's demand that citizens "hold corporations and our government accountable for the health of our communities, cultured and wild" (Williams, 2002).

Shortsighted Gains

In Rachel's view, chlorinated biocides and thalidomide represented the rashness of progress "to rush ahead and use something new without knowing what the results are going to be" (Brinkley, 2012). Vail explained how newspapers, magazines, and trade journals and the opinions of crop dusters, weed specialists, and landowners on the Great Plains reinforced a faith in biocides for promoting the American dream. Before Connecticut senator Abraham Ribicoff and the Committee on the Senate Government Operations Subcommittee on June 4, 1963, the author declared the agrarian chemical community "injudicious" in ignoring the drift factor of aerial spraying (Vail, 2018, 98). Essayist Terry Williams warned of the capitalist response: "A debate had begun: a reverence for life versus a reverence for power" derived from profits and votes (Williams, 1992, 106). At a conservation forum on May 19, 1962, Justice William Orville Douglas told an audience, "Everyone should read Rachel Carson's forthcoming book *Silent Spring* to learn what the chemical engineers are doing to our world" (Carson, "Freeman," 1962).

In a personal essay dated December 2, 1962, the author justified the compilation of *Silent Spring* in defiance of "the freewheeling use of highly dangerous chemicals" (Carson, "Reception," 1962). She also named four instances of financial grants to state universities by Diamond Black-Leaf, Shell Chemical, Velsicol, Wisconsin Canners, and Monsanto. Because of the selectivity of her polemical work, she was prepared for an industrial smear campaign, but not for what biographer Andrea Barnet called "defamation of her character—the charges that she was a Communist and a subversive" willing to destabilize the national economy and inhibit food security (Barnet, 2018, 4).

The Rebuttal

Velsicol, the Rosemont, Illinois, manufacturer of chlordane, DDT (dichlorodiphenyltrichloroethane), and heptachlor, called Rachel's research inaccurate and labeled her un–American. In a measured essay in the October 1963 *Audubon*, Rachel modestly appealed, "We ask moderation. We ask the use of other methods less harmful" (Carson, 1963, 265, 313). A year later, the company halted pesticide manufacture, but left a nine-block toxic mess in St. Louis, Michigan, that tainted milk, butter, cheese, eggs, and meat. The U.S. Environmental Protection Agency seized the manufactory in 1982 and razed the plant, but not before the effluents caused thyroid disease, miscarriages, and reproductive damage in the grandchildren of victims. In August 1988, citizens of Hardeman County, Tennessee, sued Velsicol for improper disposal of poisonous chemicals in drums and cartons in unlined 12-to-15 foot disposal trenches on Pugh Creek. Seepage polluted the watershed, surface water, soil, and sediment. The class action suit awarded $7.5 million in punitive damages.

Government agencies demanded thorough testing, labeling, and training for users of pesticides, especially farmers and herders. A growing number of companies projected a public-minded philosophy by halting use of aldrin and dieldrin. When Shell Chemical ceased to sell termiticides, only chlordane and heptachlor remained available. R.V. Carr, an employee of Velsicol, complained that chemists and vendors of urban biocides incurred suspicion and contempt from ecolawyers, neighbors, and their own children. Still, a half century after Rachel's revelations about the insidious nature of noxious hydrocarbons, Velsicol's products, spread over 54 acres in east central Michigan, continued killing bald eagles, robins, starlings, and bluebirds and threatened human health with reduced sperm counts and lowered fertility. Contaminated muck in the Pine River on the Saginaw Bay contributed to the decline in bass and carp populations.

In a foreword to Ruth Harrison's *Animal Machines*, Rachel extended her damnation of capitalistic greed to the torturous environments in which farmers raise animals for food. To prevent disease from overcrowding and befouling of pens and cages, animal keepers administered antibiotics to suppress diseases arising in artificial environments. With her standard rhetorical address, she demanded, "How can the animals produced under such conditions be safe or acceptable human food?" (Carson, 1964, viii). In a surge of "dismay, revulsion, and outrage," she accused factory farmers of creating a "menace to human consumers from the drugs, hormones, and pesticides used to keep this whole fantastic operation somehow going" (*ibid.*).

See also Carcinogens.

Sources

Barnet, Andrea. *Visionary Women: How Rachel Carson, Jane Jacobs, Jane Goodall, and Alice Waters Changed Our World.* New York: Ecco, 2018.

Bienkowski, Brian. "DDT Still Killing Birds in Michigan." *Scientific American* (28 July 2014).
Brinkley, Douglas. "Rachel Carson and JFK, an Environmental Tag Team." *Audubon* (May–June 2012), https://www.audubon.org/magazine/may-june-2012/rachel-carson-and-jfk-environmental-tag-team.
Carson, Rachel, "Foreword," *Animal Machines: The New Factory Farming Industry.* London: Vincent Stuart, 1964.
_____. "Letter to Dorothy Freeman" (20 May 1962).
_____. "Rachel Carson Answers Her Critics." *Audubon* 65 (September/October 1963): 262–265, 313–315.
Lytle, Mark Hamilton. *The Gentle Subversive: Rachel Carson, Silent Spring, and the Rise of the Environmental Movement.* New York: Oxford University Press, 2007.
Vail, David D. *Chemical Lands: Pesticides, Aerial Spraying, and Health in North America's Grasslands Since 1945.* Tuscaloosa: University of Alabama Press, 2018.
Watson, David, and A.W.A. Brown, eds. *Pesticide Management and Insecticide Resistance.* New York: Academic Press, 1977.
Williams, Terry Tempest. "One Patriot," in *Patriotism and the American Land.* Great Barrington, MA: Orion Society, 2002.
_____. "The Spirit of Rachel Carson." *Audubon* (July/August 1992): 104–107.

Climate Change

Rachel pioneered concern for climate change and its effect on an interdependent life web. In the 1950s, Rachel officially opposed scientific separations of life into strict divisions and hierarchies. She took as a personal challenge a global tutorial on holistic nature, its complexity and process. Her theory took the form of an axiom: "Nothing exists alone" (Sisson, 2018). On television in 1963, she told an audience that "the balance of nature is built on a series of relationship between living things and their environment" (*ibid.*).

In November 1951, she issued a seven-page segment of *The Sea Around Us* in *Popular Science* on global warming and resultant rising seas. The text cited the temperature and tidal charts of Swedish hydrographer and oceanographer Sven Otto Pettersson and stressed, "The frigid top of the world is very clearly warming up" (Carson, 1951, 252). She introduced the concept that ocean depths caused cyclic swings in temperature that generated flooding and drought. Her enthusiasm for "great earth rhythms" combined both threat and excitement at unavoidable shifts in the disproportion of seawater to land that could engulf the Mississippi Valley and invade the Carolinas, northern Canada, and Mexico (*ibid.*, 97). She concluded that the mysterious relationship of ocean to dry land "is the most fleeting and transitory feature of the earth" (*ibid.*).

Citing the research of Swedish oceanographer Pettersson about the moon and sun's powers to produce deep currents on the Baltic Sea, the biologist allied the commentary with alarming sketches of New York City under ice-melt. According to records from Iceland, the pattern of catastrophic tides every 18 centuries reached a height in 1433. Her calculations predicted a recurrence in 2400, causing storms, volcanic eruptions, agricultural failure, and starvation. Conversely, as the polar seas warmed, humankind enjoyed easier navigation for harvesting of fishing grounds. She introduced the interdisciplinary concept of sustainability. Social studies teachers Margaret Smith Crocco, Jay M. Shuttleworth, and Thomas Chandler defined the controversial term as "the need for contemporary human societies to figure out how to live in the world in a manner that does not jeopardize the ability of future generations to continue to live on planet earth" (Crocco, Shuttleworth, Chandler, 2016, 22).

CYCLES OF CHANGE

To substantiate her groundwork, Rachel investigated a less harmful tidal cycle of nine, 18, and 36 years and cited the calving of arctic pack ice in 1903 and subsequent melting of fossil ice and glaciers as proofs of oceanic trends. A recurrence on April 15, 1912, coincided with the sinking of the *Titanic* after its collision with a massive berg south of the Newfoundland coast. Into the 1940s, the northern hemisphere blossomed from a lengthened trading season in ice-free waters. Farmlands produced more crops and forests more pine and spruce timber in longer growing seasons.

The author revisited the subject of rising temperatures in December 1953 with a scholarly speech in Boston. Before the American Association for the Advancement of Science, her text, "The Edge of the Sea," acknowledged a "measurable warming of the Atlantic coastal waters" (Carson, 1953, n.p.). Substantiating data showed steady incline off Massachusetts shores:

Date	Lows	Average Rise
1918	28	—
1930s	32	14.3%
1953	38	18.8%
overall		35.7%

As a result, marine biologists tracked the green crab (*Carcinus maenas*) from a warming clime. They established its migration north from Cape Cod, Massachusetts, to cooler water in St. Mary's Bay, Nova Scotia, where it fed on young soft clams.

ACCEPTING CHANGE

Rachel enabled the ordinary reader to comprehend effects of climate change on small organisms. The same resistance to warmer seawater by tender larvae caused sea squirts (*Clava*) and alga (*Syncoryne*) to vacate the sea floor of Boothbay, Maine. The naturalist monitored their response to sand in specialized habitats and characterized the status of these fauna as "delicate, transparent, and minute, fragile as blown glass" (Carson, 1953, n.p.). In contrast to frail marine organisms, the narrative "The Coral Coast" prized the vigorous mangrove and its matted roots, maker of shoals into islands and islands into peninsulas. Of newly created topography, she had to admit, "A rising sea could write a different history" for the people of earth (Carson, 1955, 246).

In 1959, physicist Edward Teller spoke at the American Petroleum Institute symposium "Energy and Man." He informed oil barons that carbon dioxide can absorb infrared radiation and raise Earth's temperature. He speculated, "The icecaps will start melting and the level of the oceans will begin to rise" (McKibben, 2019, 73). A subsequent alert from the White House science adviser in 1968 warned of catastrophic alteration to the climate.

At the June 12, 1962, commencement at Scripps College in Claremont, California, Rachel's speech, "Of Man and the Stream of Time," delivered a challenge worthy of an ethicist. In token of the rhythmic variability of earth over time, she urged, "Your generation must come to terms with the environment" (Carson, 1962, 10). Of the acceptance of climate change as earth's destiny, she exalted a mature attitude toward learning as proof that humanity had reached a peak of civilization. Instead of evading hard truths about weather, natural disasters, and food security, she advocated shouldering a serious responsibility that posed "a shining opportunity" (*ibid.*). In the early 1980s, Exxon learned from James Black that loss of forests and increase burning of fossil fuels boosted carbon dioxide to dangerous levels.

    See also Fossils

Sources

Carson, Rachel. *The Edge of the Sea*. Boston: Houghton Mifflin, 1955.
_____. "The Edge of the Sea" (speech), American Association for the Advancement of Science, Boston (December 29, 1953).
_____. "Of Man and the Stream of Time." *Scripps College Bulletin,* Claremont, CA (12 June 1962): 5–10.
_____. *The Sea Around Us*. New York: Oxford University Press, 1951.
_____. "Why Our Winters Are Getting Warmer." *Popular Science* 159:5 (November 1951): 113–117, 252, 254, 256.
Crocco, Margaret Smith, Jay M. Shuttleworth, and Thomas Chandler. "Science, Media, and Civic Literacy: Rachel Carson's Legacy for the Citizen Activist." *Social Studies and the Young Learner* 28:3 (2016): 21–26.
Matthiessen, Peter, ed. *Courage for the Earth: Writers, Scientists, and Activists Celebrate the Life and Writing of Rachel Carson*. New York: Mariner, 2007.
McKibben, Bill. *Falter: Has the Human Game Begun to Play Itself Out?* New York: Henry Holt, 2019.
Sisson, Stephanie Roth. *Spring after Spring: How Rachel Carson Inspired the Environmental Movement*. New York: Roaring Book, 2018.

Clouds

    An apostle of beauty, Rachel earned a following for a lyric, poignant appreciation of earth's watery phenomena. Her integration of natural elements into scenarios stressed molecular masses at the birth of the solar system. She included sky cover, a preface to the ice ages, as a backdrop for raptors, the focus of the 1945 unpublished essay "Road of the Hawks." Like a painter sorting out visual stimuli, at the Hawk Valley Sanctuary in eastern Pennsylvania, she viewed an October day gray with clouds "heavy with unshed rain" in "an elemental landscape" under "a vast, pale, arching sky" (Carson, 1945). The setting anticipates interaction between cloud moisture and earth's crust.

    The author moved easily from lyricism to scientific objectivity. For the opening chapter of *Under the Sea Wind*, in 1941, she credited the black skimmer or flood gull (*Rynchops*) with a preference for dark, occluded nights as protection from predators. When "thick clouds lay between the water and the moon's light," the seabirds foraged safely along the shore (Carson, 1941, 12). Arctic butterflies, fearful of shadows, halted noontime flutters "when clouds stole between earth and sun" (*ibid.,* 42). The author's sensitivity to the smallest alterations of light isolated proofs of faunal adaptation to cloud cover.

Color and Shape

    During field work in June 1950 in the Florida Everglades, the writer mused over the cloud cap that shifted the tint of palmetto hammocks from gray to green. In *The*

Sea Around Us, she revisited early studies of wind and atmospheric temperature for new revelations about clouds. The narrative imagined an interglacial stage concluding with the formation of sky cover, snow clouds, and the freezing of ice sheets shielded from the sun's rays. She contextualized sky temperatures with a photo over a tropical sea, the source of heat that "[fuels] the wind systems of the globe" (Carson, 1951, 160). Her theatrical reprise of creation credited heavy cloud layers with raining down earth's first waters in a time of "swirling clouds and gloom" (*ibid.*, 22).

In another style and format, Rachel filled the liner notes of Arturo Toscanini's performance of *La Mer* with a rhapsodic intensity based on sense impressions of waters "never at rest" (Carson, 1951). The first movement credited "the thick cloud blanket that enveloped the earth" with shadowing the ocean at daybreak, adjusting color and light like God in the opening lines of Genesis I. For the after-dinner speech "The Real World Around Us" to the Theta Sigma Phi Matrix on April 21, 1954, her esthetic love for the sky's restlessness repeated a motif of evanescence: "The cloud effects were beautiful and always changing" (Carson, 1954). While introducing her foster son Roger to nature, she recommended that parents rely on the heavens for examples: "The sky—its dawn and twilight beauties, its moving clouds, its stars by night," an accessible, yet ineffable setting for learning to appreciate the universe (Carson, 1956, 46).

The Sky in Motion

For the CBS-TV broadcast on clouds for *Omnibus* on March 11, 1957, the author dated human ancestry to the Carboniferous Era (300 million years BCE). She extended lessons on moist air currents to the cycle of evaporation and condensation. In an appeal to young viewers, she scripted simple regard for water dispersal, noting, "Without clouds, all water would remain forever in the sea" (Carson, "Clouds," 1957). The narrative paid special attention to the uniqueness of cumulus clouds, the inviting "thermals" favored by prehistoric Polynesian pilots, glider fliers, hawks, and eagles (*ibid.*).

Visions of ethereal beauty eased Rachel's fears of the perversion of scientific ego and enabled her to write: "Nature was forever beyond the tampering reach of man—he might level the forests and dam the streams, but the clouds and the rain and the wind were God's" (Carson, 1958). In a rush of sensory vibes, she romanticized the shape, texture, and color of fog as "soft grey swirling mists" (*ibid.*). For "Our Ever-Changing Shore," an article for *Holiday* in July 1958, she dramatized an empty, cloudless ether, which tentatively promised change. The alteration arrived on a surge of air over the coast, which bore away clouds and sandy motes.

In the early 1960s during the planning stages of *Silent Spring,* the author idealized nature for divine control of clouds, rain, and wind. Despite the post–Sputnik fantasies of human invincibility, she characterized earthlings as psychologically ill-prepared to manage natural phenomena. On October 26, 1963, Rachel returned from an hour-long address, "The Pollution of Our Environment," to 1,500 physicians attending the Kaiser-Permanente symposium *Man Against Himself* in San Francisco. At a well-earned breather five months before her death, she visited the southern rim of the Grand Canyon to view the vast azure over the desert. Looking eastward toward home, she marveled at the mirror effect of clouds that "took on the tints of the sand reflected from below" (Carson, letter, 1963). The reflection characterized her ability to find basic science both comforting and restorative.

Sources

Carson, Rachel. "Clouds" in "Something about the Sky," CBS *Omnibus* (11 March 1957).
_____. "Help Your Child to Wonder." *Woman's Home Companion* 53 (July 1956): 25–27, 46–48.
_____. "Letter to Dorothy Freeman" (1 February 1958).
_____. "Letter to Dorothy Freeman" (26 October 1963).
_____. "Liner Notes," Claude Debussy's *La Mer*, RCA Victor, 1951.
_____. "Our Ever-Changing Shore." *Holiday* 24 (July 1958): 70–71, 117–120.
_____. "The Real World Around Us," address to the Theta Sigma Phi Matrix Table Dinner, Columbus, Ohio (21 April 1954).
_____. "Road of the Hawks," unpublished, October 1945.
_____. *The Sea Around Us*. New York: Oxford University Press, 1951.
_____. *Under the Sea Wind: A Naturalist's Picture of Ocean Life*. New York: Simon & Schuster, 1941.
Meisch, Simon. *Water, Creativity and Meaning*. New York: Routledge, 2018.

Color

The author permeated her thoughts and observations with the implications of color. After two years of writing for newspapers, she began a literary career with "Undersea," a color-rich essay for the September 1937 issue of *Atlantic Monthly*. Opening on the filtration of the spectrum by seawater, she continued summarizing changes in noon light at the ocean's surface, where "twilight blues and purples, and where the blackness of midnight is eerily aglow with the cold phosphorescence of living things" (Carson, 1937, 323). Amid shiny deep-sea beings, the essay pictured red, brown, and black as the prevalent tones of the deep, ending in a shift to violet. She drew on field work to admire the golden glow of sunrise on Canada geese, annual migrants to the Pamlico Sound in North Carolina.

In an unpublished essay, Rachel observed a warbler with his "exquisite powder-blue parole with his breast band of orange and magenta" (Matthiessen, 2007, 16–17). She admired the flashes of yellow on the Blackburnian species and the black-throated green warbler amid spruce limbs. Her oceanside survey in 1941 in *Under the Sea Wind* specified contrast in the "creamy tan" ghost crab marked by "eyes like two black shoe buttons on stalks," a stark sensory organ capable of finding beach fleas among seaweed and green sea lettuce (Carson, 1941, 25). The contrast continued at Mullet Pond with eight minnows casting "eight black shadows" on the silty bottom and the white-winged snowy egret landing his "slim black stilts" in marsh grass (*ibid.*, 26). While female crabs shielded their eggs from view with their waistline aprons, the clusters, like "bunches of miniature purple grapes," turned gray before releasing larvae from burst shells (*ibid.*, 28).

A FAR NORTH SETTING

The author chose color as the introit to an arctic spring: the perennial avens in white, saxifrage in purple, and buttercup glades yellow with petals and bees coated with golden pollen. To introduce the aging of new-hatched sanderlings, she pictured egg-stained feathers molting into a cloak of "buff and sand and chestnut," the shades that blended with the winter-hued countryside (*ibid.,* 45). Fall tinged Atlantic shores with purple rushes, green and brown meadow grass, golden brown sea oats, and the reds of swamp samphire (*Salicornia*), a flowering succulent. Over all, sandy froth masked foliage with a "brown scud" carried inland by the surf (*ibid.,* 53).

From the abyss, rising warm waters passed through the spectrum, from black to purple, deep blue, and azure. Metallic tones of bronze and silver identified menhaden and anchovies; moon jellies glowed opalescent. Amid phosphorescent plankton, starry noctiluca bubbles, and shrimp, mackerel flashed green and blue while enemy squid took on the beige of bottom sand, a useful camouflage. By February, the winter sun shed a "cold and sterile residue of blue and ultraviolet, shorn of all its warmth of reds and yellows and greens" (*ibid.,* 154). Below its rays, Rachel created a palette in the twilight zone of opal, silver, red, and orange. She cast gothic chill over "turquoise and amethyst ... green and azure" fishes at the black sea bottom "where the night had no end" (*ibid.,* 155).

American Settings

In June 1950, the author absorbed the shifting colors of clouds over a "grey sheet of water" and gray-green grass and palmetto during an exploration of the Florida Everglades (Carson, "Real," 1954). For a mesmeric gaze at shining red and pale jellyfish, *The Sea Around Us* viewed the darker ones as brick-red bells that pulsed at the ocean's surface above streaks of silver fingerlings in the "clear, deep green" dotted with motes of life (Carson, 1951, 31). Rachel typified sea basin sediments as multicolored mud in white, black, blue, green, and red. The hues of surface water ranged from green to the deep blue of the abyss. Amid "viscid, foul-smelling" algae and agile plankton, shore waters reflected brown, green, and yellow and seasonal glint of brown and red, sources of the names Red Sea and Vermilion Sea, a term for the Sea of Cortez off the Gulf of California (*ibid.,* 43).

In September 1953 off the coast of West Southport, Maine, the author made a close examination of pink coralline algae and pink baby rock barnacles, many photographed by colleague Charles Pratt. Out of respect for life, she returned the specimens to the sea at the next low tide. Seven months later, she reported memories to some 1,000 guests at the Theta Sigma Phi Matrix Table Dinner in Columbus, Ohio, of a first jaunt aboard the U.S. Fish and Wildlife trawler S.S. *Albatross III* along the Georges Bank. Mixed into the excitement of seeing the conical net arise from 600 feet with cod, anglerfish, sponges, and crabs she recollected the single electric light illuminating "men in their yellow oilskins and their bright flannel shirts," a contrast to the lonely gloom of night on the Atlantic (Carson, 1954).

Education for foster son Roger Allen Christie enabled Rachel to train him from toddlerhood in the visuals of coastal living, such as the shades of starfish and anemones. At age three, he observed the glow of moonlight on waves and the silvery moisture on evergreen needles with their "edging of crystal drops" (Carson, 1956, 27). In the incubation of *The Edge of the Sea,* she reported visiting the mangrove-infested mud flats of southwestern Florida with its rosy pink mollusks, rust and gray heron, and red egret. She favored the blue-bottle green-purple tones of the valonia algae, violet sea fan and Janthina snail, azure Portuguese man-of-war, blue-black onchidium mollusk, ethereal blue of the gooseneck barnacle, and deep cobalt of the velella, the free-floating sea raft. Off the Florida coral reef, the naturalist examined sea urchins and listed variations in spine lengths and color "ranging from deep violet to green, rose, or white," which they veiled in protective coloration within swaths of brownish-green turtle grass (Carson, 1955, 223). Other organisms—spider crabs, shrimp, cowfish, hawksbill turtles—bore a natural green that concealed them in inter-island channels.

NATURE'S LOSS

In *Silent Spring*, the author stayed true to a career of sense impressions. The prefatory "A Fable for Tomorrow" honored fall hardwood leaves for blazing in flame tones next to dark green pines. She reminded readers of the Gulf Coast presence of the "fulvous tree duck, a tawny-colored gooselike duck" (Carson, 2002, 126). Her despair at the dieback of songbirds in Michigan, Illinois, and Wisconsin filled Chapter Eight, "And No Birds Sing," with limited hope for avian nature. She tinged her writing with descriptions of sound and the colors of migrating warblers—black and white, yellow, chestnut, flame, and green. She tied their deaths in 1956–1958 to poisons sprayed over shade trees to prevent Dutch elm disease. Additional loss in Chapter Nine, "Rivers of Death," marked moribund dying carp, buffalo, drum, catfish, and gizzard shad with abnormal wine-hued gills.

Even in advanced cancer treatment and a bout of pancreatitis, the author returned home from a major speech to the Kaiser-Permanente symposium *Man Against Himself* in San Francisco on October 26, 1963, to a fall display of reds and golds in maple and dogwood canopies. Her letter that night to Dorothy Freeman reviewed the crimson declivities of the Grand Canyon and the stream valleys "flicked with a gold that could only have been the aspens" (Carson, letter, 1963). An excerpt, *The Rocky Coast,* recaptured the author's awareness of creamy anemones, pink coral, and "the delicate green and ocher-yellow of encrusting sponge, the pale pink of hydroids … , the bronze and electric blue gleams of the Irish moss, the old-rose beauty of the coralline algae," the hues that tinged her life and work (Carson, 1971, 5).

See also Clouds; *Silent Spring: Earth's Green Mantle.*

Sources

Carson, Rachel. *The Edge of the Sea*. Boston: Houghton Mifflin, 1955.
_____. "Letter to Dorothy Freeman" (26 October 1963).
_____. "The Real World Around Us," address to the Theta Sigma Phi Matrix Table Dinner, Columbus, Ohio (21 April 1954).
_____. *The Rocky Coast*. New York: McCall, 1971.
_____. *The Sea Around Us*. New York: Oxford University Press, 1951.
_____. *Under the Sea Wind: A Naturalist's Picture of Ocean Life*. New York: Simon & Schuster, 1941.
_____. "Undersea." *Atlantic Monthly* 160 (September 1937): 322–325.
Matthiessen, Peter, ed. *Courage for the Earth: Writers, Scientists, and Activists Celebrate the Life and Writing of Rachel Carson*. New York: Mariner, 2007.

Conservation

Rachel defined preservation of nature in empirical and moral terms. Her 1938 newspaper article "Fight for Wildlife Pushes Ahead" alerted readers to a sobering thought—that dwindling animal habitats equaled threats to humankind. To the editor of *Outdoor Life,* in early 1946, her article "Why America's Natural Resources Must Be Conserved" identified conservation as a vital and immediate concern. She charged humanity with arrogance toward "a universe that surely ought to impose humility and reverence" (Quaratiello, 2010, xii).

Following the example of Henry David Thoreau, John Muir, and President Theodore Roosevelt, the biologist campaigned for astute oversight of fisheries and wildlife, sustainable forestry, and global biodiversity, a topic she pursued in July 1947 in the first Fish and Wildlife pamphlet "Mattamuskeet: A National Wildlife Refuge," a principal sanctuary of the Atlantic Flyway. Her crusade for wise management called for burn-offs, plowing, and cutting of invasive brush. The methods, developed in 10,000 BCE by the swidden farmers who founded rotational agriculture in the Neolithic era, yielded clean acreage that fostered natural foods springing from "the great recurrent rhythms of nature" (Carson, 1947, 6).

JUDICIOUS PRESERVATION

Rachel based theories of outdoor life on valid science rather than sentimentality or grand schemes of exterminating plants, mammals, birds, sea life, and insects that proved inconvenient. Boston journalist Andrea Barnet applauded the author for refuting hubristic U.S. congressmen who believed "that nature could be remade to mankind's specifications, subdued, and then domesticated to serve his ends" (Barnet, 2018, 39). Mark Madison, an historian for the Fish and Wildlife Service, admired her altruism and noted her wish for fellow advocates "to conduct our work with integrity and ethics and to devote our lives to conservation in action" (Madison, 2007, 11).

In 1948, Rachel grounded the 50-page bulletin "Guarding Our Wildlife Resources" on the tragic squandering of national wildlife treasures. In reference to dwindling species, she informed readers that "wildlife, water, forests, grasslands—all are parts of man's essential environment" (*ibid.*, 51). The warning informed citizens of haphazard disposal of poisons, water quality endangerment, and chemical spills. Out of respect for democratic principles, she posted data to allow citizens to decide on accepting risks of organic chemicals or ending synthetic contamination. In a letter to the *Washington Post* protesting cronyism in the Eisenhower administration appointments, on April 22, 1953, she alerted readers to misuse of offshore oil reserves, parks, forests, and public lands. She declared: "The real wealth of the Nation lies in the resources of the earth—soil, water, forests, minerals, and wildlife…. Their administration is not properly, and cannot be, a matter of politics" (Carson, 1953, A26).

MID-CENTURY PERILS

Additional obstacles rounded out "Our Ever-Changing Shores," Rachel's six-page essay for the July 1958 issue of *Holiday.* In the final paragraphs, she regretted loss of unspoiled wilderness to the "sordid transformation of 'development,'" a decisive land use she castigated as "man's way" (Carson, 1958, 119, 120). Her diatribe against public beach clutter by snack shops and fishing shacks branched out to criticize eyesores, commercial amusements, and noise that diminished surf sounds. To restore the public trust, she urged the U.S. Park Service to purchase marine coasts.

When Rachel's stamina lessened, she dedicated herself more fully to warnings that pesticides threatened all aspects of earthly life. In a personal letter, she declared that "everything which meant most to me as a naturalist was being threatened, and that nothing I could do would be more important" (Carson, 1962). She intended to complete the tocsin in 12 months, but labored to finish it in four years. Meanwhile, during the 1960 national presidential conventions, speakers barely mentioned conservation of resources and national parks. According to David Watson, editor of *Pesticide Management and Insecticide Resistance,* Rachel's alarm resulted in overreaction and near hysteria. He stated, "Anti-intellectualism was arising, as it had not been seen since the time of Galileo" (Watson, 1977, 451).

By the 1970s, Americans suspected not just chemicals but all science and technology of causing distress to nature and human well-being. Three decades later, on Earth Day, April 29, 2000, Maine actor Kaiulani Lee performed a one-woman play, *A Sense of Wonder,* at the Camden Opera House. A resurgence of preservationism in the 200 attendees honored the famous activist and her legacy.

Sources

Barnet, Andrea. *Visionary Women: How Rachel Carson, Jane Jacobs, Jane Goodall, and Alice Waters Changed Our World.* New York: Ecco, 2018.

Bowes, Catherine. "An Evening with Rachel Carson." *Conservation Matters* 7:2 (Summer 2000): 48.

Carson, Rachel. "Letter to Dorothy Freeman" (6 January 1962).

———. "Mattamuskeet: A National Wildlife Refuge." #4. Washington, D.C.: U.S. Department of the Interior, July 1947.

———. "Mr. Day's Dismissal." *Washington Post* (22 April 1953): A26.

———. "Our Ever-Changing Shore." *Holiday* 24 (July 1958): 70–71, 117–120.

Carson, R.L. "Fight for Wildlife Pushes Ahead." *Richmond Times Dispatch Sunday Magazine* (20 March 1938): 8–9.

Madison, Mark. "Nature's Public Servant," *Fish & Wildlife News* (Spring 2007): 8–11.

Quaratiello, Arlene Rodda. *Rachel Carson: A Biography.* Amherst, NY: Prometheus, 2010.

Watson, David, ed. *Pesticide Management and Insecticide Resistance.* New York: Academic Press, 1977.

Criticism

Long after Rachel's death, her legacy continues to stir controversy. As scientist-prophet, she relied on the expertise and wisdom of colleagues, such as Cornelis Jan Briejer, a science writer in Wageningen, Holland, whom she admired, and friend and colleague E.B. White at the *New Yorker*. White concurred that humanity would be more likely to survive "if we accommodated ourselves to this planet" (Carson, 2002, n.p.). He recognized the risks Rachel undertook to disclose collusion between government, agribusiness, and industry. He admired her "skill and thoroughness" and "the courage … in putting on the gloves and going in with this formidable opponent" (Barnet, 2018, 4). For her courageous advocacy, Bill Denneen, a columnist for the *Santa Maria* (California) *Times,* called her "an eco-hooligan extraordinaire" (Denneen, 1999, A4). C. Roy Boutard, a book critic for the Pittsfield, Massachusetts, *Berkshire Eagle* viewed the uproar from Rachel's ecocentrist perspective: "She must feel flattered that the chemical companies are going to spend millions of dollars to fight her" for misquoting and slanting data (Boutard, 1962, 22).

The author's unremitting attack on the formulation and advertising of biocides earned vicious name calling and charges of fanatic cultist, arthritic spinster, semi-reclusive amateur, junk scientist, pantheist, peace nut, and priestess of nature, a veiled allusion to Wicca and witchcraft. Frank Graham, Jr., a columnist for the *Chicago Tribune,* averred that she "has been vindicated as more practical than the hard-headed businessman" (Graham, 1971, 1A). Of the eruption of aspersions, Gary Wiener, author of *The Environment in Rachel Carson's Silent Spring,* stated, "Few books have ever been more misunderstood, misinterpreted, and scurrilously attacked" (Wiener, 2012, 9). In the introduction to the 1994 edition, activist author Al Gore compared the backlash from profiteers to the demonization of Charles Darwin's *The Origin of Species* a century before to the reactions to *Silent Spring.*

Demeaning Rachel

By questioning Rachel's credibility as a scientist and academic and trivializing her emotional stability as a female, some spokesmen for agribusiness, chemical firms, and blatant polluters branded *Silent Spring* a tissue of untruths intended to raise her public renown. J. Marshall, a reviewer for the *Journal of the Entomological Society of British Columbia* in British Columbia, patronized "Miss Carson" for lacking understanding of farming: "It is to be expected that she will lose her way from time to time in that most complex of sciences.... Tut tut, Miss Carson!" (1962, 55). Pincus Rothberg, president of Montrose Chemical, charged the author with fanaticism and cultism. He based his accusations on perceptions of Rachel as a meddling amateur with tender feelings for the outdoors as opposed to the masculine adversarial views of the universe as a field of conquest. Michael B. Smith, a philosophy professor at Berry College, noted that gender issues placed her outside the "nexus of the production and application of conventional scientific knowledge" (Smith, 2001, 734). Nonetheless, her reply to detractors remained objective and controlled: Who is criticizing? What is their link to the chemical industry? What agenda do they propose? She omitted the more damning question: What profits are they protecting?

Detractors came from important professions, including Secretary of Agriculture Ezra Taft Benson and U.S. Congressman from Mississippi James Lloyd Whitten, chair of the House Appropriates Subcommittee for Agriculture, who categorized *Silent Spring* a work of science fiction, a charge echoed in *Chemical World News.* More men-only constituencies expounded opinions of Rachel and her book. On April 23, 1961, Robert J. Anderson, former chief of the Centers for Disease Control, served as the first chair of the Federal Pest Control Board, an agency set up during the Kennedy administration to review pesticide use nationwide. Members from the army and navy, farm research, forest service, and Food and Drug Administration coordinated policy with Secretary of Agriculture Orville Freeman and Secretary of the Interior Stewart Udall. A mixed message from Parke Culver Brinkley, president of National

Agricultural Chemicals Association, purported to remain neutral, but diminished the danger of toxins in food and human tissue, especially in findings from European researchers. He adopted patriotism as a cover for chem-business advocacy: "We as a nation must keep pesticides flowing freely within our borders" (Brinkley, 1966, 59).

Additional vilification derived from C. Glen King, chair of the Nutrition Foundation, nutritionist Frederick John Stare, and highway commissioners who relied on herbicides to maintain road shoulders and medians. Ronald Bailey cited the author for scare-mongering; an unsigned letter pictured a female trembling at the sight of bugs. In "The Myth of the Pesticide Menace" for *Saturday Evening Post,* Edwin Drummond labeled Rachel a faddist. Entomologist J. Gordon Edwards at San Jose State University in California accused Rachel of citing "unscientific sources" to produce "deceptions, false statements, horrible innuendoes, and ridiculous allegations" (Edwards, 1992). Perhaps the least valid, the insights of Jerry Bryan, assistant sports editor of the *Birmingham News,* lacked a single specific fault. In 2002, Marjorie Mazel Hecht accused Rachel of fraudulent data spreading disinformation leading to "menticide … anti-science ignorance" (Hecht, 2002). William J. Darby, a nutritionist at Vanderbilt University School of Medicine, emitted what historian Michael B. Smith termed "the frightened growl of cornered dogma," a reference to the Renaissance philosophy of Francis Bacon on setting man over nature (Smith, 2001, 738). Some dismissed the researcher as a "bird and bunny lover" and an unwed keeper of cats (McCrum, 2016).

Chemical companies raised the stakes against the upstart biologist. Robert White-Stevens of American Cyanamid blamed Rachel for misinformation and false assumptions. George C. Decker, an economic entomologist for the Illinois Agricultural Experiment Station labeled the author a hoaxer and writer of sci-fi. *Farm Chemicals* magazine took an anti-woman stance with a broom-mounted witch on its cover. For *Scientific American*, Cornell ecologist LaMont Cole straddled the divide between errors and integrity. Monsanto riposted with 5,000 copies of the fable "The Desolate Year," a sendup of Rachel's "A Fable for Tomorrow." The National Agricultural Chemical Association allotted a quarter million dollars towards denigrating *Silent Spring* and smearing the author.

Rachel's Vindicators

In Rachel's defense, hunters, wildlife biologists, the Garden Club of America, National Association of University Women, the National Council of Women, the National Audubon Society, and scientists at the University of Pennsylvania, Cornell, and University of California validated her work and urged the limited use of biocides. Congressman John Lindsey admired Rachel's work so much that he sent a *New Yorker* clipping to President Kennedy. Prince Philip Mountbatten bought copies of *Silent Spring* in the U.S. and ordered a circlet of red and white flowers to honor her passing. In a eulogy, the Rev. Duncan Howlett extolled Rachel's character for its serenity, insight, and strength.

Cartoonist Bill Mauldin acclaimed the biologist in the *Chicago Sun-Times.* U.S. Supreme Court Chief Justice William Orville Douglas declared her critics "merchants of poison" and compared the revolutionary effects of the book to abolitionist Harriet Beecher Stowe's *Uncle Tom's Cabin* (Brinkley, 2012). A London newspaper compared *Silent Spring* to Upton Sinclair's exposé on the meat industry in *The Jungle*. *Business Week* issued a critique under the heading "Are We Poisoning Ourselves?" Charles C. Mann's review for the *Wall Street Journal* in April 2018 characterized her diatribe as "a relentless, densely factual indictment" of organic biocides, especially DDT (dichlorodiphenyltrichloroethane) (Mann, 2018, C5).

Excerpts of Rachel's writing appeared as models in college handbooks on rhetoric, adding precise scientific terms to American language. Stewart Udall autographed a copy of *The Quiet Crisis* with high praise: "For Rachel—An educator-crusader for conservation whose stones have wide ripples" (Carson, letter, 1963). Autobiographer Sandra Steingraber admired the biologist's quiet objectivity as "less Che Guevara and more Charles Darwin" (Matthiessen, 2007, 58). Historian John Kenneth Galbraith numbered *Silent Spring* as an addition to the best of Western literary tradition. Others revered her as an oracle, saint, and mystic of nature.

See also Diction.

Sources

Barnet, Andrea. *Visionary Women: How Rachel Carson, Jane Jacobs, Jane Goodall, and Alice Waters Changed Our World*. New York: Ecco, 2018.
Boutard, C. Roy. "Review: *Silent Spring*." (Pittsfield, MA) *Berkshire Eagle* (29 September 1962): 22.
Brinkley, Douglas. "Rachel Carson and JFK, an Environmental Tag Team." *Audubon* (May–June 2012), https://www.audubon.org/magazine/may-june-2012/rachel-carson-and-jfk-environmental-tag-team.
Brinkley, Parke C. "As of Now" in the official report of the Association of American Pesticide Control Officials Incorporated, 1965–1966, 57–59.
Carson, Rachel. "Letter to Dorothy Freeman" (26 October 1963).
Denneen, Bill. "Rachel Carson Failed to Remain Silent, Thankfully." *Santa Maria* (California) *Times* (29 June 1999): A4.
Edwards, J. Gordon. "The Lies of Rachel Carson." *21st Century* (Summer 1992).
Gore, Al. "Introduction" to *Silent Spring*. Boston: Houghton Mifflin, 1994, xiii.
Graham, Frank. "Rachel Carson's Big Book." *Chicago Tribune* (31 January 1971): 1A.
Hecht, Marjorie Mazel. "Bring Back DDT, and Science with It!" *21st Century* (Summer 2002).
Mann, Charles C. "'Silent Spring & Other Writings' Review: The Right and Wrong of Rachel Carson." *Wall Street Journal* (26 April 2018): C5.
Marshall, J. "Book Review: Silent Spring, by Rachel Carson." *Journal of the Entomological Society of British Columbia* 59 (1 December 1962): 53–55.
Matthiessen, Peter, ed. *Courage for the Earth: Writers, Scientists, and Activists Celebrate the Life and Writing of Rachel Carson*. New York: Mariner, 2007.
McCrum, Robert. "The 100 Best Nonfiction Books: No 20—*Silent Spring* by Rachel Carson (1962)." *The Guardian* (13 June 2016).
Smith, Michael B. "'Silence, Miss Carson!' Science, Gender, and the Reception of *Silent Spring*." *Feminist Studies* 27:3 (Autumn 2001): 733–752.
Transactions of the Twenty-Seventh North American Wildlife and Natural Resources Conference. Washington, D.C.: Wildlife Management Institute, 1962.
Wiener, Gary. *The Environment in Rachel Carson's Silent Spring*. Farmington Hills, MI: Greenhaven, 2012.

Darwin, Charles

A century after its formulation, Darwinian theory permeated Rachel's philosophy of balance in nature. Rachel restated Darwin's theory in 1941 as an unyielding dictum of the seas: "a rule of the game of life and death which the weak play with the strong" (Carson, 1941, 36). In the 1942 memo to Mrs. Eales, the author stated the grim fact of eat or be eaten, a dictum ruling animal survival at the sea's surface. She depicted small mackerel amid their enemies: "small jellyfish with enormous appetites, little transparent worms with sharp, biting jaws, schools of small fishes that eat smaller fishes, and larger fishes that eat them" (Carson, 1942, 2). She termed the survival of only two out of 4,000,000 eggs or .0000005 percent "one of the most impressive spectacles which the sea presents" (*ibid.*). Just as Darwin theorized, the transformation of mackerel from prey to predator continued the cycle of survival of the fittest.

In the 1949 essay "Lost Worlds: The Challenge of the Islands," the author championed Darwin's experiments on migratory birds such as the Pacific golden plover and the organic components in a mud ball. From a handful of humus, he "raised 82 separate plants, belonging to five distinct species" (Carson, 1949, 182). Because of the uniqueness of biota on isolated islands, such as moas on New Zealand, flightless cormorants on the Galapagos, and dodos on Mauritius, he surmised that the appearance of one-of-a-kind beings paralleled the origination of earthly life.

THE YOUTHFUL EXPLORER

In the opening chapter of *The Sea Around Us,* in 1951, Rachel cited Darwin's observations at age 23 on his second voyage from Plymouth, England, extending from December 27, 1831, to October 2, 1836. In mid–July 1832 on a hydrographic survey of South America, he encountered an abrupt temperature rise after the H.M.S. *Beagle* left the tropical warmth of Rio de Janeiro, Brazil, to enter cool southern waters of Buenos Aires, Argentina. At Tierra del Fuego, the setting entertained the crew with porpoise antics and the noisy barking of penguins and seals. Meanwhile, he wrote in his diary that the coastline could "make a landsman dream for a week about death, peril, and shipwreck" (Carson, 1951, 117).

The author shared with Darwin a fascination for microscopic plankton, which reached a peak of luminosity in fall. She stated in *The Sea Around Us: The Restless Sea* the need for exact terms to describe oceanic phosphorescence at night. Her essay "The Birth of an Island" reprised the remarkable flora and fauna that had evolved off Ecuador on the Galapagos Islands, especially the singularity of tortoises, lizards, and sea birds. She stated, "It was from the pages of earth's history written on the lava velds of the Galapagos that young Charles Darwin got his first inkling of the great truths of the origin of species" (Carson, 1951, 91).

Because Rachel ascribed to the interconnection of all life, in 1962, *Silent Spring* vilified "Neanderthal" thinking that nature exists for human convenience and that detrimental species deserve extermination (Carson, 2002, 297). For aerating the earth, promoting drainage and root system expansion, and transforming vegetable debris into leaf mold, the narrative accredited the earthworm, a subject of Charles Darwin's final treatise, *The Formation of Vegetable Mould Through the Action of Worms* (1881). In admiration for his intense study, she extolled the world's "first understanding of the fundamental role of earthworms as geologic agents for the transport of soil" (*ibid.*, 55).

A Shared Outlook

The author identified in arsenic and other natural carcinogens, ultraviolet radiation, and the practice of aerial spraying of fields and forests the culmination of Charles Darwin's theory of survival of the fittest. *Silent Spring* declared that the Englishman "could scarcely have found a better example" than the effects of biocides on insects (*Ibid.*, 272). She found the most satisfying validation in Darwin's theorizing about small organisms:

> If Darwin were alive today the insect world would delight and astound him with its impressive verification of his theories of survival of the fittest. Under the stress of intensive chemical spraying the weaker members of the insect populations are being weeded out [Carson, 2002, 263].

By killing the weakest insects, synthetic poisons aided the proliferation of the strongest species. Thus, agribusiness defeated the purpose of removing deterrents to harvests and exterminated natural enemies, such as birds and amphibians that preyed on disease-carrying mosquitoes and flies. In one immediate result of biocides such as DDT (dichlorodiphenyltrichloroethane), the emergence of poison-resistant insects nullified the original premise that chemicals boosted profits.

In the long speech "The Pollution of Our Environment" in San Francisco to the Kaiser-Permanente symposium *Man Against Himself* on October 18, 1963, Rachel compared cavalier attitudes toward earth contaminants to the uproar that accompanied Darwin's theories of evolution of humankind from lower species. At the core, naysayers glorified *homo sapiens* and denied the placement of humankind in the web of earthly life. Surprisingly, denials in 1869 derived from public consternation as well as Darwin's learned "peers in science" (Carson, "Pollution," 1963).

See also Criticism; Evolution; *The Sea Around Us: The Restless Sea*; *Silent Spring: One in Every Four.*

Sources

Boston, Penelope J., et al. *Scientists Debate Gaia: The Next Century.* Cambridge, MA: MIT Press, 2004.
Carson, Rachel. "Lost Worlds: The Challenge of the Islands." *Wood Thrush* 4:5 (May–June 1949): 179–187.
_____. "Memo to Mrs. Eales." Rachel Carson papers, 1942.
_____. "The Pollution of Our Environment," address to the Kaiser-Permanente Symposium *Man Against Himself*, San Francisco (18 October 1963).
_____. *The Sea Around Us.* New York: Oxford University Press, 1951.
_____. *Silent Spring.* Boston: Houghton Mifflin, 40th Anniversary Edition, 2002.
_____. *Under the Sea Wind: A Naturalist's Picture of Ocean Life.* New York: Simon & Schuster, 1941.
Fuller, Robert C. *Wonder: From Emotion to Spirituality.* Chapel Hill: University of North Carolina Press, 2006.

DDT

The ubiquitous reliance on dichlorodiphenyltrichloroethane, or DDT, the A-bomb of bug killers, began in 1939 after Paul Müller, a Swiss chemist at J.R. Geigy in Basel, proved that formulation effective. It compromised the nervous system of flies, lice, ticks, fleas, mites, spruce budworms, potato beetles, scale, and gypsy moths seemingly without harming people or mammals. Cheap and easily manufactured, DDT could be emulsified in water or combined with pulverized chalk to produce a long-lived, deadly powder that shielded wool garments from moth holes and bodies from flea and tick bites. He intended his panacea to end the food shortage that gripped Europe during World War II by exterminating all insects and to aid soldiers in the Pacific War in their struggle against illness born by the anopheles mosquito.

The pesticide echoed the army tank unit's motto of search, attack, destroy. When the patent extended from Ciba-Geigy to DuPont, the military went gung-ho on DDT by dusting recruits and Balkan refugees, saturating barracks and cots, delousing air raid shelters and Tunisian prisoners of war at Bari and other parts of southern Italy, and spraying clinics, schools, and jails on Pacific islands before U.S. Marines secured the beachheads. When a typhus epidemic struck 2,000 and killed 15 in or near Naples, Italy, from November 1943 to September 1944, according to Charles M. Wheeler, head of the Typhus Commission, the U.S. Army halted the disease by powdering 1,000,000 citizens and corpses. Agents dusted clothing and bedding with DDT to kill lice, the vector of contagion.

Into the post-war era, DDT retained its reputation as an instant fix for lethal insect infestations. At the liberation in northern Germany of the Bergen-Belsen concentration camp on April 15, 1945, British delousers sprayed 20,000 inmates to rid them of lice and dusted laundry and huts. At the rate of 18,000 tons annually, the magic insect killer reputedly brought the European and Asian phases of the war to a close. The army initiated another spraying project in Japan in late 1946 by training 9,000 sanitation teams.

PEACETIME CONTROLS

For the practical use of DDT against potato beetles, Paul Müller received the 1948 Nobel Prize for physiology and medical advancement. Late into the decade, after a warning from the American Medical Association of pervasive toxicity, more spraying campaigns suppressed crickets and mosquitoes in Europe and the Americas, where malaria and yellow fever threatened lives. Six years of spraying in South Africa reduced malaria by nearly 95 percent and to nearly zero in Sardinia. For the Taiwanese, 24 years of spraying had the same effect—from 75,000 infections to only five.

By 1956, spraying for spruce budworms by the U.S. Forest Service covered 885,000 acres, unintentionally triggering an onslaught of spider mites in Montana, Idaho, Colorado, and New Mexico. The next year, the chemical industry marketed more than 6,000 products containing DDT as well as the organophosphate diazinon, a highly toxic deterrent to ants, cockroaches, fleas, silverfish, and wasps. Within a decade, further U.S. campaigns disseminated 40,000 tons of the low-cost DDT annually to suppress insect infestations in homes, lawns and birdhouses, hedgerows, forests, livestock pens, poultry houses and crops, rail lines, and utility right of ways. Homeowners bought DDT powder and dust in bags, aerosol cans, foggers, lighted coils, and liquid spray guns that obliterated crabgrass and soaked bedding to kill bedbugs.

Industrial marketers permeated shelf liner, lawn mower mufflers, paint, fabric, soap, and furniture polish with the product. Public health authorities sent spray trucks into neighborhoods threatened by encephalitis and malaria. Dry cleaners mothproofed garments with DDT. Congress investigated in 1950 and 1951 to learn how much residue affected the average head of lettuce and carton of milk. A case before the Supreme Court in 1957 won the rebuke of Justice William Orville Douglas, who declared that "the perils of DDT underline the public importance of this case" (Carson, 2002, 159).

DDT Detriments

By 1960, DDT had created resistance in 28 mosquito strains that spread malaria, encephalitis, yellow fever, and elephantiasis in the Caribbean, Central America, Eastern Europe, Indonesia, the Middle East, Southeast Asia, U.S., and West Africa. Impugned as the "DDT book," in 1962, *Silent Spring* exposed the danger of cottony cushion scale to California citrus orchards, where insecticide exterminated vedalia beetles (*Rodolia cardinalis*), a natural predator imported in 1888 from Australia and New Zealand (Wiener, 2012, 11). The narrative described the passage of the biocide up the food chain. Reckless use of the toxin caused tremors and deaths in grebes, grouse, meadowlarks, ground squirrels, sea urchins, and frogs and the feminizing effects on chickens from chemical disruption of the endocrine system, a threat to future generations of fowl. Rachel's incisive style forced readers to visualize death by DDT: twitching and spasms, quaking, self-starvation, rigid legs, and convulsions.

In a rigorous, acrimonious exposé, the biologist outlined the dangers of aerial overspray, which doomed hatchling birds, fish, and the shellfish of wetlands, such as the crabs of the Long Island salt marsh. Off the Chesapeake Bay, the horrifying demise of birds gasping for air, "their splayed claws … drawn up to their breasts in agony," drove her to rebuke American chemical companies by predicting an apocalypse for earthly life (Huckins, 1958). Loren Eiseley, an American naturalist, agreed with her charge that industrialists were irresponsible and greedy. In an essay in the October 1963 issue of *Audubon,* she struck home with patriots by warning of DDT poisoning of the American eagle and the unhatched eaglets in nests.

The opposition to *Silent Spring* insisted that DDT controlled spruce budworm as well as lice and mosquitoes, the prime carriers of typhus, elephantiasis, and malaria, a source of worldwide epidemics. In October 1962, *Monsanto Magazine* replied to her classic treatise with a six-page parody, "The Desolate Year." Company officials intended the author to admit the possibility that the prohibition of insecticides would cause epidemics and starvation as a result of insect infestation. Articles and speeches by Roland Charles Clement, an environmentalist for the National Audubon Society, defended Rachel in an essay for *Audubon* magazine and in person on June 6, 1963, before the Senate Committee on Commerce.

Despite technologists' charges of mass killing by revived insect populations, Rachel's views held sway. In 1969, state bans on DDT took effect in Wisconsin, Arizona, and Michigan. In Miramichi, New Brunswick, a continued battle for ecology pitted aerial DDT spray over threatened balsam forests against the salvaging of aquatic insects and the salmon run that thrived on them. A DDT ban incorporated in the Federal Environmental Pesticide Control Act of 1972 preceded prohibitions on aldrin and dieldrin.

See also Pesticides; *Silent Spring: And No Birds Sing; Silent Spring: Indiscriminately from the Skies; Silent Spring: Nature Fights Back; Silent Spring: Rivers of Death; Silent Spring: The Rumblings of an Avalanche;* World War II.

Sources

Carson, Rachel. "Rachel Carson Answers Her Critics." *Audubon* 65 (September/October 1963): 262–265, 313–315.
_____. *Silent Spring.* Boston: Houghton Mifflin, 40th Anniversary Edition, 2002.
"The Desolate Year." *Monsanto Magazine* 42:4 (October 1962): 4–9.
Huckins, Olga. "Letter to the Editor," *Boston Herald* (January 1958).
Souder, William. *On a Farther Shore: The Life and Legacy of Rachel Carson.* New York: Crown, 2012.
Wiener, Gary. *The Environment in Rachel Carson's Silent Spring.* Farmington Hills, MI: Greenhaven, 2012.

Death

From her first book, *Under the Sea Wind,* Rachel pondered the immutable cycle of existence. The *Atlantic Monthly* excerpt "Undersea" printed one of the author's most existential views on mortality: "The Life Span of a particular plant or animal appears not as a drama complete in itself, but only as a brief interlude in a panorama of endless change" (Carson, 1937, 325). In January 1937, the death of sister Marian Frazier Carson Williams from pneumonia at age 39 saddled the author with family responsibilities, both personal and financial. Biographer Linda Lear noted that "an altered domestic life … deprived her of privacy and drained her physical and emotional energy" (Lear, 2016, 84).

In the introduction to *Under the Sea Wind,* Lear disclosed a continuity from the current of "life in which death is only an incident" (*ibid.,* xx). She identified the biologist's primary literary themes as symbiosis of sea beings and "the concept of material immortality—the idea that the death of one creature plays a direct role in the life of another, even for the tiniest of organisms" (*ibid.,* 86). In 1941, she stood on the shore observing a tidal ebb and flow that had continued for millennia, a motif she may have gleaned from Matthew Arnold's "Dover Beach." Rather than lapse into despair, she experienced an upsurge of faith in human struggles and eventual reincarnation. From a utilitarian perspective, the narrative mused on tiny protozoa that died and contributed their shells to sea floor limestone "a thousand feet thick," the material the Egyptians used to build pyramids and the sphinx (Carson, 1941, 170).

THE IMMUTABLE CYCLE

The concept of suffering strengthened in 1947 after the death of cat Kito. A personalized glimpse of death recurred in 1951 in *The Sea Around Us,* in which Rachel viewed the endless darkness of black ocean depths "where there is no sanctuary from ever-present enemies, where one can only move on and on, from birth to death, through the darkness," which she described as a watery prison (Carson, 1951, 55). A comparison of Norwegian fjords with the Black Sea led to the conclusion that innumerable fish and invertebrate deaths created "a rich layer of organic material on the bottom" (Carson, 1951, 238).

For the speech "Design for Nature Writing," on acceptance of the Burroughs Medal on April 7, 1952, Rachel acceded to the inevitability of pain and loss. She advanced to a more mature existentialism with the statement: "For the mysteries of living things, and the birth and death of continents and seas, are among the great realities" (Carson, 1952, 254). With the certainty of Stephen Crane's assertion "it was but the great death" in *The Red Badge of Courage*, Rachel was able to affirm humanity's essential weakness. Later studies by New York conservationist Carl Safina corroborated her assertion that fish can suffer, a radical approach to typically stolid, unfeeling biological writing about lower orders of organisms. In early September 1953, the author composed a letter revealing that she and her mother Maria grieved with "tears in our hearts and sometime in our eyes" for her cat Muffie, one in a parade of felines that Rachel fostered (Carson, "Letter," 1953).

A LETHAL MALIGNANCY

The author regretted threats to her health from arthritis, ulcer, phlebitis, and radiation treatments, which brought on chest pains and inhibited walking. More than vanity, the limitations slowed her work on *Silent Spring*, a treatise she believed she owed to her generation. In fall 1960, she discussed the alarming decline with friend Dorothy Freeman. The onset of a staph infection and phlebitis in her lower limbs destroyed stamina and sleep, causing her life flame to flicker. Inclement weather and the onset of joint pain on February 12, 1963, required a six-day stay at the Washington Hospital Center, the city's largest private medical complex.

By the final months, Rachel wrote Dr. George "Barney" Crile and referred to mortality and to concern for "matters I need to arrange and tidy up" (Carson, "Letter," 1963). In correspondence with Dorothy Freeman dated March 27, 1963, the biologist hoped to live on in the memory of readers, even the ones who knew nothing personally about her. The author's thoughts veered to poetry when she hoped to commune with Dorothy and colleague E.B. White in the songs of hermit thrushes and in "moonlight on the bay—ribbons of waterfowl in the sky" (Carson, letter, 1963). The acceptance of nonbeing, like John Keats's *Ode to a Nightingale*, befuddled her thinking and forced her to welcome the beyond as a puzzle teasing human curiosity. At the death of her cat Moppet, she took comfort in the image of rivers blending with the sea, a suggestion of an oversoul to which all people belonged.

STRENGTH IN NATURE

On April 1, four days later, Rachel comforted Dorothy during a period of mourning that left an "aching emptiness" (Carson, letter, 1963). In fall, the two friends felt melancholy about the short lives of monarch butterflies. Rachel concluded from "brightly fluttering bits of life," whether insect or human, "When any living thing has come to the end of its life cycle we accept that end as natural" (*ibid.*). The acquiescence preceded her months of physical decline and death in April 1964. When her body lost stamina from cancer treatment and pelvic pain, she became immobile and had to reject an invitation to lecture at the University of Stockholm. She commiserated with earth for its debilitated seas and altered climate from global warming.

The author admitted that accepting a California speaking engagement for Kaiser-Permanente's symposium *Man Against Himself* in San Francisco on October 18, 1963, taxed her failing health from a transcontinental flight to the Pacific coast. Still, the lure of butterflies in Muir Woods and Pacific Grove perked her wonder at fragile beauty, although she required transport by wheelchair. On the flight home from San Francisco on October 21, she felt "slightly appalled at my temerity in crossing the country in this condition … at my worst physically" (*ibid.*). Her spirit revived from correspondence with Dorothy about swans. In a letter, Rachel proposed a January trip to Mattamuskeet, North Carolina, to view Canada geese, a rally of hope to view once more her beloved waterfowl.

See also Kennedy, John F.

Sources

Carson, Rachel. "Design for Nature Writing." *Atlantic Naturalist* (May–August 1952): 232–234.
_____. "Letter to Dorothy Freeman" (3 September 1953).
_____. "Letter to Dorothy Freeman" (27 March 1963).
_____. "Letter to Dorothy Freeman" (1 April 1963).
_____. "Letter to Dorothy Freeman" (10 September 1963).
_____. "Letter to Dr. George Crile," (17 February 1963).
_____. *The Sea Around Us*. New York: Oxford University Press, 1951.
_____. *Under the Sea Wind: A Naturalist's Picture of Ocean Life*. New York: Simon & Schuster, 1941.
_____, "Undersea." *Atlantic Monthly* 160 (September 1937): 322–325.
Kaza, Stephanie. "Rachel Carson's Sense of Time: Experiencing Maine." *ISLE* 17:2 (Spring 2010): 291–315.
Lear, Linda. "The Next Page: When Rachel Carson Set Sail," *Pittsburgh Post-Gazette* (21 February 2016).
Wheeler, Charles M. "Control of Typhus in Italy 1943–1944 by Use of DDT." *American Journal of Public Health* 36 (February 1946): 119–129.

Details

Rachel's skill at pinpointing the most salient data appeared early in her career. From the author's first ventures into reportage for the *Baltimore Sun* under the gender-neutral byline "R.L. Carson," her articles detailed ocean-going life. She proved agile at salting narrative with precise images: tinkers (small, young mackerel), boom (lifting arm or spar), and dory (small flat-bottomed boat). Her skills enlivened press releases, brochures, and newspaper features for average reading public:

- In January 1937, the article "The Northern Trawlers Move South" for the *Baltimore Sunday Sun* applied a visual comparison of the otter trawl net to a flat butterfly net that could scoop up eight tons of cod or haddock in one sweep.
- In articles on oyster harvesting in Chesapeake Bay for the *Baltimore Sun* in August 1938 and on whaling the next November, she specified temperatures and salinity needed for eggs and larvae to grow to edible size.

While naming and describing the function of fishing equipment, Rachel practiced the poet's skill at word pictures, a classroom essential for readers who needed to see what the writer is introducing:

- In summarizing predators on oysters, the author noted that the bivalve's "fortress of lime is of little avail" against starfish and sea snails, which bored their drills straight through to succulent meat (Carson, 1938, 2).
- Another additive to memorable prose, Rachel's knowledge of colonial American history contributed a valuable element to New England readers: A reprise of seventeenth-century shad fishing in a February 1937 essay for the Charleston, South Carolina, *News and Courier* pictured colonists importing European gear and learning Native American methods of trapping fish on river racks or in ponds by sweeping shad runs with bushes and grape vines or trapping them in brush weirs.
- In March 1939, her article for the *Baltimore Sun* ventured into avian history with "the starling equivalent of the Mayflower"—the importation of English sparrows and starlings from England in 1890 by Eugene Schieffelin, a New York ornithologist (Carson, 1939, 1).

Overall, the author favored familiarizing the newspaper audience with specifics of nature, as with "crepuscular" (at evening), "ichthyological" (concerning fish), "fathom" (six feet), and "race memory" (images and behaviors existing in one species). The exercise of diction and etymology prepared her for more complicated writing, beginning with her first literary essay, "Undersea," issued in September 1937 by *Atlantic Monthly*, displayed a sound liberal arts education. She ventured into the Greek roots of "plankton," a descriptive noting the errant nature of the sea's wanderers, and alluded to the Tyrian mollusk that Greek and Roman dye-makers boiled to extract royal purple.

The Chain of Being

In 1941, the author echoed Charles Darwin's theories by particularizing nature's chain of predation of larger creatures against smaller. She specified the ghost crab surmounting sea oat stalks "as large to it as a fallen pine" (Carson, 1941, 26). In a study of plunder in an estuary, a segment of *Under the Sea Wind* summarized the attack of eels on roe shad trapped in gill nets. The appeal, the bulging egg sacs, provoked the eel to a merciless slash releasing a worthy morsel. For the shad who underwent thorough plundering, even the soft flesh yielded to eel jaws. The narrative climaxed on the skeletal remains of gutted fish.

In balance, Rachel viewed all beings respectfully, for example, a flock of terns like "hundreds of scraps of paper flung to the wind," a suggestion of vulnerability in a constant stir of air currents (*ibid.*, 27). For Pandion the osprey, years of collected sticks and detritus filled out a six-foot nest, even incorporating cork floats, an eagle skeleton, a boot, 20 feet of seine net, and a smashed oar. The roost grew large enough to shelter a heron, owl, wreck, sparrows, and starlings, a bird condominium that the author milked for wry humor.

Rachel's interest in language enhanced her travel reports for the U.S. Fish and Wildlife department. In July 1947, she introduced a pamphlet on the 50,000-acre Mattamuskeet nature sanctuary, the largest lake in coastal North Carolina, with a reminder that Algonquin speakers named it "dry dust" (Carson, 1947, 15). Out of respect for First Peoples, she acknowledged the departure of Indians from the Outer Banks, leaving "seas of marsh grass and the only living things ... the birds and the small, unseen inhabitants of the marshes" (Carson, 1947, 1). In 1951, the second volume of Rachel's sea trilogy, *The Sea Around Us*, she filled the stave on "Mother Sea" with a scientist's knowledge of intricate animal behaviors. A history of oceanography revealed advances in diving, sounding, and photographing the sea floor and researching the effects of water pressure on creatures that regularly swam from below to the surface.

Seeing and Appreciating

Conservationist Lynn Scarlett praised Rachel's use of detail and storytelling as evidence of nature's complexity. In the speech "The Real World Around Us" on April 21, 1954, to the Theta Sigma Phi Matrix Table Dinner in Columbus, Ohio, the biologist ventured from empirical facts to a leisurely day exploring the Florida Everglades. The ramble inspired admiration for outdoor ephemera—"dew on the grass and thousands of spider webs glistening" (Carson, 1954). The style, according to Scarlett, revealed a "duality—this love of nature both as art and function. She writes at once as poet and scientist" (Scarlett, 2007, 34).

Rearing nephew Roger Christie Allen altered Rachel's language to accommodate a toddler's understanding. In one example of imagery in 1955 from *Edge of the Sea*, the marine specialist viewed moonlight as a silver edging on waves. Her metaphor combined sense impressions with the optics of heavenly light on rhythmically peaking water. The dynamics enhanced with a touch of divinity her remarks on tides and the power of the moon to regulate sea movements. In another observation, Rachel compared transparent protoplasm to "sea lace," a feminine conceit (*ibid.*).

An Aggressive Alert

As described by analyst Dianne Newell, an historian at the University of British Columbia, Rachel reached beyond staid science reports for the tone and atmosphere of apocalyptic writing and science fiction as well as verse. Critic Cheryll Glotfelty, an environmentalist at the University of Nevada, Reno, described the biologist's diction as the terminology of the Cold War and the promotion of DDT as a tool of agribusiness and the economy. In the opinion of environmentalist Julie J. Morley, author of *Future Sacred: The Connected Creativity of Nature*, Rachel's eye for detail extended the observations and grave tone of Scots nature writer John Muir with a narrative acuity derived from training in English composition.

In "Rivers of Death," Chapter Nine of *Silent Spring*, Rachel deliberately laced a steely report on DDT (dichlorodiphenyltrichloroethane) spraying of salmon runs with precise piscatory terms—grilse, redd, salmon fry, smolt--all evidence of the complexity of fish reproduction (Carson, 2002, 132–134). She concluded with a warning about modern expectations—"an explicit link between positivism—the assumption that science constitutes the only true known ... —and the modern drive for unchecked progress" (Morley, 2019, 164). Her data cited corrupt lab scientists for complicity with industry and government in "killing the planet" (*ibid.*). Her promotion of volunteerism and government regulatory agencies aided in regenerating earth's ecology before humankind wreaked irreparable damage.

See also Diction.

Sources

Carson, Rachel. "Acceptance Speech," National Audubon Society, New York (3 December 1963).
_____. *The Edge of the Sea*. Boston: Houghton Mifflin, 1955.
_____. "The Real World Around Us," address to the Theta Sigma Phi Matrix Table Dinner, Columbus, Ohio (21 April 1954).
_____. *Silent Spring*. Boston: Houghton Mifflin, 40th Anniversary Edition, 2002.
_____. *Under the Sea Wind: A Naturalist's Picture of Ocean Life*. New York: Simon & Schuster, 1941.
Carson, R.L. "The Northern Trawlers Move South." *Baltimore Sunday Sun* (3 January 1937): 6–7.
_____. "Shad Going the Way of the Buffalo." *Charleston News and Courier* (14 February 1937): 8C.
_____. "Starlings a Housing Problem." *Baltimore Sunday Sun Magazine* (5 March 1939): 1.
_____. "Walrus and Carpenter Not Oysters' Only Foe." *Baltimore Sun* (21 August 1938): 2.
_____. "Whalers Ready for New Season." *Baltimore Sunday Sun* (20 November 1938): 2.
Morley, Julie J. *Future Sacred: The Connected Creativity of Nature*. Rochester, VT: Park Street Press, 2019.
Scarlett, Lynn. "The Poetry of Truth." *Fish & Wildlife News* (Spring 2007): 34.

Diction

A meticulous wordsmith, Rachel honed each statement and read it aloud to adjust syntax, tone, alliteration, clarity, and cadence to the understanding of her audience. However, she credited readers of the 1937 newspaper article "Shad Going Way of Buffalo" with knowing that "provender" meant food and "brigands" was a synonym for thieves (Carson, 1937, 8C). In the introduction to the 1989 edition of *The Sea Around Us* from Oxford University Press, naturalist author Ann Haymond Zwinger saluted Rachel for three years of rewrites leaving "not a paragraph or a sentence out of place" and for introducing "biosphere," "balance of nature," "ecology," "ecosystem," "interdependence," and "food chain" to the common vocabulary (Zwinger, 1989, xxii, xxi). A dramatic premise declared the preformed earth "molten liquid," a "viscid tide" that gradually "congealed and hardened" before water filled the oceans (Carson, 1951, 20, 21). Ecologist H. Patricia Hynes, a former professor at the Boston University School of Public Health, described Rachel as spokesperson for the sea "for its mystery of which she was the oracle, and for its cadence and sound for which she was its voice" (Hynes, 1989, 35).

For intense sea life studies, the writer chose imaginative wording. She focused on the Darwinian concept of predation, as with the term "sortie" to militarize the attack of Rynchops the skimmer on shad trapped in estuary gill nets (Carson, 1941, 20). The migration of snow geese she imagined as a "skein," a knitting term for a loosely joined flock (*ibid.*, 25). For ravenous gulls, the narrative captured laughter and "mewing," a contrast to herring gulls, which attacked from marsh grass with jabs and screams (*ibid.*, 30). In the wintry denouement, snails glistened "like a rain of strangely shaped hailstones—daggers and spirals and cones of glassy clearness," which the author extemporized as a "ceaseless dance of life" (*ibid.*, 154).

Diction proved the author's major strength, particularly the wording of grand

and sensual observations. For the liner notes of the RCA Victor recording of Claude Debussy's symphony *La Mer,* she chose "brooding spirit" and "wind-driven processions" of waves (Carson, "Liner Notes," 1951). An outpouring of personal response resided in "streamer," "playground," "mobile," and "abyss." Verbs particularized aspects of wind on seawater—"dissolve," "intercept," "shoaling," and "surge." Her knowledge of specific locales demanded mention of Tierra del Fuego, Iceland, and the Orkney islands.

PRECISION AND DEPTH

The reviewer and author posted paragraphs and statements in articles for the *Progressive Fish-Culturist* and, for additional clarification, to specialists such as Dutch expert Cornelis Jan Biejer and Walter C. Bauer, a pathologist at the Washington University Medical School. In March 1957, Rachel's debut at scripting the TV broadcast on clouds for *Omnibus* aroused a greater exactitude with the terms "wave troughs," "lenticular," "stratus," and "portents," the kinds of details known to farmers, pilots, fishermen, and "all others who live openly on the face of the earth" (Carson, "Clouds," 1957). Unlike urban folk, outdoor laborers had reason to decode the "air ocean" that extended 600 miles into the ether. Her verb choice called for "undulate" and "surge"; for nouns, she opted for "turbulence," "momentum," and "aerial drama." Her narrative accentuated the scientific terms "foehn," "chinook," and "zonda," global descriptors of warm, dry downdrafts on mountain slopes. She summarized the endless circulation of air currents as "fleecy" and "beneficent," a brief subjective evaluation of nature.

With the aid of agent Maria Rodell, the author cultivated a guiding principle by which she bore witness to fearful changes in the intricate labyrinth of nature. Terry Tempest Williams, a preservationist of the American West, called Rachel "a conscientious and directed soul who believed in the eloquence of facts" (Williams, 2002, 32). The editor, Paul Brooks, described the unique writer "merging ... the imagination and insight of a creative writer with a scientist's passion for fact" (*ibid.*, 43). However, the urgency of *Silent Spring* aroused a sleeping giant—a shy woman's denunciation of technology for jeopardizing earthly survival. In Chapter Nine, "Rivers of Death," she poured out a biologist's knowledge of fragile life alongside the powers of DDT (dichlorodiphenyltrichloroethane) to annihilate it. In the words of literary historian Cheryll Glotfelty, an environmentalist at the University of Nevada, Reno, "When Carson's tune suddenly changed from one of gentle appreciation to one of grim alarm, people listened" (Glotfelty, 1996, 161).

THE AUTHENTIC VOICE

The procession of podia that Rachel mounted introduced her to sophisticated listeners, from gardeners to members of congress to the 1,500 scientists and medical professionals in San Francisco on October 18, 1963, at Kaiser-Permanente's symposium *Man Against Himself.* To suit the symposium's academic leanings, her speech "The Pollution of Our Environment" raised the level of vocabulary to include specifics of earth study in "geochemist," water analysis in "turbidity," and nuclear waste in "atomic fission," "Ce^{137}" "Sr^{90}" "I^{131}," "nanocuries," "radioiodine," "AEC," "gamma rays," "beta radiation," and "radioisotopes" (Carson, "Pollution," 1963). She ventured into the subject of deep-sea currents and the displacement of sediments over "continental margins," the shallowest of sea waters and those closest to land. The narrative cited Alaskan Eskimo and Scandinavian Lapps as examples of residents in the cold northern "tundra" at the far end of a contaminated food chain (*ibid.*). Of global residents unaware of mutagenic substances, the speaker delivered a humane alarm.

In a final address, a brief thank-you for the Audubon Medal at the Hotel Roosevelt in mid–Manhattan on December 3, 1963, Rachel retreated from scientific jargon to general knowledge and a gracious tone. Still insisting that the earth labored under the burden of overpopulation and the ravages of avarice and venality, she honored her forebears, the scientists and activists who had preceded her. By closing on "our privilege to contribute," she exemplified the humility that she admired in humankind (Carson, "Acceptance," 1963).

See also Details; "A Fable for Tomorrow"; *Silent Spring: The Obligation to Endure.*

Sources

Carson, Rachel. "Acceptance Speech," National Audubon Society, New York (3 December 1963).
_____. "Clouds" in "Something about the Sky," CBS *Omnibus* (11 March 1957).
_____. "Liner Notes," Claude Debussy's *La Mer*, RCA Victor, 1951.fmattam
_____. "The Pollution of Our Environment," address to the Kaiser-Permanente Symposium *Man Against Himself*, San Francisco (18 October 1963).
_____. *The Sea Around Us*. New York: Oxford University Press, 1951.
_____. *Silent Spring*. Boston: Houghton Mifflin, 40th Anniversary Edition, 2002.
_____. *Under the Sea Wind: A Naturalist's Picture of Ocean Life*. New York: Simon & Schuster, 1941.
Carson, R.L. "Shad Going the Way of the Buffalo," Charleston *News and Courier* (14 February 1937): 8C.
Glotfelty, Cheryll. "Rachel Carson" in *American Nature Writers*. New York: Charles Scribner's Sons, 1996.
Hynes, H. Patricia. *The Recurring Silent Spring*. New York: Pergamon, 1989.
Lear, Linda, ed. "Introduction" to *Lost Woods: The Discovered Writing of Rachel Carson*. Boston: Beacon Press, 1998.
Williams, Terry Tempest. "One Patriot," in *Patriotism and the American Land*. Great Barrington, MA: Orion Society, 2002.
Zwinger, Ann H. "Introduction" to *The Sea Around Us: Special Edition*. New York: Oxford University Press, 1989.

Drinking Water

With constant apprehension for humanity's survival in a corrupt ecosystem, Rachel's realistic works maintained a hold on pragmatism. In *Silent Spring,* she warned that all earth dwellers encountered dangerous substances from conception to the grave. She mocked the half-truths of authorities about the safety of naturally occurring arsenic and about fish kills that lowered quality of drinking water. From Chapter 3 to Chapter 4, she moved purposefully from "Elixirs of Death" to potable aquifers, the globe's most precious resources. Ecologist Fred Turner, on staff at Stanford University, named her book and the November 3, 1969, Cuyahoga River fire in Cleveland, Ohio, as the "turning points in the history of environmental law" (Turner, 2016, 56).

The author did not saddle nuclear physicists, farmers, and industrialists with all the fault for sullying the ecosphere with untreated waste or hydrocarbon dusts and sprays. The narrative blamed human apathy for hazards to pure, adequate supplies. Out of indifference and ignorance, citizens ignored the defilement of waterways with urban and industrial waste, medical and laboratory detritus, and radioactivity from reactors and nuclear bomb tests. To the list, she added abuse and overuse of agricultural pesticides, in particular, DDT (dichlorodiphenyltrichloroethane), which coated watersheds, river basins, and estuaries with a deadly goo.

A MAJOR EXPOSÉ

On September 27, 1962, *Silent Spring* opened on a bucolic pipe dream, "A Fable for Tomorrow," which pictured settlers building homesteads and digging wells, a basis for family life. Rachel revealed the dispersal of factory-made carcinogens permeating wells, lakes, and streams and tainting groundwater. She charged the public with responsibility for its own safety:

> A Who's Who of pesticides is therefore of concern to us all. If we are going to live so intimately with these chemicals eating and drinking them, taking them into the very marrow of our bones—we had better know something about their nature and their power [Carson, 2002, 17].

The narrative pinpointed the terrifying virulence of endrin, especially in orchards and wells. Because of the dissemination of DDD (dichlorodiphenyldichloroethane) emulsion in Clear Lake, California, in 1949 and in repeated treatment of gnats in 1954 and 1957, the bioscape suffered widespread poisoning of fish, swan grebes, and gulls. Swimmers and diners on lake fish subjected their bodies to high levels of neurotoxins, which targeted the adrenal cortex. Because of the instant backlash against *Silent Spring,* Margaret Lock, a cultural anthropologist at McGill University, concluded, "Clearly, efforts to rid the environment of such chemicals are fraught with dangers other than their toxicity" (MacClancy, 2019, 231).

On December 2, 1962, Rachel justified the timing of her jeremiad. She surveyed a troubling era of pollutants when earth could no longer heal itself from chemical damage. The writer's personal essay "On the Reception of Silent Spring" to the National Parks Association stated, "When white froth issues from his kitchen faucet instead of clear water [the average citizen] is reminded of the alarming facts of water pollution by detergents, poisons, and wastes of all kinds" (Carson, "Reception," 1962). Three days later, she informed the Women's National Press Club of DDT in fish at the Framingham, Massachusetts, reservoir, a water source for citizens west of Boston.

SOURCES OF BIOCIDES

The speaker substantiated public fears for human well-being by listing biocides that permeated water reservoirs: roadway herbicides, lawn and garden treatments, athletic field and golf course sprays, seeds soaked in fungicide, DDT (dichlorodiphenyltrichloroethane), aldrin, dieldrin, and heptachlor, a killer of fire ants. Contributing an unpredictable element, weather extremes and flooding carried hazards into local supplies. Ecofeminist writer Barbara Kingsolver explored the ramifications of such noxious waters in the novel *Animal Dreams*, in which biology students studying river samples under microscopes found no living organisms. In mid–May 1963, President John F. Kennedy's Science Advisory Committee corroborated Rachel's claims about community waterway contamination with substances not intended for use on consumables.

On June 4, 1963, the author presented a 40-minute testimony, "Environmental Hazards: Control of Pesticides and Other Chemical Poisons," to the Senate Committee on Commerce. She charged legislators with the urgent problem of nuclear explosions, radioactive waste, factory-made hydrocarbons, and hospital and laboratory detritus and the domestic use of phosphorous-rich detergent. Her speech informed elected officials of the effects of tainted drinking water in sapping human digestive systems and reducing the ability to withstand carcinogens. In the decade after Rachel's death, investigators disclosed fearful amounts of toxic hydrocarbons in aquifers beneath the heartland cornfields of Iowa and Nebraska. Her colleague, Shirley A. Briggs, warned that the severity of the problem ruled out a quick fix.

See also Fish.

Sources

Carson, Rachel. "Address," Women's National Press Club, Washington, D.C. (5 December 1962)
_____. "On the Reception of *Silent Spring*" (2 December 1962).
_____. *Silent Spring*. Boston: Houghton Mifflin, 40th Anniversary Edition, 2002.
Cook, Christopher D. "The Spraying of America." *Earth Island Journal* 20:1 (2005): 34–38.
Lock, Margaret. "Toxic Life in the Anthropocene" in *Exotic No More*. 2nd ed. Chicago: University of Chicago Press, 2019, 223–240.
Turner, Fred. "Dirty Water and Disease: A Public Health History." *National Resources & Environment* 31:1 (Summer 2016): 56.

Ecofeminism

Before the term "ecofeminism" gained credence, Rachel attempted to arouse an emotional respect for nature in readers, especially for wildflowers, birds, livestock, pets, and children. Her works awakened in readers a nurturing, healing responsibility common to the female heads of families and a reliance on collaboration rather than dominance or suppression. In an era when the world's females incurred disproportionate misery from environmental injustice and exploitation, she acquired a mystic reverence for the outdoors from her mother, who pointed out by name local plants, birds, mammals, and flowers. From Professor Mary Scott Skinker at the Pennsylvania College for Women, Rachel developed a serious respect for scholarship, especially that of female scientists.

Feminist biographer Andrea Barnet stated that the biologist broke through the era's prejudice toward technological progress and "the Cold War paranoia of her time to discuss the environment, thus winning the hearts and minds of everyday people" (Barnet, 2018, 26). As a result, urban and suburban gardeners, travelers, and vacationers valued wildlife sanctuaries for their tranquil vistas and solitude and practiced gentle sustenance of all life. Female Carson disciples were quick to write compelling letters to the editor naming specifics of pesticide abuse in their communities and proposing action against unannounced spray programs.

UP THE ACADEMIC CHAIN

Reviewers and literary historians esteemed the author for safeguarding life. Michelle Mart, a history professor at Pennsylvania State University, commended Rachel for being "the godmother of the Environmental Protection Agency, the ban on DDT and other pesticides, Earth Day, the 1972 Federal Insecticide, Fungicide, and Rodenticide Act, and indeed of Environmentalism as a philosophy and political movement" (Mart, 2009, 31). Reviewer and illustrator Charity Edwards, a lecturer at Monash University in Melbourne, Australia, regretted subsequent neglect of the author's exploration of "interrelationships between 'life' and 'work,'" which combined empathy and empowerment with laboratory objectivity toward questions of reproduction and genetics (Edwards, 2017, 209). Edwards viewed Carson's unique sensitivity as a "[blurring of] technical expertise, narrative play, and critical re-imaginings" (*ibid.*). Even though she fostered from toddlerhood her nephew, Roger Allen Christie, androcentric critics demeaned her writings as hysterical and biased by an unmarried status and love of birds, fish, and house cats. They dismissed her midwifery of ecofeminism as "other" and her views on male-dominated authority as superficial, even detrimental to research.

At Wake Forest University, English professor and environmentalist Judith Madera acclaimed Rachel's holistic, green agenda for ameliorating capitalistic and governmental sins against nature and the self. Madera saluted the naturalist's sea trilogy as a harbinger of lyric life studies and "the deep enmeshments of cohabitation" (Madera, 2017, 292). Literary critic Christine Oravec, on staff at the University of Utah, honored Rachel for obscuring "the boundaries between the self and the objective world" and aiming "to heal the artificial split between rationality and emotion" (Oravec, 1994, 73, 78). Like fellow scientists Dian Fossey and Jane Goodall and philosopher Starhawk, Rachel believed that an appreciation of transitory beauty and mysticism benefited the individual spirit.

DIRECTING ACTIVISM

Rachel's feminization of nature writing and speaking did more than spawn volunteerism in women. In January 1954, threats to Dinosaur National Monument in Colorado and Utah had her turning to garden clubs to protest the Echo Park dam project, which threatened the viewing of 11 species of fossils. Specifically, she relied on female conservators. Among them, Ruth Scott, bird chair of the Garden Club Federation of Pennsylvania, crusaded for a women's conservation lobby. In mustering additional allies, Rachel gained the trust of Agnes Meyer, owner of the *Washington Post,* and Christine Stevens, president of the Animal Welfare Institute of New York, which protected circus animals, right whales, and other at-risk species. Both women advocated Rachel's broad stance on preserving the earth's diversity.

Upon completing proofs of *Silent Spring* in January 1962, the author sent copies to the Children's Bureau, National Council of Jewish Women, National Federation of Women's Clubs, and U.S. congresswoman from Oregon Edith Starrett Green, senator from Oregon Maurine Brown Neuberger, and congresswoman Leonor Kretzer

Sullivan, the first female legislator from Missouri. Direct charges against "the man with the spray gun" in the chapter "Needless Havoc" coupled gendered misdeeds with a Cold War mentality to place blame on war-mongering males (Carson, 2002, 85). The etymology of "havoc" named a post-victory rush by soldiers to burn, steal, plunder, destroy, rape, and pillage at will.

The Gendered Touch

In summoning forces to defend nature from biocides, Rachel saluted women for being "traditionally the custodians of family welfare, the guardians of the health and happiness of their children" as well as promoters of nutrition and wellness in future generations (Carson, "Tomorrow's," 1962). She cited female protesters and letter writers—gardeners, urban bird harborers, poultry farmers, consumer advocates—for recognizing deadly threats to homes, animals, and families and for demanding consumer protection by health departments and the U.S. Food and Drug Administration. Of dangerous aerial spray of DDT (dichlorodiphenyltrichloroethane), a threat to a female chicken farmer in Texas and to Mrs. Waller in Westchester, New York, the author declared, "It is a threat that American women can help to stop" (Colson, 1962). In addition to legitimating women's concerns about ecology, Dianne Newell, a technology historian at the University of British Columbia, prized Rachel's authoritative voice for validating marginalized female scientists and activists throughout the English-speaking world.

Long after her death on April 14, 1964, the author's example popularized the concept that nature needed protection from neglect and from the inundation of pollutants and synthetic substances—smog, fertilizer, and food additives to radioactive fallout. Nature writer Peter Matthiessen, winner of a National Book Award, admired Rachel's succinct, gutsy prose, "the cornerstone of the new environmentalism" (McCrum, 2016). Her writings inspired public literacy about ecology and the interconnection of life forms. Her denunciation of biocides capable of devastating fragile ecosystems gained support worldwide. As a result of her pro-nature initiative, U.S. wildlife sanctuaries protected more than 2,000 species: 1,000 fish, 700 birds, 250 amphibians and reptiles, and 220 mammals. Out of 1,311 imperiled life forms, 280 survived on oases sheltering 59 jeopardized species.

Sources

Barnet, Andrea. *Visionary Women: How Rachel Carson, Jane Jacobs, Jane Goodall, and Alice Waters Changed Our World.* New York: Ecco, 2018.

Carson, Rachel. *Silent Spring.* Boston: Houghton Mifflin, 40th Anniversary Edition, 2002.

_____. "Tomorrow's Spring," speech to the All-Women Conference of the National Council of Women (11 October 1962).

Colson, Helen A. "'Democracy Still works…': Rachel's Song Is Loud and Clear." *Washington* [D.C.] *News* (6 November 1962).

Edwards, Charity. "Of the Urban and the Ocean: Rachel Carson and the Disregard of Wet Volumes." *Field* 7:1 (2017): 205–219.

Lear, Linda. "Introduction," *Lost Woods: The Discovered Writing of Rachel Carson.* Boston: Beacon Press, 1998.

Madera, Judith. "The Birth of an Island: Rachel Carson's The Sea Around Us." *Women's Studies Quarterly* 45:1/2 (Spring/Summer 2017): 292–298.

Mart, Michelle. "Rhetoric and Response: The Cultural Impact off Rachel Carson's *Silent Spring*." *Left History* 14:2 (2009): 31–46.

McCrum, Robert. "The 100 Best Nonfiction Books: No 20—*Silent Spring* by Rachel Carson (1962)." *The Guardian* (13 June 2016).

Newell, Dianne. "Judith Merril and Rachel Carson: Reflections on Their 'Potent Fictions' of Science." *Journal of International Women's Studies* 5:4 (2004): 31.

Nudel, Martha. "Conservation in Action." *Fish & Wildlife News* (Spring 2007): 22–25.

Oravec, Christine. "Rachel Louise Carson" in *Women Public Speakers in the United States, 1925–1993*. Westport, CT: Greenwood, 1994, 72–89.

Seager, Joni. "Rachel Carson Died of Breast Cancer: The Coming of Age of Feminist Environmentalism." *Signs* 28:3 (Spring 2003).

Ecology

A transdisciplinary philosopher in the fields of biology, ecology, oceanography, and social experience, Rachel introduced Americans to the concept of interdependence, the life force of multi-species ecosystems. For *The Edge of the Sea,* she grouped details about a transient life community into three shores—rock, sand, and coral reefs, each with indigenous flora and fauna. The narrative detailed the elements of diversity and the dependence of predators on prey. The components, she stressed, form "the universality of the sea world," a liquid ecosystem repeated around the globe on a variety of shores (Carson, 1955, xiv).

One of the biologist's most compelling essays, "Earth's Green Mantle," Chapter Six in *Silent Spring,* exposed vigorous extermination programs in Connecticut and Massachusetts that deformed oak leaves and turned the landscape brown and patchy. The narrative damned the thoughtless spraying of 75 million acres of Southwestern mesquite and 10,000 acres in northwestern Wyoming's Bridger National Forest, a stretch of wilderness in four counties that incorporates lakes and watersheds, forests, wildflowers, campgrounds, and 75 species of wildlife. The biocide wiped out mesquite and sagebrush, but it also exterminated native willows (*Salix drummondiana*) along stream beds. The loss of shady ecosystems killed waterfowl, beaver, moose, and trout and deprived the wild of natural wastewater filters, palliatives gathered by Native American healers to treat fever and malaria, and pollen and food for lace bugs, honeybees, and butterfly larva.

THEORY IN ACTION

In reference to the unintentional loss of such plants as Southwestern mesquite and Wyoming willows, Rachel viewed earth's organisms as a living, integrated network, the source of unity in her newspaper articles, *Under the Sea Wind,* and Chapter Twelve of *Silent Spring,* "The Human Price." Poet Billy Mills' literary review for *The Guardian* made a similar observation about *The Sea Around Us,* which related seas to land, air, sun, and moon. The gestalt transcended scientific prose and created a "masterpiece of ecological writing" that encouraged readers "to protect these delicate ecosystems" (Mills, 2014). In the introduction to *Lost Woods,* editor Linda Lear exclaimed, "The magnitude of Carson's impact on the public's understanding of such issues as ecology and environmental change still astonishes" (Lear, 1998, ix). As early as 1939, the conservationist questioned the wisdom of great concrete dams that left trout-spawning areas dry and challenged the effluent of West Virginia coal mines, which blackened 25 miles of the Youghiogheny River in Maryland. To solve the problem of coal-begrimed waters that smothered large-mouth bass and trout, federal investigators began sealing mines, a simple barrier method of safeguarding fish, birds, and game.

At a scholarly six-day symposium "Water for Industry" hosted by the American Association for the Advancement of Science in Boston on December 29, 1953, Rachel plunged into the matter of habitat and the parameters that enable a species to thrive and reproduce. In an introit to the "dawn age of the science of ecology," she questioned elements that welcomed animals and their spawn with a rhetorical question: "What is the nature of the ties that bind it to its world?" (Carson, 1953, n.p.). She returned to the concept of biosphere in the essay in *Good Reading* "On the Biological Sciences," which stated a truism: "It is useless to attempt to preserve a living species unless the kind of land or water it requires is also preserved" (Carson, 1956, n.p.).

With *Silent Spring* on September 27, 1962, the scientific journalist orchestrated a lifetime of research on planetary needs. Joni Seager, a feminist environmentalist at Bentley University in Boston, praised Rachel's unifying powers:

> Her prodigious feat of synthesizing a jumble of scientific and medical information into an understandable, coherent argument about health and environment was transformative. In so doing, Carson pointed the way to the key paths of inquiry, which applied scientific, industrial, and public health synergy to serious threats to earth's wellness [Seager, 2003, 959].

After *Silent Spring* reached various language groups around the world, she became a phenomenon of sense and concern for humanity. Gary Kroll, on staff at Plattsburgh State University in New York, remarked on her role in "the transition of environmentalism from a grass-roots movement to near universal consensus" (Kroll, 2001, 403).

Of the political plans for making North America more profitable, Rachel referred to a grand restructuring of salable parts of nature as "the shotgun approach" (Carson, 2002, 67). Of particular concern, the denuding of the Midwestern and Southwestern plains to exterminate sagebrush and replace it with grazing lands yielded fewer species and a sparse habitat for herders' cattle and sheep. In a similar correlation of organisms, she explained how "distinct and unrelated facts" might cause irreparable harm to humankind and "reverberate throughout the entire system to initiate changes in seemingly unrelated organs and tissues" (*ibid.*, 189).

KEEPERS OF THE PLANET

Into her last months, Rachel initiated widespread interest in what Geoffrey Norman, an essayist for *National Geographic, Forbes,* and *Outside,* called vigilance and the stewardship of the planet—"the way the natural world fit together, the pieces so tightly and inextricably bound that you could not isolate cause and effect" (Norman, 1983, 472). In a feature for *The Guardian,* Scots poet John Burnside categorized the author's "deep or radical ecology" alongside feminism and racial equality as the upsurges of liberalism in the 1960s (Burnside, 2002, 1). Comparing her philosophy of interconnectedness to a Celtic knot, he expanded on her threat to "vested interests" in government, mega-agriculture, and big business, which declared her anti-modern, anti-capitalist, and anti-progressive (*ibid.*).

Gary Kroll, an environmental historian at State University of New York at

Plattsburgh, contrasted the mindset of "technical and scientifically engineered quick-fixes" to Rachel's summoning of affirmation and humility in the human spirit (Kroll, 2002, 1). Rather than an apologia for formal science, her critical theory denounced the curriculum for allowing arrogance and absolutism to reduce and isolate nature. In rapid order, colleges and universities advanced ecology to an academic discipline debating issues of wasted resources, contaminants and toxins, and biodiversity lumped under the heading "green." Although the direction veered from Rachel's original thoughts, a new epoch of concern emerged for growing edibles and protecting citizens from degraded environments and tainted water, particularly in cities.

Sources

Burnside, John. "Reluctant Crusader." *The Guardian* (18 May 2002): 1.
Carson, Rachel. "The Edge of the Sea" (speech), American Association for the Advancement of Science, Boston (December 29, 1953).
_____. "On the Biological Sciences." *Good Reading* (July 1956).
_____. *Silent Spring*. Boston: Houghton Mifflin, 40th Anniversary Edition, 2002.
_____. "Undersea." *Atlantic Monthly* 160 (September 1937): 322–325.
Carson, R.L. "A New Trout Crop for Anglers," *Baltimore Sun* (2 April 1939): 3.
Edwards, Charity. "Of the Urban and the Ocean: Rachel Carson and the Disregard of Wet Volumes." *Field* 7:1 (2017): 205–219.
Kroll, Gary. "Rachel Carson—*Silent Spring*: A Brief History of Ecology as a Subversive Subject." *Reflections* 9:2 (2002).
_____. "The 'Silent Springs' of Rachel Carson: Mass Media and the Origins of Modern Environmentalism." *Public Understanding of Science* 10:4 (1 October 2001): 403–420.
Lear, Linda. "Introduction," *Lost Woods: The Discovered Writing of Rachel Carson*. Boston: Beacon Press, 1998.
Mills, Billy. "A Book for the Beach." *The Guardian* (28 July 2014).
Norman, Geoffrey. "The Flight of Rachel Carson." *Esquire* (December 1984): 472–479.
Quaratiello, Arlene Rodda. *Rachel Carson: A Biography*. Amherst, NY: Prometheus, 2010.
Seager, Joni. "Rachel Carson Died of Breast Cancer: The Coming of Age of Feminist Environmentalism." *Signs* 28:3 (Spring 2003): 945–972.

The Edge of the Sea

In 1955, Rachel achieved academic respect for *The Edge of the Sea*, the last of her ocean trilogy after *Under the Sea Wind* and *The Sea Around Us*. She set the parameters in 1950 in a letter to Paul Brooks, editor of Houghton Mifflin. She stated the need for a sketch of each ocean creature plus "why it lives where it does, how it has adapted its structures and habitat to its environment, how it gets food, its life cycle, its enemies, competitors, associates" (Carson, 1955, xvii). A neatly outlined aim, her plan to complete *A Guide to Seashore Life* indicated the workings of a field manual. By 1953, she trashed the original arrangement and "[freed] my style to be itself" (*Ibid.*, xviii).

With financial rewards from *The Sea Around Us,* the biologist could return to marine topics to inform readers of organisms in tide pools, shallows, granite crevices, mangrove swamps, coral reefs, estuaries, and bogs. She accepted from Rosalind Wilson, Houghton Mifflin's editor, direction on writing a guide to dispel ignorance of oceanography and pondered two possible titles: *Guide to Seashore Life on the Atlantic Coast* and *Rock, Sand, and Coral, a Beachcomber's Guide to the Atlantic Coast*. Still writing and rewriting in September 1953 at the cottage Silverledges overlooking Boothbay Harbor, Maine, the marine biologist pursued fall beachcombing and admitted to neighbor Dorothy Freeman, "Progress is—well, I may as well admit it—SLOW" on "this tyrant manuscript" (Steingruber, 2018, 330, 331).

The author highlighted evolutionary change in her philosophy and revered the liminal wet/dry marge as the "essential unity that binds all life to the earth" (Carson, 1955, viii). She opened Chapter I, "The Marginal World," on "this place of the meeting of land and water" and its "intricate fabric of life" (*ibid.*, 2). She exulted in personal favorites—the North Carolina Outer Banks, Florida Keys and Everglades, and Cape Cod, Massachusetts, the shorelines that fascinated her with natural charm and insightful revelations. With illustrator Robert "Bob" Warren Hines's windswept sketch of spume over coastal grasses, she introduced a water world dominated by serendipity, "For no two successive days is the shore line precisely the same" (*ibid.*, 1). In the wispy haze of fog and mist, she imagined an evolutionary peak—"a dim and vaporous world that might be a world of creation, stirring with new life" (*ibid.*, 42).

CREATIVE POWER

Rachel's narrative instilled in readers a regard for oceans, which cover 71 percent of earth's surface. Chapter II, "Patterns of Shore Life," returned to the mechanics of oceanography, the forces of currents, tides, and swells that bore life to land masses and determined sustainability of habitats. Sympathy with tiny larvae marked her glimpses of great surges of undersea energy. She dramatized the crushing of fossils into clay and sand sediment, which obscured records of the pre–Cambrian ocean before 541,000,000 BCE. In balance, she welcomed Maine tides ebbing to a peaceful lapse, "for the waves do not have behind them the push of the inward pressing tides" (*ibid.*, 39).

Chapters III–V—"The Rocky Shores," "The Rim of Sand," and "The Coral Coast"—interpreted the uniqueness and relevance of rock, sand, and coral as definers of seaboards. Species by species, she examined residents of coastal waters:

Example	Proper Name	Common Names	Food
alaria	(*Alaria esculenta*)	winged kelp, murlin, brown alga	____
amphithoe	(*Amphithoides*)	scud, freshwater shrimp	omnivores
barnacle	(*Semibalanus balanoides*)	acorn or rock barnacle	plankton
brittle star	(*Ophiuroidea*)	serpent star	worms, crustaceans
clava	(*Clava multicornis*)	club hydroid	worms, larvae, crustaceans
coral	(*Briareum asbestinum*)	corky sea finger	plankton, algae
coralline algae	(*Corallinales*)	red algae	algae
dog whelk	(*Nucella lapillus*)	Atlantic dogwinkle, marine snail	mussels, barnacles, tube worm
dulse	(*Palmaria palmata*)	sea lettuce, creathnach	____
golden star tunicate	(*Botryllus schlosseri*)	star ascidian	sea particles
green crab	(*Carcinus Maenas*)	shore crab	worms, crustaceans, mollusks

Example	Proper Name	Common Names	Food
horse mussel	(*Modiolus modiolus*)	clabby doo	plankton
kelp	(*Laminaria*)	tangle, brown algae, oarweed, devil's apron	____
leathesia	(*Leathesia marina*)	sea potato, sea cauliflower	moss
limpet	(*Patella vulgata*)	sea snail	algae
moon jelly	(*Aurelia aurita*)	medusa	plankton, mollusks
mussel	(*Pteriomorphia*)	moule, winkle, slug	plankton, sea particles
nereid worm	(*Nereis virens*)	ragworm, clam worm	carnivores
periwinkle	(*Littorina littorea*)	whelk, sea snail	lichen from rocks
plumed worm	(*Diopatra cuprea*)	decorator worm, tube worm	wrack
porphyra	(*Porphyra umbilicalis*)	red algae, laver	____
rockborer	(*Petricola*)	red nose	algae, kelp
rockweed	(*Fucus vesiculosus*)	bladder wrack, sea wrack	____
scale worm	(*Polynoidae*)	____	worms, crustaceans
sea anemone	(*Actiniaria*)	flower or mushroom coral	fish, crabs, mollusks, sea urchins
sea colander	(*Agarum cribosum*)	shotgun kelp	____
sea lace	(*Membranipora membranacea*)	lacy crust, sea mat	____
sea urchin	(*Echinoidea*)	____	algae
starfish	(*Astroidea*)	sea stars	sponges, snails, coral, algae

Relying on a hand lens to enlarge the smallest life forms, Rachel inspected the one-of-a-kind mangrove swamps of the Florida Everglades, the blue-green algae on coquina in St. Augustine, and a mangrove trail and living reef walls around Key Largo, home to reef fish, turtles, seahorses, sea fans, staghorn coral, lionfish, and grassy underwater meadows. The artist followed the author's penchant for curiosities with sketches of crumb-of-bread sponge, brittle stars, whelk egg strings, Portuguese man-o'-war, ghost and Jonah crabs, spirula, plumose anemone, and ramshorn shells. Upbeat in her view of Maine strands, she delighted in the power of spring tides to revive the "shining freshness, a wetness, and a sparkle" in Irish moss (*Chondrus crispus*) (*ibid.*, 95).

THE RIM OF SAND

In a perusal of New England, the Carolinas, Georgia, and Florida coastlines, the naturalist reflected on deep time and "materials ... steeped in antiquity," notably, the grit, silt, and creatures that swam from Atlantic to Pacific before the juncture of North and South America during the Tertiary Era (3,000,000 BCE) (*ibid.*, 125). Patiently, like time itself, Rachel outlined the process by which gravity, glaciers, frost, rain, and running water wore down rock into small grains, many of them quartz. She characterized shore residents as "inconceivably minute beings ... single-celled animals and plants, water mites, shrimplike crustacea, insects, and ... larvae" whose lives consisted of "eating and being eaten" (*ibid.,* 130, 135). Bob Hines's drawing on pages 164–165 pictured the contrast in shore survivors with a skate egg case, moon snail sand collar, whelk egg string, Portuguese man-o'-war, moon snail, and ghost crab.

In ruminations on beachcombing along the Florida Keys, North Carolina Outer Banks, and Cape Cod and Buzzards Bay, Massachusetts, Rachel summarized the long history of the "husks and fragments of life"—the barnacle and the wood-devouring shipworm, "the scourge of the Romans with their galleys" and of the vessels of Phoenicians, Greeks, and Dutch explorers (*ibid.,* 188, 186). Her notes concluded that the likelihood of survival on the marge increased for "detritus feeders" that burrowed into saturated sand to find stability and havens from predators (*ibid.,* 137). Known also as passive feeders, lugworms, heart urchins, sand dollars, blue and mole crabs, sea pansies, ghost shrimp, starfish, and other diggers and polyps sustained themselves on edibles sieved from seawater. Of the constant reshaping of stretches of coastline by trumpet and parchment worms, she acknowledged that "prodigious toil leavens and renews the beaches" and cleans up rotting humus (*ibid.,* 142).

THE CORAL COAST

The naturalist revered the Florida Keys for their unique warm water coastline, which "has no counterpart elsewhere in the United States" (*ibid.,* 191). Because the tropical shelf of Hawk Channel rested on the concrescence of living organisms, she appreciated the digestive tracts of sea urchins, which ground and excreted shell fragments and coral rock into sand. The powers of mangrove swamps to create new territory returned the author's thoughts to the Pleistocene Era (1,000,000 BCE). She introduced the Sangamonian interglacial stage of 125,000 BCE, when the Keys took shape from the accretion of invertebrate corals (*Anthozoa Cnidaria*), colonizers that secreted calcium carbonate. Posting a map of southern Georgia and the stub of the Florida peninsula, she explained how changes in sea levels and calcareous sedimentation continued to alter the North American coastline, especially the Everglades. Her prediction of undermining by the sulphur sponge and boring mollusks looked into the future, when waves might sever the mass constructed by the lime-secreting coral polyp and "roll [it] down the seaward face of the reef into deeper water" (*ibid.,* 199).

Curiosity drove Rachel's daily jaunts, luring her to stake out new challenges in recognizing seaside fauna, e.g., pipefish, pearl fish, sting rays, king crown conch, and gorgonian basket starfish. At Ohio Key three-quarters of the way down the island string, she examined a sea hare (*Dolabella auricularia*), a hermaphroditic marine mollusk she had first seen at Currituck on the north end of the North Carolina Outer Banks. The narrative appended a clearly differentiated view of textured organisms by placing the sea hare alongside an octopus, horse conch, cowfish, giant starfish, seahorse, and pipefish. In the reef flats, she encountered brittle stars, sand dollars, black sea urchins, and suicidal sea cucumbers, which died by self-evisceration. She typified the recyclers of the community as "links in the living chains by which materials are taken from the sea, passed from one to another, returned to the sea, borrowed again" (*ibid.*, 221).

THE ENDURING SEA

Guided by sound on the shore, the marine biologist delineated high tide on dark nights from seeing crests smashing into rocks and fog slipping among spruce, juniper, and bayberry. The resulting coastline carried fossils within a sediment "steeped in antiquity" (*ibid.*, 125). Charging herself with desecrating minuscule dwellings, she believed she "was treading on the thin rooftops of an underground city" inhabited by burrowing ghost shrimp (*ibid.*, 140). Analyst Vera Norwood, on staff at the University of New Mexico, credited Rachel's tone to "a tantalized watcher" rewarded with "surprises attendant on one who waits" (Norwood, 1993, 152). Rachel concluded that her own existence mattered little to the stream of time and terrestrial events. Looking to "some shadowy future," Chapter VI, "The Enduring Sea," pictured ocean swells pulverizing granite into sand and refurbishing "the coast to its earlier state" when the earth was still forming (*ibid.*, 249).

Reviewer Charles Poore, a literary critic for the *New York Times,* admired the author's knack for making profound science readable to middle-class America, even the appendix organizing Latin names of phyla. Analyst Charity Edwards, a biologist at Central State University in Dayton, Ohio, applauded Rachel's ability "to collapse assumed boundaries between land, life, work, and deep water" (Edwards, 2017, 216). Over a decade, versions of Rachel's book appeared in Boston, London, Paris, Munich, New York, London, and Eau Claire, Wisconsin. In 1971, the posthumous *The Rocky Coast,* a 118-page excerpt from *The Edge of the Sea*, featured 50 photos by Charles Pratt and the illustrations of fellow naturalist Bob Hines. The special edition aimed to manifest "A Magical Journey in Words and Pictures to the Timeless World Where Sea and Shore Meet." Norman John Berrill, book critic for *Saturday Review,* extolled the two enthusiasts, Rachel and Bob, "each one scientifically trained and each an artist, the one with a pen and the other with a pencil" (Berrill, 1955, 30).

See also The Rocky Coast.

Sources

Berrill, N.J. "Review: *The Edge of the Sea.*" *Saturday Review* (3 December 1955): 30.
Carson, Rachel. *The Edge of the Sea*. Boston: Houghton Mifflin, 1955.
Edwards, Charity. "Of the Urban and the Ocean: Rachel Carson and the Disregard of Wet Volumes." *Field* 7:1 (2017): 205–219.
Fellows, Valerie, and Joshua Winchell. "Returning to the Water." *Fish & Wildlife News* (Spring 2007): 26–28.
Norwood, Vera. *Made from This Earth*. Chapel Hill: University of North Carolina Press, 1993.
Steingruber, Sandra, ed. *Rachel Carson: Silent Spring & Other Writings on the Environment.* New York: Library of America, 2018.

Eels

Out of curiosity about mysterious saltwater organisms, Rachel emulated Scots naturalist John Muir, who searched the coast for eels, crabs, and seaweed. She first studied eels in summer 1929 in Baltimore at the Johns Hopkins University aquarium. She continued her research on the southeastern shore of Massachusetts at the Woods Hole marine biological laboratory, where first infused data with an imaginary plunge into the murky abyss. In Gilman Hall, she kept an eel tank. Tom Horton, a journalist for the *Salisbury* (MD) *Daily Times,* stated, "The inexplicable impulse of adult eels, after living in Chesapeake streams and ponds and rivers for years or even decades, to suddenly seek the abyss of the Sargasso Sea to spawn and die at depths still unobserved by humans, remains almost as mysterious now as in Carson's day" (Horton, 2019, A4).

Intrigued by the urge of *Anguilla rostrata* to swim downstream to spawn, Rachel focused inquiries into eel reproduction and adaptation to the effects of salinity. A friend quoted her zeal for the travels of elvers: "They migrate hundreds of miles from the seas, where they are born, into the freshwater streams and ponds of our forests" (Popkin, 2013). More details in "Shad Going the Way of the Buffalo," a February 1937 article for the Charleston, South Carolina, *News and Courier* injected a bit of whimsy by calling eels "river brigands" for robbing catches of spring shad, which they mutilated to extract roe from females caught in the mesh (Carson, 1937, 8C).

In an article for *Johns Hopkins Magazine,* author Gabriel Popkin applauded Rachel's vivid nature narratives for her inborn skill at storytelling. Her adventures in "Chesapeake Eels Seek the Sargasso Sea," an October 1938 feature for the *Baltimore Sunday Sun Magazine*, the biologist spotlighted a protagonist "half as long or as thick as a man's thumb" (Carson, 1938, 1). She expressed enthusiasm over the convergence of tiny eels at the Sargasso Sea from the Atlantic Coast as well as Greenland, Labrador, New England and the Chesapeake Bay, Mexico, the Caribbean, Scandinavia, Germany, Belgium, France, and Great Britain. Her interest in the coastal beings followed a caravan "across 1,000 miles of strange, wild waters without benefit of chart or compass" (*ibid.*).

EEL HISTORY

After consulting more than 1,000 primary sources, Rachel gave credit to eel enthusiasts of the past, particularly English biologist Henry Williams, who explored the draw of smells from the warm Gulf Stream. She padded her version of the eel's life cycle with details of Danish naturalist Johannes Schmidt's identification of the annual Sargasso breeding ground. Her melodic style pictured their speeding bodies "growing fat on shellfish, worms and water plants" as their noses scented sargassum weed (*ibid.*). The overview marveled at the "infallible homing instinct" directing American conger eels to continental waters and the 2-foot European species on the much longer migration east over the Atlantic (*ibid.*).

The author's interest in eels continued in 1941 as the focus of Book III of *Under the Sea Wind,* the first of a sea trilogy. In admiration for its size and tenacity, she proclaimed the species "without parallel in the annals of sea or land" (Carson, 1941, 4). The narrative personified Anguilla, a European species, who migrated 200 miles with her mate "in silvery wedding dress," an anthropomorphic touch to oceanic reproduction (*ibid.*, 50). Of their endurance, the foreword admired that eels "continue year in, year out, through the centuries and the ages, while man's kingdoms rise and fall" (*ibid.*, 3).

A Life Struggle

Rachel stressed the tidal flow in light and dark, which defined "the time an enemy can find you easily and the time you are relatively safe" (*ibid.*, 5). Among rocks at Herring Gull Shoal, a 15-pound conger, a lurking marauder, sized up the possibilities of a mullet run toward the open sea. Deep into wintry waters, the eastern and western eel types separated, one species swimming toward European rivers and one remaining south of Bermuda to feast among the algae. A migration into fresh water in March rounded out the life cycle. Always in motion, the launce or sand eels in *The Edge of the Sea* juggled the stalking of tidal waters with predation on fry while shadowy victimizers kept an eye toward the undulating eels.

A report of a catastrophic fish kill in Austin, Texas, over January 15–21, 1961, in *Silent Spring* connected the flushing of DDT (dichlorodiphenyltrichloroethane), lindane, chlordane, and toxaphene with fish exterminations on the Colorado River bottom. The poisonous mix killed 27 fish species, including catfish, bullhead, sunfish, carp, bass, shiner, mullet, sucker, gar, and buffalo. Collateral damage added eels to the disaster.

Sources

Carson, Rachel. *Silent Spring.* Boston: Houghton Mifflin, 40th Anniversary Edition, 2002.

_____. *Under the Sea Wind: A Naturalist's Picture of Ocean Life.* New York: Simon & Schuster, 1941.

Carson, R.L. "Chesapeake Eels Seek the Sargasso Sea." *Baltimore Sunday Sun Magazine* (9 October 1938): 1.

_____. "Shad Going the Way of the Buffalo." *Charleston News and Courier* (14 February 1937): 8C.

Horton, Tom. "Rachel Carson No Stranger to Chesapeake, Its Creatures." *Salisbury* (MD) *Daily Times* (3 November 2019): A4.

Popkin, Gabriel. "Right Fish, Wrong Pond." *Johns Hopkins Magazine* (Summer 2013).

Endangered Species

The evolution of habitats and life populations freighted Rachel's writing with an awareness of ecological destruction as inevitable as plowing virgin prairies, draining wetlands, clearcutting forests, and topsoil erosion by extremes of wind and weather. From hunting, over-harvesting, industrial and municipal pollution, and construction, North American residents lost the passenger pigeon, great auk, and heath hen and saw the decline of trumpeter swans, whooping cranes, shad, oysters, and eels, all welcome meals in the American diet. For the rescue of trumpeter swans at Montana's Red Rock Lakes Refuge, opened in 1935, government agents closely guarded nesting cover and food sources year round because "this remnant colony seems to have lost the migratory instinct of its ancestors" (Carson, 1948, 16).

When the author joined the Bureau of Fisheries, she found civil servants laboring toward more productive farms and commercial fisheries for the sake of profit, regardless of the detriment of the animal kingdom. To strip ocean floors of predators, staff proposed methods of poisoning starfish, which ravaged oysters. The Bureau of Biological Survey aimed to tip the natural order in favor of human needs for food and sport, which required the eradication of birds, vermin, coyotes, bobcats, lynx, cougars, and wolves by toxic gas, traps, or hunting. The philosophy encouraged near extinction of the American bison.

SAVING FISH

The author's knowledge of ichthyology first seized on the imperiling of fish. Her celebratory item on January 3, 1937, in the *Baltimore Sun* admitted that the extension of trawling season strained bass, croaker, flounder, and scup populations, which previously flourished off Cape Hatteras, North Carolina, in winter. Her article in the February 14, 1937, issue of the Charleston, South Carolina, *News and Courier* warned of the depletion on 80 percent of spring shad runs along the Atlantic seaboard. Conservationists for the U.S. Fish commission had opened hatcheries in 1872 to replenish shad in the Potomac. The author championed another boost to fish populations— shad runs on the Sacramento River, which spread to Monterey, California, and north to the Columbia River.

The biologist's suspicions of DDT (dichlorodiphenyltrichloroethane) grew in 1945 after the June 5 spraying of Patuxent that released an organic drift lethal to indigenous Maryland birds and 20 types of fish. The alarming extermination inspired her press releases for the U.S. Fish and Wildlife Service. Of the cogent alerts, Molly K. Murphy, on staff at Utah State University, agreed, "There is no question that Carson's arguments were bold" (Murphy, 2019, 194). Her concern grew in late January 1947, when she and artist Kay Howe tramped the Mattamuskeet refuge on the Pamlico Sound in Hyde County, North Carolina. Among teeming pintails, goldeneyes, mallards, tundra swans, snow geese, crappie, catfish, and largemouth and striped bass, she observed two dwindling waterfowl—the whistling swan and Canada geese.

RETHINKING WORLD WAR II

In the 1949 essay "Lost Worlds: The Challenge of the Islands," Rachel asserted the disappearance of some 100 avian species on islands since 1749. With a bird lover's emotion, she charged human recklessness in burning and clear-cutting territory as well as introducing rats, rabbits, pastured herds, and other alien species, which exterminated indigenous rails on the Hawaiian islet of Laysan. World War II increased carnage from bombing, artillery, swamp drainage, and construction projects, such as sea grass, vines, bats, and lizards among 3,500 species on Guam and noddies, terns, petrels, shearwaters, and the short-tailed albatross at the landing field and refueling stop on Midway featured in novelist James A. Michener's *South Pacific*. Reduced in rainforests and other habitats, endangered monkeys, pangolin, corals, sponges, clams, urchins, sharks, dolphins, monk seals, and green sea turtles added to the list of human victims. In retrospect, the biologist railed, "These island species have been created once, and only once, in all the world, the products of the slow processes of the ages" (Carson, 1949, 1).

As mentioned in *The Edge of the Sea* in 1955, Rachel's experience in Boothbay Harbor, Maine, corroborated the decline of invertebrate hydroids at Ocean Point. In *Silent Spring* in September 1962, she regretted the contamination of water in wildlife refuges. Because havens provided nesting grounds from the redhead and ruddy duck, the preservation efforts imperiled waterfowl at Lower Klamath and Tule Lake, California, from contamination by DDD (dichlorodiphenyldichloroethane), DDE (dichlorodiphenyldichloroethylene), and toxaphene. Out of loyalty to nature's esthetics, she denounced biocidal sprays that killed the swan grebe, a picturesque waterfowl that bore its fuzzy offspring on its back. Implications of thinning eggshells for future generations of the California condor alarmed readers that more organisms would add to the list of extinctions. W. Joseph Campbell, a writer for the *Hartford Courant,* declared her warning irrefutable—"the stone table, the masterpiece from the mountain" (Campbell, 1987, A33).

A Cleaner Earth

In an essay for *Audubon* in October 1963, Rachel acknowledged the mere blip of time that her generation occupied on the planet. Of the human responsibility to preserve environments that nurture biota, she challenged the polluter for profligacy. In a rhetorical question, she demanded, "Who are we to say that those who come after us may never see some of today's rare and endangered species?" (Carson, 1963, 262). She followed with more open-ended questions about toxicity. She reminded readers that each threatened plant or animal contained a "scientific record" that may answer a human need (*ibid.*). In a 40-minute address to the Committee on Government Operations on June 4, 1963, she warned that side effects of ecosystem contaminants were cumulative and often irreversible.

After Rachel's death in April 1964, the 9,125-acre Maryland strand she willed to the public shielded the piping plover, New England cottontail, wood frog, and spring peeper. On December 27, 1973, the Endangered Species Act listed more rare varieties of amphibians, fish, reptiles, insects, birds, mammals, crustaceans, flowers, grasses, and trees that required shielding. Federal oases extended protection to colonies of sea lions and polar bears, the migratory paths of bluefin and bigeye tuna and fin whale, seals and dolphins, and nesting grounds of peregrine falcons and the hawksbill and green turtle. By 1982, Rachel's foresight enabled a resurgence of the bald eagle and brown pelican. Despite some rescues, in 2015, social scientist Renee Lertzman coined the term "environmental melancholia," a pervasive mourning for earth's degradation (Lertzman, 2015, title).

See also Amphibians; Birds; Fish; History; Mammals; World War II.

Sources

Barnet, Andrea. *Visionary Women: How Rachel Carson, Jane Jacobs, Jane Goodall, and Alice Waters Changed Our World.* New York: Ecco, 2018.

Campbell, W. Joseph. "Silent Spring: A Timeless Call for Ecological Concern." *Hartford Courant* (24 May 1987): A33.

Carson, Rachel. "Environmental Hazards: Control of Pesticides and Other Chemical Poisons." Statement before the Subcommittee on Reorganization and International Organizations of the Committee on Government Operations (4 June 1963): 206–219.

_____. "Guarding Our Wildlife Resources: A National Wildlife Refuge." #5. Washington, D.C.: U.S. Department of the Interior, 1948, 1–46.

_____. "Lost Worlds: The Challenge of the Islands." *Wood Thrush* 4:5 (May–June 1949): 179–187.

_____. "Rachel Carson Answers Her Critics." *Audubon* 65 (September/October 1963): 262–265, 313–315.

Carson, R.L. "The Northern Trawlers Move South." *Baltimore Sunday Sun* (3 January 1937): 6–7.

_____. "Shad Going the Way of the Buffalo." *Charleston News and Courier* (14 February 1937): 8C.

Lertzman, Renee. *Environmental Melancholia: Psychoanalytic Dimensions of Engagement*. New York: Routledge, 2015.

Murphy, Mollie K. "Rachel Carson's Rhetorical Strategies in the *Silent Spring* Debates." *Argumentation and Advocacy* 55:3 (2019): 194–210.

Tubbs, Christopher W. "California Condors and DDT." *Endocrine Disruptors* 4:1 (2016): e1173766.

Evolution

When Rachel compiled studies in ecology, she encompassed all time, from the deep past to eons ahead. She located models in the crab of a "protracted racial drama, the evolutionary coming-to-land of a sea creature" (Carson, 1955, 159). Like Alfred Lord Tennyson in his poem "Flower in a Crannied Wall," she found no disparity between God's genesis of life and the concept of evolution, for example, the enlargement of eyes and the development of feelers in abyssal fish. To accusations that *The Sea Around Us* was atheistic, she replied in a 1952 letter to geographer James Bennet, "Believing as I do in evolution, I merely believe that is the method by which God created, and is still creating, life on earth" (Matthiessen, 2007, 6). She added that a more detailed study of nature's unfolding increased spirituality and respect for the creator's process, for example, the transformation of the chimney swift's feet into hooks for clinging to flues and hollow trees and the gradual accommodation of the winkle to seashores, her topic in an October 1951 speech to the *New York Herald-Tribune* staff.

The author's working theory about natural processes began with curiosity into the ongoing planetary developments. Notes compiled in April 1952 at Saint Simons, Georgia, reflected on the origin of "the first dry land emerging out of the ancient and primitive ocean" (Carson, 1952, n.p.). The glimpse of topography elicited greater depictions of the creep of "the first living creatures step by step out of the sea into the perilous new world of earth" (*Ibid.*). Less erudition than visual imagery, the thought illustrated how effortlessly the author's mind pictured prehistory before the amenities of plants, shade trees, and cool fresh waters. To address the Theta Sigma Phi Matrix Table Dinner on April 21, 1954, she incorporated her views on life origins in "The Real World Around Us": "Every mystery solved brings us to the threshold of a greater one," an optimistic evaluation of biological research (Carson, 1954, 325).

Hands-On Research

In 1955 for the preface to *The Edge of the Sea,* Rachel emphasized the intuition of the beachcomber who "can sense the long rhythms of earth and sea that cultured its land forms and produced the rock and sand of which it is composed" (Carson, 1955, xiii). An open-ended metaphor, the cyclical changes and adaptations "[kept] alive the sense of continuing creation and of the relentless drive of life" (*ibid.,* 2). She chose as examples the sponges that survived 300 million years of development and periwinkles, which, as described in *The Rocky Coast,* are still evolving from sea to land animals. The narrative focused on the inexplicable evolution of the rock barnacle, a stationary sea arthropod that fixed itself to a platform, secreted material for new shells, and waited for the sea to import food, "one of the riddles of zoology" (Carson, 1971, 27).

The author's correspondence revealed a constant mulling of beachcombing observations and data for significant insight. Memories from Christmas 1952 on Marcos Island and Sanibel, Florida, invaded her thoughts with impressions of mud flats slowly expanded by mangrove roots. In a letter to the president of the American Association of University Women, she characterized perusals "drawn more and more to the basic problems of life itself: What were its origins? How has it evolved? What is its future?" (Carson, "Letter," 1956).

Human Contaminants

The concern for earth's future dominated the next six years, when Rachel completed and published *Silent Spring*, particularly the relationship between synthetic chemicals and genetic deterioration or mutation in humans. At a rare halt in research to speak at the Scripps College commencement in Claremont, California, on June 12, 1962, her speech "Of Man and the Stream of Time" molded standard ecological themes into an address on human attitudes toward controlling and redirecting the universe. On the expanse of creation, she noted "biological events that represent that all-important adjustment of living protoplasm to the conditions of the external world" (Carson, 1962). She summarized evolutionary time as "millions and hundreds of millions of years" until living organisms reached "an accommodation, a balance" (*ibid.*). She feared that man-made chemicals and tampering with the atom would give protoplasm no time to adjust.

Basing the conclusion on biochemical, molecular, and genetic principles, the author believed that evolutionary mechanics bore logical explanations of life tissue, which "has come down to us through some two billion years of evolution" (Carson, 2002, 216). The narrative pictured "long eons of evolution" during which "our genes not only make us what we are, but hold in their minute beings the future—be it one of promise or threat" (*ibid.*, 208). She recognized a mutually dependent network of life, which continued to evolve through the passage of hereditary traits to developing organisms. She admitted the possibility of synthesizing live molecules, but her version of Darwinism ignored the mechanical and interpreted the mystic force that formed current and subsequent generations. In reference to genetic deterioration, she added, "To study it in detail is to increase—and certainly never to diminish—one's reverence and awe for the Creator and the process" (Quaratiello, 2010, xiii). The statement is as close as she came to acknowledging religious convictions.

In San Francisco on October 18, 1963, Rachel opened a learned consortium for Kaiser-Permanente on the subject of *Man Against Himself* with the speech "The Pollution of Our Environment." Rather than move directly into examples of contamination, she speculated on the origin of life in the solar system. A brief overview accounted for ultraviolet rays that energized the chemical synthesis of molecules, viruses, and organisms imbued with chlorophyll, the green element that absorbs light to make plant food. By following her train of thought from the planet's genesis, she deduced that earthly life is always changing. Darwin's theories, which earned the mockery of his peers in the mid–1800s, raised the hottest and most unreasonable denial for his "concept of man's origin from pre-existing forms" (Carson, "Pollution," 1963). She mused on the source of Victorian skittishness about the placement of humankind on the chain of being.

See also Darwin, Charles; Fossils.

Sources

Blum, Hester. "Bitter with the Salt of Continents: Rachel Carson and Oceanic Returns." *Women's Studies Quarterly* 45:1/2 (Spring/Summer 2017): 287–291.
Carson, Rachel. *The Edge of the Sea.* Boston: Houghton Mifflin, 1955.
_____. "Letter to Mrs. Boyette" (12 June 1956).
_____. "Of Man and the Stream of Time." *Scripps College Bulletin,* Claremont, CA (12 June 1962): 5–10.
_____. "The Pollution of Our Environment," address to the Kaiser-Permanente Symposium *Man Against Himself,* San Francisco (18 October 1963).
_____. "Rachel Carson Answers Her Critics." *Audubon* 65 (September/October 1963): 262–265, 313–315.
_____. "The Real World Around Us," address to the Theta Sigma Phi Matrix Table Dinner, *House of Life* (21 April 1954): 324–326.
_____. *The Rocky Coast.* New York: McCall, 1971.
_____. "Saint Simon Island, Georgia," unpublished 1952.
_____. *Silent Spring.* Boston: Houghton Mifflin, 40th Anniversary Edition, 2002.
_____. "Sky Dwellers." *Coronet* (November 1945).
_____. speech, *New York Herald Tribune Book Review,* Astor Hotel (1 October 1951).
Matthiessen, Peter, ed. *Courage for the Earth: Writers, Scientists, and Activists Celebrate the Life and Writing of Rachel Carson.* New York: Mariner, 2007.
McCrum, Robert. "The 100 Best Nonfiction Books: No. 20—*Silent Spring* by Rachel Carson (1962)." *The Guardian* (13 June 2016).
Quaratiello, Arlene Rodda. *Rachel Carson: A Biography.* Amherst, NY: Prometheus, 2010.

"A Fable for Tomorrow"

A masterful use of diction and tone, Rachel's pastoral fable looked beyond a harmonious Eden to a coming catastrophe for "Green Meadows," a town name she later dropped. The timeless community in America's "heart" stirred a national consciousness by its stewardship and prosperity that produced fruit and grain, the symbolic horn of plenty symbolized by poet Katharine Lee Bates's "America the Beautiful" (Carson, 2002, 1). An idyllic illustration of dogwood by zoologist Lois MacIntyre Darling and her husband, nature photographer Louis Darling, implied a prolific environment. Ironically, the corruption of the fictional pastoral haven derived, not from an invading enemy, but from a homemade disaster evoking the horrors of world war.

To rid *Silent Spring* of the sterility of a monograph, Rachel stylized a foretaste of the outdoors under assault by chemical taint, a radical form that Richard White, an historian at Stanford University, labeled "the urtext of modern American environmentalism" (White, 2017, 239). In romantic style, she dramatized assailants destroying the harbingers of spring, the annual renaissance of beauty and hope. Christine Lena Oravec, an environmental analyst from Salt Lake City, Utah, described the fable's organic construction as "layer by layer, using elements of other discursive genres and modes"—investigative journalism, dystopia, cautionary tale, polemic, jeremiad, prophecy, and scientific exposé (Oravec, 2000, 46).

A Bucolic Setting

To summon appreciation for the edenic terrain, Rachel's parable listed spring-time blooms and fall leaves alongside ferns and wildflowers, a fairy tale environment suggesting an enchanted milieu. A subtle connection between pioneers and purity pictured settlers erecting homesteads and barns and digging wells, a direct tie with core New World values. In the evaluation of literary critic Mollie K. Murphy of Utah State University, Rachel "granted the public autonomy to engage and form scientific arguments," a rhetorical strategy that mustered legions of amateur conservationists to the cause (Murphy, 2019, 194). In rebuttal, critics charged the author with romanticizing New World myth for the sake of demonizing synthetic chemicals.

The author's speculation transitioned from arcadian idyll to an apocalyptic tutorial by introducing livestock disease and human illness insidious enough to kill herds, adults, and children suddenly, inexplicably. She reflected on her urgent title with a paragraph on avian afflictions that silenced birds, ostensibly forever. Beyond the wild, farmers suffered losses of piglets and chicks, a reference to vulnerable young that recurred with young swan grebes in Chapter Four, "Surface Waters and Underground Seas." Without bees, apple trees yielded no fruit. As living organisms died, they left roadways brown and bare and streams devoid of fish. The progression of lifelessness, like the atmosphere of Ray Bradbury's story "There Will Come Soft Rains," pointed to "a white granular powder" spread by humankind over the food chain (*ibid.*, 3). To strip the narrative of futurism, the author declared that each disaster had "actually happened somewhere," a vague setting that hovered over all of North America and the globe (*ibid.*).

Libel and Praise

Critical opinion of Rachel's fable tended to extreme adjectives, from startling to sentimental. On December 30, 1962, the *St. Louis Post-Dispatch* began serializing *Silent Spring* with the fable. *Time* magazine called the work inflated; *Progressive Farmer* charged that her opening vignette included distortions and errors. At the Michigan State University Pesticide Research Center, toxicologist Fumio Matsumora blamed the author for spreading doomsday gloom. For the Jackson, Mississippi, *Clarion-Ledger,* book critic Jean Culbertson acknowledged Rachel's authenticity as a science writer, but declared her hysterical and "guilty of overstatement for the sake of emphasis (if not the best-seller lists)" (Culbertson, 1962).

The agrarian chemical industry, led by Monsanto, posed its own fable, "The Desolate Year," issued in *Monsanto* magazine in October 1962. The anonymous text depicted pigs dead from cholera, corn felled by worms, oats overrun by thistles, and children dying from diphtheria, pertussis, and scarlet fever. In 2012, reader Mark Kalinowski of Clifton, New Jersey, derogated Rachel's fable as "a wild-eyed apocalyptic scenario" and called her a propagandist and "typical leftist scaremonger" (Kalinowski, 2012, A15). Parallel to years of harsh critiques, verbal and in print, newspapers continued to venerate the famed fable at the decade mark of its publication and at incremental improvements to governmental controls of deadly chemicals. On October 25, 2019, Scott Brinton, editor of the (Baldwin, Long Island) *Herald,* revived concerns that Rachel was right about the decline of birds from contaminants. More personal sources blamed planetary threats on hubris, greed, and capitalism.

Sources

Carson, Rachel. *Silent Spring*. Boston: Houghton Mifflin, 40th Anniversary Edition, 2002.
Culbertson, Jean. "Miss Carson's 'Silent Spring': Are Pesticides Peoplecides?" (Jackson, MS) *Clarion Ledger* (14 October 1962): 7B.
Kalinowski, Mark. "Learn the Real Legacy." (Clifton, NJ) *Clifton Journal* (13 April 2012): A15.
Murphy, Mollie K. "Rachel Carson's Rhetorical Strategies in the *Silent Spring* Debates." *Argumentation and Advocacy* 55:3 (2019): 194–210.
Oravec, Christine. "An Inventional Archaeology of 'A Fable for Tomorrow.'" *And No Birds Sing*. Carbondale: Southern Illinois University, 2000.
Sideris, Lisa H. "Fact and Fiction, Fear and Wonder: The Legacy of Rachel Carson." *Soundings* 91:3/4 (Fall-Winter 2009): 335–369.
White, Richard. "Play It Again Sam: Decline and Finishing in Environmental Narratives." *Routledge Companion to the Environmental Humanities*. New York: Routledge, 2017, 239–246.

Fish

Rachel's years of work for the U.S. Fisheries Service expanded a biologist's perceptions of the beauty of waterways and shores and the fragility of spawning grounds and aquatic habitats. She saluted fisheries that released fingerlings, elvers, and young terrapins. On March 1, 1936, she earned $20 from the *Baltimore Sun* for the 4,000-word essay "It'll Be Shad Time Soon," a sedate call for protection of fish habitats in the Chesapeake Bay for the sake of biodiversity and commercial fishing. The article revealed Bureau of Fisheries monitoring of the degree to which sewage destroyed mid–Atlantic spawning grounds for shad. Of the growth of tender fauna, she acknowledged that "the ocean cradles their young in its surface waters," which she dubbed "ocean pastures" (Carson, 1937, 3). On viewing a West Indian basket fish, she wondered at its perishable beauty. To her, the tidal sweep, marsh fog, and paths of shad and eels revealed "things that are as nearly eternal as any earthly life can be," one of her oft-quoted philosophical meditations from *Under the Sea Wind* in 1941 (Carson, 1941, xiii).

The author maintained a pragmatic attitude toward fish as wonders of nature and as marketable produce. In "Numbering the Fish of the Sea," a May 24, 1936, freelance article for the *Baltimore Sun,* she analyzed the up-and-down profits of seining for mackerel, an erratic sea rover. The next year on January 3, the essay "The Northern Trawlers Move South" reported on a coastal change caused by a hurricane and the resulting deep-sea fishing: "The trawlers had at last invaded the actual sanctuary to which the fish repair when they leave the coast in the fall" (Carson, 1937, 6). She pondered why people ate shad in hotels and restaurants, but not at home and surmised that bones prohibited families from choosing shad for kitchen preparation.

A support of professional fishing caused the biologist to consider the rise and fall of species populations. In February 1937, she submitted "Shad Going Way of the Buffalo" to the Charleston, South Carolina, *News and Courier,* a report on the depletion of "important food fish which occupies a unique place on the nation's bill of fare" (Carson, 1937, 8C). She regretted that the Potomac River delicacy, which once graced the plates of President George Washington and first U.S. Chief Justice John Marshall, neared "commercial extinction" from "a century of exploitation" that reached 80 percent of shad runs (*ibid.*). To inform readers of the shad reproductive span, she cited the female production of as many as 100,000 eggs each.

THE CRITICAL ERA

In August 1938, the article "Giants of the Tide Rip Off Nova Scotia Again" moved sure-footedly into nature issues by examining oil pollution blighting waterfowl on the Chesapeake Bay and surveying the illicit sale of black bass, which she claimed to be the most prized of freshwater game fish. An essay on sport angling off Georges Bank, Nova Scotia, admired the pitting of "rod and reel against seven or eight hundred pounds of desperately fighting" bluefin tuna on its hunt for herring and mackerel (Carson, 1938, 2). The aggressive giants, famished by a long migration over the Gulf Stream to Iberia and the Azores, routed herring from the shoals and "[dispelled] illusions of 'gentle nature'" (*ibid.*). Ever on the side of the Maryland fishing industry, she concluded the survey of Atlantic Coast tournament fishing with the possibilities of tuna canneries in eastern North America.

The author turned to reviewer for the *Progressive Fish-Culturist* in September 1938 with an analysis of "Experimental Modification of Sexual Cycle in Trout by Control of Light," "Progress of Trout Feeding Experiments," and "Fish Conservation Advanced in 1937." Her readings in other academic studies examined "Production of Nutritional Cataract in Trout" in October. The November review of "Lake Management Reports, Horseshoe Lake Near Cairo, Illinois" took authors George W. Bennett and Davis H. Thompson to task for a failure to document population shifts in bass and black and white crappie. She leaped ahead of their "meager information" and flimsy conclusions with a personal surmise that the Illinois lake was "badly overstocked" (Carson, 1938, 35). Perhaps the most crucial to her later interests in fish survival occurred in December, when she reviewed publications on fish predation, trout tagging, and selenium toxicity, an acute poisoning causing fatigue, diarrhea, joint pain, nausea, and hair loss.

Rachel reprised the subject of polluted streams in "New Trout Crop for Anglers" in an April 1939 issue of the *Baltimore Sun,* which anticipated the subject of wildlife contamination in *Silent Spring.* A pair of weighty reviews of "Spawning Induced Prematurely in Trout with the Aid of Pituitary Glands of Carp" and "The Use of Hormones for the Conservation of Muskellunge, *Esox Masquinongy Immaculatus Garrard*" in the May 1940 issue of *Progressive Fish-Culturist* indicated the author's value to the academic world as an expert on pisciculture. She saluted the participants for their correction of a fish reproduction cycle halted by the dam erected in western Wisconsin on the Chippewa River. In editor Elmer Higgins' December 1941 review of *Under the Sea Wind* for the same journal, he identified in her research-based writing with the "highest merit from both a literary and technical standpoint" (Higgins, 1941, 32).

Under her full name, Rachel summarized the *Gymnodinium brevis* red tide of November 1947–January 1948 that killed herring, crabs, and shrimp and fouled waters and shores in western Florida from Naples to Boca Grande. Her article, "The

Great Red Tide Mystery," for *Field and Stream* recounted seafood loss to algal blooms for 15 miles off Fort Myers. She reported dead and malodorous small fish as well as tarpon, jewfish, black drum, grouper, mackerel, sea turtles, porpoises, and manatees, an imperiled megafauna. Again in July 1948, the lethal red tide blooms affected sport and market fishing, schools, hotels, and tourism as far away as Venice, Florida, and threatened lucrative sponge and clam beds off Tarpon Springs until a September 21 hurricane ended the scourge. A scholarly consortium debated how to suppress the cause, an overabundance of phosphorus and nitrogen in the water from the outflow of dairy farm manure and fertilizer.

In July 1949 around the Georges Banks fishing grounds 200 miles off Boston and southwest of Nova Scotia, the author shared with seasoned fishermen the excitement of net fishing from the U.S. Fish and Wildlife trawler S.S. *Albatross III.* When the clanking winch pulled a cone-shaped net up 600 feet, she craned to see bony anglerfish, goosefish, and cod among starfish, crabs, sponges, and approaching sharks. The marine biologist's survey of fish runs continued in 1951 in *The Sea Around Us* with the return of chinooks to the Columbia River, alewives to New England, salmon to the Kennebec and Penobscot rivers, and shad to the Chesapeake Sound and Connecticut and Hudson rivers. The long list of migratory fish pictured cod off Norway's Lofoten Islands and capelin in the Barents Sea. The final chapter cited the work of Swedish hydrographer and oceanographer Sven Otto Pettersson (1848–1941) in charting cyclical sea changes that influenced the formation of pack ice, a threat to Scandinavian fishing for herring and cod.

THE COMMANDING VOICE

In "Nature Fights Back," an essay in *Silent Spring,* Rachel reflected on "nature's control at work" in the dieback of millions of cod ova and the survival of just enough "to replace the parent fish" (Carson, 2002, 247, 248). The author disparaged the thoughtless spraying of sagebrush in the Bridger National Forest, where poisons killed the willows sheltering trout streams. She made direct ties between poisoned bees and dead fish from arsenic fumes in Saxony and between the contaminated caddis fly and the depleted salmon run in the Atlantic Ocean through threads of fresh water from the Miramichi River, New Brunswick. Alison Steinbach, a journalist for the *Arizona Republic,* linked the author's voice to sympathy for human traits in fish: She "grants the salmon a human-like ancestral yearning for home," the tributary of their birth for millennia (Steinbach, 2016).

In the post–*Silent Spring* months, the biologist addressed the Women's National Press Club in Washington, D.C., on December 5, 1962, on the continued poisoning of nature with toxins that accumulated in living tissue. In the eight instances she cited of fish tested from waters in Framingham, Massachusetts, all contained "ten times the legal tolerance" of DDT (dichlorodiphenyltrichloroethane) (Carson, "Address," 1962). She added that the same degree of contamination affected drinking water, a fact substantiated by President John F. Kennedy's Science Advisory Committee in mid–May 1963. Because of the aerial drift of poison, even fish organs taken far from shore revealed toxins sprayed on land, especially livers, the body's filters. Her report regretted the demise of shrimp, crabs, crayfish, oysters, and most of a 12-month production of coho salmon in British Columbia and high concentrations of DDT from fish in city waterways.

Rachel extended a concern for fish on June 4, 1963, in her testimony "Environmental Hazards: Control of Pesticides and Other Chemical Poisons" to the congressional Committee on Government Operations. She cited data from the Massachusetts Division of Fisheries and Game on DDT toxins in fish and in public water sources in Asabet, Concord, Framingham, and Sudbury at 14 times the legal tolerance of DDT for human consumption. Her commentary on food chains and the rising concentration of toxaphene at Big Bear Lake in San Bernardino County and Clear Lake, California, from plankton to trout revealed the death of trout hatchlings. She accounted for the phenomenon with data from two U.S. Fish and Wildlife biologists and anticipated the "continuous re-cycling and concentration of the more stable pesticidal compounds until they pose a real threat to man's own welfare" (Carson, "Environmental," 1963).

See also Shellfish.

Sources

Carson, Rachel. "Address," Women's National Press Club (5 December 1962), Washington, D.C.
_____. "Environmental Hazards: Control of Pesticides and Other Chemical Poisons." Statement before the Subcommittee on Reorganization and International Organizations of the Committee on Government Operations (4 June 1963): 206–219.
_____. "She Started It All—Here's Her Reaction." *New York Herald Tribune* (19 May 1963).
_____. *Silent Spring*. Boston: Houghton Mifflin, 40th Anniversary Edition, 2002.
_____. *The Sea Around Us*. New York: Oxford University Press, 1951.
_____. "Undersea." *Atlantic Monthly* 160 (September 1937): 322–325.
_____. *Under the Sea Wind: A Naturalist's Picture of Ocean Life*. New York: Simon & Schuster, 1941.
Carson, R.L., "A New Trout Crop for Anglers." *Baltimore Sun* (2 April 1939): 3.
_____. "Baltimore New Mecca for Nation's Sportsmen and Conservationists." *Baltimore Sunday Sun Magazine* (13 February 1938): 1.
_____. "Giants of the Tide Rip Off Nova Scotia Again." *Baltimore Sunday Sun* (3 August 1938): 2.
_____. "Numbering the Fish of the Sea." *Baltimore Sunday Sun* (24 May 1936): 5, 7.
_____. "Review: Lake Management Reports, Horseshoe Lake Near Cairo, Illinois." *Progressive Fish-Culturist* 5:42 (November 1938): 33–35.
_____. "Review: Spawning Induced Prematurely in Trout with the Aid of Pituitary Glands of Carp." *Progressive Fish-Culturist* 7:50 (May 1940): 48–49.
_____. "Review: The Use of Hormones for the Conservation of Muskellunge, *Esox Masquinongy Immaculatus Garrard*." *Progressive Fish-Culturist* 7:50 (May 1940): 48–49.
_____. "Shad Catches Declining as 1939 Season Opens." *Baltimore Sunday Sun* (26 March 1939): 3.
_____. "Shad Going the Way of the Buffalo." *Charleston News and Courier* (14 February 1937): 8C.
_____. "The Northern Trawlers Move South." *Baltimore Sunday Sun* (3 January 1937): 6.
Fellows, Valerie, and Joshua Winchell. "Returning to the Water." *Fish & Wildlife News* (Spring 2007): 26–28.
Higgins, Elmer. "Review: *Under the Sea Wind*." *Progressive Fish Culturist* 7: 56 (December 1941): 33–34.
Steinbach, Alison. "Metaphor and Visions of Home in Environmental Writing." https://green.harvard.edu/news/metaphor-and-visions-home-environmental-writing (21 June 2016).

Folklore

A former English composition major respectful of spoken, sung, and written sea knowledge, Rachel laced her compositions with superstitions and customs dating to the foundations of language. In 1941 in *Under the Sea Wind* with lore as old as seafaring careers, fishermen followed the seasonal elements—wind, tide, moon cycle—"as the fishermen had told it from one generation to the next" (Carson, 1941, 54). Crucial to their scanning of sky and sea, the osprey Pandion bore the name of a resolute monarch of southern India after the late 300s BCE, whose sons avenged their dynasty. The addition of Canutus—the red knot (*Calidris canutus*) of Canada, Europe, and Russia—to anthropomorphized animals incorporated a shorebird named for early 11th century Norse king Canute the Great, a wise Dane who demonstrated human weakness to his courtiers by pretending to command the tides.

The Sea Around Us exhibited the author's interest in the lifestyle of organisms into prehistory. According to analyst Judith Madera, an English professor at Wake Forest University, the encryption of oceanography "projected a lifeworld that predated human experience" (Madera, 2017, 292). Rachel's 1951 narration debunked falsehoods about the boundless oceans, particularly waters surrounding a flat terrestrial disk and hyperbole about monsters, engulfing seaweed, and the height of monster waves. Her overview of ninth century BCE Homeric lore included bottomless abysses and impenetrable fogs separating humankind from the gods and the souls of the departed. Balancing fancy with truth, she reported the Greek historian Herodotus, who recorded the Phoenician circumnavigation of Africa in the late seventh century BCE.

PREHISTORIC TALES

From girlhood, Rachel sifted lore for bits of truth. She incorporated the myth that oil calmed surf and that deep water resisted the sinking of ships, dead animals, and drowned people. Her delineation of oceanic mountain chains queried "shadowy and insubstantial" belief in the lost continents of Lemuria in the Indian Ocean, St. Brendan's Island in the North Atlantic, and Atlantis in the Mediterranean, which she credited to "racial memory," a perception present at birth (Carson, 1951, 74). Of wave recorders off coastal Cornwall and California, she compared their function to the surf observations of Pacific islanders, who developed lore identifying the swells that predicted typhoons. Similarly spooked by long surges, Irish coast watchers named the rising surf "death waves" (*ibid.,* 108).

From research in the North Atlantic Ocean, the author outlined extensive knowledge of the Sargasso Sea, its source, and the biota that flourished in its 700 × 2,000 mile ocean-within-an-ocean. In reference to folk tellings about vessels and aircraft trapped in sargassum weed (*Sargassum muticum*), Rachel neatly dismissed fantasies. Her statement that such a living snare "never existed except in the imaginations of sailors" preceded a description of "the ghosts of things that never were" (Carson, 1951, 40). In a concluding pastiche of voyage literature, she acknowledged what Kimberley Peters, a geographer at the University of Liverpool, termed "attempts … of humans to measure, record, and make sense of these mobile liquid, three-dimensional spaces" (Peters, 2017, 278).

MEMORABLE BIOTA

In 1955, Rachel continued incorporating ocean legend and lore in *The Edge of the Sea* by championing saltwater plant curatives that also served humankind and herd animals as food. A citation from Scots nature writer William Thomas Fernie's *Herbal Simples Approved for Modern Uses of Cure* celebrated "the Dulse of Guerdie" as a nutritional panacea similar to samphire and sea holly for its bromine, iodine, and sulphates (Carson, 1955, 63). Irish and Icelandic herbalists recommended the marine frond (*Iridea edulis* or *Rhodymenia palmata*) as a preventer of goiter and a cure for scrofula, a tubercular condition of the neck glands.

At Ohio Key two-thirds of the way down Florida's island chain, the author found a sea hare (*Dolabella auricularia*), a sea mollusk integral to sorcery and superstition. The narrative, adjacent to artist Bob Hines's sketch of the Gorgonians—sea whip, basket starfish, and sea fan—reviewed the snaky hair and fearful gaze of the Gorgon sisters Euryale, Medusa, and Stheno from Greek mythology, whose gaze turned men to stone. The accusation of poisoning against satirist Apuleius, author of the second-century CE Roman satire *The Golden Ass,* derived from his curiosity about the famed sea hare or marine rabbit, actually a sea slug. In 1684, Italian parasitologist and toxicologist Francesco Redi of Arezzo, a physician for the Florentine Medici household, placed the study of the sea hare on a more scientific basis.

In an overview of awe and delight in *The Sense of Wonder*, the author reflected on Italian poet Giambattista Basile's 14th century fairy tale *Sleeping Beauty* and the gifts that the infant Aurora received at birth from the lilac fairy. For Rachel's great nephew Roger Allen Christie, she wished an endless supply of fascination with the outdoors and enchantment with plants and animals. In Chapter Four of *Silent Spring*, "Surface Waters and Underground Seas," a fearful myth, the Greek story of the sorceress Medea, Jason's jealous wife, illustrated the permeation of an organism with toxins, a method of producing systemic insecticides. The author compared taints all along the food chain to the anonymous English nursery rhyme "This Is the House that Jack Built," a cumulative, progressive, or chain tale published in 1755 and based on the interrelation of farmers and their property. She concluded with a motif from Lewis Carroll's *Alice in Wonderland* by outlining the poisoning of reservoirs to remove unwanted fish. Like the satiric scenes in the children's classic, the results counter each other—public moneys underwriting toxins sprayed on water to kill fish and subsequent outlays to cleanse the water of biocides.

See also Sea.

Sources

Carson, Rachel. *The Edge of the Sea*. Boston: Houghton Mifflin, 1955.
_____. *The Sea Around Us*. New York: Oxford University Press, 1951.
_____. *The Sense of Wonder*. New York: Harper & Row, 1965.
_____. *Silent Spring*. Boston: Houghton Mifflin, 40th Anniversary Edition, 2002.
_____. *Under the Sea Wind: A Naturalist's Picture of Ocean Life*. New York: Simon & Schuster, 1941.
Madera, Judith. "The Birth of an Island: Rachel Carson's 00." *Women's Studies Quarterly* 45:1/2 (Spring/Summer 2017): 292–298.
Peters, Kimberley. "Touching the Oceans." *Women's Studies Quarterly* 45:1/2 (Spring/Summer 2017): 278–281.

Food Supply

Rachel's reportage of human well being featured sources of fresh edibles. Her works explored foods as delicate as oysters and eels and the fingerlings in tide pools, as choice as lobsters and octopus in trawler nets, as attainable as ducks and geese, as threatened as contaminated cranberries, and as rare as the Chinese swift nest, a hammock of saliva valued for soup. In March 1936, she contributed "It'll Be Shad Time Soon," an article to the *Baltimore Sun* on the cooking of planked shad under a dressing of bacon and roe. She commiserated with shad aficionados for the variance of the annual catch, which began its decline in 1886 before losing 80 percent in the market. Already attuned to the cost of civilization, she blamed destructive net-fishing, city and industrial pollutants, and the change in streams by damming and navigation. Her expansive view of life's network placed the human diet with the greater realm of all organisms.

Animals, too, flourished or declined by the availability of habitats and sustenance. In the November 1938 freelance article "Whalers Ready for New Season," she detailed the diatoms that fed parchment worms, the nitrates and phosphates that supported game fish, the crustaceans that sustained blue whales, the squid that nourished bottle-nose and sperm whales, and the "salmon-like fish" off Finland, Denmark, and Norway that fin whales pursued (Carson, 1938, 2). The report enlarged on whale calving off Africa, Australia, and South America, where mother whales suckled their newborns in the mammary style of herd mammals. Her article "New Trout Crop for Anglers" turned to trout fishing in April 1939 with an essay on the importance to a healthy stock of game fish of "one to two grams of food per square foot of bottom" from fly larvae, shrimp, sowbugs, and worms (Carson, 1939, 3). She summarized the balance of minerals and vitamins in hatchery meals to grow adult fish after their fry ceased living on stored yolks. In the author's fifth brochure of the *Conservation in Action* series, "Guarding Our Wildlife Resources: A National Wildlife Refuge," she enumerated tasks of the U.S. Fish and Wildlife Service. Her report showed photos of agents testing boat and factory sanitation, performing seafood cookery, and demonstrating "filleting, freezing, packaging, canning, or smoking fish" (Carson, 1948, 31). She credited agents with inspecting fisheries for industrial pollutants, erosion silt, dams, and the channeling of water for irrigation. Photo essays illustrated the work of fish ladders and hatcheries.

Oceanic Food

In *The Sea Around Us* in 1951, the author compared tropical and polar waters as feeding grounds for saltwater organisms. Summarized by Stephanie Kaza, an ecologist at the University of Vermont, the immense stirring of fish and birds followed "the explosions of food with the change of seasons" (Kaza, 2010, 308). Rachel noted that deeper swimming prey in the tropics offered fewer edibles for terns, gulls, and other surface feeders. In contrast, arctic and Antarctic seas fostered flocks of "shearwaters, fulmars, auks, whalebirds, albatrosses" (Carson, 1951, 36). Fur seals retained in their gullets the remains of types of deep-water fish unidentified by ichthyologists. The proliferation of mackerel, herring, whales, and seals in the Barents Sea resulted from edible biota swimming at the surface. In another teeming feeding zone in the Humboldt Current west of South America and the Benguela Current off western Africa, mineral-rich waters "[sustained] the great food chains" (*ibid.*).

In *The Edge of the Sea,* the third volume of Rachel's sea trilogy stressed the interwoven web of life that scientists call ecology. Her examination of minute sea creatures accompanied line drawings and photos that illustrated "the cycle of life—the intricate dependence of one species upon another" (Carson, 1955, 151). The reprise of deep time pictured larvae seeking food and either thriving or starving, depending on the sea's plentiful plankton and the regeneration of eroded teeth. She commiserated with herds of vegetarian snails scouting the slippery green plant cells on granite rocks. The narrative depicted their job as tireless grazers—"scraping, scraping, scraping to find food before the surf returns" (*ibid.,* 41). At the same time, carnivorous gulls thrived on evolutionary success by pacing granite ledges and, as experience taught them, probing seaweed for meals of sea urchins and crabs.

UNBALANCED NATURE

Silent Spring, Rachel's classic exposé of chemical poisons, summarized serious diebacks in lost species and their predators, a common factor in aerial spraying and drift. For examples, she cited the die-off of rabbits in Florida's salt marshes, the deaths of insects on the Miramichi River that depleted New Brunswick salmon, and the eradication of willows in the Bridger National Forest, leaving Wyoming's beaver and moose to starve. Of the extermination of sagebrush, she cited loss of habitats for the sage grouse, mule deer, and the American pronghorn antelope (*Antilocapra americana*), which provided meals for the Lewis and Clark expedition of 1804–1806. Chapter Nine, "Rivers of Death," emphasized the disappearance of aquatic insects that fed trout and salmon in New Brunswick, Yellowstone National Park, and Montana. Of a spraying for mosquitoes in Tampa Bay, Florida, on October 12, 1955, Rachel regretted the extermination of the fiddler crab, a food source for raccoons, clapper rails, and sea- and shorebirds.

Rachel achieved significant support in 1962 during the presidential campaigning of John F. Kennedy, who called for less conflict among ecologists, medical researchers, and food suppliers and more oversight of radioactive waste disposal. In a speech to the Garden Club of America on January 8, 1963, she took a more aggressive tone than usual in warning of careless permeation of seeds with the fungicide hexachlorobenzene, which caused birth defects in 5,000 Turkish children. The U.S. Food and Drug Administration feared a similar mishandling of toxic seed when leftover grains—alfalfa, barley, corn, oats, rye, sorghum, and wheat—contaminated human food and herd feeds, injuring livestock. The federal agency proposed coating grain with contrasting colors to make contaminated supplies identifiable. In the report "Use of Pesticides" issued on March 15, 1963, by 17 men and Rachel serving President John Kennedy's Science Advisory Committee, another source of poisons in starchy foods came from potatoes coated with aldrin residue, a cause of behavioral oddities, seizures, sterility, and cancer.

See also World War II.

Sources

Carson, Rachel. *The Edge of the Sea.* Boston: Houghton Mifflin, 1955.

_____. "Guarding Our Wildlife Resources: A National Wildlife Refuge." #5. Washington, D.C.: U.S. Department of the Interior, 1948, 1–46.
_____. "It'll Be Shad Time Soon." *Baltimore Sun* (1 March 1936): 6–7.
_____. "A New Chapter in *Silent Spring*." Address to the Garden Club of America, New York City (8 January 1963).
_____. *The Sea Around Us*. New York: Oxford University Press, 1951.
_____. "She Started It All—Here's Her Reaction." *New York Herald Tribune* (19 May 1963).
Carson, R.L. "A New Trout Crop for Anglers." *Baltimore Sun* (2 April 1939): 3.
_____. "Whalers Ready for New Season." *Baltimore Sunday Sun* (20 November 1938): 2.
Kaza, Stephanie. "Rachel Carson's Sense of Time: Experiencing Maine." *ISLE* 17:2 (Spring 2010): 291–315.
Pimentel, David. "Silent Spring, the 50th Anniversary of Rachel Carson's Book." *BMC Ecology* 12:20 (2012).

Forests

Rachel took a personal interest in the health of Maine forests, whether landward bands of juniper with bayberry on Indiantown Island "where the wind rustled … and at sunset the hermit thrush sang its eerie song" or offshore in "dusky, swaying plants … like the leaves of palm trees" (Carson, 1946, 1; 1955, 64). In "The Birth of an Island," an essay in *The Sea Around Us* in 1955, she regretted the introduction of goats to St. Helene, which "destroyed a magnificent forest of gumwood, ebony, and brazilwood" east of Rio de Janeiro, Brazil (Carson, 1951, 95). Without natural enemies, the herds expanded over seedlings and devoured saplings except on isolated crags and ridges. A similar casualty to goat foraging on Trinidad depleted trees, fostering erosion of "soft volcanic soils" (*ibid.*).

The author had much to say about the conservation of American woods. Laysan, a Hawaiian islet, lost fan leaf palms, sandalwood, and indigenous rails to an influx of rabbits and rats fleeing landing craft during World War II. On Lanai in 1923, pineapple farmers imported ruminant herds, which overgrazed meadows and island forests. On the Atlantic shore, deforestation and hunting exterminated the passenger pigeon, once a valuable source of meat. The pigeon contributed to the propagation of the white oak by devouring acorns of red oaks.

Rachel's reverence for trees and arboreal animals reached new levels in June 1950, when she and colleague Shirley A. Briggs traveled by swamp buggy off the Tamiami Trail into the Florida Everglades Refuge. Under the shifting gray-green of cloud cover, she identified cypress (*Taxodium ascendens*) and palmetto (*Sabal palmetto*) hammocks, strolled the uplands amid a sea of grass, and collected colorful arboreal snails. In 1955, *The Edge of the Sea* treasured an evergreen grove "that has its own peculiar enchantment" from lichens and moss and "the faint sighing of evergreen needles in the moving air" (Carson, 1955, 41). On her Maine property, she and nephew Roger Allen Christie relished roaming amid bayberry and juniper "in a wooded knoll … fragrant with spruce and balsam," an olfactory cloud that enhanced sense impressions (Carson, 1965, 22). From a naturalist's perspective, the author absorbed peace in the wild: "In such places my spirit lifted to the sight of the drifts of white clover or the clouds of purple vetch with here and there the flaming up of a wood lily" (Carson, 2002, 71).

A Personal View

The author feared that the clearing of land, draining of bogs, and pouring of concrete on urban parking lots and driveways gobbled up ages-old habitats for living creatures. In a letter to her friend Dorothy Freeman, she accused land developers of the senseless clear-cutting of forests, a profitable logging style that depletes habitats and topsoil. She hoped to save the dark, serene grove near her Southport, Maine, cottage, which she called the "Lost Woods." In an essay for *Audubon* in October 1963, she applauded Canadian foresters for researching the symbiosis of alder shrub with black spruce, which thrived from the alder's nitrogen-fixing that bolstered North America's forest soil.

In *Silent Spring,* the essay "Nature Fights Back" narrated threats to the western national forests in 1956, when the U.S. Forest Service combated spruce budworms with DDT (dichlorodiphenyltrichloroethane). A letter to the editor of the *Surrey Leader* in British Columbia stated the economic disaster in human terms: "The ultimate destruction of B.C.'s number one forest products industry, the loss of thousands of jobs, and the ruination of a billion-dollar tourist industry" (Meyers, 1977, B5). The extermination of a natural predator encouraged an outbreak of spider mites, which pierced and sucked greenery, causing foliage drop in Montana, Idaho, Colorado, and New Mexico. In the final chapter, she found hope for non-poisonous insecticides in the use of *Bacillus Thuringiensis* against budworms and gypsy moths that invaded hardwoods and evergreens in Canada, Vermont, and California. The use of natural biocides preserved "that wonderful and intricate system of checks and balances" found in forest environments (Carson, 2002, 293).

In her last six months of life, the author insisted on a wheelchair tour of Muir Woods, a 554-acre national monument northwest of San Francisco. Reviewing sightseeing on October 20, 1963, she reported to friend Dorothy Freeman six days later a desire to walk alone in the center of the redwoods (*Sequoia*), the phenomenal trees deep in a canyon beyond the Golden Gate Bridge. She regretted being confined to a wheelchair guided by a park ranger: "The thing that would have made my enjoyment complete I couldn't have" (Carson, letter, 1963).

Checks and Balances

While rethinking the state of Muir Woods, Rachel reflected on the absence of lightning strikes against trees since the 1810s and the reproduction of redwoods from young sprouts rather than seedlings. To illustrate the proliferation of California or bay laurel (*Umbellularia californica*) from old growth, she drew a horizontal tree trunk with four vertical sprouts. Around them flourished oxalis and "marvelous ferns, sword especially," an abundant Pacific coast evergreen (*ibid.*). She returned to New England to more familiar greenery—a fall bonanza of gold and red maple and deep red dogwood. Out of love for Maine, she willed 2,315 acres to the state. Supporters bought more land with federal funds.

The excerpt *The Rocky Coast,* published in 1971 nine years after Rachel's death, pinpointed stages of tree growth, from Maine's vivid balsam and spruce to down timber—"some still erect, some sagging earthward, some lying on the floor of the forest" (Carson, 1971, 7). In whatever state, silvery green and orange lichen etched their shapes above reindeer moss carpets. Away from the tidal rush in "ancient unity," she identified "the faint sighing of evergreen needles in the moving air; the creaks and heavier groans of half-fallen trees," and the bounce and ricochet of branches under a squirrel's scamper (*ibid.*, 7, 18). With an expert's attention to beauty and detail, she admired coastal evergreens for being "sharp and clean" (*ibid.*).

Sources

Carson, Rachel. *The Edge of the Sea*. Boston: Houghton Mifflin, 1955.
_____. "An Island I Remember," unpublished ode, July 1946.
_____. "Letter to Dorothy Freeman." (26 October 1963).
_____. "Rachel Carson Answers Her Critics." *Audubon* 65 (September/October 1963): 262–265, 313–315.
_____. "The Real World Around Us," address to the Theta Sigma Phi Matrix Table Dinner, Columbus, Ohio (21 April 1954).
_____. *The Rocky Coast*. New York: McCall, 1971.
_____. *The Sea Around Us*. New York: Oxford University Press, 1951.
_____. *The Sense of Wonder*. New York: Harper & Row, 1965.
_____. *Silent Spring*. Boston: Houghton Mifflin, 40th Anniversary Edition, 2002.
Meyers, Leonard. "Ecology Groups Are Oddly Silent." *Surrey* (British Columbia) *Leader* (19 May 1977): B5.

Fossils

Biographer Linda Lear introduced the 40th anniversary edition of *Silent Spring* with a summation of Rachel's passion for "the long history of the earth, in its patterns and rhythms, its ancient seas, its evolving life forms" (Carson, 2002, xii). In girlhood, she located a fossil shell in the Allegheny uplands, the start of her personal research. The biologist's summary of natural carcinogens viewed arsenic and ultraviolet radiation in the Archeozoic era (5 billion BCE), a time of primeval rains before the emergence of simple life forms in the Paleozoic Era (541,000,000 BCE) and the green coating of moss and lichen on rocks in the Silurian Era (440,000,000 BCE). Primitive development of species peaked in 300,000,000 BCE. Her broad study of "an earlier, simpler world" around the Pleistocene Era (1,000,000 BCE) viewed humankind amid reindeer, bear, elk, and mice. Long after edenic beginnings, the essay "Nature Fights Back" assumed a "highly integrated system of relationships" that suffered chaos from scientific meddling (*ibid.*, 246).

The author's references to the evolutionary past elucidated her early writings, beginning in 1941 with foraminifera, one-celled lime shells that formed the walls and labyrinths of the Egyptian pyramids. In an inquiry of global evolution in 1951 for *The Sea Around Us*, she stressed the loss of the first simple soft-tissue beings. They disappeared at the upthrust of the global crust and the extinction of trees during the volcanic formation of Ascension south of the Equator between Brazil and West Africa. She credited rocks with preserving fossils (Carson, 1951, 12). She named the Cambrian Period (541,000,000 BCE) and its invertebrates as the debut of the Paleozoic Era, the beginning of planetary life when the earth consisted of only rocks and sea.

LIFE ON LAND

By the Carboniferous period 350,000,000 years ago, the biologist imagined the creeping onto the beach of land organisms, the forefathers of butterflies, crabs, reptiles, amphibians, and lobsters and the coastal algae and coal-making trees with

trunks. By the Permian Era (270,000,000 BCE), she depicted early lacewings, predators on aphids, scale, and mites. A six-column arrangement and subsequent descriptions gleaned from her canon introduced the beings that left exoskeletons:

Cambrian	541,000,000 BCE	one-celled protozoa, trilobites, sea anemones, bacteria, jellyfish, soft-bodied creatures, basket sponges, worms, algae, larvae, starfish
Ordovician	500,000,000 BCE	squid, octopus, cuttlefish, slugs, nautilus, millipedes, brittle stars
Silurian	440,000,000 BCE	scorpions, lobsters, worms, coral, spiders, eels, moss, rock salt deposits
Devonian	400,000,000 BCE	frogs, coelacanth and other finny fish, frillsharks, coral, sponges, algae, orchids
Carboniferous	350,000,000 BCE	butterflies, crabs, snakes, lizards, bark trees, green algae
Permian	270,000,000 BCE	tortoises, turtles, mollusks, beetles, cicadas, ginkgo, fungi, lacewings, salt deposits
Mesozoic	252,000,000 BCE	seedlings borne to islands by the Equatorial Current
Triassic	225,000,000 BCE	dinosaurs, whales, small mammals
Jurassic	180,000,000 BCE	birds, crocodiles, turtles, sharks, rays, skates, plankton, shrews, ferns, conifers, palms
Cretaceous	135,000,000 BCE	flying reptiles, dinosaurs, sea urchins, bees
Tertiary	70,000,000 BCE	snails, rhinoceros, elephants, mammoths, camels, apes, sea turtles, seals, whales, sea lions, bats, moas, seed plants, grasses
Pleistocene	1,000,000 BCE	humankind, reindeer, cave bear, lions, sloths, elk, wolves, prehistoric armadillos, anteaters, mice, deer

The Cenozoic Era (65,000,000 BCE) yielded a recognizable ancestor, the horseshoe
crab. In "The Bat Knew It First," the author placed the night flier in the Eocene era
(60,000,000 BCE). For the conclusion of *Under the Sea Wind*, in 1941, she characterized the age of Bittern Pond, Canada. Epochs of change had pocked escarpments with
shark teeth, whale vertebrae, and mollusk shells.

In narratives and a two-page chart of earth's creation, she identified 500,000 BCE
as the initial preservation of skeletal remains from the geological past.

The author's overview of deep sea life incorporated analysis of whale ancestors,
formerly land mammals that browsed amid teeming fish, plankton, and squid in estuaries and along coasts. She imagined fossil salt water pools evaporated in the Permian
era (270,000,000 BCE) into caches of sodium chloride. Rachel's conservation projects included protection of national monuments in Colorado and Utah from dam
builders. She revered the area for its beauty and geological record. In a letter to Dorothy Freeman on January 21, 1954, the author feared for Dinosaur Monument: "Sub-
merging these wonderful formations and fossil beds is nothing but blind and willful
destructiveness" (Carson, "Freeman," 1954). With the aid of fossil dating in "On the

Biological Sciences," in 1956, she credited atomic physicists with crafting "a tool that has already revolutionized our concept of the age of the earth and … the problem of the evolution of man himself" (Carson, 1956).

Constant Change

By searching the evolutionary record, Rachel recognized the cycles of climate change by the imprint they left on earth. *The Edge of the Sea,* the last of her saltwater trilogy, situated humankind in the brief span of years since mammal creation in the Tertiary Era, an inconsequential blip in deep time that recedes "into the shadowy beginnings of life, or of the earth itself" (Carson, 1955, 125). She allowed introspection into nature's existence to stray beyond the Archeozoic Era after 5 billion BCE, when heat and chemistry layered topography with rocks. Her narrative linked bacteria and algae to iron sediment of the Proterozoic Era, an epoch of glaciation, oxygenated atmosphere, and the first fossilized evidence of planetary life.

The author relied on a vivid imagination, which envisioned life forms as early as earth's genesis. A foggy morning in 1958 created the sense of Paleozoic time, "when the world was in very fact only rocks and sea" (Carson, 1958, 117). According to ecologist Stephanie Kaza, the marine biologist "offered up the time scales of shorelines, ocean basins, and species evolution to set human insight in perspective" (Kaza, 2010, 304). At the end of *The Rocky Coast,* she placed herself in the great chain of being and concluded, "I … was a mere newcomer whose ancestors had inhabited the earth so briefly that my presence was almost anachronistic" (Carson, 1971, 116).

See also Evolution; History.

Sources

Boggs, Carol. "Human Niche Construction and the Anthropocene." *RCC Perspectives* 2 (2016): 27–31.
Carson, Rachel. "The Bat Knew It First." *Collier's* 20 (18 November 1944): 24, 111–112.
_____. *The Edge of the Sea.* Boston: Houghton Mifflin, 1955.
_____. "Letter to Dorothy Freeman." (21 January 1954).
_____. "Of Man and the Stream of Time." *Scripps College Bulletin,* Claremont, CA, (12 June 1962).
_____. "Our Ever-Changing Shore." *Holiday* 24 (July 1958): 70–71, 117–120.
_____. *The Rocky Coast.* New York: McCall, 1971.
_____. *The Sea Around Us.* New York: Oxford University Press, 1951.
_____. *Silent Spring.* Boston: Houghton Mifflin, 40th Anniversary Edition, 2002.
Kaza, Stephanie. "Rachel Carson's Sense of Time: Experiencing Maine." *ISLE* 17:2 (Spring 2010): 291–315.

Future

Rachel maintained a balanced view of earth's creation and the eras of change that brought about mosses and ferns, sea life, mammals, primates, and humankind. During the second year of the Korean War in September 25, 1951, at the "National Symphony Orchestra Benefit Luncheon" at Washington's Mayflower Hotel, she acknowledged post–World War II jitters without mentioning the atomic bomb or the results to A-bomb tests. At a dramatic point in chapter IV of *The Edge of the Sea,* she abandoned the great loss of life that afflicted marine organisms to salute "the intense, blind, unconscious will to survive, to push on, to expand" (Carson, 1955, 189). "Our

Ever-Changing Shore," an article for the July 1958 issue of *Holiday,* offered the tremulous citizen a grounding in "the strength and serenity and endurance of the sea," which remained ever in flux, yet always there (Carson, 1958, 120).

The author's sea trilogy incorporated the future along with commanding glimpses of earth's fractious past—epochs of glacier melt, flooding, and desert droughts as recorded in ocean floor sedimentation. In 1951, *The Sea Around Us* declared that winter's despair and hopelessness disillusioned people because of measuring by millennia rather than years the very elements of renewal. To the audience, she offered courage and uplift from tension through the contemplation of nature. At the core of earth's organic reassurance, she cited "the beauties and mysterious rhythms of the natural world," a gesture of hope in seasonal renaissance (Carson, "National," 1951).

THE PLANETARY OUTLOOK

As an adjunct to reading and study, the author perused biological research from varied sources. At the 1962 commencement address to Scripps College in Claremont, California, on June 12, she produced a 1,200-page overview of a 1955 Princeton University consortium of 70 scientists who pondered "man's role in changing the face of the earth" (Carson, 1962). The committee members concluded that most human activity had a short-range purpose and lacked a comprehensive study of the impact on the planet or on humankind.

On September 27, 1962, *Silent Spring* carried the author's most provocative warnings about human attempts to control nature for profit. In the essay "Nature Fights Back," she predicted, "We may expect progressively more serious outbreaks of insects," the result of upsetting checks and balances between organisms and their predators (Carson, 2002, 252). The alarm incorporated carriers of disease and agrarian pests— the blackfly in Ontario and cabbage aphids in England—"in excess of anything we have ever known" (*ibid.*). The explosion of bugs led government agencies to approve habitat-changing plans without figuring in perils to future generations. Rachel insisted that citizens deserved details of hazards in water, air, soil, and food for themselves and the unborn, especially chemical contaminants that altered chromosomes and mutated cells. She looked upon ecofeminism as essential to guaranteeing family well-being, ecosystems, and child physiology at birth and during breast feeding.

OPPORTUNITIES

In the October 1963 issue of *Audubon* magazine, Rachel lauded her generation's opportunities to impact the future and its concept of prosperity. Chief among occasions to improve life on earth, her peers could diagnose and treat "symptoms of an ailing world," beginning with overpopulation (Carson, 1963, 263). The essay asserted, "All is not well in the environment of man," a concealed reference to extensive research into synthetic hydrocarbon pollutants and radiation hazards in *Silent Spring* (*Ibid.*). She considered the status quo "at once the privilege and the responsibility of us who live today" (*ibid.*, 262).

To face the challenge of altered nature, the author chose optimism for sustainable recycling and stewardship over gloom that it's too late for the planet to change its ways. She urged readers to make their stand courageously: "We must have a realistic sense of values. We must decide what is worth while … the enduring realities of the long tomorrow" (*ibid.*). She added that defining values began the process, which included "defending them without fear and without apology" (*ibid.,* 265). Of the impact of Rachel's alert to human transgressions, nature essayist Ann Haymond Zwinger regretted "the dramatic transition … from the Age of Innocence to the Age of Awareness" (Zwinger, 1989, xxi).

See also Seasons.

Sources

Carson, Rachel. *The Edge of the Sea*. Boston: Houghton Mifflin, 1955.
_____. "National Symphony Orchestra Benefit Luncheon." Washington, D.C. (25 September 1951).
_____. "Our Ever-Changing Shore." *Holiday* 24 (July 1958): 70–71, 117–120.
_____. "Rachel Carson Answers Her Critics." *Audubon* 65 (September/October 1963): 262–265, 313–315.
_____. *Silent Spring*. Boston: Houghton Mifflin, 40th Anniversary Edition, 2002.
Fahrenkamp-Uppenbrink, Julia. "Envisioning a Different Future." *Science* 353:6294 (1 Jul 2016): 37–38.
Zwinger, Ann H. "Introduction." *The Sea Around Us*. New York: Oxford University Press, 1989.

"Help Your Child to Wonder"

Although critics viewed Rachel rather snidely as a barren spinster and cat lover, she reared two nieces and a great-nephew and developed methods of teaching them about the outdoors. At 204 Williamsburg Drive in Quaint Acres, Silver Spring, Maryland, the author fostered two-year-old Roger Allen Christie, son of her deceased niece Marjorie Williams. Six months before the author completed adoption papers, publication of "Help Your Child to Wonder" in the July 1956 issue of *Woman's Home Companion* stated her views on developing character depth and spirituality in youngsters. *Reader's Digest* reprinted the feature in September. She dedicated the hardback copy to Roger.

Women's studies expert Karen F. Stein, on staff at the University of Rhode Island, proclaimed the author's methods a "new pedagogy" based on "experiential learning to involve the student's fullest engagement with the subject" (Stein, 2014, 82). Beginning toddler training in Maine in mid–October 1953, the author wrapped Roger in a blanket and carried him to the coast for nightly shore strolls by flashlight, a means of limiting the field of vision to a single glowing circle. Starting with tracking "ghos" crabs, his introduction to sea life continued to age four in late winter 1956 (Carson, 1965, 10). In an article for the *Cincinnati Enquirer,* Adela Rogers St. Johns noted that the lessons contained "joyous comradeship and love of teaching so nobody noticed it was teaching" (St. Johns, 1975, 13).

REARING ROGER

Rachel varied treks in good and wet weather to view moss, fern, wildflowers, birds, mammal tracks, and fish in the stream. She made no complaint at late night jaunts producing wet feet and muddy pants. Each discovery seemed fresh and new to Roger. At home, she introduced him to the creatures of Beatrix Potter's works and played recordings of birdsong. Family plans included additional bedrooms, study, and porch for her Maine home, which she shared with her mother Maria.

The foster mom avoided weighty taxonomy and moved into sense impressions of the outdoors. With photographic slides, she sensitized Roger to types of berries and the animals they fed. His reduction of periwinkles and mussels to "winkies" and "mukkies" seemed spontaneous (Carson, 1956, 26). Integral to weather and growth cycles, seasonal change impacted Roger with new shapes and colors, such as lichen on rocks, and the springiness of saturated reindeer moss. Indoors, he gazed through a picture window at the effects of the setting moon on water and mica-flecked rock. To extend viewing with imagination, Rachel asked Roger how squirrels, woodchucks, and rabbits would select a spruce to decorate for Christmas.

Retaining Wonder

The author indicated a wish that children retain the inborn sense of awe in discovery as an antidote to "the boredom and disenchantments of later years, the sterile preoccupation with things that are artificial" (*Ibid.*, 46). To provide guidance, she recommended at least one adult mentor to preserve inborn eagerness and sensitivity. From these feelings, she expected the hypothetical child to gain "knowledge and wisdom," which spring from well prepared foundations (*ibid.*). For teaching materials, parents could rely on stars, clouds, wind, and rain viewed from a park or golf course and collections of feathers, shells, sponges, and stones. Her own experience revered "the misty river of the Milky Way flowing across the sky, the patterns of the constellations standing out bright and clear" (*ibid.*).

The essay mentioned small things equivalent in size to the child peering through a magnifying glass at a blade of grass or human hair. Within the enlarged snowflake and grains of sand, the viewer could recognize the elements of ice, water, crystal, and shell as sources of color and shape. From these adventures and similar perusals of petals or seaweed derived an appreciation of complexity in a minuscule world. Contrast also elicited comments from listening to birdsong and thunder and the joyous leap of porpoises. With the delight of a child, she suggested eavesdropping on "insects that play little fiddles in the grass" and proposed differentiating producers of sound that suggest the ethereal fairy world (Carson, 1956, 47). Essential to immersion in earthly sounds, sights, and smells and the regularity of seasonal cycles the strengths that her plan imbued reinforced children's minds for the rest of their years.

Sources

Carson, Rachel, "Help Your Child to Wonder." *Woman's Home Companion* 53 (July 1956): 25–27, 46–48.
_____. *The Sense of Wonder.* New York: Harper & Row, 1965.
Johns, Susan. "Reflections on Rachel." *Boothbay Register* (23 June 2012).
St. Johns, Adela Rogers. "'Silent Spring': Rachel Carson Wanted to Hear Birds Sing." *Cincinnati Enquirer* (26 March 1975): 13.
Stein, Karen F. "The Legacies of Rachel Carson." *English Journal* 103:6 (2014): 81–84.

History

A maven of English literature and science, Rachel spoke knowledgeably of time periods dating to the planet's birth in the Archeozoic era (5 billion BCE), the first cell division (as early as one billion BCE), and the gradual evolution around 540 million BCE of simple, Paleozoic forms. After moisture nurtured simple life forms in the Paleozoic Era (541,000,000 BCE), rocks preserved fossilized exoskeletons. The Carboniferous period (350,000,000 BCE) yielded the horseshoe crab, a coastal digger, followed in the Permian Era (270,000,000 BCE) by lacy insects. By the Mesozoic Era (252,000,000 BCE), seedlings rode ocean currents to newly formed atolls and island chains. Mammals appeared in the Cenozoic Era around 65,000,000 BCE.

Of the sea's "hoary antiquity," the biologist turned lyrical thoughts to an era of chaos and primeval rains, the fount of ocean waters and the dissolved minerals that formed brine (Carson, "Liner," 1951). To characterize terrestrial rhythms, the essay "Our Ever-Changing Shore" for the July 1958 issue of *Holiday* reported multi-million years of the rising and insurgency of seawater that flowed "across all of the coastal plain, paused for perhaps a few thousand years, and returned again to its basin" (Carson, 1948, 71). Her casual familiarity with eons of change reduced reader anxieties about natural cycles effecting vast alterations in plant and animal life, notably melted icecaps and extinctions. For the last stave of *Under the Sea Wind,* in 1941, she wrote of the longevity of Bittern Pond, Canada, where eons of change had studded cliffs with "teeth of ancient sharks, vertebrae of whales, and shells of mollusks" during an era of warm seawater inundating the coastal plateau (Carson, 1941, 138).

To typify the changes in the Northern Hemisphere over time, Rachel's February 1937 newspaper article "Shad Going the Way of the Buffalo" in the *Charleston News and Courier* compared biotic populations to pre–Columbian plenty. Colonial estimates of shad populations spoke of "the teeming abundance of life in the waters" of the Delaware and Susquehanna rivers (Carson, 1937, 8C). However, as she noted in the fifth brochure in the *Conservation in Action* series, "Early colonists had little understanding of the principles of managing a renewable source" (Carson, 1948, 25).

By the 1800s, the men of Gloucester, Massachusetts, commanded "fleet and graceful two-masters" in the search for cod and haddock to the south off Cape Cod (Carson, 1937, 6). In the articles "Ducks Are on Increase" in the January 16, 1938, issue of the *Baltimore Sunday Sun Magazine* and in "Fight for Wildlife Pushes Ahead" for the March 20, 1938, *Richmond Times Dispatch,* the author stressed the downside of land management—a century of wilderness spoilage since 1838 on North American frontiers. Throughout the Great Lakes region stocks declined in salmon, herring, alewife, shad, sturgeon, European and Canadian geese, turkeys, canvasbacks, black ducks, pintails, scaups, redheads, grouse, wild swans, antelope, and elk. The bison, America's iconic megafauna, declined from 50 million to the point of extinction; the passenger pigeon, a favorite of sport hunters, disappeared.

ATTRITION

Detective tactics dominated professional studies of where and how creatures thrived, the subject of the May 1936 feature "Numbering the Fish of the Sea." The author restated Psalm 8:8, which rejoiced in abundance: "Here is the sea, vast and wide, teeming with creatures beyond number." During the previous century, the U.S. Department of the Interior found "scarcity and depletion" (Carson, 1938, 9). Rachel's accounting of doomed species named the heath hen, redhead duck, mountain goat, grizzly bear, and moose. Enterprising fishermen, whom she hailed in the January 1937 article "The Northern Trawlers Move South," applied scientific method to the search for croaker runs, which they trailed "southward mile by mile to the vicinity of Cape Hatteras," North Carolina (Carson, 1937, 7). For *Nature* magazine in June 1939, her essay "How About Citizenship Papers for the Starling?" reprised the efforts of American ornithologist Eugene Schieffelin, who imported the bullfinch, chaffinch, nightingale, skylark, and song thrush from Europe before succeeding in 1890 with starlings, a natural gobbler of insects that harmed crops.

The author's love of the coast drew her back to Paleozoic waters in the unpublished 1945 essay "Road of the Hawks." At a time when "those ancient seas that more than once lay over all this land" reached the Appalachian highlands, they spawned life (Carson, 1945). Over millennia, "the seas receded, the mountains were uplifted" like gifts from the deep (*ibid.*). Her history tidbits recall a colonial era when settlers ate heath hens and viewed vast rushes of eels, alewives, mackerel, and shad and skies darkened by flocks of rose-breasted pigeons, a favorite meat source for hunters and cooks. Research offered data on the Native American taste for shellfish and the use of the brush weir for harvesting freshwater fish. Of the decline in whale herds, she stressed exploitation from 1900, the worst "in the thousand-year history of the industry" (Carson, 1938, 2).

Resurgent Organisms

In 1949, Rachel's essay "Lost Worlds: The Challenge of the Islands" mused on the massive loss of some 100 bird species since biologists began an accounting in 1749. She blamed despoliation of Caribbean Sea colonies since the 1500s and subsequent devastation in the Indian Ocean and Pacific rim. She visualized the stocking of bare volcanic upthrusts with reptiles, mollusks, insects, even mammals "riding on the winds, drifting on the currents, or rafting in on logs, floating brush, or trees" from the Amazon, Congo, Ganges, and Orinoco rivers (Carson, 1949, 181). Over millions of years, isolated species propagated "strange and wonderful forms" unique to specific islands, for example the giant tortoise, flightless cormorants, and black lizards of the Galapagos Islands (*ibid.*). In 1950, her eighth *Conservation in Action* bulletin, "Bear River: A National Wildlife Refuge," opened on an historic figure, mountain man Jim Bridger traveling by canoe to Utah's Great Salt Lake in fall 1824. His reports of "millions of ducks and geese" preserved for the future the wealth of wildlife in the American west before its settlement (Carson, 1950, 1). More details in 1849 from explorer John C. Frémont preceded coverage of Mormon pioneering and the laying of transcontinental rail tracks in 1869. With profitability from crops came demands for irrigation and a diversion of water from wetlands.

In October 1951 at the Astor Hotel in a speech for the *New York Herald-Tribune*, the author explored verbally her rapture in coastal scenes. The paradox of immense age and constant change reminded her of the peak of primitive evolution around 300,000,000 BCE. She stated that "the adaptation of creatures to new surroundings did not stop back in prehistoric time; they are still going on" (Carson, speech, 1951). The extension of change explained her investigation of the periwinkle (*Littorina littorea*), a sea snail in the process of adapting to land by feeding on blue-green algae and barnacles amid rocks.

HISTORIC BREAKTHROUGHS

The author made frequent references to great planetary age and to amazing phenomena—volcanic thrusts and freshwater outflows that cut the ocean bottom into mountains, cliffs, and valleys. In *The Sea Around Us,* she acknowledged climate change—huge swings in ocean temperatures that once allowed coral to flourish in polar zones and raised sea levels around the globe. The narrative speculated on Christopher Columbus's historic glimpse of the Sargasso Sea on September 20, 1492, which he recorded in two logs. He soothed his mariners' fears that the thick plant life in clear Atlantic waters did not encumber the fleet.

Rachel detailed the attempts of Portuguese explorer Ferdinand Magellan in February 1521 to measure Pacific abyssal depths and described the bathysphere and benthoscope that viewed the sea floor off Bermuda and California. From investigations as deep as 4,500 feet, biologists learned crucial facts about life forms, water pressure, salinity, temperature, and light penetration in regions left dark since earth's creation. She proposed a future investigation of vast sedimentation to determine the "dramatic and the catastrophic" from past eras of flooding, ice melts, and desert droughts.

By surveying the Cretaceous Era (135,000,000 BCE), in 1951, *The Sea Around Us* specified warpage of the earth's crust, the rise of volcanoes, and the balmy temperatures over Greenland. The same climate built up chalk skeletons on the White Cliffs of Dover, England, and deposited flint. Rachel imagined Stone Age men mining metal to use as tools, weapons, and fire starters. The narrative incorporated the dissolving of limestone to form Mammoth Cave, Kentucky, and the glacial melt that sculpted Canadian dolomite into Niagara Falls and its gorge. She dated the land connector on the Bering Strait around 200,000 BCE, around the same time that a land bridge connected India to Ceylon. At the end of extensive glaciation in the Ice Age, she pictured caves on river shores in France receding under water, concealing from anthropologists early shell middens, a source of detail on the diet and culture of indigenous residents.

SHAPING THE EARTH

For recorded history, Rachel identified the past 10,000 years as recent geologic events. She inventoried tidal and seismic waves and tsunamis and the freakish hurricanes that carved out caverns and rock stacks and demolished villages and lighthouses. A network of stations equipped with predictive powers enabled scientists to pinpoint earthquakes and the upsurge of rogue tides, such as the sudden high seas that threaten Honolulu. Her text concluded on a survey of the earliest navigation records before sailors had oceanographic equipment for reliable direction. The excerpt *The Rocky Coast* exalted tides, wind, and rain for forming "dune and beach and offshore bar and shoal," the coastal topography framing Maine's evergreen forests after sculpting by glaciers and streams (Carson, 1971, 7). The separation between North and South America allowed species to pass freely from Atlantic to Pacific waters.

The author's 1962 classic jeremiad, *Silent Spring*, reiterated past visions of cataclysmic creation. In Chapter Five, "Realms of the Soil," she depicted fiery magma and lava streaming from volcanoes and subsequent ice and frost shattering granite to turn inert material into soil. Gradually, the greening of rocks from lichens and mosses in the Silurian Era (440,000,000 BCE) preceded emergence of sea creatures on land in 300,000,000 BCE. Her summation of the North American plains as habitats drew on the diaries of Meriwether Lewis and William Clark, who on September 3, 1804, dined on a pronghorn antelope during the 1804–1806 expedition to the Pacific coast. On June 6, 1805, the expeditioners encountered the sage grouse, a species known to Indians.

Rachel created impact with the adoption of an Old Testament tone. A subtle reminder of the Assyrian king Sennacherib's assaults on Jerusalem resulted from the visual allusion "beat its plowshares into spray guns," a restatement of the Jewish prophet Isaiah's prediction of the slaughterer's loss at the sacking of Jerusalem and his assassination in January 681 BCE. The negative impact on Middle Eastern dynasties mirrored Rachel's disparaging of "the wholesale broadcasting of chemicals," for example, the dusting of aldrin pellets over greater Detroit in 1959 to kill Japanese beetles (Carson, 2002, 69). The use of a deadly biocide to quell one insect type characterized the chemical industry's commercial overreaction to a single annoyance.

See also Folklore; Literature

Sources

Carson, Rachel. "Bear River: A National Wildlife Refuge." #8. Washington, D.C.: U.S. Department of the Interior, 1950, 1–14.
_____. "Clouds" in "Something about the Sky." CBS *Omnibus* (11 March 1957).
_____. "Guarding Our Wildlife Resources: A National Wildlife Refuge." #5. Washington, D.C.: U.S. Department of the Interior, 1948.
_____. "Liner Notes." Claude Debussy's *La Mer*, RCA Victor, 1951.
_____. "Lost Worlds: The Challenge of the Islands." *Wood Thrush* 4:5 (May–June 1949): 179–187.
_____. "Our Ever-Changing Shore." *Holiday* 24 (July 1958): 70–71, 117–120.m
_____. "Road of the Hawks," unpublished, October 1945.
_____. *The Rocky Coast*. New York: McCall, 1971.
_____. *The Sea Around Us*. New York: Oxford University Press, 1951.
_____. *Silent Spring*. Boston: Houghton Mifflin, 40th Anniversary Edition, 2002.
_____. Speech, New York Herald Tribune Book Review, Astor Hotel (1 October 1951).
Carson, R.L. "Ducks Are on Increase." *Baltimore Sunday Sun Magazine* (16 January 1938): 1.
_____. "Fight for Wildlife Pushes Ahead." *Richmond Times Dispatch Sunday Magazine* (20 March 1938): 8–9.
_____. "It'll Be Shad Time Soon." *Baltimore Sun* (1 March 1936): 6.
_____. "The Northern Trawlers Move South." *Baltimore Sunday Sun* (3 January 1937): 6–7.
_____. "Numbering the Fish of the Sea." *Baltimore Sunday Sun* (24 May 1936): 5, 7.
_____. "Shad Going the Way of the Buffalo." *Charleston News and Courier* (14 February 1937): 8C.
_____. "Whalers Ready for New Season." *Baltimore Sunday Sun* (20 November 1938): 2.

Human Health

Rachel maintained a balanced interest in nature and human wellness. She highlighted the connection to humanity in descriptions of toxic plankton, mosquitoes, gnats, and ticks. In July 1937, "It's Tick Time in Maryland," a freelance article on tick bites for the *Baltimore Sun,* warned of summer outbreaks on the Atlantic seaboard of spotted fever, a difficult disease marked by a rash, aches, deafness, and amputation. She advised walkers in high grass and brush to avoid blood-sucking insects by wearing high boots and socks pulled over pants legs. Her report of high death counts in Montana and Idaho contrasted the average in Maryland, Virginia, and District of Columbia, where some 20 percent of the deceased died of tick fever. She extended the essays with commentary on dog, rabbit, and cattle ticks, the South African tsetse fly, and yellow fever- and malaria-bearing mosquitoes.

A new administration in 1962 brought the author significant support from President John F. Kennedy, who demanded cooperation and consistency from health researchers and ecologists. His Science Advisory Committee vilified aldrin and dieldrin for killing fire ants and mosquitoes, as poisonous to vertebrates because the biocides caused tremor, convulsions, and damage to the central nervous system. To alert citizens to the effects of biocidal carcinogens and threats to the liver and nervous system, on September 27, Rachel's *Silent Spring* quoted cell physiologists in Germany's Max Planck Institute located damage to enzymes, which control bodily functions, and to the cell division governing heredity.

Under profligate governmental policies, citizens lived in a nightmare of toxic fallout that surrounded them unobtrusively in soil, air, food, and water. Because people lacked data on the dangers, they made limited connection between contaminants and illness and raised few complaints. In a personal essay written on December 2, 1962, she described humanity as naively trusting in global leaders to shield the individual from "burning nostrils and bronchial distress" (Carson, "Reception," 1962). The narrative compared pesticides to the crimes of the Borgias, the Renaissance dynasty of infamous Spanish popes known for plotting murders and assassinations from 1455, notably, Cesare Borgia, an amoral power monger who provided a portrait for Machiavelli's *The Prince.*

Poisoning the Innocent

The author's letter to DeWitt Wallace, the owner of *Reader's Digest,* on January 27, 1958, alerted him to the destruction of contaminated milk by the Laboratory of Industrial Hygiene in New York. Staff findings identified child health in New Jersey, New York, and Pennsylvania as most compromised. Her detailed letter and another posted February 2, 1958, mentioned contaminated vegetables rejected for inclusion in Beechnut baby food. The wording of "Vanishing Americans," which Rachel wrote to the *Washington Post* on April 10, 1959, informed readers of the launching of post–World War II pesticides based on battlefield research into nerve gas, which disrupted transmission of impulses over nerves to organs. In a 1959 letter to William Shawn, she stated, "Every child born today carries his load of poison even at birth, for studies prove that these chemicals pass through the placenta," the filter that protects the fetus from harmful wastes (Carson, "Shawn," 1959). Feedings of breast or cow's milk continued assaulting the infant body with "DDT or other chlorinated hydrocarbons," causing premature birth, spontaneous abortion, birth defects, and infertility in the next generation (*ibid.*).

On August 30, 1960, the author learned from Marjorie Spock that 200 farm laborers and toxin handlers sought cancer treatment at the Roswell Park Memorial Institute in Buffalo, New York. The data influenced Rachel's publication of *Silent Spring* on September 27, 1962. She made a direct connection between synthetic biocides and gender mutation, mongolism, sterility, embryonic death, endocrine disruption, toxins in cord blood, leukemia, and cancer. For a model, she chose the fisherman on California's Clear Lake who ate his catch without realizing that the fish contained DDD (dichlorodiphenyldichloroethane), a destroyer of the adrenal cortex, which produces vital hormones. The pesticide proved so effective at cell destruction that doctors dosed patients suffering adrenocortical carcinoma, a rare adrenal cancer, with the same poison.

POISON RESERVES

Silent Spring emphasized the storage of synthetic toxins in human tissue and the mutation of cells from mustard gas (Bis [2-chloroethyl] sulfide) and other insecticides. She stressed the vulnerability of the young from accumulation "in the mother's milk and probably in the tissues of the unborn child" (Carson, 2002, 16). One mutation produced an extra chromosome, causing autism, mongolism, and Asperger's syndrome. Although critics skewered her for the use of "probably," subsequent research proved her right. In a 12-page retrospect in March 1987 for the *Boston Globe Magazine,* Norman Boucher summarized how petrochemicals saturate groundwater and "climb the food chain," concentrate in tissues, and damage chromosomes, the repositories of genetic codes (Boucher, 1987, 38).

In a speech to the Women's National Press Club on December 5, 1962, Rachel imparted more obvious connections between the build-up of toxins in the body and the deaths of crop-dusting pilots, a loss of life that the author's critics labeled "irrelevant" (Carson, "Address," 1962). She also cited the American Medical Association for referring patient questions about biocides to a pesticide trade association, an obvious conflict of interest. From "Use of Pesticides," the 47-page report of President John F. Kennedy's Science Advisory Committee, a concluding segment identified aldrin and dieldrin, specific to fire ants and mosquitoes, as poisonous to vertebrates. The insecticides caused tremor, convulsions, and damage to the central nervous system. The report corroborated the biologist's treatise.

Rachel launched a two-prong assault against reliance on biocides. By killing off the predators of schistosoma or blood flukes in Florida's salt marshes, organic chemicals left the flatworms to engorge the livers of cattle deer, elk, goats, rabbits, and sheep, rendering them useless for food. In December 1989, environmentalist David Steinman, in a feature for the *LA Weekly,* reported, "In the Third World, someone is poisoned by pesticides every minute of the day every day of the year" (Steinman,

1989, 36E). He concluded that, every two hours, someone dies from the effects of pesticides. Subsequent research on industrial compounds connected pesticides with the alteration of the immune system, reproductive hormones, and brain and fetal development.

Sources

Boucher, Norman. "The Legacy of *Silent Spring.*" *Boston Globe Magazine* (15 March 1987): 17, 37–47.
Carson, Rachel. "Address," Women's National Press Club (5 December 1962), Washington, D.C.
_____. "Letter to DeWitt Wallace." (27 January 1958).
_____. "Letter to Marjorie Spock." (27 September 1960).
_____. "Letter to William Shawn." (14 February 1959).
_____. "On the Reception of *Silent Spring.*" (2 December 1962).
_____. *Silent Spring.* Boston: Houghton Mifflin, 40th Anniversary Edition, 2002.
_____. "Vanishing Americans." *Washington Post* (10 April 1959): A26.
Carson, R.L. "It's Tick Time in Maryland." *Baltimore Sun* (18 July 1937): 5.
McCrum, Robert. "The 100 Best Nonfiction Books: No. 20—*Silent Spring* by Rachel Carson (1962)." *The Guardian* (13 June 2016).
Steinman, David. "Diet for a Poisoned Planet." *LA Weekly* (7 December 1989): 36A.
"Use of Pesticides," Washington, D.C.: White House, 15 March 1963, 1–25.

Humor

From the beginning of the author's writing career, she tucked bits of whimsy and drollery into newspaper articles and essays, for example, a comparison in 1955 in *The Edge of the Sea* of trumpet worms to bulldozers and the description in 1962 in *Silent Spring* of "post mortem" research after a spraying of heptachlor and dieldrin to combat fire ants (Carson, 2002, 165). She extended the image by picturing the industrious earthworm scooping sand to toss "over its shoulder" and pausing to "scrape the shovel blades clean" (Carson, 1955, 145). A celebratory essay, "The Northern Trawlers Move South," for the *Baltimore Sun* in early January 1937 credited otter trawlers for catching eight tons of scup, butterfish, trout, flounder, and bass per sweep, enough "to form a finned procession" extending from 9 a.m. to 3 p.m. as it passed "a reviewing stand at the rate of twenty fish a minute" (Carson, 1937, 6).

"Farming under the Chesapeake," a perusal of Maryland oyster harvesting for the *Baltimore Sun*, in late January 1937, joshed that oysters, "Maryland's leading aquatic citizen, led a private life in its native waters, unknown even to those gourmets most devoted to the succulent shellfish" (Carson, 1937, 6). The quip preceded scientific information about tidewater bivalves and a visual comparison of 500 oyster eggs barely reaching one inch on a ruler. Less droll, the essay "Shad Going the Way of the Buffalo" in the *Charleston News and Courier* in February 1937 bore a tinge of sorrow for one of America's most poignant eras of needless targeting of a single mammal.

Animal Jokes

The following year, the witticisms in "Whalers Ready for New Season" edged into starker terms with her biblical comparison of whales with harvesting in November 1938: "Turning the tables on the whale that swallowed Jonah, these modern vessels swallow the whale" (Carson, 1938, 44). Her anthropomorphic wit continued in

"Starlings a Housing Problem," a March 1939 article for the *Sun* on noisy invasive birds: "With no traffic cops to vex them, the starlings ... sweep down Fifth Avenue at dusk and seem to prefer sleeping quarters on the south end of the [Metropolitan Museum of Art]" (Carson, 1939, 1). *Nature* magazine published the overview of starling populations under the title "How About Citizenship Papers for the Starling?" In 1944, she issued "The Bat Knew It First," a facetious glimpse of the flying mammal during the Tertiary Era. The narrative remarks about its crashes and accidents as it evolved from a tree jumper before 60,000,000 BCE into a competent flier of the Eocene Age.

After Rachel advanced to supervisor of staff writers for the U.S. Fish and Wildlife Service, she entertained fellow writers Shirley A. Briggs and Kay Howe while she deleted atrocities in staff reports. For effect, they sat over desk lunches and ridiculed the worst of syntax. Shirley chuckled at Rachel's wry wit and zest for readable language. On October 16, 1951, in a speech at the Books and Authors Luncheon at the Astor Hotel for the *New York Herald Tribune Book Review,* Rachel teased about assumptions that the author was male or a large and intimating amazon. She described herself as a short feminine presence, "and only an average-size one at that," serving as the sea's biographer (Lear, 1997, 214). Self-deprecating comedy accompanied her speech "The Real World Around Us" on April 21, 1954, in Columbus, Ohio, to the Theta Sigma Phi Matrix Table Dinner. To 50 males assuming she would cringe at the clangor of a fishing vessel, she and chaperone Marie Rodell claimed they heard only one disturbance, a mouse, but were too sleepy to hunt for it.

Anti-woman stereotypes gave the author grist for speeches. One fact more real than she expected, a letter from a male reader addressed her as "Dear Sir" because "He had always been convinced that the males possess the supreme intellectual powers of the world" (Carson, 1954). The comment, though witty, disclosed gendered criticisms against female scientists and anticipations that they be "grey haired and venerable" (*ibid.*). On consideration of a possible beau, Rachel passed him up because of his incarceration in an insane asylum.

Gothic Glimmers

Silent Spring, Rachel's September 1962 classic, incorporated macabre humor, the dry puns and witticisms that accompanied serious threats to humankind. In the essay "The Rumblings of an Avalanche," she imagined the resistant insects in Springforbi, Denmark, dancing on DDT (dichlorodiphenyltrichloroethane), the panacea of the 1940s. Her imagery depicted the exultant organisms like runners "a lap ahead" of technology (Carson, 2002, 272). They capered like practitioners of black magic—"as much at home as primitive sorcerers cavorting over red-hot coals" (*ibid.*, 273). The diction paired with earlier intimations of alchemy in the profit-oriented chemical industry.

While writing to friend Dorothy Freeman on May 20, 1962, Rachel inserted a pun: "Another milestone (or do I mean mill stone?)" (Carson, "Freeman," 1962). Her ready badinage introduced a speech to the Women's National Press Club in Washington, D.C., on December 5, 1962. By citing a statement in the Bethlehem, Pennsylvania,

Globe Times that the county farm office disapproved *Silent Spring* without having read the book, she flayed leaders for their reactionary ignorance. A remark from the editor of the *Bennington Banner* noted refutation of author statements that she never made. She chose understatement to characterize the chemical industry as "not happy" [Carson, "Reception," 1962]. The tone of the opening paragraphs bore a controlled anger that she chose to present as satire, which she directed at a chemical that caused New York potatoes to sprout inward rather than outward.

To temper oratory expressing fearful topics, Rachel carefully inserted light-hearted phrases. In the introduction of an address on health care professionals in San Francisco by Kaiser-Permanente on October 18, 1963, on earth's contamination, she facetiously referred to humankind as "a most untidy animal" (Carson, "Pollution," 1963). She paired the insult with the Industrial Revolution, which initiated dirty, dusty manufacturing.

Sources

Barnet, Andrea. *Visionary Women: How Rachel Carson, Jane Jacobs, Jane Goodall, and Alice Waters Changed Our World*. New York: Ecco, 2018.
Carson, Rachel. "Address," Women's National Press Club (5 December 1962), Washington, D.C.
_____. *The Edge of the Sea*. Boston: Houghton Mifflin, 1955.
_____. "Letter to Dorothy Freeman" (20 May 1962).
_____. "The Pollution of Our Environment," address to the Kaiser-Permanente Symposium *Man Against Himself*, San Francisco (18 October 1963).
_____. "The Real World Around Us," address to the Theta Sigma Phi Matrix Table Dinner, Columbus, Ohio (21 April 1954).
_____. *Silent Spring*. Boston: Houghton Mifflin, 40th Anniversary Edition, 2002.
Carson, R.L. "Farming Under the Chesapeake." *Baltimore Sun* (24 January 1937): 6–7.
_____. "The Northern Trawlers Move South." *Baltimore Sunday Sun* (3 January 1937): 6–7.
_____. "Shad Going the Way of the Buffalo." *Charleston News and Courier* (14 February 1937): 8C.
_____. "Starlings a Housing Problem." *Baltimore Sunday Sun* Magazine (5 March 1939): 1.
_____. "Whalers Ready for New Season." *Baltimore Sunday Sun* (20 November 1938): 2.
Lear, Linda J. *Rachel Carson: Witness for Nature*. New York: Henry Holt, 1997.

Insects

Rachel spoke objectively of the love-hate relationship between humans and some 500,000 species of insects—ticks, gypsy moths, Japanese beetles, fire ants, mites, scale, aphids, tsetse flies, and gnats, but most of all, mosquitoes. As reported in *Silent Spring* in 1962, the worst insects on farms consisted of "blood-sucking flies that torment" grazing cattle and the screw-worm fly of the American southeast, a parasite that killed valuable herds by laying egg in open wounds (Carson, 2002, 249). Of planetary organisms, upwards of 80 percent are insects, including lacewings, which evolved in Permian times (270,000,000 BCE), and dragonflies from the Triassic period (225,000,000 BCE).

The author maintained an interest in the biota of farms, cities, and seagoing vessels. For croplands, she cited the worth of the catbird, cowbird, English sparrow, grackle, red-winged blackbird, and robin for suppressing harmful beetles and cutworms. In June 1939, her article "How About Citizenship Papers for the Starling?" endorsed the work of Eugene Schieffelin, an American ornithologist, on introducing 120 of the insect grabbers to New York's Central Park in 1890. In record time, the newcomer bug eater began destroying weevils, ground beetles, scarabaeids, cutworms, grasshoppers, millipedes, and Japanese beetles.

The naturalist esteemed the diet of the bat in "The Bat Knew It First," a November 1944 article for *Collier's*. She characterized the night feeders as acrobats "on the wing, dodging, twisting and turning in intricate aerial maneuvers" while they hunted insects from tree cover (Carson, 1944, 24). Females scoured the air in the dark for sustenance while carrying their newborn, which clung to her "fur with claws and teeth" (*ibid.*). "Sky Dwellers," a November 1945 essay for *Coronet* on the chimney swift, respected the speedy swift for being "a flying insect trap" with beak open to collect food on the wing by "straining insects out of the air" (Carson, 1945). In June 1950, she toured the Florida Everglades by swamp buggy and learned that the service patrolman, Mr. Finneran, had to sit in the dark at night "because of the terrible Glades mosquito," which clustered around lights in choking clouds (Carson 1954). Further discomfort derived from fire ants invading his bedclothes.

In 1951, *The Sea Around Us* accounted for proliferation of insects by picturing hibernation in tree bark and grasshopper eggs under snow awaiting spring emergence. Rachel inferred from data involving trunks and mats of vegetation that thistledown seed, plovers, wood-eating insects, and spiders might survive a sea or air journey from the Amazon, Congo, Ganges, and Orinoco to a barren sea island. She attested that "wood-boring insects ... of all the insect tribe, are most commonly found on oceanic islands" (Carson, 1951, 90). Those that adapted to island habitats ceased to fly because they lived "in danger of being blown out to sea" (*ibid.*, 93). The opportunistic insects of the Maine coastline found vacated barnacle shells an ideal shelter. Others took to the air to await the tidal peak.

UNIQUE ORGANISMS

With niece Marjie Louise, the author scanned the night sky to view fireflies, which she described in a letter to Dorothy Freeman on August 8, 1956. Thinking like the insect, she recognized confusion at sparkles in sea waves, which the firefly identified as fellow beings. Her outspoken support for insects raised severe objections from farmers pushing for extermination of crop destroyers. As though extending democratic principles to all organisms, she stated her concerns about insect eradication in a rhetorical question: "Who has decided—who has the *right* to decide— ... that the supreme value is a world without insects?" (Carson, 1962, 127).

A vulnerable victim of aerial spray, bugs contacted poisons in the air and on their food sources, including arsenic, an organic insecticide that killed bees. In a letter to editor Paul Brooks dated June 26, 1961, Rachel declared, "The mosquito has the last laugh, for while we have been progressively poisoning our own environment, the mosquito has been breeding a superior race ... immune to chemical attack," which she numbered at 100 species (Carson, letter, 1961). Meanwhile, the decimation of pollinators such as butterflies and dragonflies reduced plant growth by failure to spread pollen. Rachel cited as an example of food chain cycles the poisoning of caddis flies, the toxic food of salmon that killed them during annual runs. A profound loss occurred in Michigan robins. After the spraying of Dutch elms to inhibit disease, fallen leaves carried the residue to earthworms that killed the robins plucking them up for food. The World Health Organization classed insect resistance as "one of our most serious world health problems" and a potential cause of epidemic insect vector disease (*ibid.*).

INSECT CONTROL

Silent Spring reprised the concept of insect predation by the webs of forest spiders to trap flying pests and by ladybugs, caterpillars, and dragonflies as a balancer of some 700,000 species. Rachel warned: "Kill them off and the population of the prey insect surges upward" (Carson, 2002, 248). The narrative followed the carcinogenic nature of arsenic that passed from bees killed by arsenic fumes in Saxony to the fish that fed on insects. She admitted the faults of insects "as competitors for the food supply and as carriers of human disease," but hailed the use of insects to test the concept of chemical warfare in the 1940s. She outraged the Department of Agriculture by crediting fire ants with aerating and draining soil by building mounds (*ibid.*, 9). Supported by wildlife specialist Clarence Cottam and Alabama nurseryman J. Lloyd Abbot, Rachel's views took on the aura of a crusade against bureaucracy.

In response to *Silent Spring*, in 1962, the introduction of Mirex organochloride (kepone) promised control of fire ants at a low dose less harmful to vertebrates. Nonetheless, contamination of the James River by Life Sciences Product Company in Hopewell, Virginia, and illness in kepone plant workers resulted in global condemnation of the toxin. In a speech to the Garden Club of America in New York on January 8, 1963, Rachel stated another problem with biocides—the resistant species had risen in number from 12 in "pre–DDT (dichlorodiphenyltrichloroethane) days to nearly 150 today" (Carson, letter, 1963). She added that poisons also eradicated natural enemies, causing predatory insects to rebound in number and virulence.

On October 18, 1963, at a San Francisco consortium on *Man Against Himself* sponsored by Kaiser-Permanente, the author spoke on the spraying of gnats at Clear Lake, California, with DDD (dichlorodiphenyldichloroethane). The toxic build-up in plankton seriously depleted the fish-eating grebe. Tempering her thoughts from ecological catastrophe to delicate insects, she noted in September 1963 the brief era of beauty in the life of monarch butterflies. A month later, while sightseeing in Pacific Grove, California, she focused again on butterflies, an appalling contrast to the state of her body and its grueling cancer treatments. In Belvedere on the night of October 20, 1963, she lay in bed for two hours watching the flitting of monarchs past the window: "I'm sure a couple of hundred must have passed" (Carson, letter, 1963).

The anti–Carson backlash continued in 2007 with State Department analyst Dennis T. Avery's essay in the *Canada Free Press* charging the author with the deaths of 30 million African children from malaria and yellow fever spread by mosquitoes. His screed compared the loss to Hitler's extermination of Jews. Avery's logic omitted the author's warning that "the insect enemy has been made actually stronger by our efforts" (Carson, 1962, 256).

See also Islands; *Silent Spring: Nature Fights Back*; *Silent Spring: The Other Road*.

Sources

Avery, Dennis T. "Rachel Carson and the Malaria Tragedy." *Canada Free Press* (13 April 2007).
Carson, Rachel. "The Bat Knew It First." *Collier's* 20 (18 November 1944): 24, 111–112.
_____. "Letter to Dorothy and Stanley Freeman" (8 August 1956).
_____. "Letter to Dorothy Freeman" (10 September 1963).
_____. "Letter to Dorothy Freeman" (31 October 1963).
_____. "Letter to Paul Brooks" (26 June 1961).
_____. "A New Chapter in *Silent Spring*." Address to the Garden Club of America, New York City (8 January 1963).
_____. "The Real World Around Us," address to the Theta Sigma Phi Matrix Table Dinner, Columbus, Ohio (21 April 1954).
_____. *Silent Spring*. Boston: Houghton Mifflin, 2002.
_____. "Sky Dwellers." *Coronet* 39 (November 1945).
Fellows, Valerie. "On Eagle's Wings." *Fish & Wildlife News* (Spring 2007): 20–21.
Matthiessen, Peter, ed. *Courage for the Earth: Writers, Scientists, and Activists Celebrate the Life and Writing of Rachel Carson*. New York: Mariner, 2007.
Wiener, Gary. *The Environment in Rachel Carson's Silent Spring*. Farmington Hills, MI: Greenhaven, 2012.

Islands

Rachel's 1949 survey of island formation in "Lost Worlds: The Challenge of the Islands," a stand-alone essay extracted from *Under the Sea Wind*, secured admiration for the science writer. Critics appreciated her precise, yet lyrical commentary on global topography. She stressed the threat of outsiders to isolated land formations, where the introduction of such predators as rats on Lord Howe Island in the Tasman Sea and Tristan da Cunha halfway between Africa and South America wiped out indigenous birds by raiding nests and eating their young. On St. Helena east of Namibia, goats began gorging on seedlings and saplings in 1560; a similar destruction on South Trinidad in 1700 turned the area into a desert. In 1923, rabbits on Laysan, northwest of Hawaii exterminated rails, the natural predators of moths and blowflies.

Rachel's accounting of human exploitation placed profits at the center of destruction. She focused on Lanai at the center of the Hawaiian Island chain, home of the world's largest pineapple plantation, James Dole's Hawaiian Pineapple Company. Agrarian intrusion by Dole fruit farmers in 1923 introduced competing species. The importation of cattle, deer, goats, pigs, and sheep began the overgrazing of pastures, native forests, and mountain vegetation, which reached a critical pass in 1910. Careful husbandry slowed erosion on the low-moisture topography, reduced invasive species, and preserved an indigenous mint and fragrant gardenia (*Gardenia brighamii*), the few biota left of Hawaii's unique biosphere.

LANDS IN THE SEA

Additional data in *The Sea Around Us* in 1951 in the essay "Hidden Lands" accounted for the birth of island arcs from "volcanic unrest," the dynamic that shaped Barbados, Hawaii, Timor, and Bogoslof, Alaska (Carson, 1951, 69). Rachel achieved fame for "The Birth of an Island," a 13-page topographical portrait introducing island formation as "a stately geological waltz" dependent on the shift of volcanic lava, molten rock, steam, and tectonic plates (Carson, 1951, x). In December

1951, the classic nonfiction earned the $1,000 George Westinghouse Science Writing Prize for science magazines as well as reprinting in *Pageant, Reader's Digest, Saturday Review, Philadelphia Inquirer, Boston Globe,* and *Yale Review* and in the compendium *Great Undersea Adventures* (Madera, 2017, 296). By February 1952, Londoners were snapping up the book's fifth printing.

The *ad hoc* nature of island formation appealed to the author's sense of chaotic beauty. To emphasize the formation of Graham's Reef, Trinidad, Bermuda, Falcon Island, Tristan da Cunha, and Ascension by the travail of ash, pumice, and melting lava, she stated, "Thousands of years passed, and thousands of thousands," a writer's way of creating hyperbole out of repetition (Carson, 1951, 84). Her delineation of island emergence pictured millennia of deliberate, inexorable, and unhurried buildup, which she termed "the majestic pace of the process" (*ibid.,* 90).

The narrative contrasted the formation of the Rocks of St. Paul in the mid–Atlantic, an archipelago resulting from the unique upthrust of an oceanic ridge between Guinea and Brazil. In 1955, Rachel returned to the subject of tropics in *The Edge of the Sea* with lengthy descriptions of mangroves, the seed-bearing coastal archipelago builders that turned shoals into visible coastlines. She credited the Equatorial Current with transporting seedlings as far back as the Mesozoic age (252,000,000 BCE) to West Africa, Panama, Fiji, Tonga, Cocos-Keeling, Krakatoa, and Christmas Island. Securing them in global waters, strata of roots that arced out from the trunk, then downward propped each plant in a tangle firm enough to endure hurricane winds. The mat moored a grab bag of flotsam, decaying humus, shell bits, sponges, and driftwood, the rudiments of new islands and a habitat for mollusks and crustaceans. When the mangrove fringe reached out to another atoll or to the mainland, the doughty seaside tree reformed geography.

SHIELDING ISLANDS

The author shifted tone to express human onslaughts on the delicate balance of island habitats in "one of his blackest records as a destroyer" (*ibid.,* 93). Judith Madera, a teacher at Wake Forest University, credited Rachel with incorporating history in biology: "Tracking records of the wreckage humans have loosed on islands, she lists massive losses in the sixteenth century, the Golden Age of Sail" (Madera, 2017, 297). Applying the same tone as that of *Silent Spring,* Rachel repeated charges of slash-and-burn clearing and the importation of rats, hogs, goats, cattle, lantana, and other species that sped the process of extinction on Tahiti and St. Helena. She listed mynas, cardinals, doves, weavers, skylarks, and titmice as newcomers to Hawaii that displaced indigenous Laysan teal and rails and threatened to "snap the slender thread of life" (*ibid.,* 95).

Isolated bioscapes proved useful to Edward Fred Knipling, an entomologist at the U.S. Department of Agriculture. He formulated an autocidal sterilization theory that he applied in 1954 to male screw-worms in Curaçao. The irradiated insects yielded infertility in eggs and, in seven weeks, caused screw-worm eradication on the island. By extending the project to Florida, Georgia, and Alabama in February 1959, scientists performed a similar extermination.

Sources

Carson, Rachel. *The Edge of the Sea*. Boston: Houghton Mifflin, 1955.

_____. "Lost Worlds: The Challenge of the Islands." *Wood Thrush* 4:5 (May–June 1949): 179–187.

_____. *The Sea Around Us*. New York: Oxford University Press, 1951.

Madera, Judith. "The Birth of an Island: Rachel Carson's The Sea Around Us." *Women's Studies Quarterly* 45:1/2 (Spring/Summer 2017): 292–298.

Kennedy, John F.

Rachel identified leadership and wisdom in Massachusetts Senator John F. Kennedy, a supporter of the state Audubon Society. In 1959, he cosponsored a Cape Cod National Seashore bill. During his presidential run, in June 1960, she volunteered to aid the campaign. Despite treatment for breast cancer, she advised the Democratic National Committee on Natural Resources on platform issues involving recreation, parks, conservation, and banning radioactive substances from the sea. She celebrated his election on November 4 as a boost to birds, shores, forest and wetland refuges, and human health.

At Kennedy's inauguration on January 18, 1961, the author and other supporters attended a reception of Distinguished Ladies on the Washington Mall at the National Gallery of Art. First Lady Jacqueline Kennedy honored Rachel with membership in the Women's Committee for New Frontiers. On April 23, 1961, the new president appointed Robert J. Anderson, former chief of the Centers for Disease Control, to chair the Federal Pest Control Board, which monitored pesticide use nationwide. Members from the army and navy, forest service, farm bureau, and Food and Drug Administration coordinated policy with Secretary of Agriculture Orville Freeman and Secretary of the Interior Stewart Udall.

After receiving a clipping that Congressman John Lindsey removed from the *New Yorker*, the president and first lady read *Silent Spring* in 1962 and remarked on its urgency. He concurred that medical experts and federal agencies allowed complacency to compromise their study of organic chemicals in animals, fish, birds, air, water, and food. The loss of pheasants to dieldrin spraying in Donovan, Illinois, threatened the political support of sport hunters. Upon election to the White House on November 4, 1962, he delighted Rachel with formation of the Science Advisory Committee, which began work with 23 men, largely from the east coast:

Name	Title	Affiliation
Henry Stanley Bennett	dean of biological science	University of Chicago
Harvey Brooks	dean of engineering and physics	Harvard University
Kenneth Clark	dean of arts and sciences	University of Colorado
Paul Mead Doty	biochemistry professor	Harvard University
William Holland Drury	director of conservation education	Massachusetts Audubon Society
Richard Lawrence Garwin	lab research	Columbia University

Name	Title	Affiliation
Edwin Richard Gilliland	professor of chemical engineering	MIT
David Rockwell Goddard	plant physiologist	University of Pennsylvania
Donald Frederick Hornig	chemistry professor	Princeton University
James Gordon Horsfall	director of agricultural experiments	Connecticut
George Bogdanovich Kistiakowsky	chemistry professor	Harvard University
Colin Munro Macleod	professor of immunology	New York University
William David McElroy	biology department chair	Johns Hopkins University
Wolfgang Kurt Hermann Panofsky	director, accelerator center	Stanford University
John Robinson Pierce	executive director of research	Bell Laboratories
Frank Press	director of seismology	CIT
Edward Mills Purcell	physics professor	Harvard University
Frederick Seitz	president	National Academy of Sciences
John Wilder Tukey	math professor	Princeton University
James Dewey Watson	biology professor	Harvard University
Jerome Bert Wiesner	assistant to the president	White House
Jerrold Reinach Zacharias	physics professor	MIT

WORKING FOR THE PRESIDENT

On May 15, 1962, the committee began its probe of "aerial drift" over air currents (Carson, 1963). She testified that toxic pesticides aimed at fire ants, gypsy moths, Japanese beetles, and white-fringed beetles had long-lasting effects on the biosphere, especially drinking water and the reproduction systems of vertebrates. Her presentation won universal respect and the title the "Mother of Modern Environmentalism." On May 15, 1963, the presidential commission, chaired by Jerome Bert Wiesner, president of Massachusetts Institute of Technology, published "Use of Pesticides," 25 pages of troubling data about DDT (dichlorodiphenyltrichloroethane) in edible fish from urban waterways and heptachlor and dieldrin in migratory game birds. The treatise compared toxic hydrocarbons to the insidious nature of nuclear fallout.

For 40 minutes on June 4, 1963, Rachel extended concerns to toxic fish and public water reservoirs in her testimony "Environmental Hazards: Control of Pesticides and Other Chemical Poisons" to the congressional Committee on Government Operations. She was most alarmed by the 20-mile drift of the herbicide 2,4-D (Agent Orange or 2,4-Dichlorophenoxyacetic acid). The President planned to prevent industrial exploitation and to preserve coastal wetlands at Cape Cod, Massachusetts, Padre Island, Texas, Point Reyes, California, and Prime Hook, Delaware, a central point in avian migration. His leadership of federal commissions called for consistency, wise use of resources, and an absence of conflict among guardians of the environment, the food supply, and human health. The height of the commission's report took the form of official disapproval of controlling fire ants and mosquitoes with aldrin and dieldrin. The two insecticides poisoned vertebrates and afflicted people with tremor, convulsions, and damage to the central nervous system.

TANGIBLE PROGRESS

Commissioners endorsed organic agricultural methods by cultivation of insect-free areas and the medieval swidden concept, by which farmers till virgin land to evade infestation. Seasonal control began with seeding before or after pest hatching, screening windows and doors, and the draining of breeding areas in bogs. The advice suggested pairing predators with pests to eradicate scale on apples, citrus fruit, and sugar cane and the spread of myxomatosis virus to kill rabbits. In agreement with Kennedy about the profligacy of radioactivity during the Eisenhower administration, Rachel declared, "To dispose first and investigate later is an invitation to disaster" (Brinkley, 2012). In Moscow on August 5, 1963, Kennedy inked the Limited Nuclear Test Ban Treaty with Russia and Great Britain, raising optimism that the arms race would end before radioactive detritus corrupted earth's waters.

After the shooting death of President John F. Kennedy in Dallas, Texas, on November 22, 1963, Rachel grieved for months and took comfort from a late-night reading in *Under the Sea Wind*. She acknowledged the solace in nature for humans overwrought by a leader's demise. In a letter to Dutch colleague Cornelis Jan Biejer on December 2, 1963, ten days after the president's murder, she declared herself "stunned here by the terrible events and can scarcely think clearly about their impact on the future" (Carson, letter, 1963). She admired Kennedy for prioritizing implementation of the report in government departments. Her praise remarked on "his unusual grasp of problems such as this and his deep concern that steps be taken to improve conditions" (*ibid.*).

See also Science Advisory Committee.

Sources

Brinkley, Douglas. "Rachel Carson and JFK, an Environmental Tag Team." *Audubon* (May–June 2012), https://www.audubon.org/magazine/may-june-2012/rachel-carson-and-jfk-environmental-tag-team.
Carson, Rachel. "Environmental Hazards: Control of Pesticides and Other Chemical Poisons." Statement before the Subcommittee on Reorganization and International Organizations of the Committee on Government Operations (4 June 1963): 206–219.
_____. "Letter to Walter C. Bauer" (12 November 1963).
"Use of Pesticides," Washington, D.C.: White House, 15 March 1963, 1–25.

Land

Rachel revered the earth as the home of humankind and all nature. In the estimation of writer Ann H. Zwinger, "Landscape itself was the focus" of her lyrical works (Zwinger, 1989, xxv). The biologist believed that interest in land raised cultural expectations and affirmed divinity in the wild. Off St. Simons Island, Georgia, in December 1952, she jotted in her notes an apotheosis of the Carboniferous period

350,000,000 years ago: "the sea processes that brought the first dry land emerging out of the ancient and primitive ocean; or that led the first living creatures step by step out of the sea into the perilous new world of earth" (Quaratiello, 2010, 65). The unpublished 1945 essay "Road of the Hawks" revered the emergence of land in pre-history, when oceans retreated, unveiling the Appalachian Mountain chain and, in 200,000 BCE, the land bridges connecting Siberia with Alaska and India with Sri Lanka.

By reflecting constantly on the millions of years since creation, Rachel's 1955 work *The Edge of the Sea* reminded people of how much they had to lose—the shores and land forms shaped from sand and rock. Speaking for the homeowner, Rachel regretted vast re-landscaping projects that violated the American scene, national character, and individual privacy and seclusion. In the West, the near extinction of the buffalo, disappearance of the prairie hen, and the removal of sagebrush to allow the planting of grassy pasturage for sheep and cattle destroyed fragile wildflowers and the root structure of grasses. Such projects encouraged erosion and overturned the balance of the land, a subject prominent in the verse and prose of Mary Hunter Austin and the novels of Willa Cather.

The author's upholding of citizen rights subtly reminded bureaucrats that women deserved a voice at environmental hearings. To a gathering of female journalists in Columbus, Ohio, on April 21, 1954, Rachel opposed the construction of a thoroughfare through Rock Creek Park in Washington, D.C., and the cookie-cutter housing project in Levittown, Pennsylvania. On a spiritual plane, she denounced the scarring and disfiguring of land and respected "air, water, and rock" as the sources of protoplasm, the building blocks of life. In a short declaration, she emphasized humanity's foundation: "Our origins are of the earth" (Carson, 1954).

Echoing U.S. Supreme Court Justice William Orville Douglas, Rachel reviled the Forest Service for spraying 10,000 acres of sage in 1958 in Wyoming's Bridger National Forest. The thoughtless eradication, legitimized by the Forest Pest Control Act of 1947, also took willow banks, which sheltered and fed trout, moose, and beaver. The widespread soaking of wild expanses in herbicides and DDT (dichlorodiphenyltrichloroethane), she stressed, evidenced the power of male decision makers, particularly timber barons, realtors, developers, and builders of golf courses. The final decision rested on the removal of weeds, scrub, soft woods—arbitrarily labeled "bad" species—to retain plants that people deemed pleasant and remunerative to landscaping, tourism, hunting, and recreational sports. In killing off whole habitats to increase lumber profits, the Forest Service violated Wyoming's complex outdoor network.

On September 27, 1962, Rachel's blockbuster exposé *Silent Spring* honored "earth's green mantle" for sheltering the first herbivores on the planet (Carson, 2002, 53). She depicted the slow accumulation of humus, which turned disintegrating granite into soil, a mystic integration that released minerals and nitrogen to plant roots. Her concern for earth's fragility focused on archipelagos and atolls, the unique volcanic outcroppings that sprang up in the sea. She urged highway managers to leave greenery on roadsides and counseled farmers to rotate plantings and enrich soil to quell insects. The narrative outraged agribusiness and the chemical industry, which profited from the contamination of land, air, food, and groundwater. As a rebuttal, in 1965, forestry chief Ed Cliff issued "The Forest Service in a Changing Conservation Climate" exonerating agency foresters for spreading pesticides and herbicides.

See also Aerial Spraying; Islands; Maine; Soil; Topography.

Sources

Bryson, Michael A. *Visions of the Land: Science, Literature, and the American Environment.* Charlottesville: University of Virginia Press, 2002.
Carson, Rachel. *The Edge of the Sea.* Boston: Houghton Mifflin, 1955.
_____. "The Real World Around Us," address to the Theta Sigma Phi Matrix Table Dinner, Columbus, Ohio (21 April 1954).
Moore, Kathleen Dean, and Lisa H. Sideris. *Rachel Carson: Legacy and Challenge.* Albany, NY: SUNY Press, 2008.
Quaratiello, Arlene Rodda. *Rachel Carson: A Biography.* Amherst, NY: Prometheus, 2010.
Vail, David D. *Chemical Lands: Pesticides, Aerial Spraying, and Health in North America's Grasslands Since 1945.* Tuscaloosa: University of Alabama Press, 2018.
Zwinger, Ann H. "Introduction" to *The Sea Around Us: Special Edition.* New York: Oxford University Press, 1989.

Literature

Rachel's home training with nature walks and storybooks predisposed her to value narrative as a decoder of human dilemmas. An immersion in literature and classic and modern foreign languages during the first years of college stocked her memory with valuable images and citations as enduring as Plato, St. Luke, and Isaiah, as lyric as the psalmist, John Keats, Robert Frost, and John Masefield. To introduce "Undersea," Rachel's literary debut in *Atlantic Monthly,* in September 1937, she paraphrased the opening lines of Christina Rossetti's eight-line poem "Who Has Seen the Wind?," a favorite brain teaser with children. The question of knowing the deep and its denizens inspired her to escape the stranglehold of Baconian objectivity to describe from a personal stance the home of the crab and dolphin.

Long before the terror tactics of *Silent Spring,* the maritime biologist salted her rhetoric with jabs at human depravity. The May 1936 feature "Numbering the Fish of the Sea" for the *Baltimore Sunday Sun* reverted to Psalm 8:8, David's assessment of the role of humankind in creation. The verse situated *Homo sapiens* beneath a hierarchy of angels and, ultimately, beneath the Almighty. In a February 1937 article for the *Charleston News and Courier,* she alluded to American frontier lore with the nostalgic title "Shad Going the Way of the Buffalo," a subtle reminder that animals survived well in the wild until the post–Columbian intrusion of bloodlust and arrogance.

In an August 1938 article on undersea predators for the *Baltimore Sun,* the author chose the title "Walrus and Carpenter Not Oysters' Only Foe" from a narrative poem in Lewis Carroll's *Alice in Wonderland* (Carson, 1938, 2). Because Carpenter and Walrus plot a shore dinner on the oysters, the episode ends in silence, a hint at Rachel's fears for sea life. With a more lugubrious view of the gobbling of nature, she returned to Carroll's satire of Victorian England on September 27, 1962, in *Silent Spring.* Although a longtime federal employee, the author derided the U.S. Food and Drug Administration for "deliberately poisoning our food, then policing the result" (Carson, 2002, 183). The charge illustrated Alice's belief that, by the inverted standards of Wonderland, she had to run her hardest to remain in one place. In the view of Terrell Dixon, a specialist in literature and environment at the University of Houston, the author's perception of planetary threat "shaped the critical first stage in the contemporary literature of toxicity" (Dixon, 1996, 238).

TUTORIAL WRITING

In composing a rhetoric of mistrust, the author recognized the instructive value of storytelling, fable, legend, and myth. Narrative remained especially dear to the average reader brought up on accounts of cave man, Christopher Columbus, Indian tribes, and pioneers. In a U.S. Fish and Wildlife pamphlet in July 1947, she portrayed the 50,000-acre Mattamuskeet nature sanctuary, the largest lake in coastal North Carolina, as oral Algonquin lore had characterized it in pre–Columbian times. One version outlined the burning of peat bogs to shape a round depression. A second origin myth recalled the fall of meteors that scored out four local lakes. The literature of First Peoples suggested that the acts of God were both extreme and purposeful.

Classical allusions frequently aided Rachel's wording of complex concepts. Her 1937 Walrus and Carpenter essay pictured the birth of myriad sea snails as "the horde of troubles which streamed from under the lid of Pandora's box," the source of human ills in Greek mythology that blamed primeval woman for earthly miseries (Carson, 1938, 2). A subconscious expiation of females for universal sin, the image tugged at the elbows of male scientists, who pushed intelligent women to the rear of professionalism. In March 1939, a tongue-in-cheek comment on intrusive flocks in "Baltimore starling hostelries" for the *Baltimore Sunday Sun Magazine* suggested a nursery rhyme about "four-and-twenty blackbirds … encased in pastry and set before a king" (Carson, 1939, 1). The metaphor reimagined James I and the printing of the King James Bible in 1611 in the era's 24-letter alphabet. Because Rachel grew up in the Scots Presbyterian tradition, she had reason to revert to scriptural imagery to substantiate her philosophy.

SCIENCE AND ART

When Rachel made her way to the top of twentieth-century nonfiction writing and oratory, she expressed a symbiotic view of the arts. At the acceptance speech for the National Book Award for Nonfiction in January 1952, she claimed all aspects of life as the purview of art and science. Without waver, she declared, "There can be no separate literature of science," an indirect censure of cold, fact-filled reports compiled for an audience of short-sighted experts and devoid of human outcomes (Carson, "National," 1952). In the estimation of biographer Linda Lear, Rachel considered popular science and nature nonfiction "vehicles of human redemption" for a multitude of sins (Lear, 1997, 221).

On the question of style, the author allowed the topic and her imagination to guide diction and syntax. For "The Real World Around Us," an address to the Theta Sigma Phi Matrix Table Dinner in April 1954 at Columbus, Ohio, she recited Emily Dickinson's quatrain "I never saw a moor," an acknowledgment of the role of imagination in illuminating logic. Daniel Woolf's *The Education of Rachel Carson* pictured her "extrapolating from what she could see, relying on her sense of wonder, believing in the mystery as much as the science" ("Education," 2009, G6). The following April 1952, she acclaimed the example of great nature writers—Henry David Thoreau, W.H. Hudson, Richard Jefferies, and John Burroughs—and the emergence of "a new type of literature as representative of your own day as was their own" (Carson, "Design," 1952, 232). The post–World War II, post–Hiroshima ethos recognized universal threat from the split atom and from a button-popping military-industrial complex in love with nuclear power.

ESTABLISHING WORTH

The author accepted the public role of scientist-prophet by redirecting Americans to apply core values to an ecocidal apocalypse. In 1962 during the Cold War, her interpretation of scripture underscored combat examples in *Silent Spring*, notably, Isaiah's anti-war preaching and Jesus's parable "The Good Samaritan" (Luke 10:25–37). To demean contractors who offered cheap substitutes for roadside mowing, her anti-herbicide parody fabricated sales pitches urging local authorities to "beat its plowshares into spray guns" (Carson, 2002, 69). The witty rephrasing of Jewish prophet Isaiah's call on Judah and Jerusalem in Isaiah 2:4 around 700 BCE exerted moral solutions to the problem of weaponization, an existential issue dating to the Assyrian king Sennacherib's besieging of the Hebrews.

More references to literature indicated connections between Rachel's thinking about living organisms and her respect for naturalist writers. In the chapter "And No Birds Sing," she referred to the destiny of bluebells in Henry Major Tomlinson's essay "The Lost Wood," in which carts and engines of the Industrial Revolution crushed tender blossoms. Rachel's last chapter, "The Other Road," recalled an American favorite, Robert Frost's "The Road Not Taken," a meditation on the outcome of choices. Rather than evoke a choice for earth's survival, the writer stipulated that ecological oversight may be "our last, our only chance" for rejuvenating earth (*ibid.*, 277).

See also Folklore; *Silent Spring: Needless Havoc*.

Sources

Carson, Rachel. "Design for Nature Writing." *Atlantic Naturalist* (May–August 1952): 232–234.
_____. "Mattamuskeet: A National Wildlife Refuge." #4. Washington, D.C.: U.S. Department of the Interior, July 1947.
_____. "National Book Award Acceptance Speech." *House of Life* (27 January 1952): 127–129.
_____. "The Real World Around Us," address to the Theta Sigma Phi Matrix Table Dinner (21 April 1954), Columbus, Ohio.
_____. *Silent Spring*. Boston: Houghton Mifflin, 40th Anniversary Edition, 2002.
_____. Speech, *New York Herald Tribune Book Review*, Astor Hotel (1 October 1951).
_____. "Undersea." *Atlantic Monthly* 160 (September 1937): 322–325.
Carson, R.L., "Starlings a Housing Problem." *Baltimore Sunday Sun Magazine* (5 March 1939): 1.
_____. "Walrus and Carpenter Not Oysters' Only Foe." *Baltimore Sun* (21 August 1938): 2.
Dixon, Terrell. "The Literature of Toxicity from Rachel Carson to Ana Castillo." *Interconnections Between Human and Ecosystem Health*. Dordrecht, Holland: Springer, 1996, 237–258.
"The Education of Rachel Carson." *Pittsburgh Post-Gazette* (2 May 2006): G6.
Lear, Linda J. *Rachel Carson: Witness for Nature*. New York: Henry Holt, 1997.

Maine

Rachel reveled in the natural beauty of Maine's pine groves, roadside fern and wildflowers, and the Atlantic shore, which she surveyed as a natural marine laboratory. In the words of ecologist Stephanie Kaza, a former professor of the University of Vermont, compared to living in greater Washington, D.C., the Maine shore provided "the perfect idyllic 'other,' where nature predominated and human impact was far less intrusive" to her sense of wholeness (Kaza, 2010, 303). In *The Sense of Wonder*, Rachel named wet weather as her favorite time to hike the woods and view moss, lichens, and evergreens. To her neighbor Dorothy Freeman, on December 15, 1952, she proclaimed, "I have loved the Boothbay Harbor area for years and do look forward to having a summer place to write in such beautiful surroundings" (Carson, letter, 1952). Frank M. Meola, a travel writer for the *New York Times,* stated that "Carson, keen-eyed and patient, would sometimes stay for an entire tide cycle" (Meola, 2012, TR.5).

Before Dorothy and Stanley Freeman could arrive at Silverledges, Rachel's family cottage, in early August 1956, she bubbled with excitement over high tide—"lots of swell and surf and noise all day … all my rocks crowned with foam, and long white crests" (Carson, letter, 1956). At Pemaquid Point, Cape Newagen, and Ocean Point, she spent hours each summer barefoot in tide pools, gathering specimens and examining found treasures—sea colander, dogwinkles, mussels, kelp—under the microscope and in Stanley Freeman's photos and slides of gulls. At leisure, she chatted with locals at the general store, dined with friends at the Newagen Seaside Inn on Colony Road, walked the hotel grounds to view migrating monarchs, and sat writing in the porch rockers.

A WRITER'S HABITAT

Details of Maine's rugged granite shoreline, arctic kelp, and the unshielded island of Monhegan filled the author's notes and, in 1955, influenced the writing of *The Edge of the Sea*. The colors of spruce, bayberry and junipers reflected a tone in green urchins that clung to rock surfaces shaped by glacial debris and flexible crust pressures as far east as Nova Scotia. She identified the saltwater estuaries of the Damariscotta, Kennebec, and Sheepscot rivers as the result of ocean sculpting. Cul-de-sacs retained a considerable amount of sand, gravel, shell fragments, and even boulders deposited by stormy crests.

"Our Ever-Changing Shore," an essay in the July 1958 issue of *Holiday,* opened with praise for northern New England's "immediate presence, compelling, impossible to ignore" (Carson, 1958, 70). Her retrospect narrated a 1,000 year cycle begun by a sea influx that covered hills, leaving a surface of evergreens and a granite-lined shore. She was delighted to investigate the bunchberry (*Cornus canadensis*), an edible ground cover in the dogwood family. Other joys—sea urchins, coralline algae, luminarias, barnacles, worms, and Irish moss—permeated her letters. As anti-cancer radiation sapped her body, leaving her susceptible to arthritis, ulcers, and phlebitis, in fall 1960, she wrote in her notebook, "I moan inside—and I awake in the night and cry out silently for Maine" (Kaza, 2010, 293).

THE VIOLATED LAND

During the composition of *Silent Spring*, the author deplored erosive spraying of Maine roadsides and the killing of bayberry and huckleberry. She loathed denuded land for its own sake and commented wisely on the loss of tourist dollars in New England from foolish land use projects. Chapter Nine, "Rivers of Death," charged industrialists with choking salmon habitats with logs and polluting watersheds. She extended the list of lost plant species to Connecticut, where chemical poisons had stripped roadways of viburnum, shadbush, azalea, laurel, winterberry, chokecherry, blueberry, and wild plums. Along with bushes, citizens lost the enjoyment of Queen Anne's lace, black-eyed Susan, daisies, goldenrod, and aster.

Out of love for state residents, on October 26, 1963, Rachel praised a local doctor for his reduced bill of $42 for diagnosing and treating her pancreatitis and a 10 day regimen for "little Moppet," her nickname for nephew Roger Allen Christie (Carson, letter, 1963). She exulted, "Where except in Maine could that happen" (*ibid.*). Shared with photographer Charles Pratt, her passion for the states' rugged shoreline rested on the "actuality" of his pictures, especially for her favorite tide pool in the fairy cave and the coastline's "elusive and indefinable boundary" (Carson, 1971, x; 1955, 1). Her last writings and speeches bridled with anger and disgust at the desecration of New England and the former beauties "worth traveling far to see" (Carson, 2002, 70).

See also Forests; *The Rocky Coast;* Sense Impressions.

Sources

Carson, Rachel. *The Edge of the Sea*. Boston: Houghton Mifflin, 1955.
_____. "Letter to Dorothy and Stanley Freeman" (8 August 1956).
_____. "Letter to Dorothy Freeman" (15 December 1952).
_____. "Letter to Dorothy Freeman" (26 October 1963).
_____. "Our Ever-Changing Shore." *Holiday* 24 (July 1958): 70–71, 117–120.
_____. *The Rocky Coast*. New York: McCall, 1971.
_____. *The Sense of Wonder*. New York: Harper & Row, 1965.
Hecht, David K. "Rachel Carson and the Rhetoric of Revolution." *Environmental History* 24:3 (July 2019): 561–582.
Kaza, Stephanie. "Rachel Carson's Sense of Time: Experiencing Maine." *ISLE* 17:2 (Spring 2010): 291–315.
Meola, Frank M. "Rachel Carson's 'Rugged Shore' in Maine." *New York Times* (19 August 2012): TR.5.

Mammals

Within extensive writings about birds, small forest dwellers, and sea creatures, Rachel's perception of the place of large and small animals in the scheme of biodiversity offered grist for a literary career that began with newspaper features. Her 1938 article on whales for the *Baltimore Sun* identified two American vessels, the *Frango* off Australia and the *Ulysses,* in pursuit of profit in the Antarctic and Ross seas during a 90-day season. Statistics identified the need for an international treaty to halt the killing of 19,000 whales per year for the rendering of some 6,000,000 gallons of meat, ambergris as a perfume fixative, and marketable oil for face cream, soap, margarine, lard, and lubricants. She contrasted Herman Melville's fictional account of 19th-century whaling on the *Pequod* to the "floating factories" of her own time, notably, Norway's 24 company ships in the Antarctic (Carson, 1938, 44). In self-effacing style, she disclosed that scientists have no knowledge of how whales follow teeming prey to their spawning sites.

The author's early writing stressed the behaviors of forest and field fauna with the vivid terms "burrow," "prowl," "forage," and "probe." She saluted the resilience of animals with a summation of mammoth and rhinoceros fossils from the Pleistocene Age (1,000,000 BCE) on the Dogger Bank east of Great Britain. Her alarm at the *Gymnodinium brevis* red tide, which spread from Boca Grande, Florida, south to Naples from November 1947 to January 1948, advised readers of *Field and Stream* of the loss of fish, sea turtles, manatees, and porpoises.

Rachel's fifth brochure, "Guarding Our Wildlife Resources: A National Wildlife Refuge," for the U.S. Department of the Interior in 1948 recapped American mammal history and restocking efforts: "Forests were cut down, prairies were transformed into cultivated lands, plains became grazing lands for domesticated stock" as settlers depleted the wilderness (Carson 1948, 13). The "often wanton slaughter" reduced 50,000,000 bison to 500 animals by 1890. Elk suffered a similar loss by 1910 to 60,000, while pronghorn antelope, black bear, and grizzlies neared extinction. In 1951, she added to fish and bird surveys in *The Sea Around Us* the migration of fur seals from the Bering Sea, where they had spent the summer months reproducing and rearing young. When fall approached, they departed from the rocky Aleutian Island to subsist on deep sea fish.

ENDANGERING SPECIES

Silent Spring pinpointed the devastation wrought by persistent organic pollutants, the poisons that accumulate in wildlife and humans. She noted the torment of grazing cattle by "blood-sucking flies" and the role of fish at the large end of the food chain for mink and raccoons and the loss of owls, shrews, raccoons, and moles in 1956 to the spraying of DDT (dichlorodiphenyltrichloroethane) to control Dutch elm disease (Carson, 2002, 249). Illustrators Lois and Louis Darling opened Chapter Seven, "Needless Havoc," with whitefish and birds alongside a rabbit, beaver, opossum, squirrel, and two raccoons. In a lengthy analysis of sagebrush as fodder, the narrative identified as residents of the habitat the sage grouse, mule deer, and fleet-footed pronghorn antelope (*Antilocapra americana*), which provided meat for the Meriwether Lewis and William Clark expedition of 1804–1806. Government projects replacing sage with grass threatened the existence of Rocky Mountain mammals as well as herds of cattle and sheep that investors hoped to raise. For Chapter Six, "Earth's Green Mantle," artists Lois and Louis Darling stressed small, crouching squirrels, raccoon, beaver, and opossum and set apart a harmless rabbit as a model of vulnerability. In a reprint of Rachel's "Rivers of Death" on January 4, 1963, the *St. Louis Post-Dispatch* surrounded print with the drawings.

The biologist spotlighted the hazards of upsetting nature's balance, particularly the spraying of Florida's salt marshes to the detriment of ruminants and rabbits, victims of schistosoma or blood flukes, and the eradication of coyotes, natural predators of field mice. The extermination of puma and wolf in Arizona left Kaibab deer to overproduce and die of starvation. Chemical inundation of 10,000 acres of Wyoming's

Bridger National Forest killed the sage as well as the willows that nourished beaver and moose. The general spraying of roadsides destroyed vines and shrubs, the sources of food, burrows, cover, and nesting grounds for birds, bees, and small animals. Widespread use of TCP or 2,4,5-T (2,4,5-Trichlorophenol) and 2,4-D or Agent Orange (2,4-Dichlorophenoxyacetic acid) produced a strange effect on grazing animals, causing pigs, lambs, and cattle to seek out sweetened cocklebur, thistle, wild cherry, and ragwort for forage. In South Africa, dependence on lindane resulted in a resurgence of the blue tick, a killer of cattle. Rachel accused sprayers of "breaking the threads that bind life to life" (*ibid.*, 73). Commentary on suppressed reproductive systems alerted readers to the withering of testes and suppressed sperm counts in mice, guinea pigs, bulls, and deer. Thickened skin and anomalies in nose, liver, and gut in deer, horses, cows, goats, sheep, and pigs disclosed early links between arsenic and cancer.

WILD AND DOMESTIC VICTIMS

In "A New Chapter in *Silent Spring*," a speech to the Garden Club of America on January 8, 1963, Rachel warned of unforeseen damage from the pelleted insecticide dieldrin. Because of a battle against Japanese beetles in a game preserve in East St. Louis, Illinois, the biocide killed hundreds of rabbits. When the same extermination of small animals occurred in Sheldon, Illinois, a state agriculture specialist denied that the pellets were a threat to mammals. Another falsification of dangers in Norfolk by the Virginia Department of Agriculture misled the public. Authorities had stated that the biocide would enter soil through drilling, but instead, the application emerged from blowers, seeders, and helicopters, a method similar to the one that killed pastured sheep and polluted pastureland nourishing dairy cows in Illinois. In the concluding section of "Use of Pesticides," the 47-page report of President John F. Kennedy's Science Advisory Committee on May 15, 1963, data corroborated the death of all pups born to female dogs poisoned with dieldrin and a reduction in conception and births of rats.

As models of food chains, Rachel decried the pollution of tiny nutrients and their passage into the tissue of predators, as with the toxaphene-contaminated plankton that exterminated the western grebe and pelicans in California. In a description of food-chain pollutants to the Kaiser-Permanente symposium on *Man Against Himself* in San Francisco's Fairmont Hotel on October 18, 1963, she enhanced the model to microorganisms and fish that carry radioisotopes from atomic waste dumps in deep-sea waters to fish and their mammal predators, seals and whales. On sightseeing ventures through Muir Woods at Golden Gate Park two days later, she observed sea lions sleeping on rocks, a reassuring image. Of the devaluation of animals, in the foreword to Ruth Harrison's *Animal Machines,* the author blamed human greed: "The modern world worships the gods of speed and quantity, and of the quick and easy profit, and out of this idolatry monstrous evils have arisen," her depiction of the caging and torment of animals for food (Carson, 1963, vii). To preserve 9,125 acres of her beloved Maine coast, she willed a sanctuary intended to protect otters, raccoons, bear, moose, vole, squirrel, mink, deer, skunk, fox, beaver, muskrat, porcupine, woodchuck, weasel, mole, and coyote. At the merger of salt marsh and beach, the refuge welcomed three species of seals. Refuge manager Ward Feurt respected Rachel for being "a fulcrum to leverage a movement" (Feurt, 2007, 35).

Sources

Carson, Rachel. "Foreword." *Animal Machines: The New Factory Farming Industry.* London: Vincent Stuart, 1964.

_____. "Guarding Our Wildlife Resources: A National Wildlife Refuge." #5. Washington, D.C.: U.S. Department of the Interior, 1948, 1–46.

_____. "A New Chapter in *Silent Spring.*" Address to the Garden Club of America, New York City (8 January 1963).

_____. "The Pollution of Our Environment," address to the Kaiser-Permanente Symposium *Man Against Himself,* San Francisco (18 October 1963).

_____. *The Sea Around Us.* New York: Oxford University Press, 1951.

_____. *Silent Spring.* Boston: Houghton Mifflin, 40th Anniversary Edition, 2002.

_____. "Use of Pesticides," Washington, D.C.: White House, 15 March 1963, 1–25.

Carson, R.L. "Whalers Ready for New Season." *Baltimore Sunday Sun* (20 November 1938): 2.

Feurt, Ward. "A Living Trust." *Fish & Wildlife News* (Spring 2007): 35.

Jepson, Paul D., and Robin J. Law. "Persistent Pollutants, Persistent Threats." *Science* 352:6292 (2016): 1388–1389.

Mutagens

Rachel researched cell damage from multiple sources as ubiquitous as epoxide, a highly reactive toxic plasticizer, coating, adhesive, and detergent. Dumping of radioactive waste in deep ocean waters as early as 1946 extended her worry that leaks could contaminate the food chain that fed humankind. During the Korean War, she feared the warping of organisms by atomic blast, a proposed end to the conflict. "Design for Nature Writing," a speech delivered in Washington, D.C., in spring 1952 at her receipt of the John Burroughs Medal from the American Museum of Natural History in New York expressed her foresight that "more experiments for the destruction" of the world could result in human bone cancer or leukemia from strontium-90, a lethal byproduct of nuclear fission (Carson, 1952, 332). In July 1962, five bomb tests in the Nevada desert released gamma rays and wind-borne radioactive particles that placed at risk citizens in Idaho, Nevada, and Utah.

On September 27, 1962, *Silent Spring* jumpstarted ecological concern about reproduction effects of mutagenic-carcinogenic chemical agents. The text warned of contaminants powerful enough to alter coding in chromosomes, the reproductive elements in plants and animals from yeast to amoeba to giant sequoia. A terrifying concept, gene mutation by gamma rays or synthetic chemicals caused Rachel to rebuke military and laboratory tinkerers for formulating and marketing "something so trivial as … an insect spray" (Carson, 2002, 8). She chose the verb "distorted" to characterize short-sightedness among the scientific decision makers whom twentieth-century media extolled as brilliant.

CAUSES OF MUTATION

In Chapter Thirteen, "Through a Narrow Window," the author probed discoveries of altered reproductive cells in a variety of organisms, including the sperm of crop dusters who disseminated DDT (dichlorodiphenyltrichloroethane). In birds, the insecticide caused errors in protein sequencing that prevented cell division. She listed major scientific research—on irradiated tissue at the University of Texas in 1926 and, in the early 1940s at the University of Edinburgh, on fruit flies in the presence of mustard gas (Bis [2-chloroethyl] sulfide), an alkylate that produced the first chemical mutagen. Subsequent research on such defoliants and biocides as 2,4-D or Agent Orange (2,4-Dichlorophenoxyacetic acid), BHC (benzene hexachloride), phenol, and urethane revealed similar effects on chromosomes, which contained the genes that encoded heredity.

Agent Orange, formulated by Dow, Monsanto, and Diamond Shamrock, damaged and mutated human and animal cells and eradicated species of birds and mammals. Exposure to spray or consumption of contaminated fish, dairy food, and eggs caused Parkinson's disease, porphyria, diabetes, sterility, embryonic death, miscarriage, spina bifida, cleft palate, extra appendages, and other prenatal defects. In mongolism, an extra chromosome caused an irreversible malformation and mental defect. In decades-long class action suits against manufacturers, company authorities denied that the biocide deserved its toxic legacy.

The Future at Risk

The biologist reserved her strongest language to warn of mutagenic hydrocarbons that disrupted enzyme in endocrine systems and caused genetic deterioration. Damaged DNA altered heredity in subsequent generations, a violation that historian Mark Madison referred to as "our children's natural inheritance" (Madison, 2007, 11). Biographer Andrea Barnet honored Rachel for exposing organic chemicals as dangerous as radioactive fallout from the A-bomb. DDT had "the same capacity to alter our genetic makeup in grave and irreversible ways" (Barnet, 2018, 4).

Rachel posted as models of foresight the Austrians and English who had already outlawed the environmental poisons that altered chromosomes. While the author gathered data from experts, she wrote John Irvin McClurkin, a biologist at Memphis State College, to ask about gene mutations in frogs. She requested identification of biocides that might have caused six-legged frogs in the same way that radiation confounded genetic structure. More troubling, the industrial chemicals that mutated anatomy could slip through the mother's placenta into the fetus and appear in the body decades after ingestion. In her October 18, 1963, oration "The Pollution of Our Environment" to the Kaiser-Permanente Symposium *Man Against Himself* in San Francisco, she enlarged on the lethal capability of beta radiation to enter human tissue.

See also Carcinogens; Darwin, Charles; *Silent Spring: The Obligation to Endure.*

Sources

Barnet, Andrea. *Visionary Women: How Rachel Carson, Jane Jacobs, Jane Goodall, and Alice Waters Changed Our World*. New York: Ecco, 2018.
Carson, Rachel. "Design for Nature Writing." *Atlantic Naturalist* (May–August 1952): 232–234.
_____. "Letter to J.I. McClurkin" (28 September 1956).
_____. "The Pollution of Our Environment," address to the Kaiser-Permanente Symposium *Man Against Himself*, San Francisco (18 October 1963).

_____. *Silent Spring.* Boston: Houghton Mifflin, 40th Anniversary Edition, 2002.
Madison, Mark. "Nature's Public Servant." *Fish & Wildlife News* (Spring 2007): 8–11.

Nature

From the publication of "Undersea" in the *Atlantic Monthly* in September 1937, Rachel's writing career on biota took firm shape. Biographer Andrea Barnet pictured the author fleeing the mundane editing of her government job and "probing deeper into the unseen machinery of primordial realms" (Barnet, 2018, 43). The essay viewed the continental shelf as a version of earth's topography. Amid underwater meadows and hillocks, she disclosed sudden abysses formed at the birth of the planet. The narrative instructed readers on seasonal rhythms and intricate networks that impact all life, including the work of fishers and whalers who figured in her newspaper features for the *Baltimore Sun.* Author Stephanie Roth Sisson honored Rachel's organic concept of earth for giving "a voice to nature and an awareness of peoples' connection to our fragile planet" (Sisson, 2018).

For *The Sea Around Us* in 1951, the author examined emergent topography in "The Birth of an Island," an essay on models of evolution. Like a blank canvas, volcanic atolls and archipelagos gave the planet an opportunity to "prove her incredible versatility" by evolving endemic plants and animals (Carson 1951, 92). As a biologist, she exulted in findings "peculiar to [the island] alone and ... duplicated nowhere else on earth," a description of the Rocks of St. Paul in the mid–Atlantic and of Ecuador's Galapagos Islands (*ibid.*). Of the uniqueness of birds, lizards, and tortoises on the latter, Charles Darwin labeled the habitat a "mystery of mysteries—the first appearance of new beings on earth" (*ibid.*).

A Bird's Eye View

Rachel viewed landscapes through an avian perspective. By way of introduction to the editor of *Outdoor Life,* in 1946, she declared herself an ornithology hobbyist. She added, "I am always willing to get up in the middle of the night or to get wet, cold, or dirty. I like to travel, especially in wild country, with a strong preference for the seacoast" (Steingruber, 2018, 318). She displayed her eagerness to ramble the outback by hiking national wildlife refuges, beachcombing the shoreline of her Maine property, and studying nesting grounds off Cape Cod, the North Carolina Outer Banks, and the Florida Everglades and Keys. At the end of her strength in 1963, she explored the birds and forests of the Muir Woods outside San Francisco by wheelchair.

Rachel's receipt of the Burroughs Medal on April 7, 1952, gave her an opportunity to express fears for humankind. Her acceptance speech described hubris as the illusion of power and a will to experiment with man-made devices threatening earth organisms. She urged the audience to approach nature with humility and reverence and to ally scientific writing with all civilization. In an unassuming meditation in *This Week,* "The Exceeding Beauty of the Earth—Words to Live By," in May 1952, the author appreciated the healing power of such seasonal cycles as bird migrations, a consolation she needed to face family troubles. As a warning to the profligate, she stated: "Man's endeavors to control nature by his powers to alter and to destroy would inevitably evolve into a war against himself, a war he would lose unless he came to terms with nature" ("Rachel Carson: A Conservation Legacy").

Enjoying Beauty

Publication of "Help Your Child to Wonder" in the July 1956 issue of *Woman's Home Companion* placed the author in a new realm of nature advocacy, generated in part by maternal feelings for nephew Roger Allen Christie and his education. She stated a non-academic pleasure that adults could bestow on children in their most receptive years. The author declared such satisfaction "available to anyone who will place himself under the influence of earth, sea and sky" (Carson, 1956, 48). A gentle reminder in a commencement speech at Scripps College on June 12, 1962, urged the audience to "be quiet and listen to what she has to tell us," a return to the notion of maternal remonstrance from the Earth Mother. The line rephrased the psalmist David's advice, "Be still and know that I am God" (Psalm 46:10). At its core, her suggestion implied that humanity needed to absorb more of the outdoors without disturbing or tampering with its uniqueness.

With issuance of *Silent Spring* on September 27, 1962, according to author Anil Narine, on staff at the University of Toronto, "Carson made a powerful plea for a reassessment of nature's sanctity" (Narine, 2015, 8). Carson believed that, in a constant state of adaptation, the life dynamic remained as fragile as it was in the Pleistocene Era—"a complex, precise, and highly integrated system of relationships between living things which cannot safely be ignored" (Carson, 2002, 246). Her narrative followed the pattern of large organisms devouring smaller organisms "in an endless cyclic transfer of materials from life to life" (*ibid.,* 46). Convinced of a universal unity, she asserted in Chapter Four, "In nature nothing exists alone" (*ibid.,* 51).

See also Islands; Weather.

Sources

Barnet, Andrea. *Visionary Women: How Rachel Carson, Jane Jacobs, Jane Goodall, and Alice Waters Changed Our World.* New York: Ecco, 2018.
Carson, Rachel. "The Exceeding Beauty of the Earth—Words to Live By." *This Week* (25 May 1952): 5.
_____. "Help Your Child to Wonder." *Woman's Home Companion* 53 (July 1956): 25–27, 46–48.
_____. *The Sea Around Us.* New York: Oxford University Press, 1951.
_____. *Silent Spring.* Boston: Houghton Mifflin, 2002.
Narine, Anil, ed. *Eco-Trauma Cinema.* New York: Routledge, 2015.
"Rachel Carson: A Conservation Legacy." https://www.fws.gov/rachelcarson/#bio.
Sisson, Stephanie Roth. *Spring after Spring: How Rachel Carson Inspired the Environmental Movement.* New York: Roaring Book, 2018.
Steingruber, Sandra, ed. *Rachel Carson: Silent Spring & Other Writings on the Environment.* New York: Library of America, 2018.

"Of Man and the Stream of Time"

For the commencement class of 1962 at Scripps College in Claremont, California, the author composed "Of Man and the Stream of Time," a meditation delivered at the invocation of the college president Charles Frederick Hard, a Shakespeare scholar. At 2:00 p.m. on June 12 on Elm Tree Lawn, she described the past decade as a personal learning experience that informed her of the mounting arrogance and lack of humility in "man's attitude toward nature … the part of the world that man did not make" (Carson, 1962). For an audience of 47 female graduates, most born during World War II, the scientist set the example of the confident woman professional at the beginning of Second Wave Feminism. She developed a pervasive theme in her canon, the likelihood that human immaturity and irresponsibility could destroy the race. She observed, "Man has long talked somewhat arrogantly about the conquest of nature—now he has the power to achieve his boast" (*ibid.*, 6).

Through a series of rhetorical questions, the speaker followed the evolution of *Homo sapiens* from a tree climber and cave dweller to a modern thinker and planner. She cited her colleague E.B. White, a writer for the *New Yorker,* in describing human thought as "too ingenious for its own good" (*ibid.*). By skimming across world history, mentioning Norsemen and Polynesians, she arrived at the Judeo-Christian concept of the first human as master of an Eden created for his domination. The philosophy had grounded the Victorian era until Charles Darwin issued *On the Origin of Species* in 1859. She quoted conservationist John Muir's painful drollery of the conquest of whales for their oil and the harvesting of hemp to braid hangman's ropes. Her diction—"recklessness," "arrogantly," "boast"—deflated post–World War II overconfidence in conquest.

To substantiate a belief that the wild exists outside commercialism, Rachel quoted English mystic Francis Thompson's couplet uniting all creation, flower and star. A sudden segue alerted graduates to threats to earth's viability in their own time—the bombing of Hiroshima on June 6, 1945, and the dumping of nuclear waste in the sea, beginning in 1946. She extended a warning to the radiation emitted by bomb tests and the designer chemicals fouling air, food, soil, and water, a violation of Albert Schweitzer's credo of "reverence for life" (*ibid.*). For impact, her speech heightened accusatory diction to "feverish," "madness," "fateful," and "destructive" (*ibid.*). By ramping up the tone, she left Scripps graduates with a challenge to rescue the environment from "ignorance and evasion of truth," a two-edged threat to planetary survival (*ibid.*).

Sources

Carson, Rachel. "Of Man and the Stream of Time." *Scripps College Bulletin,* Claremont, CA (12 June 1962): 5–10.
"Rachel Carson Speaker at Scripps College." *South Pasadena Review* (6 June 1962): 7.
Rockwood, Larry, Ronald Stewart, and Thomas Dietz, eds. *Foundations of Environmental Sustainability.* New York: Oxford University Press, 2008.

Pesticide

Insecticides for household use have marked the American domestic lifestyle since the 1920s in what Rachel called "squirt-gun control of insects" with arsenic and mercury, both toxic metals (Carson, letter 1958). In 1923, Standard Oil issued mineral oil under the label "Flit." Home builders could choose Trimz, a wallpaper soaked in DDT (dichlorodiphenyltrichloroethane) to prevent roach and ant infestations; the Whirl-a-Way vacuum cleaner attachment diffused anti-moth gas throughout the house. Rachel's research into biocides extended to synthetic toxins formulated in developed countries during World War II to control vermin, fish, mollusks, worms, insects, animals, algae, broad-leaf weeds, fungi, viruses, and bacteria. For combat in Italy, North Africa, and the Pacific, these new organic products filled in gaps left from a wartime dearth of pyrethrins, a natural insecticide that caused sneezing, itching, dermatitis, and runny nose. Soldiers could easily rub DDT on skin, boots, uniforms, bedding, and tents.

After the war, the Eisenhower years magnified progress and the unlimited growth of science, technology, and the economy. In part, Rachel agreed on the convenience of organic chemicals, but crusaded for control of biocides and their wise application to specific problems affecting cotton, soybeans, and peanuts. She warned that sprays bestowed a false sense of power over insect pests. In the words of David D. Vail, an historian at the University of Nebraska, the organic chemicals, especially DDT, "poisoned much more than they protected" (Vail, 2018, 95). In February 2, 1958, she compiled data on organic poisons from the Conservation Foundation, National Audubon Society, National Wildlife Federation, U.S. Food and Drug Administration, and U.S. Public Health Service. Meanwhile, in July 1962, England's farming, fishing, and food ministry banned aldrin, dieldrin, and heptachlor for springtime use against the wheat bulb fly because of the increasing bird kill. Authorities admitted the threat of DDT, endrin, lindane, and methoxychlor, but left them unregulated.

Keen Detective Work

To her credit, according to ethnobiologist Edward O. Wilson, at the pinnacle of Cold War politics, Rachel collected evidence from varied researchers to report to academics, farmers and farm laborers, and ordinary citizens the ecological damage of unrestricted pollution. She was most alarmed by the modification of reproduction by mutagenesis. Historian Mark Madison referred to *Silent Spring* as "a stinging rebuke to those who would diminish and degrade our children's natural inheritance" (Madison, 2007, 11). Rachel warned of the herbicide 2,4-D or Agent Orange (2,4-Dichlorophenoxyacetic acid) and aldrin, a granulated chlorinated hydrocarbon that killed Japanese beetles. The weed killer caused neuritis, paralysis, non–Hodgkin's lymphoma, and brain tumors and, on reshaping chromosomes and altering cells, it generated miscarriages and birth defects.

The biologist found a simple way to word alerts about indiscriminate suppression of pests. On the CBS special on April 3, 1963, she spoke in elementary rhetoric: "Pesticides are nonselective; they kill everything" (Kroll, 2001, 414). Critics dismissed her as an unqualified female lacking in patriotism, but suburbanites began worrying about soil and plant residue on play areas, pets, lawns, gardens, cars, and ponds. Many agreed with Rachel that the intrusion of bug sprays violated property rights. On a personal level, parents read damning evidence that biocides disrupted avian reproductive cycles, leaving birds sterile and nestlings moribund.

COMMON POISONS

Rachel stressed the dangers of drifting gaseous poisons and of surfactants that coated leaves as well as soil and streams. Unlike historical chemical compounds of calcium, copper, and silica, modern formulas soaked the environment in "biologically potent" compounds to which nature had never adapted (Carson, 1962). Because biocide use burgeoned 50 times within a decade and became an element of foreign policy, the loss to nature included fish-eating birds. For some organisms that failed to metabolize or excrete poisons, biomagnification (or bioaccumulation) caused toxins to build up in living tissue, including the plants, animals, birds, and fish that feed humankind. Interaction with barbiturates and muscle relaxers intensified toxicity. The dangers varied:

Name/Dates	Target	Health Hazards
aldrin (1962–1987)	Japanese beetles, termites, chiggers	hyperactivity, seizures, cancer, gastric upset, twitching, sterility in pheasants, rats, dogs, respiratory irritation in Detroit, Michigan; dead songbirds in Blue Island, Illinois
aminotriazole (1972–1987)	grass, marsh weeds, poison ivy	throat and thyroid cancer, liver damage, disruption to endocrine system and reproductive organs
atrazine (1969–1989)	chickweed, clover, henbit, wiregrass	hormone and reproduction disruption, birth defects, low birth weight, cancer
BHC (beta-hexachlorocyclohexane) (1963–1987)	lice, scabies, bacteria, weevils, nematodes, flies	Alzheimer's disease, Parkinson's disease, cancer
chlordane (1967–1987)	termites, flies, crabgrass, ticks, mosquitoes, roaches	diabetes, lymphoma, breast and testicular cancer, lung infection, seizures, liver necrosis
chlordecone (Kepone) (1963–1987)	roaches, ants, leaf eaters, flies	seizures, tremor, prostate and liver cancer, oral and renal carcinoma
(DDD) dichlorodiphenyldichloroethane (1971–1983)	gnats, brush, leaf rollers	destruction of the adrenal gland, tumors of the lung, liver, and thyroid, skin irritation, vomiting, diarrhea, anorexia, weakness, swollen breasts
(DDE) dichlorodiphenyldichloroethylene (1948–1987)	weeds, rats, insects	limited lactation, premature infants, growth variance, cancer, liver tumors in rodents

Name/Dates	Target	Health Hazards
(DDT) dichlorodiphenyltri-chloroethane (1948–1987)	spruce budworm, spiders, roaches, codling moths, rat flea, Culex mosquitoes, mites, thrips, caterpillars, leaf hoppers, moths, ticks, potato bugs, cabbage bugs, wireworms, bedbugs	nerve damage, infertility, premature infants, spontaneous abortion, birth defect, autism; reproductive and thyroid imbalance, pancreatic and liver cancer, spasm, leukemia, death; inedible fish in Massachusetts; dead and unhatched eagles; an outbreak of spider mites in the western national forests
Diazinon (1970–1988)	silverfish, ants, roaches, fleas, wasps	convulsion, neuropathy, breathing difficulty, pancreatic damage, non–Hodgkin's lymphoma, blood pressure anomalies, heart rate disruption
dieldrin (1970–1988)	fire ants, mites, mosquitoes, Japanese beetles, crabgrass, tortricid moth, banana borer, tent caterpillars	convulsions, seizures, coma, liver necrosis, memory loss; death of songbirds, pheasant, quail, rabbits, and squirrels in southern Illinois and Michigan
(DNP) dinitrophenol (1984–1998)	grass, fungi, rodents, fish broadleaf weeds	cataracts, skin lesions, weakness, hypothermia, disruption of nerves and heart, birth defects, death
endrin (1969–1986)	roaches, fish, rodents	vomiting, muscle spasm, seizure, brain damage, death in fish, birds, dogs, and cattle
heptachlor (1957–1989)	fire ants, root weevils, tent caterpillars, mites	birth defects, cancer, death; poisoned woodcock in New Brunswick; tremor, compromised nervous system and immunity in infants, convulsion, cancer; liver and kidney damage, dead fish, muskrats, opossums, and rabbits in Joliet, Illinois
hexachlorobenzene (1971–1984)	fungi	porphyria, birth defects, arthritis, kidney cancer, liver and thyroid tumors
lead arsenate (1976–1988)	gypsy moths, mosquitoes, potato beetles	neuropathy, anemia, kidney failure, skin legions, lung cancer, tremor, death
lindane (benzene hexachloride) (1979–1983)	lice, scabies, seed treatment, moths, blue tick	weak nervous system, compromised kidneys and liver, disrupted endocrine system, tumors, anemia, seizures, leukemia, death
malathion (1969–1987)	mosquitoes, lice, scabies, Mediterranean fruit fly	muscle weakness, hyperactivity, gastric upset, seizures, cancer, mental illness, death

Name/Dates	Target	Health Hazards
methoxychlor (1980–1997)	fruit flies, mosquitoes, roaches, chiggers	leukemia, disrupted sperm production, kidney and liver damage, leukemia, growth inhibition, heart and endocrine disruption, low birth weight
methylated naphthalene (1973–2006)	moths, roaches	leukemia, eye and organ damage, seizures, anemia, jaundice, kidney failure, confusion, diarrhea, vomiting, coma, convulsions, liver failure, death
methylmercury (1966–1989)	larvae, spiders, plankton, gnats, locusts	birth defects, cardiovascular disease, autoimmune deficiency, loss of speech and coordination, damaged hearing and sight, death
mustard gas (Bis [2-chloroethyl] sulfide) (1917–1993)	fruit flies	blistered skin and lungs, mutated chromosomes, cancer, temporary blindness, fluid in the lungs
orthene (1982–1987)	aphids, white flies, mealybugs, grasshoppers, ants, weevils, lace bugs	confusion, paralysis, death
nicotine sulphate (1954–1989)	aphids, thrips, spider mites	irregular cardiovascular system, loss of sight and hearing, coma, death
parathion (1986–1989)	mosquitoes, potato beetles	vomiting, blindness, convulsions, coma, tremor, lung edema, brain damage, weakness, paralysis, cancer
(PCB) polychlorinated biphenyl (1954–1989)	aquatic weeds, ants	acne and cysts, disrupted immunity and menstruation, melanoma, cervical and uterine cancer, dermatitis, liver dysfunction
(PCP) pentachlorophenol (1967–2016)	algae, fungi, moss, wood borers, bacteria defoliation	organ damage, loss of sight, cancer, anemia, coma, hypothermia
phenol (1973–1989)	gypsy moth, fungi	weight loss, vertigo, diarrhea, damage to blood and liver, burns, eye damage, skin rash, shock, heart arrhythmia
phenothiazine (1940–2015)	flies, cattle parasites, hornworm, Mexican bean beetles, weevil, flea hopper, coddling moth, borers	anemia, abdominal pain, skin irritation, liver and kidney damage
rotenone (1966–1987)	insects, fish lice, mites	Parkinson's disease, death
schradan (1968–1987)	aphids, squash bugs, milkweed bug	nausea, edema, vomiting, diarrhea, convulsion, liver damage, respiratory arrest, coma

Name/Dates	Target	Health Hazards
sodium arsenite (1973–1989)	fungi, bacteria, rodents, termites, aquatic weeds	tumors, dermatitis, depigmentation, vomiting, diarrhea, convulsion, weakness, neuropathy, paralysis
toxaphene (1973–1983)	lice, ticks, fleas, fish, mites, mange	lung and kidney damage, bronchial cancer, respiratory failure, seizures, death
TCP (2,4,5-T) 2,4,5-Trichlorophenol (1973–2013)	fungi, nettles, ticks, dock, broad-leafed plants	corneal and throat injury, dermatitis, pulmonary fibrosis, cancer
(2,4-D or Agent Orange) 2,4-Dichlorophenoxyacetic acid (1974–1992)	aquatic weeds, plantain, clover, chickweed, dandelion	neuritis, paralysis, birth defects, miscarriage, non–Hodgkin's lymphoma, brain tumor, chromosomal damage, mutated cells
Urethane	fungus, termites, rodents	headache, vomiting, dizziness, fainting, mutated cells, lung cancer, kidney and liver damage

In July 1962, the U.S. Department of Agriculture acknowledged the theories that misapplication of organic biocides posed danger to people and animals. In a warning about roadside spraying in Connecticut and Maine, Rachel lamented that chemical plant killers were "turning our roads into barren, unsightly wastes" devoid of blossoms, berries, and ferns (Carson, 1963, 263). She agreed with tourists and travelers who grieved the loss of beauty and the habitats for small animals, birds, and wild pollinators.

In her last year of life, Rachel advocated vigilance against profiteers and complacency about chemical pesticides. In November 1963, although wheelchair dependent and ill with cancer and pancreatitis, she wrote to Walter C. Bauer, a scholar at Washington University in St. Louis, Missouri, on the feasibility of forming a catalog of pesticides similar to his Committee for Nuclear Information, which she admired as a model of organization. To assure control of dangerous spraying, she insisted that "the burden of proof lies with those who would use these chemicals to prove the procedures are safe" (Carson, 1962, 265).

Sources

Cansler, Clay. "The DDT Collector." *Distillations* (Fall 2014/Winter 2015).
Carson, Rachel. "Letter to Edwin Teale" (12 October 1958).
_____. "Letter to Marie Rodell" (2 February 1958).
_____. "Letter to Walter C. Bauer" (12 November 1963).
_____. "Rachel Carson Answers Her Critics." *Audubon* 65 (September/October 1963): 262–265, 313–315.
_____. *Silent Spring*. Boston: Houghton Mifflin, 1962.
Kroll, Gary. "The 'Silent Springs' of Rachel Carson: Mass Media and the Origins of Modern Environmentalism." *Public Understanding of Science* 10:4 (1 October 2001): 403–420.
Madison, Mark. "Nature's Public Servant." *Fish & Wildlife News* (Spring 2007): 8–11.
McCrum, Robert. "The 100 Best Nonfiction Books: No. 20—*Silent Spring* by Rachel Carson (1962)." *The Guardian* (13 June 2016).
Sarathy, Brinda, Vivien Hamilton, and Janet Farrell Brodie. *Inevitably Toxic: Historical Perspectives on Contamination, Exposure, and Expertise*. Pittsburgh, PA: University of Pittsburgh Press, 2018.

Vail, David D. *Chemical Lands: Pesticides, Aerial Spraying, and Health in North America's Grasslands Since 1945*. Tuscaloosa: University of Alabama Press, 2018.

Pesticide Alternatives

Rachel favored compromise over all-or-nothing resolutions to liquid biocides, such as DDT (dichlorodiphenyltrichloroethane) suppressants of the spruce budworm that threatened Montana forests and trout and salmon habitats and the spraying of fire ants from Florida to Texas with heptachlor and dieldrin. The concept of natural or organic pest control gained credence in 1872 with the successful importation to California of an Australian beetle to annihilate citrus scale. To obliterate corn borers in Illinois, the U.S. government tested 24 insect parasites, but ruined the project with lethal spraying. The author began exploring natural insect control in July 1937 in "It's Tick Time in Maryland" and in March 1939 with "Starlings a Housing Problem," two articles for the *Baltimore Sun*. She cited the U.S. Department of Agriculture's evaluation of the starling as "one of the most effective bird enemies of terrestrial insect pests" (Carson, 1939, 1).

The biologist impugned government policies grounded in the economics of greater, more profitable harvests from such chlorinated hydrocarbons as DDT (dichlorodiphenyltrichloroethane). She warned of long-term consequences of biocides, which altered the cellular structure of living organisms and their offspring. In June 1939, *Nature* magazine published her essay on starlings and their "diet of injurious insects" as a boon to farmers (Carson, 1939, 317). In an April 1939 *Baltimore Sun* article "New Trout Crop for Anglers," she advocated chemical baths at trout hatcheries to rid fish of epidemic disease. A November 1944 feature, "The Bat Knew It First" for *Collier's,* continued her perusal of organisms that thrived on insects.

Worst of the Worst

From grubs, weevils, cutworms, beetles, and hibernating pests, Rachel advanced to the Japanese beetle. For its voracious appetite, she depicted it as "this Oriental despoiler of foliage for breakfast, lunch and dinner as a daily diet" (*ibid.*). She cited a U.S. Fish and Wildlife departmental summation that starlings snacked on more beetles and other insects than "the robin, the catbird, the redwing blackbird, the grackle, the cowbird and the English sparrow" (*ibid.*). When the starling became a nuisance in large buildings, nonviolent methods of removal ranged from shooting to floating balloons, aiming lights from trees, shaking upper branches with ropes, screening, and placing boards on sloped ledges.

For an alternative to routine spraying of synthetic killers, in February 1960, Rachel proposed organic farming and biological pest control. She recommended replacing manmade biocides with harmless strategies, such as mulch for weeds, mongooses to catch rats, fungi to control nematodes, and natural enemies to dispatch aphids, gypsy moths, and hornworms. Marine predators showed promise of shielding plant-eating krill, sea snails, crabs, sea urchins, flamingos, and parrotfish and of consuming algae and seaweeds on coral reefs. Other herbivorous predators included koalas, lemurs, hedgehogs, shrews, possums, honeycreepers, bees, fig wasps, citrus ants, and ladybugs. Oddly, beetles, aphids, and termites appeared on both lists of pests and natural predators.

To control moths and flies, gardeners could choose a deep-soil bacterium, *Bacillus Thuringiensis;* another, *Paenibacillus popillae,* killed the larva of Japanese beetles. Viruses lessened spread of gypsy moths; mold and mosquitofish destroyed mosquito larva. Bean vines eliminated invasive grasses and witchweed, a parasite that robbed cereal grains of water and nitrogen. On the domestic level, she advocated "unglamorous methods of good community housekeeping: eliminating standing water in ditches, under porches, in basements; turning tubs, pails, boats, or wheelbarrows upside-down, draining clogged gutters, stocking ornamental pools with fish" (Carson, letter, 1961).

Defeating Industrial Poisons

Silent Spring, issued on September 27, 1962, spoke positively about an integrated ecological means of controlling invasive insects. To avoid the creation of Frankensteinian superbugs, the narrative proposed coexisting with insects rather than eradicating them. To halt the accumulation of toxins in the food chain, she endorsed biopesticides—the organism-against-organism method, for example, the use of the bacterium *Bacillus thuringiensis* as a natural predator of corn borers. The essay "Nature Fights Back" in *Silent Spring* dramatized the bug-on-bug predation that reduced pests, particularly the "browsing caterpillar," dragonflies, and ladybugs that employed "little fires of energy" to gorge on aphids and scale (Carson, 2002, 250). In October 1963, "Rachel Carson Answers Her Critics," an essay in *Audubon,* suggested replacing expensive blanket spraying with selective extermination of young trees and tall shrubs, a method developed in Connecticut by Right-of-way Resources of America. The stabilizing of ferns, wildflowers, and low shrubs prevented tree invasion for a period up to three decades, thus sparing the community treasury and preventing mass poisoning with herbicides.

Writer Emmy Nicklin summarized Rachel's methods as "integrated management: using a minimum of chemicals combined with biological and cultural controls," including viral and microbial affliction of insects, alarming sounds, hormone adjustment, and chemical attractants (Nicklin, 2019). Central to wise land management, farmers rotated crops and diversified plantings to enrich soil and exterminate infestations. In 1959, the author wrote William Shawn, editor of the *New Yorker,* on a positive note—the control of insects via hormonal manipulation to halt their maturation. She had to admit, "This Utopia, if it ever materialized, is a long way off" (Carson, letter, 1959). More recent discoveries proposed using radioactive cobalt to produce sterile male mosquitoes and screwworms, the fly larvae or maggots that eat live tissue on herd animals throughout the Western Hemisphere. A subsequent experiment baited flies with synthetic odors of wounded animals to exterminate screwworms.

LESS DESTRUCTIVE CONTROLS

Silent Spring reported on do-it-yourself methods—the interplanting of roses with marigolds to eradicate nematodes, removal of diseased elms in New York, and the posting of nesting boxes to draw insectivore bats, owls, and woodpeckers to forests—and the more scientific luring of insects with sex attractants. Rachel approved the importation of enemy parasites—a Korean wasp, milky spore bacterium, European beetles—to defeat the Klamath weed, which reduced the weight of cattle and sheep, and to lessen Japanese beetle infestations in Connecticut, Delaware, Maryland, New Jersey, and New York. The narrative gave multiple examples of one-on-one controls, including the quarantining and deliberate importation of 13 parasites in New England, which curbed the gypsy moth by 1955.

A less poisonous reduction of fire ants across the U.S. South in Chapter Ten, "Indiscriminately from the Skies," involved direct treatment of ant mounds at a low cost of 6.6 cents per acre. For ant mounds in parks, lawns, meadows, pastures, and plowed fields, baiting each site and pouring ant killer on it reduced the damage done by broadcasting poison. For homeowners, a single dousing in boiling water sometimes sufficed. A more severe loss in Australia, lands choked with prickly pear (*Opuntia stricta*) did not respond to chemical sprays. Entomologists launched the Argentine moth, which killed the spiny cactus and restored 60 million desert acres to use.

In Part IV of "Use of Pesticides," a May 15, 1963, report from President John F. Kennedy's Science Advisory Committee, contributors listed chemical-free agricultural methods, beginning with planting in areas free of pests and rotation to virgin land to evade infestation. Seasonal management involved sowing in periods before or after pest manifestation, covering windows with screens, and draining marshes to rid insects of breeding areas. The advice reiterated pairing predators with pests to eradicate scale on apples, citrus fruit, and sugar cane and the implementation of myxomatosis virus to kill rabbits.

See also Silent Spring: Dreams of the Borgias; Silent Spring: Nature Fights Back; Silent Spring: The Other Road.

Sources

Carson, Rachel. "How About Citizenship Papers for the Starling?" *Nature* 32 (June/July 1939): 317–319.
_____. "Letter to Paul Brooks" (26 June 1961).
_____. "Letter to William Shawn" (14 February 1959).
_____. *Silent Spring.* Boston: Houghton Mifflin, 40th Anniversary Edition, 2002.
Carson, R.L. "Starlings a Housing Problem." *Baltimore Sunday Sun Magazine* (5 March 1939): 1.
McCrum, Robert. "The 100 Best Nonfiction Books: No 20—*Silent Spring* by Rachel Carson (1962)." *The Guardian* (13 June 2016).
Meiners, Roger, Pierre Desrochers, and Andrew Morriss, eds. *Silent Spring at 50: The False Crises of Rachel Carson.* Washington, D.C.: Cato Institute, 2012.
Nicklin, Emmy. *What We Owe to Rachel Carson.* https://www.cbf.org/blogs/save-the-bay/2019/03/what-rachel-carson-gave-us.html.
"Use of Pesticides," Washington, D.C.: White House, 15 March 1963, 1–25.
Weigert, Andrew J. "Pragmatic Thinking about Self, Society, and Natural Environment: Mead, Carson, and Beyond." *Symbolic Interaction* 31:3 (Summer 2008): 235–258.

Pollutants

Rachel wanted to extend conservation concerns beyond birdwatching, wild-flower photography, and snow skiing to concerns of all citizens. As reported in Daniel Wolff's "The Education of Rachel Carson" in the book *How Lincoln Learned to Read*, the biologist grew up outside Pittsburgh within smell of the Franklin Glue Works, which simmered animals' bones, hide, ears, and tails into gelatin. The Pittsburgh Plate Glass factory and coal mines contributed to the death of the Allegheny River, which sustained "not a mussel, not a crawfish, nor a fish" for 30 miles ("Education," 2009, G6). In 1909, a report on regional ecology declared the river "possibly the greatest variety of pollution of any of the streams in the state" (*ibid.*). In addition, clearcutting and chemical forestry control reduced woodlands to the "Allegheny Brush-patch" (*ibid.*)

In adulthood, the author found work for the U.S. Bureau of Fisheries in Baltimore and supplied the *Baltimore Sun* with features charging industrial effluents with contaminating oyster beds on the Chesapeake Bay. She stated the connection between empty skies, forests, and streams with a planet "not likely to be fit habitat for man himself" (Carson, 1963, 263). Aware that hydrocarbons accumulate in bone, blood, fat, and muscle, she proposed an article for *Reader's Digest* in 1945 warning of chemical poisons, particularly DDT (dichlorodiphenyltrichloroethane), the darling of farm and domestic pest killers. In the introduction to *Silent Spring*, her biographer, Linda Lear, cited the author's belief that chemical pollution was "the ultimate act of human hubris, a product of ignorance and greed" (Carson, 2002, xiv).

THE PROPHET'S VOICE

Fortunately for humanity, Rachel assumed the role of futurist, not for personal gain, but out of compunction to warn that pollutants were irreversible. Her visions of toxic buildup in living tissue ridiculed the notion of "safe" doses of biocides. She informed parents of the dangers of mercury in food fish and of strontium-90 in milk, both the results of unconscionable dumping of industrial residue in the ocean. Biologists determined that chemical pollutants ranked third in exterminating species after environmental devastation and competition from alien species. To stop the destruction of organisms, by 1973, legislators saw the wisdom of the Endangered Species Act. Nonetheless, the U.S. continued exporting DDT to Ecuador, Ethiopia, Mexico, South Africa, and Venezuela, primarily countries battling malaria and leishmaniasis.

Global response to Rachel's alarm resulted in new regulations and prohibitions of contaminants. German vegetarians and organic farmers lionized her candor and responded with outrage at a Sandoz warehouse fire in Basel on November 1, 1986, that killed salmon, eels, and river organisms on the Rhine. In England, the presence of Shell Oil's formulations—aldrin, dieldrin, and heptachlor—in human fat as well as in butter, beef, and mutton incited debate that ended in bans on agricultural poisons. The Dutch discussed the growth of insect resistance to chlordane, dieldrin, lindane, parathion, malathion, and DDT (dichlorodiphenyltrichloroethane), and a drop in raptor populations. Because of Swedish radio broadcasts warning of DDT in human breast milk, the term "biocide" entered the Finnish and Swedish languages.

MIXED RESPONSE

In Soviet states, Ireland, Italy, and Spain, *Silent Spring* made a small impact on the post–World War II scene. By August 1972, however, the Australian Agricultural Council entered the international revolt against DDT. Attitudes shifted toward green following oil spills, the Chernobyl accident, ejected industrial waste in Love Canal, and chemical factory explosions that threatened Europeans with polluted shores, toxic dioxin, and radiation. Literary historian Patricia Hynes acknowledged *Silent Spring* as an economic and political force altering global thinking about profiteering: "No one since would be able to sell pollution as the necessary underside of progress so easily or uncritically" (Hynes, 1989, 3).

Despite threats of lawsuits from capitalists, Rachel's treatise became a literary classic for its trenchant message, reaching even rural China. In 2018, marine biologist Sylvia Earle contributed a new introduction to *The Sea Around Us* that warned of more recent assaults on global waters: "By the twenty-first century, it is likely that large-scale fishing will collapse and that bits of plastic will outnumber what fish remain" (Carson, 2018, xvi). David Rosner, a professor of medicine and history at Columbia University, concluded a graver concern: "*All* of us are toxic dumps.... We have become walking, talking biohazards, and we don't even know it" (Rosner, 2015, 11).

See also "The Pollution of Our Environment."

Sources

Brinkley, Douglas. "Rachel Carson and JFK, an Environmental Tag Team,. *Audubon* (May–June 2012), https://www.audubon.org/magazine/may-june-2012/rachel-carson-and-jfk-environmental-tag-team.

Carson, Rachel. "Rachel Carson Answers Her Critics." *Audubon* 65 (September/October 1963): 262–265, 313–315.

_____. *The Sea Around Us.* New York: Oxford University Press, 2018.

_____. *Silent Spring.* Boston: Houghton Mifflin, 40th Anniversary Edition, 2002.

"The Education of Rachel Carson." *Pittsburgh Post-Gazette* (2 May 2006): G6.

Hynes, H. Patricia. *The Recurring Silent Spring.* New York: Pergamon, 1989.

Rosner, David. "Swimming Upstream: Probing the Problem of Pollution." *Milbank Quarterly* (March 2015): 8–11.

"The Pollution of Our Environment"

On October 10, 1963, Rachel detailed the next Black Death of humankind and a chilling apocalypse of global environment. She opened the Seventh Annual Kaiser Foundation Hospitals and Permanente Medical Group symposium to "an informed and intelligent audience" of 1,500 physicians on the subject of *Man Against Himself*. Her keynote oration, "The Pollution of Our Environment," informed listeners of the risks of a contaminated earth (Carson, "Pollution," 1963). To the managed care consortium and guests at San Francisco's Fairmont Hotel, she spoke for an hour, 50 percent longer than her usual 40-minute texts. Directing remarks to company president Clifford H. Kramer Keene, a surgeon-philanthropist, she introduced a strong topic sentence asserting that "man could be working against himself," a statement that hedged her accusation with the use of "could be" (*ibid.*). Connecting hubris with the atomic age, her theme noted the lapse of wisdom and responsibility toward complex life dynamics.

By reciting a synopsis of life's origin, the speaker connected evolutionary shifts to the constant changes on earth, which she characterized as "action and interaction" (*ibid.*). The ongoing alteration, dynamics that she called "ecosystems" and "ecology," required study by a network of specialists. Her address introduced examples of waste disposal, including rubbish, fumes, smoke, and atomic waste. She charged humankind with profligacy, a predicament that biologist Barry Commoner, the founder of modern ecology, had amplified at the Air Pollution Conference in Washington, D.C., in December 10–12, 1962. For an everyday example, she chose the indestructibility of detergent used in clothes and dishwashers.

Deadly Taint

Rachel's three-stage warning about pollutants began with amounts of contaminants at large over the globe and advanced to pollution mobility and the interactions of biocides with living organisms. She enhanced the definition of "drift," explaining how more than 50 percent of pesticides moved along air currents to unknown places, some as far away as the Arctic Circle and deep-water oceans. Her text reiterated testimony to congress the previous June 4, 1963, about unimaginable concentrations of toxaphene in California among pelicans at Big Bear Lake and in the western grebe at Clear Lake. By citing losses to Kaiser-Permanente's home state, her address deepened the impact of troubling data.

At a climactic point in the oration, Rachel moved on to atomic waste, which nuclear physicists failed to consider when they first split the atom. The emerging knowledge of oceanic currents and dynamics introduced the possibility that dumping of radioisotopes in the sea did not secure deposits at one spot. The transporter, tiny plankton, carried radioactivity vertically and horizontally, feeding fish, seals, and whales on migratory routes far from the original disposal. To stress human links to radioactive contamination, she cited the absorption in Alaskan Eskimos, Norwegians, and Finnish and Swedish Lapps, the indigenous people who reside at the far end of a food chain consisting of lichens, caribou, and reindeer, and who eat venison. She chose the term "burden" to describe the pollutant concentrated in each human body (*ibid.*).

Radiation and DNA

In presenting facts about radioactive iodine, the speaker's last public address before her death aired a sophisticated analysis of science in the early 1960s. She admitted that experts acted on faulty conclusions that the radiation in "hot spots" was short-lived (*ibid.*). Passed through milk into infants and children, contaminated iodine accumulated in thyroid glands and presented a danger of cancer. More hazardous, gamma rays penetrated human tissue, mutating DNA. Because of five bomb tests in Nye County, Nevada, in July 1962, the Utah Department of Health established methods of diverting milk from tainted dairy cows. Further study in 1963 by the Committee for Nuclear Information warned that local milk threatened populations in Idaho, Nevada, and Utah with the effects of iodine 131, a radioisotope lethal enough to treat thyroid cancer. Nonetheless, the U.S. Public Health Service declared the contaminated milk safe for human intake. Rachel's nonjudgmental conclusion reminded listeners that science was disseminating deadly materials without understanding long-term effects.

In Rachel's view of future technological advancement, the American citizen deserved input on biocidal contaminants that entered his food and body and "to prudent and necessary measures that ought to be taken" to defend the unborn (*ibid.*). She itemized the perils of militarization of atomic power as well as underground testing, hazardous waste disposal, and accidents releasing radiation. An alarming possibility, the hereditary damage to subsequent generations by mutagenic substances received her most acute concern. She derided simplistic reports on fish kills that declared tainted water safe for drinking. At the core of lack-logic thinking, she charged her generation with the same recoil from evolution that the Victorian public and some of his colleagues felt in 1865 at Charles Darwin's theories. Because the English recovered from their disbelief, she hoped that the atomic era could accept the place of humankind in the environment.

See also Darwin, Charles; Diction; Speeches.

Sources

Carson, Rachel. "The Pollution of Our Environment," address to the Kaiser-Permanente Symposium *Man Against Himself*, San Francisco (18 October 1963).

Gerwig, Kathy. "Kathy Gerwig Highlights Kaiser Permanente's Environmental Work in Congressional Testimony." webcache.googleusercontent.com/search?q=cache:RJ4UAYzARooJ:https://share.kaiserpermanente.org/article/kathy-gerwig-highlights-kaiser-permanentes-environmental-work-in-congressional-testimony/+&cd=1&hl=en&ct=clnk&gl=us, 26 February 2009.

Magdoff, Fred, and Chris Williams. *Creating an Ecological Society: Toward a Revolutionary Transformation.* New York: New York University Press, 2017.

Petrina, Stephen. "Critique of technology." *Critique in Design and Technology Education.* Singapore: Springer, 2017, 31–49.

Predators

Rachel's essays and freelance newspaper articles stressed relationships within the life cycle—the long migration of elvers from fresh waters to the Sargasso Sea, the coyote's reduction of field mice populations, the paralyzing effect of glowworm poison on snails, and the starvation of Arizona's Kaibab deer from a loss of predators. In the estimation of analyst Susan Power Bratton, chair of environmental science at Baylor University, the author believed that "predation is part of the natural order" (Bratton, 2004, 9). Bratton explained marine checks and balances: "The sea is the domain of unfulfilled life goals, and even at the top of the food chain the losses are brutal [with] natural mortality" (*ibid.*, 13).

The biologist's enthusiastic reportage of fish cataloging in the May 1936 essay "Numbering the Fish of the Sea" for the *Baltimore Sunday Sun* detailed the chancy lives of Atlantic mackerel. Against cold and storms, small fry also suffered attacks by "small, predacious monsters, the comb jellies and the glass worms," which diminished the fish population (Carson, 1936, 7). She summarized loss as "infantile disasters," a term suggesting the vulnerability of the young (*ibid.*). A variant perspective in "Undersea," a lyrical essay for the September 1937 issue of *Atlantic Monthly,* gentled the image of saltwater mayhem with the reminder that "wandering fish prey and are preyed upon," a balanced take on nature's amorality (Carson, 1937, 322).

Nature's Dynamic

In the July 1937 *Baltimore Sun* article "It's Tick Time in Maryland," the author indicted wild rodents for carrying ticks. For campsites threatened by abundant ticks, she recommended spraying with creosote oil, a natural preservative distilled from coal tar and petroleum. Her upbeat features on nature's balance exonerated owls and hawks for eating mice and other wild rodents, the vectors of ticks. In a later essay on nurturing young trout, she praised stream and lake fish for gobbling sowbugs, stone-flies, shrimp, caddis flies, aquatic worms, and mayflies, carriers of nematodes.

After introducing the life cycle of oysters in the *Richmond Times Dispatch* in April 1937, Rachel returned to bivalves for the *Baltimore Sun* in August 1938 with a graphic description of attacks on mollusks. Two exploiters, starfish and sea snails, drilled into shells and ate the oysters alive. With a ghoulish quip on predator manners, she added, "Several of them may creep between shells of the dying oysters to banquet uninvited" (Carson, 1938, 2). A reverse of undersea fortunes allowed scavenger fish to scarf up a meal of both oyster and snail. Subsequent articles for the *Sun* accounted for rat forays on turtle eggs in Beaufort, North Carolina, and for herring and mackerel runs enticing predatory bluefin tuna off the Georges Bank and Liverpool, Nova Scotia. When herring leaped skyward to escape, they ran afoul of the next layer of attackers—"swooping, screaming gulls which are never far away" (Carson, 1938, 2).

Motherly Protection

For maximum tension in *Under the Sea Wind,* in 1941, the writer spotlighted female birds shielding their eggs and downy fledglings from bigger birds and "a thousand dangers, formless and without name" (Carson, 1941, 45). The gyrfalcon's seizure of a new-fledged longspur in the Arctic tundra terrified the heroine, Silverbar, who harbored "fear of all wild things for the safety of their helpless young" (*ibid.*, 43). The mother-and-child motif revered quick maternal action to conceal egg shards. Millennia of instinct emboldened her to lure a fox out of range of tender sanderlings. The narrative featured shining eyes and twitching nostrils as proofs of the predator's sensory perceptions.

In Chapter Two, entitled "The Gull's Way," the late summer story of eat-or-be-eaten spotlighted mackerel larvae, microscopic young armed with pincers. Immature fry fought off fearsome stalkers, notably, "cilium-studded mouths of the drifting green or golden cells of the diatoms," the flickering ctenophores or comb jellies, and ravenous squid, who bit into the spinal cord of its prey (*ibid.*, 74). A blazing attack scenario pictured Scomber, the immature mackerel, in an anchovy school beset by a bluefish. With one bite, he dismembered two anchovies, leaving their tails and heads to float away in "a sea of death" (*ibid.,* 84). A mad scramble of lesser fish caused leaps above the surface into the mouths of gulls, a fight for survival that Rachel termed "carnage ... clouded with a spreading stain," a sibilant equivalent of "blood" (*ibid.,* 82).

ANIMAL FABLES

The narrative packed action equal to a bloody Western. Startled by slaughter, Scomber sank 30 feet into deep sea murk and launched his own massacre of minuscule crustaceans, a pattern of survival he quickly embraced. With sympathy for his naiveté, Rachel followed his first encounter with a slippery, spasming comb jelly and recorded an unforeseen rescue by a sea trout. Sounds of gull laughter complemented the terror of launce or sand eels stranded on shore, "an abundance for all" (*ibid.,* 93). A brief glimpse of porpoises described their killing mackerel for sport.

Rachel's memories of a first voyage aboard the U.S. Fish and Wildlife trawler S.S. *Albatross III* retrieved glimpses of the predatory shark and anglerfish of Georges Bank. South of Nova Scotia, she viewed "slender shapes of sharks moving in to the kill" (Carson, 1954, n.p.). As nets arose from the deep, she witnessed the appetite of the anglerfish, which appeared with "the tails of two or three large cod ... protruding from their mouths" (*ibid.*). In the opening chapter of *Under the Sea Wind*, she featured the rat's sleek villainy as "lust for blood," an instinctive appetite for seabird eggs and their unfledged young. In a bid for balance, the narrative carried the shore hunt to the rat's meal of young terrapin and the blue heron's beak spearing a rat. In a tie to human behavior, the narrative commiserated with the roe shad, which struggled in a net before slowly strangling. Simultaneously, robber eels feasted on the "taste of fish blood," the plunder of gill nets (Carson, 1941, 19).

Sources

Bratton, Susan Power. "Thinking like a Mackerel: Rachel Carson's *Under the Sea-Wind* as a Source for a Trans-Ecotonal Sea Ethic." *Ethics and the Environment* 9:1 (April 2004): 1–22.

Carson, Rachel. "Memo to Mrs. Eales." Rachel Carson papers, 1942.

_____. "The Real World Around Us," address to the Theta Sigma Phi Matrix Table Dinner, *House of Life* (21 April 1954): 324–326.

_____. *Silent Spring.* Boston: Houghton Mifflin, 40th Anniversary Edition, 2002.

_____. *Under the Sea Wind: A Naturalist's Picture of Ocean Life.* New York: Simon & Schuster, 1941.

_____. "Undersea." *Atlantic Monthly* 160 (September 1937): 322–325.

Carson, R.L., "Giants of the Tide Rip Off Nova Scotia Again." *Baltimore Sunday Sun* (3 August 1938): 2.

_____. "It's Tick Time in Maryland." *Baltimore Sun* (18 July 1937): 5.

_____. "Numbering the Fish of the Sea." *Baltimore Sunday Sun* (24 May 1936): 5, 7.

_____. "Walrus and Carpenter Not Oysters' Only Foe." *Baltimore Sun* (21 August 1938): 2.

Presidential Medal of Freedom

On Monday, June 9, 1980, President Jimmy Carter presented the Medal of Freedom posthumously to Rachel Carson 16 years after her death. In company with photographer Ansel Adams, soprano Beverly Sills, actor John Wayne, and novelists

Eudora Welty and Robert Penn Warren and eight other recipients living and dead, the biologist held her own in public appeal and gratitude for her career. Carter commented that the medal was "the highest civilian award given in this nation" ("Freedom," 1980, 9). A white star mounted on a red and gold ensign and suspended from a blue grosgrain ribbon, the citation, instituted in 1963 by President John F. Kennedy's Executive Order 11085, acknowledged meritorious contributions to American culture and life and to the security and national concerns of citizens.

In a procession of 14 honorees or their proxies to the White House south lawn and a reception and lunch in the East Room, 28-year-old Roger Allen Christie represented his aunt and foster mother. President Carter accredited the 14 Americans with "broadening the scope of our vision" in varying endeavors and lauded their passion and commitment to deals of tolerance, literacy, and love ("Fourteen," 1980, 1). Ironically, Rachel's fame for ecological protest contrasted that of Admiral Hyman Rickover, father of the U.S. nuclear navy. In an editorial comment, Ernest B. Ferguson, writing for the *Baltimore Sun,* characterized the medal as "a handy way for a president to touch political or cultural constituencies he may have been neglecting" (Furgurson, 1980, K5). The editor noted the ridicule that industrialists heaped on a "mystical" female. He continued his encomium with "Rachel Carson was the catalyst … she was so right" (*ibid.*).

Sources

"Fourteen Received Medals of Freedom." *Salt Lake Tribune* (10 June 1980): 1.
"Freedom Medals Given." (Newport News, VA) *Daily Press* (June 10, 1980): 9.
Furgurson, Ernest B. "Another Spring." *Baltimore Sun* (15 June 1980): K5.

Radiation

From the Trinity project, the first A-bomb test outside Alamogordo in south central New Mexico, at 5:29 a.m. on July 16, 1945, Rachel feared the out-of-control advance of plutonium implosions. Beginning after World War II in February 1946, the military conducted 23 nuclear detonations at Bikini Atoll in Micronesia, which required the relocation of 167 islanders to safety. The subsequent use of ocean depths for disposing of contaminated waste alarmed the author for the government's flimsy investigation into safe ways to package hazardous materials to prevent leaks or breakage. During the Eisenhower administration, she mulled over the convergence of atmospheric blasts at Enewetak Atoll in the Marshall Islands on November 1, 1952, and falling radioactive residue on homes, land, organisms, and water. Most fearful, wild-eyed proposals to use nuclear power to dredge harbors and to carve a new canal across Panama gave no thought to harming the natural world.

At the onset of the nuclear arms race, the media shocked readers with reports of herd animals dying near hot zones and milk from dairy animals contaminated with radiation. Anticipating long-delayed cancers, birth defects, and endocrine and genetic harm from radioactive buildup in human tissue, Rachel charged government and science with folly in risking all life on earth on an experimental weapon, an international situation in Margaret Atwood's novel *The Handmaid's Tale.* By 1958, follow-up reports found fallout impacting the food chain and all who ate from it. She felt an urge to close her thinking to the insidious nature of atomic power, but she chose the role of oracle of the truth. Her candid writings and speeches angered industrialists and the scientific elite who minimized their responsibility and escalated jitters among middle-class Americans.

The Earth's Waters

In 1961, the author developed a new preface for the revised edition of *The Sea Around Us.* Of greatest concern, the dumping of atomic waste in the ocean's depths seemed ill-conceived considering the length of time sealed containers would continue to hold lethal by-products. She conjectured that using the sea as a dumping ground risked "rending the earth uninhabitable" (Carson, 1961, xi). Her appeal to female activists energized an ecological movement among ecofeminists concerned with the welfare of children and future generations.

In September 1962, Rachel opened *Silent Spring,* her censure of earth's contaminators, with carefully honed diction. She linked adjectives in a condemnation of the "irrecoverable ... chain of evil" that wreaked "irreversible" damage on living organisms (Carson, 2002, 6). The next sentence paired radiation with "sinister" chemicals, both of which permeated the human skeleton for life (*ibid.*). Extending the murky implications of "alchemy," she characterized synthetic chemicals as "devils" in a citation from Albert Schweitzer, the revered German ethicist and recipient of the 1952 Novel Peace Prize for his reverence for life.

A Moral Decision

In a personal essay dated December 2, 1962, the scientist justified her publication of *Silent Spring* in an era when nations tested atomic weapons. The treatise fused concern over pesticides with denunciation of reckless use of radioactive substances, both insidious violators of living tissue. She regretted the routine tone of fallout level listings in the daily press, which posed "an ominous meaning not only for [the average citizen] but for his children and generations to come" (Carson, "Reception," 1962). In testimony to congress on June 4, 1963, she theorized that the convection of air currents could carry radioactive debris as well as aerial spray unpredictable distances.

Rachel's equating of biocidal and radioactive threats pictured both as invisible assassins accumulating in human tissue at the whim of the hubristic military-industrial complex. Reprising the subject in an hour-long keynote address to 1,500 attendees of the Kaiser-Permanente symposium *Man Against Himself* in San Francisco on October 18, 1963, she identified more thoroughly "the byproducts of atomic fission" (Carson, "Pollution," 1963). She again stressed the planetary threat of the reckless deposit of radioactive tailings and pharmaceutical waste in the seas, even at their deepest points. From her jeremiad grew the field of ecotoxicology, which reviewed the effects of vapor and solvent, heavy metals, dioxin, pesticides and other carcinogens, radiation, and radioactive materials on environmental health.

See also World War II.

Sources

Carson, Rachel. "Environmental Hazards: Control of Pesticides and Other Chemical Poisons." Statement Before the Subcommittee on Reorganization and International Organizations of the Committee on Government Operations (4 June 1963): 206–219.

_____. "On the Reception of *Silent Spring*" (2 December 1962).

_____. "The Pollution of Our Environment," address to the Kaiser-Permanente Symposium *Man Against Himself*, San Francisco (18 October 1963).

_____. *The Sea Around Us: Revised Edition.* New York: Oxford University Press, 1961.

_____. *Silent Spring.* Boston: Houghton Mifflin, 40th Anniversary Edition, 2002.

Rome, Adam. "Rachel Carson and the Challenge of Greening Technology" in *Technology in America: a History of Individuals and Ideas.* Third ed. Cambridge: Massachusetts Institute of Technology, 2018.

Zaretsky, Natasha. *Radiation Nation: Three Mile Island and the Political Transformation of the 1970s.* New York: Columbia University Press, 2018.

Reproduction

With a motherly concern for animal survival, Rachel stressed the crucial connection between organisms and their nesting and spawning grounds. For models, she chose the hermaphroditic sea hare, a mollusk that extrudes 100,000 eggs in the wavy turtle grass off the Florida Keys, and the North American sage grouse, a plains bird dependent on Western sagebrush for spring nesting, egg incubation, and cover. To account for an 80 percent depletion of Atlantic coast shad, her February 1937 article "Shad Going Way of the Buffalo" for the Charleston, South Carolina, *News and Courier* outlined a perilous exuding of 100,000 eggs on muddy estuary basins, where "many fail to be fertilized, some are buried under mud" and others developed lethal fungus (Carson, 1937, 8C). Artificial egg fertilization on the Atlantic and Pacific coasts boosted commercial catches, especially in California. However, she concluded that "artificial propagation is ineffective" in halting shad reduction (*ibid.*).

In 1941, for the opening chapter of *Under the Sea Wind,* Rachel followed a mother diamondback terrapin along the high-tide line to Maytime egg laying in soft sand. In the post-nesting swim off the North Carolina Outer Banks, the freshwater amphibian refreshed herself with crabs and snails, paddling silently between a blue heron's legs. Behind the female, feeble hatchlings fed on egg yolks while the mother laid a new generation of young. The author contrasted the terrapin's procreative style with that of shad females, which deposited 100,000 roe in successive years in low salinity estuaries shadowed by cypress clumps. By Darwin's law of survival of the fittest, only one or two fish survived.

The Tender Young

The author's theme of vulnerability continued in the introduction to a spring blizzard on the Arctic barrens. "Six little owls-to-be" expired when their "pulsating red sacs" ceased to function (Carson, 1941, 36). Silverbar, the sanderling protagonist, had more luck padding a nest with willow leaves and standing guard over four eggs, which she observed during hatching. The phalarope, a slender shorebird, shaped a similar home of willow leaves and catkins, where the male bird warmed the young for two and a half weeks. Rachel built suspense at the coarse sounds of jaegers, the "scourge of all the tundra," who threatened a brood of snow bunting eggs (*ibid.,* 41). Birds ceased their calls as a means of concealing hatchlings from the enemy.

Chapter Two, "The Gull's Way," emphasized the unique spawning season of the mackerel Scomber, the author's favorite Atlantic species. In meticulous coverage of birthing, she pictured offshore grounds from Chesapeake Bay to Nantucket, Massachusetts, clouded by the outpouring of "hundreds of trillions" of fertilized eggs (*ibid.,* 72). In a territory patrolled by comb jellies, glassworms, and other raveners, the infant fish drifted "helplessly wherever the sea takes them" (*ibid.,* 75). The author specified a period of "furious activity" during growth, cell division, and the production of tissue and organs in the embryos. To offer the reader a microscopic view, on day three, she detailed the formation of cartilage into a spine, a bulging head, fins, and digestive system. Affectionately, she summarized the growth of the "tiny fishlets" to one-twentieth of an inch (*ibid.,* 78). Out of concern for his immature mouth and gill, she identified the yolk sac as a temporary food supply. Within three days, Scomber, still immature, learned to wiggle and float through the ocean currents.

The summation of earth's formation in *The Sea Around Us* pursued a useful comparative—the "miniature ocean within [the] mother's womb" that swathed land animals before birth (Carson, 1951, 28). The essay "The Moving Tides" introduced precise timing of animal spawning and reproduction and rising sea levels. As though cued by the orchestra leader, regeneration awakened in simple saltwater plants, alerting small fauna to "their own burst of multiplication" (*ibid.,* 30). For examples of profusion, the narrative cited European oysters, North African sea urchins, California grunion, and the palolo worms of Japan and Samoa, which release so many eggs that they discolored surface waters.

SURVIVING TO ADULTHOOD

In 1955, Rachel's reflections on marine turtles pinpointed the Tortugas, the Carolinas, Georgia, and Cape Sable in the Florida Everglades as the chief spawning grounds. Her descriptions of shore cycles incorporated high tide and foaming surf into the propagation of the periwinkle and horseshoe crab. In "The Rocky Shore," a chapter of *The Edge of the Sea,* she summarized the viviparous gestation and birth of the periwinkle from a cocoon that protects and feeds the young until its emergence as a mature mollusk. With maternal simplicity, the July 1958 essay "Our Ever-Changing Shore" for *Holiday* magazine pictured the female horseshoe crab's "burden of eggs, hundreds of tiny balls of potential life. An attending male fertilizes them" (Carson, 1958, 117). As though tucking infants into their cradles, the sea packed the embryos with sand, "grain by grain" and returned a month later to split egg membranes and set baby crabs free "in a mysterious and magical way" as they had for "a million—or a hundred million years" (*ibid.*).

The author's concern for regeneration inspired a 1959 letter to the editor of the *Washington Post* revealing the effects of aerial spraying on robins. Dispersal of deadly hydrocarbons on soil and vegetation killed songbirds and left survivors sterile. She altered her writing style in 1962 with a classic allegory "A Fable for Tomorrow," in which she envisioned farm conditions under which "hens brooded, but no chicks hatched" and pigs produced small litters that died within days (Carson, 2002, 2). Her jeremiad alerted readers to behavioral and chromosomal disruption in animals and adverse shifts in their population because of the dispersal of chemical pesticides that impaired reproduction.

In September 1962, at the beginning of Chapter Nine in *Silent Spring,* the author described the meticulous preparation by female salmon of spawning trenches in the Miramichi River, New Brunswick, and the birthing of half-inch salmon fry, which survived on nutriments from the yolk sac. Residue from a 1953 spraying of DDT (dichlorodiphenyltrichloroethane) to quell the spruce budworm killed the young salmon along with trout and birds. Her treatise warned of the decimation of greenery: "Clean cultivation and the chemical destruction of hedgerows and weeds are eliminating the last sanctuaries of … pollinating insects and breaking the threads that bind life to life" (Carson, 2002, 73). Ironically, critics labeled the biologist an overly emotional spinster. Chemical companies considered her ill equipped to speak for future generations or to critique reproduction abnormalities and environmental politics concerning neurodevelopment and the survival of the species.

See also "A Fable for Tomorrow."

Sources

Carson, Rachel. "Our Ever-Changing Shore." *Holiday* 24 (July 1958): 70–71, 117–120.
_____. *The Sea Around Us.* New York: Oxford University Press, 1951.
_____. *Silent Spring.* Boston: Houghton Mifflin, 2002.
_____. *Under the Sea Wind: A Naturalist's Picture of Ocean Life.* New York: Simon & Schuster, 1941.
_____. "Vanishing Americans." *Washington Post* (10 April 1959): A26.
Carson, R.L. "Shad Going the Way of the Buffalo." *Charleston News and Courier* (14 February 1937): 8C.
Ensor, Sarah. "Spinster Ecology: Rachel Carson, Sarah Orne Jewett, and Nonreproductive Futurity." *American Literature* 84:2 (2012): 409–435.
Lakhman, Sukhwinder S., and Arjun Dutta. "Endocrine Disruptive Chemicals: Silent Poison for Human Health." *EC Pharmacology and Toxicology* 7 (2019): 62–63.

Reptiles

Rachel's familiarity with reptiles and their embryo derived from lengthy research. She began work in August 1929 at age 22 in the Johns Hopkins University laboratory. At the suggestion of an adviser, she assembled specimens of semiaquatic turtles and crocodiles and dissected the heads of lizards and rattlesnakes, which she ordered by mail. During the year, the examination of cranial nerves, sensory organs, and brain tissue in the pit viper (*Crotalus horridus*) stalled, forcing her to change thesis topics. Thus, for the purpose of achieving an advanced degree in two years, the biologists altered the focus of a proposed master's thesis to squirrels. She finally settled on "The Development of the Pronephros during the Embryonic and Early Larval Life of the Catfish (*Ictalurus punctatus*)," to kidney development in embryonic rayfish obtained from hatcheries. Nonetheless, reptiles remained prominent in her writing career, especially consumers of contaminated insects, fish, snails, and small organisms in the food chain.

Field Work

The network of shore life in *Under the Sea Wind,* issued in 1941, incorporated the diamondback terrapin, a quiet resident who nested beyond the high-tide boundary. A startling *Gymnodinium brevis* red tide from November 1947 to January 1948, which killed large fish and sea turtles, energized "The Great Red Tide Mystery," her article for *Field and Stream.* In June 1950, she studied alligator holes, rocky caves among the willows in the Florida Everglades, where she sped over the wetlands by swamp buggy to survey tropical organisms. A year later in *The Sea Around Us,* she acknowledged the kinship of reptiles, amphibians, and fish to birds, mammals, and humankind, each of whom "carries in our veins a salty stream in which the elements sodium, potassium, and calcium are combined" (Carson, 1951, 13).

The interconnectivity of creation dominated Rachel's philosophy, reaching its acme in her classic treatise, *Silent Spring.* Her crowning achievement, released on September 27, 1962, recognized the threat of agrochemicals—aerial DDT (dichlorodiphenyltrichloroethane) spray, water treatments with DDD (dichlorodiphenyldichloroethane), dieldrin and heptachlor pesticides, and herbicides and fertilizers in city runoff. All liquid and powder poisons impacted groundwater and fouled reptile habitats in ponds and wetlands, making it nearly impossible for herpetologists to find uncontaminated specimens in the wild. The situation worsened during the Vietnam War from Agent Orange and napalm dispersal.

Rachel's Prophecy

Because of the effects of organic compounds on water, after 1970, aquatic creatures faced limited reproduction and species extinction at the rate of 60 percent of lizards and iguanas, anoles, geckos, skinks, salamanders, chameleons, crocodiles, alligators, frogs and toads, snakes, tortoises, and sea and freshwater turtles. Most seriously threatened, unique species in the lower Mississippi valley and Gulf Coast states faced total eradication. The American Society of Ichthyologists and Herpetologists warned that many organisms "occupy only small areas and therefore might readily be completely exterminated" (Carson, 2002, 141).

After the author died in April 1964, the 9,125-acre Maryland sanctuary she willed to the public shielded the sunfish, creek chub, American eel, trout, skate, piping plover, New England cottontail, wood frog, and spring peeper (*Pseudacris crucifer*), a favorite chirping chorus frog. The Rachel Carson National Wildlife Refuge incorporated diverse habitats on the rocky shore, vernal pools, tidal estuary, dunes, barrier strands, wetlands, pine bogs, and salt marshes. The natural homes provided a haven and sustenance for painted and snapping turtles, garter and redbelly snakes, and eastern black racers. Despite activist efforts, between 1970 and 2010, reptiles and other organisms decreased in population, with only 48 percent thriving.

See also Turtles.

Sources

Carson, Rachel. "The Development of the Pronephros during the Embryonic and Early Larval Life of the Catfish (*Ictalurus punctatus*)," master's thesis, Johns Hopkins University, 1932.

_____. *The Sea Around Us.* New York: Oxford University Press, 1951.

_____. *Silent Spring.* Boston: Houghton Mifflin, 40th Anniversary Edition, 2002.

_____. *Under the Sea Wind: A Naturalist's Picture of Ocean Life.* New York: Simon & Schuster, 1941.

Fellows, Valerie. "On Eagle's Wings." *Fish & Wildlife News* (Spring 2007): 20–21.

Rattner, Barnett A. "Wildlife and Environmental Pollution." *Animals and Human Society* 18 (September 2017): 472–482.

The Rocky Coast

In 1971, McCall Publishing issued an excerpt from Rachel's *The Edge of the Sea* as *The Rocky Coast,* a timeless study of nature's colors, shapes, textures, and movements. It featured the line drawings of artist Robert Warren "Bob" Hines, an Ohio native and employee of the U.S. Fish and Wildlife Service, and 50 photos—25 in color— by Charles Pratt, who also illustrated *The Sense of Wonder.* Seven years after Rachel's death from breast and bone cancer and a heart attack, the work appeared with a dedication to Dorothy and Stanley "Stan" Freeman, her Maine neighbors. During her 12 summer pilgrimages to Southport, she treasured the Freemans for sharing the allure of "the low-tide world" (Carson, 1971, v). Pratt's note on p. x admired the author's fervor for the Maine shore.

The narrative confirmed award-winning novelist Jim Lynch's description of the late author as "a passionate beachcomber … a hyper observant loner as well as an underdog" (Matthiessen, 2007, 39). She thrilled to the metamorphosis of the tide—"a place of unrest" on the surge and the peaceful ebb (Carson, 1971, 3). Of the illustrations, Phelps Dewey, a book reviewer for the *San Francisco Examiner & Chronicle,* admired Pratt's skill at picturing the "intricacy and sheer ingenuity of the struggle for life" (Dewey, 1972, 34).

WORDS AND PICTURES

The pairing of Pratt's first two illustrations contrasts striated rock ledges with the grandeur of rushing swells "leaping high over jutting rocks and running in lacy cascades of foam over the landward side of massive boulders" (Carson, 1971, 3). From rock and surf to wet shore, his lens captured the curious sandpiper browsing for food, one of Rachel's favorite avian beachcombers. Pratt introduced color in a profile of gray-green bearded lichen (*Usnea longissima*), a sturdy drape that veiled the green and yellow surfaces of rocks lying higgledy-piggledy among gravel. Long fronds of saltwater flora suggested combed green tresses, "stringy as mermaids' hair," outlining the ridges beneath them (*ibid.,* 5). The chartreuse limpet and red sphaerella, a low-level fungal plant, extended Pratt's palette to yellow and rust-red tones.

Essential to the photographer's tonal variations from glinting sea to multicolored stones, sea urchins, starfish, and smooth-sided crags patterned in Irish moss, algae, and gaping mussels and barnacles, careful light settings suggested odes to the sea. Amid group shots, the artist set portraits, such as the five legs of the brittle star, the evanescence of moon jelly, and the exploration of periwinkle in rockweed. The narrative ventured beyond the author's usual succinct descriptions to the puzzling larval stages of the rock barnacle, which eventually attached itself to a stationary rough surface "after a period of seeming deliberation" (*ibid.*, 30). J. Earle Bowden, a reviewer for the *Pensacola News*, admired the "mysterious, intensely alive world, showing exactly how the tides, the waves and the ocean current [revealed] patterns that go back for thousands of years" (Bowden, 1971, 4D).

SALTWATER PORTRAITS

Pratt's combination of a sloping granite ledge with serene waters emphasized the shore's longevity, ringed by concentric circles that Rachel made by wading through the surface. The layout inserted a glimpse of a human viewer, a head-and-shoulders pose of Rachel seated between forest and coast. The geometrics captured her solitary musings on seashore and land, stressing a lone scientist's contentment at a fairy cave on the Maine coast. The site hosted the marine specialist along with nephew Roger Allen Christie, who learned about ocean creatures from hands-on training in infancy and toddlerhood.

Robert Warren "Bob" Hines's articulate drawings added scientific authenticity to the narrative, especially the satellite formation of the crumb-of-bread sponge, the tubal habitat of the worm (*Potamilla reniformis*), and the symbiosis of skeleton shrimp with branching tubularia, a tufted hydroid that resembled a Christmas ornament. His portraits of sea squirts heightened the drama of open mouths awaiting food ferried in by the tide; a kelp's holdfast pictured root-like tentacles clinging to sea matter and remaining steady amid the pounding surf. A detailed sketch of emerging dog whelks disclosed the intricacy of seaside propagation. The hydroid clava, like a tussy-mussy of woods violets, demonstrated the flower shape of miniature fauna that clustered in blossoming colonies.

Sources

Bowden, J. Earle. "Review: *The Rocky Coast.*" *Pensacola News Journal* (26 September 1971): 4D.
Carson, Rachel. *The Rocky Coast.* New York: McCall, 1971.
Dewey, Phelps. "Review: *The Rocky Coast.*" *San Francisco Examiner & Chronicle* (2 January 1972): 34.
Matthiessen, Peter, ed. *Courage for the Earth: Writers, Scientists, and Activists Celebrate the Life and Writing of Rachel Carson.* New York: Mariner, 2007.
"Review: *The Rocky Coast.*" *Detroit Free Press* (5 December 1971): 5B.

Science Advisory Committee

In her last year of life, Rachel composed an overview of President John F. Kennedy's 46-page Science Advisory Committee report, "Use of Pesticides," issued May 15, 1963. Members of the committee included specialists from Harvard, Johns Hopkins, Connecticut Agricultural Experiment Station, Massachusetts Audubon Society, Bell Laboratories, and the universities of Chicago, Colorado, New York, Stanford, and Pennsylvania. The outline classed hydrocarbon compounds as hazards, described distribution and biological effects, and specified toxicity of compounds that impacted quality foodstuffs in a period of "rapid population growth" ("Use of," 1963, 5).

Committee members, led by Chairman Jerome B. Wiesner, a professor of electrical engineering at MIT, vindicated the charges published in the author's *Silent Spring* and heatedly debated by industrialists and the media. Appointees recommended urgent research and comprehensive study into side effects of each formula, especially to water and wildlife. In addition, they required sensible safeguards to minimize risk: education in pesticide use, marketing controls, warning labels, improved equipment, and publication of tolerance levels. According to the *Journal of Science Policy and Governance*, the "sea change" in opinion policy "spawned massive growth in the government's science-based regulatory apparatus" (Berman & Carter, 2018, 4).

NATIONAL EMERGENCY

At a time when 75 children and 75 adults per year died from pesticide poisoning, California, the largest user of agrochemicals by state, reported 1,100 worker illnesses. The final tabulation of compounds reached nearly 500 in "54,000 formulations," ranging from the less dangerous nicotine, pyrethrum, and rotenone to the toxic heavy metals arsenic, copper, and lead (*ibid.*, 9). The fact that the chief adviser rated toxic residues, whether a single type or multiple sources, more dangerous than nuclear fallout gave Rachel hope that citizens would awaken from complacency and combat the drift of poisons in air, water, and animal movements. She impugned the evidence concerning moth-proofing and garden toxins, which derived from the U.S. Department of Agriculture rather than a bureau of human health.

Rachel's data helped to shape policy. She demanded immediate registration of toxins and interim protection until a consortium of government agencies could complete a comprehensive program. She especially necessitated a control on the amount of poison allowed in consumables, such as dairy products and fresh fruit and vegetables. She extolled publication of corroborating evidence attesting to gradual build-up of DDT (dichlorodiphenyltrichloroethane) and other contaminants in the body, and promoted toxicology and poison diagnosis in medical training.

ADVISABLE REMEDIES

Straddling the line between extreme positions, the president's appointees approved use of insecticides only against vectors of human disease. The 23 men declared the failure of past extermination strategies to control black-headed budworm, fire ants, gypsy moths, Japanese beetles, and white-fringed weevils, a threat to citrus, grapes, sweet potatoes, plums, and cotton and other farm and garden crops throughout the Western Hemisphere as far south as Argentina. To stem the dangers of indiscriminate spread of poisons, the president prepared "legislative and technical proposals" for congress ("Use of," 1963, 4).

White House recommendations called for more monitoring and data collection and inter-departmental cooperation between agriculture, interior, and health, education and welfare. The president requested data on human tolerance to aldrin, chlordane, dieldrin, heptachlor, lindane, methoxychlor, and parathion, a cause of blindness, convulsions, coma, brain damage, paralysis, and cancer. Rachel declared herself satisfied with the report for its scrupulous objectivity and coverage of the issues and appreciative of the president's involvement and concern for the environment.

See also Kennedy, John F.; Pesticides.

Sources

Berman, Emily, and Jacob Carter. "Policy Analysis: Scientific Integrity in Federal Policymaking Under Past and Present Administrations." *Journal of Science Policy and Governance* 13:1 (2018).

Carson, Rachel. "Letter to Walter C. Bauer" (12 November 1963).

_____. "She Started It All—Here's Her Reaction." *New York Herald Tribune* (19 May 1963).

Nieves Autumn. "Rachel Carson: Proving the Competency of Femininity." *Women Leading Change* 3:2 (10 October 2018).

"Sound Pesticides Report." (Staunton, VA) *News Leader* (20 May 1963): 4.

"Use of Pesticides." Washington, D.C.: White House, 15 March 1963, 1–44.

Sea

Rachel Carson earned renown as poet laureate of earth's watery mantle, which she saluted as mutable, yet unconquerable and enduring. From more than 1,000 print materials and a decade of correspondence with prominent specialists, she formulated essays that integrated diverse scientific topics, some released from secret World War II government documents on oceanography. In the estimation of analyst Neil W. Browne, an ecological writer, her sea trilogy—*Under the Sea Wind* (1941), *The Sea Around Us* (1951), and *The Edge of the Sea* (1955)—surveyed "an astonishing interface of ecosystems" (Browne, 2007, 86).

At a gathering of the *New York Herald Tribune* in October 1951 at the Astor Hotel, the speaker cherished intriguing ocean mysteries and hoped that they would never be solved. In the last year of college, she wrote a class essay imagining the grandeur and boom of "long lazy swells that rolled in on the shallow beach" and "the menacing reefs beneath" (Sterling, 1970, 45). The astonishingly accurate sense impressions preceded field experience in June 1929 on Cape Cod, Massachusetts, at the Woods Hole Biological Laboratory, where science students had collaborated since 1871 on the mysteries of the deep. In a February 1937 article on shad depletion along the Atlantic seaboard for the Charleston, South Carolina, *News and Courier,* she admitted that movements of freshwater shad to salt water "is a secret known only to themselves," one of multiple mysteries locked in the oceans (Carson, 1937, 8C).

In July 1937, Rachel ventured out of comfortable anonymity as R.L. Carson to mail to *Atlantic* the article "Undersea," previously called "World of Waters." She introduced the four-page précis with a comparison of explorations of Antarctica and Mount Everest to surveys of the oceans. She warned, "The sea knows how to guard its secrets well," an indirect reference to the data she had researched (Carson, 1937, 322). For added mystery, she referred to earth's waters as *mare incognita,* the Latin for "unknown sea." An admirer, historian Henrik Willen van Loon, compared his enjoyment of her essay to a reading of Jules Verne's fantasy *20,000 Leagues under the Sea.*

At Beaufort, North Carolina, in fall 1938, the biologist, accompanied by her mother and nieces Marjorie and Virginia, rented a cottage among dunes, ponds, and wetlands pools, which she explored at night by flashlight. Rachel viewed the museum and aquarium, read surveys of aquaculture and commercial fishing, and toured the Shackleford Banks barrier islands and salt marshes on the Cape Lookout National Seashore. On her own time, she chatted with pier fishermen and gathered details of an interdependent coastal environment comprising sea-dwelling flora and fauna. Moved by mystic beauty, she concluded "that no single marine creature or its habitat could be understood in isolation" (Barnet, 2018, 25).

Oceanic Revelations

In the Foreword to *Under the Sea Wind,* Rachel formed a world of sound, color, and thrilling new life in three liquid locales—seashore, open water, and bottom of the abyss. She extolled a pervasive stretch of open water—"various, strangely beautiful and wholly unknown to all but a fortunate few" (Carson, 1941, 4). The narrative followed changes in a Massachusetts harbor as August gave way to September and mackerel sought depths "sharply salt and clean and cold" (*ibid.,* 97). Introducing Scomber, an anthropomorphic mackerel, and his fellow sea characters to waters oxygenated by surging, throbbing currents, Rachel added percussion to her words. In tune with the entourage into the deep, her tone took on a melodic edge as "the abyss, the primeval bed of the sea" where icy waters creep, "deliberate and inexorable as the flow of time itself" (*ibid.,* 156).

For *The Sea Around Us,* in 1951, the author took a maternal persona based on global myth. From the "all-providing, all-embracing mother sea," she researched the value of marine resources for providing food and minerals, regulating tides, and offering health, recreation, knowledge, heritage, and inspiration (Carson, 1951, 23). Her psalm to primeval earth and the upheaval yielding its first mountain ranges took on the sonority and gravity of Genesis 1. For structure, she divided ages of earth's formation into geologic epoch, which recur throughout her canon:

Cambrian	600,000,000 BCE	calcium-rich oceans fluctuate, inundating most of North America
Ordovician	500,000,000 BCE	saltwater covers over half of North America
Silurian	440,000,000 BCE	shallow seas engulf eastern North America, forming Niagara Falls
Devonian	400,000,000 BCE	quartz rock forms; ice erodes as vascular plants invade land
Carboniferous	350,000,000 BCE	oceans invade central North America
Permian	270,000,000 BCE	saltwater engulfs Germany and western North America
Triassic	225,000,000 BCE	upthrusts shape the Appalachian Mountain chain
Jurassic	180,000,000 BCE	seawater inundates California and Oregon and deposits thick salt layers on the ocean floor
Cretaceous	135,000,000 BCE	England's chalk cliffs and the Hawaiian island chain form while the rest of Europe and half the Western Hemisphere and northern Africa lie under water

Tertiary	70,000,000 BCE	the Himalayas, Alps, Andes, and Rocky Mountains emerge; limestone and the island of Bermuda form. The Gulf Stream begins flowing around 60,000,000 BCE
Pleistocene	1,000,000 BCE	glaciers alter sea levels at the Grand Banks of Newfoundland and Dogger Bank, forming deep canyons and valleys and the mid–Atlantic island of Ascension.

Constant changes in sea levels and division into temperature zones forced life forms to adapt or die. Human bodies retained in their circulatory and skeletal systems the proportions of calcium, potassium, and sodium that filled the sea. Of the availability of elements, she declared, "Nothing is wasted in the sea; every particle of material is used over and over again, first by one creature, then by another" (*ibid.,* 42).

PLANETARY UNITY

Biographer Andrea Barnet outlined Rachel's coming-to-knowledge, at age 31, of the holistic study of nature. At the heart of her environmental ethic lay earth's waters and its denizens. In a January 27 speech accepting the 1952 National Book Award from the National Book Foundation, she justified her melodic prose: "No one could write truthfully about the sea and leave out the poetry" (Carson, "National Book Award," 1952). Aboard the agency trawler S.S. *Albatross III* in July 1953, the esthetic of marine splendor caused her to observe, "Ours is a water world, dominated by the immensity of the sea" (Carson, 1953).

At the issuance of *The Sea Around Us,* Rachel's preface declared global seas "the last great frontier of Earth," an echo of "our last outpost" from the chapter "Our Ever-Changing Shore" (Carson, 1951, xvii; 1958, 119). The speaker relayed to the American Association of University Women on June 22, 1956, an innate love of the watery world: "That fascination was always there, calling me, even long before I had ever seen the ocean" ("Rachel," 1956, 19). She spoke straightforward imperatives about saltwater journeys: "An ocean voyage, or a trip to the shore means so much more if you know a few things about the sea" (Lear, 1997, 202).

UNDERWATER RESEARCH

With data including photos of a coring tube from the Lamont Geological Observatory, a mountain 9,600 feet above the Gulf of Alaska, the Lydonia Canyon off Georges Bank, and the U.S. Navy bathyscaphe *Trieste* after page 64 in *The Sea Around Us,* Rachel gathered data and theories in the mid-to-late 1940s concerning the existence of life on the sea floor. From the soundings of fathometers, she looked ahead to the invention of deep-water cameras and the correlation of photos such as the image of starry creatures and tracks following p. 64 with echograms, sonograms of the ocean's abyssal. In 1947, evidence of thick lava plains southeast of Sri Lanka defied coring missions. She anticipated the evidence obtained by future seine and core samples, dredging, and television cameras and acknowledged the gradual sounding of deep trenches around the globe, particularly the Mindanao trench east of the Philippines and the Tuscarora off Japan. Cartographers gathering the measurements pieced together details of declivities and volcanic islands, aiming toward "an accurate and detailed relief map of the ocean basins," especially for the Arctic realm (Carson, 1951, 64).

Through imagination, the biologist allowed readers to think like marine creatures and thus to identify with an aqua-centric life. Among her main apprehensions, she feared that post–World War II irresponsibility with radioactive waste since 1946 despoiled a global "chemical reservoir" in sedimentation that took millennia to dissolve (Carson, 1951, 81). Her concern for the pillaging caused by trawlers and whaling and the fouling of oceans by cruise ships, oil spills, and garbage scows caused critics to label her writing over-anxious and shrill, evidence of stereotypical femininity. In "Nature Fights Back," a 1962 essay in *Silent Spring,* the wonder of barnacles on shore rocks and the "pulsing, ghostly forms" of a jellyfish swarm retrieved from field work her awe at the fecundity of sea life. Lack of the macho will to control nature and set it to work for profit indicated her disinterest in politics and personal empowerment.

See also Darwin, Charles; Ecology; *Under the Sea Wind*; Waves.

Sources

Barnet, Andrea. *Visionary Women: How Rachel Carson, Jane Jacobs, Jane Goodall, and Alice Waters Changed Our World.* New York: Ecco, 2018.
Browne, Neil W. *The World in Which We Occur: John Dewey, Pragmatist Ecology, and American Ecological Writing in the Twentieth Century.* Tuscaloosa: University of Alabama Press, 2007.
Carson, Rachel. "National Book Award Acceptance Speech." (29 January 1952), New York.
_____. "Our Ever-Changing Shore." *Holiday* 24 (July 1958): 70–71, 117–120.
_____. "Preface." *The Sea Around Us,* 2nd ed. New York: Oxford University Press, 1961, xvii–xxiv.
_____. "The Real World Around Us," address to the Theta Sigma Phi Matrix Table Dinner (21 April 1954), Columbus, Ohio.
_____. *The Sea Around Us.* New York: Oxford University Press, 1951.
_____. *Silent Spring.* Boston: Houghton Mifflin, 40th Anniversary Edition, 2002.
_____. Speech, *New York Herald Tribune Book Review,* Astor Hotel (1 October 1951).
_____. *Under the Sea Wind: A Naturalist's Picture of Ocean Life.* New York: Simon & Schuster, 1941.
_____. "Undersea." *Atlantic Monthly* 160 (September 1937): 322–325.
Carson, R.L. "Shad Going the Way of the Buffalo." *Charleston News and Courier* (14 February 1937): 8C.
Lear, Linda J. *Rachel Carson: Witness for Nature.* New York: Henry Holt, 1997.
"Rachel Carson Wins Achievement Award." *AAUW Journal* (October 1956): 19.
Sterling, Philip. *Sea and Earth: The Life of Rachel Carson.* New York: Crowell, 1970.

The Sea Around Us

Drawing on oceanographic methods developed during World War II, Rachel achieved what Billy Mills, a literary critic for the London *Guardian,* described as "the first, and still perhaps the best science bestseller … a quiet tour de force" (Mills, 2014). The 1951 blockbuster and a second edition in 1960 presented sea life via dynamic rhetoric, citations from Genesis and Job, maps, and photos. Human dependence on the oceans motivated her research into sandy stretches, coral reefs, undersea mountain ranges, and rocky shorelines. With a personalized approach, she abandoned biological hierarchy to introduce readers to nature's rhythms, especially lunar cycles, which govern tides.

The author pondered various titles—*Empire of the Sea, Sea Without End, Return to the Sea, The Story of the Ocean*—before settling on *The Sea Around Us.* The text examined the beginnings and geological bases of oceans and divided the survey into "Mother Sea," "The Restless Sea," and "Man and the Sea about Him." Natural history writer Ann Haymond Zwinger declared the watery expanse the star of a classic work of the New Wave: "She made Ocean itself the persona, and she its amanuensis" (Zwinger, 1989, xxiv). Out of admiration for the author, Robert Williams, a book reviewer for the Paterson, New Jersey, *Morning Call,* placed the work "on a plane with the sublime" (Williams, 1952, 16).

A Theatrical Tone

Epic drama dominated Rachel's biography of earth. Setting earth's foundation in the solar system at two and a half billion years ago, the narrative pictured the moon as the result of a universal cataclysm—a "great tidal wave of earthly substance, torn off into space" (Carson, 1951, 20). With a naturalist's self-restraint, Rachel stopped short of declaring the planetary upheaval the source of earth's oceans and continents. The splendor of creation produced centuries of rain, a source of dissolved minerals that made terrestrial basins "ever more bitter with the salt of the continents" (*ibid.,* 22). For the work's engrossing reportage, the *Boston Globe* printed excerpts in its July 25 and 26, 1951, issues.

Readers of excerpts in the June 1951 *New Yorker* bombarded the office with more letters than any former article had generated. Anticipation mounted in the public, including radio announcer Walter Winchell, a Carson fan. On July 1, 1951, the *New York Times* reviewed *The Sea Around Us* as its lead story under the title "And His Wonders in the Deep; A Scientist Draws an Intimate Portrait of the Winding Sea and Its Churning Life." In the opinion of Jonathan Norton Leonard, science reviewer for *Time* magazine, the author combined the accuracy of a scientist with the lush prose of a poet. The *New York Times* rated the book the outstanding work of the year. Oxford University Press issued a reprint on July 2, 1951. Book-of-the-Month Club selected *The Sea Around Us* for the June alternate.

Rachel's Notoriety

On April 14, 1952, *Life* magazine featured an 18-page excerpt entitled "The Edge of the Sea." Baltimore artist Rudolph Freund illustrated the text with glimpses of a diamondback terrapin, eels, spawning shad, sanderlings, a snowy egret, petrel and jaeger, and a dramatic view of gulls swooping over inlets, ponds, and sand bars. Freund's presentation of a blue heron capturing a rat enacted the author's concept of the chain of life, the theme of a subsequent image of gulls devouring shad, a bald eagle diving for a mullet, and a channel bass dining on a ghost crab. The article concluded that mortality results in recycling: "One dies, another lives, as the precious elements of life are passed on and on in endless chains" (Carson, 1952, 81).

In 1961, the reissue of *The Sea Around Us* became a bestseller with 40,000 pre-publication copies reserved. Within two decades, Rachel's work appeared in translation on five continents:

Assen, Holland	London, England
Belgrade and Koper, Yugoslavia	Helsinki, Finland
Tehran, Iran	Reykjavik, Iceland
Rangoon, Burma	Stockholm, Sweden
Sao Paulo, Brazil	Copenhagen, Denmark
Lahore, West Pakistan	Cairo, Egypt
Gutenberg, Switzerland	Tel Aviv, Israel
Madras, Tamil	Bangkok, Thailand
New Delhi, India	Athens, Greece
Florence and Turin, Italy	Warsaw, Poland
Mexico City, Mexico	Amsterdam, Holland
Paris, France	Stuttgart and Munich, Germany
Rome, Italy	Seoul, Korea
Tokyo, Japan	

Young adult versions met the needs of tweens in New York, London, Stockholm, Paris, Milan, Copenhagen, Antwerp, Mexico, and Ravensburg, Germany. A subsequent excerpt, "Moving Tides," appeared in the July 1963 edition of *Motor Boating*. Rachel anthologized her work in an omnibus, featuring *Under the Sea-Wind, The Sea Around Us,* and *The Edge of the Sea* in publication from London in 1964, 1967, and 1968. Forty years later, editors Roger Meiners from the University of Texas, Pierre Desrochers at the University of Toronto, and Andrew Morriss at the University of Illinois lionized *The Sea Around Us* as a precursor and energizer of the ecological movement (Meiners, Desrochers, Morriss, 2012).

Sources

Carson, Rachel. "The Edge of the Sea." *Life (*14 April 1952): 64–81.
_____. *The Sea Around Us*. New York: Oxford University Press, 1951.
Fellows, Valerie, and Joshua Winchell. "Returning to the Water." *Fish & Wildlife News* (Spring 2007): 26–28.
Meiners, Roger, Pierre Desrochers, and Andrew Morriss, eds. *Silent Spring at 50: The False Crises of Rachel Carson*. Washington, D.C.: Cato Institute, 2012.
Mills, Billy. "A Book for the Beach." *The Guardian* (28 July 2014).
Williams, Robert. "Review: *The Sea Around Us*." (Paterson, NJ) *Morning Call* (26 January 1952): 15–16.
Zwinger, Ann. "Introduction" to *The Sea Around Us: Special Edition*. New York: Oxford University Press, 1989.

The Sea Around Us: Man and the Sea About Him

In the third section of *The Sea Around Us*, Rachel's most didactic chapter introduced an erudite purity that called humankind to task for trivializing oceanography. Her views on reshaping of ocean currents dismissed notions of redirecting inland the warmth of the Gulf Stream, one of a host of pipe dreams that placed humankind in dominion over creation. She explained the essentials of seawater absorption and radiation of solar heat and valued sea currents as stabilizers of temperature and creators of the Atacama and Kalahari deserts. The regulation of heat and cold accounted for the lichens and mosses that survived in the Antarctic and explained the reduction of megafauna to birds, mosquitoes, flies, and mites.

Rachel contrasted Arctic summers and temperatures warm enough to support flowers on the tundra, "a world apart from the Antarctic" (Carson, 1951, 162). She abridged the theories of Swedish hydrographer and oceanographer Sven Otto Pettersson (1848–1941), who graphed the currents of the Baltic and North seas and their effects on weather and herring fisheries, the Pettersson family business. Herring had supplied the oily forage meat from 3000 BCE for fermenting, curing, pickling, smoking, drying, or eating raw. From observations at his laboratory at Gulmarfiord on the southwestern coast, he hypothesized that deep moon waves from the North Atlantic established tides every 12 hours. In 1912, he theorized that climatic cycles influenced human history, notably, the rise of the Vikings in the late 700s CE and Eric the Red in the late 900s and the routes of their 14 boats to southwestern Greenland in 986.

NARRATING DEEP TIME

Much of the author's storytelling incorporates earthly cataclysm that marked evolutionary epochs. In southern Europe, drastic shifts in climate precipitated famine, storms, and death. In the north, warmer temperatures drew yellowlegs, albatross, orioles, crossbills, warblers, and cliff swallows while suppressing seasonal influxes of larks, plovers, and sandpipers. Likewise, shifts in climate enticed to Greenland's shores cod-like ling fish, haddock, and bottom-feeding cusk, an endangered species. As earth warmed from the last Pleistocene glaciation around 1,000,000 BCE, glaciers and snowfields shrank.

The narrative demonstrated the dispersal of vanadium, iodine, bromine, magnesium, lithium, potassium, sodium, and borax via flooding, brines, and winds carrying cyclic salt, a source of chlorine in sea foam blown into river water. She cited as examples the monsoons bearing granules inland to northern India's Sambhar Salt Lake west of Jaipur and the bitter salts left in Israel's Dead Sea in the Jordan Rift Valley. The same weather patterns deposited petroleum in the Black Sea and Norwegian fiords and under Oklahoma oilfields and salt domes along the Gulf of Mexico in Louisiana and Texas. Extraction of precious oil reserves from ocean basins and under arctic ice required sophisticated equipment.

EARLY SEA LITERATURE

The final chapter surveyed early topographical writings and fragments about seafaring. Rachel highlighted from the list the voyages of Greek geographer and explorer Pytheas of Marseilles, who traveled Europe's Atlantic in 325–300 BCE as far north as northern Great Britain, Ireland, the Baltic Sea, and the Arctic Circle. She named Ottar, the ninth-century Viking sea pilot from far northern Halogaland, Norway, as the next credible sea venturer, whaler, and walrus hunter on the White Sea. As early as 3000 BCE, Polynesian pilots sailing by the stars preceded the voyager Captain James Cook, who observed boobies and an albatross off Madagascar in 1776 for clues to navigation.

Critics extolled Rachel's second sea book for its splendid narration of earth's story and her tutorial on movements of the waters. Philip Burnham, book editor for *Commonweal,* declared *The Sea Around Us* "a work of radical simplification, organization and popularization" (Burnham, 1951, 388). The cohesion and energy of Rachel's sea biography preceded her greatest achievement. Poet Billy Mills, in a book review for the London *Guardian,* declared, "Without *The Sea Around Us, Silent Spring* might never have been written" (Mills, 2014).

See also Folklore.

Sources

Burnham, Philip. "Review: *The Sea Around Us." Commonweal* 54 (27 July 1951): 387–389.
Carson, Rachel. *The Sea Around Us.* New York: Oxford University Press, 1951.
Mills, Billy. "A Book for the Beach." *Guardian* (28 July 2014).
Zwinger, Ann. "Introduction" to *The Sea Around Us: Special Edition.* New York: Oxford University Press, 1989.

The Sea Around Us: Mother Sea

Rachel's penchant for storytelling reached a high point in the opening stave of *Mother Sea,* which she entitled "The Gray Beginnings." By positioning a chart and follow-up details of evolution, she drew readers into the spectacle of life's progressions, from protoplasm to variant beasts and the plants that feed them. The second stave, "The Pattern of the Surface," turned to novelist Herman Melville's apothegm for description of soulful stirrings in the deep before introducing the pulsing colors of myriad jellyfish. For verification, she cited Norwegian ethnographer Thor Heyerdahl, whose summer 1947 Pacific raft adventure *Kon-Tiki: Across the Pacific in a Raft* echoed her fascination at myriad diatoms and plankton pursued by leaping squid.

With a blend of the physical with a supernal notion of a universal mother, the author related a creation story on a par with that of Japan, Hawaii, and plains Indians. She chose identifiable marvels that differentiated an expansive water world into the memorable life centers of Oceanus. Each owed its existence to the planet and "parent sun" (Carson, 1951, 2). Her narrative implied the management of a higher power, which she called the "all being" (*ibid.,* 7). She stated, "The continents had no life. There was little to induce living things to come ashore, forsaking their all-embracing, all-providing mother sea" (*ibid.,* 8). She pictured the creation of the placid Sargasso Sea north of Bermuda from "the great currents of the North Atlantic that encircle it" and the accumulation of 10 million tons of seaweed, in which hid the sargassum fish pictured after p. 64 (Carson, 1951, 38).

A SHELTERING HOME

In tandem with the Gulf Stream, the Sargasso became what Judith Madera, a literary expert on staff at Wake Forest University, characterized as a "drifting biome that reorients continental bearings" (Madera, 2017, 294). The mass sheltered flying fish, eels, sea slugs, and vulnerable microorganisms that relied on the sargassum weed for sustenance and shelter. Part of their success required skillful mimicry of fronds and berries to disguise them from predators. Rachel offered more than one theory about the source of seaweeds, some from as far away as Florida and the Caribbean.

In an inspection of the deep in "The Sunless Sea," Rachel envisioned waters stratifying in liquid tiers, each stratum capable of supporting specific biota. On the way to the abyss, she concluded that "the food supply is different and in general poorer than for the layer above" (*ibid.,* 59). A few anachronisms—frillsharks (*Chlamydoselachus anguineus*) and coelacanths (*Latimeria menadoensis*)—retained their anatomical features from the Devonian Era extending from 400,000,000–350,000,000 BCE. A photo of a fossilized trilobite detailed the finely ribbed shape of an ancient crustacean of the Cambrian Era from 541,000,000 BCE.

The author's musings about the Pleistocene Age (1,000,000 BCE) revealed theories about undersea declivities carved out by ice melt, freshwater, and mud outflows from global deltas at the Hudson, San Francisco, Salinas, Mississippi, Columbia, Congo, Indus, and Ganges rivers. She marveled at the ages of sedimentation of sand, mud, rocks, shells, meteoric debris, skeletons, and volcanic dust in "so enormous an amount in the life of earth and sea" (*ibid.,* 77). The impression of great alluvial weight preceded her supposition that "the crust of the earth sagged under its load" (*ibid.,* 79).

UNIQUE BIOSPHERES

The final staves informed readers of the fragility of island habitats and the alternating effects of rising seas from increased sedimentation and the lowering of estuary levels by glaciation, which isolated water in great ice slabs. Her most famous segment, "The Birth of an Island," investigated the singularity of small habitats and the types of flora and fauna occupying them. English fabulist Jacquetta Hawkes, in a respectful review for the London *Observer,* admired the narrative grace of the "slow, incalculable peopling" of islands through "the agency of currents, winds, birds, and men" (Hawkes, 1951, 7). With an ecofeminist touch, the author probed human ignorance of biospheric fragility, especially the species that existed nowhere else but a single atoll.

The introduction of exotic animals and plants and exploitive sheep, goats, cattle, cats, and rodents accounted for the rapid extinction of one-of-a-kind island birds and plants. At chapter's end, Rachel revealed her zeal for ongoing research and for the variant theories of how currents chiseled water courses in sea basins. Her curiosity about "tides so vast they are invisible and uncomprehended by the senses of man" revealed an insight into geologic eras grounded in scientific readings and her scholarly surmise (*ibid.,* 106). Jack Scott, a British Columbian columnist for the *Vancouver Sun,* lauded Rachel's intuitive love of the sea and her sensitivity to "the long vistas of its history in which the existence of man is but a moment of time" (Scott, 1953, 2).

See also Fossils; History; Islands; Sea; Topography.

Sources

Carson, Rachel. *The Sea Around Us.* New York: Oxford University Press, 1951.
Deaton, Thomas. "Spirituality and the Environment: Learning from People of the Whale." *Ashen Egg* 7 (2019): 10–18.

Hawkes, Jacquetta. "Mother Sea." London *Observer* (11 November 1951): 7.

Madera, Judith. "The Birth of an Island: Rachel Carson's The Sea Around Us." *Women's Studies Quarterly* 45:1/2 (Spring/Summer 2017): 292–298.

Scott, Jack. "Mother Sea." *Vancouver Sun* (29 July 1953): 2.

Seager, Joni. "Radical Observation." *Women's Studies Quarterly* 45:1/2 (2017): 269–277.

The Sea Around Us: The Restless Sea

In the second section, "The Restless Sea," of *The Sea Around Us,* Rachel tackled deep time, high seas, and folklore about oceans. Gaining momentum with specific examples, she reviewed the one-of-a-kind qualities of the Bay of Fundy, Gulf Stream, Chesapeake Bay, and Humboldt Current. To dramatize the thunderous effects of surf strong enough to engulf villages and to hurl boulders and smash piers and lighthouses, the narrative examined the constant erosion of Cape Cod and the dwindling coastline of Great Britain. Photos on p. 160 displayed the damage a seismic wave on April 1, 1946, did to the Scotch Cape Light at Unimak, Alaska's largest Aleutian island. The panorama summarized evidence of power that refused human efforts to harness or control it.

The pedagogical quality of *The Sea Around Us* reached a significant height in the author's introduction of sea currents, tidal oscillation, and planetary influences on ocean levels and creature reproduction, especially the power of both sun and moon. Essential to the author's introduction of sea motility, details examined specifics. She outlined the nature and causes of swells and identified land masses off northern Scotland—the Orkney and Shetland islands—as the world's most treacherous waters to navigate because of clashing currents. Allied with tossing waves, seismic upheavals, and fearful hurricanes and monsoons, she inserted the result of grinding, leveling crests on cliffs, coral rock, and sea caves, a pounding she pictured on p. 160.

High surfs became a fierce reshaping force on Morocco, St. Helena, and the Aleutian Islands. Admitting the limitations of science in 1951, Rachel stated, "We can only sense that in the deep and turbulent recesses of the sea are hidden mysteries far greater than any we have solved," a fact that piqued her curiosity (Carson, 1951, 124). The frank assessment endeared the narrative to readers who declined overconfident texts that concealed the holes in oceanography. Instead of hiding behind the sesquipedalian vocabulary of the sciences to characterize the mystique of nighttime phosphorescence, she agreed with Norwegian adventurer Thor Heyerdahl and English philosopher Charles Darwin that "the dark sea prompts catachresis, a need for new languages" (Madera, 2017, 295).

Crucial to the author's frank overview, data on temperature and Benjamin Franklin's charting of the Gulf Stream engendered an academic atmosphere without squelching a tone of upbeat investigation. Contrasts with Atlantic and Pacific features answered reader questions about the nature of regions around island clusters and at each end of the Panama Canal. The contrasts posed reasons why the seas maintained variant reputations for ease of navigation and coastal bird life. Academic respect for the cause and direction of tides brought to a conclusion perhaps her most scholarly writing about water movement and their effects on planetary health. Philip Burnham, an owner, editor, and book reviewer for *Commonweal,* viewed the pacing and tone of *The Sea Around Us* as "a rather dreamy narcotic to minds and consciences overburdened with the earthy concerns of day to day" (Burnham, 1951, 387).

See also Tides; Weather.

Sources

Burnham, Philip. "Review: *The Sea Around Us*." *Commonweal* 54 (27 July 1951): 387–389.
Carson, Rachel. *The Sea Around Us*. New York: Oxford University Press, 1951.
Madera, Judith. "The Birth of an Island: Rachel Carson's *The Sea Around Us*." *Women's Studies Quarterly* 45:1/2 (Spring/Summer 2017): 292–298.

Seasons

Like early humankind, Rachel found reassurance and solace in natural cycles for their dependability. For the opening chapter of *Under the Sea Wind*, in 1941, she focused on the changes and their effects on "all the movements of birds, fish, shrimp, and other water creatures" (Carson, 1941, 4). By May, diamondback turtles initiated annual nesting, which yielded young each August. Essential to survival, the "food-stuffs—the starches and the fats—had been stored away in the seeds to nourish the precious embryos," constituting a parent's summer task to feed the future (*ibid.*, 46). She perceived the spreading of pollen and energizing of chlorophyll as completed by fall, when summer began to wither and the colors mutated from green to red and yellow.

In token of snowy months to come, the narrative pictured thickening caribou coats and the metamorphosis of the weasel pelt from brown to a white-haired cam-ouflage. Eyes followed flocks moving south from rime "down the coastlines of two continents, finding the way by inherited memory" (*ibid.*, 47). The statement revealed a mystery—how nature encoded animal expectations of cyclical change.

Rachel reaffirmed life rhythms, which existed "before ever man stood on the shore of the ocean ... they continue year in, year out, through the centuries and the ages, while kingdoms rise and fall" (*ibid.*, xix). Analyst Susan Power Bratton, an envi-ronmentalist at Baylor University, contrasted the complexities of the seasonal shad run described in *Under the Sea-Wind* with the attempts of bottom fishers to profit from seining. Because of imperfect understanding of ocean food chains, humans miscalculated fish migrations and misunderstood the total picture of sea life, thus disrupting reproductive cycles and over-harvesting the year's yield.

Seasons of Plenty

In 1947, Rachel's first *Conservation in Action* brochure, "Chincoteague: A National Wildlife Refuge," summarized the regulation of North American avian life by seasons. Along the Atlantic flyway from November to late March, brant, Canada geese, black ducks, and snow geese found safe migration routes, breeding areas, and ample marshland for wintering, depending on the whims of weather. By April, water-fowl departed, leaving the 250-acre Chincoteague to shore birds. The second bro-chure, "Parker River: A National Wildlife Refuge," examined a sanctuary outside

Boston, where "you begin to get the feel of real black duck country" on salt marshes in September and October (Carson, 1947, 5). By May 15, the ducklings enlarged the nest population by three or four, except where drainage had spoiled the habitat.

In "Mattamuskeet: A National Wildlife Refuge," a July 1947 pamphlet for the U.S. Fish and Wildlife department on a coastal North Carolina sanctuary, the author campaigned for natural foods to fatten swans, geese, ducks, and herons. She depicted their diet each spring focusing on "fresh green shoots of ... sedges, bulrushes, and salt grass" (Carson, 1947, 7). She revered summer for its "recuperative powers" to supply the Atlantic Outer Banks with forage for waterfowl (*ibid.*). By fall, shorebirds had their choice of green tips, seeds, and roots that kept them alive through winter.

A BROAD VIEW

In 1948, the author's pamphlet series developed a strong tutorial tone by #5, "Guarding Our Wildlife Resources: A National Wildlife Refuge." She surveyed the Western Hemisphere year round, from North to Central America, the Caribbean to South America, and identified the flights of the white-winged dove as far south in winter as Guatemala and El Salvador. Of the annual bird flights, she articulated a long route: "In their migrations between summer and winter homes they freely cross international boundaries, and some range all the way ... to the shores of the Arctic Ocean" (Carson, 1948, 3). Suitable places to feed, shelter, and breed marked their paths, which took them over agricultural fields and grazing lands.

Rachel enhanced *The Sea Around Us,* her 1951 oceanic portrait, with a gesture toward spring vigor, which revitalized the Northern Hemisphere with the green-up of dormant plants, the budding of blossoms, and exodus of flocks. The narrative offered a thanksgiving for the "seasonal abundance of certain forms containing reddish or brown pigments," the source of the Red Sea (Carson, 1951, 21). For the elements that grew biota, she saluted the warming sea floor and its rich store of minerals—phosphorus for marine plants and silica for diatoms to beget a seasonal resurgence. In fall, she sensed the majesty of a "fresh blaze of phosphorescence, when every wave crest is aflame" (Carson, 1951, 45). She concluded that, whatever the date, "day by day and season by season, the ocean dominates the world's climate" (*ibid.*, 162). Mike Hulme, a geography professor at Cambridge commented on the varied spans in Rachel's discourse: "Winter and summer, freeze and thaw cycles, monsoons, heatwave or hurricane seasons, rhythms of drought and flood ... provide a scaffold for human existence and offer the possibility of fruitful human action" (Hulme, 2018, 3).

UNCHANGING CYCLES

Seasonal uniqueness marked Rachel's script for the March 11, 1957, CBS *Omnibus* program. Her summation of a wintry snow vivified the severe substratospheric cold of the sky, "far below zero summer and winter" (Carson, 1957). Gelid temperatures yielded the "deep, soft, sound-absorbing blanket bringing a great quiet to the earth," the source of moisturizing runoff in spring (*ibid.*). For the essay "Our Ever-Changing Shore" in the July 1958 issue of *Holiday* magazine, the author stressed summer's end in misty mornings, hints of frost, and stretches of red, yellow, white, and purple on Maine's beaches. She looked heavenward to the mythic "Orion and his dogs hunt in the sky," a celestial token of autumn (Carson, 1958, 71).

In *The Sense of Wonder,* an education manual completed in 1965, the author encouraged teaching appreciation of the outdoors to young children. She explained the power of the seasons: "There is something infinitely healing in the repeated refrains of nature—the assurance that dawn comes after night, and spring after winter" (Carson, 1965, 100). The statement not only accentuated optimism, but, at the same time, lumped her into the population of ordinary joes who rely on the wild for stability.

Rachel's final work, *Silent Spring,* issued in September 1962, opened on a pastoral allegory, "A Fable for Tomorrow," and grounded a discussion of disrupted ecology on diurnal patterns, birdsong, and animal voices. With a mature gravitas, she worded concern for the death of spring robins from the spraying of elm trees. In the American West, she lamented the eradication of Wyoming's sagebrush to appease demanding cattle and sheep herders. *Artemisia tridentata* had for millennia fed sage grouse, mule deer, and pronghorn antelope during the heavy snowfalls of winter. Extermination of sage violated the natural balance and doomed animals to slow starvation.

See also Reproduction.

Sources

Bratton, Susan Power. "Thinking Like a Mackerel." *Ethics & the Environment* 9:1 (2004): 1–22.
Carson, Rachel. "Chincoteague: A National Wildlife Refuge." #1. Washington, D.C.: U.S. Department of the Interior, 1947.
_____. "Clouds" in "Something about the Sky." CBS *Omnibus* (11 March 1957).
_____. "Guarding Our Wildlife Resources: A National Wildlife Refuge." #5. Washington, D.C.: U.S. Department of the Interior, 1948, 1–46.
_____. "Mattamuskeet: A National Wildlife Refuge." #4. Washington, D.C.: U.S. Department of the Interior, July 1947.
_____. "Our Ever-Changing Shore." *Holiday* 24 (July 1958): 70–71, 117–120.
_____. "Parker River: A National Wildlife Refuge." #2. Washington, D.C.: U.S. Department of the Interior, 1947, 1–14.
_____. *The Sea Around Us.* New York: Oxford University Press, 1951.
_____. *The Sense of Wonder.* New York: Harper & Row, 1965.
_____. *Under the Sea Wind: A Naturalist's Picture of Ocean Life.* New York: Simon & Schuster, 1941.
Hulme, Mike. "Weather-Worlds of the Anthropocene and the End of Climate." *Weber* 34:1 (Fall 2018): 1–12.

Sense Impressions

Beyond the demands of biological classification and analysis, Rachel joyed in the wild earthscape and confided to friend Dorothy Freeman, "I am visual minded" (Carson, letter, 1962). She accounted for an immersion in the outdoors from early life: "If there is any simple explanation I think it is that my sensory impressions of, and emotional responses to, the experiences of nature date from earliest childhood.... I had felt at home with wild creatures all my life" (Carson, letter, 28 September 1953). In June 1929 on the author's first view of the ocean beyond Eel Pond at Woods Hole at the southwestern end of Cape Cod, she delighted in "that wonderful place of whirlpools and eddies and swiftly racing water" (Carson, 1954, n.p.). She characterized an instant love of the deep in Massachusetts as "sensory and emotional" (Carson, speech, 1951).

Newspaper articles dating to March 1, 1936, previewed the author's bent for simile, metaphor, onomatopoeia, and image. With the publication of "Undersea" in the September 1937 issue of *Atlantic Monthly,* she indulged an innate skill at sense impressions that framed her passion for ocean depths of six miles. The opening paragraph pictured "the recesses of the abyss, where reign utter silence and unvarying cold and eternal night" in "all-pervading water" (Carson, 1937, 322). Diction swelled the atmosphere of shadowy byways that remained unchanged from their creation. For *Nature* magazine in June 1939, she championed the "incessant chitter-chatter" of the starling over cityscapes echoing "raucous hooting of impatient traffic" (Carson, 1939, 319). Her comment subtly riposted to urban dwellers of Baltimore, Maryland, and Harrisburg, Pennsylvania, who preferred man-made furor to the sound of birds.

Experiencing the Wild

At her summer home in West Southport, Maine, Rachel let unfettered senses peruse the pink fronds of coralline algae and baby rock barnacles. The personal ode "An Island I Remember," composed in July 1946, strayed from pure science to pure joy in birdsong, a diving seal, and "the heady, aromatic, bitter-sweet fragrances compounded of pine and spruce and bayberry" (Carson, "Island," 1946). Farther south, the sounds of Canada geese flocking over the Pamlico Sound in North Carolina paralleled "wild music, rising at times to a great, tumultuous crescendo, and dying away again to a throbbing undercurrent" (Carson, 1947, 2).

For *The Sea Around Us,* the author indulged the reader in what essayist Ann Haymond Zwinger termed "a whole scene into which we submerge, sentience raised and mind pleasured" (Zwinger, 1989, xx). A swamp buggy ride over the Florida Everglades filled her with curiosity about tree snails, dew on spider webs, and "glowing hordes of alligators in the ponds" (Carson, 1954). In September 1953, her letters spoke of lying in bed listening to "open-ocean rollers … trampling in over our ledges" (Steingruber, 2018, 330). The pulsing crashes piqued her imagination about the creatures that lived in roiling surf. In 1955, she exulted in *The Edge of the Sea,* "We can sense the long rhythm of earth and sea that sculptured its land forms and produced the rock and sand of which it is composed" (Carson, 1955, vii). After a storm off South Carolina, she perceived a bone-chilling wind that turned the swells "a cold leaden hue," the result of obscured sunlight (*ibid.,* 175).

Holistic Learning

In the magazine tutorial "Help Your Child to Wonder," Rachel, the foster mother of grand-nephew Roger Allen Christie, advised selection of simple, yet wondrous sense experiences to satisfy a child's curiosity. She listed sky, stars, rain, and wind as stimuli "opening up the disused channels of sensory impression" in eyes, ears, nose, and fingers (Carson, 1956, 47). For the March 11, 1957, CBS program "Clouds" for *Omnibus,* her thoughts turned to the importance of vision in introducing the individual to moist clusters in the sky and their constantly shifting outlines, a foggy "veil through which the earth is seen dimly, like the shallow bottom of a bay" (Carson, 1957).

The impact of natural forces returned to Rachel's personal correspondence on January 6, 1962, as she listened to "rain on the roof and now and then strong gusts off wind [on] a cozy night" (Carson, letter, 1962). For "Nature Fights Back," an essay in September 1962 for *Silent Spring*, she recounted the wonder of cultivating paramecia in the lab and viewing the praying mantis at night by flashlight to see "the drama of the hunter and the hunted" (Carson, 2002, 249). Her esthetic response to monarch butterflies in September 1963 allowed her to accept a short life span in an insect that brought her joy. Still perusing biology the next month during treatment for pancreatitis, she reveled in sightseeing among giant redwoods, oxalis, palmetto, and sword ferns in Muir Woods. An excerpt, *The Rocky Coast*, depicted the marine biologist's sense of smell in sulphur sponges, iodine rockweed, and the salty rime on granite rocks. Thinking over her chances of surviving metastatic cancer, she declared faith that "the eye will let me stumble along somehow until I 'come out into the light,'" a cliché she may have meant as a symbol of eternity (Carson, letter, 1962).

See also Aeriall Spraying; Color.

Sources

Carson, Rachel. "Clouds" in "Something About the Sky." CBS *Omnibus* (11 March 1957).
_____. *The Edge of the Sea*. Boston: Houghton Mifflin, 1955.
_____. "Help Your Child to Wonder." *Woman's Home Companion* 53 (July 1956): 25–27, 46–48.
_____. "How About Citizenship Papers for the Starling?" *Nature* 32 (June/July 1939): 317–319.
_____. "An Island I Remember," unpublished ode, July 1946.
_____. "Letter to Dorothy Freeman" (28 September 1953).
_____. "Letter to Dorothy Freeman" (6 January 1962).
_____. "Mattamuskeet: A National Wildlife Refuge." #4. Washington, D.C.: U.S. Department of the Interior, July 1947.
_____. "Our Ever-Changing Shore." *Holiday* 24 (July 1958): 70–71, 117–120.
_____. "The Real World Around Us," address to the Theta Sigma Phi Matrix Table Dinner, Columbus, Ohio (21 April 1954).
_____. *The Rocky Coast*. New York: McCall, 1971.
_____. *Silent Spring*. Boston: Houghton Mifflin, 40th Anniversary Edition, 2002.
_____. speech, *New York Herald Tribune Book Review*, Astor Hotel (1 October 1951).
_____. "Undersea." *Atlantic Monthly* 160 (September 1937): 322–325.
Peters, Kimberley. "Touching the Oceans." *Women's Studies Quarterly* 45:1/2 (Spring/Summer 2017): 278–281.
Steingruber, Sandra, ed. *Rachel Carson: Silent Spring & Other Writings on the Environment*. New York: Library of America, 2018.
Zwinger, Ann. "Introduction." *The Sea Around Us*. New York: Oxford University Press, 1989.

The Sense of Wonder

According to the introduction to *The Sense of Wonder*, Rachel prized experiential education. The delight of her own introduction to wildflowers by her mother remained gratifying in college laboratory experiments on the rapid reproduction of paramecia. The author viewed childhood innocence with the same appreciation as William Wordsworth's *Intimations of Immortality:* "Trailing clouds of glory do we come from God, who is our home: Heaven lies about us in our infancy." She intended an awe-inspired walk in the woods to defeat apathy toward nature and instill a love of mystery and discovery, a credo fostered by religious groups and dramatized in the title character's introduction to the sea in Avi's *The True Confessions of Charlotte Doyle* and the prowling of 15-year-old Wil Neuton in Gary Paulsen's YA novel *The Island*. She fostered phenomena and life processes pictured by photographers Charles Pratt and Nick Kelsh of Philadelphia as everyday miracles amid hectic life.

The parenting of baby Roger Allen Christie in mid–October 1953 afforded the biologist a compelling opportunity of viewing the outdoors, which included the tow-path of the 184-mile C&O Canal. Taking the toddler to the coast at age 20 months, she began the lifetime task of introducing an innocent babe to the Maine shoreline and the daily wonders of tide pools and surf. On their way, they passed clusters of spring peepers, which she tape recorded and introduced by mail to friends. In mid–February 1956, she and the three-year-old dressed in oilskin and sou'wester to tramp springy lichens in wet thickets in search of a deer or fox. The Christmas tree game, an open-ended imagination activity, encouraged the boy to think of spruces according to animals of proportionate size who might decorate each tree for yuletide.

CREATING MEMORIES

Rachel surmised that her nephew's education in nature was successful at age four because of his memory of bunchberry and whelks and respect for periwinkles and mussels. The narrative imparted the evocative side of his upbringing near "a thousand diamonds in the rocks on the shore as the light strikes the flakes of mica embedded in them" (Carson, 1965, 22). The author hoped that his awe at natural beauty would be "so indestructible that it would last throughout life" (*ibid.,* 43).

As Maine grew in population and urbanism, Rachel valued inspiration and pleasure in the wild as antidotes to modernity, with its artificiality, ennui, and disenchantment. She identified emotion and first impressions with fertile soil on which to plant seeds of knowledge. From significant moments with cricket symphonies, sky, constellations, light, weather, and wind and from "opening up the disused channels of sensory impression," she predicted a "magical release for your thoughts" and "inner contentment" (*ibid.,* 52, 49, 88).

ENLIVENING AWARENESS

Analyst Kathleen Dean Moore, an environmental activist at Oregon State University, accounted for fascination with marvels—sights, sounds, smells, tastes, and textures—as a bridge linking facts with values. She advocated a mystic awareness of living things as "an antidote to the view that the elements of the natural world are commodities to be disdained or destroyed" (Moore, Sideris, 2008, 12). By living a pro-life creed, Rachel turned wonder into a virtue alongside wholeness, reverence, decency, and self-control.

In November 1968, actor Helen Hayes, a conservator of the Hudson River Valley, narrated excerpts from *The Sense of Wonder* and *The Edge of the Sea* that dramatized the author's intimacy with the natural beauty of city, desert, forest, and coast. She admired Rachel for thoroughness: "I've always had an enormous respect for people who trouble to explore things" ("Actress," 1968, 4). Executive producer Jules Power commented to the *Los Angeles Times* on the significance of the pictorial documentary: "A child has a natural curiosity about nature, but this is nearly always lost when that child becomes an adult" (Laurent, 1968, 22). He intended the TV filming at Boothbay, Maine, to arouse interest in the outdoors and joy in being alive.

See also Sense Impressions.

Sources

"Actress Offers 'Message' in a Nov. 13 TV Special." *La Cross* (WI) *Tribune* (26 October 1968): 4.
Carson, Rachel. *The Sense of Wonder*. New York: Harper & Row, 1965.
Gross, Alan G. *The Scientific Sublime*. Oxford, UK: Oxford University Press, 2018.
Laurent, Lawrence. "Bringing Country to City Dwellers." *Los Angeles Times* (13 November 1968): 22.
Martin, Maria Angeles, and Connie Lasher. "Nature as a School of Wonder." *Human* 4 (2016).
McCrum, Robert. "The 100 Best Nonfiction Books: No 20—*Silent Spring* by Rachel Carson (1962)." *The Guardian* (13 June 2016).
Moore, Kathleen Dean, and Lisa H. Sideris. *Rachel Carson: Legacy and Challenge*. Albany, NY: SUNY Press, 2008.

Shellfish

Rachel probed sea organisms as models of ingenuity and fecundity, as with the conception of myriad oysters and the spread of barnacles over rocks on the Maine shore. In "Farming under the Chesapeake," an article for in January 1937 the *Baltimore Sun* on undersea cultivation and dredging, she declared oysters second only to salmon in value to the U.S. diner, who tended to eat them whole. She reprised propagation methods in ancient China, pre–Christian Rome, and native American beds in Maine on the Damariscotts River. Her feature summarized the production of Maryland oysters from 1880 to 1934, when the total fell from 47.5 percent to 19.6 percent.

The author filled journalistic writings with the causes of change. The article blamed the declining numbers on competition from 10,000 acres of public beds as opposed to Virginia's "privately leased and operated beds" (Carson, 1937, 6). With skill in visualization, she pictured a quart bottle of oyster eggs yielding a 20,000,000-bushel crop. The essay speculated on the upper limit of oyster productivity by picturing the survival of some 500,000,000 eggs per female. A bonanza could result in a "layer of oysters over thirty feet deep" over the whole country (*ibid.*).

SETTLING IN

Rachel personified larvae as wanderers who settled to the sea bottom "to take up the sedentary existence of the adult," a wording geared to appeal to literal-minded readers, especially children (*ibid.*). The Ordovician Era (500,000,000 BCE) evolved the first shelled nautilus, squid, and cuttlefish. She pictured the successful Chesapeake Bay bivalve living in appropriate salinity and attaching to Massachusetts's clean rocks and shells by exuding cement. Her development of possible bonding sites near clam rock and crabbing bottoms added humor by naming seabed garbage—"old boots, spectacles, false teeth, bottles and lanterns" (*ibid.*). Dredgers also pulled up old shells, starfish, and snail borers.

For the sake of a healthy oyster harvest, Massachusetts gleaners adhered to a process. By returning old shells to established beds, watermen ensured suitable spawning locales. The Federal Bureau of Fisheries improved survival rate by providing cement partitions situated in stacks. A photo illustrated harvesting in Seattle, Washington, where oystermen built dikes to hold seawater over beds at low tide.

For the 36-page conservation bulletin "Fish and Shellfish of the Middle Atlantic Coast," issued June 1, 1945, as part of the "Food from the Sea" series for the U.S. Department of the Interior, the biologist moved into academic turf by identifying types—mussels, bay scallops, sea scallops, hard-shelled clams, and surf clams. Defining shellfish boundaries from Cape Cod, Massachusetts, to Cape Hatteras on the North Carolina Outer Banks, the narrative valued oysters as the best-known and best-selling seafood for all times, dating to the settlement of Maryland's Chesapeake Bay by Nanticoke, Piscataway, and Powhatan tribes originating from paleo–Indians of 7000 BCE. She intended the brochure to popularize lesser-known food fish and stem over-harvesting of the most popular mollusks and crustaceans—oysters, clams, crabs, and shrimp.

Seafood Perils

The marine biologist remained alert to the endangerment of seafood. In 1951, *The Sea Around Us* listed the evolution in deep time of sea organisms, which secrete their shells from dissolved calcium salts in their mantles. She placed the arthropods— ghost crab, snails, and lobsters—in the Silurian Epoch (440,000,000 BCE). Mollusks from the Permian Era appeared around 270,000,000 BCE, long before the snails of the Tertiary period in 70,000,000 BCE. Of the survival of oysters and mussels, she credited the effect of tides on sessile organisms, which brought food that sedentary shellfish could not hunt. Their reproductive cycles depended on moon cycles. Vigorous sweeps of seawater could dislodge the bivalves from their silky threads and carry them to their death. Only lima crabs and scallops could swim to safety.

Poisonous plankton known as Gonyaulax toxified mussels in summer and fall, filling shellfish with a substance like strychnine. To protect tribes, Pacific coast Indians posted sentinels to alert outsiders of the danger. Rachel warned that the migration of crustaceans from the deep at night to feed on diatoms left them open to industrial profiteers, who seined indiscriminately.

On September 27, 1962, *Silent Spring* denounced the aerial spraying of DDT (dichlorodiphenyltrichloroethane), which affected mussels and clams as well as the animals and people who fed on them. Likewise, crustaceans, especially fiddler crabs, fell victim to dieldrin, a treatment for fire ants, Japanese beetles, moths, and crabgrass. Endrin, a lethal roach killer, reduced shrimp populations by half. Herbicides caused the most damage to young mollusks, which devoured poisoned plankton from coastal wetlands. For people who ate shellfish raw, the concentration of biocides in clam and oyster tissues made them especially toxic. Yuki Masami, a socio-environmentalist at Kanazawa University, credited Rachel with "[demonstrating] how easily a web of life turns into a web of death once an environment is contaminated with toxic pollutants" (Masami, 2017, 58).

Sources

Carson, Rachel. *The Sea Around Us*. New York: Oxford University Press, 1951.
Carson, R.L., "Farming under the Chesapeake." *Baltimore Sun* (24 January 1937): 6–7.
Cumbler, John T. *Cape Cod: An Environmental History of a Fragile Ecosystem*. Boston: University of Massachu-
     setts Press, 2014.
Fellows, Valerie. "On Eagle's Wings." *Fish & Wildlife News* (Spring 2007): 20–21.
Masami, Yuki. "Meals in the Age of Toxic Environments." *The Routledge Companion to the Environmental
     Humanities*. New York: Routledge, 2017, 56–63.

Silent Spring

Rachel's moral classic initiated frank inquiry into a new technological era. Editor Edward O. Wilson labeled the treatise a "galvanic jolt"; Mark Madison, a historian for the U.S. Fish and Wildlife Service, called the book a "chemical indictment"
(Carson, 2002, 357; Madison, 2007, 11). A period of critical thinking began in autumn
1957 with her intense research into the effects of synthetic pesticides, a result of
agrarian intensification. Among the pioneering scientists, she consulted Beatrice
Trum Hunter, organic foods maven. The task changed Rachel from the lyric author
of *The Edge of the Sea* to a trenchant, fearful Jeremiah. To prepare scientists for the
onslaught of criticism, Houghton Mifflin editor Paul Brooks sent pre-publication
copies of *Silent Spring* to ready them for media grilling,

Frank Graham, a columnist for the *Chicago Tribune,* noted that Rachel's "reverence for life was expressed not in awe but in anger" in a "living document" still cogent
because the problems remain unsolved (Graham, 1971, 1A). Natural history essayist Ann Haymond Zwinger crystallized the metamorphosis of a twentieth-century
alarmist: "Gone is the easy charm of style, replaced by the crisper voice of an authoritative, well-informed, angry woman" (Zwinger, 1989, xxv). The biologist denounced
mutagenic-carcinogenic chemicals, but her focal target remained the ubiquitous
DDT (dichlorodiphenyltrichloroethane), the post–World War II pest killer. Graham
concurred with Rachel: "To turn against life in all its variety a barrage of long-lasting,
nonspecific poisons is barbaric" (Graham, 1971, 1A).

Tentatively entitled "The Control of Nature," "Dissent in Favor of Men," "At War
with Nature," "The War Against Nature," "How to Balance Nature," and "Man Against
the Earth," the literary tocsin profited from the mystic imagery of a sibilant, two-word
title, *Silent Spring,* the suggestion of editor Brooks. The choice revived the human cel-
ebration of spring as a renaissance of the outdoors and wildlife, enhanced by the line
drawings of environmentalist illustrators Louis and Lois Darling. Rachel drew on
reader familiarity with the 19th-century theories of English naturalist Charles Darwin for the bases for her arguments. The philippic created pre-publication demand
for 40,000 copies. By late September 1962, *Silent Spring* had sold two million books
and continued selling at the rate of 25,000 per year.

Habitats of All Life

Four years earlier in the essay for *Good Reading* "On the Biological Sciences,"
Rachel had grounded an ecological stance on good sense: "It is useless to attempt

to preserve a living species unless the kind of land or water it requires is also preserved" (Carson, 1958). Her editor warned that selling the idea of pesticide control to the world would require "something of a crusade" (Brinkley, 2012). She altered her melodic imagism, according to Minneapolis landscape architect Adam Regn Arvidson, to suit the serious tone of a masterwork: "It's not a stretch to say that the sea trilogy is poetic while *Silent Spring* is analytical" (Arvidson, 2011). Donald Edward Worster, a founder of environmental history at the University of Kansas, considered Rachel delphic for her gifts of prophecy and political insight. When the book reached the public on September 27, 1962, editor Brooks and the Houghton Mifflin staff hosted a party in New York in Rachel's honor.

With prefatory storytelling, "A Fable for Tomorrow," the author used allegory to inform the public of their kinship with all life. Her letter to the *Washington Post* had alerted readers to global degradation from "highly poisonous hydrocarbons and organic phosphates allied to the nerve gases of chemical warfare," a reminder of the devastation unleashed by two world wars (Carson, 1959, A26). She denounced the contamination of cranberries in the 1957, 1958, and 1959 harvests from illegal use of aminotriazole. The carcinogenic herbicide contributed to throat cancer and damaged the liver, endocrine system, and reproductive organs. The cranberry scare extended to a widespread concern about all American foodstuffs and to the citizens themselves in the path of "an amazing rain of death upon the surface of the earth" (*ibid.*). The explicit charge against the makers of biocides produced what reviewer Claas Kirchhelle, a historian at Oxford University, called "a cultural breakup with pesticides" (Kirchhelle, 2018, 222).

READER RESPONSE

The public readily consumed *Silent Spring* because the author "gently led her audience through the complexities of natural systems and the need for balance" (*ibid.*). Biographer Linda Lear declared the author "a trusted voice in a world riddled by uncertainty" (Carson, 2002, xiv). An advocate of non-proliferation of nuclear energy, she dedicated the book to philanthropist-physician Albert Schweitzer, winner of the 1952 Nobel Peace Prize for his philosophy of reverence for life. He earned her respect in December 1956 for warning the International Union for Conservation that insecticide killed bees, the pollinators of food plants.

The classic text stirred readers to write members of congress, the U.S. Department of the Interior, and the public health service. Farm researchers for the U.S. Department of Agriculture riposted to *Silent Spring* with the film *Fire Ant on Trial*, which exonerated the dangers of dieldrin and heptachlor in exchange for control of the fire ant (*Solenopsis invicta*), an invasive subterranean pest with the species name meaning "unconquered." Concerns over radioactive fallout and the presence of strontium-90 in a baby tooth in St. Louis, Missouri, contributed to controversy over contaminants that endanger the young. To keep up with the media and correspondence, Rachel hired Jeanne Vance Davis, a medical research aide, as secretary and researcher at the National Institutes of Health.

Jonathan Norton Leonard, a journalist for the *New York Times,* called the author's eco-polemic an "apocalyptic word picture" (Leonard, 1964). The book created a furor in Brazil, Britain, China, Denmark, Finland, France, Germany, Holland, Hungary, Iceland, Israel, Italy, Japan, Korea, Norway, Portugal, Slovenia, Spain, Sweden, Thailand, Turkey, and Yugoslavia. Support from Swedish ornithologist Erik Rosenberg, Secretary of the Interior Stewart Udall, Dow research lab, the Audubon society, and the *New York Times* countered disinformation, evasion, and propaganda from a $300,000,000 industry headed by American Cyanamid, DuPont, Monsanto, Montrose, and Velsicol.

FACTS VS. SLANDER

Ad hominem attacks, mostly from male adversaries, declared Rachel first of all a suspect scientist for being female. Protesters called her a Communist, sinister scaremonger, fanatic, cultist, zealot, and idealistic flag-waver. Experts in the field accused her of distorting data with experimental, unsupported evidence that would lessen America's ability to feed its citizens. One critic linked her with "a noisy, misinformed group of 'organic-gardening faddists and other beyond-the-fringe groups'" (Lawlor, 2014, 31). The critique in *Chemical & Engineering News* by William Jefferson Darby, on staff at the Vanderbilt University School of Medicine, declared her ignorant.

Reviewers who combed the work for explicit phrases tended to repeat the author's most famous salute to the ocean from *The Sea Around Us*: "For all at last returns to the sea—to Oceanus, the ocean river, like the everflowing stream of time, the beginning and the end" (Carson, 1951, 204). As biblical as David's psalms, the line imparted sanctity to nature as well as to Greek mythographers, who declared Oceanus a primordial, earth-encircling spirit, the divine offspring of earth and sky. Support poured in from Trout Unlimited, Izaak Walton League of America, Outdoor Writers Association, Citizens Natural Resources Association of Wisconsin, and the Sport Fishing Institute. The sentiment so intimidated state lawmakers across America that, by December 31, 1962, they had introduced 40 bills advocating restraint in pesticide use.

Op-ed pieces varied, notably "Fact and Fancy," a parody of the Kennedys as fancy, and a vague riposte from the National Agricultural Chemicals Association that pesticides increase mammal and bird populations. From the Panama City, Florida, *News-Herald*, columnist Bill Lowther cited sports fishermen who supported Rachel's anti-chemical writings. In opposition, Edwin Diamond, the provocative senior editor of *Newsweek*, charged Rachel with emotional exaggeration and mythmaking. For nearly a decade, versions of Rachel's treatise in 22 languages appeared in Paris, Helsinki, New York, Tokyo, Amsterdam, Lisbon, Stockholm, Copenhagen, Munich, Milan, London, Barcelona, Israel, and Norway as well as Ljubljana, Yugoslavia, and Sao Paulo, Brazil. Receipt of the Dutch translation on October 26, 1963, amused the author with its title—*Dode Lenten* (Carson, letter, 1963).

Rachel's pragmatic methodology gained attention for connecting data and relating case studies to her claim that synthetic toxins, like radiation, threatened earthly biota. From her scholarly application of facts to ecology came a new dynamic for social protest of what literary critic Perry Parks, a journalism specialist at Michigan

State University, termed "a hyper-technologized and profit-oriented society" (Parks, 2017, 1218). *Silent Spring* awakened the U.S. Public Health Service to chemical threats and earned from U.S. Supreme Court Justice William Orville Douglas an accolade for being "the most important chronicle of this century for the human race" (Offit, 2017, 170). Both the New York Public Library and the *New York Times* named the work one of the century's 100 most important books. Historian John Kenneth Galbraith ranked the text among the top in Western literature. In 2018, Charles C. Mann, a writer for the *Wall Street Journal,* proclaimed the treatise "an impressive piece of work—and a deserving candidate for the Library of America series" (Mann, 2018, C5). After panning her book, *Time* magazine later recanted and proclaimed her one of the century's most influential people for questioning threats to quality of life.

See also "A Fable for Tomorrow"; Pesticides.

Sources

Arvidson, Adam Regn. "Nature Writing in America: The Power of Rachel Carson." *Nature & Science* 2:9 (September 2011).

Brinkley, Douglas. "Rachel Carson and JFK, an Environmental Tag Team." *Audubon* (May–June 2012), https://www.audubon.org/magazine/may-june-2012/rachel-carson-and-jfk-environmental-tag-team.

Carson, Rachel. "Letter to Dorothy Freeman" (26 October 1963).

_____. "On the Biological Sciences." *Good Reading* (July 1956).

_____. "On the Reception of *Silent Spring*." (2 December 1962).

_____. *The Sea Around Us.* New York: Oxford University Press, 1951.

_____. *Silent Spring.* Boston: Houghton Mifflin, 40th Anniversary Edition, 2002.

_____. "Vanishing Americans." *Washington Post* (10 April 1959): A26.

Fellows, Valerie, and Joshua Winchell. "Returning to the Water." *Fish & Wildlife News* (Spring 2007): 26–29.

Graham, Frank. "Rachel Carson's Big Book." *Chicago Tribune* (31 January 1971): 1A.

Kirchhelle, Claas. "Toxic Tales—Recent Histories of Pollution, Poisoning, and Pesticides (ca. 1800–2010)." *NTM* 26:2 (June 2018): 213–229.

Lawlor, Laurie. *Rachel Carson and Her Book That Changed the World.* New York: Holiday House, 2014.

Leonard, Jonathan Norton. "Obituary." *New York Times* (15 April 1964).

Madison, Mark. "Nature's Public Servant." *Fish & Wildlife News* (Spring 2007): 8–11.

Mann, Charles C. "'Silent Spring & Other Writings' Review: The Right and Wrong of Rachel Carson." *Wall Street Journal* (26 April 2018): C5.

Offit, Paul A. *Pandora's Lab: Seven Stories of Science Gone Wrong.* Washington, D.C.: National Geographic Partners, 2017.

Parks, Perry. "*Silent Spring,* Loud Legacy: How Elite Media Helped Establish an Environmentalist Icon." *Journalism and Mass Communication Quarterly* 94:4 (December 2017): 1215–1238.

Zwinger, Ann. "Introduction." *The Sea Around Us.* New York: Oxford University Press, 1989.

Silent Spring: And No Birds Sing

Retaining the commoner's perspective on backyard bird deaths, Rachel opened Chapter Eight with a letter from an unidentified Hinsdale, Illinois, housewife. A failed attempt to control the fungal spores and beetles causing Dutch elm disease with DDT killed cardinals, chickadees, nuthatches, downy woodpeckers, and robins, America's beloved harbingers of spring. A woman in Alabama reported the same eradication of songbirds. Supported by the National Audubon Society and the U.S. Fish and Wildlife Service, the report of missing land birds in Alabama, Illinois, Louisiana, Mississippi, and West Virginia exposed "an incredible reduction" in 90 avian species, a loss that alarmed and saddened residents (Carson, 2002, 104).

The author indicated how multiple pesticide programs in Lansing, Michigan, could attack gypsy moths, mosquitoes, and the bark beetle (*Hylurgopinus rufipes*) responsible for spreading Dutch elm disease. Although DDT makers denied fault, the attack on avian nervous systems precipitated grisly deaths. A test of earthworms, typical robin food, on crayfish and a snake corroborated the 1958 writing by Roy Baker at Urbana, Illinois, who identified the worms as "biological magnifiers" of harm (*ibid.*, 108). The reduction of robins on the Michigan State University campus from 370 to three dozen exterminated over 90 percent of the resident birds. A fearful suppression of reproduction resulted from fewer eggs and the loss of baby chicks before and immediately after hatching. Similar studies in Wisconsin totaled a mortality rate in robins up to 88 percent.

Mass Death

Rachel's narrative identified demise of the woodcock and a dieback of Wisconsin's warblers and kinglets from a late spraying of DDT and heptachlor in spring 1956. Treatment with DDT of the beetles and fungal spores causing Dutch elm disease yielded a decline in thrushes, owls, hawks, swallows, phoebes, cardinals, wrens, catbirds, and sparrows as well as shrews, raccoons, and moles, possibly from feeding on poisoned worms, birds, and mice. Loss of insect-eating chickadees, brown creepers, woodpeckers, and nuthatches allowed opportunistic insect species to flourish. Thus, a plan to save the elm increased insect populations by killing birds, "nature's safeguards" (*ibid.*, 113). A Milwaukee woman posed a more positive methodology: "Isn't it possible to help the balance of nature without destroying it?" (*ibid.*, 114).

The author, as profiled in the *London Times* in 1994, was "no negative cassandra" ("When," 1994). She balanced a dismal beginning of balanced John Keats's dismal line "And No Birds Sing" with a New York success story. For scrupulous sanitation, arborists located beetles breeding in elms and destroyed their wood. In Buffalo, Westchester County, and Syracuse, the proactive system reduced elm loss by over 99 percent. Scientists proposed hybridizing the elm to resist further infestation. A variant proposal urged planting an array of elm species rather than limit an area to only one type.

Authoritarian Poisoners

Rachel returned to the subject of bird loss with the prospects of the imperiled bald eagle, an American icon of majesty and independence. Tracing August–September migratory patterns from Prince Edward Island, Canada, to the U.S. South, she disclosed reproductive problems from the female eagle's failure to ovulate to eggs that failed to hatch and the death of hatchlings. Similar research into American quail and pheasant mortality and the demise of Belgian and French partridges and English chaffinches and linnets linked low bird count to DDT, heptachlor, aldrin, and dieldrin. She cited a daunting fact about insecticides and reproduction: they affect "a generation once removed from initial contact" (*ibid.*, 121).

More outcomes emerged from mid-twentieth century research. Rachel remonstrated with chemical manufacturers for conducting lab tests but no field work in the wild to substantiate safety to a broader selection of organisms. She revealed use of parathion by Indiana farmers to rid cornfields of blackbirds, a "chain of devastation" that the *Boston Globe* reprinted in January 1963 (Carson, 1963, 12). The poison also targeted raccoons, rabbits, and opossums and felled farm workers. Summoning pity for innocent animals, she questioned how individuals had the right to poison "the ordered world of nature" with impunity (*ibid.*, 127). With a journalist's skill, she ended the chapter with a periodic sentence concluded with "imperative," a nudge for the uninvolved to take action (*ibid.*).

Sources

Carson, Rachel. "Exit the Elm ... and Birds." *Boston Globe* (25 January 1963): 12.
_____. *Silent Spring*. Boston: Houghton Mifflin, 40th Anniversary Edition, 2002.
Foote, Bonnie. "The Narrative Interactions of *Silent Spring*: Bridging Literary Criticism and Ecocriticism." *New Literary History* 38:4 (Autumn 2007): 739–745, 747–753, 777.
"When the Sedge Withers and No Birds Sing." *London Times* (14 February 1994).

Silent Spring: Beyond the Dreams of the Borgias

The tone of Chapter 11, "Beyond the Dreams of the Borgias," advanced from alarming to terrifyingly sarcastic, especially mention of "a pocket-sized insecticide dispenser" for use during recreation (Carson, 2002, 175). Rachel referred to the status of hazardous pesticides as a "birth-to-death contact with dangerous chemicals" portending disaster (*ibid.*, 173). Her subtitle summoned the infamous Hispano-Italian dynasty during the Italian Renaissance known for sexual promiscuity, corruption, and poisoning with arsenic, aconite, and strychnine. The *Sioux City Journal* credited the author with issuing "a smashing indictment of the chemical mass-warfare" ("Hour," 1969, A4). Newspapers snapped up the intriguing title of her essay and issued reprints in the *Minneapolis Star, Detroit Free Press,* and North Hills, Pennsylvania *News Record*.

The Borgias' clandestine poisoning offered the writer a trope for unwarranted contaminants. The recondite nature of the era's biocides obscured from citizens the gradual accumulation in human tissue of such deadly substances as DDD, DDT, chlordane, lindane, endrin, parathion, malathion, heptachlor, and dieldrin. Many solved household invasions by permeating shelf paper, floor wax, fly strips, and garden and fogger sprays, which Rachel declared "a public menace" (*ibid.*, 176). She surmised, "We are in little better position than the guests of the Borgias," a terrifying prospect that Harvey Levenstein, a history professor at McMaster University, dubbed "death on a plate" (*ibid.*, 184; Levenstein, 2016, 16).

The author's confrontational style contrasted mundane advertisements and ambiguous labels for chlorinated hydrocarbons with alerts from the U.S. Food and Drug Administration (FDA) and Department of Agriculture. She revealed a conclusion from the U.S. Public Health Service that most edibles have contained DDT since its patenting in 1942, especially the meals served in prisons and hospitals and in all butter and dairy products. She charged farmers with exceeding safe levels of DDT, application of multiple toxins, spraying ripe produce at harvest time, and ignoring label warnings. Other sources of contamination, transportation in treated vessels, and storage in warehouses, increased hazards. Researchers had to move beyond civilization to the Arctic realm in Alaska to find diets free of toxicity.

Rachel confided that the FDA employed only enough agents to analyze under one percent of foods crossing state lines. She questioned the concept of tolerances and added that provisos for acceptable amounts of toxins in the body ignored buildup in fatty tissue. Formulators of safe limits based their cases on inadequate or outdated facts, such as those certifying aminotriazole in cranberries, which could cause throat cancer, liver damage, and disruptions to endocrine system and reproductive organs. The biologist called for a more vigilant FDA force and the elimination of tolerances of chlorinated hydrocarbons, organic phosphates, and other biocidal residues. In their place, she advocated plant-based insecticides—pyrethrin from African daisies, rotenone from jicama vines, and ryania from willows. The *Detroit Free Press* and the *Miami News* reprinted the chapter in December 1962; it appeared in the *Minneapolis Star* in February 1963 and in the North Hills, Pennsylvania *News Record* in September 1963.

Sources

Carson, Rachel. *Silent Spring*. Boston: Houghton Mifflin, 40th Anniversary Edition, 2002.
"The Hour Glass." *Sioux City Journal* (6 July 1969): A4.
Levenstein, Harvey. "Death on a Plate." *How Canadians Communicate VI*. Edmonton: Athabasca University, 2016, 297–312.

Silent Spring: Earth's Green Mantle

In the mode of a canny classroom teacher, Rachel introduced Chapter Six, "Earth's Green Mantle," by restating data on the need of all life for water, soil, sunlight, and vegetation. She rebuked humankind for an arrogant tendency toward cosmetic insect and weed reduction, the impetus to a vast chemical industry growing rich off profits from DDT (dichlorodiphenyltrichloroethane). For a tutorial model, the narrative typified life in the Rocky Mountains after their formation in the Tertiary Era (70,000,000 BCE) during extremes of blizzard, drought, and wind. The heroic plant that survived the onslaught, sagebrush (*Artemisia tridentata*), a deep-rooted evergreen, survived to carpet the Western plains and become Nevada's state flower. According to journalist Rebecca Renner, the chapter introduction "weaves her most vivid images," an optical springboard to serious thoughts on ecology (Renner, 2018).

Not typically drawn to large animals, the author described the plains as a habitat for sage grouse (*Centrocercus urophasianus*) and pronghorn antelope (*Antilocapra americana*). She focused on the food value of sagebrush, an aromatic forage that nourished the antelope through deep winter. The grouse and antelope shared perennial bunch grass and the evergreen shrubs, which also fed mule deer and livestock herds. She credited a vigorous "shotgun approach" of sage eradication for selling grass seed and heavy machinery (Carson, 2002, 67).

The downside of the political clout of cattle and sheep herdsmen lay in lack of evidence that sparse rainfall could support grasslands "once the moisture-holding sage is gone" (*ibid.*). Overall, she castigated planners for sabotaging a centuries-old "fabric of life" (*ibid.*). Analyst Michael B. Smith, a technical writer, stated that Rachel "indicts the dictatorial nature of science and its star chamber of practitioners who make decisions that effect everyone, destroying a part of the world without consent" (Smith, 2001, 745).

THE SAGEBRUSH FIASCO

Rachel's descriptions of foolish manipulation of ecology credited the U.S. Forest Service with yielding to herder's demands by spraying 10,000 acres of Wyoming's Bridger National Forest to oust sagebrush, a proposal issued in Laramie on October 8, 1960. The domino effect destroyed willows along streams and disrupted the ecosystems of beaver, moose, trout, and waterfowl. The biologist's narrative followed with a staggering view of brush spraying by utility companies and the herbicidal control of 75 million acres of Southwestern mesquite (*Prosopis*), a shrubby pod producer that flourished in pasturage. Additional goals—weeding out hardwoods from conifers and treating lowlands, parks, golf courses, and family yards for weeds—resulted in the agrarian engineering term "chemical plowing" (Carson, 2002, 69).

As happened to income in Jackson Hole, Wyoming, the author warned of lost tourism in Maine from permanently disfigured land and the extermination of bayberry, fern, huckleberry, and wildflowers. C. Roy Boutard, a book reviewer for the *Berkshire Eagle* (Pittsfield, MA), smirked, "Presumably this is done to make you see the road better and sneeze less," but he described the aerial assault as "ruthless devastation" (Boutard, 1962, 22). Zealous spraying in Massachusetts resulted in the arsenic poisoning of a dozen cattle. In Waterford, Connecticut, in 1957, synthetic herbicides deformed oak trees and killed branches. Of the effects, Rachel called the scarred landscapes a "sterile and hideous world" (*ibid.*, 71). She reacted emotionally to loss of "delicate and transient" loveliness—purple vetch, white clover, and the red wood lily (*ibid.*, 72). Justice William Orville Douglas equated threats to the esthetic enjoyment of the countryside with theft of the nation's precious gold and copper.

POISONOUS HERBICIDES

Rachel reported a heightening of sugars in 2,4,5-Trichlorophenol (TCP or 2,4,-5-T) and 2,4-Dichlorophenoxyacetic acid (2,4-D)--together the formula of Agent Orange. The taste drew pigs, lambs, and cattle to poisoned foliage of smartweed, spiderwort, lamb's quarters, pigweed, sorghum, spiderwort, and sunflowers and caused herd deaths from anoxia or suffocation. The same danger destroyed sheep, goats, deer, and antelope. The release of nitrates extended to silos, where gases caused rapid respiratory arrest in farm workers. She introduced alternatives to such pesticides to preserve useful broad-leafed plants and cited corroboration from Dutch entomologist C.J. Briejèr, who recommended planting marigolds near roses to kill nematodes naturally.

The biologist stressed the reverse effects of some herbicides, which actually propagate such pests as opportunistic crabgrass and ragweed, a source of human allergies. Instead of obliterating species, she advocated "managing vegetation as a living community" (*ibid.,* 81). She chose as a model the use of European beetles to attack and control the poisonous Klamath weed (or St. John's wort), which choked out range plants and threatened the lives of cattle, sheep, goats, horses, dogs, and cats. She cited a model of the prickly pear (*Genus Opuntia*) that overran 60 million acres of Australia and the chemical controls that failed to retrieve the land for use. In 1920, entomologists completed the job by introducing Argentine moths (*Cactoblastis cactorum*), a cheap alternative to synthetic poisons. The chapter appeared in reprint in November 1962 in the *Detroit Free Press, Ottawa Journal,* and *Philadelphia Inquirer* and in December 1962 in the *Miami News.*

Sources

Boutard, C. Roy. "Review: *Silent Spring.*" (Pittsfield, MA) *Berkshire Eagle* (29 September 1962): 22.
Carson, Rachel. *Silent Spring. Boston: Houghton Mifflin,* 40th Anniversary Edition, 2002.
Renner, Rebecca. "*Silent Spring* Is More Than a Scientific Landmark: It's Literature." https://lithub.com/silent-spring-is-more-than-a-scientific-landmark-its-literature/, (20 April 2018).
Smith, Michael B. "'Silence, Miss Carson!': Science, Gender, and the Reception of *Silent Spring.*" *Feminist Studies* 27:3 (Fall 2001): 733–752.

Silent Spring: Elixirs of Death

In Chapter Three of *Silent Spring,* Rachel's skillful rhetoric moved swiftly to the heart of her argument. The subtitle returned to the diction of alchemy, a medieval source of panaceas and potions. By choosing a passive verb, "is now subjected," she implied a faceless, nameless specter spreading factory-made toxins "virtually everywhere" (Carson, 2002, 15). She dated the onslaught to 1942, stating a connection between pesticide residues and the sarin nerve gas that the Nazis researched in World War II that preceded commercialization of biocides. To enhance the argument with the theme of vulnerability, she cited chemical contamination of women's breast milk and of fetal tissue. She linked the contaminants to global conflict by extending the trope of susceptibility to "a child of the Second World War" (*ibid.,* 16). Subsequent examples focused on children disabled or killed by toxins and presaged similar images of vulnerable waterfowl in Chapter Four, "Surface Waters and Underground Seas."

Diction heightened the author's implication of evil doing with laboratory "manipulation of the molecules," a hint at pernicious formulation (*ibid.*). She contrasted pre-war insect control via arsenic, nicotine sulphate, pyrethrum, and rotenone with the post-war proliferation of chlorinated hydrocarbons and organic phosphates. To build on a combat theme, she described how toxins destroyed protective enzymes and altered cells from benign to malignant as "a battery of poisons of truly extraordinary power" (*ibid.,* 20). The U.S. chemical industry so valued the new "agents of death" that, in 13 years, factories ramped up production by 256,703 tons, an increase of 500 percent (*ibid.,* 18). The target of escalation became not control of nature, but millions in profits.

THE SILENT KILLERS

Striking directly at the wanton dissemination of DDT (dichlorodiphenyltrichloroethane), Rachel's overview warned of its accretion in body tissue, especially the liver, and its perils to farmers, sprayers, pilots, and employees of insecticide factories. She outlined passage through the food chain:

alfalfa → hens → eggs
hay → milk cows → dairy food

an impurity that the U.S. Food and Drug Administration banned from interstate shipping. Ironically, no agency could prohibit the permeation of the human fetus with DDT. The author emphasized that the potential hazard to human well-being has "no such parallel ... in medical history" (*ibid.,* 23).

Authorial drama introduced chlordane, the most poisonous biocide, which could kill on contact or after a long buildup in human organs. She detailed the creation of aldrin, dieldrin, and endrin, "the most violently poisonous of all the hydrocarbons" (*ibid.,* 25). Research into human health factors in 1962 failed to document fully citizen jeopardy. Of aldrin, she introduced the effects of biocides on reproduction in pheasants, rats, and dogs, but added that no one had calculated the effects of the toxin on humans. She concluded the triad of killers with endrin, a poisoner of well water and killer of fish, birds, and cattle. Through an extensive coverage of brain damage of an American child in Venezuela, the author returned the narrative to the most defenseless life stage.

An Array of Poisons

Rachel's chapter on poisons gained intensity with introduction of the lethal alkyls parathion and malathion, common home insecticides. Specific jobs—orchard pickers, crop dusters, physicians, launderers—placed handlers of toxins in immediate danger of seizure, coma, and death, especially when users combined alkyls in sprays or consumed alkyls in food. She emphasized insidious poisons in systemic insecticides, the deterrents that lodge in the stems, roots, and leaves of plants. By emulating the effects of natural selenium in wheat fields, entomologists created "built-in insecticides," such as seeds treated to ward off aphids and the flea killers that inhabit cat and dog blood (*ibid.,* 33).

Rachel's provocative and sobering introduction to herbicides debunked beliefs that animals were immune to plant killers, such as sodium arsenite, a suppressor of bacteria, aquatic weeds, fungi, termites, and rodents. In an apocalyptic style that ecologist Jennifer Schell, on staff at the University of Alaska, called "unsparing, blunt prose," the author stressed carcinogenic and mutational effects and the actions of authorities in England and Austria to outlaw the poisons (Schell, 2015, 58). With a rhetorical question, the author concluded the chapter with a reminder that both chemicals and radiation can alter human genes, a disheartening prospect.

See also DDT; Pesticides.

Sources

Bryson, Michael A. "Nature, Narrative, and the Scientist-Writer: Rachel Carson's and Loren Eiseley's Critique of Science." *Technical Communication Quarterly* 12:4 (Fall 2003): 369–387.
Carson, Rachel. *Silent Spring.* Boston: Houghton Mifflin, 40th Anniversary Edition, 2002.

Laakkonen, Simo, Richard P. Tucker, and Timo Vuorisalo, eds. *The Long Shadows: A Global Environmental History of the Second World War.* Corvallis: Oregon State University Press, 2017.

Schell, Jennifer. "Polluting and Perverting Nature: The Vengeful Animals of *Frogs.*" *Animal Horror Cinema.* London: Palgrave Macmillan, 2015.

Silent Spring: The Human Price

Chapter Twelve, "The Human Price," a short, but provocative essay, awakened readers to multiple physical ills caused by exposure to one or more organic killers. As she did with "Elixirs of Death" and "Needless Havoc," Rachel continued to pelt her audience with unavoidable terrors—radiation and industrial chemicals engulfing the world, spawning drastic changes in human health. Because unobtrusive effects "depend on the sum of the exposures," humankind may not suffer the damage for decades (Carson, 2002, 188).

Anatomical details about fat-soluble biocides warned of storage in lipids and a compromise to the liver's protection from disease and its detoxification of poisons from hepatitis and cirrhosis. Tests on staff at the British Royal Navy Physiological Laboratory linked a series of symptoms—lethargy, fatigue, tremor, achy joints and extremities, insomnia, anxiety, headache, irascibility, lack of vigor—with damage from DDT (dichlorodiphenyltrichloroethane) to the central nervous system, particularly in youths and women. The gradual destruction of anatomical systems created what she termed indirect death, a slow dissolution of body safeguards.

By comparing ecological risks to epidemic plague, cholera, and smallpox and by picturing pervasive pollutants in soil, water, and edibles, she preceded haunting thoughts of human obsolescence on a par with the annihilation of dinosaurs. She revealed that anatomical effects of DDT could outlast a decade. According to David Kinkela, a specialist in environmental politics at State University of New York at Fredonia, "Accidental poisoning, cancers, and chromosome abnormalities spoke of landscapes that were far from sanitized, and were, in fact, dangerous" (Kinkela, 2009, 916).

Rachel also disclosed the effects of mating two or more synthetic substances: "A chemical of supposedly innocuous nature can be drastically changed by the action of another" (*ibid.*, 195). When paired with organic phosphates, food additives and dyes, or pharmaceuticals, chlorinated hydrocarbons could cause greater damage to nerves or liver. During post–Carson global testing of the concept, medical researchers identified anomalies, for example, sick building syndrome and chemical sensitivity to cosmetics, sunscreen, perfumes, and skin cleansers.

In concurrence with Rachel's findings, in the 1960s, teachers and technical writers in Kerala, India, formed the People's Science Movement to re-plot and redirect technological research to real life in human societies, for example, projects in recycling, energy, agroecology, and transforming pure science into technology, such as the solar hot box rice cooker. The anti–DDT campaign picked up speed in July 1969, when the U.S. Department of Agriculture banned use of DDT and the Federal Aviation Agency agreed that dieldrin spray around the National Airport threatened organisms along the Potomac River. In Sweden the same year, a two-year moratorium on DDT reflected response to Rachel's concern for human wellness. As a result, in 1969, the Scranton *Tribune* and Baltimore *Evening Sun* excerpted Chapter Twelve.

Sources

Baratta, Chris. "'Interdisciplinarity' Achieved: A Brief Look at Interdisciplinary Environmentalism in the 1960s." *Interdisciplinary Literary Studies* 18:3 (2016): 301–324.
Carson, Rachel. *Silent Spring*. Boston: Houghton Mifflin, 40th Anniversary Edition, 2002.
Kinkela, David. "The Ecological Landscapes of Jane Jacobs and Rachel Carson." *American Quarterly* 61:4 (December 2009): 905–929, 997.
Smith, Adrian, Mariano Fressoli, Dinesh Abrol, Elisa Arond, and Adrian Ely. *Grassroots Innovation Movements*. London: Routledge, 2016.

Silent Spring: Indiscriminately from the Skies

In the opening sentence of Chapter Ten, Rachel advanced from "Rivers of Death" to "rain of death," a visual image of liquid toxins that inspired her compilation of *Silent Spring* (Carson, 2002, 155). Diction enhanced the fear of organic poisons with "sinister," "reckless," "blunderingly," "drenching," and "misgivings," an indication that the American public no longer rubber-stamped dispersal of organic biocides to kill fire ants (*Solenopsis geminata*) and gypsy moths (*Lymantria dispar dispar*). The author vigorously opposed an unnecessary urban DDT spraying in 1956 for moth eradication in Michigan, New Jersey, New York, and Pennsylvania.

The author demeaned the slap-dash method of applying poisons from planes, an insane sullying of streams that earned the scorn of Pennsylvania fishermen. Analyst David D. Vail, an historian at the University of Nebraska, characterized dissemination from aloft as "done without much thought to long-term dangers and with little regard for precision" (Vail, 2018, 3). The spew from the sky against gypsy moths coated ponds, marshes, dairies, pastures, and truck gardens, killing birds, crabs, fish, bees and other beneficial insects, and one unlucky horse. In view of the moth's forest habitat, the author ridiculed mass biocidal application as "the height of absurdity," a violation of landowners' constitutional rights (Carson, 2002, 158). In rebuttal, Eleanor Duke, a biologist at Texas Western College, called the "scare-type book" unfortunate (Duke, 1962, 4). Leonard N. Sime, a Phoenix writer for the *Arizona Republic*, opened his attack on the essay with the gendered accusation "A woman author, Rachel Carson, wrote a book recently" (Sime, 1963, B11).

Superficial Protections

Rachel's alert failed to stop the tainting of green produce, meat, eggs, honey, and milk, to which U.S. Food and Drug Administration agents offered halfhearted interstate monitoring. She cited lawsuits covering loss of leaf crops and honeybees. The narrative noted the public's suspicions that federal bureaus wasted money on ineffective and superfluous spraying that "had in reality accomplished nothing at all" (Carson, 2002, 161). By 1957, faceless, nameless government mimeograph machines resumed cranking out press releases, this time in Alabama and 19 other Southern states alerting citizens to the fire ant, a "sales bonanza" for biocide factories (*ibid.*,

162). The author's implications of unscrupulous profiteering upped the impact with the terms "damned," "propaganda," and "detrimental" and the rhetorical question, "Just how sound were these claims?" (*ibid.,* 163). To broaden the lack of veracity and current findings, the narrative listed beneficial acts of fire ants—killing boll weevil larvae and draining and aerating soil—while contrasting the sting of bees and wasps as more adverse to human well-being.

The treatment of a million acres from Texas to Florida with dieldrin and heptachlor in 1958, silently condoned by Secretary of Agriculture Ezra Benson, wiped out cattle, goats, horses, hogs, chicks, and pets as well as wild turkeys, raccoons, opossums, armadillos, kingbirds, larks, quail, and blackbirds. Because of the mass poisoning, Georgia veterinarian Otis L. Poitevint questioned feeding children milk from local dairy animals defiled with poison. In answer to damning questions, health officials in Alabama, Louisiana, and Texas authorized no tests on milk to determine the presence of biocides.

Alerting the Public

On September 27, 1962, the author's influence on public awareness of toxins burgeoned with the publication of *Silent Spring.* In November and December 1962, the *Ottawa Journal, Detroit Free Press,* and *Miami News* reprised "Indiscriminately from the Skies"; the *Boston Globe, St. Louis Post-Dispatch, Minneapolis Star, Des Moines Register,* and *Shreveport Times* reprinted the essay in January, February, and March 1963. In the aftermath, farmers applied deterrents directly to ant mounds at a reduction in cost of 93.4 percent of the original outlay. David D. Vail, author of *Chemical Lands,* credited Rachel's "ability to connect complex toxicological data to the real-world consequences of agricultural chemicals in common language" (Carson, 2002, 2). The controversy spread from farmers and parents to President John F. Kennedy.

Academic support indicated that Rachel had located a core threat to life on earth from aerial sprays to kill a single organism. Instead, she and other biologists proposed non-toxic control with predators rather than an uncontrolled aerosol that produced overspray and drift, which could spread for miles. Analysts René I. Alfaro, an Ottawa forester, and Edmonton entomologist David Langor, writers for the *Canadian Entomologist,* credited the author with creating "a demand and opportunities for new approaches for pest management in forestry and agriculture" (Alfaro and Langor, 2016, 10). For its trenchant message, the *Ottawa Journal* reprinted the essay in November 1962 and the *Miami News* a month later. The Santa Rosa, California, *Press Democrat, Boston Globe,* and *St. Louis Post-Dispatch* reprised the chapter in January 1963, the *Minneapolis Star* in February, and the *Des Moines Register* and the Shreveport, Louisiana, *Times* in March 1963.

See also DDT.

Sources

Alfaro, René I., and David Langor. "Changing Paradigms in the Management of Forest Insect Disturbances." *Canadian Entomologist* 148 (August 2016): S7–18.

Carson, Rachel. *Silent Spring.* Boston: Houghton Mifflin, 40th Anniversary Edition, 2002.
Cox, Jeff. "DDT Spraying Is Attacked." (Stroudsburg, PA) *Pocono Record* (9 May 1963): 15.
Duke, Eleanor. "Review: *Silent Spring."* *El Paso Herald-Post* (3 November 1962): 4.
Sime, Leonard N. "Bug Killers in Arizona Discriminate." *Arizona Republic* (8 September 1963): B11.
Vail, David D. *Chemical Lands: Pesticides, Aerial Spraying, and Health in North America's Grasslands Since 1945.* Tuscaloosa: University of Alabama Press, 2018.

Silent Spring: Nature Fights Back

In the introduction to Chapter 15, "Nature Fights Back," Rachel credited living organisms with the ability to resist chemical control. In the words of Montreal reviewer Sarah O. Cross, on staff at the *Gazette,* pesticides "have begun to boomerang" (Allen, 1962, 29). Throughout *Silent Spring,* she stressed that "nature controls her own" (Carson, 2002, 249). The narrative described pesticides as "self-defeating" and visualized the perils of tampering with nature with the image of a man perched on a cliff (*ibid.*, 246). Because of the shifting of nature's balance, insects originally faced an "internecine warfare" from predators and climate and weather conditions (*ibid.,* 247). Synthetic controls tended toward overkill—wiping out all insects, regardless of their relationship with pests.

The essay corroborated the author's precepts with a list of insects feeding on their own kind—aphids, yellowjackets, wasps, flies, ladybugs, caterpillars, dragonflies, lacewings, and "blood-sucking flies" (*ibid.,* 248). To account for damage from DDT (dichlorodiphenyltrichloroethane) spraying, Rachel cited replacements in nature—spruce budworms with spider mites and appleworms with leaf rollers and codling moths. The author stressed American agrarian enemies—Japanese beetles, corn and sugarcane borers, fire ants—and the trading of one scourge for a worse one. In Sudan, the cotton-destroying bollworm flourished in the Gash River Delta. The Belgian Congo and Uganda incurred voracious pests in coffee bushes. Truman Twill, editor of the East Liverpool, Ohio, *Evening Review,* stated, "We'll live and learn by watching death and damage" (Twill, 1962, 4).

Rachel turned boomerang effects of biocides into illustrative stories of chemical failures. According to Sarah Cross, the "distortions are apt to be nightmarish," such as "an inadvertent combination of substances that will interact disastrously" (Cross, 1962, 29). In eastern Florida, biocides killed fish and crabs in salt marshes, but left unhindered aquatic snails. Because the mollusks carried schistosoma (blood flukes), people swimming or fishing in the water or drinking it risked schistosomiasis from an infestation of the flatworms, which caused diarrhea, spleen enlargement, liver and kidney damage, infertility, bladder cancer, and death. The flukes also infested the livers of cattle deer, elk, goats, rabbits, and sheep, making their meat inedible to humans. Because of the essay's urgent message, editors reprinted it in the *Des Moines Register, Shreveport Times, St. Louis Post-Dispatch, Minneapolis Star,* Santa Rosa *Press Democrat,* and the North Hills, Pennsylvania, *News Record.*

Sources

Carson, Rachel. *Silent Spring.* Boston: Houghton Mifflin, 40th Anniversary Edition, 2002.
Cross, Sarah O. "What Price a World without Bird Song." Montreal *Gazette* (6 October 1962): 29.
Twill, Truman. "Let Us Spray." *East Liverpool Review* (3 November 1962): 4.

Silent Spring: Needless Havoc

In the seventh chapter of *Silent Spring*, the tone developed a keener edge after Rachel crafted what analyst Chad Montrie, a historian at the University Massachusetts-Lowell, termed "a methodical indictment of synthetic pesticides," particularly DDT (dichlorodiphenyltrichloroethane) (Montrie, 2018, 1). Skewering irresponsibility, she charged "the man with the spray gun" with raining havoc on nature (Carson, 2002, 85). By choosing a military term for post-combat marauding, she attributed destruction to corporate profiteers and the "control men in state and federal government" (*ibid.*, 86). Her rhetoric indicted males governed by a Cold War mentality. Analyst Joni Seager, a global environmentalist at Bentley University, restated Rachel's manifesto against "the boosters' embrace of militarized, 'miracle of science' definitions of 'progress,' in which nature is reduced to spoils of war" (Seager, 2014, 67–68).

With the authority of a bible reader, the writer implied a connection to "The Good Samaritan," Jesus's parable of charity in Luke 10:25–37. She identified the heartless priest and Levite in the story with careless and collateral deaths in the animal kingdom. Similar in purpose to "A Fable for Tomorrow," the allegory that opened *Silent Spring*, the reference invested a discussion of broad range insecticide spraying with morality. Just as Jesus presented the parable to define relationships between neighbors, the author's allusion reminded citizens of their obligations to other Americans, including hunters and fishers, explorers, gardeners, and bird watchers. For her cogent style, Chad Montrie called her "the single-most important galvanizing force behind an emergent environmental movement" (Montrie, 2018, 2).

Fearful Details

The author salted her writing with specific examples of haphazard poisoning from the air, beginning with the dusting of Detroit suburbs in 1959 with aldrin pellets to kill Japanese beetles, a project funded by the U.S. Department of Agriculture. Under the aegis of state and federal agrarian agencies, purveyors of chlorinated hydrocarbons spread the killer by air in Michigan as well as Kentucky, Illinois, Iowa, Indiana, and Missouri. Their choice of aldrin reflected its low price rather than its efficacy against the beetle. The Illinois state legislature provided $375,000 for spraying, but only $6,000 or .016 percent of the outlay for field research.

Swiss chemist Franz Froelicher characterized Rachel as "a soldier in the movement that said what science produces in Frankensteinian evil" (Chapman, 2001, D3). She recognized lies and disinformation about its safety, but gave perpetrators the benefit of the doubt: rather than deliberately conceal their error, the Detroit Department of Parks and the Federal Aviation Agency lacked information on aldrin poison from the U.S. Fish and Wildlife Service and the U.S. Public Health Service. Nonetheless, the state Audubon Society warned that the clay and aldrin pellets constituted "a possible death potion" to birds, squirrels, dogs, cats, and humankind (*ibid.*, 90).

LETHAL TREATMENTS

A similar lethal dusting in Blue Island south of Chicago, Illinois, left only 20 percent of songbirds alive. Farther south in Sheldon, Illinois, in 1954–1961, aerial eradication of Japanese beetles with dieldrin exposed birds to poisoned grubs. A collateral loss—the adulteration of grackles, meadowlarks, pheasants, robins, starlings, and brown thrashers—left survivors sterile. The animal world lost cattle, sheep, cats, fox squirrels, rabbits, and muskrats. Similar extermination of cats in Java and Venezuela resulted from haphazard dissemination of dieldrin.

According to Spanish ecologist Joandomènec Ros, on staff at the University of Barcelona, the author "forced Americans to consider an environmental drama too terrible to disregard" (Ros, 2012, 30). Instead of terrorizing, she proposed an alternate to pesticide, a coating of milky spore bacterium to control Japanese beetle larvae. Because the bacterium required only a single application, it proved cheaper and less cumbersome than self-perpetuating sprays of dieldrin, which Rachel demeaned as "nightmare excesses" (*ibid.,* 99). She accused civilization of waging an immoral war on nature, which she exemplified with the protracted death throes of the meadowlark and ground squirrel. From such unethical banes, she posed a rhetorical question: "Who among us is not diminished" by needless havoc (*ibid.,* 100).

Sources

Carson, Rachel. *Silent Spring.* Boston: Houghton Mifflin, 40th Anniversary Edition, 2002.

Chapman, Dan. "Dusting Off DDT's Image." *Atlanta Constitution* (9 September 2001): D1, D3.

Montrie, Chad. *The Myth of Silent Spring: Rethinking the Origins of American Environmentalism.* Oakland: University of California Press, 2018.

Payne, James L. "Misreading Rachel Carson's *Silent Spring.*" https://fee.org/articles/misreading-rachel-carson-s-silent-spring/, (12 August 2019).

Ros, Joandomènec. "Rachel Carson, Sensitive and Perceptive Interpreter of Nature." *Contributions to Science* 8:1 (2012): 23–32.

Seager, Joni. *Carson's Silent Spring: A Reader's Guide.* London: Bloomsbury Academic, 2014.

Silent Spring: The Obligation to Endure

To introduce a serious assessment of technological advancement by overspecialized scientists, "The Obligation to Endure," Chapter Two of Rachel's alarum defined and touted environmental citizenship for all. Reviewer Karen F. Stein, on staff at the University of Rhode Island, stated that the biologist "challenges our belief that science and technology can control the natural world, for this assumption leads us to imagine ourselves apart from nature rather than a part of nature" (Stein, 2014, 83). To draw attention to serious threats against earth, Rachel opened *Silent Spring* with a foreboding construct, "A Fable for Tomorrow." From the allegory, she moved expertly into broad concepts of time, creation, and the ability of earth to adapt to change.

Introducing the dangers of radiation to living organisms, the first chapter employed allusive diction—"alchemy" and "brewed" alongside "impetuous, heedless, unnatural, barrage, escalation, and crossfire." The medieval trope of the sorcerer's black magic carried over to the author's first insertion of data to create awareness of 500 new formulations streaming from laboratories into the U.S. marketplace. She tagged 200 nonselective insecticides as post–World War II patents applied freely in residences, yards and gardens, farms, and forests. The wanton killers concerned her for their indiscriminate spread over foliage, water, and soil.

CHEMICAL KILLER

Rachel's choice of "biocide" as a genus name pinpointed DDT (dichlorodiphenyltrichloroethane) as a creator of a super race of insects, a throwback image to Nazi Germany. Following 19th-century English naturalist Charles Darwin's theory of survival of the fittest, she explained how pesticides actually replenished the insect world with stronger, more resilient strains. Like the escalation of weaponry among super powers during the Cold War, the propagation of invasive insects required more research, newer patents, and the production of more pernicious brands of insecticides. To amplify the notion of kill power, she introduced a key concept—the biomagnification of biocides in living tissue and in the reproductive cells of plants and animals.

The one-by-one defeat of futurists revealed the biologist at her best. She claimed that U.S. farms yielded surplus foodstuffs, thus requiring creation in 1956 of the Soil Bank, a federal diversion of land use to promote conservation and a stable economy. Her narrative acknowledged the success of widespread chemical control, but added that the pesticide industry "threatens to worsen the very conditions that it is intended to curb" (Carson, 2002, 10). She complained of monocrop farming and the limiting of street shade to elms, which fell victim to a single beetle, *Xanthogaleruca luteola*. To champion the expanding science of ecology, she cited the principles of British scientist Charles Sutherland Elton, winner of the Royal Society Darwin Medal, on the need to balance rather than annihilate animal communities as a means of preventing invasions.

ETHICAL CONTROL

At chapter's end, Rachel ramped up diction once more on human disregard of empirical alternatives to "the chemical death rain" of synthetic pesticides (*ibid.*, 12). Citing Missouri-born ecologist Paul Shepard on unsound thinking, she berated entomologists who arbitrarily chose species to exterminate. To the chagrin of her peers, according to Calum Marsh, a Canadian writer for the *National Post*, Rachel questioned the intelligence, accountability, and honesty of trusted scientists. Her diatribe blasted them for amoral leadership and unconscionable profiteering.

By stipulating constitutional rights to "be secure against lethal poisons," Rachel returned to subtle reminders of "our forefathers" and the faults of the modern chemical industry for threatening the U.S. populace with toxins (*ibid.*, 12–13). Inundated with half-truths, citizens tended to accept faulty reassurances. Rachel riposted with a citation of French humanist philosopher Jean Edmond Cyrus Rostand that demanded "full possession of the facts" about synthesized poisons (*ibid.*, 13). In the estimation of semantic scholar Andrew J. Weigert, a professor emeritus at the University of Notre Dame, Rachel's pragmatism generated "changes in personal gestalts, institutional paradigms, cultural worldviews, and projected futures in the United States and beyond" (Weigert, 2008, 241).

See also DDT; Radiation; World War II.

Sources

Carson, Rachel. *Silent Spring*. Boston: Houghton Mifflin, 40th Anniversary Edition, 2002.

Marsh, Calum. "In the Beginning Was the Book; How Rachel Carson's *Silent Spring* Inspired the First Earth Day—and How Hard the Powers That Be Fought to Stop It." (Don Mills, Ont.) *National Post* (20 April 2019): WP6.

Stein, Karen F. "The Legacies of Rachel Carson." *English Journal* 103:6 (2014): 81–84.

Weigert, Andrew J. "Pragmatic Thinking about Self, Society, and Natural Environment: Mead, Carson, and Beyond." *Symbolic Interaction* 31:3 (Summer 2008): 235–258.

Silent Spring: One in Every Four

Reprising the earth's story before 541,000,000 BCE, Chapter 14, "One in Every Four," found carcinogens in pre–Paleozoic nature, notably ultraviolet radiation and arsenic. In perhaps the most popular chapter of *Silent Spring*, Rachel characterized human adaptation to hazards in Darwinian terms—the weak died, leaving the strong to thrive. Humankind added synthetic hazards by altering the biosphere with such carcinogens as the soot of pre–Industrial Age smokestacks, which caused scrotal cancer in chimney sweeps. In Great Britain and Europe, more examples appeared in Cornish and Welsh smelters of tin and copper, Saxon cobalt miners, and Bohemian uranium extractors. Into the 1800s, more connections appeared between Saxon lignite workers, Scots shale laborers, and skin cancer.

The mid–1900s generated disturbing data on malignancies in lymph and blood. *Silent Spring* emphasized that prenatal tumors derived from carcinogens passed through the mother's placenta to the unborn, one of the author's many references to the young and defenseless. Rachel listed five or six pesticides that directly caused cancer, beginning with arsenic, the source of anomalies in the liver, skin, and nervous and digestive systems in smelting operations in Saxony and naturally occurring contaminants in Cordoba, Argentina.

The author cited cancer studies that proved irreversible the main culprit—interrupted cell respiration. She connected bone cancer in factory workers who painted with radium, the weed killer aminotriazole with thyroid cancer, and agrarian arsenic with tobacco farms, orchards, and blueberry bush country. The Mayo Clinic provided data on leukemia and its link to spraying with DDT (dichlorodiphenyltrichloroethane), benzene, chlordane, lindane, and petroleum distillates.

Out of normal controls, precancerous cells could wildly reproduce, especially in young children. Despite efforts to rid the biosphere of hazards, the "great reservoirs of carcinogenic agents" continued growing as science attempted greater control of natural phenomena (Carson, 2002, 241). Orville Freeman, Secretary of Agriculture, concurred with her urging that chemical pesticide purchasers should select substances "for use in the right way at the right time" (Gavzer, 1963, C6).

Rachel proposed that prevention rather than cure offered more hope for mitigation of the disease, which occurred in complex variations. In reference to the author's treatment for breast and bone cancer beginning April 4, 1960, according to University of British Columbia author Neshma Mattu, the subtitle "One in Every Four" was "well thought-out…. She intended to be objective, yet intimate" (Mattu, 2017). In an interview with Associated Press feature writer Bernard Gavzer, Rachel declared her writing free of guile: "I'm not a muckraker…. If there was sensationalism, it was in the facts" (Gavzer, 1963, C6.).

Sources

Carson, Rachel. *Silent Spring*. Boston: Houghton Mifflin, 40th Anniversary Edition, 2002.
Gavzer, Bernard. "Pesticides: Boon or Harm." *Bridgeport Sunday Post* (24 March 1963): C1, C6.
Mattu, Neshma. "The Marriage of Science and Art within Rachel Carson's *Silent Spring*." https://artsone.arts.ubc.ca/2017/06/06/the-marriage-of-science-and-art-in-carsons-silent-spring/ (May 2017).
ten Have, Hank. *Wounded Planet: How Declining Biodiversity Endangers Health and How Bioethics Can Help*. Baltimore: Johns Hopkins University Press, 2019.

Silent Spring: The Other Road

With a nod to American poet Robert Frost, Rachel's last chapter, "The Other Road," gave one option for rescuing earth from the devastation wreaked by organic poisons. Listing the contributors to "a new science of biotic controls," the narrative identified farms as the first pioneers by suppressing insects with natural enemies (Carson, 2002, 278). The author acclaimed Edward Fred Knipling, an American entomologist with the U.S. Department of Agriculture, for a unique idea: the sterilization of male screw-worms with X-ray. The production of infertile eggs rid the test island of Curaçao of the insects and aided Florida, Alabama, and Georgia in annihilating a similar killer of cattle. Rachel extolled Knipling's strategy for its practicality. Successful applications of the method on Rhodesian tsetse flies and Hawaiian melon flies influenced scientists to attempt sterilization of Chilean mosquitoes and to create a chemical sterilant to eradicate the housefly and gypsy moth.

Lest the wrap-up argument sound too idealistic, the biologist warned that anti-sterilants—the destroyers of metabolism and chromosomes—could be cancer-causing and mutagenic. An alternate avenue, the use of insect secretions such as juvenile hormones and sex attractants proved overwhelming to Hessian flies, tobacco hornworms, fruit flies, and melon flies. Another possibility, electronic and ultrasonic sound repulsion and attraction agitated moths, sawflies, cutworms, blowflies, mealworms, mosquitoes, and corn and wood borers.

Rachel extended the list of non-poisonous microorganisms with an introduction to bacteria and viruses, such as milky spore disease to kill Japanese beetles and *Bacillus thuringiensis* to paralyze and kill the flour moth in the larval stage. The author reported success in France, Germany, Yugoslavia, and Russia and the exploitation of protozoa to reduce reproduction of Czech corn borers. Closer home, bug diseases prevailed in the evergreen forests of Canada and Vermont and in California vegetable and alfalfa plots. The major selling point of microbial control was specific details— the nature of each disease and the life cycle of the target insect. She summarized advantages of a biotic method: "it is relatively inexpensive, it is permanent, it leaves no poisonous residues" (*ibid.*, 292).

Advancing to the animal world, the chapter unfolded natural forest protectors—woodpeckers and owls to pick caterpillars off tree trunks and spiders to trap flying insects in webs. Canadians valued voles, shrews, and mice for obliterating sawflies by eating their cocoons. By abandoning organic pesticides, which Rachel likened to "the cave man's club," the feeding styles of small mammals replaced "unnatural manipulations" that worked temporarily on "insect hordes" and that jeopardized birds and other organisms essential to ecology (*ibid.*, 297, 296).

The provocative conclusion to *Silent Spring* received accolades from journalists at the London *Guardian, Berkshire Eagle, Rutland Daily Herald,* and *St. Louis Globe-Democrat* and reprints in the *Detroit Free Press, Santa Rosa* (California) *Press Democrat, St. Louis Post-Dispatch, Philadelphia Inquirer, Minneapolis Star,* and *Shreveport Times.* Justin Dillon, an environmentalist at the University of Exeter, encapsulated Rachel's message as a questioning of the definition of "progress." She demonized control of nature by reckless chemists, yet exonerated biologists for using nature to control itself. French marine biologist Daniel Pauly, on staff at the University of British Columbia, and research scientist Dirk Zeller warned that Rachel's "other road" required self-control, patience, and sacrifice, but it offered a positive future for humans and the wild (Pauly and Zeller, 2016, xiii).

Sources

Carson, Rachel. *Silent Spring.* Boston: Houghton Mifflin, 40th Anniversary Edition, 2002.
Davis, Frederick Rowe. "Pesticides and the Perils of Synecdoche in the History of Science and Environmental History." *History of Science* (24 June 2019).
Dillon, Justin. *Towards a Convergence Between Science and Environmental Education.* New York: Routledge, 2017.
Pauly, Daniel, and Dirk Zeller, eds. *Global Atlas of Marine Fisheries.* Washington, D.C.: Island Press, 2016.

Silent Spring: Realms of the Soil

Chapter Five of *Silent Spring* limited the space the book devoted to soil contaminants, a subject largely neglected in scientific studies, but Rachel did not skimp on punch. Her holistic ecological text addressed major themes—connectivity in nature from the earliest eras of evolution and cause and effect of tainting. Because animals relied on food plants, she concluded that soil had been a life foundation dating to genesis. Without naming the Silurian Age (440,000,000 BCE), she built mystery around the green-up of crushed granite from lichens and mosses, the simplest plants. Sustained by flora, which she honored as "earth's green mantle," the title of Chapter Six, the first creepers from the sea introduced plant eaters to the land (Carson, 2002, 53).

To encourage the mid–twentieth century generation to reassess its place in the outdoors, the author demonstrated regeneration by humus that kept loam alive, fragrant and productive. Promoting a mystic image of underground strands, she introduced the motifs of decomposition, the work of bacteria, algae, and fungal threads that supply nitrogen and minerals to flora. The softening and infiltration of vegetation resulted in ground aeration and drainage, a dual process advanced by earthworms, a subject introduced by English naturalist Charles Darwin in 1881 in his last treatise, *The Formation of Vegetable Mould Through the Action of Worms.*

TREATING THE LAND

By connecting the largely invisible work of subterranean organisms with pesticides, Rachel questioned the dangers of soil sterilants and biocides sprayed on woods, orchards, and plowland. The broadcasting of poisons killed targeted fungi and insects as well as beneficial organisms. She attached a gender to contaminators by calling them "control men" who "insult" the land, especially sandy soils (*ibid.,* 56). She cited the interruption of the nitrogen cycle in Florida by the all-purpose insecticide DDT (dichlorodiphenyltrichloroethane), the herbicide 2,4-D (Dichlorophenoxyacetic acid *or* agent orange), the anti-termite agent aldrin, the gnat spray DDD (dichlorodiphenyldichloroethane*)*, the fire ant deterrent heptachlor, the neurotoxin lindane, and BHC (beta-hexachlorocyclohexane), a treatment for lice, scabies, nematodes, weevils, and bacteria in rice paddies and a cause of Alzheimer's and Parkinson's disease.

To build a case against disrupting nature's balance, the author cited long-lived pesticides—aldrin, dieldrin, toxaphene, heptachlor, BHC, chlordane—that can remain in soil for more than a decade. Serious accumulations of lead arsenate in tobacco fields and DDT in potato and corn fields, orchards, and cranberry bogs derived from modest annual spraying. Toxicity in food crops, particularly carrots, reduced the value of fruits and vegetables for baby food, which manufacturers held to a high standard of purity. BHC tainted South Carolina sweet potatoes and peanuts from southern states. In Idaho and Washington, heptachlor in hops resulted in long-term virulence in soil that progressed to the mouths of cigar and cigarette smokers.

A FAVORITE READ

Rachel's essay on soil built suspense as to unknown banes of agriculture and the barrage of lethal agents in the land, notably DDT. German industrial and technological historian Joachim Radkau characterized the threat of chlorinated hydrocarbons as eternal—"a latent crisis zone that could never be entirely mastered" (Radkau, 2002, 33). For the naturalist's attempt to rescue the planet from chemical peril, Radkau compared her to Joan of Arc.

"Realms of the Soil" proved one of the author's most popular writings. The essay appeared in the *Ottawa Journal* and *Detroit Free Press* in November 1962 and, the next month, in the *Miami News,* In January 1963, the *Boston Globe,* Santa Rosa, California *Press Democrat, St. Louis Post-Dispatch,* and *Minneapolis Star* reprinted the chapter. The *Shreveport Times* and *Des Moines Register* published it in March 1963, the North Hills, Pennsylvania, *News Record* the following August.

See also Soil.

Sources

Carson, Rachel. *Silent Spring.* Boston: Houghton Mifflin, 40th Anniversary Edition, 2002.

Radkau, Joachim. *Nature and Power: A Global History of the Environment.* New York: Cambridge University Press, 2002.

Silent Spring: Rivers of Death

For Chapter 9, "Rivers of Death," the author related gripping events of 1953 in Miramichi, New Brunswick, which resulted in a mass wipeout of eastern Canadian fish, insects, and birds over 11.5 million acres. At a cost of $10 million, the aerial dispersal of DDT in oil over balsam forests, streams, and watersheds killed birds, caddis fly and blackfly larvae, midges, and mayfly and stonefly nymphs and left brook trout and salmon depleted from hunger. By August, the Canadian Fisheries Research Board could estimate that all salmon fry died and the second generation dropped by 33 percent. Fishermen gained no reprieve in the ensuing decade because the black-headed spruce budworm (*Choristoneura fumiferan*) resurged to greater numbers and required "drenching forests" in poison to rescue woodlands integral to the lumber and paper industries (Carson, 2002, 135).

Out of love for Maine, Rachel moved down the map from New Brunswick to New England to report effects of a 1958 spring spraying of oily DDT film that killed minnows, trout, and suckers, a long-lived fish species that appeared about 33,900,000 BCE. After a coating of 1,700,000 acres in Yellowstone National Park and Montana, the author detailed a 1956–1957 dieback of brook and brown trout, suckers, and whitefish and the loss of 90 percent of aquatic fauna that fed them. After 80 percent of game fish died, even more expired later after they began accessing contaminated fat stored for energy.

DEBATED APPLICATIONS

The U.S. Forest Service and the Montana Fish and Game Department tussled over the greater good for industry, tourism, recreation, and commercial and sport fishing. Even with concessions as to amounts of poison and locations of application, four streams lost all their salmon. Willing to compromise, the author proposed a pragmatic use of natural parasites—microorganisms that attacked and killed spruce budworms.

The author's careful compilation of fish die-offs extended cross-country and incorporated interaction in 1958 between the U.S. Department of Agriculture and the American Society of Ichthyologists and Herpetologists. Data from the late 1950s pinpointed agriculture and aquaculture as prime sources of biocide spills:

State	Poison	Pest	Crop	Collateral Damage
Alabama	heptachlor/dieldrin (1949–1953)	fire ant	cropland	fish, crabs, shrimp
	toxaphene (1950)	boll weevil		white crappies, bass,

State	Poison	Pest	Crop	Collateral Damage
	DDT	shiners	ponds	sunfish, catfish, drum, shad, carp, buffalo fish
California	dieldrin	leaf miner	rice	blue gill, sunfish
Florida	heptachlor/epoxide	fire ant	farms	sunfish, bass, frogs
	dieldrin (1955)	sandfly larvae	tourists, recreation venues	snook, mullet, gambusia, mojarra, crustaceans, crabs, snails
	dieldrin (1955)	mosquitoes	residences	fish, fiddler crabs
Louisiana	endrin (1960)	borers	sugarcane	sunfish
New Jersey	DDT (1945)	mosquitoes	residences, beaches	fiddler crabs, laughing gulls
Oklahoma	2,4-D (1961)	weeds	cropland, ponds	bees
Pennsylvania	endrin (1962)	mice, voles	orchards	glass shrimp, oysters, fathead minnows
Philippines	DDT (1960s)	mosquitoes	milkfish ponds	milkfish
Rhodesia	DDT (late 1940s)	mosquitoes	ponds	bream
Texas	heptachlor/dieldrin (1958)	fire ant	cropland in general	birds, fish, crabs
	DDT, lindane, chlordane, toxaphene (1961)	insects		catfish, bullhead, sunfish, carp, bass, shiner, mullet, sucker, gar, eels, buffalo
Western Plains	chlordane (1953)	grasshopper	grassland	stream fish, bees

The disastrous January 15–21, 1961, fish kill in Austin and La Grange, Texas, from industrial dumping of chlordane, lindane, DDT, and toxaphene required major restocking of the Colorado River from state hatcheries and acceptance of permanent loss of certain species. Rachel left as an unknown the outflow of biocides among organisms in the Gulf of Mexico.

FISHERS VS. FARMERS

Response to Rachel's diatribe was immediate. On November 22, 1962, Christopher Young, editor of the *Ottawa Citizen,* summarized her conclusion in a timely aphorism: "Much is suspected, but not enough known" (Young, 1962, 6). From November 1962 to late 1963, the *Ottawa Journal, Philadelphia Inquirer, Baltimore Evening Sun, St. Louis Post-Dispatch*, and Santa Rosa, California, *Press Democrat* excerpted "Rivers of Death"; *Outboard Boating* repeated the chapter in the September–October 1963 issue. The following March, Leon Terriere, a biochemist at Oregon State University, rebutted Rachel's findings by reminding the public of successful battles against sleeping sickness and malaria from insect control. In June 1963, the *Chicago Tribune* reported that the American Fishing Tackle Manufacturers distributed reprints of "Rivers of Death," which readers found informative and disturbing, especially sport fishers of Iroquois County, Illinois.

Because Rachel considered irreconcilable the clash between nature and the impact of agribusiness and the chemical industry on the economy and public health, "Rivers of Death" became a touchstone of advocacy for sensible pest control. On March 3, 1965, Rupert Cutler, editor of *National Wildlife,* revived interest in the chapter before Pennsylvanians sprayed DDT to combat cankerworms. In April 1984, Elton J. Gissendanner, director of the Florida Department of Natural Resources and a guest columnist for the Fort Myers *News-Press* excerpted "Rivers of Death" in opposition to chemical control of mosquitoes. In 2019, David K. Hecht, an historian of science at Bowdoin College, concluded that the author "carefully constructed her argument in ways that facilitated its initial acceptance" (Hecht, 2019, 582).

See also Pesticides.

Sources

Carson, Rachel. *Silent Spring.* Boston: Houghton Mifflin, 40th Anniversary Edition, 2002.

Hecht, David K. "Rachel Carson and the Rhetoric of Revolution." *Environmental History* 24:3 (July 2019): 561–582.

McNally, Tom. "Woods and Waters." *Chicago Tribune* (16 June 1963): 2–7.

Milewski, Inka. "Rivers of Death Revisited." https://www.elements.nb.ca/theme/artists/inka/milewski.htm (June 2000).

Young, Christopher. "Pesticides and *Silent Spring.*" *Ottawa Citizen* (22 November 1962): 6.

Silent Spring: The Rumblings of an Avalanche

For a summation on unprecedented assaults on nature and human health by deadly synthetic substances, Rachel returned to her deference to the Darwinian theory of survival of the fittest. Chapter Sixteen, "The Rumblings of an Avalanche," noted that inorganic insecticides formulated to subdue orchard scale began to fail in Clarkston, Washington, a grain export nexus. In California, hydrocyanic acid produced resistance in the codling moth, which preys on apples, apricots, chestnuts, cherries, peaches, pears, plums, and walnuts.

The author reported the rise of resistant insect species in 1960 to 137, a serious concern for farmer and foresters and for potential victims of encephalitis, dysentery, malaria, yellow fever, typhus, sleeping sickness, and eye disease. In a September 1962 newspaper feature for the Louisville *Courier-Journal,* William M. Clay, chair of the biology department at the University of Louisville, cited generously from Rachel's words and examples. Two years later, Pete Perschbacher, a journalist for the Hillsdale, Michigan, *Daily News,* honored *Silent Spring* as the "Paul Revere alarm to the nation" (Perschbacher, 1964, 3)

Critics tended to ignore the biologist's statement that "No responsible person contends that insect-borne disease should be ignored," especially carriers of malaria, plague, and typhus on every continent and most islands (Carson, 2002, 266). Throughout the mid-to-late 1940s, new chlorinated hydrocarbons combatted mosquitoes and flies in Italy, Sardinia, Egypt, Denmark, and the Tennessee Valley. At the development of insect resistance in 1949, authorities turned to organic phosphates. To stress the dangers of irresponsible use of organic poisons, the author's illustrator grouped grapes, green beans, a pumpkin, milk bottle, and daisies alongside a spray can of DDT (dichlorodiphenyltrichloroethane).

At mid-century, greater insect resistance spread round the world, carrying epidemic conjunctivitis, elephantiasis, encephalitis, malaria, and yellow fever. Rachel warned of the swarms of black mosquitoes (*Aedes taeniorhynchus*) in Florida's salt marsh, rendering wetlands uninhabitable for tourism, commerce, and recreation. Additional mosquito infestation affected California, Massachusetts, New Jersey, and Ohio at the same time that brown dog ticks (*Rhipicephalus sanguineus*), overran New York and Connecticut. A similar resistance in 65 agrarian pests and in house roaches left exterminators with few choices of suppressants. The author repeated Charles Darwin's views on survival of the fittest and acknowledged that insects sped "a lap ahead" of technology by laying eggs on DDT and raising healthy young that were immune to the poison (*ibid.*, 272). Another insect coping measure, the application of a fly enzyme to detoxify DDT resulted in DDE (dichlorodiphenyldichloroethylene), a less harmful substance with no practical use.

Political analyst Christopher Bosso, on staff at Northeastern University, summarized Rachel's issues as a moral and economic dilemma. Because the governance of biocides raised technical and ethical complexities, there were few overlaps in opinions.

- Ecologists wanted a prohibition of biocides.
- Insecticide profiteers wanted to cash in on their investments.
- Meanwhile, agribusiness sought a cheap pesticide that could raise crop yields.
- For different reasons, health authorities sought ways to curb insect-borne disease.

Conflicts pitted the public against strategies that raised food costs and elevated threats of cancer.

See also World War II.

Sources

Carson, Rachel. *Silent Spring*. Boston: Houghton Mifflin, 40th Anniversary Edition, 2002.
Clay, William M. "Is Man Poisoning Himself in His Battle Against Bugs?" Louisville, Kentucky *Courier-Journal* (23 September 1962): 4:3.
Killingsworth, M. Jimmie, and Jacqueline S. Palmer. *Ecospeak: Rhetoric and Environmental Politics in America*. Carbondale: Southern Illinois University Press, 1992.

Silent Spring: Surface Waters and Underground Seas

In Chapter Four of *Silent Spring*, Rachel segued from "Elixirs of Death" to subsurface aquifers, a Gothic take on essential, salubrious liquid threatened by toxic waste and agricultural runoff. Seeping into streams, the watershed, and public reservoirs, the invisible pesticides spread poison evenly across the land, eluding the vigilance of water departments and the U.S. Public Health Service. From a 1960 U.S. Fish and Wildlife Service report, she acquired redoubtable evidence that groundwater bore DDT (dichlorodiphenyltrichloroethane), a killer of harmful mosquitoes, gnats, and flies as well as beneficial organisms, such as dragonflies, which eat midges, moths, and mosquitoes.

From an initial study, the author deduced, "It is not possible to add pesticides to water anywhere without threatening the purity of water everywhere" (Carson, 2002, 42). The balance of "anywhere" with "everywhere" condemned the people of earth to a perpetual scourge from alien agents in its "dark, subsurface sea" (*ibid.*). Advancing from motifs introduced in *The Sea Around Us,* the author sprinkled the narrative with examples of increased concentrations in biocides in regions across the United States: Tennessee, Pennsylvania, Alabama, Colorado, California, and, Oregon. Environmental historian Gary Kroll surmised, "Rachel Carson's *Silent Spring* played a large role in articulating ecology as a 'subversive subject'—as a perspective that cuts against the grain of materialism, scientism, and the technologically engineered control of nature" (Kumar, 2014, 303).

INDIVIDUAL EXAMPLES

Rachel located one of her most astounding cases of contaminated water in Colorado. Seepage from a defunct war arsenal near Denver spread non-selective biocides into nearby farms from 1943 to the early 1960s, sickening herds and killing corn crops in a nine-mile radius. An eerie fact astounded groundwater researchers for the U.S. Public Health Service—the mix of discharge spontaneously formed the herbicide 2,4-D (Dichlorophenoxyacetic acid or agent orange), a cause of neuritis, paralysis, birth defect, miscarriage, and non–Hodgkin's lymphoma. She surmised that the impromptu synthesis of carbon-based substances derived energy from air, sunlight, or ionizing radiation.

By citing the fisherman and tourist's annoyance by gnats at Clear Lake in north central California, Rachel exemplified concern for toxic insecticides that permeate other sources of water and sediment. Targeted in 1949 with a DDD (dichlorodiphenyldichloroethane) emulsion at the rate of one part to 70,000,000 parts water, the obnoxious midge began disappearing. A second application in 1954 and a third in 1957 inadvertently killed the swan grebe, a graceful glider on the lake surface, "the body riding low, white neck and shining black head held high" (*ibid.*, 47). By picturing a dignified elegance in an innocent bird, the author advanced a subtext of concern for the defenseless.

TOXIC WATERS

The author's deliberate creation of mental images imprinted on readers' minds a vicious killer of wildlife that struck indiscriminately, a hint that humans shared the threat. The image of a fluffy gray hatchling nestled under a parent's wing echoed Rachel's concern for the very young, a controlling metaphor of the opening allegory "A Fable for Tomorrow." Analysis of the fish that fed grebes introduced one of her major theories, the biomagnification of taint along the food chain, a "house-that-Jack-built sequence," an allusion to the nursery rhymes of childhood (*ibid.*, 48).

The writer concluded the chapter with a conundrum of funding from public coffers: The wholesale poisoning of reservoirs to exterminate unwanted fish required water treatment to spare citizens the contaminants in food fish and drinking supplies. At the National Cancer Institute in Bethesda, Maryland, Wilhelm Carl Hueper, a German expert on environmental carcinogens, alerted the public to mounting hazards from toxic drinking water. A Dutch study a decade before the writing of *Silent Spring* established that citizens have a lower cancer risk from well water than from public cisterns dependent on rivers, which commonly carried naturally occurring arsenic as well as synthetic chemicals. According to analyst Jen Hill, a writer and illustrator of children's works, Rachel's description universalized the menace of water-borne pesticides and "[enabled] us to think transnationally and ecologically" about a global issue (Hill, 2017, 284). A reprint appeared in a November 1962 *Detroit Free Press* and *Philadelphia Inquirer*, December 1962 *Miami News* and *St. Louis Post-Dispatch*, January 1963 *Minneapolis Star*, and March 1963 *Des Moines Register.*

Sources

Carson, Rachel. *Silent Spring.* Boston: Houghton Mifflin, 40th Anniversary Edition, 2002.

Dimock, Wai Chee. *Through Other Continents: American Literature across Deep Time.* Princeton, NJ: Princeton University Press, 2006.

Elliott, Melanie. "Carson's Landmark Book Still Has Relevance Today." *Saskatoon Sun* (16 December 2007): 22.

Hill, Jen. "Surfaces and Depths." *Women's Studies Quarterly* 45:1/2 (Spring/Summer 2017): 282–286.

Kumar, Sunita Vijay. "Ecocentricism and Environmentalism. Stewardship of the *Silent Spring*." *Research Scholar* 2:4 (November 2014): 297–303.

Perschbacher, Pete. "Sounds Rumblings of Avalanche." *Hillsdale* (Michigan) *Daily News* (8 April 1964): 3.

Silent Spring: Through a Narrow Window

Opening on an optical trope of peering through a slim aperture, Rachel's Chapter Thirteen, "Through a Narrow Window," focused on destruction of cells by "foreign chemicals," a phrase implying alien or intrusive substances (Carson, 2002, 200). By picturing the little fires that spark the body's energy and the ever-turning wheel of chemical changes, the narrative created the image of mitochondria, the well-stocked factory machines that energize muscle, reproductive, and nerve cells. The author's experience at classroom teaching visualized for the reader the danger to mitochondria through uncoupling by radiation, DDT (dichlorodiphenyltrichloroethane), or phenol, a petroleum byproduct.

The complexity of uncoupling threatened the readability of much of the essay, especially information about enzymes, the catalysts that generate biochemical actions. Rachel listed DDT, malathion, methoxychlor, and phenothiazine as biocides that starve the cell of oxygen. Data on congenital malformations and fetal death indicated oxygen deprivation to ova in frogs and sea urchins during cell division.

With a compassionate reflection on defunct eggs of eagles, pheasants, chickens, and robins, she restored some lyricism and canceled the effects of too much biological terminology.

A Fearful Conclusion

Connecting human welfare to the web of life, the author stated a grim fact: that insecticide contamination in "any species should therefore disturb us, suggesting comparable effects in human beings" (*ibid., 207*). She warned of huge amounts of synthetic chemicals in the reproductive organs of pheasants, mice, guinea pigs, robins, bulls, and deer. Her alarm progressed to the withering of testes and suppressed sperm production in crop dusters who spread DDT.

Rachel alerted readers to the death or mutation of chromosomes, human hereditary material altered by radiation or synthetic chemicals to cause malformed fetuses. With a touch of drama, she stressed the importance of mitosis: "Neither man nor amoeba, the giant sequoia nor the simple yeast cell can long exist without carrying on this process of cell division" (*ibid.,* 210). The narrative cited opinions that durable mitosis depended on accurate passage of coded genes from one generation to another.

Menaces to Health

The science of genetics impressed Rachel with its research into the risks of contaminating cells with weed killers and insecticides such as 2,4-D or Agent Orange (2,4-Dichlorophenoxyacetic acid), phenol, BHC (benzene hexachloride), and urethane. She listed cell alteration, gender mutation, mongolism, sterility, leukemia, malignancy, endocrine disruption, and embryonic death as possible outcomes. She reported insect evolution into "gynandromorphs—part male and part female" (*Ibid.,* 212). Her conclusion called for preservation of genetic integrity, especially by testing synthetic chemical effects beyond one generation.

Nearly a half century after publication of *Silent Spring,* the prophecy proved true. Biologist Patricia M. DeMarco, a research professor at Carnegie Mellon University, reported in 2010 a Centers for Disease Control discovery of mutagens, carcinogens, and toxins in the cord blood of newborns. In 2017, over a half century after publication of *Silent Spring,* DeMarco applauded Rachel's efforts to "support precaution in manmade intrusions into the living world" (DeMarco, 2017, 130).

See also Human Health; Mutagens.

Sources

Carson, Rachel. *Silent Spring.* Boston: Houghton Mifflin, 40th Anniversary Edition, 2002.
DeMarco, Patricia M. "Every Day Earth Day." *Pittsburgh Post-Gazette* (22 April 2010): B7.
_____. "Rachel Carson's Environmental Ethic—A Guide for Global Systems Decision Making." *Journal of Cleaner Production* 140:1 (1 January 2017): 127–133.
Richmond, Marsha L. "Women as Public Scientists in the Atomic Age: Rachel Carson, Charlotte Auerbach, and Genetics." *Historical Studies in the Natural Sciences* 47:3 (June 2017): 349–388.

Soil

Rachel revered planetary growing matter as the basis of the wild. She stated, "Our Origins are of the earth" (Carson, 2002, 88). In 1951, *The Sea Around Us* contrasted the fertile salt depths with a pre-evolutionary stony land, "bleak and hostile … a continent without soil" shadowed by clouds and pelted with rain and wind (Carson, 1951, 3). Throughout her career, she gathered data on modern land use, including clearcutting of rainforests that caused topsoil to erode, soil fumigation to eradicate fungi, and the spraying of herbicides, particularly Agent Orange (2,4-Dichlorophenoxyacetic acid), a cause of human and animal chromosome damage, mutated cells, miscarriage, and birth defects.

The biologist activated her research in the 1920s and developed into a voice for holistic science. By 1935, she warned that the plowing of prairie grass caused erosion of topsoil, a concern of President Franklin D. Roosevelt until passage of the Soil Conservation Act to replace lost loam from Ontario to Mexico. She reported that, for two decades, from the end of World War II in 1945 to 1965, government agencies, farmers, and domestic users spread 675,000 tons of DDT (dichlorodiphenyltrichloroethane) over the land. In 1959 alone, the dissemination reached its peak at 40,000 tons. Rachel's friends, Olga and Stuart Hutchins, wrote of the aerial sprayers invading the air space and permeating the soil of their two-acre refuge at Powder Point in Duxbury, Massachusetts, with dangerous hydrocarbons.

LIFE'S FOUNDATION

Just as Rachel revered evolution and regeneration, she honored soil as the foundation of life. In *Silent Spring: Realms of the Soil,* she stated the constant interconnection of humus with air, minerals, sunlight, and water. She inferred that the land "exists in a state of constant change, taking part in cycles that have no beginning and no end" (Carson, 2002, 53). Her speech to the Federation of Homemakers in Bethesda, Maryland, on January 8, 1963, proposed a letter-writing blitz to congressmen complaining of soil contamination, which migratory birds carried as far north as the Arctic Circle at Yellowknife. On June 4, 1963, she appeared before Secretary of Health, Education, and Welfare Abraham Ribicoff and a Senate subcommittee to state a fundamental precept of nature: "The world of air and water and soil supports not only the hundreds of thousands of species of animals and plants, it supports man himself" (Vail, 2018, 97). Her testimony asserted that humankind carelessly ignores the connection.

At a height of oratorical success, on October 18, 1963, the writer participated in the symposium *Man Against Himself,* which convened 1,500 physicians in San Francisco. To envision the unity of soil with air and water, the author spoke frankly to experts at the Kaiser-Permanente conference about the fallout from bomb tests in Nye County, Nevada, in July 1962. Her hour-long speech, "The Pollution of Our Environment," enlarged on toxic drift to pastures in Utah and Idaho and the tainting of cow's milk with radioactive particles of iodine 131. The text targeted the unlikely tie between polluted soil and babies dependent on milk feedings.

ECHOES OF RACHEL

A posthumous excerpt of *The Edge of the Sea*, in 1971, *The Rocky Coast*, exalted the scaly rock lichens of the Maine shore, the earth's earliest plant life. Their hairy tentacles infiltrated crevices and exuded acid that broke down granite into soil. By intensifying the ongoing creation of loam, she alerted readers to the need to maintain earth's purity and to support the natural tillage of humus by earthworms.

The narrative urged shielding land from chlordane, a toxic chlorinated hydrocarbon sprayed in yards and around buildings to kill termites. On October 18, 1972, the Clean Water Act drew on Rachel's wise counsel to address pollution of ground sources. As a result, the shores of Washington's Potomac River improved enough to thrive as a bird and fish habitat.

See also Silent Spring: Realms of the Soil

Sources

Carson, Rachel. "The Pollution of Our Environment," address to the Kaiser-Permanente Symposium *Man Against Himself*, San Francisco (18 October 1963).

_____. *The Rocky Coast*. New York: McCall, 1971.

_____. *The Sea Around Us*. New York: Oxford University Press, 1951.

_____. *Silent Spring*. Boston: Houghton Mifflin, 2002.

Fellows, Valerie. "On Eagle's Wings." *Fish & Wildlife News* (Spring 2007): 20–21.

Vail, David D. *Chemical Lands: Pesticides, Aerial Spraying, and Health in North America's Grasslands Since 1945*. Tuscaloosa: University of Alabama Press, 2018.

Speeches

Literary historians tend to reduce Rachel's canon to four major works, but her output included pamphlets, press releases, articles, personal essays, professional and personal correspondence, and public addresses. Ranging in style and delivery from informative to provocative, her oratory emerged from notes written in strict outline and in poetic spacing. To explain how a mainlander learned to love the sea, Rachel quoted American poet Emily Dickinson's "I Never Saw a Moor." Even on an odyssey through the Florida Everglades in June 1950, she had calculated the ancient effects of tides on the formation of a swamp, leaving it "trackless … as the sea" (*ibid.*). She detailed the talk with memories of a gator, sea snails, the mysteries of seeds, and an archeological dig of prehistoric Seminole sites predating the 16th century CE.

For lay audiences, Rachel revealed personal delights and quirks by stressing monosyllabic action verbs that allowed listeners to imagine underwater adventures of sea creatures. On January 9, 1952, becoming the first woman to achieve the Henry Grier Bryant Gold Medal from the Geographical Society of Philadelphia, she quoted Algernon Swinburne's "Laus Veneris" (Praise of Venus) and his view of white caps, which challenged listeners to meld imaginative with scientific thinking. In "The Real World Around Us," delivered conversational style on April 21, 1954, to the Theta Sigma Phi Matrix Table Dinner in Columbus, Ohio, she described the usual assembly as 10 people rather than a "sea of faces … $10 \times 10 \times 10$" (*ibid.*). She crafted candid oratory about the "unanswerable questions" that emerged in research and piqued curiosity (Carson, "Real," 1954). Personal remarks to attending journalists characterized her as a "reporter and interpreter of the natural world" and elicited chuckles at her self-deprecating wit (*ibid.*).

She recounted a first research voyage in July 1953 to Georges Banks south of Massachusetts, a love-at-first-sight experience of trawling for fish. To Theta Sigma Phi, she championed the affinity of humankind for outdoor beauty "in the spiritual development of any individual or any society," a child development theme that recurred in the posthumous meditation *The Sense of Wonder* (*ibid.*). In a letter to Maine neighbor Dorothy Freeman on June 23, 1956, Rachel reported staying at Washington's Sheraton-Park Hotel and wearing a shell pin and pink carnation corsage to address an assemblage of the American Association of University Women. In receipt of $2,500, she delivered a brief thank-you. She described the event to Dorothy: "My own little talk went off all right and—here she goes being shameless again—there were some very satisfying comments about it" (Carson, letter, 1956). In the speech "Man and Nature in a Chemical Age" to the Association of Librarians on May 28, 1962, she reminded herself in podium notes to create an image of pageantry and spectacle of an elusive world open to all comers. In early November 1962, as reported in the *Richmond Times-Dispatch*, Rachel set up a graphic picture of chemical industries "hurling brute force against the delicate web of natural relationships" (Ellyson, 1962).

"Of Man and the Stream of Time"

On June 12, for the commencement class of 1962 at Scripps College in Claremont, California, the author presented "Of Man and the Stream of Time." The meditation stressed human over-confidence and a careless "attitude toward nature … the part of the world that man did not make" (Carson, "Of Man," 1962). Her commentary directed audience thought toward a terrifying possibility that irresponsibility could end life on earth, a message later issued in *Silent Spring*. She charged the evolving race with too many smarts but not enough caution.

In a summary of global history, Rachel depicted Victorians as purveyors of belief in man's supremacy over the rest of creation. Introducing aftereffects of the bombing of Hiroshima on June 6, 1945, she inveighed against the disposal of nuclear tailings at sea. In defense of philanthropist Albert Schweitzer's credo of "reference for life," she emphasized the risks of radioactive contaminants and designer chemicals, which fouled air, land, food, and water. By heightening the tone of address to graduates, she sent them on their way from Scripps with a challenge to overcome rampant "ignorance and evasion of truth," a common deception mounted by greedy chemical firms and agribusiness (*ibid.*).

"Address" to the Women's National Press Club

On December 3, 1962, to the Women's National Press Club, Rachel opened with witty remarks on criticisms of *Silent Spring* by Pennsylvanians who had not read the book and by Vermont readers who defied claims that she didn't make. Countering the naysayers, she cited heaps of mail to her office, newspapers, and federal agencies (Carson, "Reception," 1962). Revelation of propaganda from the agrarian and chemical industries implied a defensive tactic to shore up pesticide sales rather than formulation of a wise method of pest control.

The speaker charged critics of *Silent Spring* with unscientific thinking and lies that her data were out of touch. With a newswoman's aplomb, she listed eight accidents with the biocides aldrin, dieldrin, DDT (dichlorodiphenyltrichloroethane), and heptachlor and faulty application of highway herbicides, lawn sprays, and seeds permeated with fungicide. By linking DDT-poisoned fish in Framingham, Massachusetts, with contaminated drinking water, she brought home a disturbing message. Additional reportage on freakish potato that sprouted inside rather than outside condemned use of biocides on consumables.

Sharpening in tone and detail, Rachel's oration alerted listeners to the deaths of cattle, crop dusters, and citizens in California, Florida, India, and Japan. She asserted that reliable educators at Johns Hopkins University had prepared her for a career in marine biology. She developed thoughts about higher education to cover university grants backed by chemical firms. With dramatic enhancement, she posed rhetorical questions: "Whose voice do we hear—that of science? or of the sustaining industry?" (*ibid.*). By linking monetary inducements with a scientific report on wildlife dispatched by the National Academy of Sciences, she alerted journalists to an obvious conflict of interest. Her conclusion charged capitalism with corrupting truth.

ANIMAL WELFARE INSTITUTE

On January 7, 1963, in receipt of the Albert Schweitzer Medal from the Animal Welfare Institute in Washington, D.C., Rachel acknowledged the credo of a group promoting life-sustaining habitats in air, water, and earth. Specifically, she celebrated the famed Alsatian ethicist-physician for his concept of "Reverence for Life" (Carson, 1963, 223). His credo derived from an insightful moment on the way in September 1915 from the compound at Lambaréné in west central Gabon to save the life of Madame Pelot at N'Gomo, a Swiss mission downriver from his hospital. Rachel chose storytelling as a method of dramatizing an altruist's aid to African Christians. Traveling east on a 160-mile trip along the Ogooué River that crosses Gabon, he adapted the Jain concept of non-violence into an obligation to safeguard all organisms.

Rachel characterized Schweitzer's observation of hippopotami at sunset as an "aha" experience, a sudden apotheosis that reflected ethical insights into the unity of life. Her own reflection of a crab in a North Carolina swamp dwarfed by incoming Atlantic swells symbolized the adjustment of small organisms to overwhelming powers in the environment. Her brief text stressed human defense of all beings as a foundation of civilization. She condemned "needless destruction and suffering" as detrimental to enlightenment and to the refinement of the sacred in human attitudes (*ibid.*).

GARDEN CLUB OF AMERICA

Although seriously depleted by cancer treatment since November 1960, Rachel carefully honed her oratory to another audience on January 8, 1963, the day after her address to the Animal Welfare Institute in Washington. To the Garden Club of America in New York City, the speech "A New Chapter in *Silent Spring*" tailored alarming rhetoric to a learned, committed listener in the same style as her rhetoric to the National Women's National Press Club. Moving directly to the reckless use of biocides, she called for a "sane policy for controlling unwanted species," whether they be weeds, insects, or rodents (Carson, "New Chapter," 1963). By condemning broad spraying as one of the "crude methods of a rather low scientific order," she implied that entomologists should aid the U.S. Department of Agriculture. She called for a more direct and efficient method of control such as the sterilization of the screwworm or blowfly, a devourer of living flesh (*ibid.*). Less exacting methods only launched new problems, particularly the spider mite infestations, which burgeoned after the eradication of predatory spruce budworms by sprays of DDT.

Overall, Rachel outlined a regimen of vigilance to gardeners that generated excitement for activism. She targeted situations where state and district spray programs rejected input from citizens, the case in Norfolk after a decision by the Virginia Department of Agriculture to target the white fringed beetle with dieldrin. She urged citizens to remain wary of propaganda from chemical firms, corrupt agricultural colleges, the U.S. Congress, lobbyists, biased research, and industry as a whole. Her example, the manufacturer's permeation of wheat seed in Turkey with hexachlorobenzene, a cause of freakish birth defects in 5,000 children, demonized irresponsible users of chemicals.

Including herself as a concerned citizen, the author personalized the democratic ideal. She demanded accountability by lobbyists and formulators of biased or misleading reports: "We must continue to challenge and to question, we must insist that the burden of proof is on those who would use these chemicals" (*ibid.*). She denounced the chemical industry for double dealing by seeking tax relief on the cost of lobbying against regulation. Her speech sought reduced obstacles on tax-exempt garden clubs and Audubon societies for influencing congress. As a guide to testing for truth, she inquired, "Who speaks?—And why?" (*ibid.*).

KAISER-PERMANENTE

On October 10, 1963, Rachel opened a Kaiser-Permanente symposium in San Francisco on *Man Against Himself,* by informing 1,500 physicians on global contamination. Her hour-long address, "The Pollution of Our Environment," asserted a fearful possibility—that "man could be working against himself" (Carson, "Pollution," 1963). She advised on the need for wisdom and responsibility toward complex life forms and connected constant changes on earth to ecology. Detailed examples of waste disposal and detergent use linked pollutants to the homeowner.

Rachel declared that over half of pesticides traveled at large on air currents as far as the Arctic Circle and deep seas. She cited as an example the spread of toxaphene at Clear Lake, California, to the detriment of pelicans and the western grebe. She progressed to the migration of atomic waste via plankton, the food of fish, seals, and whales. Tainted sea animals further sullied the meals of Alaskan Eskimos, Norwegians, and Finnish and Swedish Lapps.

The speaker acknowledged that scientists acted on faulty conclusions about radioactive particles. Iodine 131, a product of nuclear fission found in milk, accumulated in thyroid glands and presented a danger of cancer to infants and children. More hazardous, radioactive rubble and gamma rays from five bomb tests in Nye County, Nevada, in July 1962 mutated DNA. Westerly winds carried fallout that threatened residents of Idaho, Nevada, and Utah with tumors and cancer. In addition, bomb tests centered explosions underground, where released energy from plutonium and uranium compromised aquifers. She asserted that some government agencies approved deadly materials without understanding the menace to citizens and future generations. She hoped that the modern military would recognize its perilous role in polluting the environment.

Audubon Medal

Although literary historians declared the Kaiser-Permanente keynote oration Rachel's last speech, she made a subsequent thank-you address at the Hotel Roosevelt in New York. In accepting the Paul Bartsch Medal from the National Audubon Society on December 3, 1963, she chose standard terms about achievement and pride. Via personal example, she asserted, "the National Audubon Society *is* my country—I belong to it…. The earth will be better for our efforts" (Carson, "Acceptance," 1963). Her text reminded members that conservation efforts never end—the responsibility is ongoing.

Rather than cite alarms about pesticides and radiation, Rachel praised Stewart Udall's even-handed survey of earth preservation in his book *The Quiet Crisis*. At the heart of her commentary, she maintained that nature is finite, "not inexhaustible" (*ibid.*). Profligacy at the hands of "timber barons and the land grabbers," greedy, shortsighted profiteers jeopardized the national legacy, especially the extermination of wildlife and clearcutting of forests (*ibid.*). The growth of population resulted in "less clean water, less uncontaminated air; there are fewer forests, fewer unspoiled wilderness areas" (*ibid.*). The speech ended with dignity and gratitude for the privilege of defending the earth.

See also "Address" to the Women's National Press Club; Diction; "The Pollution of Our Environment."

Sources

Carson, Rachel. "Acceptance Speech," National Audubon Society, New York (3 December 1963).
_____. "Address," Women's National Press Club (5 December 1962), Washington, D.C.
_____. "Letter to Dorothy Freeman" (23 June 1956).
_____. "A New Chapter in *Silent Spring*," address to the Garden Club of America, New York City (8 January 1963).
_____. "Of Man and the Stream of Time." *Scripps College Bulletin*, Claremont, CA (12 June 1962): 5–10.
_____. "The Pollution of Our Environment," address to the Kaiser-Permanente Symposium *Man Against Himself*, San Francisco (18 October 1963).
_____. "Rachel Carson Speaks on Reverence for Life." *Information Report, Animal Welfare Institute* 12:1 (January–February 1963): 223.
_____. "The Real World Around Us," address to the Theta Sigma Phi Matrix Table Dinner, Columbus, Ohio (21 April 1954).
Ellyson, Louise, "'Let Nature Work for You,' Author Rachel Carson Says." *Richmond Times-Dispatch* (2 November 1962).

Sport Hunting

Rachel's incorporation of American history into biological overviews included gamesmen who fished for salmon and hunted bison and passenger pigeons, two losses to colonial species. In January 1938, "Ducks Are on Increase, But the Short Hunting Season Will Continue," her evaluation of the 1937 waterfowl shooting season for the *Baltimore Sunday Sun Magazine,* even-handedly viewed bag limits, open season, and the dip in duck and geese populations in 1933 and 1934. Her explanation of flyways and breeding grounds on the prairies of Quebec, Ontario, and the Great Lakes covered canvasbacks, pintails, redheads, and scaups and their struggles against "the plow and the dredge" (Carson, 1938, 1).

The author reprised the draining of the North American grain bowl in 1922 from Manitoba, Alberta, and Saskatchewan into the U.S., where drought from the Dust Bowl further depleted lakes and marshes. Federal sanctuaries in the Dakotas in 1936 produced an uptick in waterfowl populations, but the author named Canada as the key to plentiful fowl. She concluded that "Restoration of the southern Canadian area is ... of primary importance" to plentiful geese and ducks (*ibid.*). In mid–February 1938, she gathered more details on threats to hunters' quarry at the Third North American Wildlife Conference sponsored by the American Wildlife Institute at the Lord Baltimore Hotel in south central Baltimore. Speakers informed her about the status of waterfowl market hunting, night shooting, and illegal trapping of canvasback ducks.

RAVAGING THE WILD

In 1939, "Starlings a Housing Problem," the author's article on perching birds for the *Baltimore Sunday Sun Magazine* reported that the Maryland Sportsmen's Club had sponsored a 1934 law allowing police to shoot the messy birds from tall buildings, an unwise pest control method. In more forceful commentary on whaling, she approved treaties that limited the reduction of earth's dwindling supply of pods, especially regulations protecting mothers and their young. Two years later, a tinge of nostalgia in *Under the Sea Wind* recalled a time when flocks of golden plover cloaked the Arctic skies on their way 2,000 miles south for the winter. She named bird shooters "gunners" who "picked off" seabirds. The article briefly mentioned "eskimos and trappers and traders" of Hudson Bay, Canada, who furthered the destruction of avian life out of "the fancied pleasure of stopping in full flight a brave and fiercely burning life" (Carson, 1941, 48, 49).

In essays on declining avian populations, Rachel recognized the complexity of bird loss. Her essay "Sky Dwellers," a salute to the chimney swift in the November 1945 issue of *Coronet,* esteemed the zippy flier for combing clear air for insects, which they fed to their nestlings. Mindful that the heron took only enough for a meal, she recoiled from human predations—the shooting of shorebirds by sport hunters and the plucking of feathers from egrets to provide plumage for women's hats, boas, and fans. Her 1947 pamphlet "Chincoteague: A National Wildlife Refuge" for the U.S. Department of the Interior, warned of historical periods of heavy gunning, such as the 1890s to 1900s, when shore birds face annihilation from sportsmen and commercial hunters.

The biologist acknowledged the devastation from sports and differentiated types of hunting and killing animals for food, recreation, and pleasure. In 1948, her fifth addition to the *Conservation in Action* series, "Guarding Our Wildlife Resources: A National Wildlife Refuge," credited gunners with financing sanctuaries through a "federal tax on sporting arms and ammunition" (Carson, 1948, 18). At the time, the population of large game animals reached 8,250,000. Through revenues from 12 million hunters, the U.S. Department of the Interior could inventory megafauna by airplane and could restore and restock refuges with "game birds and mammals" (*ibid.*). Planes also delivered salt blocks and feed, especially during blizzards.

Speaking for the Wild

In the eighth brochure, "Bear River: A National Wildlife Refuge," Rachel reported on waterfowl hunting in Box Elder County, Utah, by settlers, many of them Mormon pioneers arriving in 1860 eager to bag mule deer for meat. By 1900, market gunners and residents had increased the annual kill to 200,000 ducks to ship east. To their credit, sportsmen attempted to halt the loss by organizing outdoors fraternities to purchase and shield marsh habitats. In 1901, the Bear River Club secured 8,000 acres at North Bay. The original preserve preceded federal refuge land in 1928 of some 65,000 acres "as an inviolate sanctuary for such migratory birds" (Carson, 1950, 5).

In 1952, while researching food fish around the Georges Banks to the east off Cape Cod, Massachusetts, Rachel observed the crew of the U.S. Fish and Wildlife trawler S.S. *Albatross III* shooting sharks for sport, a pastime she characterized as moronic. A more brutal assault on mammals appeared in Aldo Leopold's *Round River*. In September 1953, Rachel identified "a state of cold anger that I haven't experienced in many a day" over the author's hypocrisy about conservation (Steingruber, 2018, 327). To an executive at Oxford University Press, she railed at Leopold's admiration of wild beasts for the purpose of torturing and slaying while declaring himself a naturalist and humanist. A detailed list of his sins ranged from using a live cormorant for baiting a bobcat trap and the casual skinning of a raccoon and shooting of a squirrel and snowshoe rabbit with a slingshot. She stated Leopold's purpose in conserving nature—"to provide fodder for their guns" and "moronic delight in killing" (*ibid.*, 328).

Rachel remained informed about chemical spraying on forest acreage, particularly in Midwestern states, and the effects of eating game fish and animals contaminated with pesticides. With *Silent Spring,* she reminded hunters that they owed fairness and a respect for the wild to explorers, fishers, bird watchers, and gardeners. Hunting clubs defended her crusade to limit use of biocides. In Wyoming's Bridger National Forest, suppression of sagebrush killed the willows that shaded trout and provided greenery and habitats for waterfowl, beaver, and moose. President John F. Kennedy's Science Advisory Committee reported DDT in fish from urban waterways and heptachlor and dieldrin in migratory game birds. The loss of pheasants to dieldrin spraying in Donovan, Illinois, threatened the survival of sport hunting.

See also History; Whales; Waterfowl.

Sources

Carson, Rachel. "Bear River: A National Wildlife Refuge." #8. Washington, D.C.: U.S. Department of the Interior, 1950, 1–14.

_____. "Chincoteague: A National Wildlife Refuge." #1. Washington, D.C.: U.S. Department of the Interior, 1947, 1–19.

_____. "Guarding Our Wildlife Resources: A National Wildlife Refuge." #5. Washington, D.C.: U.S. Department of the Interior, 1948, 1–46.

_____. "She Started It All—Here's Her Reaction." *New York Herald Tribune* (19 May 1963).

_____. *Silent Spring.* Boston: Houghton Mifflin, 40th Anniversary Edition, 2002.

_____. *Under the Sea Wind: A Naturalist's Picture of Ocean Life.* New York: Simon & Schuster, 1941.

Carson, R.L. "Ducks Are on Increase." *Baltimore Sunday Sun Magazine* (16 January 1938): 1.

Steingruber, Sandra, ed. *Rachel Carson: Silent Spring & Other Writings on the Environment.* New York: Library of America, 2018.

Storytelling

A skilled writer of clear, untechnical greenspeak, Rachel championed the power of the arts to inspire, uplift, and console. The London *Times* credited her with being "a self-confident controversialist" for questioning the patenting of 200 chemical biocides ("When," 1994). She harnessed historic tales and scientific data to news clips to connect oral lore to academic writing as sources on happenings in the wild, particularly the migrations of fish and birds. For "Fight for Wildlife Pushes Ahead" for the March 20, 1938, *Richmond Times Dispatch,* the essay depicted the carnage of pioneers against North American wildlife since 1838. Her amalgamations of stories about bison, sage grouse, grebe, heath hen, mountain goat, redhead duck, moose, grizzly bear, and passenger pigeon produced an urgent narrative that revolutionized conservation.

The biologist began highlighting good stories in her newspaper articles, starting with "Chesapeake Eels Seek the Sargasso Sea," an October 1938 feature for the *Baltimore Sunday Sun Magazine.* The June 1939 issue of *Nature* magazine featured the three-page essay "How about Citizenship Papers for the Starling?," which dramatized the huddled bodies of birds trying to keep warm. In an evaluation of literary strategies in *Under the Sea Wind,* analyst Amanda Hagood, an assistant academic dean at Eckerd College in St. Petersburg, Florida, identified Rachel's 1941 fish story as "a new kind of ecological literacy" featuring "creature-driven perspective" (Hagood, 2013). "Our Ever-Changing Shore" for the July 1958 issue of *Holiday* presented a millennia-old episode in the sea's evolution. Frank Pemberton, a book critic for the Providence, Rhode Island, *Journal,* praised the narrative method as a means of interpreting for the average reader the orderly cycles of the wild.

THE CLASSIC TALE

On September 27, 1962, the author's advocacy of bioethics reached a height of prophecy in *Silent Spring* with the prefatory allegory "A Fable for Tomorrow."

A dystopic horror tale, the view of unhatched eggs, dead farm animals, and un-pollinated apple trees launched a jeremiad unnerving enough to start a global revolution. Apocalyptic metanarratives condemning the wayward use of toxins stressed the rhetor's ability to draw readers into a significant occurrence, particularly the aerial spraying of dieldrin pellets in Illinois. She extended the range of protest to the faulty judgment of sprayers in Michigan, Wisconsin, New England, and the South about the safety of DDT (dichlorodiphenyltrichloroethane), aldrin, and heptachlor. Through rhetorical strategies incorporating metaphor, allusion, regionalism, and a variety of genres, she made accessible to the non-scientist a perspective on imminent danger from the outdoors and themselves.

Much of the book's reception reflected the zeitgeist—a post–World War II angst proceeding from A-bomb tests and John Hersey's *Hiroshima* (1946), a journalistic inquiry into the medical catastrophe among survivors of the U.S. bombings of Hiroshima and Nagasaki, Japan. Rachel's reminders that birds can no longer fly skies replete with aerial poisoning alluded to a world war conducted significantly from the air and a Cold War based on fear of Russian missile strikes. With John Keats's epigraph "And No Birds Sing" for Chapter Eight of *Silent Spring,* she incorporated the ghastly results of enchantment of an errant knight by a merciless *femme fatale.* The scientific dabbling in insecticides and governmental funding for chlorinated hydrocarbons enhanced the apocalyptic quality of a kiss-of-death story repeated across the U.S. and Europe.

Story's End

The rhetoric of Chapter Nine, "Rivers of Death," moved inexorably from the Keatsian subtitle to appalling examples of "moribund" conditions, such as the symptoms of nerve damage on October 12, 1955, in fiddler crabs in Tampa Bay, Florida, following spraying of poison (Carson, 2002, 135). Her sensitivity to suffering assembled action verbs: "all dead or sick, quivering, twitching, stumbling, scarcely able to crawl" (*ibid.*, 148). Graphic descriptions of moribund trout, minnows, and suckers trying to swim extended the near-death condition to erratic swimming, gasping, trembling, and spasms.

The author carried her tale of murder in the wild to a lugubrious end. Too weak to migrate, "blind and dying trout … appeared floating passively downstream," a pathetic condition caused by aerial spraying of DDT (*ibid.*). For emphasis, the reportage of widespread death segued to proof that fingerling trout were too sluggish and blind to escape. The coho salmon that survived retained a film over their eyes, a touching conclusion to the narrative. On April 3, 1963, Eric Sevareid, news anchor for *CBS Reports,* seated Rachel in a rocking chair for a one-hour TV portrait depicting her as a patient prose artist. Ecologist Lynn Scarett, in a tribute issued in *Fish & Wildlife News,* saluted the author's control of narrative and detail to instruct readers on nature's complexity. On May 11, 2016, the Illinois Grand Prairie Master Naturalists screened a documentary, "The Power of One Voice: A 50-Year Perspective on the Life of Rachel Carson."

See also Birds; "A Fable for Tomorrow"; History; Speeches.

Sources

Carson, Rachel. *Silent Spring*. Boston: Houghton Mifflin, 40th Anniversary Edition, 2002

Foote, Bonnie. "The Narrative Interactions of *Silent Spring*: Bridging Literary Criticism and Ecocriticism." *New Literary History* 38:4 (Autumn 2007): 739–745, 747–753, 777.

Hagood, Amanda. "Wonders with the Sea: Rachel Carson's Ecological Aesthetic and the Mid-Century Reader." *Environmental Humanities* 2:1 (2013): 57–77.

Pemberton, Frank. "Along the Seaboard." Providence (RI) *Journal* (13 April 1952).

Scarlett, Lynn. "The Poetry of Truth." *Fish & Wildlife News* (Spring 2007): 34.

Twidle, Hedley. "Rachel Carson and the Perils of Simplicity: Reading *Silent Spring* from the Global South." *Ariel* 44:4 (October 2013): 49–88.

"When the Sedge Withers and No Birds Sing." *London Times* (14 February 1994).

Temperatures

Rachel's biocentric prose related the importance of heat and cold to living organisms, particularly streams chosen for stocking trout. During the displacement of warm currents in the deep as cold surface waters sank to the sea floor, even a drop of one degree could scatter sea creatures to more hospitable climes. For "Farming under the Chesapeake," a January 1937 article on oysters for the *Baltimore Sun,* she depicted the fertilizing of eggs in warm Maryland waters between 68 and 75 degrees Fahrenheit, which occurred from July to mid–September. A month later, her essay "Shad Going the Way of the Buffalo" reported in the Charleston, South Carolina, *News and Courier* on the spawning of major food fish, which temperatures limited to 56 to 66 degrees. She later connected global warming and rising temperatures to the migration of fish north of Cape Cod as far as the Arctic Circle and shouldered a moral duty to alert humankind to vast ecological dangers.

An upbeat report on Atlantic coast trawling, "The Northern Trawlers Move South" for the *Baltimore Sunday Sun,* remarked on the need for monitoring water temperatures, "the key to fish movements," a topic important to the U.S. Bureau of Fisheries sea creatures census (Carson, 1937, 7). The author cited as examples sea bass, which preferred 46–47 degree waters, and scup, a short panfish that could thrive only at 45 degrees. The facts visualized a warm ribbon of water in winter confined fish "as securely as though they were penned up behind a rail fence" (*ibid.*). In September 1937, her essay "Undersea" in *Atlantic Monthly* differentiated the conditions of sea water: "temperature, saltiness, and pressure, that forms the invisible barriers that confine each marine type within a special zone of life" (Carson, 1937, 322). She listed the three dominant strata as coastline, declivities of the continental shelf, and mid-depths of ocean.

For a description of the diamond-back terrapin in 1938, the author respected the U.S. Bureau of Fisheries for building heated houses at Beaufort, North Carolina, to increase the yield of turtle eggs and young for holiday eating. Another reminder of consistent water temperature in the August 1938 article "Giants of the Tide Rip Off Nova Scotia Again" for the *Baltimore Sunday Sun* surmised that bluefin tuna possibly travel in "the mysterious Sargasso Sea" or "migrate from Italy and the Azores to Norway, keeping in the Gulf Stream drift in waters of about the same temperature" (Carson, 1938, 2). In a salute to starling intelligence, in the June 1939 issue of *Nature* magazine, the three-page essay "How About Citizenship Papers for the Starling?"

covered the flocks that chose warm skyscrapers for housing. On "long ledges, balconies and towers … the starling may huddle, wing to wing, sharing the warmth of each other's bodies" (Carson, 1939, 1). A more appealing roost developed from lights in trees meant to scare off birds in Washington, D.C. Instead of fleeing, the starlings roosted on the light bulbs.

LAYERED SEA DEPTHS

For *Under the Sea Wind* in 1941, the author focused on the passage of seasons in the Arctic and the arrival of the first rime frost, a signal for seabirds to flock south over Labrador and Nova Scotia to South America. Avian instinct gauged subtle changes in light and air temperature in autumn, when fall rains began "chilling the water and driving the fish to the warmer sea" (Carson, 1941, 51). Pandion the osprey pursued warm air streams to coast on rigid wings. On their way out to the Atlantic depths on September tides, shrimp, sensitive to "warm shallows," found a haven and ample pantry (*ibid.*). In the style of a raconteur, she recounted migrations to comfort zones, the instinctual clustering of animals at transition points in the ocean's depths.

Aboard the U.S. Fish and Wildlife trawler S.S. *Albatross III* around the Georges Banks fishing grounds 200 miles southeast of Boston and south of Nova Scotia, in July 1949, Rachel tabulated a fish census. To explain a dearth of cod, she charted water conditions, which she itemized in 1951 in *The Sea Around Us,* a model of non-anthropocentric views. Details identified certain ranges comfortable for fish: "to warm water or cold water, to clear or turbid water, to water rich in phosphates or in silicates," often shifting abruptly (Carson, 1951, 34). She viewed the constant movement as sinister and concluded that the oceans would survive climate shifts, but "the threat is rather to life itself" (*ibid.,* xxv).

Similarly, data undergirded "The Edge of the Sea," a December 1953 speech to the American Association for the Advancement of Science in Boston, where she commented on the exodus of animal populations according to prevailing temperatures. Data listed the Persian Gulf as the hottest and polar waters as the coldest, leading her to conclude, "Change of temperature is probably the most important single condition" in sea life distribution (*ibid.,* 35). For one reason, tropical waters sped reproduction, allowing life to regenerate at a faster rate than in arctic seas. For another, the clash of variant temperatures caused agitation that summoned food for marine creatures.

NATURE'S POWERS

The narrative outlined ocean changes in spring as warm waters brought dissolved minerals from the offshore shelf. She scoffed far-fetched notions of rechanneling the Gulf Stream closer inland, ostensibly to create warmer winters. Her version of temperature control derived from simple gravity, by which chilled seawater "becomes so heavy that it will plunge downward … the first act in the drama of spring" (Carson, 1951, 36). The escalation of sun rays at the surface and the rise of chemical stimulants quickened the diatoms, the food of much sea life.

For the meditation "The Real World Around Us," delivered to the Theta Sigma Phi Matrix Table Dinner in April 1954, Rachel added details of fog banks "where the cold water and the warm air from the Gulf Stream are perpetually at war at that season of the year" (Carson, 1954). Of the effects of seasonal changes, Rachel declared, "For the globe as a whole, the ocean is the great regulator, the great stabilizer of temperatures" (*ibid.*, 158). *The Sea Around Us* highlighted the role of stable streams within oceans: "Currents, modifying temperature and distributing the larval stages of sea creatures, create still another world" (Carson, 1955, 13). More than other elements, currents shaped the climate of the deep, forcing some creatures to hibernate to escape ice.

The author addressed the 1962 graduating class of Scripps College in Claremont, California, on periods of adaptation during evolution, which accommodated "extremes of temperature, background radiation in rocks, and atmosphere" (Carson, 1962). In early 1963, the author turned her attention to a rise in sea tides and cycles of warmer temperatures. Her knowledge of convection informed her testimony to the U.S. Congress about drift from aerial spraying of pesticides: "This force could lift the very fine particles of spray materials to an altitude at which strong horizontal winds could" transport the poisons over long distances (Carson, "Environmental," 1963). Unlike earlier reports of temperature changes, her incorporation of heat and cold with biocidal drift alerted legislators to the uncontrollable shifts in nature that spread agrochemicals to the four winds.

See also Climate Change; Seasons; *Silent Spring: Through a Narrow Window.*

Sources

Carson, Rachel. *The Edge of the Sea.* Boston: Houghton Mifflin, 1955.
_____. "The Edge of the Sea" (speech), American Association for the Advancement of Science, Boston (December 29, 1953).
_____. "Environmental Hazards: Control of Pesticides and Other Chemical Poisons." Statement before the Subcommittee on Reorganization and International Organizations of the Committee on Government Operations (4 June 1963): 206–219.
_____. "How About Citizenship Papers for the Starling?" *Nature* 32 (June/July 1939): 317–319.
_____. "Of Man and the Stream of Time." *Scripps College Bulletin,* Claremont, CA (12 June 1962): 5–10.
_____. *The Sea Around Us.* New York: Oxford University Press, 1951.
_____. "Undersea." *Atlantic Monthly* 160 (September 1937): 322–325.
_____. "Why Our Winters Are Getting Warmer." *Popular Science* 159:5 (November 1951): 113–117, 252, 254, 256.
Carson, R.L. "Farming Under the Chesapeake." *Baltimore Sun* (24 January 1937): 6–7.
_____. "Giants of the Tide Rip Off Nova Scotia Again." *Baltimore Sunday Sun* (3 August 1938): 2.
_____. "The Northern Trawlers Move South." *Baltimore Sunday Sun* (3 January 1937): 6–7.
_____. "Starlings a Housing Problem." *Baltimore Sunday Sun Magazine* (5 March 1939): 1.
Howe, Joshua P. *Making Climate Change History: Documents from Global Warming's Past.* Seattle: University of Washington Press, 2017.

Testimony to Congress

On June 4, 1963, Rachel presented to the Senate Committee on Commerce a 40-minute testimony "Environmental Hazards: Control of Pesticides and Other Chemical Poisons." Her unemotional opening in the Senate hearing room before a standing-room audience prodded legislators and committee chair Abraham A.

Ribicoff to action to repair earth cycles: "The problem you have chosen to explore is one that must be solved in our time ... in this session of Congress" (Lear, 1997, 4). The bold beginning of a 15-page text highlighted reactor waste, contaminants from laboratories and hospitals, nuclear explosion, domestic outflow from urban areas, and factory chemicals. She included non-toxic detergents, which polluted drinking water and weakened human gut linings and their ability to withstand carcinogens.

The biologist charged a technologically advanced society with ignoring interactions and side effects of contaminants, especially those in drinking water. She singled out the American Medical Association for relaying biased trade reports that spread false information about toxins in food and clothing fibers. A distressing fact, the tainting of drains with DDT (dichlorodiphenyltrichloroethane) on Prince of Wales Island, Alaska, and of waterfowl and their young in Yellowknife, Canada, recorded the harm of a poison never used in the areas. She puzzled over the presence of DDT in the oil of deep-sea halibut and tuna far off the shores of Asia, Europe, and the Americas and compared drift to the dissemination of radioactive debris, making pesticide poisoning "a new kind of fallout" (Carson, "Environmental," 1963). Her testimony stressed the immense concentration of biocides as they pass up the food chain. She cited the deaths of eagles, osprey, and robins from biocides and the dangers posed to people by the spraying of gypsy moths in New York State.

PROS AND CONS

The witness wisely admitted the hidden cost of reduced pesticide use and the downside to farm profits and efficiency. The time span between biocide dispersal and effects on the environment tended to quell fears of long-lasting contaminants. Another clever turn of phrase called legislators' attention to the rights of Americans to be safe from "the intrusion of poisons applied by other persons," a basic guarantee of the Constitution (*ibid.*). She specified losses to persons, pets, horses, and dairy cows, which produced tainted, unmarketable milk, and recommended the right of redress through lawsuits. A Long Island court suit pondered the homeowner's quandary at aerial spraying for gypsy moths without advance notice. Too late to demand a halt, the citizen deserved "appropriate redress" for inconvenience and the damaging incursion on private property (*ibid.*).

Rachel's testimony moved to another area of concern, the lack of information from medical research and insufficient physicians' training on toxicology and diagnosis of poisoning by such dangerous substances as lindane and malathion, a cause of seizures, cancer, mental aberrations, and death. She continued with corroborative evidence of medical concerns about acute and latent biocide poisoning—the resolution passed by the Illinois Medical Society on March 17, 1963, calling for "wise and effective controls" to toxicants (*ibid.*). From her own research, Rachel asked for laws restricting pesticide proliferation, sale, and use and required registration of domestic chemicals found in floor wax, mothproofing, and home and garden dusts and sprays. Her specifics demanded reduction of dependence on long-lived residues and warnings to communities in advance of state and federal spraying projects. She proposed a minimum of agricultural aviation for specific objectives and called for a moratorium on crop dusting except during extreme emergencies.

Swaying the Public

Beyond the U.S. Congress, Rachel's presence and reasoned arguments had global powers to stimulate recovery and improve farm health. Shy and soft-spoken, she refused to riposte against her detractors and chose to let data speak the truth. With one of her disturbing rhetorical questions, she asked in the *New York Times*: "Have we fallen into a mesmerized state that makes us accept as inevitable that which is inferior or detrimental, as though having lost the will or the vision to demand that which is good?" (Carson, 1962, 28).

Action at high levels began weaning Americans from their dependence on hydrocarbon killers. According to environmentalist Michael B. Smith, "A presidential commission and congressional investigation into the dangers posed by pesticides led to stricter guidelines about the testing, labeling, and application of pesticides" (Smith, 2001, 752). In a live demonstration, senators pondered the effectiveness of scent lures to rid areas of cockroach infestation. In Washington State, the U.S. Forest Service cancelled a DDT spraying project against the hemlock looper caterpillar because of the threat to oyster beds. On June 7 during hearings on Rachel's testimony, Senator Ribicoff charged the U.S. Agriculture Department with concealing the names of lindane, Algimycin, Neodane, and Perma-Guard seed treatment, which imperiled crops, animals, and people from hepatitis, cancer, and leukemia in children. He gave the department one day to release the list and promised to insert the names in the *Congressional Record.*

A week after Rachel's congressional testimony, Margaret L. Wyatt, publisher and editor of the *Brown County* (Indiana) *Democrat,* questioned helicopter flights spraying vines and weeds along power lines. Reports from British Columbia corroborated Rachel's data on the wipeout of coho salmon in four Port Hardy streams tainted with DDT at a time when foresters debated spraying Vancouver Island. On June 16, the Izaak Walton League saluted Rachel with its Founders Award for "alerting the people of the world to the real, and also the unknown, dangers resulting from the indiscriminate uses of insecticides and pesticides" (Izaak, 1963, *23*). In *Fish & Wildlife News,* specialist Jerry Novotny esteemed Rachel for "quiet, but effective leadership" that moved the United States and "industrialized nations to join the conservation movement" (Novotny, 2007, 18).

See also Fish.

Sources

Carson, Rachel. "Environmental Hazards: Control of Pesticides and Other Chemical Poisons." Statement before the Subcommittee on Reorganization and International Organizations of the Committee on Government Operations (4 June 1963): 206–219.

_____. "Rachel Carson's Warning," editorial, *New York Times* (2 July 1962): 28.

"Izaak Walton League Honors Rachel Carson." *La Crosse* (WI) *Tribune* (16 June 1963): 12.

Lear, Linda J. *Rachel Carson: Witness for Nature.* New York: Henry Holt, 1997.

Novotny, Jerry. "A Quiet Leader." *Fish & Wildlife News* (Spring 2007): 18.

Smith, Michael B. "'Silence, Miss Carson!': Science, Gender, and the Reception of *Silent Spring*." *Feminist Studies* 27:3 (Fall 2001): 733–753.

Vail, David D. *Chemical Lands: Pesticides, Aerial Spraying, and Health in North America's Grasslands Since 1945*. Tuscaloosa: University of Alabama Press, 2018.

Tide Pools

Rachel's fascination with tide pools began in January 1928 with biology courses under Mary Scott Skinker. The curriculum introduced the author to shoreline shellfish and fin fish as well as deep water seagrass and dulce, an edible seaweed. Into adulthood, she continued beach combing in bare feet for sea plants and tide pool invertebrates. Because of her love for southern Maine, she longed to own a beach cottage with its own access to kelp, mussels, dogwinkles, crabs, and sea colander. In "Undersea," a lyrical debut in the September 1937 issue of *Atlantic Monthly,* she typified the coming together of land life with tidal influx and the "[pools] forgotten by the retreating sea in recess of sand and rock" (Carson, 1937, 323). In 1941, she wrote *Under the Sea Wind,* which reviewed the evaporation of salt water pools into salt ponds during the Permian era (270,000,000 BCE) and frosted rock pools among snowy hummocks.

Yearning for littoral property in the intertidal zone resulted in purchase of acreage on the Maine coast. In a speech to the Books and Authors Luncheon at New York's Astor Hotel on October 17, 1951, Rachel imagined the elusive, indefinable tide pools of the Silurian Era (440,000,000 BCE) as homes to the sea's original beach organisms. The next July, she began serious investigation of rock pool insects, barnacles, and worms for *The Edge of the Sea* and continued research down the North Carolina Outer Banks to Florida's mangrove swamps. In July 1953, the biologist's interest extended to tutorials of her nephew, Roger Allen Christie, whom she guided on long walks on the Maine shore from toddlerhood. The two explored fingerlings, oysters, and elvers and collected shells.

The Writer's Passion

The completion of *The Edge of the Sea* in 1955, the third in her saltwater trilogy, revisited reefs, fens, estuaries, and tide pools, which she recorded with an Exakta camera. A miniature of ocean depths, the marginal backwaters held sponges, starfish, moss, and sea anemones, which she described on May 13 at a fund raiser for the Lincoln County Cultural and Historical Association in Wiscasset, Maine. Alongside, slugs and tube worms created grainy residences forming a "glistening mosaic" amid "brown, leathery weed" (*ibid.*). She expounded on the "Lilliputian beings" in *The Edge of the Sea* with a list of spaces, crevices, and burrows in which the smallest could survive (Carson, 1955, 2).

Exploring with fingertips the Irish moss and dulse in the hidden chamber, the biologist experienced a timelessness common to the naturalist's sense of awe, which she shared with Maine photographer Charles Pratt. In the posthumous narrative *The Rocky Coast,* she wondered how "creatures of such extreme delicacy … can exist in

this cave when the brute force of some surf is unleashed within its confined space"
(Carson, 1971, 114). By comparing the time span that the simplest sea species existed,
she admired the longevity of creatures that "came out of the sea in those ancient eras
of the Paleozoic, 300 million years ago" (*ibid.*, 116).

Color and Shape

With deft staging of an August sunrise over Georgia, Rachel approached an
intertidal "fairy pool" to view "heavy-surf fauna"—oarweed, green sponge, and a
community of sea squirts, primitive vertebrates known as tunicates, organisms that
lost their ancient segmentation (Carson, 1955, 3; 1971, 112). The emerging drama
introduced an "elfin starfish" suspended over a reflective surface (*ibid.*). Like infant
nurseries, the basins of larvae elicited reflection on the next season's saltwater creatures. The image spawned a poignance at ephemeral beauty in the fluffy pink *Tubularia indivisa,* which swayed like a flower stalk.

In an artful mood, the author imagined primeval earth contained in the microcosm of a single ghost crab, which she illuminated by flashlight. She shared with
Maine photographer Charles Pratt a passion for a hidden world beneath giant granite clusters that "[formed] its floor and walls and roof" (Carson, 1971, 109). Peering through small niches at these microcosmic communities sustained by the tides,
she valued green-carpeted tidal pools as places of "color and form and reflection"
(*ibid.,* 101). She referred to "illusions of depth" from escarpments, forests, and drifting clouds overhead as well as the shapes of seaweed under the surface in constant
movement (*ibid.,* 107). She absorbed the moods of shore pools and the "infusion and
distillation of light ... with its glowing radiance," which "[created] the illusion of
another world" (*ibid., 108,* 101*)*. For the author's "love and concern for nature's artistry in rock and kelp and tidewater pool," the *Detroit Free Press* book editor chose
The Rocky Coast as an ideal Christmas gift ("Review," 1971, 5B).

See also Maine.

Sources

Carson, Rachel. *The Edge of the Sea.* Boston: Houghton Mifflin, 1955.
_____. *The Rocky Coast.* New York: McCall, 1971.
_____. "Undersea." *Atlantic Monthly* 160 (September 1937): 322–325.
Coughlin, Maura. "Biotopes and Ecotones: Slippery Images on the Edge of the French Atlantic." *Landscapes*
    7:1 (2016): 1–23.
Hessler, Stefanie, and Bruno Latour. *Prospecting Ocean.* Cambridge, MA: MIT Press, 2019.
"Review: *The Rocky Coast.*" *Detroit Free Press* (5 December 1971): 5B.

Tides

During the composition of *Under the Sea Wind* in 1941, the author trained her
thoughts on oceanic rhythms that ruled underwater life and impacted the day-to-day
labors of watermen. In Chapter Two, she acknowledged the timing of twice-daily
floods that pushed plankton and other edibles into the path of larger creatures,
which swept "into the harbor by the interplay of currents" and "the incoming flood"

(Carson, 1941, 87). As though swimming along with the tide, Rachel exulted in motion that "sucked and swirled ... and raced in whirlpools and eddies and broke over the rocks in white rips" (*ibid.*). The grandeur of constant, unpredictable tumbling and rippling by wind and wave paralleled the undersea gutting of small beings by larger.

In 1942, Rachel reflected on the effects of oceans rhythms on the shorebird. Its "measure of time is not an hour, but the rise and fall of the tides," the forces that provided food (Carson, "Memo," 1942). In a 1951 speech at the Astor Hotel sponsored by the *New York Herald-Tribune,* she acknowledged her first contact with the sea at Woods Hole Biological Laboratory in Cape Cod, Massachusetts. She revealed a coastal pastime: "I never tired of watching the tidal currents pouring through the Hole, and the waves breaking on Nobska Point after a storm" (Carson, speech, 1951). The statement identified her reliance on sense impressions as well as scientific research.

The Sea Trilogy

The author incorporated planetary history in much of her prose. The orchestration of epic creation in *The Sea Around Us* pictured unfettered solar tides during "the period of the free oscillation of the liquid earth" and the resultant formation of the moon from "a great wave ... torn away and hurled into space" (Carson, 1951, 21). At the conclusion of the second chapter, Rachel connected tidal sculpting of undersea basins to "the fiery center of the earth" and uncharted spaces of the universe (*ibid.,* 106). In "The Global Thermostat," she imagined the inundation of tidal cycles under arctic ice and the alterations to "the winds, the rainfall, and the air temperatures" in Europe's climate (*ibid.,* 167).

With "The Moving Tides," the marine biologist targeted a segment of *The Sea Around Us* to maximum and minimum ocean levels, which have gradually declined since the planet's birth. The author's pedagogical talent clarified confusing aspects of moon and sun cycles, tidal oscillation, and diurnal rhythm, in part by contrasting cosmic variances in the Bay of Fundy, Chesapeake Bay, and the Gulf of Maine. She credited the differences to topography—"the slope of the bottom, the depth of a channel, or the width of a bay's entrance" (*ibid.,* 144).

The Sea's Minutia

For *The Edge of the Sea,* in 1955, Rachel admired worms and crabs—tough, vital, and adaptable creatures. They flourished in a mutable habitat "that brings transforming change to their world" at the point of metamorphosis, "that brief and magical hour of the tide's turning" (Carson, 1955, 73, 95). She characterized their experience in terms of the gravitational forces of ebb tide and flood tide rather than the human temporality of night and day. As though transforming sandy strands with magic, the tides withdrew, leaving a shoal, "a dull velvet patch" that gradually rose into view (*ibid.,* 146). The formation became her invitation to wade in ankle-deep water and examine small organisms.

Rachel shared with foster son Roger Allen Christie a magnetism toward the tides. In the wee hours of August 8, 1956, they left her cat Jeffie slumbering while they viewed "the spring tides of the new moon," a perennial celestial draw (Carson, 1956). She imagined diamonds and emeralds of light and absorbed the colored kaleidoscope of underwater phosphorescence. In subsequent scenarios, she enjoyed lacy foam, striated rocks, salty smell, marsh sparrows, and the powerful tide cycles in wetlands and estuaries that comforted her last days. Her ability to dramatize and enlarge on tidal mysteries made her the "poet of the seas."

See also Tide Pools; Time.

Sources

Carson, Rachel. *The Edge of the Sea*. Boston: Houghton Mifflin, 1955.
_____. "Letter to Dorothy and Stanley Freeman" (8 August 1956).
_____. "Memo to Mrs. Eales." Rachel Carson papers, 1942.
_____. *The Sea Around Us*. New York: Oxford University Press, 1951.
_____. Speech, New York Herald Tribune Book Review, Astor Hotel (1 October 1951).
Kaza, Stephanie. "Rachel Carson's Sense of Time: Experiencing Maine." *ISLE* 17:2 (Spring 2010): 291–315.
Meola, Frank M. "Rachel Carson's 'Rugged Shore' in Maine." *New York Times* (19 August 2012): TR.5.

Time

Rachel repeatedly linked the rocky heights, littoral strands, and watery depths of the planet to perpetual planetary fluctuations. In 1951 in *The Sea Around Us,* she declared of the oceans: "The alternation of day and night, the passage of the seasons, the procession of the years, are lost in its vastness, obliterated in its own changeless eternity" (Carson, 1951, 41). In the next sentence she presented the sea's surface as an ever-shifting cache of light, shadow, and color engendered by wind and tide. Over time, the particles eroded—disintegrated, blown, flooded, and ground by the forces of water, ice, and wind to become sand grains, each a marker of planetary time.

After removal of a breast tumor on September 21, 1950, Rachel became more concerned for mortality and the time she had left to write. In notebooks, she preserved bird tracks vanishing into the sea and remarked, "Time itself is like the sea, containing all that came before us, sooner or later sweeping us away on its flood and washing over and obliterating the traces of our presence" (Carson, 1998, 126). *The Sea Around Us* reminded readers that, compared to marine organisms, "Man has occupied a mere moment of time," which she had previously described as "centuries into ages of geologic time" (Carson, 1952, 15; 1937, 323). A sensual evaluation of Claude Debussy's sympathy *La Mer* inspired the author to reflect on earth's timelessness, "The passage of the years and the centuries and the eons are lost in time itself" (Carson, "Liner Notes," 1951).

A Philosopher's Mind

For the London *Guardian,* literary critic John Burnside remarked that Rachel's abandonment of human measurements of time became "the biggest risk that she had decided to take" (Burnside, 2014, 54). A detachment from earthly life in *The Edge of the Sea* enabled her to reminisce on mud flats in southwestern Florida and the constant interchange of land and sea as tides come and go. Imagining the beating down of coastal escarpments over the ages, she pictured "a shifting, kaleidoscopic pattern in which there is no finality, no ultimate and fixed reality" (Carson, 1955, 250). Reverencing the image of constant flux, she described global fluidity as the equivalent of seawater—"never static, never quite the same from year to year" (*ibid.*). In the haunting, elusive microcosm of rock barnacles and protozoa, she envisioned the source of life's mystery.

At Scripps College in Claremont, California, on June 12, 1962, the author used her dwindling strength to deliver a commencement speech, "Of Man and the Stream of Time." For the all-female class, she meditated on "the flowing stream of time, unhurried, unmindful of man's restless and feverish pace" (Carson, 1962). Within the stream, she acknowledged the brief blip that made up human history. Of her busy schedule, she justified to friend Dorothy Freeman the risk of exhaustion by flying to California for the speech, citing "a desire to live more affirmatively, making the most of opportunities when they are offered, not putting them off for another day" (Freeman, 1995, 332). The statement combined death anxieties with her appreciation of earth's demands on mortals.

Earthly Rhythms

Stephanie Kaza, an ecologist at the University of Vermont, conducted an unusual study of Rachel's structured nature writing and grouped time elements into daily tides, seasons, geologic eras, and the evolutionary epoch. Kaza summarized the approach to "deep time" as a "great arc of creativity and destruction surging through all life and physical form," a self-discipline that kept the beleaguered marine biologist humble and anchored in patience (Kaza, 2010, 291). Issued on September 27, 1962, the opening chapter of *Silent Spring* stated Rachel's concept of the planetary pace as a delineator of change. She viewed the totality of existence "in millennia—life adjusts, and a balance has been reached" (Carson, 2002, 6). Of the hellish tampering with radiation, "brewed in ... laboratories," she warned, "Time is the essential ingredient; but in the modern world, there is no time" (*ibid.*, 7).

In an analysis of Rachel's catalytic impact on environmentalism, Lisa H. Sideris, a religion professor at Indiana University, and Kathleen Dean Moore, an environmentalist at Oregon State University, contemplated a world view unlimited by history. Rachel believed that "we are not isolated and alone. Our lives, like the lives of all animals, are braided into the complex interactions of water, chemicals, and time" (Sideris & Moore, 2008, 9). Thus, the profligate dispersal of poisonous hydrocarbons threatened not just the present, but generations to come by compromising earth's regenerative powers. She reminded readers that those powers incorporated human reproduction and the well-being of future children fed on contaminated breast milk.

See also Fossils; *Under the Sea Wind*.

Sources

Burnside, John. "A Fish Called Wonder." *Guardian* 143:5205 (11–17 April 2014): 54–55.

Carson, Rachel. "Liner Notes." Claude Debussy's *La Mer,* RCA Victor, 1951.

_____. "Of Man and the Stream of Time." *Scripps College Bulletin,* Claremont, CA (12 June1962): 5–10.

_____. *The Sea Around Us.* New York: Oxford University Press, 1951.

_____. "Undersea." *Atlantic Monthly* 160 (September 1937): 322–325.

Freeman, Martha, ed. *Always, Rachel: The Letters of Rachel Carson and Dorothy Freeman, 1952–1964.* Boston: Beacon Press, 1995.

Kaza, Stephanie. "Rachel Carson's Sense of Time: Experiencing Maine." *ISLE* 17:2 (Spring 2010): 291–315.

Sideris, Lisa H., and Kathleen Dean Moore, eds. *Rachel Carson: Legacy and Challenge.* Albany: State University of New York, 2008.

Topography

In a significant study of the North Carolina Outer Banks in "The Rim of Sand" and of the Florida Keys in "The Coral Coast," chapters in *The Edge of the Sea,* Rachel objectified the connection between earth's contours and the biota they nurtured. She shared with Southwestern poet Mary Hunter Austin, author of *The Land of Little Rain,* an ecocentric prospect: "To understand the fashion of any life, one must know the land it is lived in" (Lear, 1997, 8). For September 1937 issue of *Atlantic Monthly,* the writer contributed a detailed land study in "Undersea," which pictured the ocean floor "scarred with deep ravines, perhaps the valleys of drowned rivers, and dotted with undersea plateaus ... submerged islands" (Carson, 1937, 323).

From there, the author imagined a gradual descent that revealed crevasses some 600 feet below the surface before the continental shelf dropped away a mile below to "an inky void that is the abyss" (*ibid.*). During her first voyage aboard the U.S. Fish and Wildlife trawler S.S. *Albatross III* east of Boston and south of Nova Scotia, she created an image of the sea floor of Georges Bank: "a small mountain resting on the floor of a surrounding deeper sea" (Carson, 1954). The ship's nets dragged the mountain sides all the way to the plateaus, collecting denizens of the mid-ocean.

Cold Lands

In January 1937, the author's feature "The Northern Trawlers Move South" for the *Baltimore Sunday Sun* explained the migration of coastal Atlantic fish in cold weather. At the littoral rim, "The fish begin to move out across the continental shelf into deeper waters less affected by the cooling of the air" (Carson, 1937, 6). She added, "This continental slope borders the great depths of the ocean, where extremely cold temperatures prevail throughout the year" (*ibid.*). The temperature and water pressure determined what creatures could survive so far from sunlight and shore.

The foreword of *Under the Sea Wind* in 1941 introduced the gentle declivity of the Atlantic shelf, "the steep descent of the continental slopes, and finally the abyss" beyond North Carolina's Outer Banks (Carson, 1941, 4). The narrative leap-frogged from balmy Carolina shores and dunes to the Arctic barrens, where a blizzard whitened the "ice-strewn sea edge across miles of tundra, even far south to the fringe of the forests, the undulating hills, and the ice-scoured valleys" (Carson, 1941, 35). Her study of unrelenting cold pictured a vicious wind over land masses, a ravine, and a willow copse where owl chicks died in the shell, some of the defenseless victims of unpredictable seasonal chill.

In Chapter Two, "The Gull's Way," Rachel defined "the true sea," a depth freighted with 600 feet of water and a darkness limiting view of "escarpments and deep palisades," a textured sea floor similar in shape to mountain ranges (Carson, 1941, 69). A decade later, she returned to the topic of deep water sounding and viewing in *The Sea Around Us,* which remarked on the lack of details of "hidden contours" in the ocean ooze (Carson, 1951, 64). Her concentration on continental shelves in "Hidden Lands" emphasized the downgrade as sources of fossil fuel, human and livestock food, fertilizer, dye, coatings, mulch, explosives, and pharmaceuticals. In 1955, for the opening paragraph of *The Edge of the Sea,* she simplified the piling of sediment on the global crust as "continental margins [that warp] up or down in adjustment of strain and tension," a deliberately human image (Carson, 1955, 1). In the six-page essay "Our Ever-Changing Shore" for the July 1958 issue of *Holiday,* she pondered the glacial shaping of Buzzards Bay, Massachusetts, into a rocky beach studded with barnacles.

HUMAN TOPOGRAPHY

Imagery of wind on sand accentuated a pervasive fact in Rachel's writing—that humankind makes little lasting imprint on the universe. Picturing "footprints, toiling up slopes and plunging down into valleys," she captured the mystic shapelessness of sand dunes, forever drifting and sliding (Carson, 1958, 117). When the winds altered, they formed impermanent ridges and curves, all devoid of human tracks. Her subtle comparison concluded that "man came but yesterday" (*ibid.,* 118). A swamp buggy ride over the Florida Everglades in July 1951 cast an eerie view of the sea floor on land forming "the thinnest veneer over this underlying platform of the ancient sea" (Carson, 1954).

Throughout her mature years, Rachel celebrated the mounting scientific perception of earth's shape. In the preface to *The Sea Around Us,* she credited the world's naval powers for increasing oceanographic data during World War II: "Instruments and equipment, most of which had been born of urgent necessity, gave oceanographers the means of tracing the contours of the ocean bottom" and sampling the sea's cellar (Carson, 1951, xviii). Her curiosity wandered to sedimentary mountains "uplifted, tilted, compressed, and broken by the vast earth movements" and the rapid declivity of marine shelves and sub-level canyons and valleys, which formed the Grand Banks of Newfoundland and Dogger Bank east of England in the Pleistocene Era around 1,000,000 BCE (*ibid.,* 79). With lyric precision, she envisioned the Pacific basin "aquiver with earthquakes and fiery with volcanoes, some frequently active, some extinct, some merely sleeping" (*ibid.,* 73). While describing tectonic shifts in *The Edge of the Sea,* she explained the shaping of Long Island, Maine, and Nova Scotia as terrestrial crusts pressed beneath the waters by glaciers.

LIFETIME VIEWS

On a trip to the Arizona desert on October 26, 1963, six months before Rachel's death, the Grand Canyon's southern rim exhilarated her failing stamina. She followed the Colorado River toward Lake Mead to examine the coloration of red walls and the tree-topped plateaus. Nine days later, the author detailed a jaunt by wheelchair in the Muir Woods northwest of San Francisco. Of the drive from the Golden Gate Bridge, she reveled in "smooth, brown hills, so much of the road lined with eucalyptus trees" (Carson, letter, 26 October 1963). The descent over tight curves took her to a red-wood forest in the canyon. Her knowledge of natural phenomena accounted for few lightning strikes against trunks deep in the declivity.

In 1971, the posthumous excerpt *The Rocky Coast* revisited Rachel's delight in Maine's Atlantic shore at Bar Harbor and its dramatic names—Thunder Hole, Schooner Head, and Anemone Cave, the residence of myriad sea creatures. The illustrated narrative reviewed earth formations of the Carboniferous Era (350,000,000 BCE)— the glacial grinding of pebbly beaches and the crashing tides and their reduction of sandstone and marl into "marine stacks, caves, chimneys, and archways" (Carson, 1971, 13). The pictures honored the extent of her career in marine biology and the writings that characterized earth's surface.

Sources

Carson, Rachel. *The Edge of the Sea.* Boston: Houghton Mifflin, 1955.
_____. "Letter to Dorothy Freeman" (17 October 1963).
_____. "Letter to Dorothy Freeman" (26 October 1963).
_____. "Our Ever-Changing Shore." *Holiday* 24 (July 1958): 70–71, 117–120.
_____. "Preface." *The Sea Around Us,* 2nd ed. New York: Oxford University Press, 1961, xvii–xxiv.
_____. "The Real World Around Us," address to the Theta Sigma Phi Matrix Table Dinner, *House of Life* (21 April 1954): 324–326.
_____. *The Rocky Coast.* New York: McCall, 1971.
_____. *Under the Sea Wind: A Naturalist's Picture of Ocean Life.* New York: Simon & Schuster, 1941.
_____. "Undersea." *Atlantic Monthly* 160 (September 1937): 322–325.
Carson, R.L., "The Northern Trawlers Move South." *Baltimore Sunday Sun* (3 January 1937): 6.
Lear, Linda J. *Rachel Carson: Witness for Nature.* New York: Henry Holt, 1997.

Under the Sea Wind

In the compilation of *Under the Sea Wind: A Naturalist's Picture of Ocean Life,* at age 33, Rachel revered the endurance of age-old tides, surf, fogged-in marshes, and bottom ooze to create a transcendent wonder and aesthetic reflection. On oceanographic inquiry completed aboard the U.S. Fish and Wildlife Service's trawler S.S. *Albatross III,* she concentrated on sea creatures by displacing humankind from the central role. Her research focused on imagining elements of underwater life that no one had seen or documented. For the sake of didacticism, she admitted to deliberately humanizing the prose with expressions by animal protagonists that more pedantic science writers would avoid.

Rachel's innovative writing in 1941 introduced a new genre of nature prose that, for decades, influenced nonfiction. Her style, according to Swedish essayist Hakan Sandgren, a lecturer at the University of Queensland, made "life underwater appear as something alien, otherworldly" (Sandgren, 2017, 262). According to biographer Linda Lear, Rachel's prevalent theme "was very much a product of its time and reflected both anxiety about the future and optimism about nature's resilience" (Lear, 2016).

A SEA TUTORIAL

In the author's view, research introduced unending deep sea cycles of birth, feeding, warding off predators, and brutally quick deaths. She named the three chapters "Edge of the Sea," "The Gull's Way," and "River and Sea." Simon & Schuster introduced the book on November 1, 1941. John Burnside, on staff at the London *Guardian,* explained its appeal to the reader's mind: "She animates our imaginations so that what could have seemed alien to the reader—and so inconsequential—becomes humanly vivid" (Burnside, 2014, 55).

Influenced by English author John Richard Jefferies's rustic nature rhapsodies in the essay *The Pageant of Summer,* Rachel's foreword embraced the grandeur and mystery of "things that are as nearly eternal as any earthly life can be" (Carson, 1941, 3). She spoke confidently of the titanic creation of earth from molten iron, an evolutionary landmark she reiterated in the book's resolution. Liberated from human constraints, she declared, "Time measured by the clock or the calendar means nothing" to ocean fauna (*ibid.,* 4). Rather, tides and sunlight regulated the struggle for food and safety from predators for mature creatures and their young. To enhance intricacy, she orchestrated the totality of nature—climate, winds, light, and animal instincts alongside their daily calls and signals of distress.

ANTHROPOMORPHIC CREATURES

Opening on the surge of waves over boulders and sand during the May bird migration, the author chose a compellingly wild setting at Ship's Shoal and Mullet Pond on North Carolina's Outer Banks. The strip of barrier islands sheltered the eastern side of the Albemarle and Pamlico sounds from the pounding Atlantic during seasonal hurricanes. As explained in a memo in 1942, she stripped the narrative of personal bias by focusing the action on "a sandpiper, a crab, a mackerel, an eel" and other representative species. With a sense of time and danger, she animated the cast like the pseudo-humans in Aleut animal tales and Aesop's fables (Carson, "Memo," 1942).

Character	Species	Common Name
Anguilla	(*Anguilla anguilla*)	eel
Aurelia	(*Aurelia aurita*)	moon jellyfish
Blackfoot	(*Calidris alba*)	sanderling
Cynoscion	(*Cynoscion nebulosus*)	sea trout
Kigavik	(*Falco rusticolus*)	gyrfalcon
Lophius	(*Lophius piscatorius*)	angler fish or monkfish
Mugil	(*Mugil cephalis*)	gray flathead mullet
Nereis	(*Alitta succinea*)	clamworm
Ookpik	(*Bubo scandiacus*)	snowy owl
Pandion	(*Pandion haliaetus*)	osprey
Rynchops	(*Rynchops niger*)	skimmer or flood gull

Character	Species	Common Name
Scomber	(*Scomber scombrus*)	mackerel
Silverbar	(*Calidris alba*)	sanderling
Tullugak	(*Corvus corax*)	raven
Uhvinguk	(*Muridae arvicolinae*)	lemming mouse
White Tip	(*Haliaeetus albicilla*)	sea eagle

Readers responded to the anthropomorphic cast of characters like children viewing a cartoon. The imaginative story, set among dunes and sea marshes, in surface waters, and in the deep, drew them into the network of abyssal residents and the dominating feature, "the ocean itself" (*ibid.*).

Competing with the catastrophe that Japanese inflicted at Pearl Harbor, Hawaii, on December 7, 1941, the new book struggled, selling only 1,348 copies. As of June 1942, *Under the Sea Wind* earned Rachel only $689.17. It went out of print the following August. Although the publisher had the narrative translated into braille, she abandoned Simon & Schuster for life and gave up book writing for the more lucrative magazine article. Eventually, her sea trilogy found readership on high school, college, and university required reading lists. At the same time that she popularized oceanography and beach combing into new passions, she initiated skepticism that scientific advancement bettered life on earth.

See also Tides; Time.

Sources

Burnside, John. "A Fish Called Wonder." *Guardian* 143:5205 (11–17 April 2014): 54–55.
Carson, Rachel. "Memo to Mrs. Eales." Rachel Carson papers, 1942.
_____. *Under the Sea Wind: A Naturalist's Picture of Ocean Life*. New York: Simon & Schuster, 1941.
Higgins, Elmer. "Review: Under the Sea Wind." *Progressive Fish Culturist* 56 (December 1941): 33–34.
Lear, Linda. "The Next Page: When Rachel Carson Set Sail." *Pittsburgh Post-Gazette* (21 February 2016).
Sandgren, Håkan. "Life Under Water: Narratives of Deep Sea Counternatures." *Contesting Environmental Imaginaries: Nature and Counternature in a Time of Global Change*. Leiden, Netherlands: Brill, 2017, 260–282.

Under the Sea Wind: Edge of the Sea

In Chapter One of *Under the Sea Wind: A Naturalist's Picture of Ocean Life*, a 1941 classic marine fauna biography, Rachel adopted deceptively simple diction to express environmental wisdom and complexity. In the critique of John Burnside, a literary analyst for the London *Guardian*, the author "[flirted] with anthropomorphism ... and her success in treading that thin line is one of the great triumphs" (Burnside, 2014, 54). The narrative initiated for a privileged audience a cast of characters to act out natural cycles of feeding, reproducing, and migrating. She chose Rynchops, the tropical skimmer or flood gull (*Rynchops niger,* literally "black beak-face"), as a main character because of his high-flying inspection of the waterside. Her summary of parenting valued the mother wader for concealing eggshells and fledglings from predators and the playacting of a phalarope couple at feeding in the marshy pool until a pursuing fox gave up stalking hatchlings.

Character studies yielded a compellingly nonhuman narrative featuring the sanderlings (*Calidris alba*) named Blackfoot and Silverbar. The couple made 60,000-mile migrations from Patagonia, Argentina, along the Atlantic Flyway over Yucatan and the Carolinas to the Arctic tundra. Alert to sand-burrowing hippa crabs, the crafty pair timed their feedings on the rise and onrush of breakers. Like a World War II dogfighter, Silverbar eluded a marauding tern, producing low-level theater that continued out to sea. The author empathized with their struggles in prose that reviewer Elmer Higgins, editor-in-chief of the *Progressive Fish-Culturist,* termed "factually sound, technically accurate, and free from the artificialities and sentiment so often found in nature books of this sort" (Higgins, 1941, 33).

STAGING THE CAST

The introduction of Uhvinguk, Ookpik, Tullugak, and Kigavik—the Eskimo names for a lemming mouse, male snowy owl, raven, and gyrfalcon—personalized the author's scan of the Hudson Bay marine community. In a two-day blizzard during "the short, gray night of the Arctic spring," the creatures were vulnerable to hunger and to the white fox, wolf, and owl (Carson, 1941, 36). Intensifying the effects of deep drifts and unavailable seed plants, snails, and insects, Rachel vivified the cycle of pillage that killed baby owls, ptarmigans, and sanderlings and drove the ravens to pick a caribou skeleton for winter sustenance.

By adding the osprey Pandion (*Pandion haliaetus*) to her *dramatis personae,* the author incorporated Greek mythology featuring a series of semi-historical Athenian monarchs. Less poetic, Mugil (*Mugil cephalis*) bore the Greco-Roman designation of the gray flathead mullet, Pandion's afternoon meal. Rachel evened out threats with the predatory White Tip (*Haliaeetus albicilla*, Greco-Roman for "white-tipped sea eagle"). His unyielding sortie in air snatched Pandion's second catch, a catfish that White Tip wolfed down at his leisure on a pine perch.

ABOVE AND UNDER THE SEA

The author's familiarity with seagoing careers elicited sympathy for mullet netters, who waited out the tide before launching skiffs into the surf. A muscular task, seining forced men to brace their legs at the thwarts or crossbars and lean into rowing. Meanwhile, their fellow crewmen waded out waist deep to steady guy ropes from the shores. By pitting determined, leaping fish against the netters, the narrative reiterated the motif of predator and catch, including the by-catch tossed aside as unsaleable and inedible.

With respect for the process, Rachel applied its meaning to earthly mortality. She concluded, "One dies, another lives," a gesture toward the chain of being that included human eaters of seafood (*ibid.,* 65). Analyst Susan Bratton exulted that, in comparison to Rynchops and his fellow birds, "Watermen … are neither fully competent predators, nor can they coordinate with each other the way the skimmers can" because humans lack the instinct of marine ecology (Stratton, 2004, 10).

Sources

Bratton, Susan Power. "Thinking like a Mackerel: Rachel Carson's *Under the Sea-Wind* as a Source for a Trans-Ecotonal Sea Ethic." *Ethics and the Environment* 9:1 (April 2004): 1–22.
Burnside, John. "A Fish Called Wonder." *The Guardian* 143:5205 (11–17 April 2014): 54–55.
Carson, Rachel. *Under the Sea Wind: A Naturalist's Picture of Ocean Life.* New York: Simon & Schuster, 1941.
Higgins, Elmer. "Review: Under the Sea Wind." *Progressive Fish Culturist* 7:56 (December 1941): 33–34.

Under the Sea Wind: The Gull's Way

In Chapter Two of *Under the Sea Wind: A Naturalist's Picture of Ocean Life*, the most challenging section to write, Rachel distanced consciousness from self. With stagy drama, she immersed the text in a marine organism, a unique resident of a watery world. She shifted the atmosphere to a tender mackerel called Scomber (*Scomber scombrus*), a Greek-named pelagic (mid-depth) or open sea rover whom she humanized in her imagination.

After hatching at the water's surface, Scomber idled from fall until April off the Virginia coast. Nature foresaw his need to draw energy from stored fat in its egg yolk while developing gills, mouth, and fins. Analyst Susan Power Bratton summarized the focus on the mackerel and its milieu as an introduction of human readers to a complex and alien marine ecosystem. With her usual circumspection, Rachel warned of the threat of overfishing during creature migrations.

Into Adulthood

As though adopting Scomber for a pet, the author cheered the fry on his way after a near miss with the jaws of an anchovy and a squid. She exulted in his retreat: "In a fraction of a second he would have been seized and eaten" (Carson, 1941, 81). By dramatizing the fish's reaction to a trawl seine, she claimed to have initiated "something that I do not believe has been done before" (*ibid.,* 3). Critic Amanda Hagood identified the conflict between fish and net as "a violent anthropogenic interruption," an encounter framed by human expansionism and its thirst for profit from a fragile ecosystem (Hagood, 2013, 58).

With a lilting view of early fall, Rachel pictured mystic zodiacal changes: "The sun passed through the constellation of the scales (Libra); and September's moon waned to a thin ghost of itself" (Carson, 1941, 97). Her anthropomorphic procession received Nereis the clamworm, whom Baltimore illustrator Howard Frech drew among waving eel-grass fronds. An epic face-off between Scomber and 400 yards of trawl net depicted mackerel judging man-made perils beyond their experience. Susan Bratton described the survivors as "tricksters who thwart the fishermen's ventures" and the sea harvesters as "disruptive and inept" villains in the drama (Bratton, 2004, 10).

Instinctive Self-Preservation

In reference to the fish-waterman relationship, Bratton declared that "Fishers who spend their entire lives making a living from the sea do not perceive or fully understand what is transpiring underneath their keels ... between the terrestrial and hydric realms" (*ibid.*, 6, 7). Rachel's narrative inserted serendipity into an ecocentric cycle fraught with unpredictable obstacles, some created by humankind. Only the ripping jaws of dogfish, a *deus ex machina,* saved Scomber, who swam through a hole in the mesh.

In a heart-pounding conclusion, the author characterized the sea as both dangerous milieu and salvific home. In retrospect, she claimed *Under the Sea Wind* as evidence of her creative composition on natural phenomena. Her trilogy, *Under the Sea Wind, The Sea Around Us,* and *The Edge of the Sea,* and the 1971 excerpt *The Rocky Coast,* became the sources of a surge of public interest in oceanography and the web of life.

See also Predators; Reproduction; Seasons; Sport Hunting.

Sources

Bratton, Susan Power. "Thinking like a Mackerel: Rachel Carson's *Under the Sea-Wind* as a Source for a Trans-Ecotonal Sea Ethic." *Ethics and the Environment* 9:1 (April 2004): 1–22.
Carson, Rachel. "The Edge of the Sea." *Life* (14 April 1952): 64–81.
_____. "Memo to Mrs. Eales." Rachel Carson papers, 1942.
_____. *Under the Sea Wind: A Naturalist's Picture of Ocean Life.* New York: Simon & Schuster, 1941.
Hagood, Amanda. "Wonders with the Sea: Rachel Carson's Ecological Aesthetic and the Mid-Century Reader." *Environmental Humanities* 2:1 (2013): 57–77.

Under the Sea Wind: River and Sea

The final stave of *Under the Sea Wind* moved with certainty toward its conclusion, an intimate perusal of animal communities. The narrative opened in autumn on Bittern Pond south of Newfoundland, where elvers swam some 200 miles from the sea in transition from fresh to saline habitats. In the creation of an earth ethic, Rachel admired the histories of saltwater beings "as ageless as sun and rain, or as the sea itself" (Carson, 1941, 4).

For focus, the author set the stage with a single swimmer. Introducing the well-traveled eel Anguilla, which had ventured 1,000 miles as a fingerling, the narrative probed the mystic summons of instinct to migrate from fresh water feeder creeks to the saline Atlantic. On the way, excitement grew in restless eels "pressing on downstream with fevered haste" toward an unknown destiny, a future meant to evoke reader sympathy (*ibid.*, 137).

EEL METAMORPHOSIS

As the adult swimmers moved shoreward to marshy islands at the coast, to mark a natural physiological change, Rachel's fish saga represented olive brown bodies altering to silver bellies and black spines. Significant to the shift in habitat, rising salinity required some adaptation when the eels rode the tide down the channel. Over breakers, they approached "a great water which each had known in the beginning of life" (*ibid.*, 139).

The author echoed the theme of temperature change and its effect on water organisms. Seasonal timing put the eels out to sea before the first blizzard, which edged the bay in ice. Book critic Estelle C. Tappen, in a review for the *Verona-Cedar Grove* (NJ) *Times,* noted Rachel's views on Darwinian determinism: "Story after story reveals how creatures of land and sea meet enemies, succumb, or rise to victory" (Tappen, 1952, 16).

Human Fishers

The narrative linked the perils of sea life with human loss by inserting a view of the fishing schooner *Mary B.,* which a strong tide ran aground at McNab's Island southwest of Halifax, Nova Scotia, on December 14, 1882. In its shadow, the angler fish trapped victims in its broad mouth, gulping an eider duck whole that nourished him for days to come. Rachel's seasonal scenario followed creatures 600 feet deeper into winter grounds toward the warm Gulf Stream.

The saltwater saga ended on the daily toil of trawler crews and, in February, the mysterious disappearance of slick, wiggly eels into the abyss. They remained in the deep until rising temperatures returned them to freshwater estuaries and the whole cycle of reproduction and growth. In retrospect, Alfred C. Ames, a literary critic for the *Chicago Tribune,* acknowledged the author's focus on a watery cosmos: "Human beings figure only incidentally, as occasional setters of nets. If mankind were to vanish quietly, the processes told here would be little affected" (Ames, 1952, 4:3).

Sources

Ames, Alfred C. "More about the Strange Sea Around Us." *Chicago Tribune* (6 April 1952): 4:3.
Carson, Rachel. *Under the Sea Wind: A Naturalist's Picture of Ocean Life.* New York: Simon & Schuster, 1941.
Feneja, Fernanda Luísa. "'To What End Is Nature?'—Rachel Carson's *Under the Sea Wind* and Environmental Literature." *Anglo-Saxónica* 3:12 (2016): 59–82.
Tappen, Estelle C. "Review: *Under the Sea Wind.*" *Verona-Cedar Grove* (NJ) *Times* (5 June 1952): 16.

Vegetation

The author's immersion in seaside habitats found delight in plants—the aromatic sagebrush of the North American plains and huge anemones and urchins at the West Southport shore of Maine. Her early biological writing incorporated Irish moss, purple laver, dulse, "coralline algae spreading a rose-colored crust," and sea grasses gripping loose sand with their roots (Carson, 1955, 17). In 1941, *Under the Sea Wind* explained the cycle of the sinking cold currents of snow-melt and the rising of warm waters, rich in nitrates and phosphates to fertilize plants. The swap of cold for warm waters produced "pale, green shoots and swelling buds" in a "rich pasturage" that fed crustaceans (Carson, 1941, 70). Still musing on abundance, Rachel pictured rich plateaus, pale-blossomed anemones, and green meadows of mossy creatures and hydroids, which formed colonies that attached to parents.

In a retrospect on the evolution of the planet's flora, Rachel agreed with English naturalist Charles Darwin that development took "millions upon millions of years" (Carson, 1963, 262). In 1951, her perusal of primeval beginnings of earth in *The Sea*

Around Us pictured "mysterious borderline forms that were not quite plants, not quite animals" living on inorganic elements rather than chlorophyll activated by sunlight, carbon dioxide, and seawater (Carson, 1951, 23). Few underwater plants could locate rays to nourish life below 66 fathoms and none at 100 fathoms, a cut-off point she compared to the timberline of high rocky mountain chains.

THE LIFE OF SEA PLANTS

For *The Edge of the Sea,* the biologist explored the varied microplants, mosses, and sea fronds that commonly sway in the current on the Maine coastline around Southport. In "The Coral Coast," she differentiated types of ocean meadows along the reef flats of Florida's Keys. Unlike algae of the Cambrian age (541,000,000 BCE), "the earth's oldest plants," the seed plants—turtle grass, shoal grass, manatee grass—date to 60,000,000 BCE in the Tertiary period alongside sea turtles and snails. Unlike lightly attached algae, the seeded grasses rooted securely in sand and protected the marine bottom from erosion much as dune grass anchored sandy strands from wind and tide.

In the chapter "The Rocky Shore," the naturalist's admiration for dulse derived from folklore that urged Scots to eat the oceanic greenery for health and longevity. The passage also explored a "fantastic jungle, mad in a Lewis Carroll sort of way" of sea tangle (*Laminaria saccharina*), rockweed (*Fucus vesiculosus*), and winged kelp (*Alaria esculenta*), edible parts of New England's undersea copse that resembled palm groves (Carson, 1971, 50). She continued a study of the tides in September 1953 with examination of deep-water luminaria or kelp, a type of brown alga or sea fern with long strappy leaves. For "Our Ever-Changing Shore," a July 1958 essay for *Holiday* magazine, her thoughts turned to "the dry swish of beach grass writing, writing its endless symbols in the sand" (Carson, 1958, 117). The anthropomorphic scribe continued the animation of coastal creatures she began in *Under the Sea Wind.*

ENDANGERING EARTH'S EDEN

By the time Rachel began *Silent Spring,* she was certain that vegetation evolved over "a long period of trial and error" to survive on an inhospitable rocky terrain (Carson, 2002, 64–65). She sought clarification of issues from independent plant scholar Frank Edwin Egler, who pioneered the study of tolerance limits and herbicides in multidimensional vegetation systems in utility rights-of-way and landscape management. On January 29, 1962, she queried him about southwestern sagelands and the role of sage in keeping soil moist and in shading bunch grass. Her curiosity included questions about the extermination of hardwoods with herbicides to maintain conifer forests and the use of 2,4-D or Agent Orange (2,4-Dichlorophenoxyacetic acid) to kill blueberries. Her dismay at autocratic decisions to exterminate sagebrush on the North American plains to placate herdsmen noted the absence of serious investigation of annual rainfall to keep grass pasturage alive. Even in Maine, roadside maintenance denuded the landscape of fern, bayberry, huckleberry, and wildflowers.

Rachel expanded on the use of herbs, trees, brush, and shrubs, which fed wild mammals and grazing stock. She described willow blooms, vetch, goldenrod, mustard and dandelion as sources of pollen for bees. To limit the extermination of valuable organisms, she urged the selective spraying of woody plants rather than blanket spraying that killed everything. In her last year, the author wrote of being bedfast and admiring from her window the emergence of spring in daffodils and roses. At Rachel's death in 1964, when 60.9 percent of wildflowers entered endangered lists, her prophecies proved true.

See also Silent Spring: Earth's Green Mantle.

Sources

Burgess, Robert L., "Resolution of Respect: Frank Edwin Egler, 1911–1996." *Bulletin of the Ecological Society of America* 78 (1997): 193–194.
Carson, Rachel. "Letter to Frank E. Egler" (29 January 1962).
_____. "Our Ever-Changing Shore." *Holiday* 24 (July 1958): 70–71, 117–120.
_____. "Rachel Carson Answers Her Critics." *Audubon* 65 (September/October 1963): 262–265, 313–315.
_____. *The Sea Around Us.* New York: Oxford University Press, 1951.
_____. *Silent Spring.* Boston: Houghton Mifflin, 40th Anniversary Edition, 2002.
_____. *Under the Sea Wind: A Naturalist's Picture of Ocean Life.* Boston: Houghton Mifflin, 1955.
Steingruber, Sandra, ed. *Rachel Carson: Silent Spring & Other Writings on the Environment.* New York: Library of America, 2018.

Waterfowl

The author promoted waterfowl for their beauty and use as game birds, photography subjects for bird watchers, and food. Her contribution of hunting data in the late 1930s indicated a style equitable to both shooters and conservationists. For the article "Ducks Are on Increase" for the January 16, 1938, issue of the *Baltimore Sunday Sun Magazine,* she gathered facts about the Canadian-U.S. Migratory Bird Treaty restricting gunners at flyways on the Gunpowder, Honga, and Susquehanna rivers in Maryland. By limiting calendar days and bag limits and prohibiting bait and decoys, government officials for the U.S. Biological Survey hoped to shield waterfowl populations across Central and North America as far south as Cuba and Puerto Rico during seasonal migrations. Rachel identified limitations as a way to defeat overshooting and the loss of nesting areas to dredging, plowing wheat fields, the Dust Bowl, and bog drainage in Alberta, Manitoba, and Saskatchewan.

Essential to Rachel's reportage, a tutorial on where ducks and geese migrate for reproduction relieved hunter ignorance of the big picture. Her knowledge of waterfowl aggregates on the Mackenzie River and Great Bear Lake in the North Territories of Canada accounted for the proliferation of ducks in Minnesota, Nebraska, and North and South Dakota, the location of 75 percent of game birds in the Northern Hemisphere. Congressional investment in 1933 restored breeding grounds at 220 sanctuaries and designated resting places during migration. She made a startling comparison of U.S. land priorities: 140,000,000 acres for herd grazing as opposed to 7,500,000 acres for wildlife. She attested that an avian epidemic in southern Canada could deplete waterfowl throughout the continent.

A WATER BIRD THEME

Rachel focused on waterfowl in the first of *Conservation in Action,* a series of informational pamphlets on nature sanctuaries for the U.S. Fish and Wildlife Service. "Mattamuskeet: A National Wildlife Refuge," a nine-page brochure issued in July 1947, reported on the uniqueness of the whistling swan, an endangered water bird. The Arctic species, once native to ancestral Algonquin territory, wintered on the Pamlico Sound on North Carolina's Mattamuskeet sanctuary and ate large amounts of foliage. Of flocks of 500 swans, she described the host as "magnificent in their gleaming white plumage" (Carson, 1947, 4).

In 1950, the author again concentrated on waterfowl in the eighth brochure, "Bear River: A National Wildlife Refuge." She described the collapse of a population of millions of ducks and geese after New World settlers directed water to agricultural irrigation and drained swamps. Contributing to the decimation, "Gunners had slaughtered [waterfowl] by the thousands; and many others had fallen prey to diseases" (Carson, 1950, 1). Only federal conservation in Utah enabled the nation to enjoy skies "patterned with millions of wings," the result of restocking and restoring habitats (*ibid.*).

FATAL TOXINS

For a masterwork, *Silent Spring,* issued on September 27, 1962, Rachel denounced the use of organochlorines in bird country, especially DDT (dichlorodiphenyltrichloroethane). She reflected on the central California wildlife refuges on the Oregon border at Lower Klamath and Tule Lake. For their teeming wildlife, she treasured "an original waterfowl paradise of marshland and open water" (Carson, 2002, 45). Unfortunately, in summer 1960, drainage of irrigation waters from farmlands killed fish-eaters—grebes, gulls, herons, and pelicans—from outflow contaminated with DDD (dichlorodiphenyldichloroethane), DDE (dichlorodiphenyldichloroethylene), and toxaphene. The latter, a fish killer, caused lung and kidney damage, bronchial cancer, neurological anomalies, respiratory failure, seizures, and death.

The biologist noted the irony of stewardship efforts to protect natural hydrology at the convergence of the Pacific Flyway. Contrasting strands intended to gratify duck hunters and "everyone to whom the sight and sought of drifting ribbons of waterfowl across an evening sky are precious" (*ibid.,* 45). For accuracy, she identified the redhead and ruddy duck as endangered species further imperiled by toxin-laced water. Her melodic prose contrasted lakes and streams polluted with DDD and the beauty that it threatened. Idyllic images depicted the gliding adult swan grebe and its young "clothed in soft gray down" that piggybacked on its parents' bodies under the wing (*ibid.,* 47). The metaphor suggested the need for conservation in nesting grounds.

Rachel's classic work decried the wholesale alteration of Rocky Mountain flyways, which offered saline lakes, wetlands, and grasslands in the Dakotas and Montana, Colorado River Basin, the Great Salt Lake, and the Rio Grande and as far south as Belize. To the north, the spraying of Bridger National Forest by the U.S. Forest Service annihilated Wyoming sagebrush, a source of nesting, feeding, and cover for the sage grouse. Collateral riparian damage killed the shady willows along streams and reduced the prolific waterfowl, beaver, moose, and trout populations that promoted recreation, hunting, and fishing. In exasperation, she concluded, "The living world was shattered" (*ibid.*, 68).

See also Endangered Species; Waterways.

Sources

Carson, Rachel. "Bear River: A National Wildlife Refuge." #8. Washington, D.C.: U.S. Department of the Interior, 1950, 1–14.
_____. "Mattamuskeet: A National Wildlife Refuge." #4. Washington, D.C.: U.S. Department of the Interior, July 1947.
_____. *Silent Spring.* Boston: Houghton Mifflin, 40th Anniversary Edition, 2002.
Carson, R.L. "Ducks Are on Increase." *Baltimore Sunday Sun Magazine* (16 January 1938): 1.
Tesfahunegny, Weldemariam. "Impact of Pesticides on Birds from DDT to Current Fatality: A Literature Review." *Journal of Zoology Studies* 3:2 (2016): 44–56.

Waterways

Rachel's relationship to U.S. waterways never strayed from appreciation of a crucial earth element. In 1938, she regretted the draining of the 25 × 8 mile Klamath Lake in south central Oregon for agrarian use. The failure of farming in alkaline soil and subsequent prairie fires ended the experiment intended to repurpose the land for irrigation. She noted subsequent plans to re-flood the marshes and wetlands to restore waterfowl to the Pacific Flyway and to halt the Dust Bowl, a section of Midwestern plowland that once relied on stability from prairie grass roots. In a statement simple enough for a child to understand, her script for "Clouds," a CBS-TV program for *Omnibus* on March 11, 1957, summarized the eternal unity of evaporation and condensation over waterways: "from sea to air—from air to earth—from earth to sea" (Carson, "Clouds," 1957).

In 1941 in the Foreword to *Under the Sea Wind,* the writer particularized the "far tributaries of a coastal river," the home of adult eels, one of her focal water creatures (Carson, 1941, 4). The narrative continued its perusal of seaside mysteries by picturing the gliding of shad through varying degrees of salinity as they left the ocean. The unique species traveled the spawning grounds in an estuary, "broad and sluggish, little more than an arm of the sound" (*ibid.*, 16). The journey preceded a pilgrimage to the Arctic tundra.

From Fresh to Salt

The narrative returned to the familiar Ship's Shoal and Mullet Pond on North Carolina's Outer Banks and traced incoming tides that formed a narrow slough flecked with ocean spume. As though answering the starting gun, shrimps, eels, and minnows followed the spate of seawater, "leaping and racing, foaming and swirling," from freshwater ponds and wetlands "on their wild dash to the sea" (*ibid.*, 53). With a touch of alliteration, the narrative suffused with bliss the exodus of saltwater organisms to their motherland, an hour-long free-for-all in the "rollicking, roistering, rough-and-ready tide" (*ibid.*).

While accounting for ridges, valleys, and coasts in topography, in 1955 in *The Edge of the Sea,* Rachel pictured the beauties of Maine's ragged shoreline and the saltwater estuaries, home to birds and fish on the Damariscotta, Kennebec, and Sheepscot rivers. From a more aggressive stance, the biologist's speeches to Audubon clubs decried blood sport and the poisoning of lakes to improve fishing. After missing the Water Pollution Conference on November 18, 1960, at Michigan State University, Ann Arbor, because of a bout of influenza, in early 1961, she gained information secondhand from the Welder Wildlife Foundation in Sinton, Texas, about DDD (dichlorodiphenyldichloroethane) residues in plankton specimens from Clear Lake, California. She also requested research on biocides in KIamath Lake, Oregon, and Tule Lake, California, where toxic DDE (dichlorodiphenyldichloroethylene) caused the deaths of pelicans, cormorants, and waterfowl from eating tainted fish.

LIVING WITH POISONS

On September 27, 1962, Rachel returned to the essentials of waterways in *Silent Spring* by accounting for the natural production of methane. A source of global warming, the atmospheric marsh gas arises from the rotting of humus under water, particularly in wetlands. More serious to life, in Chapter Nine, "Rivers of Death," she regretted the intentional poisoning of "inshore waters—the bays, the sounds, the river estuaries, the tidal marshes—an ecological unit of the utmost importance" (Carson, 2002, 149). Janine Kitson, an Educator at National Trust of Australia in Adelaide, reiterated the biologist's chief concern: "Chemicals poisoned the waterways, air and soil and harmed living things as the toxification intensified up the food chain harming insects, birdlife, wildlife" (Kitson, 2017, 29). Without conservation of natural resources, Rachel warned, Americans could no longer eat fish, mollusks, and crustaceans, including lobster, crab, oysters, and shrimp.

In an intense statement about poisons to the U.S. Congress on June 4, 1963, Rachel noted that evaporation of DDT (dichlorodiphenyltrichloroethane) from water surfaces created a separate form of chemical contamination from methane. According to data from the U.S. Public Health Service, rain rinsed spray from land, forming runoff into "ponds, streams, and rivers" and on to oceans and the upper atmosphere (Carson, "Environmental," 1963). She reprised the model on October 18, 1963, in the speech "The Pollution of Our Environment" before a San Francisco symposium *Man Against Himself* hosted by Kaiser-Permanente. The example stressed the permeation of ground and surface water with pesticides and evidence of contamination in river systems and drinking water. She alarmed the 1,500 physicians in attendance with specifics: at Clear Lake, California, toxaphene remained so interwoven in flora and fauna that effects emerged with each new generation. In a flight home from the California speech on October 21, 1963, the author viewed desert lands and thought "about water in relation to the landscape—or especially the lack of it!," a prophetic statement of need recognized into the 21st century (Carson, letter, 1963).

See also Fish.

Sources

Carson, Rachel. "Clouds" in "Something about the Sky." CBS *Omnibus* (11 March 1957).
_____. "Environmental Hazards: Control of Pesticides and Other Chemical Poisons." Statement before the Subcommittee on Reorganization and International Organizations of the Committee on Government Operations (4 June 1963): 206–219.
_____. "Fight for Wildlife Pushes Ahead." *Richmond Times Dispatch Sunday Magazine* (20 March 1938): 8–9.
_____. "Letter to Clarence Cottam" (4 January 1961).
_____. "Letter to Dorothy Freeman" (21 October 1963).
_____. "The Pollution of Our Environment." Address to the Kaiser-Permanente Symposium *Man Against Himself*, San Francisco (18 October 1963).
_____. *Silent Spring*. Boston: Houghton Mifflin, 40th Anniversary Edition, 2002.
_____. *Under the Sea Wind: A Naturalist's Picture of Ocean Life*. New York: Simon & Schuster, 1941.
Kitson, Janine. "Marie Byles and Rachel Carson: Two exceptional Women Who Loved Nature." *Nature New South Wales* 61:1 (2017): 29.
Norwood, Vera. *Made from This Earth*. Chapel Hill: University of North Carolina Press, 1993.

Waves

The motions of seawater mesmerized Rachel, inspiring the opening paragraph of "Undersea," her 1937 debut into the literary world for the *Atlantic Monthly*. She pictured the "lilt of the long, slow swells of mid-ocean," a calming, reassuring rhythm that dominated her early career (Carson, 1937, 322). Four years later, sound in the first chapter of *Under the Sea Wind* romanticized the silencing of breakers into "a sigh, a sort of rhythmic exhalation as though the sea, too were asleep" (Carson, 1941, 15). The sibilance anticipates her skill at allying human needs and responses with the cycles of oceans.

As a contrast to gentle water noises, in 1951 in *The Sea Around Us,* photos of powerful crests sculpting coral accompanied two pictures of serious damage: the tsunami on April 1, 1946, that smashed an Alaskan lighthouse at Scotch Cap on Unimak Island and killed five crewmen. Seven waves subsequently damaged shores at Kauai and Hilo Bay, Hawaii. The author summarized the hypnotic pull of a mystic "water world" and a "horizon ridged and furrowed by waves," a power that intruded on the continents (Carson, 1951, 30). In the introduction to the 1989 edition, essayist Ann Haymond Zwinger applauded Rachel for "[making] of waves a romance, whence they came, how they came, why they were the shape they were, how they bring 'the feel of the distant places' interwoven with solid scientific data" (Zwinger, 1989, xx).

Seawater in History

In the initial paragraphs of "The Restless Sea," the third and last chapter of *The Sea Around Us,* Rachel heightened oceanic drama. She summarized most waves as "the result of the action of wind on water" or, less often, the rare crests generated by underwater volcanoes (*ibid.,* 109). The narrative championed the gathering of data from the western extremes of the Atlantic via instruments off Lands End, England. Meticulous meteorology recounted "the life histories of the waves" that rolled up out of the salty abyss from wind and storms as far away as 6,000 miles (*ibid.,* 107).

In a gesture to period studies of the 1940s, Rachel substantiated wave data recording since World War II in California, Cornwall, and the Atlantic coast of North

America. Beyond the pier at Long Branch in east central New Jersey, electric graphing informed the Army Corps of Engineers on the source of beach erosion. In flights over Africa, the British surveyed coastal colonial outposts by photographing the advance of crests. More serious monitoring aided vessels approaching Scotland at Sumburgh Head, Duncansby Bore, and the Merry Men of Mey off Pentland Firth, a treacherous stretch of tidal race.

In late September 1951, the writer ventured away from intellectual writing to compose the liner notes for an RCA recording of Claude Debussy's classic symphony *La Mer,* which debuted in October 1905. In lyric mode, she portrayed "a world of water and sky, crossed by the hurrying forms of waves and holding endless converse with the great winds" (Carson, "Liner," 1951). Her bestselling *The Sea Around Us* incorporated bright protozoa and phosphorescent microphyla in a swirl of flash and tints igniting cresting waves into glitter and flame.

Diagnosing oceanic surface symptoms required the ability "to read the language of the sea" (Carson, 1951, 45). Crimson streaks warned First Peoples of an abundant plankton bearing a poison similar to strychnine. The perusal of ocean basins and upthrust mountain chains credited "the push and pull and drag of even the heaviest of storm waves" with wearing down deep sea peaks (*ibid.*, 73). A worse upheaval, the explosion of Krakatoa in north central Indonesia on August 17, 1883, generated a rogue wave that struck the Sunda Strait, Indian Ocean, Cape Horn, and the English Channel, killing 36,417 from magma impact, fire, steam, and tsunamis.

Sea Lyrics

For a sea story for *The Edge of the Sea,* the author respected the occasional tall wave that overshadowed lesser swells. She reported personal views of limpets, whose "shells have developed in myriad shapes to resist the pounding of the waves" (Carson, 1955, 232). In "Our Ever-Changing Shore," an essay for the July 1958 issue of *Holiday* magazine, she imagined a "muted whisper" of sea influx "when the heated air shimmers above the sand and the sky is without clouds" (Carson, 1958, 71). She interpreted the susurration as a "tentativeness that suggests that something is about to happen" (*ibid.*).

More challenging sounds and motions rocked Rachel's first sea voyage in July 1953 aboard the U.S. Fish and Wildlife trawler S.S. *Albatross III.* Under white light, she stared into dark waters to view "the great shapes of waves" that kept the craft in constant motion (Carson, 1954). The sea's artistry permeated her remarks on the Lost Woods, a beloved expanse on Southport Island, Maine, between Deep Cove and Dogfish Head. On the mile-long shoreline, the currents and "storm surf" formed "deep chasms" and piled up driftwood, trunks, logs, and stumps, the detritus that she explored for hidden sea life (Carson, letter, 1956).

See also Sea; Sense Impressions.

Sources

Carson, Rachel. *The Edge of the Sea.* Boston: Houghton Mifflin, 1955.
_____. "Letter to Curtis and Nellie Lee Bok" (12 December 1956).

_____. "Liner Notes." Claude Debussy's *La Mer,* RCA Victor, 1951.
_____. "Our Ever-Changing Shore." *Holiday* 24 (July 1958): 70–71, 117–120.
_____. "The Real World Around Us," address to the Theta Sigma Phi Matrix Table Dinner, *House of Life* (21 April 1954): 324–326.
_____. *The Sea Around Us.* New York: Oxford University Press, 1951.
_____. *Under the Sea Wind: A Naturalist's Picture of Ocean Life.* New York: Simon & Schuster, 1941.
_____. "Undersea." *Atlantic Monthly* 160 (September 1937): 322–325.
Irwin, Virginia. "Author of Best Sellers about the Sea." *St. Louis Post-Dispatch* (16 July 1952): 3F.
Zwinger, Ann H. "Introduction." *The Sea Around Us.* New York: Oxford University Press, 1989.

Weather

Rachel acknowledged the power of wind and weather to impact history. In a freelance article in January 1937 for the *Baltimore Sun,* she announced a change in the Atlantic coast: "When the sea, driven by the August hurricane of three years ago, cut an inlet into Sinepuxent Bay, the first step was taken toward giving Maryland a port of entry for the Atlantic fleet" (Carson, 1937, 6). Nature's intrusion provided the state's deep seas fishermen with a new industry—"winter trawling for saltwater fish" with "pound nets and haul seines" (*ibid.*). The alteration brought southern harvests of butterfish, croaker, flounder, scup, sea bass, and grey and sea trout at the rate of eight tons of fish from one pass of the watermen's boat. Additional catch—lobster, squid, scallops—satisfied distinct tastes.

The author respected rogue weather patterns for endangering professional fishers. A year later, the August 1938 article "Giants of the Tide Rip Off Nova Scotia Again" for the *Baltimore Sunday Sun* accounted for the heroism of fishermen from northwestern England. In heavy mist, strong currents, rip tides, and gales, they landed huge bluefin tuna, a valuable commercial seafood. She warned, "By the mouth of the Mersey River at Liverpool, fogs blanket the water with dangerous suddenness at this time of year and small boats are often lost" (Carson, 1938, 2).

Coastal Rigors

For *Under the Sea Wind,* in 1941, Rachel varied settings from the breezy North Carolina Outer Banks to the Arctic tundra, where solid ice slabs "moved, straining and groaning, with the tides" (Carson, 1941, 32). With "winter ... yet to die," the fickle climate thinned the snow blanket (*ibid.,* 33). Each afternoon, it frosted rock pools. She pitied Silverbar the sanderling, who warmed four fledglings under her wings "when sudden gusts of rain drove across the barrens" (*ibid.,* 45). Because of the limited window of survival, the author cautioned a seasonal threat: "Only the kernel of life, fortified and protected," finished out the cold, dark Arctic winter (*ibid.,* 41).

In *The Sea Around Us,* the author summarized forces driving waves and boulders and questioned glib generalizations about the most treacherous waters. Against claims that Tierra del Fuego and the Juan de Fuca straits encountered the most formidable blasts, she posited Icelandic storms battering the Orkney and Shetland islands beyond Scotland in the North Sea. The text substantiated the choice with a citation from the *British Islands Pilot,* which warned of seasonal gales. Measured by mid–19th-century Scots engineer Thomas Stevenson's wave dynamometer, the scale corroborated freakish gales and torrents battering capes and lighthouses. As described in *The Edinburgh Review,* a storm in fall 1840 mustered enough pneumatic pressure to rip a door off its hinges from inside the Eddystone Light, a 72-foot landmark southeast of Cornwall at Rame Head, England.

The tutorial quality of *The Sea Around Us* emerged from personal experience. Aboard the U.S. Fish and trawler S.S. *Albatross III* around the Georges Banks in mid–July 1949, she viewed the constant rise of fog from the warmth of the Gulf Stream. She characterized its effect off Labrador as "a thick, blanketing whiteness that is the atmospheric response to the Gulf Stream's invasion of the cold northern seas" (Carson, 1951, 129). Her explanation of clockwise and counterclockwise currents explained variance in the Indian Ocean as the result of "capricious monsoons" (Carson, 1951, 126). Commentary in *Silent Spring* alerted readers to climate change and the extreme weather conditions to come. Shelley Choi, a South Korean environmentalist, stated the value of the author's weather essays: "By weaving seemingly unrelated incidents and facts into a coherent, science-based narrative, Carson allowed the public to easily grasp the state of affairs while urging them towards action" (Choi, 2018, 121).

See also Climate Change; Temperature; Waves; Wind.

Sources

Carson, Rachel. *The Sea Around Us.* New York: Oxford University Press, 1951.
_____. *Under the Sea Wind: A Naturalist's Picture of Ocean Life.* New York: Simon & Schuster, 1941.
Carson, R.L., "Giants of the Tide Rip Off Nova Scotia Again." *Baltimore Sunday Sun* (3 August 1938): 2.
_____. "The Northern Trawlers Move South." *Baltimore Sunday Sun* (3 January 1937): 6–7.
Choi, Shelley. "'Smart' Surveillance of Dusty Behavior: Illuminating the Relationship Between Particulate Matter and the Atmosphere." *Computational Water, Energy, and Environmental Engineering* 7:03 (2018): 119–126.

Wetlands

At a time when urbanization, recreation, agriculture, and industrialization rapidly used up wild acreage, Rachel's literary career favored watery settings for prolific animal life. She spoke often of land conditions favoring living things, such as wetlands as the home of clams, huge reptiles, and dragonflies, whose young fed on aquatic larvae of mosquitoes. In September 1938, she wrote "Mass Production for Diamond-Back Terrapins," an article for the *Baltimore Sunday Sun* on government propagation of diamond-back terrapin eggs from Beaufort, North Carolina, for release of some 2,600 young in the salt marshes of six coastal states. The author revealed that the amphibians had a lengthy history in the American South. Before the Civil War, coastal planters fed slaves on plentiful turtle meat. The U.S. Bureau of Fisheries attempted to increase populations in 1904 by experimenting with wood hatcheries on North Carolina's Pamlico Sound. By the 1920s, supply in Maryland had fallen to a mere 823 pounds.

Land management for birds provided nesting sites, wintering grounds, and rests above high tide along Atlantic coast avian flyways. In her pamphlet for the U.S. Department of the Interior "Parker River: A National Wildlife Refuge," issued in 1947, she amassed active verbs—forested, restrained, carpeted, filled, bordered—to advocate experimental topographic shaping on a "northern coastal march—building up potential nesting sites in the marshes by creating artificial islands" (Carson, 1947, 9). In "Chincoteague: A National Wildlife Refuge," she retreated to North American history: "This is the kind of country the ducks knew in the old days, before the white man's civilization disturbed the face of the land. This is the kind of country that is rapidly disappearing except where it is protected in wildlife sanctuaries" (Carson, 1947, 2).

UTAH'S WETLANDS

In 1950, the author returned to marshland in the brochure "Bear River: A National Wildlife Refuge," the eighth in a series called *Conservation in Action*. The text featured Utah's swamps, some drained by settlers or directed to crop irrigation by farmers. She noted the outlines of "ancient Lake Bonneville, a large inland sea that covered some 20,000 square miles" during the Pleistocene Era (1,000,000 BCE) (Carson, 1950, 1). She honored the borderless, liminal expanses as "a shifting kaleidoscopic pattern in which there is no finality, no ultimate and fixed reality—earth becoming blood as the sea itself" (*ibid.*)

The author advertised the flying duck symbol of the National Forest Refuge and reminded readers, "Wild Creatures, like men, must have a place to live" (*ibid.*). After marshland developed, for centuries, aborigines of the Anasazi and Fremont Culture depended on waterfowl for food. The bogs supported thousands of ducks and geese in 1824, when mountain man and fur trader Jim Bridger, the first white frontiersman to view the Great Salt Lake, guided his bull boat along Bear River in search of an egress to the Pacific Ocean. In 1843, John Charles Frémont, an explorer of alternates to the Oregon Trail, surveyed the north end of the delta and ate heartily of "a delicious supper of ducks, geese, and plover" (*ibid.*, 3).

FIELD SURVEYS

In June 1950, Rachel made her own trek off from Florida's Tamiami Trail to view the "trackless, roadless" extremes of the Everglades (Rachel, 1954). Traveling by a crude, noisy glades buggy, she investigated sawgrass, shrubs, and thickets. Subsequent experience in a North Carolina swamp with a single crab inspired her acceptance speech to the Animal Welfare Institute on January 7, 1963. Her composition of *The Sea Around Us* in 1951 recounted sunken lands and peninsulas, including the Dogger Bank east of England, a former wetland rich in prehistoric mammoth and rhinoceros, bison, wolves, hyenas, wild ox, moor peat bogs, willow and birch trees, fern, and moss.

In 1962, the essay "Nature Fights Back" in *Silent Spring* detailed the results of spraying DDT (dichlorodiphenyltrichloroethane) in eastern Florida's salt marshes, which left schistosoma (blood flukes) without enemies. The free ranging flatworms invaded the skin of swimmers and fishermen or entered the body of vacationers through drinking water. Infestation in humans produced vomiting and intestinal complaint, infertility, spleen and liver enlargement, kidney damage, bladder, and death. In ruminants, rabbits, elk, and deer, the parasites made the meat dangerous for consumption. Of fishers and other watermen, Caterina Scaramelli, an anthropologist at Boston University, warned "This is their life, their home, and their everyday work, all seemingly at the precipice of destruction" (Scaramelli, 2018, 54).

Sources

Carson, Rachel, "Bear River: A National Wildlife Refuge." #8. Washington, D.C.: U.S. Department of the Interior, 1950, 1–14.
_____. "Chincoteague: A National Wildlife Refuge." #1. Washington, D.C.: U.S. Department of the Interior, 1947, 1–19.
_____. "Parker River: A National Wildlife Refuge." #2. Washington, D.C.: U.S. Department of the Interior, 1947, 1–14.
_____. "The Real World Around Us," address to the Theta Sigma Phi Matrix Table Dinner (21 April 1954), Columbus, Ohio.
_____. *The Sea Around Us*. New York: Oxford University Press, 1951.
_____. *Silent Spring*. Boston: Houghton Mifflin, 40th Anniversary Edition, 2002.
Carson, R.L., "Mass Production for Diamond-Back Terrapins." *Baltimore Sunday Sun Magazine* (13 September 1938): 1.
Scaramelli, Caterina. "Fish, Flows, and Desire in the Delta." *Anthropology News* 59:2 (2018): 51–56.

Whales

Rachel's admiration for megafauna added grandeur to her first literary essay, "Undersea," published in the September 1937 issue of *Atlantic Monthly*. Of the 37-yard expanse of the blue whale, she extolled its place among earth's beasts as "the largest animal that ever lived" (Carson, 1937, 323). Its remains were among the few prehistoric bones to survive in the oozy bottom. For the sake of size comparison, she contrasted the whale to minuscule diatoms, unicellular alga that may be no longer than 2 micrometers. In an accounting for the popularity of whaling in the 1940s, the author cited wartime shortages of beef as a reason for the Japanese consumption of foul-smelling whale meat.

More upbeat references to whales in 1941 in *Under the Sea Wind* noted the following of the phalarope, a sparrow-size shorebird that marks the whale route to sample "ever-drifting clouds of whale food" and sea lice on whale backs (Carson, 1941, 42). The glossary named the pteropod, slender launce, and common menhaden, which schools from Brazil to Nova Scotia, as common food of the finback whale. Another entry pictured the gutsy orca or killer whale swimming in packs on the ocean surface and terrifying walruses, dolphins, seals, and whales with their attacks.

THREATS TO SURVIVAL

The author's fifth pamphlet in the *Conservation in Action* series for the U.S. Department of the Interior, "Guarding Our Wildlife Resources: A National Wildlife Refuge," summarized the work of factory whalers in some 30 nations. She honored the profession as an industry dating to the mid–900s CE, when area by area declined from the over-harvesting of whale pods. By 1900, the only virgin banks left for exploitation bordered the Antarctic Ocean. Her summation contributed rules for legal size and protections for endangered species and females with calves.

In 1951 in *The Sea Around Us*, orcas and whales returned to the author's perusal of echo sounding of the abyss by fathometers in the 1920s. The text marveled that spring spawning dives of a half mile caused "pressure of a half a ton on every inch of body" of the baleen whale (Carson, 1951, 66). She admired seals, fish, and whales for "[migrating] over enormous distance," some to the Antarctic whaling ground, where mineral-rich waters sustained enough food for huge animals (*ibid.,* xiii).

The narrative pictured krill swarms as the magnet, drawing whales "from no one knows where, by no one knows what route" (*ibid.,* 43). In the North Atlantic, she depicted "the distant sudden spurt and lazy drift of a whale's spouting, [which lends] life to the water" (*ibid., 32*). Along the way, they fed their massive bodies on "fishes, shrimps, or on some of the smallest of the plankton creatures" (*ibid., 26*). The radioactive deposits that nations began dropping in 1946 affected whales, which carried radiation around the globe. She concluded, "The sea, though changed in a sinister way, will continue to exist; the threat is rather to life itself" (*ibid.,* 109).

Whales in History

Rachel traced sea lions, seals, sea elephants, and whales to the Tertiary Era (70,000,000 BCE). She surmised that prehistoric whales foraged on land before adapting to marine existence, which cost them hind appendages and turned their front legs into flippers. During a speech on October 1, 1951, at the Astor Hotel to the New York Herald Tribune Book Review, she treated listeners to hydrophone recordings of whale sounds, which navy technicians monitored during World War II at they searched for enemy submarines.

On September 27, 1962, a brief accolade to the "great blue whale" in *Silent Spring* extolled the "incredible diversity" of creation, which ranged downward in size to bacteria (Carson, 2002, 18). The Afterword, by biographer Linda Lear, acclaimed the 1973 Endangered Species Act for restoring the gray whale along with the alligator and brown pelican. The author noted, "All were imperiled forty years ago, and all are now considered relatively safe" (Carson, 2002, 362).

Sources

Blum, Hester. "Bitter with the Salt of Continents: Rachel Carson and Oceanic Returns." *WSQ: Women's Studies Quarterly* 45:1 (Spring/Summer 2017): 287–291.
Carson, Rachel. "Guarding Our Wildlife Resources: A National Wildlife Refuge." #5. Washington, D.C.: U.S. Department of the Interior, 1948.
_____. *The Sea Around Us.* New York: Oxford University Press, 1951.
_____. *Silent Spring.* Boston: Houghton Mifflin, 40th Anniversary Edition, 2002.
_____. Speech, New York Herald Tribune Book Review, Astor Hotel (1 October 1951).
_____. *Under the Sea Wind: A Naturalist's Picture of Ocean Life.* New York: Simon & Schuster, 1941.
_____. "Undersea." *Atlantic Monthly* 160 (September 1937): 322–325.
Carson, R.L. "Whalers Ready for New Season." *Baltimore Sunday Sun* (20 November 1938): 2.

Wind

Rachel's scan of dunes, woods, weather, and tides returned repeatedly to changes in wind direction and their effects on shore plants and birds. In *Under the Sea Wind,* after a passing storm at Mullet Pond on North Carolina's Outer Banks in 1941, Rachel viewed the rush of waters into the inlet while "air currents came fresh again and the wind blew clean and steady from the southwest" (Carson, 1941, 31). Unlike the balmy South, Arctic winds bore "a bitter air that turned to mist as it moved, swirling, over the warmer plains" and penetrating protective feathers and fur (*ibid.*, 33). Sanderlings instinctively shouldered together to share body heat during a blizzard. The gust of north wind forced a mass movement from Herring Gull Shoal into deeper sun-warmed waters and hurled a mist of sand above dune grasses, an icing on the cake that shape topography.

An undeniable force, ocean air currents dominated seasonal changes in *The Sea Around Us*. Rachel, a skywatcher from childhood, viewed the coming winter gales as sources of gigantic storms and crests "lashing the water foam and flying spray" (Carson, 1951, 46). For literary comparison, the narrative quoted Joseph Conrad's *The Mirror of the Sea,* a first-person memoir of life aboard ship. A photo on p. 160 declared Rachel's lyric contrast: "Clouds draw heat energy from tropical seas to fuel the wind systems of the globe," empowering the world's weather (*ibid.*, 160).

Activating Nature

In "River and Sea," the third stave, the writer credited winds with motivating organisms to follow instinctive urges. She represented an unpredictable fall breeze in Newfoundland over Bittern Pond, northeast of Nova Scotia, that mounted from evening to midnight into a gale force. The driving air set the tone of migration to the sea and the instinctive trek of eels from fresh water to salt. For less dramatic times, she contrasted winter sounds of rustling leafless branches with the whisper of wind through branch and foliage.

Solitude on Saint Simon Island, Georgia, on April 17, 1952, gave Rachel a long sandy stretch to investigate. As darkness approached, she contrasted the sound of water over shore with wind on water. Among the dunes, she imagined the winds like unfettered companions—"roaming down into the valleys and leaping in little, unexpected gusts over the crests of the sand hills" (Carson, 1952). As though inspiring a duet, the air currents stirred dune grass into gentle swishes that she termed "scribblings," which she interpreted as the geological history of "earth building" (*Ibid.*).

Air Powers

On March 11, 1957, for the CBS-TV program "Clouds" in "Something about the Sky," Rachel reiterated the impact of air currents on earth. With clouds as the visual proof, she summarized sky observation and its alerts to downdrafts and ocean conditions. From mountain peaks, gales as rigorous as 300 miles per hour generated "strong wave motion which extends out over miles of valley on the lee side" (Carson, 1957, 178). She referred to the massive change in atmosphere as "spectacular features of the aerial drama" that carries to earth snow, fog, and mist (*ibid.*, 179). Birds, her favorite actors, rode soaring thermal updrafts like glider pilots.

While musing on the dual purpose of gusts over slopes, gullies, and ridges at Kitty Hawk, North Carolina, Rachel's essay "Our Ever-Changing Shore" for the July

1958 issue of *Holiday* magazine concluded that "the winds seemed bent on destroying the very dunes they had created" (Carson, 1958, 71). On the opposite shore of North America, she credited western winds with forceful heavy surf on the Pacific beaches and with sculpting Monterey cypresses by pelting buds with sea salt. In 2019, energy economist Brandon N. Owens credited Rachel with "kick-starting the modern environment movement" that preceded wind power technology (Owens, 2019, 129).

See also Weather.

Sources

Carson, Rachel. "Clouds" in "Something About the Sky." CBS *Omnibus* (11 March 1957).
_____. "Our Ever-Changing Shore." *Holiday* 24 (July 1958): 70–71, 117–120.
_____. "Saint Simon Island, Georgia," unpublished 1952.
_____. *The Sea Around Us.* New York: Oxford University Press, 1951.
_____. *Under the Sea Wind: A Naturalist's Picture of Ocean Life.* New York: Simon & Schuster, 1941.
Owens, Brandon N. "Wind Power's Silent Decade." *The Wind Power Story: A Century of Innovation that Reshaped the Global Energy Landscape.* Hoboken, NJ: Wiley, 2019: 129–141.

Woods Hole Biological Laboratory

Rachel profited from centering field research in coastal New England. In 1942, she composed her first memories of experiencing the ocean at Woods Hole, the famous Marine Biological Laboratory in Cape Cod, Massachusetts. The cooperative scientific center opened in 1881 as a permanent research station for the U.S. Fish Commission. At one of the top North American settings for marine seaside study, the complex drew on major universities for talent to engage in serious inquiry into the environment. The first course focused in invertebrate neurology.

On a six-weeks fellowship at one of the few laboratories that accepted women, the author, at age 22, arrived at the lab in August 1929 and lived on Chesapeake Bay while studying fish, eels, and swans. She recalled "a little dredging boat" in which she would "steam up and down Vineyard Sound or Buzzards Bay southeast of New Bedford" (Carson, 1942). Sea organisms pulled up in the dredge introduced her to unfamiliar rocks, shells, weeds, and animals and found their way into press releases and reports by the information officer. Prior to transferring to biology and physiology courses at Johns Hopkins University in Baltimore in fall, she acquired further training from Woods Hole professors, seminars, and readings in the campus library. She recorded in personal notes that Woods Hole was the place where she favored imagination to envision the holistic environment of sea creatures.

A Pied-à-Terre

In 1937, Rachel returned to the laboratory to serve as junior aquatic biologist for the oceanographic institute. Two years later, she spent the summer beachcombing at Woods Hole Station and researching harbor and wharf for data on saltwater organisms. By June, she advanced to assistant aquatic biologist and her first publication in *Nature* magazine. In July 1940, she joined the U.S. Fish and Wildlife Service, returned to the Woods Hole wetlands, and sailed Buzzards Bay and Vineyard Sound aboard a research dredger, the SS *Phalanthrop*, to observe mackerel and squid for her 1941 publication, *Under the Sea Wind: A Naturalist's Picture of Ocean Life*.

In the winter of 1947–1948, the institute participated in a consortium of oceanographers in helping the U.S. Fish and Wildlife Service determine the cause of sequential red tides off Sanibel and Captiva Islands on Florida's Gulf Coast. The effort included shellfish biologist Paul S. Galtsoff and Bostwick Ketchum from Woods Hole and investigators from the Scripps Institute of Oceanography, University of Miami, and U.S. Food and Drug Administration. They sampled the water for chemical analysis and autopsied herring, mackerel and other game fish, shrimp, eels, manatee, turtles, and porpoises killed by natural poisoning.

A SCIENCE WAYSTATION

Rachel profited from a close association with female scholars. The consortium concluded that some 60,000,000 Gymnodinium overproduced on five to ten times normal phosphorus, causing slimy water in the Gulf of Mexico, a gas irritant to eyes and throat, and red granules. Galtsoff proposed aerial spraying of Madeira Beach in August 1947 with calcium hypochlorite or copper sulphate to suppress the phosphorus. Rachel posted a press release on December 21, 1947, offering explanations for the abnormal red tide bloom.

In July 1951, the author used Woods Hole as a base of marine research on tides and waves, subjects of *The Sea Around Us*. A year later, a sabbatical anchored in Cape Cod enabled her to compose *The Edge of the Sea*, a summation of avian life in shallows, marshland, and tide pools. The classic marine narrative rounded out her oceanographic trilogy. At a peak of popularity, for a speech to *New York Herald Tribune Book Review* at the Astor Hotel on October 1, 1951, she borrowed hydrophone recordings from the Woods Hole laboratory to illustrate a lecture on the evolution of global seas. She credited the famous laboratory for "my first impressions of the sea" (Carson, 1951, 77). In July 2013, a seated likeness of Rachel sculpted by David Lewis adorned Woods Hole Waterfront Park.

Sources

Carson, Rachel. "The Great Red Tide Mystery." *Field and Stream* (February 1948): 15–18.
_____. "Memo to Mrs. Eales." Rachel Carson papers, 1942.
_____. Speech, *New York Herald Tribune Book Review,* Astor Hotel (1 October 1951).
Cullen, Vicky. *Down to the Sea for Science.* Cape Cod, MA: Woods Hole Oceanographic Institution, 2005.
Egerton, Frank N. "History of Ecological Sciences, Part 53: Organizing Ecologists before 1946." *Bulletin of the Ecological Society of America* 96:2 (April 2015): 239–311.

World War II

Employed by the Department of the Interior during the early 1940s, Rachel gradually compiled data on a global change, the stockpiling of "significant power to alter the nature of [the] world" (Carson, 2002, 5). She endowed period technology with a wartime magic that saved armies and civilians. While composing *Under the Sea Wind* in 1941, she expressed the misgivings of an era in which the military objectified living organisms in secret dispatches, inveighed against shipworms, and restricted use of fathometers to measure ocean depths. Meanwhile according to reflections by Dan Chapman, a journalist for the *Atlanta Constitution*, "The bug boys were under orders by the military to develop new pesticides" because "every U.S. theater of operation, from Burma to Italy, was under bug-borne siege" (Chapman, 2001, D3).

In the interim, the biologist expanded her knowledge of first aid, air strikes, and the topography, weather, and economics of sea life, especially the extraction of magnesium from the sea floor for the aviation and ammunition industries. Nonetheless, she felt powerless to help the war effort. Busy with government assignments concerning scarcity of fish on the Georges Bank east of Boston and south of Nova Scotia, she limited freelance writing to magazine submissions. She reported in "Guarding Our Wildlife Resources: A National Wildlife Refuge," the fifth brochure in her *Conservation in Action* series for the U.S. Department of the Interior, that fishery specialists attacked "the problem of increasing supplies of protein foods" when "critical wartime conditions made increased local production of foodstuffs a necessity" (Carson, 1948, 43).

In the preface to *The Sea Around Us,* the author stated the wartime inadequacy of oceanography to guide shipping and U.S. Navy surveillance crews to detect enemy submarines at a time when "the ability to predict the actions of tides and currents and waves might easily determine the success or failure of military undertakings" (Carson, 1961, xvii). In addition, the navy used hydrophones to study sound and recorded the calls of porpoises, whales, shrimp, and fish. Rachel's reportage on the Chesapeake Bay in the early 1940s covered the role of croakers in overwhelming submarine detection and puzzling crackles, whistles, squeals, and clucking from sea creatures in the St. Lawrence Seaway. Additional study of organic poisonous hydrocarbons identified malathion and parathion as weapons of mass biocide. Simultaneously with these dire topics, she edited *Progressive Fish-Culturist* and prepared 12 brochures on the topic of affordable meat in the series "Food from the Sea." To replace rationed meat and poultry, the pamphlets encouraged families to rely on cheap protein from some 100 fish species, such as the undersold wolffish.

CAREER ADVANCEMENT

Concise, accurate advocacy of little-known seafood earned the author a promotion in May 1943 to aquatic biologist for the U.S. Fish and Wildlife Service, but did not satisfy her longing to perform more significant defense work. In the essay "Lost Worlds: The Challenge of the Islands" for the May–June 1949 edition of *Wood Thrush,* she identified the assault of bombs and artillery as killers of rails (*Ralidae*) on the Ulithi Atoll in the Carolines. This period devastated the Midway atolls and wiped out sooty terns, shearwaters, albatrosses, and petrels. She attested in *The Sea Around Us* that, in 1944, rats from naval vessels and landing craft introduced predators that exterminated the Laysan rail (*Porzana palmeri*), an irreplaceable flightless seabird that fed on moth larvae and blowflies.

Because of gas rationing, Rachel reported that Marine Studios had drained the Oceanarium at Marineland, Florida, in 1942. In 1944, near war's end, she returned to study fishes and mammals sharing 850,000 gallons of water at the world's first indoor marine habitat. She sought corroborating information at the Library of Congress and, in March, composed "Ocean Wonderland" for *Transatlantic* magazine. Three months later, *This Month* reprinted the article under the title "Indoor Ocean." To satisfy post-war interest in the sea, the topic focused on bio networks and the cause of predation among underwater species.

Dangerous Signs

Of the sudden killing of shorebirds and herd animals, Rachel warned that casual murder of species diminished humankind. She flourished at writing and editing into summer 1945, when she gained a promotion to staff supervisor of the U.S. Fish and Wildlife division. From editing scientific essays and issuing press releases, she gleaned crucial data for freelance writing, such as the tally of some 100 avian species lost to combat and the leveling of topography for landing strips.

To aid the U.S. Navy in submarine detection, the author explored the sources of "a most extraordinary uproar … [a] tumult of undersea voices" from living creatures and radar, a topic of the August 1945 *Reader's Digest* article "The Bat Knew It First" (Carson, speech, 1951). The bombing of Hiroshima and Nagasaki, Japan, on August 6 and 9, 1945, ended the Pacific war, but burdened Rachel with more pressing concerns for earth's survival of invisible radiation. Within the year, she opposed atmospheric testing of thermonuclear weapons on Bikini Atoll as outgrowths of imperialism, greed, and unsubstantiated trust in militarized science to eradicate anything annoying or inconvenient. As a result of bioaccumulation, the region absorbed vast amounts of radioactivity, a dire pollutant that shaped her later philosophy of earth's sustainability.

Wartime Experiments

Rachel summarized in *The Sea Around Us* the weather recordings of surf approaching coastal California, Cornwall, and Long Branch, New Jersey. The methods served meteorologists as warnings of storms arising in remote expanses, "lonely, unvisited parts of the ocean, seldom crossed by vessels, off the normal routes of the air lines" (Carson, 1951, 108). Electronic graphs of the Atlantic coast studied crests that eroded the New Jersey shoreline, of particular concern to the U.S. Army Corps of Engineers. The data, still lacking practical application, preceded the invasions of European and African shores.

An awareness of the ping-pong effects of DDT (dichlorodiphenyltrichloroethane) galvanized the author into writing a series of articles intended to alert general interest readers to the inefficacy of aerial spraying. By July 1944, the petrochemical industry had begun the manufacture of organic compounds formulated from natural gas and oil byproducts, a death-dealing synthesis that she called "a child of the Second World War" (Carson, 2002, 16). She learned of a dismaying outcome— DDT resistance in houseflies (*Musca domestica*) and the *Culex* mosquito in Italy and Sardinia. The World Health Organizations supplemented DDT with chlordane, a biocide causing lymphoma, breast cancer, seizures, and liver necrosis. The replacement of DDT with dieldrin introduced a biocide "40 times as toxic," which increased her concern for human health after sprayers died of convulsions (Carson, 2002, 25).

The essay "The Rumblings of an Avalanche" in *Silent Spring* reported the Allied Military Government's dusting of Italian soldiers' bodies in 1943 with synthetic insecticides developed as military weapons against the fleas, lice, and mosquitoes that spread typhus and malaria. On Nissan Island between Papua New Guinea and the Solomon Islands, spraying killed off mosquitoes as well as their predators. After the war, the disease-bearing mosquito rebounded in Denmark and Egypt. The dusting of two million people in Japan and Korea in 1945 quelled body lice. A similar assault on lice failed during a typhus outbreak in Spain in 1948 and during the resurgence of malaria in Greece from the *Anopheles* mosquito in 1949. In Korea and Japan, a new dissemination of DDT in 1950 increased the spread of body lice. Similarly in Egypt, Jordan, and Syria, the insecticide lost efficacy, as it did in Afghanistan, Chile, Ethiopia, France, Iran, Mexico, Peru, South Africa, Tanganyika, Turkey, Uganda, West Africa, and Yugoslavia.

Post-War Arrogance

In the post-war job boom, Rachel endeavored to educate citizens on the status of mid–1940s deep-sea core sampling and seismology. Simultaneously, she warned of the self-glorification of the American military-industrial complex, which sought to harvest petroleum from the abyss, desalinate water, and spur the use of radar, sonar, and nuclear submarines for defense of a new frontier. Her career profited in 1946 from promotion to federal information specialist and in 1949 from advancement to marine biologist and chief editor. In the estimation of David D. Vail, an historian at the University of Nebraska, "cultural, scientific, and economic legacies of World War II" influenced her attitudes toward twentieth-century science, especially the formulation of chlorated hydrocarbon pesticides (Carson, 2002, 4).

During a crucial retrospect on war damage to the Pacific by Americans and Japanese, the founding of the Koror Island laboratory in the Palau Islands east of the Philippines introduced the specific conservation of fragile island ecosystems and old growth forests. At heightened risk, Hawaii's Laysan albatross lost strength in their wings from exposure to lead paint. Out of concern for wildlife, the U.S. Navy established a sanctuary for Micronesian wildlife on Saipan in 1948. Avian specialists scanned the Marianas mallard (*Anas oustaleti*) in the fern thickets and wetlands of Guam, Saipan, and Tinian, where engineers had drained swamps and built military complexes. Parallel research into rhythmic sounds from the Pacific depths disproved beliefs that no life existed in the sea ooze, but left unsolved the types of plankton, fish, or squid that inhabited "the sea's phantom bottom" (Carson, 1951, 51).

By studying the invention of the scuba by Jacques-Yves Cousteau and Frederic Dumas, Thor Heyerdahl's documentary *Kon-Tiki,* and the research of biologist Barry Commoner and oceanographer Roger Revelle, Rachel perceived the possibility of permanent mutagenic alteration of nature and total destruction of life by atomic blasts, a proposed threat during the Korean War. On September 25, 1951, her attention to citizen anxiety became the topic of an oration to the National Symphony Orchestra Benefit Luncheon in Washington, D.C. The Burroughs Medal Acceptance Speech "Design for Nature Writing" in April 1952 extended her fears for "more experiments for the destruction" of the world (Carson, 1952, 332). Post-Hiroshima threats continued plaguing her in 1961 with alarm for the sickening of people from strontium-90, a byproduct of nuclear fission, and by the dumping of radioactive contaminants in drums into the sea, a practice that began in 1946. She identified this detritus as "the most dangerous materials that have ever existed in all the earth's history" (Carson, 1951, xx).

A child of world war, Rachel retreated often to a monumental era of experimentation. On September 27, 1962, for *Silent Spring*, she gathered data for the chapter "Surface Waters and Underground Seas" at mid-war from the Rocky Mountain Arsenal of the Army Chemical Corps at Denver. Recycled from war material manufacturer to insecticide plant, the facility discharged a host of lethal effluents into its cisterns, ranging from arsenic to chlorides, phosphoric acid salts, chlorates, and fluorides. From human ills, crop deaths, and livestock maladies came proof that groundwater had carried the seepage an unknown distance. In the chapter "Indiscriminately from the Skies," she identified surplus military planes with the aerial spraying of chlorinated hydrocarbon pesticides. Critic Andrew Wadsworth, an administrator at Arizona State University at Tempe, stated that, "By drawing on the rhetoric of World War II and the Cold War, Carson imbues readers with a sense of patriotic duty, the responsibility to defend life and freedom" (Wadsworth, 2016).

See also Aerial Spraying; DDT.

Sources

Burnham, Philip. "Review: *The Sea Around Us*." *Commonweal* 54 (27 July 1951): 387–389.
Carson, Rachel. "Design for Nature Writing." *Atlantic Naturalist* (May–August 1952): 232–234.
_____. "Guarding Our Wildlife Resources: A National Wildlife Refuge." #5. Washington, D.C.: U.S. Department of the Interior, 1948.
_____. "Lost Worlds: The Challenge of the Islands." *Wood Thrush* 4:5 (May–June 1949): 179–187.
_____. "Preface." *The Sea Around Us*, 2nd ed. New York: Oxford University Press, 1961, xvii–xxiv.
_____. "The Real World Around Us." Address to the Theta Sigma Phi Matrix Table Dinner, *House of Life* (21 April 1954): 324–326.
_____. *The Sea Around Us*. New York: Oxford University Press, 1951.
_____. Speech, *New York Herald Tribune Book Review*, Astor Hotel (1 October 1951).
_____. *Silent Spring*. Boston: Houghton Mifflin, 40th Anniversary Edition, 2002.
_____. "Vanishing Americans." *Washington Post* (10 April 1959): A26.
Chapman, Dan. "Dusting Off DDT's Image." *Atlanta Constitution* (9 September 2001): D1, D3.
DeMarco, Patricia M. "Rachel Carson's Environmental Ethic–A Guide for Global Systems Decision Making." *Journal of Cleaner Production* 140 (1 January 2017): 127–133.
Quaratiello, Arlene Rodda. *Rachel Carson: A Biography*. Amherst, NY: Prometheus, 2010.
Richmond, Marsha L. "Women as Public Scientists in the Atomic Age: Rachel Carson, Charlotte Auerbach, and Genetics." *Historical Studies in the Natural Sciences* 47:3 (June 2017): 349–388.
Vail, David D. *Chemical Lands: Pesticides, Aerial Spraying, and Health in North America's Grasslands Since 1945*. Tuscaloosa: University of Alabama Press, 2018.
Wadsworth, Andrew. "Carson's Christianity and Environmental Crises." *Criterion* 9:1 (2016).

Appendix I: Glossary

accipiter a general term for the hawk ("Chicoteague: A National Wildlife Refuge," 1947).

adipose capable of storing fat (*Silent Spring*, 1962).

AEC Atomic Energy Commission, a federal agency empaneled in 1945 to oversee nuclear materials in military and domestic use ("The Pollution of Our Environment," 1963).

alchemy magic (*Silent Spring*, 1962).

alga a nonflowering seaweed or other aquatic plant that lacks roots, stems, and leaves (letter to Dorothy Freeman, 1953).

alkylate a toxic agent such as mustard gas that damages DNA (letter to Marjorie Spock, 1960).

ambergris a waxy substance obtained from the bile ducts of sperm whales and used in food, incense, and medicines ("Whalers Ready for New Season," 1938).

amphipod a soft segmented swimmer of fresh or salt water (*Under the Sea Wind*, 1941).

antivivisectionist an opponent of experimental surgery on living bodies (*Silent Spring*, 1962).

Archeozoic the geologic period in which rocks, algae, and bacteria evolved ("Liner Notes," 1951).

atomic fission the splitting of an atom to release energy ("The Pollution of Our Environment," 1963).

atrophy shrinkage (letter to Morton S. Biskind, 1959).

back siphonage the draining of a liquid from a higher to a lower source (*Silent Spring*, 1962).

basalt volcanic rock (*The Sea Around Us*, 1951).

beam to the wind the trawler's prow facing into the wind ("The Northern Trawlers Move South," 1937).

beta radiation a particle capable of intense penetration of human tissue causing genetic mutation ("The Pollution of Our Environment," 1963).

biocide a toxic substance that eradicates all life ("A New Chapter in *Silent Spring*," 1963).

biosphere areas of land, air, and water occupied by living beings ("Introduction," *The Sea Around Us*, 1989).

bivalve a water mollusk encased in a two-part hinged shell ("Farming under the Chesapeake," 1937).

blanket spraying spreading pesticide over an entire property ("Rachel Carson Answers Her Critics," 1963).

brant European goose ("Fight for Wildlife Pushes Ahead," 1938).

brush weir a fish dam that traps marine fish as they advance upriver ("It'll Be Shad Time Soon," 1936).

buck brush a flowering shrub ("Review: Lake Management Reports, Horseshoe Lake Near Cairo, Illinois," 1938).

Bugula a tree-like sea animal that grows in arboreal colonies ("Our Ever-Changing Shore" 1958).

byssus a slender fiber or filament that binds mollusks to solid surfaces. *cf.* holdfast (*Under the Sea Wind*, 1941).

Cambrian dating to 500,000 million years ago, the beginning of the Paleozoic Era (*The Sea Around Us*, 1951).

CCC Civilian Conservation Corps ("Lost Worlds: The Challenge of the Islands," 1949).

Ce^{137} chemical notation for cesium 137 ("The Pollution of Our Environment," 1963).

chara green alga (*Under the Sea Wind*, 1941).

Charybdis a whirlpool personified in Homer's *The Odyssey* (*The Sea Around Us*, 1951).

chinook a warm, dry air current on the lee side of the Rocky Mountains ("Clouds," 1957).

chitin a fibrous sugary mouth lining in periwinkles (*The Rocky Coast*, 1971).

chiton a hard-shelled mollusk named for a Greek tunic (*Under the Sea Wind*, 1941).

chlorinated hydrocarbon an organic compound used as a pesticide having profound impact on the nervous system and liver (letter to Beverly Knecht, 1959).

chlorophyll the green element that absorbs light to make plant food ("The Pollution of Our Environment," 1963).

cilia hair-like appendages, such as the fringe surrounding oyster larvae ("Farming under the Chesapeake," 1937).

cobalt a natural element useful in the production of gamma rays (letter to William Shawn, 1959).

cochineal a scale insect that yields carmine dye for food and cosmetics (*Silent Spring*, 1962).

commensal symbiotic organisms that share food (*The Edge of the Sea*, 1955).

continental margin the shallow shelf that outlines a coast ("The Pollution of Our Environment," 1963).

convection the rise of hot, lightweight material through a fluid and the fall of cooler, heavier substances ("Environmental Hazards: Control of Pesticides and Other Chemical Poisons," 1963).

copepod small plankton ("The Edge of the Sea," 1953).

coracoid process a bony stabilizer of the shoulder joint ("Letter," 1963).

cortin an energy-producing hormone of the adrenal gland (*Silent Spring*, 1962).

crepuscular appearing in twilight ("Undersea," 1937).

crustacea terrestrial or aquatic animals with segmented bodies ("Whalers Ready for New Season," 1938).

cull choose or select ("Farming under the Chesapeake," 1937).

cypris the final larval stage of a barnacle as it chooses a place to attach itself (*The Rocky Coast*, 1971).

cytochrome oxidase a protein complex controlling metabolism (letter to Morton S. Biskind, 1959).

derrick a crane, hoist, or lifting mechanism ("Whalers Ready for New Season," 1938).

diatom single-celled alga ("Environmental Hazards: Control of Pesticides and Other Chemical Poisons," 1963).

diurnal daily (*The Sea Around Us*, 1951).

dory a narrow fishing boat with high sides ("Giants of the Tide Rip Off Nova Scotia Again," 1938).

duff the forest floor (*Silent Spring*, 1962).

dynomometer a device gauging the output of power (*The Sea Around Us*, 1951).

echogram a sonogram of the ocean bottom (*The Sea Around Us*, 1951).

ecologist an expert in the relations of organisms to habitats and each other (*Silent Spring*, 1962).

ectocrine a hormone exuded onto larvae to influence development and behavior ("The Edge of the Sea," 1953).

eddy whirlpool ("Preface," *The Sea Around Us*, 1951).

elver an immature eel ("Chesapeake Eels Seek the Sargasso Sea," 1938).

enzyme natural proteins that speed chemical reactions in the body (*Silent Spring*, 1962).

epoxide a toxic coating, surfactant, plasticizer, or detergent that can cause asthma, endocrine disruption, cancer, or genetic mutation (letter to Morton S. Biskind, 1959).

estuary the tidal mouth of a river ("Preface," *The Sea Around Us*, 1951).

evisceration gutting, disemboweling (*The Edge of the Sea*, 1955).

eyrie a predator's nest built on a treetop or cliff (*Under the Sea Wind*, 1941).

fallout particles ejected from nuclear explosion ("On the Reception of *Silent Spring*," 1962).

fallow unplanted, uncultivated (*Silent Spring*, 1962).

fathom six feet ("The Northern Trawlers Move South," 1937).

fathometer a sounding device that measures ocean depths (*The Sea Around Us*, 1951).

fauna animals (*Silent Spring*, 1962).

FIFRA Federal Insecticide, Fungicide, and Rodenticide Act ("Address to the Women's National Press Club," 1962).

foehn wind a warm, dry air current on the lee side of a mountain ("Clouds," 1957).

foraminifera unicellular plankton covered in carbonated lime shells (*The Sea Around Us*, 1951).

freshet a stream of snowmelt or rain in a river ("Farming under the Chesapeake," 1937).

gamma ray a high energy wave of electromagnetism that breaks down cells ("The Pollution of Our Environment," 1963).

geochemist a specialist in the minerals and rocks that compose earthly soil ("The Pollution of Our Environment," 1963).

germ plasm genetic material ("Of Man and the Stream of Time," 1962).

gill net a fishing net that snares fish by their gills ("It'll Be Shad Time Soon," 1936).

glasswort a salt marsh plant yielding soda ash for making soap and glass ("Our Ever-Changing Shore" 1958).

gneiss granite formed at high temperatures into dark and light colored striations (*The Rocky Coast*, 1971).

graminoid grass-like sedges related to rushes (letter to Frank E. Egler, 1962).

grilse a year-old salmon on return to fresh water from the sea (*Silent Spring*, 1962).

guano seabird and bat feces sold as fertilizer (*The Sea Around Us*, 1951).

gunwales reinforcing bands at the top of boat sides (*Under the Sea Wind*, 1941).

haul seine a weighted snare that traps a school of fish ("It'll Be Shad Time Soon," 1936).

holdfast a root or stalk that stabilizes attachment of kelp or alga to another surface (*Under the Sea Wind*, 1941).

humus living matter that decays in soil (*Silent Spring*, 1962).

hydrocarbon an organic compound found in nature that provides ignitable fuel ("Vanishing Americans," 1959).

hydrographer a scientist who measures and describes the features of bodies of water (*The Sea Around Us*, 1951).

hydroid a colonial water animal such as jellyfish that reproduces by budding ("Of Man and the Stream of Time," 1962).

hydrophone a listening device to detect underwater sound (*The Sea Around Us*, 1951).

ianthina sea slug ("Undersea," 1937).

ichthyological relating to the study of fish ("Numbering the Fish of the Sea," 1936).

ilmenite a titanium-iron ore found in igneous rock. *See also* rutile (*The Edge of the Sea*, 1955).

I^{131} chemical notation for iodine 131 ("The Pollution of Our Environment," 1963).

inflorescence blossoming ("Undersea," 1937).

intensivism specialism in farming intended to increase profits by adopting crop pesticides and animal antibiotics and hormones ("Foreword," *Animal Machines: The New Factory Farming Industry*, 1964).

Keewatin a Canadian district north of Ontario (*Under the Sea Wind*, 1941).

knots sandpipers (*Under the Sea Wind*, 1941).

Krebiozen a useless cancer drug comprised largely of creatinine from horse blood and mineral oil (letter to Dorothy Freeman, 1963).

lamellibranch a bivalve, including clams, scallops, and oysters ("The Edge of the Sea," 1953).

Laurentian concerning the geological core of North America from 458,000,000 years ago (*The Sea Around Us*, 1951).

lee sheltered side ("Clouds," 1957).

lenticular curved on both sides ("Clouds," 1957).

lichen slow-growing mossy plants ("The Pollution of Our Environment," 1963).

Lysenkoism a faux scientific attack on genetics in Russian agriculture ("Address to the Women's National Press Club," 1962).

macerate soften or chew (*Silent Spring*, 1962).

marl loosely consolidated mudstone consisting of clay, lime, and silt (*The Rocky Coast*, 1971).

mesentery fat-storing tissue surrounding the intestines (*Silent Spring*, 1962).

metabolite a substance formed during digestion ("Environmental Hazards: Control of Pesticides and Other Chemical Poisons," 1963).

milt fish semen ("It'll Be Shad Time Soon," 1936).

mitochondria a subunit of a cell that produces energy (letter to Dorothy Freeman, 7 December 1959).

mitosis cell division that passes encoded genes to two new cells (*Silent Spring*, 1962).

Mohorovicic discontinuity the divide between earth's light crust and the mantle covering the hot core ("Preface," *The Sea Around Us*, 1961).

mollusk a soft aquatic invertebrate, including the mussel, octopus, slug, and snail ("Walrus and Carpenter Not Oysters' Only Foe," 1938).

molt shed exoskeleton, hair, or feathers (*Silent Spring*, 1962).

monadnock a single hill arising on a level plain (*The Edge of the Sea*, 1955).

monograph a detailed treatise on a single subject (*Silent Spring*, 1962).

monosaccharide the simplest form of sugar, found in fructose and glucose (letter to Dorothy Freeman, 1963).

moraine a ridge of sediment and rocks pushed downhill by a glacier (*Under the Sea Wind*, 1941).

moribund in a fatal decline; dying (*Silent Spring*, 1962).

motor cortex brain tissue that plans and executes movement (*Silent Spring*, 1962).

mutagenic causing change in DNA and future generations ("The Pollution of Our Environment," 1963).

nanocurie a unit of radioactivity equal to 10^{-9} curies ("The Pollution of Our Environment," 1963).

NAS National Academy of Sciences "Address," Women's National Press Club, 1962).

nauplius the one-eyed, unsegmented larva of a barnacle (*The Rocky Coast*, 1971).

neap tide a weak, low tide generated at the beginning of the second and fourth quarters of the moon (letter to Dorothy Freeman, 1953).

necrosis death of living tissue (*Silent Spring*, 1962).

nitrogen-fixing conversion of atmospheric nitrogen for plant use ("Rachel Carson Answers Her Critics," 1963).

nummulites fossils of ancient coiled marine protozoa (*The Sea Around Us*, 1951).

obsolescence worthlessness, uselessness (*Silent Spring*, 1962).

opercula gill flaps or covers ("Our Ever-Changing Shore" 1958).

otter trawler a method of catching fish in a drag net ("The Northern Trawlers Move South," 1937).

Oyashio a nutrient-rich Arctic current that flows toward Japan (*The Sea Around Us*, 1951).

oyster drill an appendage in a small mollusk that devours oysters through a hole in the shell ("Walrus and Carpenter Not Oysters' Only Foe," 1938).

parole titmouse (unpublished essay).

pentachlorophenol an insecticide that causes organ damage, blindness, cancer, and anemia (letter to Morton S. Biskind, 1959).

phaeocystis an algae that grows in colonies (*The Sea Around Us*, 1951).

phosphate a chemical derived from phosphoric acid that can disrupt the nervous system ("Vanishing Americans," 1959).

phosphorescence glow ("Our Ever-Changing Shore," 1958).

phosphorylation the activation of enzymes (letter to Morton S. Biskind, 1959).

pinions primary flight feathers (*Under the Sea Wind*, 1941).

placenta a multipurpose organ feeding and protecting the unborn fetus (*Silent Spring*, 1962).

polysaccharide a complex sugar, such as starch and cellulose (letter to Dorothy Freeman, 1963).

poult young edible fowl (*Silent Spring*, 1962).

protoplasm the life source in a cell ("It'll Be Shad Time Soon," 1936).

pteropod winged sea snail ("Undersea," 1937).

purpurin a bromine compound in whelks that yields purple dye (*The Rocky Coast*, 1971).

purse net a fishing seine that opens and shuts like a pocketbook ("It'll Be Shad Time Soon," 1936).

putrefaction decay or rot (*Silent Spring*, 1962).

race memory images and behaviors passed down by organisms in a biological family ("Farming under the Chesapeake," 1937).

radioiodine a carcinogenic product of fallout that accumulates in the thyroid ("The Pollution of Our Environment," 1963).

radioisotope a variant form of an unstable atomic nucleus ("The Pollution of Our Environment," 1963).

radiolaria single-cell sea creatures protected by a shell ("Undersea," 1937).

radula a toothed appendage extending from the mouth of a mollusk for scraping plants from rocks or boring holes in shells

("Walrus and Carpenter Not Oysters' Only Foe," 1938).

ray fungi branching filaments of bacteria that decompose plant matter in the soil (*Silent Spring*, 1962).

redd a trench that a female salmon sweeps in a stream bottom to receive her eggs (*Silent Spring*, 1962).

rock tripe an edible lichen valued as famine food (*The Rocky Coast*, 1971).

rookery a dense nesting and breeding ground for birds (*Under the Sea Wind*, 1941).

rumen the first of four stomachs in a grazing animal (*Silent Spring*, 1962).

rutile titanium oxide ore found in igneous rock (*The Sea Around Us*, 1955).

serrate zigzag ("An Island I Remember," 1946).

sessile immobile ("Undersea," 1937).

Silurian a short geologic era after 443,000,000 BCE, when bony fish emerged (speech to the *New York Herald Tribune Book Review*, 1951).

smolt salmon fry on their first migration to the sea (*Silent Spring*, 1962).

sou'wester a foldable waterproof rain hat ("Help Your Child to Wonder," July 1956).

spat young oysters ("Farming under the Chesapeake," 1937).

spindrift salty sea spray (*The Edge of the Sea*, 1955).

Sr^{90} chemical notation for strontium 90 ("The Pollution of Our Environment," 1963).

stipe a stalk or stem of seaweed (*The Rocky Coast*, 1971).

substratospheric of the area 3.5 miles above earth ("Clouds," 1957).

symbiosis a mutually beneficial relationship between two organisms ("The Edge of the Sea," 1953).

syncoryne algae ("The Edge of the Sea" 1953).

synthesis the creation of chemical compounds from simple substances ("The Pollution of Our Environment," 1963).

3-edge, 4-square stem type of sedges and marsh reeds ("Mattamuskeet: A National Wildlife Refuge," 1947).

tonger an oyster gatherer equipped with tongs ("Farming under the Chesapeake," 1937).

toxicology the scientific study of poison, its effects, and its detection ("She Started It All—Here's Her Reaction," 1963).

trawl net a mechanized dredge reaching as deep as 600 feet ("The Northern Trawlers Move South," 1937).

trilobite an extinct hard-shelled sea invertebrate that flourished after 521,000,000 BCE ("Our Ever-Changing Shore," 1958).

trying out rendering oil from whale fat ("Whalers Ready for New Season," 1938)

tundra cold Arctic lands above the treeline ("The Pollution of Our Environment," 1963)

turbidity the murkiness of water caused by agitation of particles ("The Pollution of Our Environment," 1963).

ultraviolet light extra-high frequency sun rays ("The Pollution of Our Environment," 1963).

understory greenery living beneath a forest canopy (letter to Dorothy Freeman, 1963).

vector carrier of a pathogen (*Silent Spring*, 1962).

vernal spring (*The Sea Around Us*, 1951).

vitreous glassy (*Under the Sea Wind*, 1941).

viviparous nurturing offspring inside the parent's body until birth (*The Rocky Coast*, 1971).

water boatmen aquatic water skaters (*Under the Sea Wind*, 1941).

watershed an upland that channels snowmelt and rainfall to streams and rivers (*Silent Spring*, 1962).

winch a device that adjusts tension on a rope ("Whalers Ready for New Season," 1938).

zonda a warm, dry air current on the lee side of the Andes Mountains in Argentina ("Clouds," 1957)

Appendix II:
A Guide to Writing, Art and Research Topics

1. Discuss the effectiveness of the following rhetorical and linguistic devices:
- *controlling metaphor* the long snowfall. (*The Sea Around Us*, 1951)
- *alliteration* unknown to all but a fortunate few. (*Under the Sea Wind*, 1941)
- *rhetorical question* Whose voice do we hear—that of science? or of the sustaining industry? ("Address," Women's National Press Club, 1962)
- *metaphor* these sea gypsies appear suddenly. ("Numbering the Fish of the Sea," 1936)
- *anthropomorphism* marsh grasses waded boldly out into dark water. (*Under the Sea Wind*, 1941)
- *characterization* the sea itself must be the central character. (Foreword, *Under the Sea Wind*, 1941)
- *fable* There was once a town… (*Silent Spring*, 1962)
- *sibilance* the soft sell, the soothing reassurances. ("Address to the Women's National Press Club," 1962)
- *hyperbole* jet streams … written in the clouds. ("Clouds," 1957)
- *periodic sentence* Starlings are credited with considerable intelligence. ("Starlings a Housing Problem," 1939)
- *subjectivity* a beneficent process, bringing the continents to life. ("Clouds," 1957)
- *contrast* dispose first and investigate later. ("Preface," *The Sea Around Us*, 1961)
- *ode* "An Island I Remember," 1946.
- *cliché* a dime a dozen. ("Address to the Women's National Press Club," 1962)
- *repetition* gloriously tired, gloriously happy ("My Favorite Recreation," 1922)
- *visual contrast* drifts of white clover or the clouds of purple vetch with here and there the flaming cup of a wood lily. (*Silent Spring*, 1962)
- *allusion* Charybdis of classical fame. (*The Sea Around Us*, 1951)
- *simile* bluefish, like roving buccaneers. ("Undersea," 1937).
- *passive voice* the oceans are made one. (*The Sea Around Us*, 1951)
- *citation* Darkness was upon the face of the Deep. (*The Sea Around Us*, 1951)
- *fragment* Substances that are highly capable of entering into biological reactions with living organisms. ("The Pollution of Our Environment," 1963)

- *dramatis personae* the central character is Anguilla. (*Under the Sea Wind*, 1941)
- *balanced sentence* Sometimes a lone bird rode the air currents; sometimes several at a time. ("Road of the Hawks," 1945)
- *assonance* his pen dipped in acid. ("Of Man and the Stream of Time," 1962)
- *parallelism* exposed to heat and cold, to wind, to rain and drying sun. ("The Marginal World," 2006)
- *understatement* the industry press was not happy. ("Address to the Women's National Press Club," 1962)
- *drama* How portentous a moment! ("Of Man and the Stream of Time," 1962)
- *consonance* columns of cumulus. ("Clouds," 1957)

2. Compare Rachel Carson's essay "The Marginal World" or television script "Clouds" to the nature writing of one of these authors:

Jacquetta Hawkes	Barbara Kingsolver	Isabella Bird
Loren Eiseley	John Steinbeck	Joy Adamson
Ursula Le Guin	Mary Hunter Austin	Henry David Thoreau
John Muir	Gary Paulsen	Jacques Cousteau
Dian Fossey	Jane Goodall	Thor Heyerdahl
Navarre Scott Momaday	Ernest Hemingway	

3. How do individual authors incorporate humor to ease serious or dismaying topics?

4. Apply Rachel Carson's rationale about the indiscriminate spread of radioactivity and biocides to the situations in John Hersey's *Hiroshima,* Nevil Shute's *On the Beach,* Cormac McCarthy's *The Road,* Ray Bradbury's "There Will Come Soft Rains," or Barbara Kingsolver's *Animal Dreams.*

5. Compare biographies of Rachel Carson to the fictional character of Sylvie in Sarah Orne Jewett's story "A White Heron." Why does the hunter fail to understand Sylvie's values? What did the killing of birds mean to Rachel? to Sylvie?

6. Summarize the poem "Power" by Adrienne Rich. What did the poet mean by "wounds"? Why is the title appropriate? How did the brief verse characterize the work and lives of Marie Curie, Dian Fossey, Jane Goodall, Joy Adamson, Isabella Bird, Mary Hunter Austin, and Rachel Carson?

7. What did Rachel reveal about eels in her wildlife essay, written in 1944? How did her attitude change toward marine biology in subsequent brochures and speeches? Why did she incorporate the word "wonder" in writings about children, the outdoors, and scientific education?

8. Summarize Rachel's speaking style. What do her speeches have in common with the essays of Henry David Thoreau, Margaret Sanger, Jacques Cousteau, Margaret Mead, and John Muir? How did she establish a unique, passionate presentation for the middle-class American?

9. Outline the common elements of a child's environment that reveal damage, alteration, and threats of taint or extinction. How does classroom science elevate respect for the fragility of food, potable water, clean air, birds, fish, amphibians, and bees?

10. What aspects of Rachel's education and career made her a generalist rather than a specialist on one area of biology, such as oceanography, ichthyology, geology, or ornithology?

11. In a short speech, compare public response to Rachel's *Silent Spring* to media evaluations of these works:

> Al Gore's *Earth in the Balance*
> Henry David Thoreau's *Walden*
> Charles Darwin's *Origin of Species*
> Thor Heyerdahl's *Kon-Tiki*
> Dian Fossey's *Gorillas in the Mist*
> Paul Monette's *Borrowed Time*
> Jane Goodall's *My Friends the Wild Chimpanzees*
> John Muir's *My First Summer in the Sierra*
> Harriet Beecher Stowe's *Uncle Tom's Cabin*
> Jacques Cousteau's *Life at the Bottom of the World*

12. Compile a list of technical details from Rachel's literary career for hunters, whalers, and fishers. Incorporate terms such as tagging, dredge, flyway, purse net, brush weir, phosphorescent, crustacean, fathom, beam, continental shelf, emulsion, leeward, milt, food fish, spout, barnacle, and trawling.

13. Propose a glossary and locations of place names that have special meaning in Rachel's career: Woods Hole, Cape May, Chesapeake Bay, Sheepscot River, Muir Woods, Buzzards Bay, North Carolina Outer Banks, Florida Everglades, Humboldt Current, Yellowstone National Park, Gulf Stream, Acadia National Park, Sargasso Sea, Georges Bank, Cape Cod, Gulf Coast, Vineyard Sound, prairie states, Barents Sea, Hudson Bay, continental shelf, Delaware Bay, Orkney Islands, Marianas Trench, Clear Lake, Colorado River, and Cape Hatteras.

14. Compare the subjectivity of Gerard Manley Hopkins's poems "Inversnaid" and "The Windhover" to Rachel's immersion in the water cycle in "Clouds." How do both authors illustrate beneficence? natural phenomena?

15. Why do biologists like Rachel Carson bolster their training with studies in geology? hydrology? biochemistry? fossil fuels? agronomy? genetics? astronomy? meteorology? global history? In which subsets does Rachel appear most informed, particularly ornithology, ichthyology, and marine biology?

16. Summarize "The Eruption of Vesuvius" by Pliny the Younger. What details would Rachel add to express disruption of nature and topography?

17. Explain the fear of Tennesseans in Jerome Lawrence and Robert E. Lee's play *Inherit the Wind*. What is their understanding of biblical creation? evolution? classroom curriculum? student curiosity?

18. Compose a speech on the Sargasso Sea or Gulf Stream explaining its value to sea life. Choose citations from Rachel's sea trilogy to account for the uniqueness of temperature and motion.

Bibliography

Primary Sources

Books

Always, Rachel: The Letters of Rachel Carson and Dorothy Freeman: An Intimate Portrait of a Remarkable Friendship. Boston: Beacon Press, 1995.

The Edge of the Sea. Boston: Hobiughton Mifflin, 1955.

Food from the Sea: Fish and Shellfish of New England. London: Forgotten Books, 2018.

Lost Woods: The Discovered Writing of Rachel Carson. Boston: Beacon Press, 1998.

The Rocky Coast. New York: McCall, 1971.

The Sea Around Us. New York: New American Library, 1960.

The Sea Around Us. New York: Oxford University Press, 1951.

The Sea Around Us. New York: Oxford University Press, 2018.

The Sea Around Us: A Special Edition for Young Readers. New York: Simon & Schuster, 1958.

The Sea Around Us: Revised Edition. New York: Oxford University Press, 1961.

The Sea Around Us: Special Edition. New York: Oxford University Press, 1989.

The Sense of Wonder. New York: Harper & Row, 1965.

Silent Spring. Boston: Houghton Mifflin, 1962.

Silent Spring. Boston: Houghton Mifflin, 25th Anniversary Edition, 1987.

Silent Spring. Boston: Houghton Mifflin, 40th Anniversary Edition, 2002.

Under the Sea Wind: A Naturalist's Picture of Ocean Life. New York: Simon & Schuster, 1941.

Under the Sea Wind: A Naturalist's Picture of Ocean Life. Boston: Houghton Mifflin, 1955.

Short Works

"Acceptance Speech." Cullum Medal from the American Geographical Society (5 December 1963).

"Acceptance Speech." National Audubon Society, New York (3 December 1963).

"Acceptance Speech for the Schweitzer Medal of the Animal Welfare Institute." *House of Life* (7 January 1963): 315–316.

"Ace of Nature's Aviators." Unpublished, 1944.

"Address." Women's National Press Club, Washington, D.C. (5 December 1962); reprint, "Housewives Today," *British Housewives' League* (October 1963).

"Address at Audubon Dinner." Audubon Naturalist Society (5 October 1962).

"Address to the National Council of Women of the United States." *House of Life* (11 October 1962): 301–302.

"Baltimore New Mecca for Nation's Sportsmen and Conservationists." *Baltimore Sunday Sun Magazine* (13 February 1938): 1.

"The Bat Knew It First." *Collier's* 20 (18 November 1944): 24.

_____. *Reader's Digest* 34 (August 1945): 45–46.

"A Battle in the Clouds." *St. Nicholas* 45:11 (September 1918): 1048.

"Bear River: A National Wildlife Refuge." #8. Washington, D.C.: U.S. Department of the Interior, 1950, 1–14.

"A Beetle Scare, Spray Planes and Dead Wildlife." *Audubon* (November-December 1962).

"Beyond the Dreams of the Borgias." *National Parks* (October 1962).

"The Birth of an Island." *Yale Review* 40:1 (September 1950): 112–126; *Pageant* (January 1952).

"Books and Authors Luncheon." https://www.wnyc.org/story/148408-rachel-carson-1951/ (16 October 1951).

"Broken Lamps." *Englicode* (27 May 1927).

"Chesapeake Eels Seek the Sargasso Sea." *Baltimore Sunday Sun Magazine* (9 October 1938): 1.

"Chesapeake Oystermen See Stars and They Don't Like It." *Baltimore Sunday Sun* (28 March 1937).

"Chincoteague: A National Wildlife Refuge." #1. Washington, D.C.: U.S. Department of the Interior, 1947, 1–19.

"Clouds" in "Something about the Sky." CBS *Omnibus* (11 March 1957). "Conservation

Pledge," second place award, *Outdoor Life* (October 1946).

"Design for Nature Writing." Burroughs Medal Acceptance Speech (7 April 1952), New York; reprint, "Design for Nature Writing," *Atlantic Naturalist* (May-August 1952): 232–234.

"The Development of the Pronephros during the Embryonic and Early Larval Life of the Catfish (*Ictalurus punctatus*)." Master's thesis, Johns Hopkins University, 1932.

"Ducks Are on Increase." *Baltimore Sunday Sun Magazine* (16 January 1938): 1.

"The Edge of the Sea" (lecture). Cranbrook Institute of Science, Bloomfield Hills, Michigan (9 April 1954).

"The Edge of the Sea." *Life* 32:15 (14 April 1952): 64–81.

"The Edge of the Sea." *New Yorker* 27:27 (20 August 1955; 27 August 1955).

"Environmental Hazards: Control of Pesticides and Other Chemical Poisons." Statement before the Subcommittee on Reorganization and International Organizations of the Committee on Government Operations (4 June 1963): 206–219.

"The Exceeding Beauty of the Earth—Words to Live By." *This Week* (25 May 1952): 5.

"Exit the Elm ... and Birds." *Boston Globe* (25 January 1963): 12.

Factory Farming: The Experiment That Failed (introduction). Washington, D.C.: Animal Welfare Institute, 1987.

"A Famous Sea Fight." *St. Nicholas* 46 (August 1919): 951.

"Farming Under the Chesapeake." *Baltimore Sun* (24 January 1937): 6–7.

"Fight for Wildlife Pushes Ahead." *Richmond Times Dispatch Sunday Magazine* (20 March 1938): 8–9.

"Fish and Shellfish of New England." #33. Washington, D.C.: U.S. Department of the Interior, 1943.

"Fish and Shellfish of the Middle Atlantic Coast." #38. Washington, D.C.: U.S. Department of the Interior, 1945.

"Fish and Shellfish of the Middle West." #34. Washington, D.C.: U.S. Department of the Interior, 1943.

"Fish and Shellfish of the South Atlantic and Gulf Coasts." #37. Washington, D.C.: U.S. Department of the Interior, 1944.

"Foreword." *Animal Machines: The New Factory Farming Industry.* London: Vincent Stuart, 1964.

"Giants of the Tide Rip Off Nova Scotia Again." *Baltimore Sunday Sun* (3 August 1938): 2.

"The Global Thermostat." *Vogue* (October 1950).

"The Great Red Tide Mystery." *Field and Stream* (February 1948): 15–18.

"Guarding Our Wildlife Resources: A National Wildlife Refuge." #5. Washington, D.C.: U.S. Department of the Interior, 1948, 1–46.

"The Harbor." *Falmouth Enterprise* (16 May 1952): C1.

"Help Your Child to Wonder." *Woman's Home Companion* 53 (July 1956): 25–27, 46–48; reprint, "Help Your Child to Wonder," *Reader's Digest* (September 1956): 19–22.

"How About Citizenship Papers for the Starling?" *Nature* 32 (June/July 1939): 317–319.

"Indoor Ocean." *This Month* (June 1946): 31–35.

"Interview." *Washington Post* (4 July 1951): 3B.

"An Island I Remember." Unpublished ode, July 1946.

"It Is a Wholesome and Necessary Thing for Us to Turn Again to the Earth." *EarthSong Journal* 3:2 (Autumn 2016): 16–17.

"It'll Be Shad Time Soon." *Baltimore Sun* (1 March 1936): 6–7.

"It's Tick Time in Maryland." *Baltimore Sun* (18 July 1937): 5.

"Keeping Alive the Sense of Wonder." *National Wildlife* (April-May 2007).

"The Land Around Us." New York *Herald-Tribune* (25 May 1952).

"Letter to the Editor." *Boothbay Register* (27 July 1961): 5.

"Lifesaving Milkweed." *This Week* (4 September 1944).

"Liner Notes." Claude Debussy's *La Mer*, RCA Victor, 1951.

"Long-Range Bird Migration." *Holiday* (1948).

"The Lost Woods." Letter to Curtis and Nellie Lee Bok (12 December 1956).

"Lost Worlds: The Challenge of the Islands." *Wood Thrush* 4:5 (May-June 1949): 179–187.

"Make Spring Silent." *News,* Garden Club Federation of Pennsylvania (March 1963).

"Man and Nature in a Chemical Age." Association of Librarians (28 May 1962).

"Man's Great Peril—Pesticide Poisons." Chicago *Sun-Times* (26 May 1963).

"The Marginal World" in *Bedrock: Writers on the Wonders of Geology.* San Antonio, TX: Trinity University Press, 2006, 224–227.

"Mass Production for Diamond-Back Terrapins." *Baltimore Sunday Sun Magazine* (13 September 1938): 1.

"The Master of the Ship's Light." *Englicode* (1928).

"Mattamuskeet: A National Wildlife Refuge." #4. Washington, D.C.: U.S. Department of the Interior, July 1947.

"Memo to Mrs. Eales." Rachel Carson papers, 1942.

"A Message to the Front." *St. Nicholas* 46 (February 1919): 375.

Michel, Hedwig, "Ideas and Ideals Are Not Lost." Fort Myers, FL *News-Press* (19 April 1964): 27.

"Miss Carson Goes to Washington." *American Forests* (October 1963).

"Mr. Day's Dismissal." *Washington Post* (22 April 1953): A26; *Reader's Digest* (August 1953).

"Mother of Life" in "The Living Ocean." *World Book Encyclopedia Yearbook,* Chicago, 1963: 52–64.

"Moving Tides." *Motor Boating* (July 1963): 20–23.

"My Favorite Recreation." *St. Nicholas* 49 (July 1922): 999.

"The Mystery of Life at the Seashore." *Reader's Digest* (September 1956).

"National Book Award Acceptance Speech." *House of Life* (27 January 1952): 127–129.

"National Symphony Orchestra Benefit Luncheon Speech." Washington, D.C. (25 September 1951).

"A New Chapter in *Silent Spring.*" Address to the Garden Club of America, New York City (8 January 1963); reprint, "A New Chapter," *Silent Spring. Bulletin of the Garden Club of America* (May 1963).

"A New Trout Crop for Anglers." *Baltimore Sun* (2 April 1939): 3.

"The Northern Trawlers Move South." *Baltimore Sunday Sun* (3 January 1937): 6–7.

"Numbering the Fish of the Sea." *Baltimore Sunday Sun* (24 May 1936): 5, 7.

"Ocean Wonderland." *Transatlantic* (March 1944): 35–40; reprint, *This Month* (June 1946).

"Of Man and the Stream of Time." *Scripps College Bulletin,* Claremont, CA (12 June 1962): 5–10.

"On the Biological Sciences." *Good Reading* (July 1956).

"On the Reception of *Silent Spring.*" *National Parks Association Magazine* (2 December 1962).

"The Origins of *Silent Spring.*" National Parks Association (29 June 1962).

"Our Ever-Changing Shore." *Holiday* 24 (July 1958): 70–71, 117–120.

"Oyster Dinners at the Bottom of the Chesapeake." *Richmond Times Dispatch Sunday Magazine* (25 April 1937).

"Parker River: A National Wildlife Refuge." #2. Washington, D.C.: U.S. Department of the Interior, 1947, 1–14.

"Parker River—A New England Conservation Project." *Massachusetts Audubon Society Bulletin* 31:2 (1947): 51–61.

"Poisoned Waters Kill Our Fish and Wildlife." *Audubon* (September-October 1962).

"The Pollution of Our Environment." Address to the Kaiser-Permanente Symposium *Man Against Himself,* San Francisco (18 October 1963).

"Preface." *The Sea Around Us,* 2nd ed. New York: Oxford University Press, 1961, xvii–xxiv.

"A Profile of the Sea." *New Yorker* 2:9 (16 June 1951).

"Rachel Carson Answers Her Critics." *Audubon* 65 (September/October 1963): 262–265, 313–315.

"Rachel Carson Receives Audubon Medal." *New Englander* (April 1963): 13, 36; *Audubon* 66 (March 1964): 98–99.

"Rachel Carson Speaks on Reverence for Life." *Information Report,* Animal Welfare Institute 12:1 (January-February, 1963): 223.

"The Real World Around Us." Address to the Theta Sigma Phi Matrix Table Dinner, *House of Life* (21 April 1954): 324–326.

"Review: Experimental Modification of Sexual Cycle in Trout by Control of Light." *Progressive Fish-Culturist* 5:36 (September 1938): 34.

"Review: Fish Conservation Advanced in 1937." *Progressive Fish-Culturist* 5:36 (September 1938): 35.

"Review: Fish Predation Investigation." *Progressive Fish-Culturist* 5:39 (December 1938): 46.

"Review: Lake Management Reports, Horseshoe Lake Near Cairo, Illinois." *Progressive Fish-Culturist* 5:42 (November 1938): 33–35.

"Review: Production of Nutritional Cataract in Trout." *Progressive Fish-Culturist* 5:37 (October 1938): 27.

"Review: Progress of Trout Feeding Experiments." *Progressive Fish-Culturist* 5:40 (September 1938): 48.

"Review: Selenium Poisoning in Fishes." *Progressive Fish-Culturist* 5:39 (December 1938): 44.

"Review: Some Results of Trout Tagging in Massachusetts." *Progressive Fish-Culturist* 5:39 (December 1938): 44.

"Review: Spawning Induced Prematurely in Trout with the Aid of Pituitary Glands of Carp." *Progressive Fish-Culturist* 7:50 (May 1940): 48–49.

"Review: The Use of Hormones for the Conservation of Muskellunge, Esox Masquinongy Immaculatus Garrard." *Progressive Fish-Culturist* 7:50 (May 1940): 48–49.

"Road of the Hawks." Unpublished, October 1945.

"Saint Simon Island, Georgia." Unpublished 1952.

"Scientists' Findings on Florida Red Tide Reported." U.S. Fish and Wildlife Service (21 December 1947).

"The Sea." *Johns Hopkins Magazine* 12:8 (May-June 1961): 6–20.

"The Sea Frontier." Presentation to the American Association for the Advancement of Science Symposium, The Hub Hotel, Boston (29 December 1953).

"A Sense of Values in Today's World." Address to the New England Wildflower Preservation Society (17 January 1963).

"The Sense of Wonder." *McCall's* (June 1965).

"Sentiment Plays No Part in the Save the Shad Movement." *Baltimore Sunday Sun* (28 February 1937).

"Shad Catches Declining as 1939 Season Opens." *Baltimore Sunday Sun* (26 March 1939): 3.

"Shad Going the Way of the Buffalo." *Charleston News and Courier* (14 February 1937): 8C.

"Shallow Waters." *Cape Cod Compass* (April 1953).

"The Shape of Ancient Seas." *Nature* 44:5 (May 1951): 233–238, 272–273.

"She Started It All—Here's Her Reaction." *New York Herald Tribune* (19 May 1963).

"Silent Spring." *New Yorker* (June 16, June 23, June, 30, 1962): 16; 99; 64.

"Sky Dwellers." *Coronet* 39 (November 1945).

"Something About the Sky." CBS *Omnibus,* https://publicism.info/environment/woods/24.html, March 11, 1957.

Speech, Drexel Institute of Technology luncheon, Philadelphia (14 June 1952).

Speech, Geographical Society of Philadelphia (9 January 1952).

Speech, New York Herald Tribune Book Review, Astor Hotel (1 October 1951).

Speech, New York Zoological Society, Barclay Hotel, Philadelphia (14 January 1953).

Speech, Quaint Acres Citizens Association, Maryland (11 June 1959).

"Starlings a Housing Problem." *Baltimore Sunday Sun Magazine* (5 March 1939): 1.

"Testimony Before a Senate Committee on Environmental Hazards." *House of Life* (4 June 1963): 308–309.

"Testimony to Ribicoff Committee" (5 June 1962).

"To Understand Biology." *Humane Biology Projects.* Washington, D.C.: Animal Welfare Institute, 1960, i–iv.

"Tomorrow's Spring." the All-Women Conference of the National Council of Women (11 October 1962).

"A Treasure Chest of Favorite Sea Books." *Washington Post* (2 December 1951).

"Undersea." *Atlantic Monthly* 160 (September 1937): 322–325.

"Vanishing Americans." *Washington Post* (10 April 1959): A26.

"Walrus and Carpenter Not Oysters' Only Foe." *Baltimore Sun* (21 August 1938): 2.

"Wealth from the Salt Seas." *Science Digest* (October 1950).

"Whalers Ready for New Season." *Baltimore Sunday Sun* (20 November 1938): 2.

"Why America's Natural Resources Must Be Conserved." *Outdoor Life* (29 July 1946).

"Why Our Winters Are Getting Warmer." *Popular Science* 159:5 (November 1951): 113–117, 252, 254, 256.

"A Young Hero." *St. Nicholas* 46 (January 1919): 280.

Letters

"Letter to Beverly Knecht" (12 April 1959).
"Letter to Clarence Cottam" (4 January 1961).
"Letter to Correspondents" (2 August 1962).
"Letter to Curtis and Nellie Lee Bok" (12 December 1956).
"Letter to DeWitt Wallace" (27 January 1958).
"Letter to Dr. George Crile" (17 February 1963).
"Letter to Dorothy and Stanley Freeman" (8 August 1956).
"Letter to Dorothy and Stanley Freeman" (7 October 1956).
"Letter to Dorothy Freeman" (15 December 1952).
"Letter to Dorothy Freeman" (3 September 1953).
"Letter to Dorothy Freeman" (28 September 1953).
"Letter to Dorothy Freeman" (21 January 1954).
"Letter to Dorothy Freeman" (23 June 1956).
"Letter to Dorothy Freeman" (1 February 1958).
"Letter to Dorothy Freeman" (12 June 1958).
"Letter to Dorothy Freeman" (28 June 1958).
"Letter to Dorothy Freeman" (August 1958).
"Letter to Dorothy Freeman" (19 November 1959).
"Letter to Dorothy Freeman" (7 December 1959).
"Letter to Dorothy Freeman" (January 1960).
"Letter to Dorothy Freeman" (6 January 1962).
"Letter to Dorothy Freeman" (20 May 1962).
"Letter to Dorothy Freeman" (27 March 1963).
"Letter to Dorothy Freeman" (1 April 1963).
"Letter to Dorothy Freeman" (10 September 1963).
"Letter to Dorothy Freeman" (21 October 1963).
"Letter to Dorothy Freeman" (17 October 1963).
"Letter to Dorothy Freeman" (26 October 1963).
"Letter to Edwin Teale" (12 October 1958).
"Letter to Frank E. Egler" (29 January 1962).
"Letter to J.I. McClurkin" (28 September 1956).
"Letter to Lois Crisler" (8 February 1962).
"Letter to Marie Rodell" (2 February 1958).
"Letter to Marjorie Spock" (27 September 1960).
"Letter to Morton S. Biskind" (3 December 1959).
"Letter to Mrs. Boyette" (12 June 1956).
"Letter to Paul Brooks" (26 June 1961).
"Letter to Walter C. Bauer" (12 November 1963).
"Letter to William Shawn" (14 February 1959).

Secondary Sources

Archer, Jules. *To Save the Earth: The American Environmental Movement.* New York: Simon & Schuster, 2016.

Barnet, Andrea. *Visionary Women: How Rachel Carson, Jane Jacobs, Jane Goodall, and Alice Waters Changed Our World.* New York: Ecco, 2018.

Beston, Henry. *The Outermost House: A Year of Life on the Great Beach of Cape Cod.* New York: Holt, 2003.

Bonta, Marcia Myers. *Women in the Field: America's Pioneering Women Naturalists.* College Station: Texas A & M University Press, 1991.

Boston, Penelope J., et al. *Scientists Debate Gaia: The Next Century.* Cambridge, MA: MIT Press, 2004.

Brooks, Paul. *The House of Life: Rachel Carson at Work.* Boston: Houghton Mifflin, 1972.

_____. *Rachel Carson: The Writer at Work.* San Francisco, CA: Sierra Club, 1998.

_____. *Speaking for Nature: How Literary Naturalists from Henry Thoreau to Rachel Carson Have Shaped America.* San Francisco, CA: Sierra Club, 1983.

Browne, Neil W. *The World in Which We Occur: John Dewey, Pragmatist Ecology, and American Ecological Writing in the Twentieth Century.* Tuscaloosa: University of Alabama Press, 2007.

Bryson, Michael A. *Visions of the Land: Science, Literature, and the American Environment.* Charlottesville: University of Virginia Press, 2002.

Cullen, Vicky. *Down to the Sea for Science.* Cape Cod, MA: Woods Hole Oceanographic Institution, 2005.

Dillon, Justin. *Towards a Convergence Between Science and Environmental Education.* New York: Routledge, 2017.

Dimock, Wai Chee. *Through Other Continents: American Literature across Deep Time.* Princeton, NJ: Princeton University Press, 2006.

Dunlap, Thomas R. *DDT, Silent Spring, and the Rise of Environmentalism.* Seattle: University of Washington Press, 2008.

Ehrlich, Amy. *Rachel: The Story of Rachel Carson.* San Diego, CA: Harcourt, 2003.

Fabiny, Sarah. *Who Was Rachel Carson?* New York: Penguin, 2014.

Felder, Deborah, G. *The 100 Most Influential Women of All Time.* New York: Citadel Press, 1996.

Fletcher, Marty. *Who on Earth is Rachel Carson?: Mother of the Environmental Movement.* Berkeley Heights, NJ: Enslow, 2009.

Free, Ann Cottrell. *Since "Silent Spring": Our Debt to Albert Schweitzer and Rachel Carson.* Washington, D.C.: Flying Fox, 1992.

Freeman, Martha, ed. *Always, Rachel: The Letters of Rachel Carson and Dorothy Freeman, 1952–1964.* Boston: Beacon Press, 1995.

Fuller, Robert C. *Wonder: From Emotion to Spirituality.* Chapel Hill: University of North Carolina Press, 2006.

Gartner, Carol B. *Rachel Carson.* New York: Ungar, 1983.

Goldbert, Jake. *Rachel Carson.* New York: Chelsea, 1992.

Gottlieb, Robert. *Forcing the Spring: The Transformation of the American Environmental Movement.* Washington, D.C.: Island Press, 2005.

Gow, Mary. *Rachel Carson: Ecologist and Activist.* Berkeley Heights, NJ: Enslow, 2005.

Graham, Frank. *Since Silent Spring.* Boston: Houghton Mifflin, 1970.

Gross, Alan G. *The Scientific Sublime.* Oxford, UK: Oxford University Press, 2018.

Harrison, Brian. *Seeking a Role: The United Kingdom.* Oxford, UK: Oxford University Press, 2009.

Henricksson, John. *Rachel Carson: The Environmental Movement.* Brookfield, CT: Millbrook, 1991.

Hessler, Stefanie, and Bruno Latour. *Prospecting Ocean.* Cambridge, MA: MIT Press, 2019.

Hile, Lori. *Rachel Carson: Environmental Pioneer.* Chicago: Heinemann, 2015.

Howe, Joshua P. *Making Climate Change History: Documents from Global Warming's Past.* Seattle: University of Washington Press, 2017.

Hustad, Douglas. *Environmentalist Rachel Carson.* Minneapolis, MN: Lerner, 2017.

Hynes, H. Patricia. *The Recurring Silent Spring.* New York: Pergamon, 1989.

Jameson, Conor Mark. *Silent Spring Revisited.* London: A&C Black, 2013.

Jezer, Marty. *Rachel Carson: Biologist and Author.* New York: Chelsea House, 1988.

Killingsworth, M. Jimmie, and Jacqueline S. Palmer. *Ecospeak: Rhetoric and Environmental Politics in America.* Carbondale: Southern Illinois University Press, 1992.

Knopf-Newman, Marcy Jane. *Beyond Slash, Burn, and Poison: Transforming Breast Cancer Stories into Action.* Piscataway, NJ: Rutgers University Press, 2004.

Kohlstedt, Sally Gregory, and David Kaiser, eds. *Science and the American Century: Readings from "Isis."* Chicago: University of Chicago Press, 2013.

Kudlinski, Kathleen V. *Rachel Carson: Pioneer of Ecology.* New York: Puffin, 1989.

Lantier-Sampon, Patricia. *Rachel Carson: Fighting Pesticides and Other Chemical Pollutants.* New York: Crabtree, 2009.

Latham, Jean Lee. *Rachel Carson: Who Loved the Sea.* Champaign, IL: Garrard, 1973.

Lawlor, Laurie. *Rachel Carson and Her Book That Changed the World.* New York: Holiday House, 2014.

Lear, Linda J. *Rachel Carson: Witness for Nature.* New York: Henry Holt, 1997.

Lertzman, Renee. *Environmental Melancholia: Psychoanalytic Dimensions of Engagement.* New York: Routledge, 2015.

Levine, Ellen. *Rachel Carson: A Twentieth-Century Life.* New York: Viking, 2007.

Locker, Thomas, and Joseph Bruchac. *Rachel*

Carson: Preserving a Sense of Wonder. Golden, CO: Fulcrum, 2004.

Lytle, Mark Hamilton. *The Gentle Subversive: Rachel Carson, Silent Spring, and the Rise of the Environmental Movement.* New York: Oxford University Press, 2007.

Macgillivray, Alex. *Understanding Rachel Carson's Silent Spring.* New York: Rosen, 2010.

Magdoff, Fred, and Chris Williams. *Creating an Ecological Society: Toward a Revolutionary Transformation.* New York: New York University, 2017.

Marco, Gino J., et al., eds. *Silent Spring Revisited.* Washington, D.C.: American Chemical Society, 1987.

Matthiessen, Peter, ed. *Courage for the Earth: Writers, Scientists, and Activists Celebrate the Life and Writing of Rachel Carson.* New York: Mariner, 2007.

McCay, Mary A. *Rachel Carson.* New York: Twayne, 1993.

McKibben, Bill. *Falter: Has the Human Game Begun to Play Itself Out?* New York: Henry Holt, 2019.

Meiners, Roger, Pierre Desrochers, and Andrew Morriss, eds. *Silent Spring at 50: The False Crises of Rachel Carson.* Washington, D.C.: Cato Institute, 2012.

Meisch, Simon. *Water, Creativity and Meaning.* New York: Routledge, 2018.

Montrie, Chad. *The Myth of Silent Spring: Rethinking the Origins of American Environmentalism.* Oakland: University of California Press, 2018.

Morley, Julie J. *Future Sacred: The Connected Creativity of Nature.* Rochester, VT: Park Street Press, 2019.

Murphy, Priscilla Coit. *What a Book Can Do: The Publication and Reception of Silent Spring.* Amherst: University of Massachusetts Press, 2005.

Musil, Robert K. *Rachel Carson and Her Sisters: Extraordinary Women Who Have Shaped America's Environment.* New Brunswick, NJ: Rutgers University Press, 2014.

Musser, Charles. "Trauma, Truth, and the Environmental Documentary" in *Eco-Trauma Cinema.* New York: Routledge, 2015.

Norwood, Vera. *Made from This Earth.* Chapel Hill: University of North Carolina Press, 1993.

Offit, Paul A. *Pandora's Lab: Seven Stories of Science Gone Wrong.* Washington, D.C.: National Geographic Partners, 2017.

Oravec, Christine. "Rachel Louise Carson" in *Women Public Speakers in the United States, 1925–1993.* Westport, CT: Greenwood, 1994, 72–89.

Oreskes, Naomi, and Erik M. Conway. *Merchants of Doubt: How a Handful of Scientists Obscured the Truth on Issues from Tobacco Smoke to Global Warming.* New York: Bloomsbury, 2010.

Pauly, Daniel, and Dirk Zeller, eds. *Global Atlas of Marine Fisheries.* Washington, D.C.: Island Press, 2016.

Pemberton, Frank. "Along the Seaboard." Providence (RI) *Journal* (13 April 1952).

Petrina, Stephen. "Critique of Technology." *Critique in Design and Technology Education.* Singapore: Springer, 2017, 31–49.

Pimentel, David, and Hugh Lehman. *The Pesticide Question.* New York: Chapman & Hall, 1993.

Quaratiello, Arlene Rodda. *Rachel Carson: A Biography.* Amherst, NY: Prometheus, 2010.

Radkau, Joachim. *Nature and Power: A Global History of the Environment.* New York: Cambridge University Press, 2002.

Reef, Catherine. *Rachel Carson: The Wonder of Nature.* Frederick, MD: Twenty-First Century Books, 1992.

Rockwood, Larry, Ronald Stewart, and Thomas Dietz, eds. *Foundations of Environmental Sustainability.* New York: Oxford University Press, 2008.

Rome, Adam. "Rachel Carson and the Challenge of Greening Technology" in *Technology in America: A History of Individuals and Ideas.* Third ed. Cambridge: Massachusetts Institute of Technology, 2018.

Sarathy, Brinda, Vivien Hamilton, and Janet Farrell Brodie. *Inevitably Toxic: Historical Perspectives on Contamination, Exposure, and Expertise.* Pittsburgh, PA: University of Pittsburgh Press, 2018.

Seager, Joni. *Carson's Silent Spring: A Reader's Guide.* London: Bloomsbury Academic, 2014.

Shea, George. *Rachel Carson: Founder of the Environmental Movement.* Detroit, MI: Blackbirch, 2006.

Sideris, Lisa H., and Kathleen Dean Moore, eds. *Rachel Carson: Legacy and Challenge.* Albany: State University of New York, 2008.

Sisson, Stephanie Roth. *Spring after Spring: How Rachel Carson Inspired the Environmental Movement.* New York: Roaring Book, 2018.

Smith, Adrian, Mariano Fressoli, Dinesh Abrol, Elisa Arond, and Adrian Ely. *Grassroots Innovation Movements.* London: Routledge, 2016.

Souder, William. *On a Farther Shore: The Life and Legacy of Rachel Carson.* New York: Crown, 2012.

Stauber, John, and Sheldon Rampton. *Toxic Waste Is Good for You! Lies, Damn Lies, and the Public Relations Industry.* Monroe, ME: Common Courage Press, 1995.

Stein, Karen F. *Rachel Carson: Challenging Authors.* Rotterdam: Sense, 2012.

Steingruber, Sandra, ed. *Rachel Carson: Silent*

Spring & Other Writings on the Environment. New York: Library of America, 2018.

Sterling, Philip. *Sea and Earth: The Life of Rachel Carson.* New York: Crowell, 1970.

ten Have, Hank. *Wounded Planet: How Declining Biodiversity Endangers Health and How Bioethics Can Help.* Baltimore: Johns Hopkins University Press, 2019.

Transactions of the Twenty-Seventh North American Wildlife and Natural Resources Conference. Washington, D.C.: Wildlife Management Institute, 1962.

Tremblay, E.A. *Rachel Carson: Author/Ecologist.* Philadelphia: Chelsea House, 2003.

Vail, David D. *Chemical Lands: Pesticides, Aerial Spraying, and Health in North America's Grasslands Since 1945.* Tuscaloosa: University of Alabama Press, 2018.

Van Emden, H.F., and David B. Peakall. *Beyond Silent Spring.* Berlin: Springer, 1996.

Venezia, Mike. *Rachel Carson: Clearing the Way for Environmental Protection.* Danbury, CT: Children's Press, 2010.

Waddell, Craig, ed. *And No Birds Sing: Rhetorical Analyses of Rachel Carson's Silent Spring.* Carbondale: Southern Illinois University Press, 2000.

Watson, David, and A.W.A. Brown, eds. *Pesticide Management and Insecticide Resistance.* New York: Academic Press, 1977.

Wiener, Gary. *The Environment in Rachel Carson's Silent Spring.* Farmington Hills, MI: Greenhaven, 2012.

Winston, Mark L. *Nature Wars.* Cambridge, MA: Harvard University Press, 1997.

Zaretsky, Natasha. *Radiation Nation: Three Mile Island and the Political Transformation of the 1970s.* New York: Columbia University Press, 2018.

Periodicals

"Actress Offers 'Message' in a Nov. 13 TV Special." *La Cross* (WI) *Tribune* (26 October 1968): 4.

Adams, Val. "CBS Reports Plans a Show on Rachel Carson's New Book." *New York Times* (30 August 1962): 42.

Alexander, James E. "Disturbing Book about Poisons around Us." *Pittsburgh Post-Gazette* (29 September 1962).

Alfaro, René I., and David Langor. "Changing Paradigms in the Management of Forest Insect Disturbances." *Canadian Entomologist* 148 (August 2016): S7–18.

Alsop, Joseph. "My Turtle and Rachel Carson." *Boston Globe* (26 May 1963).

Ames, Alfred C. "More about the Strange Sea Around Us." *Chicago Tribune* (6 April 1952): 4:3.

"And Was It a Silent Spring." *Popular Mechanics* (June 1963).

Arvidson, Adam Regn. "Nature Writing in America: The Power of Rachel Carson." *Nature & Science* 2:9 (September 2011).

Atkinson, Brooks. "Rachel Carson's 'Silent Spring' Is Called 'The Rights of Man' of Our Time." *New York Times* (2 April 1963): 44.

Avery, Dennis T. "Rachel Carson and the Malaria Tragedy." *Canada Free Press* (13 April 2007).

Bailey, Ronald. "*Silent Spring* at 40: Rachel Carson's Classic Is Not Aging Well." *Reason* (12 June 2002).

Baratta, Chris. "'Interdisciplinarity' Achieved: A Brief Look at Interdisciplinary Environmentalism in the 1960s." *Interdisciplinary Literary Studies* 18:3 (2016): 301–324.

Bates, Marston. "Review: *Silent Spring.*" *Nation* (6 October 1962): 202.

Bauers, Sandy. "'Under the Sea Wind' Takes Listeners on a Rich Journey." *Orlando Sentinel* (31 January 2001): E6.

Baum, Rudy M. "Rachel Carson." *Chemical & Engineering News* (4 June 2007).

Beebe, William. "Review: *Under the Sea Wind.*" *Saturday Review* (27 December 1941): 5.

Bell, Elizabeth S. "The Language of Discovery: The Seascapes of Rachel Carson and Jacques Cousteau." *CEA Critic* 63:1 (Fall 2000): 5–13.

Berman, Emily, and Jacob Carter. "Policy Analysis: Scientific Integrity in Federal Policymaking Under Past and Present Administrations." *Journal of Science Policy and Governance* 13:1 (2018).

Berrill, N.J. "Review: *The Edge of the Sea.*" *Saturday Review* (3 December 1955): 30.

Beston, Henry. "Review: *The Sea Around Us.*" *Freeman* (3 November 1952): 100.

Bethune, Brian. "Was Rachel Carson Wrong?'" *Maclean's* (4 June 2007): 42–43.

Bienkowski, Brian. "DDT Still Killing Birds in Michigan." *Scientific American* (28 July 2014).

Blum, Hester. "Bitter with the Salt of Continents: Rachel Carson and Oceanic Returns." *Women's Studies Quarterly* 45:1/2 (Spring/Summer 2017): 287–291.

Boggs, Carol. "Human Niche Construction and the Anthropocene." *RCC Perspectives* 2 (2016): 27–31.

Boucher, Norman. "The Legacy of *Silent Spring.*" *Boston Globe Magazine* (15 March 1987): 17, 37–47.

Boutard, C. Roy. "Review: *Silent Spring.*" (Pittsfield, MA) *Berkshire Eagle* (29 September 1962): 22.

Bowden, J. Earle. "Review: *The Rocky Coast.*" *Pensacola News Journal* (26 September 1971): 4D.

Bowes, Catherine. "An Evening with Rachel

Carson." *Conservation Matters* 7:2 (Summer 2000): 48.

Bratton, Susan Power. "Thinking like a Mackerel: Rachel Carson's *Under the Sea-Wind* as a Source for a Trans-Ecotonal Sea Ethic." *Ethics and the Environment* 9:1 (April 2004): 1–22.

Briggs, Shirley. "Remembering Rachel Carson." *American Forests* (July 1970): 9–11.

Brinkley, Parke C. "As of Now" in the official report of the Association of American Pesticide Control Officials Incorporated, 1965–1966, 57–59.

Brooks, Paul. "Courage of Rachel Carson." *Audubon* (January 1987): 14.

Bryson, Michael A. "Nature, Narrative, and the Scientist-Writer: Rachel Carson's and Loren Eiseley's Critique of Science." *Technical Communication Quarterly* 12:4 (Fall 2003): 369–387.

Buhs, Joshua Blu. "The Fire Ant Wars." *Isis* 93:3 (September 2002): 377–400.

Burgess, Robert L., "Resolution of Respect: Frank Edwin Egler, 1911–1996." *Bulletin of the Ecological Society of America* 78 (1997): 193–194.

Burnham, Philip. "Review: *The Sea Around Us.*" *Commonweal* 54 (27 July 1951): 387–389.

Burnside, John. "A Fish Called Wonder." *The Guardian* 143:5205 (11–17 April 2014): 54–55.

_____. "Reluctant Crusader." *The Guardian* (18 May 2002): 1.

Cafaro, Philip. "Rachel Carson's Environmental Ethics." *Worldviews* 6:1 (2002): 58–80.

_____. "Rachel Carson's Environmental Ethics." *Linking Ecology and Ethics for a Changing World.* Berlin: Springer, 2013, 163–171.

Campbell, W. Joseph. "Silent Spring: A Timeless Call for Ecological Concern." *Hartford Courant* (24 May 1987): A33.

Carleton, Milton. "*Silent Spring* Merely Science Fiction Instead of Fact." *Chicago Sunday Sun-Times* (23 September 1962).

Chapman, Dan. "Dusting Off DDT's Image." *Atlanta Constitution* (9 September 2001): D1, D3.

Clay, William M. "Is Man Poisoning Himself in His Battle Against Bugs?" Louisville (KY) *Courier-Journal* (23 September 1962): 4:3.

Colson, Helen A. "'Democracy Still works. .': Rachel's Song Is Loud and Clear." *Washington* (D.C.) *News* (6 November 1962).

Compton, A.H. "Review: *Under the Sea-Wind.*" *Scientific Book Club Review* (October 1941): 1.

Cone, Marla. "The Unbroken Chain." *Columbia Journalism Review* 44:2 (2005): 65–68.

Cook, Christopher D. "The Spraying of America." *Earth Island Journal* 20:1 (2005): 34–38.

Coughlin, Maura. "Biotopes and Ecotones: Slippery Images on the Edge of the French Atlantic." *Landscapes* 7:1 (2016): 1–23.

Cowen, Robert. "Review: *Silent Spring.*" *Christian Science Monitor* (27 September 1962): 11.

Cox, Jeff. "DDT Spraying Is Attacked." (Stroudsburg, PA) *Pocono Record* (9 May 1963): 15.

Crocco, Margaret Smith, Jay M. Shuttleworth, and Thomas Chandler. "Science, Media, and Civic Literacy: Rachel Carson's Legacy for the Citizen Activist." *Social Studies and the Young Learner* 28:3 (2016): 21–26.

Cross, Sarah O. "What Price a World without Bird Song." Montreal *Gazette* (6 October 1962): 29.

Culbertson, Jean. "Miss Carson's 'Silent Spring': Are They Pesticides or Peoplecides?" (Jackson, MS) *Clarion Ledger* (14 October 1962): 7B.

Darby, William J. "Silence, Miss Carson." *Chemical & Engineering News* (1 October 1962): 60–62.

Davis, Frederick Rowe. "Pesticides and the Perils of Synecdoche in the History of Science and Environmental History." *History of Science* (24 June 2019).

Deaton, Thomas. "Spirituality and the Environment: Learning from People of the Whale." *Ashen Egg* 7 (2019): 10–18.

DeMarco, Patricia M. "Every Day Earth Day." *Pittsburgh Post-Gazette* (22 April 2010): B7.

_____. "Rachel Carson's Environmental Ethic—A Guide for Global Systems Decision Making." *Journal of Cleaner Production* 140:1 (1 January 2017): 127–133.

Denneen, Bill. "Rachel Carson Failed to Remain Silent, Thankfully." *Santa Maria* (CA) *Times* (29 June 1999): A4.

"The Desolate Year." *Monsanto Magazine* 42:4 (October, 1962): 4–9.

Dewey, Phelps. "Review: *The Rocky Coast.*" *San Francisco Examiner & Chronicle* (2 January 1972): 34.

Diamond, Edwin. "The Myth of the 'Pesticide Menace,'" *Saturday Evening Post* 136 (28 September 1963): 16, 18.

Doffey, Philip M. "Environment, Two Decades after *Silent Spring.*" *Rutland Daily Herald* (29 May 1982): 17.

Dreier, Peter. "How Rachel Carson and Michael Harrington Changed the World." *Contexts* 11:2 (Spring 2012): 40–46.

Druckenbrod, Andrew. "The Sound of Silence." *Pittsburgh Post-Gazette* (12 February 2012): E1, E3.

Duke, Eleanor. "Review: *Silent Spring.*" *El Paso Herald-Post* (3 November 1962): 4.

Durgin, Cyrus. "Overnight Miss Carson Has Become Famous." *Boston Globe* (20 July 1951): 1, 4.

"The Education of Rachel Carson." *Pittsburgh Post-Gazette* (2 May 2006): G6.

Edwards, Charity. "Of the Urban and the Ocean:

Rachel Carson and the Disregard of Wet Volumes." *Field* 7:1 (2017): 205–219.

Edwards, J. Gordon. "The Lies of Rachel Carson." *21st Century* (Summer 1992).

Egerton, Frank N. "History of Ecological Sciences, Part 53: Organizing Ecologists before 1946." *Bulletin of the Ecological Society of America* 96:2 (April 2015): 239–311.

Eiseley, Loren. "Review: *Silent Spring*." *Saturday Review* (29 September 1962): 18.

Elliott, Melanie. "Carson's Landmark Book Still Has Relevance Today." *Saskatoon Sun* (16 December 2007): 22.

Ellis, Henry. "Review: *The Edge of the Sea*." *Christian Science Monitor* (10 November 1955): 8

_____. "Review: *The Sea Around Us*." *Christian Science Monitor* (5 July 1951): 7.

Ellyson, Louise, "'Let Nature Work for You,' Author Rachel Carson Says." *Richmond Times-Dispatch* (2 November 1962).

Ensor, Sarah. "Spinster Ecology: Rachel Carson, Sarah Orne Jewett, and Nonreproductive Futurity." *American Literature* 84:2 (2012): 409–435.

Faust, Joan Lee. "Around the Garden: Will Spring Be Silent?" *New York Times* (7 October 1962): 25.

Fellows, Valerie. "On Eagle's Wings." *Fish & Wildlife News* (Spring 2007): 20–21.

_____, and Joshua Winchell. "Returning to the Water." *Fish & Wildlife News* (Spring 2007): 26–29.

Feneja, Fernanda Luísa. "'To What End Is Nature?'—Rachel Carson's *Under the Sea Wind* and Environmental Literature." *Anglo-Saxónica* 3:12 (2016): 59–82.

Feurt, Ward. "A Living Trust." *Fish & Wildlife News* (Spring 2007): 35.

Foote, Bonnie. "The Narrative Interactions of *Silent Spring*: Bridging Literary Criticism and Ecocriticism." *New Literary History* 38:4 (Autumn 2007): 739–745, 747–753, 777.

"Fourteen Received Medals of Freedom." *Salt Lake Tribune* (10 June 1980): 1.

Free, Ann Cottrell, "Rachel Carson Book Stirs Congress." *Baltimore Evening Sun* (7 January 1963): 14.

_____. "Silent Spring Stir: 'I Never Thought Uproar Would Be So Tremendous,'" *Baltimore Evening Sun* (8 January 1963): A17.

"Freedom Medals Given." (Newport News, VA) *Daily Press* (June 10, 1980): 9.

Furgurson, Ernest B. "Another Spring." *Baltimore Sun* (15 June 1980): K5.

Galton, Lawrence. "The Great Debate over Pests—And Pesticides." *New York Times* (14 April 1963): 42.

Gavzer, Bernard. "Pesticides: Boon or Harm." *Bridgeport Sunday Post* (24 March 1963): C1, C6.

Glotfelty, Cheryll. "Rachel Carson" in *American Nature Writers*. New York: Charles Scribner's Sons, 1996.

Gore, Al. "Introduction." *Silent Spring*. Boston: Houghton Mifflin, 1994, xiii.

Griswold, Eliza. "How *Silent Spring* Ignited the Environmental Movement." *New York Times Magazine* (21 September 2012).

Hagood, Amanda. "Wonders with the Sea: Rachel Carson's Ecological Aesthetic and the Mid-Century Reader." *Environmental Humanities* 2:1 (2013): 57–77.

Hawkes, Jacquetta. "Mother Sea." London *Observer* (11 November 1951): 7.

_____. "Review: *The Edge of the Sea*." *New Republic* (23 January 1956): 17–18.

Hazard, Nancy. "Rachel Carson and the Biodiversity Crisis." *Greenfield Recorder* (13 March 2019).

Hazlett, Maril. "'Woman vs. Man vs. Bugs': Gender and Popular Ecology in Early Reactions to *Silent Spring*." *Environmental History* 9:4 (Oct. 2004): 701–729.

Hecht, David K. "Rachel Carson and the Rhetoric of Revolution." *Environmental History* 24:3 (July 2019): 561–582.

Hecht, Marjorie Mazel. "Bring Back DDT, and Science with It!" *21st Century* (Summer 2002).

Higgins, Elmer. "Review: *Under the Sea Wind*." *Progressive Fish Culturist* 7:56 (December 1941): 33–34.

Hill, Jen. "Surfaces and Depths." *Women's Studies Quarterly* 45:1/2 (Spring/Summer 2017): 282–286.

Hines, Bob. "The Woman Who Started a Revolution: Remembering Rachel Carson." *Yankee Magazine* (June 1991): 62–67.

"Hiss of Doom?" *Newsweek* 60 (6 August 1962): 55.

Horton, Tom. "Rachel Carson No Stranger to Chesapeake, Its Creatures." *Salisbury* (MD) *Daily Times* (3 November 2019): A4.

"The Hour Glass." *Sioux City Journal* (6 July 1969): A4.

"How to Poison Bugs ... But NOT Yourself." *Popular Science* (June 1962).

Howard, Jane. "The Gentle Storm Center: A Calm Appraisal of *Silent Spring*." *Life* 53:5 (12 October 1962): 105.

Hubbell, Sue. "Introduction." *The Edge of the Sea*. Boston: Mariner, 1998.

Huckins, Olga. "Letter to the Editor." *Boston Herald* (January 1958).

Hulme, Mike. "Weather-Worlds of the Anthropocene and the End of Climate." *Weber* 34:1 (Fall 2018): 1–12.

Hunter, Marjorie. "U.S. Sets Up Panel to Review the Side Effects of Pesticides." *New York Times* (31 August 1963): 9.

Ingram, Janet. "Rachel Carson" in *Scribner Encyclopedia of American Lives: The 1960s*. New York: Charles Scribner's Son, 2003.

Irwin, Virginia. "Author of Best Sellers about the Sea." *St. Louis Post-Dispatch* (16 July 1952): 3F.

"Izaak Walton League Honors Rachel Carson." *La Crosse* (WI) *Tribune* (16 June 1963): 12.

Jackson, J.H. "Review: *The Sea Around Us*." *San Francisco Chronicle* (3 July 1951): 14.

Jepson, Paul D., and Robin J. Law. "Persistent Pollutants, Persistent Threats." *Science* 352:6292 (2016): 1388–1389.

Johns, Susan. "Reflections on Rachel." *Boothbay Register* (23 June 2012).

Johnson, Lyndon B. "Remarks by President Johnson upon Signing the Clean Air Act Amendments and the Solid Waste Disposal Act" in *Health, Education, and Welfare Indicators*. Washington, D.C.: U.S. Government Printing Office, 1965.

Kalinowski, Mark. "Learn the Real Legacy." *Clifton* (NJ) *Journal* (13 April 2012): A15.

Kaza, Stephanie. "Rachel Carson's Sense of Time: Experiencing Maine." *ISLE* 17:2 (Spring 2010): 291–315.

Kinkela, David. "The Ecological Landscapes of Jane Jacobs and Rachel Carson." *American Quarterly* 61:4 (December 2009): 905–929, 997.

Kirchhelle, Claas. "Toxic Tales—Recent Histories of Pollution, Poisoning, and Pesticides (ca. 1800–2010)." *NTM* 26:2 (June 2018): 213–229.

Kitson, Janine. "Marie Byles and Rachel Carson: Two Exceptional Women Who Loved Nature." *Nature New South Wales* 61:1 (2017): 29.

Klinger, David. "Rachel Carson's Hidden Treasures." *Fish & Wildlife News* (Spring 2007): 33.

Koehn, Nancy F. "From Calm Leadership, Lasting Change." *New York Times* (27 October 2012).

Kraft, Virginia. "Life-Giving Spray." *Sports Illustrated* 19 (18 November 1963): 22–25.

Kroll, Gary. "Rachel Carson—*Silent Spring*: A Brief History of Ecology as a Subversive Subject." *Reflections* 9:2 (2002).

_____. "The 'Silent Springs' of Rachel Carson: Mass Media and the Origins of Modern Environmentalism." *Public Understanding of Science* 10:4 (1 October 2001): 403–420.

Kuchment, Olga. "Rachel Carson, Science Editor." *Science Editor* 32:2 (March-April 2009): 39–42.

Lakhman, Sukhwinder S., and Arjun Dutta. "Endocrine Disruptive Chemicals: Silent Poison for Human Health." *EC Pharmacology and Toxicology* 7 (2019): 62–63.

La Monte, Francesca. "Review: *The Sea Around Us*." *New York Herald Tribune Book Review* (5 July 1951): 3.

Laurent, Lawrence. "Bringing Country to City Dwellers." *Los Angeles Times* (13 November 1968): 22.

Lear, Linda J. "Bombshell in Beltsville: The USDA and the Challenge of *Silent Spring*." *Agricultural History* 66:2 (Spring 1992): 151–170.

_____. "The Next Page: When Rachel Carson Set Sail." *Pittsburgh Post-Gazette* (21 February 2016).

Lee, John M. "'Silent Spring' Is Now Noisy Summer." *New York Times* (22 July 1962): 87.

Leonard, Jonathan Norton. "And His Wonders in the Deep; A Scientist Draws an Intimate Portrait of the Winding Sea and Its Churning Life." *New York Times* (1 July 1951).

_____. "Obituary." *New York Times* (15 April 1964).

Lepore, Jill. "The Right Way to Remember Rachel Carson." *New Yorker* (19 March 2018).

_____. "The Shore Bird: Rachel Carson and the Rising of the Seas." *New Yorker* (26 March 2018): 64–66, 68–72.

Levenstein, Harvey. "Death on a Plate." *How Canadians Communicate VI*. Edmonton: Athabasca University, 2016, 297–312.

Levinton, Jeffrey S. "Afterword." *The Sea Around Us: Special Edition*. New York: Oxford University Press, 1989.

Lewis, Jack. "The Birth of EPA." *EPA Journal* (November 1985).

_____. "Rachel Carson." *EPA Journal* (May/June 1992): 60–62.

Lock, Margaret. "Toxic Life in the Anthropocene." *Exotic No More*. 2nd ed. Chicago: University of Chicago Press, 2019, 223–240.

Lockwood, Alex. "The Affective Legacy of *Silent Spring*." *Environmental Humanities* 1:1 (2012): 123–140.

Loy, David R. "The Nonduality of Ecology and Economy." *Tikkun* (September-October 2009): 31–32, 84–85.

Lutts, Ralph H. "Chemical Fallout: Rachel Carson's *Silent Spring*, Radioactive Fallout, and the Environmental Movement." *Environmental Review* 9:3 (Autumn 1985): 210–225.

Madera, Judith. "The Birth of an Island: Rachel Carson's *The Sea Around Us*." *Women's Studies Quarterly* 45:1/2 (Spring/Summer 2017): 292–298.

Madison, Mark. "Nature's Public Servant." *Fish & Wildlife News* (Spring 2007): 8–11.

Mann, Charles C. "'Silent Spring & Other Writings' Review: The Right and Wrong of Rachel Carson." *Wall Street Journal* (26 April 2018): C5.

Marsh, Calum. "In the Beginning Was the Book; How Rachel Carson's *Silent Spring* Inspired the First Earth Day—and How Hard the Powers That Be Fought to Stop It." (Don Mills, Ont.) *National Post* (20 April 2019): WP6.

Marshall, J. "Book Review: *Silent Spring,* by Rachel Carson." *Journal of the Entomological Society of British Columbia* 59 (1 December 1962): 53–55.

Mart, Michelle. "Rhetoric and Response: The Cultural Impact of Rachel Carson's *Silent Spring.*" *Left History* 14:2 (2009): 31–46.

Martin, Maria Angeles, and Connie Lasher. "Nature as a School of Wonder." *Human* 4 (2016).

Masami, Yuki. "Meals in the Age of Toxic Environments." *The Routledge Companion to the Environmental Humanities.* New York: Routledge, 2017, 56–63.

Mather, Kirtley F. "Review: *The Sea Around Us.*" *American Scientist* 39:4 (October 1951).

Matthiessen, Peter. "Environmentalist Rachel Carson." *Time* (29 March 1999): 187.

Mattill, John. "Looking Anew at *Silent Spring.*" *Technology Review* (November-December 1984): 72–73.

McCrum, Robert. "The 100 Best Nonfiction Books: No. 20—*Silent Spring* by Rachel Carson (1962)." *The Guardian* (13 June 2016).

McNally, Tom. "Woods and Waters." *Chicago Tribune* (16 June 1963): 2–7.

Meola, Frank M. "Rachel Carson's 'Rugged Shore' in Maine." *New York Times* (19 August 2012): TR.5.

"Midcoast Actress Brings Rachel Carson's Life to State." *Portland Press Herald* (15 September 2007).

Mills, Billy. "A Book for the Beach." *The Guardian* (28 July 2014).

Milne, Lorus, and Margery Milne. "There's Poison All Around Us Now." *New York Times* (23 September 1962): 24.

Moore, Kathleen Dean. "The Truth of the Barnacles: Rachel Carson and the Moral Significance of Wonder." *Environmental Ethics* 27:3 (Fall 2005): 265–277.

Murphy, Mollie K. "Rachel Carson's Rhetorical Strategies in the *Silent Spring* Debates." *Argumentation and Advocacy* 55:3 (2019): 194–210.

Murphy, Tom. "Are You Being Poisoned?" (De Kalb, IL) *Daily Chronicle* (2 June 1965): 20.

Newell, Dianne. "Judith Merril and Rachel Carson: Reflections on Their 'Potent Fictions' of Science." *Journal of International Women's Studies* 5:4 (2004): 31.

Nieves, Autumn. "Rachel Carson: Proving the Competency of Femininity." *Women Leading Change* 3:2 (10 October 2018).

Nixon, Rob. "Rachel Carson's Prescience." *Chronicle of Higher Education* 59:2 (2012).

Norman, Geoffrey. "The Flight of Rachel Carson." *Esquire* (December 1983): 472–474.

Novotny, Jerry. "A Quiet Leader." *Fish & Wildlife News* (Spring 2007): 18.

Nudel, Martha. "Conservation in Action." *Fish & Wildlife News* (Spring 2007): 22–25.

Oravec, Christine. "An Inventional Archaeology of 'A Fable for Tomorrow,'" *And No Birds Sing.* Carbondale: Southern Illinois University, 2000.

Orlando, Laura. "From Rachel Carson to Oprah." *Dollars & Sense* 240 (March/April 2002): 26–30.

Osmundsen, John. "Man Against Nature: Our Synthetic Environment." *New York Times,* May 19, 1963.

Owens, Brandon N. "Wind Power's Silent Decade." *The Wind Power Story: A Century of Innovation that Reshaped the Global Energy Landscape.* Hoboken, NJ: Wiley, 2019: 129–141.

Parke, Richard. "Connecticut Urged to Establish Board to Control Pesticide Use." *New York Times* (17 April 1963): 43.

Parks, Perry. "*Silent Spring,* Loud Legacy: How Elite Media Helped Establish an Environmentalist Icon." *Journalism and Mass Communication Quarterly* 94:4 (December 2017): 1215–1238.

Perschbacher, Pete. "Sounds Rumblings of Avalanche." *Hillsdale* (MI) *Daily News* (8 April 1964): 3.

"Pesticide Inquiry Is Sought in House." *New York Times* (3 May 1963): 18.

Peters, Kimberley. "Touching the Oceans." *Women's Studies Quarterly* 45:1/2 (Spring/Summer 2017): 278–281.

Pimentel, David. "Silent Spring, the 50th Anniversary of Rachel Carson's Book." *BMC Ecology* 12:20 (2012).

Poore, Charles. "Review: *The Edge of the Sea,*" *New York Times* (26 October 1955): 29.

Popkin, Gabriel. "Right Fish, Wrong Pond." *Johns Hopkins Magazine* (Summer 2013).

"Rachel Carson." *Calliope* 21:4 (January 2011): 32–33.

"Rachel Carson Answers Her Critics." *Audubon* (September 1963).

"Rachel Carson Centennial Anniversary." *Fish & Wildlife News* (Spring 2007): 2–45.

"Rachel Carson Honored." *New York Times* (20 June 1963): 30.

"Rachel Carson National Wildlife Refuge." Washington, D.C.: U.S. Fish & Wildlife Service, 2001.

"Rachel Carson Speaker at Scripps College." *South Pasadena Review* (6 June 1962): 7.

"Rachel Carson Wins Achievement Award." *AAUW Journal* (October 1956): 19.

"Rachel Carson's Warning." *New York Times* (2 July 1962): 28.

Ramirez, Pedro. "Everything Is Connected." *Fish & Wildlife News* (Spring 2007): 16.

Rattner, Barnett A. "Wildlife and Environmental

Pollution." *Animals and Human Society* 18 (September 2017): 472–482.

"Review: *The Edge of the Sea.*" *Christian Science Monitor* (December 1955).

"Review: *The Lost Woods.*" *Publishers Weekly* (28 September 1998).

"Report on 'Silent Spring,'" *New York Times* (9 October 1962): 39.

"Review: *The Sea Around Us.*" *Kirkus* (1 June 1951): 285.

_____." *New York Times* (27 April 1952): 8.

"Review: *The Sense of Wonder.*" *Kirkus* (6 October 1965).

"Review: *The Rocky Coast.*" *Detroit Free Press* (5 December 1971): 5B.

"Review: *Silent Spring.*" *Christian Century* (19 December 1962): 1564.

_____. *Economist* (23 February 1963): 711.

_____. *Time* (28 September 1962): 45–48.

Reynolds, Susan Salter. "It's the End of the World As We Know It." *Los Angeles Times* (25 February 2007): R4.

Richmond, Marsha L. "Women as Public Scientists in the Atomic Age: Rachel Carson, Charlotte Auerbach, and Genetics." *Historical Studies in the Natural Sciences* 47:3 (June 2017): 349–388.

Rohr, J.R. "Atrazine and Amphibians: A Story of Profits, Controversy, and Animus." *The Encyclopedia of the Anthropocene.* Oxford: Elsevier, Vol. 5 (2018): 141–148.

Ros, Joandomènec. "Rachel Carson, Sensitive and Perceptive Interpreter of Nature." *Contributions to Science* 8:1 (2012): 23–32.

Rosenberg, Tina. "What the World Needs Now Is DDT." *New York Times Magazine* (11 April 2004).

Rosner, David. "Swimming Upstream: Probing the Problem of Pollution." *Milbank Quarterly* (March 2015): 8–11.

Rothlisberger, John D. "The Gentle Subversive: Rachel Carson and the Rise of the Environmental Movement." *Western North American Naturalist* 69:1 (2009): 144–146.

Rothman, Joshua. "Rachel Carson's Natural Histories." *New Yorker* (27 September 2012).

Routhier, Ray. "Documentary Looks at Life, Work of Rachel Carson." *Portland* (ME) *Press Herald* (22 January 2017): E5.

St. Johns, Adela Rogers. "'Silent Spring': Rachel Carson Wanted to Hear Birds Sing." *Cincinnati Enquirer* (26 March 1975): 13.

Sandgren, Håkan. "Life Under Water: Narratives of Deep Sea Counternatures." *Contesting Environmental Imaginaries: Nature and Counternature in a Time of Global Change.* Leiden, Netherlands: Brill, 2017, 260–282.

Scaramelli, Caterina. "Fish, Flows, and Desire in the Delta." *Anthropology News* 59:2 (2018): 51–56.

Scarlett, Lynn. "The Poetry of Truth." *Fish & Wildlife News* (Spring 2007): 34.

Schmeck, Harold M., Jr. "U.S. Panel Urges $2.5-Billion to Curb Pollution." *New York Times* (13 June 1967): 1.

Scott, Jack. "Mother Sea." *Vancouver Sun* (29 July 1953): 2.

Seager, Joni. "Rachel Carson Died of Breast Cancer: The Coming of Age of Feminist Environmentalism." *Signs* 28:3 (Spring 2003): 945–972.

_____. "Radical Observation." *Women's Studies Quarterly* 45:1/2 (2017): 269–277.

Seely, Ron. "Nature Is Giving Us Dire Warnings." *Wisconsin State Journal* (3 November 1996): 3C.

Sevareid, Eric. "Pests vs. Men: The Big Battle Is Raging Agains; Is Pesticide Use Tinkering with Nature Balance?" *Los Angeles Times* (23 September 1962).

Sherman, Jerome L. "Environmentalist Rachel Carson's Legacy Remembered on Earth Day." *Pittsburgh Post-Gazette* (23 April 2006).

Sideris, Lisa H. "The Ecological Body: Rachel Carson, *Silent Spring,* and Breast Cancer." *Soundings* 85:1/2 (2002): 107–120.

_____. "Fact and Fiction, Fear and Wonder: The Legacy of Rachel Carson." *Soundings* 91:3/4 (Fall-Winter 2009): 335–369.

Sime, Leonard N. "Bug Killers in Arizona Discriminate." *Arizona Republic* (8 September 1963): B11.

Smith, Michael B. "'Silence, Miss Carson!' Science, Gender, and the Reception of *Silent Spring.*" *Feminist Studies* 27:3 (Autumn 2001): 733–752.

"Sound Pesticides Report." (Staunton, VA) *News Leader* (20 May 1963): 4.

Stare, Frederick John. "Some Comments on *Silent Spring.*" *Nutrition Reviews* 21 (January 1963): 1, 4.

Stein, Karen F. "The Legacies of Rachel Carson." *English Journal* 103:6 (2014): 81–84.

Steinman, David. "Diet for a Poisoned Planet." *LA Weekly* (7 December 1989): 36A.

Sterne, J.R.L. "Silent Spring." *Baltimore Sun* (10 January 1991): 8A.

Sullivan, Walter. "Books of the Times." *New York Times* (27 September 1962): 35.

Sutton, G.M. "Review: *Under the Sea Wind.*" *Books* (14 December 1941): 5.

Tallock, Gordon. "Of Mites and Men." *National Review* 13 (20 November 1962): 398–399.

Tappen, Estelle C. "Review: *Under the Sea Wind.*" *Verona-Cedar Grove* (NJ) *Times* (5 June 1952): 16.

Temple, Stanley A. "Rachel Carson and a Childhood Sense of Wonder." *Wisconsin Academy of Sciences, Arts & Letters* (Summer 2015).

Tesfahunegny, Weldemariam. "Impact of

Pesticides on Birds from DDT to Current Fatality: A Literature Review." *Journal of Zoology Studies* 3:2 (2016): 44–56.

Thomson, Candus. "Love, Dread Drove Carson." *Baltimore Sun* (22 April 2007).

Thurston, Harry. "Sing to Me of the Oceans, Muse: The Poetry of the Sea." *The Future of Ocean Governance and Capacity Development.* Leiden: Brill Nijhoff, 2018. 498–502.

Toth, Robert. "Pesticide Study Found Difficult." *New York Times* (7 December 1962): 41.

_____. "Scientists Urge Wider Control over Pesticides." *New York Times* (16 May 1963): 1.

Tubbs, Christopher W. "California Condors and DDT." *Endocrine Disruptors* 4:1 (2016): e1173766.

Tudge, Colin. "The Great Green Book." *New Statesman* (19 April 1999): 35–36.

Turner, Fred. "Dirty Water and Disease: A Public Health History." *National Resources & Environment* 31:1 (Summer 2016): 56.

Twidle, Hedley. "Rachel Carson and the Perils of Simplicity: Reading *Silent Spring* from the Global South." *Ariel* 44:4 (October 20213): 49–88.

Twill, Truman. "Let Us Spray." *East Liverpool Review* (3 November 1962): 4.

"Use of Pesticides." Washington, D.C.: White House (15 March 1963): 1–25.

Vail, David D. "Toxic Fables: The Advertising and Marketing of Agricultural Chemicals in the Great Plains, 1945–1985." *Endeavour* 36:4 (December 2012): 165–173.

Van Loon, Hendrik, letter, 10 September 1937.

Vijver, Martina G. "The Choreography of Chemicals in Nature; Beyond Ecotoxicological Limits." *Chemosphere* 227 (2019): 366–307.

Wadsworth, Andrew. "Carson's Christianity and Environmental Crises." *Criterion* 9:1 (2016).

Walker, Martin J. "The Unquiet Voice of *Silent Spring*." *Ecologist* (August/September 1999): 322–325.

Walsh, Bryan. "How *Silent Spring* Became the First Shot in the War over the Environment." *Time* (25 September 2012).

Wange, Zuoyue. "Responding to *Silent Spring*: Scientists, Popular Science Communication, and Environmental Policy in the Kennedy Years." *Science Communication* 19 (December 1997): 141–163.

Wareham, Wendy. "Rachel Carson's Early Years." *Carnegie Magazine* 58:6 (November 1986).

Watson, Bruce. "Sounding the Alarm." *Smithsonian* (September 2002): 115–117.

Weigert, Andrew J. "Pragmatic Thinking about Self, Society, and Natural Environment: Mead, Carson, and Beyond." *Symbolic Interaction* 31:3 (Summer 2008): 235–258.

Wheeler, Charles M. "Control of Typhus in Italy 1943–1944 by Use of DDT." *American Journal of Public Health* 36 (February 1946): 119–129.

Wheeler, Timothy B. "Debate on Pesticides Lingers." *Baltimore Sun* (27 September 2002): 2A.

"When the Sedge Withers and No Birds Sing." *London Times* (14 February 1994).

White, Richard. "Play It Again Sam: Decline and Finishing in Environmental Narratives." *Routledge Companion to the Environmental Humanities.* New York: Routledge, 2017, 239–246.

Williams, Robert. "Review: *The Sea Around Us.*" (Paterson, NJ) *Morning Call* (26 January 1952): 15–16.

Williams, Terry Tempest. "One Patriot." *Patriotism and the American Land.* Great Barrington, MA: Orion Society, 2002.

_____. "The Spirit of Rachel Carson." *Audubon* (July/August, 1992): 104–107.

Woods, Bruce, Philip Johnson, and Valerie Fellows. "Sounding the Alarm." *Fish & Wildlife News* (Spring 2007): 12–13.

Woodwell, George. "Broken Eggshells: The Miracle of DDT Was Short-lived, But It Helped Launch the Environmental Movement." *Science* (November 1984): 115–118.

Young, Christopher. "Pesticides and *Silent Spring*." *Ottawa Citizen* (22 November 1962): 6.

Zubrin, Robert. "The Truth about DDT and *Silent Spring*." *New Atlantis* (27 September 2012).

Zwinger, Ann H. "Introduction" to *The Sea Around Us: Special Edition.* New York: Oxford University Press, 1989.

Electronic

Brinkley, Douglas. "Rachel Carson and JFK, an Environmental Tag Team." *Audubon* (May-June 2012), https://www.audubon.org/magazine/may-june-2012/rachel-carson-and-jfk-environmental-tag-team.

Curwood, Steve. "Living on Earth," *PRI Environmental News Magazine* (22 April 2005).

Doyle, Jack. "Power in the Pen," https://www.pophistorydig.com/topics/tag/rachel-carson-senate-hearings/ (22 February 2012).

Gerwig, Kathy. "Kathy Gerwig Highlights Kaiser Permanente's Environmental Work in Congressional Testimony," webcache.googleusercontent.com/search?q=cache:RJ4UAYzA-RooJ:https://share.kaiserpermanente.org/article/kathy-gerwig-highlights-kaiser-permanentes-environmental-work-in-congressional-testimony/+&cd=1&hl=en&ct=clnk&gl=us, 26 February 2009.

Kroll, Gary. "Rachel Carson—*Silent Spring*: A Brief History of Ecology as a Subversive," http://www.onlineethics.org/cms/9174, 2002.

Mattu, Neshma. "The Marriage of Science and Art within Rachel Carson's *Silent Spring*," https://artsone.arts.ubc.ca/2017/06/06/the-marriage-of-science-and-art-in-carsons-silent-spring/ (May 2017).

Milewski, Inka. "Rivers of Death Revisited," https://www.elements.nb.ca/theme/artists/inka/milewski.htm (June 2000).

Nicklin, Emmy. *What We Owe to Rachel Carson.* https://www.cbf.org/blogs/save-the-bay/2019/03/what-rachel-carson-gave-us.html.

Payne, James L. "Misreading Rachel Carson's *Silent Spring*," https://fee.org/articles/misreading-rachel-carson-s-silent-spring/ (12 August 2019).

Popova, Maria. "Undersea: Rachel Carson's Lyrical and Revolutionary 1937 Masterpiece Inviting Humans to Explore Earth from the Perspective of Other Creatures," www.brainpickings.org/2017/02/28/undersea-rachel-carson/

_____. "The Writing of *Silent Spring*: Rachel Carson and the Culture-Shifting Courage to Speak Inconvenient Truth to Power," https://www.brainpickings.org/2017/01/27/rachel-carson-silent-spring-dorothy-freeman/

"The Power of One Voice: A 50-Year Perspective on the Life of Rachel Carson," www.powerofonevoicefilm.com.

"Rachel Carson," *Bill Moyers Journal,* https://www.pbs.org/moyers/journal/09212007/profile.html (21 September 2007).

"Rachel Carson: A Conservation Legacy," https://www.fws.gov/rachelcarson/#bio.

"Remembering Rachel," https://www.fws.gov/rachelcarson/resources/FWS_perspectives.pdf.

Renner, Rebecca. "*Silent Spring* Is More Than a Scientific Landmark: It's Literature," https://lithub.com/silent-spring-is-more-than-a-scientific-landmark-its-literature/ (20 April 2018).

Stafford, Jeff. "Rachel L. Carson as Interpreted by Irwin Allen," *Streamline,* http://moviemorlocks.com/2011/02/20/rachel-l-carson-as-interpreted-by-irwin-allen/, 20 February 2011.

Steinbach, Alison. "Metaphor and Visions of Home in Environmental Writing," https://green.harvard.edu/news/metaphor-and-visions-home-environmental-writing (21 June 2016.

Steingraber, Sandra. "Living Downstream," www.LivingDownstream.com.

Index

Numbers in **bold** indicate main entries